THE MOST DANGEROUS BOOK EVER PUBLISHED: DEADLY DECEPTION EXPOSED!

“

"They are safe as long as they are not discovered that is their method of survival; keep us asleep, keep us selfish, keep us sedated."
They Live, 1988

”

KP
Korsgaard Publishing
www.korsgaardpublishing.com
ISBN 978-87-93987-14-2

PUBLISHING HISTORY
First edition: 2020

Cover design by Søren Roest Korsgaard.
Book editor: Søren Roest Korsgaard

ALSO BY KORSGAARD PUBLISHING

America's Jack The Ripper: The Definitive Account of the Zodiac Killer (Søren Roest Korsgaard, 2020).

The Düsseldorf Vampire (Karl Berg, foreword by Søren Roest Korsgaard)

US-Imposed Post-9/11 Muslim Holocaust & Muslim Genocide (Dr. Gideon Polya, forewords by Søren Roest Korsgaard and Dr. Kevin Barrett)

TABLE OF CONTENTS

DR. PAUL CRAIG ROBERTS

JAMES CORBETT

DR. REINER FUELLMICH

PREFACE

This book is composed of almost eighty essays that address a variety of subjects and issues deemed *verboten* by mainstream media and government. For example, "whitewashed" holocausts, subversive information about the never ending wars on terror and drugs, the legitimacy of taxation, the systematic elimination of freedoms and rights, the purported threat to humanity of COVID-19, the dangers of technology, and several more.
The viewpoints and evidence found in this book have been rendered invisible by censorship. For example, Jerry Day, one of the United States' foremost orators and advocates of civil and human rights, publishes his speeches on YouTube. The view count of his channel has steadily decreased as the administration of YouTube has implemented more and more draconian algorithms that effectively eliminate content that contradicts or poke holes in official narratives. Since it is likely only a matter of time before his channel is deleted, transcripts of his videos are found in this book.
I wish to express my gratitude to James Corbett, John Remington Graham, Jerry Day, Dr. Gideon Polya, Dr. Paul Craig Roberts, and Dr. Reiner Fuellmich. My gratitude also extends to Lady Jane Emefa Addy, Caroline Cheruiyot, and Oluwafunmilayo Elizabeth Bamidele.

Søren Roest Korsgaard
Germany, 2020.

ABOUT THE AUTHORS

Søren Roest Korsgaard is a social critic, humanitarian, entrepreneur, and author. He serves as the editor-in-chief of www.CrimeAndPower.com, and is the webmaster of www.PaulCraigRoberts.org and many other sites. Søren is also the CEO and founder of the editorially independent, pro-free speech publishing house, Korsgaard Publishing (KP). The mission of KP is to advance high quality books that challenge dangerous and false dogmas.

Dr. Gideon Polya is a Melbourne-based biochemist, writer, humanitarian activist, and artist. Over the last two decades, he has published numerous articles on the human consequences of neoliberalism, war, mainstream media deception, and climate change. Evidently, as a consequence of his carefully researched writing, he has been honored by being rendered invisible in look-the-other-way, US-dominated Australia. His latest book is, "US-Imposed Post-9/11 Muslim Holocaust & Muslim Genocide" (Korsgaard Publishing 2020).

John Remington Graham has practiced law for over fifty years, working as a public defender, public prosecutor, and law professor. He has extensive experience in forensic science and medicine. He has secured judicial findings in three cases, which link water fluoridation with human cancer, and published key works on this environmental danger with Pierre Morin and Dean Burk, both world renowned researchers in the field. He has also produced massive volumes on British, American, and Canadian constitutional law and history. His latest book is, "Free, Sovereign, and Independent States: The Intended Meaning of the American Constitution" (Pelican Publishing 2009).

Jerry Day is an Emmy-winning media producer in Southern California with millions of views on his freedom and rights themed videos on YouTube under the name "minivanjack." Jerry Day also maintains the websites www.FreedomTaker.com and www.EMFhelpcenter.com to assist people with solutions to the excess wireless radiation now flooding our living environments and causing widespread illness and death.

James Corbett, a lecturer and award-winning investigative journalist, is the architect of the incomparable Corbett Report (www.CorbettReport.com), an independent, listener-supported alternative news source. It operates on the principle of open source intelligence and provides podcasts, interviews, articles, and videos about breaking news and important issues from 9/11 Truth and false flag terror to the Big Brother police state, eugenics, geopolitics, the central banking fraud, and more.

Dr. Paul Craig Roberts was the Assistant Secretary of the Treasury in the Reagan administration, associate editor and columnist for the Wall Street Journal, columnist for Business Week, the Scripps Howard News Service, and Creators Syndicate. He has testified before Congress on 30 occasions. He was awarded the US Treasury's Meritorious Service Award as well as the French Legion of Honor by the Mitterrand government. Roberts has held academic appointments in six universities, including Stanford and the William E. Simon Chair in Political Economy, Center for Strategic and International Studies, Georgetown. His unparalleled website, www.PaulCraigRoberts.org, has millions of visitors every year.

Dr. Reiner Fuellmich is a consumer protection trial lawyer in Germany and California. He is one of four members of the German Corona Investigative Committee who are now working with an international network of lawyers who will argue the biggest tort case ever, the Corona Fraud Scandal, which has meanwhile unfolded into probably the greatest crime against humanity ever.

One World Digital Dictatorship

Søren Roest Korsgaard

Introduction

Dystopian classics are back into the spotlight, like Aldous Huxley's Brave New World and George Orwell's 1984. They have roared back onto bestseller lists due to whistleblowers' exposés of government imperialism and totalitarian surveillance of their citizens and foreigners. While the kakistocracy and dystopian surveillance state depicted in 1984 undoubtedly reflected, to some extent, contemporary sociopolitical realities, Orwell extrapolated worst-case scenarios set as warnings for future generations. Nonetheless, his book and implicit warnings seem to have been ignored as an authoritarian surveillance state is now a reality for most people in first and second world countries. In lieu of accountability for criminal mass-surveillance or these revelations deterring or limiting the prying eyes of government-sponsored spy programs, the establishment in conjunction with their media platforms has used it to their full advantage, almost as if they, themselves, masterminded the leaks. Rather than being dismantled, the establishment has openly added advanced surveillance technology to their arsenal in their cataclysmic War on Truth. The mainstream media now parallels Orwell's Ministry of Truth that broadcasts official explanations, while it effectively neutralizes those who venture outside the parameters of government-approved thinking, which so often equates to threatening their interests. While the current Western population control via advanced surveillance technology and social engineering is unparalleled in history, China has nevertheless rolled out a system that sets new standards for government control, the so-called social credit system. In a few decades from now, if the Chinese government succeeds, those who are imprisoned by the social crediting system will have no reference point or conception of freedom;

digital tyranny will have become the norm. To some extent, Western policymakers have been apprehensive of the Chinese program, but as we shall see, it is nevertheless evident that they themselves are working diligently behind the scenes to implement the same technology that makes the Chinese digital prison possible.

The Social Credit System

The Chinese Communist Party implemented the world's first social crediting system in 2014, a dystopian and Orwellian surveillance-based program that rates citizens according to a set of rules defined by the government; for example, one will be punished for playing too much video game, eating food in the metro, criticizing the government, failing to sort personal waste correctly, swearing in public, and other offenses. On the other hand, one will be rewarded for spying on one's fellow citizens and reporting to the authorities if people use profane language. At this time, the system has been rolled out in selected cities and declared a success by the government. Before the end of 2020, the Chinese government intends to have assigned a credit score to all of China's citizens and private businesses, and, at this time, there is, therefore, some variability in the imposed set of regulations and rewards.

If you lose too many points, you become a "blacklisted" individual. Violations, for example, red-light violations, caught on video and mugshots, and personal information of those who are blacklisted are openly displayed on LED screens in public, and even in cinemas as a substitute for commercials. Chinese authorities have also released an app showing "a map of deadbeat debtors" within a 500-meter radius [1]. Users of the app are then encouraged to report if they think a particular debtor could repay his outstanding loans. Rules and regulations cover almost every aspect of human behavior and interaction. For example, if dog owners forget to keep their pet on a leash, disturb other people, or if their leftovers are not removed by the owner for a total of three times, government employees will forcefully remove the dog, and the person will be banned from keeping any dog for five years [2]. Senior citizens may sue their children if they do not visit them regularly; the courts can force the family members to visit them more often [3]. Violations can result in blacklisting. Blacklisted individuals become personae non-gratae: they and their children are banned from a long list of services, like getting out of the country, from specific schools, have their banking accounts frozen, and other people will by force not associate with them as it causes their rating to drop [4]. It is evident that getting blacklisted puts restrictions on movements to such an extent that it effectively amounts to house arrest. It, therefore, seems likely that a blacklisted individual could suffer from starvation and malnutrition as a result of the imposed restrictions. It is important to note that the punishments can – as all other government rules and laws – be changed at any time for the worse. Individuals who have a high credit ranking can receive a list of rewards, including a greater chance of employment, a variety of discounts, and less waiting time at hospitals.

The social crediting system is made possible by extensive and intrusive surveillance, such as video-surveillance and facial recognition technology. The newest technology being rolled out to isolate, control, and modulate people's behavior parallels science-fiction action thrillers from the 20th century, such as John Carpenter's They Live from 1988. State-of-the-art technology currently being deployed includes gait recognition technology (they can identify you by the way you walk), robotic birds that hover in the sky monitoring people on the ground, and facial recognition sunglasses for police officers [5]. The surveillance is taken to such an extreme that by 2022 the total number of CCTV installments is projected to increase to 2.76 billion [6]. The Internet also plays a vital role in the edification, the alleged rationale behind the social crediting system, as it is subjected to oppressive control by the Internet Police, a sophisticated unit which monitors online behaviors and punishes government critics, people who watch porn, or somehow else violates the thousands of rules. The Chinese authorities have a well-developed profile of each citizen to the extent that they can find out how often you open your refrigerator, go to the toilet, when you get up in the morning and go to bed as smart meters installed in people's homes give them that capability. The data is submitted to a variety of analyses, including predictive and behavioral analytics. The end result is a dynamic profile of each citizen. Government workers and artificial intelligence can, at any time, access a file and impose restrictions.

In a blatant propaganda piece on the social credit system by the American NBC News, it was stated that "it pushes you to become a better citizen" and "you are not going to be punished if you haven't done anything wrong [7]." The terms used in this sentence are obviously subjective; a good citizen from the perspective of the social crediting system is one who never questions authority, always follows the rules, in essence, an aspiring drone controlled by a set of external rules that may at any time be changed. There is no room for individuality, liberty, and creativity within the digital prison. The second assertion has religious connotations as it assumes that the Chinese government and its social crediting system are all fair and just, which is provably false. The Chinese government and judiciary system are notorious for their criminality, blood lust, corruption, and extreme bias. In 2013, Chinese prosecutors had a conviction rate of 99.93%, yet it was a typical year for them [8]. Provably wrongful convictions and executions are abundant. In 1989, a Chinese executioner put a rifle to the head of Teng Xingshan and pulled the trigger for the murder of Shi Xiaorong. In 2005, however, Shi resurfaced, alive and well. In 1996, 18-year-old Hugjilt was executed 68 days after sentencing despite an abundance of evidence attesting to his innocence. When the Chinese courts finally had to admit that the state had executed an innocent teenager, they compensated the parents with 30,000 Yuan ($4300) [9]. The US justice system is likewise notorious for executing innocent people and forcing innocent people to plea bargain to avoid an overly harsh sentence; in fact, 97% of federal criminal convictions end in a plea bargain while state criminal convictions are at 94% [10, 11]. Nonetheless, in 2015 the average US death row inmate waited 15 years between sentencing and execution, allowing plenty of time for further analysis of the alleged crime committed, and many innocent individuals have been released from death row [12]. In China, execution sometimes takes place immediately after sentencing [13].

Capital punishment is a lucrative business, as organs from executed prisoners are harvested and sold to the highest bidder. For years, the Chinese government denounced the allegations but admitted in 2005 that organ harvesting indeed took place, but asserted in January 2015, they had stopped this practice. Their claim has been met with intense skepticism. The Independent Tribunal into Forced Organ Harvesting from Prisoners of Conscience in China (China Tribunal) has disputed this claim, and presented evidence to the UN that there is "no evidence that the significant infrastructure associated with China's transplantation industry has been dismantled [14]." The tribunal concludes, "Forced organ harvesting is of unmatched wickedness even compared – on a death for death basis – with the killings by mass crimes committed in the last century [14]." The International Coalition to End Transplant Abuse in China has concluded that the number of organ transplants may exceed the official government statistics by 1000% [15].

The organ harvesting industry is not only targeting executed prisoners, but is also aimed at "prisoners of conscience," such as Falun Gong, Uyghurs, Tibetans, and House Christians, and has been "practiced for a substantial period of time involving a very substantial number of victims [14]." In 2001, a whistleblower, Dr. Wang Guoqi, gave testimony to the US House Committee on International Relations. He described in detail how he had been paid $40 for every prisoner he had stripped of organs. He had, however, quit the job in 1995 when he had observed doctors removing the kidneys from a man who was still alive. He had survived his execution. Dr. Wang Guoqi had then inquired whether "the man should be shot again," but he was informed that it was not necessary "because the man would die after the organ harvest anyway [16]."

Many of China's "prisoners of conscience" are kept in "concentration camps," allegedly for re-education purposes; eyewitness testimony and evidence from a variety of sources, however, suggest otherwise [17]. Human rights lawyer Arsalan Iftikhar has called their concentration camps, "a completely Orwellian system of ethnic cleansing, where China is acting as big brother [18]."

Considering China's long history of causing harm when no harm was merited, it is a distinct possibility that the social crediting system will be used to harvest organs of dissenters who have lucrative, well-kept organs and rare blood types as medical and dental records are a part of each citizen's digital profile.

Big Brother is Watching You

Government officials who have commented on China's social credit system have offered mild criticism of it. For example, in 2018, US Vice President Mike Pence, surrounded by teleprompters, stated, "China has built an unparalleled surveillance state," but his main point seemed to be that they allegedly often had used US technology to achieve their "Orwellian" state [19]. Deputy Prime Minister of Russia, Maxim Akimov, has stated that Russia "currently" has "no such projects [20]." The adverb, "currently," signifies that the situation may change in the future.

However, there is no need to analyze their statements rigorously, as the evidence is abundant that governments have systematically and deliberately undermined our liberties and secretly geared up their respective states for a tyrannical, digital prison. As will be shown in this article, the same types of surveillance technology deployed in China are being set up by government agencies or in conjunction with private companies, in numerous countries, such as USA, France, Australia, Germany, Canada, India, United Kingdom, Russia, and soon they will have the capability to create a digital prison. Additionally, there exists an unmistakable propensity toward crediting systems by private companies. Dr. Gerd Gigerenzer, a director at the Max Planck Institute for Human Development and researcher of the Chinese social crediting system, has warned that western countries are sleepwalking in the same direction, and we are much closer to an Orwellian social crediting system than what it may appear [21]. A variety of crediting systems gauging citizens' trustworthiness have already been put in place. For instance, Germany is using the universal credit rating system, SCHUFA, which is analogous to FICO, an American version, affecting the majority of those populations and millions of companies. SCHUFA tracks your entire credit history, and by means of classified algorithms, they give you a score. Additional variables also come into play. One of these is "geo-scoring," meaning that neighbors' credit ratings can affect yours [21]. If the score is below a certain threshold, you will not be able to acquire a loan, get a phone subscription, etc. This trustworthiness record follows "you everywhere as [a]consumer in your everyday life [22]." Dr. Gigerenzer has warned, "If we don't do anything, then one day a corporation or a government institution will pull all the information from different data banks together and come up with a social credit score," and "at the end, we will be in the same state as the Chinese [21]." He concludes, "We live in a world where judgment is being replaced by numbers – by scores that calculate the value of a human being, with the help of algorithms," and "It would be tragic if somebody's life was destroyed just because others put blind faith in a commercial algorithm [21]."

In 2018, the Moscow Times reported that by 2025 four out of five Russians will have received a "personal development trajectory [23]," a digital file which Dmitry Kuznetsov, head of IT at Russia's Pension Fund, has clarified will contain, "Every achievement in a person's life – the misses, mistakes, big projects [23]." This personal digital file is a part of Russia's multibillion-dollar program that aims to digitize the economy and roll out digital technologies nationwide. One of these is fifth-generation wireless technology (5G) that is expected to cover 80% of the population by 2025 [24]. Despite overwhelming safety concerns with numerous scientific studies pointing to cancer and other adverse effects at levels "well below most international and national guidelines," 5G is being rolled out in most advanced countries across the globe [25]. If governments are to create a "smart" or "digital" prison for all of us, it follows that as much as possible of human behavior and interaction with physical devices must be readily quantifiable and internet accessible, preferably connected to large databases; this is often referred to as the Internet of Things (IoT). Government agencies that can process vast amounts of data, such as the National Security Agency (NSA), will then intercept the data to evaluate our interaction with the world. 5G network technology is essential for IoT. One of the devices that can transform physical activity into quantifiable data is a smart meter [26]. Country after country has embraced smart meters and, despite evidence that these devices can be hazardous and carcinogenic, often made their installment compulsory [27]. A smart meter digitizes nearly everything in your household by registering when you do what, for example, when you turn on your computer and when it is off. Old-fashioned measuring devices of electricity were limited to measuring the aggregate consumption of energy, but smart meters can collect data every minute, allowing for "consumer profiling" with high accuracy [26].

Surveillance is essential for the workings of a social credit system, in particular, facial recognition technology or biometric face scanners and similar technology [28]. Numerous governments have embraced the technology. In addition to facial recognition technology, governments have successfully implemented several other types of live surveillance technology such as automated license plate readers, which are mounted on street poles, streetlights, highway overpasses, and attached to police cars. These devices record your license plate, and thus governments will have a well-developed profile of your regular movement pattern, irregularities, where you are, and at what time [29].

Although the implementation of biometric face scanners has been challenged and banned to some extent in a few US cities, the FBI has been working diligently behind the scenes by scanning millions of drivers' license photos from DMV databases, and in all probability from social media accounts and other sources [30]. According to a report from Georgetown Law's Center on Privacy and Technology, "law enforcement face recognition affects over 117 million American adults. It is also unregulated. A few agencies have instituted meaningful protections to prevent the misuse of the technology. In many more cases, it is out of control [31]." In March 2017, President Donald Trump issued an executive order mandating a "biometric entry-exit system" for top 20 US airports by 2021 [32]. According to a declassified report by the Department of Homeland Security, all travelers, including US citizens, will be subject to facial recognition technology and other methods of identification [33].

A British court ruled in 2019 that biometric face scanners do not violate privacy and human rights, and it is acceptable that the police use them [34]. Private stores, totaling hundreds if not thousands, use facial recognition technology to scan their customers to detect "subjects of interest" and determine if customers are old enough to buy beer and cigarettes [35]. In August 2019, Big Brother Watch, a British civil liberties and privacy campaigning organization, issued a statement that they had uncovered a "collusion between police and private companies [36]." Law enforcement had allied themselves with private companies, such as the owners of the Sheffield's Meadowhall, one of England's largest shopping centers, and secretly used facial recognition technology to scan an estimated two million visitors [36]. One year prior to this revelation, it was revealed that the owners of the Trafford Centre, another popular shopping mall, had in collusion with the Greater Manchester Police scanned around 15 million visitors [37]. Big Brother Watch has characterized the situation as an "epidemic," and the organization has warned that "facial recognition surveillance risks making privacy in Britain extinct [36]."

The usage of automated live identification systems in Canada is similar to the other countries described in this article, but with one exception. Wei Chengyi, the owner of the Foody Mart grocery chain, has stated that the company is planning to introduce "payment by Chinese-made facial recognition devices [38]." Rather than using a credit card or cash, the facial recognition system identifies the customer and links his face to his account, enabling the person to make purchases by simply looking into a camera.

Reportedly, "Russia is building one of the world's largest facial recognition networks" and that "according to some projections, it may even be bigger than China's [39]." In particular, strategical places are targeted since the Russian government knows that people will enter these facilities or use these services at some point, like social security payments and passport renewals, to ensure that virtually no one can escape having their face measured, analyzed, and recorded in an instant.

France has launched a nationwide ID app that strongly parallels one of the most essential aspects of China's social crediting system. The app gives access to a host of public services; however, you can only access them if you let it scan, analyze, and store your facial characteristics. The only way to verify your identity is by means of a facial recognition scan, which is then compared to your passport photo, and undoubtedly used for a wide range of other classified purposes [40]. The usage of facial recognition technology is similarly on the rise in Germany, and from 2010 to 2017, its usage by law enforcement increased by over 1600% [41].

For years, the government of Australia has been creating a massive database of photographic material from a variety of sources, such as passport photos. The database will be available for "government agencies and private businesses to access facial IDs held by state and territory traffic authorities, and passport photos held by the foreign affairs department [42]." The Australian Privacy Foundation has voiced its concerns and stated that Australia is just steps away from "automated and real-time surveillance of public spaces [43]." Measures strongly paralleling China's surveillance system were taken in 2019, when the government proposed that facial recognition software should be used to verify users' identity on certain websites [44].

In 2019, the National Crime Records Bureau (NCRB), an Indian government agency, released a 172-page document. It was announced that the NCRB had started working toward making India the world's epicenter of facial recognition software, permeating the country's 29 states [45]. The document urges private companies to submit a proposal to help them build the system. When the contract has been signed, it has been ambitiously estimated that it will take less than one year for the system to go live in the world's second most populated country [46]. Eventually, there will be a single, centralized database comprised of images from "social media accounts, newspapers, CCTV cameras, passport photos, publicly available pictures, and criminal records. Even artists' sketches of suspects will be part of the database [47]." Law enforcement will be equipped with "hand-held mobile devices enabling them to capture a face in the field and search it instantly against the national database, through a dedicated app [48]." According to the NCRB, "This is an effort in the direction of modernizing the police force, information gathering, criminal identification, verification and its dissemination among various police organizations and units across the country [45]." On the other end of the spectrum, Apar Gupta, a lawyer and the Executive Director of the Internet Freedom Foundation, has voiced strong concerns over India's plans to roll out a national facial recognition database, saying, "political opponents, civil rights activists, government critics, and journalists could become potential targets for surveillance [47]." In January 2009, India launched Aadhaar, which has become the world's largest biometric ID system, containing details of more than 1.2 billion Indians as of October 2019. Gupta fears that the national facial recognition network might be linked up to Aadhaar, resulting in India becoming a "total, permanent surveillance state [49]." Gupta concludes, "These kinds of technologies will be used not toward satisfying the needs of national security, but to enforce a system of social control, like in China" [47].

In addition to the type of technology that is engineered to identify you swiftly, like biometric face scanners, massive data centers are essential to a social crediting system or digital prison. These centers harvest the most private and sensitive data and use it to create individual profiles that include people's call history, medical records, school records, employment history, purchase history, network of friends via social media monitoring, movement history through GPS signals, and through sophisticated analyses, it is determined whether or not a person is a threat. Newer cell phones give the user the option to lock and unlock it using one's fingerprint, or via a facial recognition scan, such data is also collected by these data centers. Additionally, smart TVs, computers, iPads, cell phones, which are present in millions of homes, record user activity, conversations, movements, and certain video games employ facial recognition software. It has been shown that this data is being intercepted by western governments [50]. The NSA is well known at this time due to the media-friendly whistleblower Edward Snowden who revealed that the US engages in the activities specified above. Specifically, the NSA is the American part of the Five Eyes Alliance, a conspiratorial network designed to intercept data, share it between them, and thus commit espionage on as many people and governments as possible [51]. The other four countries are the United Kingdom, Canada, New Zealand, and Australia. These countries are the main players, but governments have also formed the Nine and Fourteenth Eyes Alliances comprising major and minor European countries [52].

Collectivism and Censorship

While the technology is already available or will soon be to most advanced countries, it can be argued that its availability does not necessitate a rollout of a digital prison. However, for years governments have preconditioned the masses with the ideological underpinnings paramount to a totalitarian digital prison, namely collectivism and the related idea of free-speech restraints via political correctness, brute force, and censorship. By preconditioning the masses, they will slowly be guided into acceptance or compliance with such a system as it is being gradually rolled out.

The Chinese social crediting system is rooted in collectivism and thereby is individualism sacrificed at the expense of the "greater good." The collectivistic notions that underline this system are similar to these ideas: "A social crediting system is to help us all become better citizens," and "We need government to protect us." While collectivistic propaganda runs rampant in socialistic/communistic countries, like Denmark, Sweden, Norway, and many others, it has similarly been integrated into the legal framework, culture, and public awareness of supposedly "liberal" countries like the USA. For example, vaccination has successfully been transformed into an aggressive collectivistic idea by the psychopharmaceutical complex with the assistance of a government-enforced monopoly [53]. While inoculation used to be a personal choice, it has now become mandatory by law in numerous countries and States, and in those places where an individual choice is still possible, dissenters and those who even question the safety of vaccines are targeted for harassment and exclusion. Mandatory vaccination is a collectivistic and social crediting related concept. Another important collectivistic idea is that of "gun control," but only for the masses, not for the government personnel (law enforcement, military, etc.). Removing firearms or making them extremely difficult to be obtained has been achieved in numerous socialistic/communistic countries, and effective strategies have been implemented in supposedly "liberal" countries [54]. In a digital prison, it is important that the citizens are unarmed in order to make the population virtually powerless.

Silencing whistleblowers, government critics, and free thinkers is an essential component of any tyrannical regime in order to terrorize the public into compliance, and to keep them isolated from information that runs contrary to official dogmas; the greater the ignorance of human rights violations the lower is the chance of resistance and opposition. The digital revolution has equipped us with lightning speed communication, but ruling elites have weaponized the digitization to control, manipulate, and destroy information that is contrary to their interests. For example, as far back as 2003 and 2004, Internet activists were tracked down, and Chinese judges imposed extremely harsh sentences [55]. With its massive resources, China conducts real-time Internet censoring through artificial intelligence and their cyber police squads. Western governments are no better and spy on their citizens in blatant violation of privacy rights, all enabled by the events of September 11, 2001. Subsequent to September 11, the US government launched the draconian PATRIOT Act, limiting and nullifying laws governing civil liberties [56]. England, France, Germany, and other countries followed in the American footsteps and implemented similar laws [57]. These legislative steps served as the first steps toward an Orwellian digital prison.

In addition to imposing restrictions via legislation, governments have also allied themselves with the corporate juggernaut of Facebook, Google, Twitter, and YouTube for the purpose of censorship and social engineering. YouTube's CEO, Susan Wojcicki, admitted in 2019 that 10,000 Google employees and artificial intelligence had succeeded in reducing the "amount of time Americans watch controversial content by 70%" and that instead of referring users to "controversial content" they would be directed to government-approved sources, like CNN [58]. Furthermore, there has been a strong move toward punishing intellectuals and public figures for voicing dissent of official narratives and a variety of ideologies, such as questioning the official 9/11 dogma and the transgender ideology, to the extent that such criticism has been codified into law as a criminal offense [59]. Diversity of thought, especially notions that exist outside of the imaginary boundaries established by governments, is no longer accepted in supposedly advanced countries. Even more illuminating is that whistleblowers have been severely punished, tortured, and made an example of in blatant violation of international law, sending a clear message to potential whistleblowers that exposing government corruption might entail grave consequences. For instance, Chelsea Manning (born Bradley Manning) leaked documents exposing horrendous US war crimes, and for her service, she was sent to prison while the perpetrators walked free [60]. The editor-in-chief of WikiLeaks, Julian Assange, despite protests from human rights organizations and the public, has been subjected to arbitrary confinement, harassment, humiliation, and torture, not for spreading false information, but for exposing government corruption, war crimes, and other information. Professor Nils Melzer, the UN's Special Rapporteur on torture and other cruel, inhuman or degrading treatment or punishment, and a team of medical experts visited the Wikileaks editor in a UK prison. From their examination, it was clear that Assange displayed "all the symptoms typical for prolonged exposure to psychological torture [61]." Melzer subsequently sent an appeal to the UK government demanding that they adhere to international law, immediately release him, and bar his pending extradition to the US. However, in their considerably delayed response, the UK government "flatly rejected" the appeal, "without indicating any willingness to consider my recommendations, let alone to implement them, or even provide the additional information requested," Malzer later said [61].

The Special Rapporteur on torture concludes:
"While the US Government prosecutes Mr. Assange for publishing information about serious human rights violations, including torture and murder, the officials responsible for these crimes continue to enjoy impunity [61]."

And:

"The blatant and sustained arbitrariness shown by both the judiciary and the government in this case suggests an alarming departure from the UK's commitment to human rights and the rule of law. This is setting a worrying example, which is further reinforced by the Government's recent refusal to conduct the long-awaited judicial inquiry into British involvement in the CIA torture and rendition programme [61]."

And:

"In my view, this case has never been about Mr. Assange's guilt or innocence, but about making him pay the price for exposing serious governmental misconduct …. Unless the UK urgently changes course and alleviates his inhumane situation, Mr. Assange's continued exposure to arbitrariness and abuse may soon end up costing his life [61]."

Cognitive Spyware

Surveillance technology follows the trend of other computing technologies, and its cost will decrease while accuracy, size, and speed will improve concomitantly. Governments prioritize control of the masses, and unless significant changes happen to the status quo, scientific development will continue unabated due to sizable government grants. Advanced cameras will eventually reach a size that is nearly unperceivable to the human eye, but even more important is the opportunities advances in technology will provide in regards to monitoring people. Today's most advanced cameras can monitor physical activity, identify a person, and via advanced algorithms, cameras can outline general characteristics of a person's appearance, detect if someone is in possession of a gun, and even "detect motions that are commonly used to commit a crime [62]." Although advanced, cameras are nonetheless limited to the physical realm, and while the behavior of a person will reveal a lot about that person's intentions, mannerisms, etc., the person's mind can nevertheless hold secrets, engage in "thought crimes," and plot and outline "crimes" against government or others. In the near future, the mind might not be the refuge it has been hitherto.
A long list of studies found in the PubMed literature deal with decoding human brain activity, for example, by extracting images or thoughts. As early as 2011, Professor Jack Gallant et al. were able to decode brain activity associated with watching movies on YouTube and digitally reconstruct the dynamic

mental images using fMRi technology and advanced algorithms [63]. Gallant would later say, "We are opening a window into the movies in our minds [64]." In 2016, in the Journal of Neuroscience, Hongmi Lee and Brice A. Kuhl showed that they could decode information from neural activity in the angular gyrus, a region of the brain associated with memory, and digitally reconstruct a face a person had been instructed to think about [65]. Neuroscientist Divya Chander concludes, "We can now look into the brain and actually see what it is you are seeing," and "imagine where this technology is taking us ... We can now read brains without opening them [66]."

During that same year, Dr. Toshimasa Yamazaki and his team of the Kyushu Institute of Technology in Japan found a connection between sound waves and brainwaves, and they were able to read certain words from people's minds without them saying anything [67]. Yamazaki has stated that this technology could empower people who are speech impaired. He did not address the more sinister potential of the technology that governments will have the potential to spy on people's minds. We may call this type of intrusive surveillance for "cognitive spyware." In the future, cognitive spyware will likely be able to decode intent before an action has been undertaken, and thus we could be punished for thought crimes and crimes without any physical component based on intent.

At the University of California, researchers have developed a "Brain Decoder Device [68]." Although the device is far from being rolled out globally, the objective is clear: it is to monitor what people are thinking. The lead author of the study, Dr. Brian Pasley, has stated, "If you're reading text in a newspaper or book, you hear a voice in your own head," and "We're trying to decode the brain activity related to that voice [69]."

The Defense Advanced Research Projects Agency, or DARPA, has been given considerable government grants to develop Next-Generation Nonsurgical Neurotechnology. Although the majority of their projects are kept in the dark, it has been revealed that they are working on "a nonsurgical interface between the human brain and technology [70]." The goal is to develop a way for humans to "brain control" machines, i.e., an interface between humans and artificial intelligence in order to control robots, cybersecurity systems, weapons systems, drones [70].

In addition to large corporations and the military, Tesla founder Elon Musk through his company Neurolink is also working toward creating a brain-machine interface system, connecting the human brain to an external device via implants. Musk envisions that brain implants could lead to a future of "superhuman intelligence" by means of symbiosis with artificial intelligence [71]. "Over time I think we will probably see a closer merger of biological intelligence and digital intelligence [72]," he has also said. As animal experimentation has been successful, and monkeys can now control computers with their brains, human trials will begin in 2020 [73]. Elon Musk has warned that super-powerful computers could soon overtake humans, and in order to safeguard us against such a scenario, human biology must be merged with artificial intelligence [74]. Facebook, Inc. is similarly investing heavily in this domain. One of the projects they are working on is "smart glasses" that "superimpose computer-generated images over the real world" [75]. Mark Zuckerberg has stated, "The goal is to eventually make it so that you can think something and control something in virtual or augmented reality [76]." Eventually, this type of technology will enable us to control devices with our minds rather than, for example, type a message on a smartphone or check emails on a laptop. Perhaps smartphones will even be replaced entirely by wearable technology.

If we can control machines with our minds, we are approaching a domain in which machines may also control our minds directly or indirectly. It is well established that people change their behavior when they know or believe there is a chance they are being monitored. It follows that people will modulate their thinking patterns and thoughts if they know or expect that government agencies are eavesdropping on their minds.

Albeit brain decoding technology is still considered "extremely primitive [77]," in some years or decades from now, it will most likely mature, and the cost, efficiency, and accuracy will diminish considerably. When or if that happens, police officers may start to be equipped with "cognitive spyware" glasses, just as today where Chinese police officers wear glasses with facial recognition software. Thought reading software might even become as abundant as cameras are today and perhaps be integrated into smart glasses, smartphones, and found on light poles, in airports, on street corners, in government buildings, etc. Thought reading software is simply an extension of the technology embraced by the majority today. For example, Microsoft's digital assistant, Cortana, is enabled on millions of computers and smartphones. The digital assistant will appear and be ready to assist whenever its name is said in proximity to the device [78]. In order to accomplish this task, it registers all sounds and conversations.

Getting the majority to embrace new technology and even pay for their own surveillance does not appear to be difficult. Usually, certain benefits are offered by using a particular technology. These benefits are often a veneer covering the true intentions behind the software. In the case of the Pokémon GO game, a highly successful surveillance software, millions of people were actually paying for their own surveillance; surveillance can be made trendy if disguised as a game [79]. Smart meters are touted as devices that are more accurate than analog meters; in reality, a smart meter can act as a surveillance system [80]. The success in regards to smartphones is unparalleled, and billions of people now have one. Surveillance cameras and other equipment are advertised as needed for capturing criminals, but regular people are treated as criminals, and the technology can be used for excessive mental and physical control. The efficiency of a social crediting system largely depends on advanced technology. It follows that advances in brain decoding technology and other types of spying equipment will be integrated into social crediting systems to monitor as much of physical and mental activity as possible.

Blockchain Technology

Cryptocurrencies are reported on in the mainstream news on a daily basis, and most people have heard of bitcoin and possibly even ethereum, the second-largest cryptocurrency by marketcap. The obscure, underlying technology of cryptocurrencies is called blockchain technology or distributed ledger technology. Chinese President Xi Jinping has called the technology for an "an important breakthrough" and allocated extra funding for it [81]. A growing list of countries, China, Russia, Venezuela, Estonia, Japan, and others, has announced their intention of launching a national cryptocurrency [82]. Futurists have predicted that blockchain technology will have a considerable impact upon a long list of industries, including banking, real-estate, healthcare, voting, copyright information, and journalism. Some have ambitiously touted it to be the "new Internet [83]." Blockchain technology eliminates the need for a middleman and trusting a centralized management, as protocols, computer code, and cryptography ensure trust in the network. With middlemen eliminated, blockchain technology enables people to interact with large peer-to-peer networks, and it has the capability to transform and reshape society and economy by making the world more decentralized.

A blockchain is a digital concatenated record of transactions. The name derives from the fact that information is stored in a series of blocks, whereas a block typically contains a predetermined amount of data, for instance, one megabyte of transactions. These blocks of data are connected to form a chain, hence the name "blockchain." A peer-to-peer network of computers validates transactions against the previous blocks. This means that to alter a particular record, for example, in order to put a spurious bitcoin into existence, it would require altering all subsequent blocks. Because data is spread out over a peer-to-peer network, single points of failure are eliminated; thus, blockchains are decentralized.

The concept of blockchain was put onto paper by a person or group using the name Satoshi Nakamoto, and in 2009 he or they created bitcoin, a decentralized and pseudo-anonymous cryptocurrency that has since become extremely valuable [84]. Cryptocurrencies have provided an outlet for circumventing the conventional banking system and government restrictions. However, a public cryptocurrency is simply one implementation of blockchain technology, and it appears to be an ideal tool for enabling totalitarianism, especially if IoT, blockchain technology, and a social credit system are combined. Blockchain technology, if embraced by world governments, may become an integrated part of social crediting systems through tokenization and monetary control. For instance, the

Chinese government may create a national, digital currency, and by means of facial recognition linked to one's virtual cryptocurrency wallet, the need for physical cash is eliminated. Proponents of a cashless society could argue that it would eliminate a country's shadow economy, and put an end to funding of illegal activities and terrorism as every record of every transaction is stored in the blockchain. A government-enabled blockchain-permeated society also fosters social engineering as dissenters, lawbreakers, and others could, in an instant, be cut off from services, if they venture outside the government established parameters.

Blockchain tokenization is a process by which real-world objects or certain types of behaviors can be digitally represented on a blockchain. For instance, a $30 million real estate property was tokenized in 2018 [85]. A token is a unit of value that is recorded on the blockchain. A token economy may be introduced in a social credit system to "build vibrant ecosystems through the use of tokens that can incentivize behavior [86]." Blockchain technology could, therefore, "create something that might enable the coordination of human activity at a much larger scale than has been possible before [86]." For example, a climate token where anyone who engages in climate-friendly behavior is rewarded, and those who do not contribute to the maintenance and provision of the climate are punished by losing tokens. Unemployed people could receive unemployment tokens for carrying out certain activities, but also have tokens removed from their digital wallet for not sending out enough job applications, etc. Perhaps a certain amount of tokens needs to be earned before a person is qualified for certain jobs. The applications of blockchain technology are considerable as even industry leaders BMW, Mercedes-Benz, Ford, and Toyota are developing blockchain technology for their products, especially for autonomous vehicles [87]. In 2018, Daimler AG, the parent firm of Mercedes Benz, experimented with a small-scale token-based rewards system to encourage eco-driving. Those who followed the rules were rewarded with MobiCoins, which the driver could then use for a variety of services, like VIP access to DTM Race events [88]. Token economies open up for a combination of blockchain technology, IoT, and a social credit system. Modern blockchains are fast, efficient, and operating in real-time, and are considered superior to traditional methods of storage. Therefore, if blockchain technology is connected to IoT, the result could be a near-complete, digital record of one's interaction with the world. In conclusion, blockchain technology may enable decentralized and autonomous totalitarianism.

Centralized Government

In favor of a social crediting system, it can be argued that extensive surveillance may reduce violent crime and overall improve people's moral character, and if the rules, regulations, and punishments are codified into law by a democratically elected government, then a social crediting system is sound. However, as we shall see in the following section, these arguments do not stand scrutiny or justify a totalitarian regime. Murders and other violent crimes committed outside the law are relatively rare phenomena compared to the violence meted out by governments. In fact, history profusely demonstrates a distinct correlation between the power of a government and atrocities [89]. The more powerful a government is, the more capable it is, and more likely it is to kill its own citizens or foreigners. Throughout history, Chinese governments, like most other governments, have systematically killed their own or other populations through violence or deprivation. For the past century alone, Dr. Rudolph Rummel, whose specialty was democide or death by government, has calculated that the Chinese governments murdered more than 80,000,000 unarmed civilians, while governments murdered 262,000,000 worldwide [90]. This massive and staggering figure is nonetheless deceptively conservative as Rummel ignored numerous democides by successive US governments and other governments he favored, such as the approximate 30% of the North Korean population that was killed by US bombing and chemical warfare [91]. The reason for this neglect can presumably be traced to his palpable American jingoism and his unshakable adoration for democracy. Having not learned from studying the history of government-sanctioned democides, genocides, and holocausts, Rummel vehemently supported President George Bush, who told 935 lies about Iraq between 9/11 and the war of aggression against Iraq in March 2003 [92].

Notwithstanding this "technicality" and that the Iraq war violated international and US law, he labeled the War on Terror, "George Bush's democratic peace foreign policy [93, 94]." He, furthermore, advocated destabilizing the North Korean regime through assassinations and military force, even if it would kill a million people, in order to democratize the country [95]. Thus, in 2014 when it was well known that the War on Terror had killed millions through violence and war-imposed deprivation, Rudolph Rummel died as a warmonger and as an inciter and intellectual facilitator of genocides and democides [96]. Rummel, despite having a profound knowledge of state-sanctioned violence, never questioned the institution of government and naively went along with the fallacious and widespread notion that we need democracy and elect the right people in order to prevent wars, genocides, holocausts, and democides [97]. In any event, Rummel's overall conclusion cannot be challenged: "Power kills, absolute power kills absolutely [98]."

Governments, whether they are democratic or dictatorial, have a monopoly on violence, lawmaking, and money printing. Corporations, in particular, the top players of what constitutes the psychopharmaceutical complex and the industrial-military/security complex, control by economic means the force of government in order to create or protect their monopolies. Corporations are able to bribe, coerce, or manipulate governments into granting them unparalleled powers, which without government would not have been possible, for instance, the power to enforce fluoridation and vaccination by law, and inflate military spending and in the process make war and related matters very profitable businesses. In 2018, the world's military expenditures approximated two trillion dollars worldwide [99]. War is so profitable that the British have invaded 193 countries, Australia 85, France 82, the US 72 (52 after WW2), Germany 39, Japan 30, Russia 25, Canada 25, and Israel 12 [100]. The so-called democratic peace theory, which holds that liberal democracies exercise peaceful foreign relations, is empirically false. While war is profitable for corporations, governments force taxpayers to give up their property in order to finance wars. Government is a control mechanism used to extract wealth from the masses. The wellbeing of voters or humanity, in general, is not a priority of governments. For instance, since September 11, 2001, about 29 million Americans have died avoidably from "all kinds of 'life-style' or 'socio-political choice' reasons (smoking, vehicle crashes, alcohol, etc.);" yet, US governments have spent about $6 trillion on wars in Iraq and Afghanistan [100, 101]. In lieu of trying to save the lives of 29 million Americans at home, the industrial-military/security complex has been enriched, and millions have been murdered in the Middle East and North Africa.

Even if elected officials paid heed to the opinion of the majority (an impossibility due to diversity of opinions), their existence is nonetheless illegitimate as it is made possible through taxation without consent, which enables them to maintain power. However, taxation is never a sufficient revenue source for governments, so massive loans are necessary. In 2019, the total world government debt surpassed $70 trillion, around $10,000 for every person in the world [102]; government is the most economically irresponsible institution in history. Taxation without consent is theft as it violates people's property rights, but becomes robbery when the instrument of force is introduced. In an essay on taxation, professor of philosophy, Michael Huemer, describes what it means when a government "taxes" citizens: "[It means] that the government demands money from each citizen, under a threat of force: if you do not pay, armed agents hired by the government will take you away and lock you in a cage [103]." Lysander Spooner, a 19th-century philosopher, is noted for saying, "If taxation without consent is not robbery, then any band of robbers have only to declare themselves a government, and all their robberies are legalized [104]." In his book The Constitution of no Authority, he elaborated on taxation as robbery regardless of the pretensions and number of people involved: "Taking a man's money without his consent, is also as much robbery, when it is done by millions of men, acting in concert, and calling themselves a government, as when it is done by a single individual, acting on his own responsibility, and calling himself a highwayman. Neither the numbers engaged in the act, nor the different characters they assume as a cover for the act, alter the nature of the act itself [105]."

When we take a closer look at taxation, it becomes clear that it is the greatest single facilitator of most democides, genocides, and wars as these are primarily financed through taxation or even used as the active agent to starve populations to death. For example, under British occupation, the Indians were overtaxed and "despite a very high birth rate, the Indian population did not increase between 1860 (292 million) and 1934 (292 million)," and it has been estimated that 745 million Indians died avoidably from deprivation in this period [106]. It gets worse because the British occupation started in 1757 and ended in 1947, during which "1.8 billion Indians died avoidably from egregious deprivation" pursuant to Dr. Gideon Polya, one of the world's leading experts on avoidable mortality [106]. Similarly, through taxation, world governments have financed their obsession with holocaust-weapons. In 1986, governments had an estimated 70,300 active nuclear weapons ready to be launched enough to kill all humans on earth multiple times; taxation is not for the benefit of the people, but for the enrichment of the elite [107].

Making matters worse is that governments are dedicated to secrecy. For example, between October 1, 2013, and September 30, 2014, the Obama administration classified 77.5 million documents, despite promises of transparency [108]. Similar trends are apparent in other countries, with the difference being that the US is relatively forthcoming regarding their secrecy. You will never fully know or understand what your government is doing behind the scenes.

With the possible exception of religion, if any other institution had murdered more than 262,000,000 people in one century alone (democide only concerns unarmed civilians, not soldiers), it would have been abandoned by now; yet, people ignore the atrocious history of governments that continues to the present and proclaim their faith in elected officials to solve problems, the most dangerous of all beliefs.

If we make the false assumption that democratic governments represent the prevailing opinion of their respective populations, then the people should, technically speaking, be held accountable for actions undertaken by these officials. For example, in 2016, the US dropped at least 26,171 bombs (a "low" estimate admittedly) in Iraq, Syria, Afghanistan, Libya,

Yemen, Somalia, and Pakistan [109]. These 2016 atrocities were committed under the authority of Barack Obama, the 2009 Nobel Peace Prize winner who during his presidency oversaw the bombing of "wedding parties, funerals, kid's soccer games, hospitals, schools, people in their homes and walking their streets, and farmers tilling their fields [110-115]." If populations started being personally responsible for the actions of state officials, such as spending time in prison for war crimes, then the institution of government would presumably be abandoned rapidly.

Governments' abysmal humanitarian track record should be ample evidence for us to conclude that a social crediting system will, with little doubt, lead to atrocities. If, on the other hand, we believe that our elected government can and will solve problems for the benefit of the masses, an absurd belief, then as Voltaire said, "we shall commit atrocities [116]."

Originally published as "One World Digital Dictatorship," crimeandpower.com, January 2020.

References

1. "Chinese app offers map of "deadbeat debtors" near you"
https://boingboing.net/2019/01/24/chinese-app-offers-map-of-de.html
2. "Forget to leash your dog? Chinese credit scoring system for owners means you could lose your pet"
https://www.scmp.com/tech/policy/article/2170400/forget-leash-your-dog-chinese-credit-scoring-system-owners-means-you
3. "上海新规：子女拒不回家看看或影响当事人信用"
www.finance.sina.com.cn/sf/news/2016-04-07/101626350.html
4. "Debtors in China are placed on a blacklist that prohibits them from flying, buying train tickets, and staying at luxury hotels"
https://www.businessinsider.com/chinas-tax-blacklist-shames-debtors-2017-12?r=US&IR=T
5. "China launches 'spy bird' drone to boost government surveillance"
https://www.independent.co.uk/life-style/gadgets-and-tech/news/china-spy-bird-drone-government-surveillance-a8415766.html
6. "IDC predicts China to have 2.76 billion surveillance cameras by 2022"
https://kr-asia.com/idc-predicts-china-to-have-2-76-billion-surveillance-cameras-by-2022
7. "A Look Inside China's Social Credit System | NBC News Now"
https://www.youtube.com/watch?v=0cGB8dCDf3c
8. "China scored 99.9 percent conviction rate last year"
https://www.washingtonpost.com/news/morning-mix/wp/2014/03/11/china-scored-99-9-percent-conviction-rate-last-year/
9. "Executed Chinese teenager found innocent 18 years on"
http://www.hurriyetdailynews.com/executed-chinese-teenager-found-innocent-18-years-on-75633
10. Gross et al. "Rate of false conviction of criminal defendants who are sentenced to death." National Academy of Sciences (2001)
https://doi.org/10.1073/pnas.1306417111
11. "Prisons are packed because prosecutors are coercing plea deals. And, yes, it's totally legal." https://www.nbcnews.com/think/opinion/prisons-are-packed-because-prosecutors-are-coercing-plea-deals-yes-ncna1034201
12. "The National Registry of Exonerations"
https://www.law.umich.edu/special/exoneration/Pages/Exonerations-in-the-United-States-Map.aspx
13. "Immediate executions follow 15 death sentences in China"
https://www.irishtimes.com/news/immediate-executions-follow-15-death-sentences-in-china-1.439360
14. "SHORT FORM of THE CHINA TRIBUNAL'S JUDGMENT"
https://chinatribunal.com/wp-content/uploads/2019/06/Short-Form-Conclusion-China-Tribunal.pdf
15. "The International Coalition to End Transplant Abuse in China"
https://endtransplantabuse.org
16. "Doctor Says He Took Transplant Organs From Executed Chinese Prisoners" https://www.nytimes.com/2001/06/29/world/doctor-says-he-took-

transplant-organs-from-executed-chinese-prisoners.html
17. "China putting minority Muslims in 'concentration camps,' U.S. says" https://www.reuters.com/article/us-usa-china-concentrationcamps-idUSKCN1S925K
18. "Secret papers reveal workings of China's Xinjiang detention camps" https://www.aljazeera.com/news/2019/11/secret-papers-reveal-workings-chinas-xinjiang-detention-camps-191125004212642.html
19. "Remarks by Vice President Pence on the Administration's Policy Toward China" https://www.whitehouse.gov/briefings-statements/remarks-vice-president-pence-administrations-policy-toward-china/
20. "Chinese-Style Social Credit System Is a 'Threat' to Russia, Deputy PM Says" https://www.themoscowtimes.com/2018/11/12/chinese-style-social-credit-system-is-threat-to-russia-deputy-pm-says-a63462
21. "Germany edges toward Chinese-style rating of citizens" https://www.handelsblatt.com/today/politics/big-data-vs-big-brother-germany-edges-toward-chinese-style-rating-of-citizens/23581140.html?ticket=ST-33429918-GVpfKPrTyukpP07CqGGM-ap1
22. "What is SCHUFA: your credit record" https://www.settle-in-berlin.com/what-is-schufa/
23. "80% of Russians Will Have State-Gathered 'Digital Profiles' by 2025, Official Says" https://www.themoscowtimes.com/2018/09/28/80-percent-russians-will-have-state-gathered-digital-profiles-by-2025-official-says-a63027
24. "Russia Spending Billions on National Digital Economic Development Programs" https://www.russia-briefing.com/news/russia-spending-billions-national-digital-economic-development-programmes.html/
25. "Scientists warn of potential serious health effects of 5G" https://ehtrust.org/wp-content/uploads/Scientist-5G-appeal-2017.pdf
26. Ramyar Rashed Mohassel et al., "A Survey on Advanced Metering Infrastructure," International Journal of Electrical Power & Energy Systems. http://www.sciencedirect.com/science/article/pii/S0142061514003743
27. " Health Experts Caution About Smart Meters " https://www.saferemr.com/2015/02/health-experts-caution-about-smart.html
28. "FIND FACE" https://findface.pro/en/
29. "In just two years, 9,000 of these cameras were installed to spy on your car" https://qz.com/1540488/in-just-two-years-9000-of-these-cameras-were-installed-to-spy-on-your-car/
30. "FBI, ICE find state driver's license photos are a gold mine for facial-recognition searches" https://www.washingtonpost.com/technology/2019/07/07/fbi-ice-find-state-drivers-license-photos-are-gold-mine-facial-recognition-searches/
31. "Unregulated Police Face Recognition in America" https://www.perpetuallineup.org
32. "Executive Order Protecting The Nation From Foreign Terrorist Entry Into The United States" https://www.whitehouse.gov/presidential-actions/executive-order-protecting-nation-foreign-terrorist-entry-united-states-2/

33. "Biometric Entry-Exit Program" https://epic.org/foia/dhs/cbp/biometric-entry-exit/Concept-of-Operations.pdf
34. "Police Use of Facial Recognition Is Accepted by British Court" https://www.nytimes.com/2019/09/04/business/facial-recognition-uk-court.html
35. "Almost 30% of retailers use facial recognition technology to track consumers in store" https://www.computerweekly.com/news/4500253499/Almost-30-of-retailers-use-facial-recognition-technology-to-track-consumers-in-store
36. "Facial Recognition 'Epidemic' in the UK" https://bigbrotherwatch.org.uk/all-media/facial-recognition-epidemic-in-the-uk/
37. "Greater Manchester Police monitored every visitor to Trafford Centre for SIX MONTHS using controversial technology until they were told to stop" https://www.manchestereveningnews.co.uk/news/greater-manchester-news/gmp-trafford-centre-camera-monitored-15278943
38. "Businessman with Beijing ties looks to bring face-recognition tech to Canadian stores" https://nationalpost.com/news/pay-with-your-face-ontario-grocery-chain-looks-at-paying-via-facial-recognition
39. "Russia Is Building One of the World's Largest Facial Recognition Networks" https://www.themoscowtimes.com/2019/11/12/russia-building-one-of-worlds-largest-facial-recognition-networks-a68139
40. "France to become first EU country to use nationwide facial recognition ID app" https://www.telegraph.co.uk/news/2019/10/03/france-become-first-eu-country-use-nationwide-facial-recognition
41. "German police expand use of facial recognition software: report" www.xinhuanet.com/english/2018-03/21/c_137055203.htm
42. "Plan for massive facial recognition database sparks privacy concerns" https://www.theguardian.com/technology/2019/sep/29/plan-for-massive-facial-recognition-database-sparks-privacy-concerns
43. https://twitter.com/apf_oz
44. "Australia proposed using facial recognition technology for online gambling and pornography age verification" https://www.privateinternetaccess.com/blog/2019/11/australia-proposed-using-facial-recognition-technology-for-online-gambling-and-pornography-age-verification/
45. "Request For Proposal To procure National Automated Facial Recognition System (AFRS)" ncrb.gov.in/TENDERS/AFRS/RFP_NAFRS.pdf
46. "India is trying to build the world's biggest facial recognition system" https://edition.cnn.com/2019/10/17/tech/india-facial-recognition-intl-hnk/index.html
47. "India setting up world's biggest facial recognition system" https://www.dw.com/en/india-setting-up-worlds-biggest-facial-recognition-system/a-51147243
48. "India aims to build world's biggest facial recognition system: Report" https://www.bgr.in/news/india-aims-to-build-worlds-biggest-facial-recognition-system-report-854992/

49. "India is trying to build the world's biggest facial recognition system" https://edition.cnn.com/2019/10/17/tech/india-facial-recognition-intl-hnk/index.html
50. "Vault 7: Projects" https://wikileaks.org/vault7/
51. "5 Eyes, 9 Eyes And 14 Eyes Alliance Explained" https://www.privacyend.com/5-eyes-9-eyes-14-eyes-intelligence-alliance/
52. "Five Eyes, Nine Eyes, 14 Eyes – Explained" https://restoreprivacy.com/5-eyes-9-eyes-14-eyes/
53. "Mandatory vaccinations: The international landscape" https://www.ncbi.nlm.nih.gov/pmc/articles/PMC3216445/
54. "Timeline of Gun Control in the United States" https://www.thoughtco.com/us-gun-control-timeline-3963620
55. "Communication in China: political economy, power, and conflict" https://books.google.dk/books/about/Communication_in_China.html?id=WUMcAQAAIAAJ&redir_esc=y
56. "Text of the USA PATRIOT Act" https://www.aclu.org/other/text-usa-patriot-act
57. "Exporting the Patriot Act? Democracy and the 'War on Terror' in the Third World" https://www.jstor.org/stable/20454977?seq=1
58. "YouTube CEO Wojcicki: We've Cut Amount Of Time Americans Watch "Controversial Content" By 70%" https://www.realclearpolitics.com/video/2019/12/02/youtube_ceo_wojcicki_weve_cut_amount_of_time_americans_watch_controversial_content_by_70.html
59. "NYC Commission on Human Rights Announces Strong Protections for City's Transgender and Gender Non-Conforming Communities in Housing, Employment and Public Spaces" https://www1.nyc.gov/office-of-the-mayor/news/961-15/nyc-commission-human-rights-strong-protections-city-s-transgender-gender
60. "Bradley Manning sentenced to 35 years in WikiLeaks case" https://www.washingtonpost.com/world/national-security/judge-to-sentence-bradley-manning-today/2013/08/20/85bee184-09d0-11e3-b87c-476db8ac34cd_story.html
61. "UN expert on torture sounds alarm again that Julian Assange's life may be at risk" https://www.ohchr.org/EN/NewsEvents/Pages/DisplayNews.aspx?NewsID=25249&LangID=
62. "Gun Detection" https://athena-security.com/gun-detection
63. "Reconstructing Visual Experiences from Brain Activity Evoked by Natural Movies" https://www.ncbi.nlm.nih.gov/pmc/articles/PMC3326357/
64. "Scientists use brain imaging to reveal the movies in our mind" https://news.berkeley.edu/2011/09/22/brain-movies/
65. "Reconstructing Perceived and Retrieved Faces from Activity Patterns in Lateral Parietal Cortex" https://www.jneurosci.org/content/36/22/6069.long
66. "Brain-Computer Interfaces and Neuroscience " https://www.psychologytoday.com/us/blog/the-future-brain/201808/brain-computer-interfaces-and-neuroscience
67. "Japanese scientists claim 'mind-reading' ability in fresh study"

https://www.rt.com/news/328052-japanese-read-thoughts-words/

68. "Reading Mind Technology" www.nanostuffs.com/blog/?p=4701

69. "Penny for your thoughts? Scientists develop mind-reading "brain decoder" that reveals our inner thoughts using sound waves" https://www.cityam.com/mind-reading-possible-new-brain-decoder-can-translate-your-inner-voice-using-sound-waves/

70. "Mind Control of Machines Isn't Brain Surgery Any More" https://www.afcea.org/content/mind-control-machines-isnt-brain-surgery-any-more

71. "Elon Musk's Secretive Brain Tech Company Debuts a Sophisticated Neural Implant" https://www.scientificamerican.com/article/elon-musks-secretive-brain-tech-company-debuts-a-sophisticated-neural-implant1/

72. "Elon Musk: Humans must merge with machines or become irrelevant in AI age" https://www.cnbc.com/2017/02/13/elon-musk-humans-merge-machines-cyborg-artificial-intelligence-robots.html

73. "Elon Musk says he's tested his brain microchip on monkeys, and it enabled one to control a computer with its mind" https://www.businessinsider.com/elon-musk-neuralink-brain-microchip-tested-on-monkeys-2019-7?r=DE&IR=T

74. "Elon Musk Wants To Connect Human Brains Directly To Computers Next Year" https://www.thedailybeast.com/elon-musk-unveils-neuralink-brain-computer-interface-wants-to-have-human-trials-in-2020

75. "Facebook working on smart glasses with Ray-Ban, code-named 'Orion'" https://www.cnbc.com/2019/09/17/facebook-enlists-ray-ban-maker-luxottica-to-make-orion-ar-glasses.html

76. "Mark Zuckerberg says brain-reading wearables are coming, but certain functions may require implanted devices" https://www.cnbc.com/2019/10/10/zuckerberg-says-brain-reading-wearables-come-before-implantables.html

77. "New commentary on neuroethics published in Nature" https://gallantlab.org/papers/nature-neuroethics-commentary/

78. "What is Cortana?" https://support.microsoft.com/en-us/help/17214/cortana-what-is

79. "iPhone Users: Pokémon GO Can Spy On Your Entire Google Account — UPDATED " https://www.forbes.com/sites/thomasbrewster/2016/07/11/pokemon-go-google-privacy-disaster/#391e326a3cde

80. "Calif. utilities yield energy-use data" https://www.sfgate.com/business/article/Calif-utilities-yield-energy-use-data-4611159.php

81. "Crypto Markets Pump As President Xi Calls Blockchain a 'Breakthrough'" https://bitcoinist.com/china-president-xi-blockchain-breakthrough/

82. "List Of Countries That Have Plans To Roll Out Their Own Cryptocurrencies" https://coinsutra.com/national-cryptocurrencies/

83. "Why are people referring to Blockchain as the New internet?" https://www.blockchain-council.org/blockchain/why-are-people-referring-to-blockchain-as-the-new-internet/

84. "Bitcoin: A Peer-to-Peer Electronic Cash System" satoshinakamoto.me/bitcoin.pdf

85. "A First For Manhattan: $30M Real Estate Property Tokenized With Blockchain " https://www.forbes.com/sites/rachelwolfson/2018/10/03/a-first-for-manhattan-30m-real-estate-property-tokenized-with-blockchain/#4c25381e4895

86. "Blockchain Technology Explained (2 Hour Course)" https://www.youtube.com/watch?v=qOVAbKKSH10

87. "Real-life Blockchain Use Cases in Automotive" https://openledger.info/insights/blockchain-use-cases-automotive-industry/

88. "Car Manufacturer Daimler AG Launches Crypto Coin as a Reward for Eco-Friendly Drivers" https://interestingengineering.com/car-manufacturer-daimler-ag-launches-crypto-coin-as-a-reward-for-eco-friendly-drivers

89. "Freedom, Democracy, Peace; Power, Democide, and War" https://hawaii.edu/powerkills/welcome.html

90. "20TH CENTURYDEMOCIDE " https://hawaii.edu/powerkills/20TH.HTM

91. "KNOW THE FACTS: North Korea lost close to 30% of its population as a result of US bombings in the 1950s" https://www.globalresearch.ca/know-the-facts-north-korea-lost-close-to-30-of-its-population-as-a-result-of-us-bombings-in-the-1950s/22131

92. Lewis, Charles (2014). 935 Lies: The Future of Truth and the Decline of America's Moral Integrity. PublicAffairs.

93. "American Monster: Chris Kyle, the American Sniper" https://www.crimeandpower.com/2019/09/28/american-monster-chris-kyle-the-american-sniper/

94. "All novels/books DOWNLOADABLE and FREE in PDF" https://hawaii.edu/powerkills/NH.HTM#SUPPLEMENT

95. "The Democidal Famine In North Korea" https://www.orthodoxytoday.org/articles4/RummelKorea.php

96. "Paris Atrocity Context: 27 Million Muslim Avoidable Deaths From Imposed Deprivation In 20 Countries Violated By US Alliance Since 9-11" https://www.countercurrents.org/polya221115A.htm

97. "The Democratic Peace" https://hawaii.edu/powerkills/MIRACLE.HTM

98. "POWER KILLS" https://www.hawaii.edu/powerkills/PK.CHAP1.HTM

99. "World military expenditure grows to $1.8 trillion in 2018" https://www.sipri.org/media/press-release/2019/world-military-expenditure-grows-18-trillion-2018

100. "Ongoing Global Avoidable Mortality Holocaust and Horrendous Human Carnage from War and Hegemony" https://www.crimeandpower.com/2019/12/09/ongoing-global-avoidable-mortality-holocaust-and-horrendous-human-carnage-from-war-and-hegemony/

101. "American Holocaust, Millions Of Untimely American Deaths And $40 Trillion Cost Of Israel To Americans" https://www.countercurrents.org/polya270813.htm

102. "World Debt Clock" https://commodity.com/debt-clock/

103. "Is Taxation Theft?" https://www.libertarianism.org/columns/is-

taxation-theft

104. "Lysander Spooner" https://www.goodreads.com/quotes/1240517-if-taxation-without-consent-is-not-robbery-then-any-band

105. "The Constitution of no Authority" https://en.wikisource.org/wiki/No_Treason/6#16

106. "Britain Robbed India of $45 Trillion & Thence 1.8 Billion Indians Died From Deprivation" https://www.crimeandpower.com/2019/10/27/britain-robbed-india-of-45-trillion-thence-1-8-billion-indians-died-from-deprivation/

107. "Status of World Nuclear Forces" https://fas.org/issues/nuclear-weapons/status-world-nuclear-forces/

108. "The Government Is Classifying Too Many Documents" https://www.thenation.com/article/the-government-is-classifying-too-many-documents/

109. "How Many Bombs Did the United States Drop in 2016?" https://web.archive.org/web/20170106155853/https://blogs.cfr.org/zenko/2017/01/05/bombs-dropped-in-2016/

110. "Obama The War Criminal Butcherer of Women and Children" https://www.paulcraigroberts.org/2017/01/11/obama-the-war-criminal-butcherer-of-women-and-children/

111. "The Wedding That Became a Funeral: U.S. Still Silent One Year on From Deadly Yemen Drone Strike" https://www.newsweek.com/wedding-became-funeral-us-still-silent-one-year-deadly-yemen-drone-strike-291403

112. "Doctors Without Borders Hospital Bombing: Witnesses Recount Strikes" https://www.nbcnews.com/news/world/doctors-without-borders-hospital-bombing-witnesses-recount-strikes-n438506

113. "U.S. Drone Strike Said to Kill 60 in Pakistan" https://www.nytimes.com/2009/06/24/world/asia/24pstan.html

114. " Victim of Obama's first drone strike: 'I am the living example of what drones are' " https://www.theguardian.com/world/2016/jan/23/drone-strike-victim-barack-obama

115. "Most US drone strikes in Pakistan attack houses" https://www.thebureauinvestigates.com/stories/2014-05-23/most-us-drone-strikes-in-pakistan-attack-houses

116. "Voltaire > Quotes > Quotable Quote" https://www.goodreads.com/quotes/544453-if-we-believe-absurdities-we-shall-commit-atrocities

Public Enemy Number One: Government, not Drugs!

Søren Roest Korsgaard

Governments have learned that laws can be used as revenue and control measures by criminalizing more and more of human activity. Indeed, the term "criminal" is now meaningless as law enforcement has become a greater threat to ordinary people than actual "criminals."

At an accelerating rate, western governments are criminalizing victimless trivialities for profit and control of the masses. In Denmark, the laws governing unemployment benefits are more than 36,000 pages and grow by almost seven pages daily on average. A massive 20,000 laws have been formulated to control ownership and use of guns in the US. The taxfoundation.org has shown that in order to understand and comply with US tax laws one must go through about 80,000 pages. The UK is more moderate as the British tax code is only in excess of 17,000 pages. On the other hand, the Old Testament's 613 laws that are spread over 929 chapters appear quite moderate to the totalitarian conditions created by governments. As it is impossible for a person to peruse all the required pages in order to comply with the laws, we are all probable criminals. Thus, the word "criminal" has effectively lost its meaning.

Regardless of which country you find yourself in, the government of that country is everyday criminalizing previously conceived normal behavior in which there is no victim. However, as we shall see in the following, such laws produce millions of victims and "new criminals" who hitherto were law-abiding citizens. Lawmakers and power brokers inform us that without these laws society would explode into chaos and fury, and to ensure order and social control, laws governing every aspect of human behavior must be enacted. They often fail to mention, however, that Nazi Germany was an orderly society kept in place by thousands of laws. As philosopher Jerry Day has observed, "Order may be nothing more than evidence of tyranny. Order may be nothing more than the prohibitions on freedom, the elimination of rights and the suppression of liberty. You are just as unsafe when things are too orderly as when they are disorderly [1]."

Coercive monopoly is a term that is mostly used in economics to describe an organization that maintains its status as the exclusive supplier of a certain good or service via the threat of force (legal or non-legal). It is clear that governments exercise coercive monopoly of legislation. They ban competitors from entering the market and are in full control of definitions, design, and implementation of legislations. As we shall see via example, this has been a disaster for millions of people in full agreement with the American economist Murray Rothbard who observed that "a coercive monopolist will tend to perform his service badly and inefficiently [2]."

Public Enemy Number One

A good example to illustrate the disastrous consequences of government coercive monopoly of legislation is that of drug laws. Most governments worldwide have formulated thousands of laws for a variety of arbitrarily chosen substances and waged war on private persons who want to use and distribute these. President Nixon set an example to the world by launching the US War on Drugs in 1971.

While Nixon declared that drugs are "public enemy number one [3]," history has shown that anti-drug policies of governments have resulted in millions of incarcerations, one trillion dollars in tax revenue have been used on a war that is failing and –as we shall see – hundreds of thousands of people have been murdered by reckless anti-drug governments worldwide. The official rationale for launching drug wars is the notorious concept of deterrence. Drug policy initiatives are intended to deter production, distribution, and consumption. Notwithstanding the rationale, numerous detailed reports attest to direct US government involvement in illicit production and distribution of drugs. For example, San Jose Mercury investigative reporter Gary Webb found an abundance of evidence for CIA involvement in drug trade and how they had helped foster the crack epidemic of the 1980s [4]. The Mercury published his findings, after which the CIA used its media assets, such as the Washington Post, to carry on a campaign against Webb to discredit him. Investigative reporters got the message and have not looked into the CIA's presence in the Afghan opium drug trade despite the massive growth under US occupation of Afghanistan's opium share of the world market. The Taliban had suppressed the opium trade, but under US occupation the percentage of the world market supplied by Afghanistan rose from about 6% in 2001 to 93% in 2007 [5].

Opium poppy cultivation in Afghanistan, 1994-2017 (Hectares)

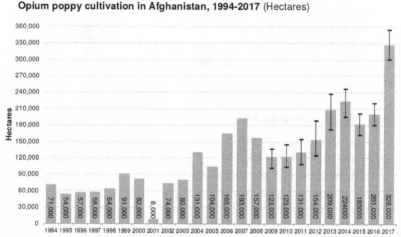

Opium poppy cultivation in Afghanistan, 1994-2017 [6] (the vertical lines represent upper and lower bounds of the 95% confidence interval).

Drug Legislation is a Business Model

An explosion in drug laws and incarcerations saw the light of the day after President Nixon launched the US War on Drugs in 1971. After 50 years of stable incarceration rates, the number of US prisoners went from 161 per 100,000 population in 1972 to 767 per 100,000 in 2007, almost a five-fold increase. In 2007, federal and state prisons and local jails held nearly 2.3 million inmates (over 20% of the world's prisoners), but if parolees and probationers are included, the total US correctional population exceeded 7 million [7]. If all of them lived in a single city, only New York would have more residents.

Prisoners have become integrated into the corporate world as privately owned prisons and forced labor have become big businesses. Corporations who owe their low labor cost to prison labor have a vested interest in harsh sentences and expansion of the already seemingly infinite number of laws. Criminalization of virtually everything is furthermore a necessity for the continued operation and expansion of inflated states, and consequently governments on a global scale collect billions of dollars in revenue from penalties and fees. In many countries, the tax burden cannot be significantly increased any further (e.g. in Denmark it is effectively 80%) and the state's survival and growth are becoming increasingly dependent upon revenue from penalties. Thus, more laws need to be written and enacted.

The Drug War is a Designed Failure

Prohibition of drugs does not deter people from using them. If harsh drug laws deterred people from drugs, not many offenders would be found in correctional facilities with a drug offense on their rap sheet. If we consider the 2015 statistics for people on probation and parole, 25% and 31% respectively had a drug charge as their most serious offense, a total of 1,217,305 people [8]. In 2016, 47% and 15% respectively of federal and state prisoners were in prison for drug violations, their most serious offense [8]. In 2017, federal agents and state police made 1,632,921 arrests for drugs violations whereof 85.4% of these arrests were for possession [9]. These numbers clearly show that harsher sentences do not deter people from drugs. This was also echoed in a study by the Pew Research Center which showed that drug use, drug arrest, and overdose death had no statistically significant relationship with drug imprisonment. That is, higher incarceration rates did not deter people from drugs [10].

Moreover, prohibition leads to secondary crimes as indicated by a study that showed "17% of state and 18% of federal prisoners committed their crimes to obtain money for drugs [8]." If cigarettes, alcohol, and chocolate were outlawed tomorrow, prices would rise, vicious syndicates would appear and people would commit real crimes, including robbery and theft in order to get their preferred stimulant. Prohibition of alcohol in the US and elsewhere produced a new class of criminal activity. It should come as no surprise that a study by Coyne et al concluded that "prohibition is not only ineffective, but counterproductive, at achieving the goals of policymakers both domestically and abroad … the domestic War on Drugs has contributed to an increase in drug overdoses and fostered and sustained the creation of powerful drug cartels [11]."

Getting access to drug war expenditures is notoriously difficult, but a 2010 estimate showed that one trillion dollars in tax revenue have been spent on the War on Drugs since 1971 [12]. Nevertheless a multiyear study, published in the British Medical Journal by Werb et al, concluded that "expanding efforts at controlling the global illegal drug market through law enforcement are failing [13]." It appears that the US War on Drugs has been a disaster for the average American, but has enriched certain powerful organizations.

Governments are the Biggest Drug Dealers

Some governments not only participate in the illegal drug trade, but also approve the production and sale of addictive drugs by private businesses. In the following, the focus is on the US although the dynamics are not much different elsewhere.

Many of the drugs that can be purchased on the street from your average drug dealer have been approved by the FDA, including amphetamines, MDMA, opioids, psilocybin, and methamphetamine. One of these drugs is called Adzenys which is a formulation of amphetamine, even so it has been approved by the FDA for children. This amphetamine drug comes in "great-tasting" fruit and candy flavors for children who do not like taking pills. Possible side effects include addiction, heart attack, and death.

Large pharmaceutical corporations which have deep financial ties to policymakers produce and distribute these drugs on a grand scale. The US government cashes in on the drugs via taxation and through campaign contributions from these multibillion dollar industries. Transparency International concludes: "Pharmaceutical companies can unduly influence national political systems through their large spending power. Pharmaceutical companies often fund candidates that support their position on key issues. Outside of elections, the pharmaceutical industry spends vast sums of money lobbying [14]."

Professor Peter Gøtzsche, former director of the independent Nordic Cochrane Centre, shows in his book, Deadly Medicines and Organised Crime: How Big Pharma Has Corrupted Healthcare, that legalized drugs kill at least 200,000 Americans and also 200,000 Europeans every year [15]. Half of those people take their drugs as prescribed, the other half die because of contraindications and accidental overdoses. Data from the CDC show that in 2017, heroin and cocaine killed 15,482 and 13,942 Americans respectively. However, 88,000 died from alcohol related causes, over 480,000 from tobacco, but zero died from a cannabis overdose [16]. With these numbers in mind it is clear that the motivational forces behind the War on Drugs are not humanitarian.

The Filipino Holocaust

While it is well-known that the US is the world's leader in imprisonment of drug users and sellers, it is lesser known that the US War on Drugs has resulted in thousands of killings by police officers and federal agents as well as by other means. As police are seldom held accountable for their crimes, the legal and constitutional protections of citizens are being lost. Drugwarrant.com lists some of these deaths. In 1999, police officers murdered Ismael Mena when they raided his house looking for drugs. They had the wrong address. In 2000, Curt Ferryman sat in his car when a Drug Enforcement Administration officer knocked on the window with his pistol to get his attention. The gun went off killing Curt. In 2003, Alberta Spruill was getting dressed for work when police officers who acted on a tip related to drugs threw a grenade into her apartment. She had a heart attack and died. It was the wrong address.

In Asia, some policymakers have gone one step further and have systematically exterminated alleged drug lawbreakers. It has been reported that China executes drug offenders, sometimes immediately after sentencing. Rodrigo Duterte, the president of the Philippines who has an admitted history of drug use, directed his armed forces and officers in 2016 to indiscriminately murder alleged drug offenders without due process. It has been demonstrated in the Journal of Genocide that Duterte policies satisfy Gregory H. Stanton's eight stages of genocide: "symbolization, dehumanization, organization, polarization, preparation, extermination and denial [17]." A New York Times photojournalist, Daniel Berehulak, has reported that police officers heeded Duterte's call to "slaughter them all" and shot "anyone suspected of dealing or even using drugs [18]." One eyewitness to the ongoing carnage told him that "they are slaughtering us like animals [18]."

It was reported in 2017 that drug law enforcers and death squads directed by Duterte were dumping truckloads of corpses of alleged drug users and distributors at hospitals. Doctors said that the condition of the bodies indicated they had been executed. Duterte has expressed his genocidal intent and disregard for human rights on numerous occasions in a manner that has few historical precedents. He has said: "If you know of any addicts, go ahead and kill them yourself as getting their parents to do it would be too painful [19]," and "I don't care about human rights, believe me [20]." He has even compared his actions to those of Hitler: "Hitler massacred three million Jews [sic]. Now there are three million drug addicts … I'd be happy to slaughter them [21]."

Chito Gascon, the chairman of the Commission on Human Rights of the Philippines, stated in December 2018 that the death toll could be as high as 27,000 due to the drug war [22]. Assuming the figure is reasonably accurate and the murders continue at a constant rate, simple extrapolation shows that the drug war will approach 1,000,000 victims by 2100. Duterte will not live that long, but considering his popularity among other policymakers it is not unlikely that the war will continue unabated, especially if the systematic slaughter becomes integrated into the corporate world. While human rights groups and activists have condemned Duterte's methods, powerful policymakers have, perhaps not surprisingly, perceived it in quite a different light. In 2016, US President Trump and Duterte talked about the drug war among other things. Before Trump is quoted, it is advisable to think of the incredible carnage and horror taking place while they were talking: Execution of children, bodies being hurled onto trucks, mothers crying out hysterically and having nightmares over the loss of their loved ones. Trump told Duterte that you are doing it "the right way [23]."

President Maithripala Sirisena of Sri Lanka has similarly praised Duterte's war on drugs, saying "the war against crime and drugs carried out by you is an example to the whole world, and personally to me [24]." He added, "Drug menace is rampant in my country and I feel that we should follow your footsteps to control this hazard [24]."

The Mexican Holocaust

This article has briefly looked at the US and Philippine drug wars, but it is worth dedicating a footnote to the Mexican drug war. The government of Mexico decided in 2006 to go tough on drug offenders and militarized the conflict. The murder rate of Mexico had been declining since the 1990s and significantly declining from 2000 to 2007. As a consequence of the war, the homicide rate exploded soon after and reached a record high in 2018 [25]. Depending on which source is relied on, the homicide rate was 9.5 or as low as 7.9 in 2007 per 100,000 inhabitants while statisticians have informed us to deal with a new record high of 29 murders per 100,000 inhabitants in 2018 [26].

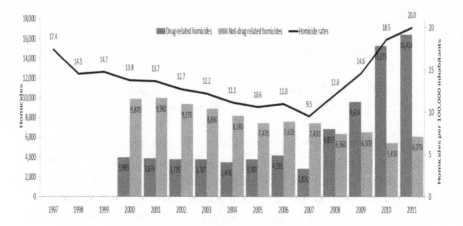

The above figure shows the number of homicides cases and homicides rates by type (1997 – 2011) [25]. Note that the drug-related homicides increased from 2,826 to 16,414 between 2007 and 2011. Drugpolicy.org estimates that the Mexican drug war has caused over 200,000 deaths since 2006. No one has ever assumed the task of estimating the all-time death toll of drug policies (indirect and direct death), but it is reasonable to assume that on the global scene, millions have perished.

The Portugal Approach

As opposed to eradication and imprisonment of alleged drug users and smugglers, Portugal decided in 2001 to decriminalize drug use (but not distribution) and made the decision to handle the problem as a social one rather than as a criminal one. For example, people with drug addiction would not be sent to prison, but would instead be directed to a panel of social workers, psychologists, legal advisers and then offered treatment. The government also made many other initiatives including anti-drug campaigns.

In a 2011 paper by Jordan Woods at the University of Arkansas, he showed that problematic drug use, such as intravenous drug use, dropped after 2001 while increasing in neighboring countries. This suggests that "decriminalization may have reduced the most harmful forms of drug use in Portugal [27]." Furthermore, Woods showed that Portugal was unparalleled in the EU in the number of drug related AIDS cases and had the second highest number of HIV cases among drug users. New

AIDS cases were increasing while decreasing in France, Spain and Italy. However, "drug-related disease" including new incidents of HIV and AIDS have "declined substantially" post decriminalization [27]. In the years preceding decriminalization, the number of acute drug-related deaths increased every year. From 1989 to 1999, drug related deaths increased more than tenfold, but this death rate declined significantly after decriminalization.

Is Anyone Safe?

There is no reasonable and objective method to assess what constitutes a "drug;" thus, cigarettes are legalized in most places despite the fact that "more deaths are caused each year by smoking tobacco than by all deaths from HIV, illegal drug use, alcohol use, motor injuries, suicides, and murders combined [28]." Smoking cannabis and other plants might get you imprisoned or massacred in the Philippines, but you can safely walk into a cafe in Amsterdam and smoke, drink or eat cannabis. Legal and moral relativity prevail. Governments in their criminalization schemes might change their definitions tomorrow and start to punish, kill, and terrorize former law abiding citizens. The problem is not drugs, but government overall and especially governments who perceive your body as their property.

Although this article has primarily focused on drug laws and wars. The discussion could revolve around a long list of topics, such as taxation. The universal axiom that nobody has the right to take or molest your property, without your consent, puts the practice of taxation into question. Tax evasion usually results in a lengthy prison sentence or a hefty fine. Recently, China executed tax evaders. If we take into consideration the complexity and length of China's tax regulations, it would appear that perceived tax evasion could easily stem from mix-ups and misunderstandings (85 million Chinese are illiterate). If taxation violates people's property rights, i.e. theft, as have been demonstrated in numerous papers, it shows that there is no limit as to what can be criminalized. Civil forfeiture is a non-controversial example of government approved theft. Civil forfeiture allows the US government to seize property (cash, cars, real estate, etc.) based on a subjective suspicion of criminal activity. The statistics are mind-boggling: In 80% of the cases charges are never filed against those who have had their property confiscated [29]. You are presumed guilty and you have to prove your own innocence – an almost impossible task for citizens who cannot afford superb legal assistance. A leaked memorandum from 1990 demonstrates the deliberate and criminal nature of civil forfeiture. The US Attorney General stated, "We must significantly increase forfeiture production to reach our budget target .... Every effort must be made to increase forfeiture income [30]."

Many will undoubtedly object to the data and arguments presented here, and simply put the blame on a few bad apples. In this regard, American economist, Dr. Robert Higgs, had this to say:

"We need not enumerate what proportion of cops appears to be good or listen to someone's anecdote about his uncle Charlie, an allegedly good cop. We need only consider the following:
a. A cop's job is to enforce the laws, all of them;
b. Many of the laws are manifestly unjust, and some are even cruel and wicked;
c. Therefore every cop has to agree to act as an enforcer for laws that are manifestly unjust or even cruel and wicked.
There are no good cops [31]."

Conclusion

At any time can harmless activities like smoking a certain plant or any other behavior you consider being a part of your daily activities, e.g. practicing a certain religion, be criminalized and police and federal agents will target you and destroy your existence. Every day governments define the word "criminal" more and more broadly. Eventually, by existence alone we will all be criminals.

Originally published as "Public Enemy Number One: Government, not Drugs!," CrimeAndPower.com, 2018.

References

1. "How Much Criminalization Will You Tolerate From Your Government?" https://www.youtube.com/watch?v=EZTMKfTP6P0
2. Rothbard, M. The Ethics of Liberty. New York University Press, 2002, p. 161.
3. "Public Enemy Number One: A Pragmatic Approach to America's Drug Problem" https://www.nixonfoundation.org/2016/06/26404/
4. Dark Alliance: The CIA, the Contras, and the Crack Cocaine Explosion, by Gary Webb. New York: Seven Stories Press, 1998.
5. "United Nations Office on Drugs and Crime: Afghanistan Opium Survey 2007 Executive Summary" https://www.unodc.org/documents/crop-monitoring/AFG07_ExSum_web.pdf
6. "United Nations Office on Drugs and Crime: Afghanistan Opium Survey 2017 Cultivation and Production" https://www.unodc.org/documents/crop-monitoring/Afghanistan/Afghan_opium_survey_2017_cult_prod_web.pdf
7. Parole and probation have grown far beyond resources allocated to support them www.theconversation.com/parole-and-probation-have-grown-far-beyond-resources-allocated-to-support-them-98372
8. "Drugs and the Correctional System (Prisons, Jails, Probation and Parole)" https://www.drugwarfacts.org/chapter/drug_prison
9. "Total Annual Arrests in the US by Type of Offense" https://www.drugwarfacts.org/node/235
10. "More Imprisonment Does Not Reduce State Drug Problems" https://www.pewtrusts.org/en/research-and-analysis/issue-briefs/2018/03/more-imprisonment-does-not-reduce-state-drug-problems
11. Coyne, Christopher J. and Hall, Abigail, Four Decades and Counting: The Continued Failure of the War on Drugs (April 12, 2017). Cato Institute Policy Analysis No. 811. Available at SSRN: https://ssrn.com/abstract=2979445
12. "AP IMPACT: After 40 years, $1 trillion, US War on Drugs has failed to meet any of its goals" https://www.foxnews.com/world/ap-impact-after-40-years-1-trillion-us-war-on-drugs-has-failed-to-meet-any-of-its-goals
13. "The temporal relationship between drug supply indicators: an audit of international government surveillance systems." https://www.ncbi.nlm.nih.gov/pubmed/24080093
14. "Corruption in the Pharmaceutical Sector" https://www.transparency.org.uk/publications/corruption-in-the-pharmaceutical-sector/
15. Deadly Medicines and Organised Crime: How Big Pharma Has Corrupted Healthcare, by Peter Gotzsche. Radcliffe Publishing Ltd, 2013.
16. Overdose Death Rates https://www.drugabuse.gov/related-topics/trends-statistics/overdose-death-rates
17. Is the Philippine "War on Drugs" an Act of Genocide? https://www.tandfonline.com/doi/abs/10.1080/14623528.2017.1379939
18. 'They Are Slaughtering Us Like Animals' https://www.nytimes.com/interactive/2016/12/07/world/asia/rodrigo-duterte-philippines-drugs-killings.html

19. Philippines president Rodrigo Duterte tells people to 'go ahead and kill' drug addicts https://www.independent.co.uk/news/world/asia/philippines-president-rodrigo-duterte-tells-people-to-go-ahead-and-kill-drug-addicts-a7116456.html

20. Rodrigo Duterte: 'I don't care about human rights' https://www.aljazeera.com/news/2016/08/rodrigo-duterte-human-rights-160806211448623.html

21. "Duterte: Hitler killed millions of Jews, I will kill millions of drug addicts" https://www.washingtonpost.com/news/worldviews/wp/2016/09/29/duterte-hitler-killed-3-million-jews-i-will-kill-3-million-drug-dealers/?noredirect=on

22. CHR chief: Drug war deaths could be as high as 27,000 https://news.abs-cbn.com/focus/12/05/18/chr-chief-drug-war-deaths-could-be-as-high-as-27000

23. Duterte: Trump says Philippines tackling drug problem 'the right way' https://www.edition.cnn.com/2016/12/03/politics/trump-duterte-phone-call/index.html

24. Duterte drug war 'an example to the whole world': Sri Lanka president https://news.abs-cbn.com/news/01/17/19/duterte-drug-war-an-example-to-the-whole-world-sri-lanka-president

25. Income Inequality and Violent Crime: Evidence from Mexico's Drug War documents.worldbank.org/curated/en/236161468299090847/pdf/WPS6935.pdf

26. Number of murders committed per 100,000 inhabitants in Mexico from 2009 to 2018 https://www.statista.com/statistics/714113/mexico-homicide-rate/

27. Woods, Jordan Blair, "A Decade after Drug Decriminalization: What can the United States learn from the Portugese Model?" University of the District of Columbia Law Review (Washington, DC: The University of the District of Columbia David A. Clarke School of Law, 2011) Volume 15, Number 1, pp. 19-20.

28. James E. White. Contemporary Moral Problems. Florence, KY: Thomson Wadsworth, 2009

29. "Asset Forfeiture Reform" www.drugpolicy.org/issues/asset-forfeiture-reform

30. "Seized Property In Crime Cases Causes Concern" https://www.nytimes.com/1993/05/31/us/seized-property-in-crime-cases-causes-concern.html

31. "There are no good cops. – Robert Higgs" https://www.reddit.com/r/quotes/comments/3zvx8r/there_are_no_good_cops_robert_higgs/

The United States is the Largest Prison Camp in the World

Introduction by Paul Craig Roberts

The United States has the highest incarceration rates in the world. The US not only has a far higher percentage of its population in prison than allegedly "authoritarian" governments, but also has a larger total number of citizens imprisoned than China, a country with four times the US population. The US is by far the largest prison camp in the world.

The conditions, such as solitary confinement, in which many US prisoners are kept are strictly illegal under international law, but that means nothing to "freedom and democracy America." Solitary confinement, especially confinement inside tiny cells, is like being buried alive. Yet, "freedom and democracy America" is subjecting more than 100,000 citizens to this horror as I write. We hear so much about "America's moral conscience," but where is this conscience?

Other prisoners are used as a cheap work force for US military and consumer industries. Prison labor and the privatization of prisons have created an enormous demand for prisoners. American citizens are shoveled into the profit-making prison system regardless of innocence or guilt.

There is no doubt that a large percentage of US prisoners are innocent or imprisoned for victimless crimes, such as drug use. According to official US government statistics, 97 percent of all felonies are settled with plea bargains. Consequently, the police evidence and prosecutor's case are never tested in court. Not even the innocents want a trial, because the jurors are brainwashed and biased against everyone charged, and the punishments that result from trial conviction are much harsher than those given to a compliant defendant who agrees to a plea bargain. Despite the US Constitution's prohibition of self-incrimination, the US prison population consists of people coerced into self-incrimination. There is no justice whatsoever in the US criminal justice (sic) system. See: The Tyranny of Good Intentions: How Prosecutors and Law Enforcement Are Trampling the Constitution in the Name of Justice.

"Law and order conservatives" have fantasy ideas about US prisoners lounging around watching TV all day, playing sports in the open air, and studying in prison libraries for law degrees—a life of leisure at public expense. Søren Korsgaard, editor of [CRIME and POWER], tells us what life inside an American prison is really like.

The United States Criminal Justice System Violates Human Rights

Søren Roest Korsgaard

The US criminal justice system has a long history, continuing to this day, of systematically violating prisoners' human rights and, hence, international law. Although it has moved away from executions of those who committed their crimes as minors, the justice system still condones wrongful executions as evidenced by a study from 2014, published in the Proceedings of the National Academy of Sciences, in which it was concluded, conservatively, that at least 1 in 25 of US death row inmates is innocent of the crime for which they were sentenced to death. Even though this figure, along with facts related to dubious executions, is readily available for public consumption, a massive 55-60% of the US population still supports the death penalty.

Considering that such polls are conducted, it is safe to say that most have given the death penalty some thought; however, the conditions of US prisons are evidently a rare topic of reflection or conversation, except that most informed citizens are, at least, somewhat acquainted with the practices associated with the Guantanamo Bay detention camp and other so-called 'black sites.' These practices, of course, include detention without charge or trial, various methods of torture, isolation, and indefinite imprisonment of minors in flagrant violation of international law. What is lesser known is that equally criminal human rights abuses take place in US maximum security facilities, so-called supermax prisons, and it is therefore essential that the conditions of these are put into the spotlight. In fact, as will be shown in this article, these supermax prisons have been specifically built for torture in the form of prolonged solitary confinement, which goes by many names including isolation, administrative segregation, management control units, protective custody, restrictive housing, and special needs units. What is solitary confinement? It is typically defined as the physical and social isolation of individuals who are confined to their cells for 22 to 24 hours per day. According to a detailed report by Amnesty International, the US "stands virtually alone in the world in incarcerating thousands of prisoners in long-term or indefinite solitary confinement," as more than 40 states operate supermax facilities, collectively housing over 25,000 inmates that are kept in near-constant solitary confinement. In other prisons, an additional 80,000 inmates are at any time kept in isolation for variable periods. Solitary confinement has become the first resort in many prisons, and it has been shown that even absurdities can lead to years in isolation. For example, men and women have been placed in isolation for "months or years not only for violent acts but for possessing contraband, testing positive for drug use, ignoring orders, or using profanity …. or report rape or abuse by prison officials." Perhaps the most absurd example concerns a group of Rastafarian men who were placed in solitary confinement, some for more than a decade, for refusing to cut their hair as it was fundamental to their faith. Human rights organizations have for a long time discouraged nations from using solitary confinement. For example, when UN's Special Rapporteur on torture and other inhuman punishment, Juan E. Méndez, delivered his report before the UN's General Assembly about solitary confinement, he absolutely condemned the use of prolonged isolation and equated it with torture. He added that it should only be used under "exceptional circumstances, for as short a time as possible." After citing various scientific studies, which showed that "lasting mental damage" can result from even a "few days of social isolation," he stated that "indefinite and prolonged solitary confinement" should be absolutely prohibited. Méndez also urged nations to end the practice of solitary confinement in pre-trial detention. Méndez's recommendations were later codified in the United Nations Standard Minimum Rules on the Treatment of Prisoners, known as the "Mandela Rules." Extremely harsh sentences and absurdities leading to isolation have also not gone unnoticed by the UN, especially in the context of underage offenders. Among others, Méndez has scolded the US for "being the only country in the world that continues to sentence children to life in prison without parole," a practice which violates international law as it is considered a "cruel and inhumane punishment" in accordance with article 37(a) of the Convention on the Rights of the Child, which states that "no child [below 18 years of age] shall be subjected to ... capital punishment nor life imprisonment without possibility of release ...." During the production of the report on torture and isolation, US officials had openly opposed Méndez's investigation by restricting his access to prisons and various types of documentation; for example, the number of prisoners in solitary confinement is an estimate as such documentation is not available to the public or even the UN. ADX, a supermax, was one of the prisons that US authorities did not want Mendez to inspect and scrutinize. It is located in Florence, Colorado, and has gained a notorious reputation, even internationally, and it is guarded by secrecy and censorship. The former warden has described it as a "clean version of hell," and that "it's far much worse than death."

Pursuant to Amnesty International's report, "Entombed: Isolation in the US Federal Prison System," the vast majority of ADX prisoners are kept in their cells for 22-24 hours per day "in conditions of severe physical and social isolation." The designers of ADX (as well as other supermax prisons) had that specific purpose in mind as thick steel-reinforced concrete walls prevent inmates from having contact with those in adjacent cells, and "most cells have an interior barred door as well as a solid outer door, compounding the sense of isolation." When prisoners are not confined to their cells for 24 hours per day due to understaffing and other issues, they can leave their cells for a few hours per week to "exercise" in a "bare interior room or in small individual yards or cages, with no view of the natural world." Cells are equipped with a shower and toilet, minimizing the need for leaving them. The inmates are almost invariably separated from other humans, and even "checks by medical and mental health staff, take place at the cell door and medical and psychiatric consultations are sometimes conducted remotely, through teleconferencing."

It is no surprise that under these conditions, suicide attempts, self-mutilations, and acute psychoses are rampant among the inmates. Amnesty International concludes that "the conditions of isolation at ADX breach international standards for humane treatment and, especially when applied for a prolonged period or indefinitely, amount to cruel, inhuman or degrading treatment or punishment in violation of international law."

According to the official policy of the Bureau of Prisons, mentally ill inmates are not kept in isolation. It has, however, been profusely documented that inmates with serious psychiatric disorders are kept in isolation and many inmates with no diagnosis have become seriously mentally deranged. Many of these instances have been detailed in various lawsuits. In one lawsuit against ADX, it was detailed that many inmates "suffer from chronic mental illness and some routinely smear themselves and their cells with their own [feces], howl or shriek continuously or bang their metal showers at all hours of the day or night." This lawsuit also detailed several specific instances of inmates deteriorating mentally during solitary confinement at ADX, one of whom was John Powers. He was originally placed in the Control Unit (the most isolated part of ADX), but he was frequently transferred to the federal medical facility at Springfield after numerous incidents of self-mutilation. Upon being 'stabilized' with various pharmaceuticals, he was promptly returned to the CU at ADX. His medical records showed that he had lacerated his scrotum, bit off his finger, inserted staples into his forehead, and slashed his wrists. Originally, he was ordered to serve 60 months in the Control Unit, but because he did not comply with the behavioral requirements, he spent an unfathomable ten years and five months in that unit before finally being transferred to the lesser restricted General Population Unit (GPU). In the GPU, officials continued to deprive him of mental health care, and subsequently he sliced off his earlobes, sawed through his Achilles tendon, and mutilated his genitals. In 2013, he was transferred to another high-security facility and reportedly "rammed his head into an exposed piece of metal in his cell, causing a skull fracture and brain injury .... [later he was found inserting] metal into his brain cavity through the hole that remain[ed] in his skull."

Considering the humanitarian aspects and that prolonged solitary confinement is a breach of international law, it is striking that the US continues to enforce it upon its convicts as well as those awaiting trial. It appears that inmates are perceived as objects that need to be dealt with in the most efficient way possible for prison staff regardless of international regulations and recommendations.

The Fluoride-Induced American Holocaust Continues Unabated

Introduction by Paul Craig Roberts

For liberals, fluoridation of water became a cause to advance government intervention in behalf of improving dental health. After decades of fluoridation numerous unrefuted studies have established not only that fluoridation is damaging to teeth, but also is associated with a wide range of health and cognitive issues ranging from cancer to ADHD and lower IQ scores. Despite the evidence the Center for Disease Control (CDC), the fluoride lobby and associated bought scientists continue to proclaim the unproven benefits of fluoridation. Søren Korsgaard concludes his report on the real evidence with the suggestion that those responsible for the immense adverse health effects of fluoridation be brought before the International Criminal Court for crimes against humanity. This is a very important readable scientific report. Read it and see the total absence of concern for public health by the CDC.

Søren Roest Korsgaard

Seventy-four long years have passed since the US government decided to start community water fluoridation of a few selected cities. Back then when fluoride was first added to water supplies, asbestos was the preferred fireproofing material, PCBs were used as insulation and in pesticides, and the notoriously "safe and effective" DDT was sprayed in schools and from airplanes over large populations, killing tens of thousands of people from cancer and other diseases. All of these chemicals have been banned, except fluoride. Since 1945, the US fluoridation program has expanded massively and now encompasses over 70% of all community water supplies while the majority of the world has rejected or banned it (only 5% of the world, US included, consumed artificially fluoridated water in 2012). Fluoride is allegedly added to water supplies and most commercial toothpaste to strengthen teeth and hence reduce cavities. Until recently, US water supplies contained 1.0-1.2 ppm of fluoride i.e. around one milligram per liter of water. In 2015, the US government lowered the recommended amount of fluoride to 0.7 ppm.

The Food and Drug Administration classifies fluoride as a prescription drug; yet, there is no control of the intake. Athletes, people living in warmer climates and the elderly who cannot excrete fluoride to the same extent as younger generations are obviously overexposed. Fluoride is, among others, also absorbed by plants and animals making it increasingly difficult to avoid. Ethically, fluoridation deprives people of informed consent to medication. On the other hand, the Center for Disease Control (CDC) has proclaimed that water fluoridation is "one of public health's greatest success stories" and "one of 10 great public health achievements of the 20th century." The CDC proclaims to work "24/7 to protect America from health, safety and security threats, both foreign and in the U.S." The veracity of these statements by the CDC is for the readers to judge in the pages that follow.

Intelligence

While the CDC and many other organizations praise and glorify water fluoridation on their respective websites and at conferences, they omit a massive body of peer-reviewed studies that correlate fluoride exposure with reduced IQ in humans. In fact, 61 studies that included a total of 22,176 children and 245 adults have documented this link. Many of these studies examined fluoride levels equivalent to or lower than the concentration found in most US water supplies, and adjusted for relevant variables such as socio-economic status and other toxins that affect IQ. These mainstream experts also omit numerous animal studies that have thoroughly established that fluoride can produce cognitive impairment in animals and bring about "anxiety-depression-like behaviors in mice" (Liu et al., 2014). Here are quotations from a small sample of these studies. Bartos and associates concluded in 2019 that "the present study

reveals that exposure to [fluoride] in early stages of rat development leads to impairment of memory in young offspring." Another rat study revealed that "the learning and memory of rats in [the fluoride] group significantly decreased" (Zheng et al., 2016). Jetti et al showed in their 2016 study that "the rats that received fluoride water exhibited impairment in their spatial learning and memory deficits." In 2014, a study led by Jiang S. reached the conclusion that "fluoride and arsenic, either alone or combined, can decrease learning and memory ability in rats." Chioca and coworkers concluded in their 2008 study, which was published in the European Journal of Pharmacology, that "moderate intoxication with sodium fluoride has potentially deleterious effects on learning and memory." Dozens of animal studies have shown adverse cognitive affects in animals as well as many other issues not covered to any degree in this article, including cancer, infertility, loss of bone strength, and genetic damage, each topic requiring lengthy dissertations to cover. Now we will briefly summarize the conclusions of a few selected epidemiological studies. In 2009, Sudhir and coworkers studied 1000 schoolchildren exposed to several degrees of fluoride: <0.7 ppm, 0.7-1.2 ppm, 1.3-4.0 ppm, and >4.0 ppm. Sudhir and his research team observed that the "number of intellectually impaired children were gradually increased with the increase in fluoride concentration in the drinking water" and "high fluoride environment adversely affects the development of intelligence in children."
Ding and coworkers examined low fluoride levels, between 0.24 and 2.84 ppm, and how they had affected 331 children. They showed that 1 mg of fluoride present in urine was associated with a 0.59-point decrease in IQ. Their study, which was published in 2011 in the Journal of Hazardous Materials, reached the conclusion that "low levels of fluoride exposure in drinking water had negative effects on children's intelligence and dental health and confirmed the dose-response relationships between urine fluoride and IQ scores as well as dental fluorosis." Excessive fluoride intake produces easily seen damage to tooth enamel, called dental fluorosis. In its most severe form, the enamel begins to erode and crumble, often giving the appearance that the teeth are "rotten," resulting in severe psychological problems, especially among children.

Dental fluorosis becomes especially concerning when we consider the CDC's own study on dental fluorosis. In the period 1999–2004, the prevalence of dental fluorosis in adolescents, aged 12–15, was 40.6%. For children and adolescents, aged 6-19, a total of 37% had dental fluorosis. A follow-up study by Eman Behbehani that focused on the period 2011-2012 showed that the number of affected had increased to 57% for those aged 6 to 19.

Contrary to mainstream experts, fluoridation not only destroys health but also teeth and does so irreversibly. Furthermore, numerous large-scale studies have demonstrated that populations with unfluoridated water do not have a higher incidence of cavities than in the US and, thus, fluoridation is ineffective. Even data collected by the World Health Organization shows that several unfluoridated countries have fewer cavities on average than the US, including Denmark, Germany, Netherlands, Belgium, Switzerland, Sweden, and Italy.

In 1999, Dr. Mansfield gathered urine-fluoride data in England from people living in artificially fluoridated areas. The water-fluoride-level in these areas is equivalent to the level in the US before 2015. Conservatively, we may assume that the urine-fluoride levels are similar in the US; however, they are most likely higher as only a small percentage of England is fluoridated and thus food and drinks likely contain lower levels of fluoride than in the US. In the West Midlands, 31.3% had between 1.7 ppm and 4 ppm of fluoride in their urine; the mean urine-fluoride concentration was determined to be 1.46 ppm. According to the CDC, the number of people who "benefit" from fluoridation continues to grow. Their data show that 74.4% of all community water supplies were fluoridated in 2014, which translates into 211,393,167 people receiving fluoridated water. The CDC admits on their website that they are working diligently to ensure that nearly 80% of people on public water systems will receive fluoridated water by 2020. By invoking the data from the aforementioned study by Ding, it can be shown that fluoridation in the US is associated with a loss of 182 million IQ points. As we shall see, this figure underestimates the true nature of the carnage. In 2019, a major study was published in JAMA Pediatrics, titled, "Association Between

Maternal Fluoride Exposure During Pregnancy and IQ Scores in Offspring in Canada." This study, which had been founded by the U.S. National Institute of Environmental Health Science and by the Canadian government, demonstrated that an increase of 1 mg of fluoride in urine among pregnant women resulted in a 4.5-point decrease in IQ among boys, and collectively for both genders, a drop of 3.66 IQ-points could be documented – i.e. a higher loss than estimated by Ding and coworkers.

Since 1997, the FDA has required that all fluoride containing toothpastes carry a poison label: "If you accidentally swallow more than used for brushing, seek professional help or contact a poison control center immediately."

Notwithstanding the profound criminality by successive profluoridation US governments and ruthless lobbyists and scientists who have been working tirelessly to ensure that the IQ holocaust continues, it gets much worse. The US government approved and secretly installed "fluoridators" in schools across the US in the 1960s, and possibly earlier, and continued until the 1990s to adjust fluoride levels to as high as 5.4 ppm. In 1992, over 100,000 school children were exposed to this horror. Murphy's law dictates, "If something can go wrong it will." Not surprisingly dozens of fluoride accidents have occurred, poisoning an untold number of people. One of these accidents took place in 1972 in the Northeast Bradford Elementary School, Rome, Pennsylvania, where students and teachers were poisoned with fluoride levels as high as 230 ppm due to faulty equipment. Dr. Philippe Grandjean of the Harvard School of Public Health, who has published several papers on fluoride, stated in 2014, "Fluoride seems to fit in with lead, mercury, and other poisons that cause chemical brain drain."

In a presentation on fluoride, renowned neurosurgeon, Dr. Russell Blaylock, asked, "If you've demonstrated [that fluoridation] doesn't reach its objective - that is reducing cavities ... Why is it still being added to the water? If it has these profound health effects, why is it still being added to the water? ... Either they're incredibly stupid and incompetent or criminal or they are doing it on purpose."

Other Health Effects

While this article has briefly looked at a few selected studies
showing that fluoride affects IQ, the problem does not end
there. Fluoride causes havoc in the body. For example,
fluoridation can damage the male reproductive system (see for
example Freni et al., 1994), and studies from China, India,
Mexico, and Russia have shown that high fluoride exposure can
reduce male testosterone levels (see for example Peizhong et al.,
1997). Those who live in fluoridated areas are well advised to
filter all of their water (even that which is used for showering).
Inexpensive water filters removing fluoride are easily accessible
(e.g. ZeroWater). Toothpaste without fluoride is readily
available in health stores and online.
Dr. Dean Burk, one of the most famous and decorated cancer
research scientists in the world during the 20th century, and Dr.
John Yiamouyiannis, president of the Safe Water Foundation,
compared in a 1975 epidemiological survey the cancer mortality
rate of central cities that were either fluoridated or
unfluoridated. Prior to fluoridation, the cancer death rate
remained identical for both sets of cities, but subsequent to
fluoridation the cancer death rate skyrocketed in the fluoridated
cities, but not in the unfluoridated ones. In 1976, Dr. Burk was
asked: "Is this conclusive evidence that fluoride kills because of
cancer?" He replied as follows: "It is one of the most conclusive
bits of scientific and biological evidence that I have come across
in my 50 years in the field of cancer research." He added,
"[fluoridation] amounts to public murder on a grand scale."
The explosive findings were a thorn in the side of the pro-
fluoridation policy of the US government, and the study was
criticized, with the main contention being that the association
could be explained away by demographic changes. In 1977,
Burk and Yiamouyiannis addressed the criticism in another
survey. They showed that sex, race, and age did not explain the
significant cancer death correlated to fluoride. The cancer-
fluoride survey led to three historic trials in Pennsylvania,
Illinois, and Texas in 1978-1982. Although pro-fluoridation
scientists from the National Cancer Institute, the National
Academy of Sciences, the Royal Statistical Society, and the

Royal College of Physicians attempted to dispute the evidence, three veteran trial judges in three different States found that water fluoridation causes cancer and other ailments in man. In each of the trials, it had been shown that the US government or their surrogates had attempted to conceal laboratory studies showing that fluoride causes cancer, and left out available and pertinent data in their demographic adjustment of surveys linking fluoridation and human cancer (Graham et al., 1999). These findings were never disturbed on appeal. After the judicial findings, Dr. Burk and co-workers published more expansive adjustments of demographic factors in epidemiological data in 1984 and 1988, thereby showing that the evidence presented in court was too conservative. Specifically, Burk, Graham, and Morin showed in 1988 that "artificial fluoridation appears to cause or induce about 20-30 excess cancer deaths for every 100,000 persons exposed per year after about 15-20 years." Using this data it can easily be shown that at least a million excess cancer deaths in the United States have been caused or promoted by water fluoridation since this measure was endorsed by the government of the United States in 1951.

Fluoride also affects behavior. Following extensive peer-review in 1995, Mullenix and coworkers published their study into the possible neurotoxicity of fluoride in rats. In order to eliminate bias, Mullenix had utilized a computer-pattern-recognition-system to detect if fluoride had an effect on behavior. Strikingly, it was discovered that fluoride produced life-long changes in behavior. If young rats were exposed to fluoride in their drinking water for a few weeks of the rat's lifetime it produced hypoactivity; Mullenix would later say, "they became slower, 'couch potatoes' if you like." They also gave a one-time subcutaneous injection of fluoride into pregnant rats. As the offspring of those rats grew up they became distinctly hyperactive, indicating that fluoride affects different regions of the brain depending on what time exposure takes place. Mullenix and her team also discovered that "there was major accumulations of fluoride in all the regions of the brain, and that some areas looked like there were greater accumulations than others, that were sex-determinant." Several other animal and epidemiological studies have supported the conclusions drawn by Mullenix, including Jennifer Anne Luke's PhD dissertation from 1997, which showed that fluoride accumulates in the pineal gland affecting melatonin production and results in accelerated onset of sexual maturation in female gerbils. In regard to hyperactivity, a 2015 study demonstrated that "state prevalence of artificial water fluoridation in 1992 significantly positively predicted state prevalence of ADHD in 2003, 2007 and 2011, even after controlling for socio economic status .... Each 1% increase in artificial fluoridation prevalence in 1992 was associated with approximately 67,000 to 131,000 additional ADHD diagnoses from 2003 to 2011" (Malin et al., 2015). Pursuant to Dr. Blaylock, the effects of fluoridation and other environmental toxins are immense:

"We're seeing a society that not only has a lot more people of lower IQ, but a lot fewer people of higher IQ. In other words: a dumbing down, a chemical dumbing down of society. So everyone is sort of mediocre. That leaves them dependent on government, because they can't excel. We have these people of lower IQ who are totally dependent. Then we have this mass of people who are going to believe anything they are told because they can't really think clearly—and very few people of a very high IQ have good cognitive function who can figure this all out. And that's what they want."

Successive US government officials, academics, mainstream experts, dentists, and journalists continue to cover-up fluoridation's profoundly hazardous effects. The responsible parties must be hurled before the International Criminal Court for crimes against humanity.

Originally published as "The Fluoride-Induced American Holocaust Continues Unabated," www.paulcraigrobert.org, October 2019.

The Notion of Evil Killer Genes Examined

Søren Roest Korsgaard

Introduction

Scientists from the Karolinska Institute in Sweden have reported an association between violent crime and genes (a low-activity MAOA genotype and the CDH13 gene), labeled evil killer genes by the mainstream press. Supposedly, having these genes makes one more likely to commit profoundly immoral acts such as murder. This article examines the genetic hypothesis and the broader implications. It is demonstrated that the genetic hypothesis is oversimplified and that situational attributions (e.g. culture, environment) are far more important than dispositional attributions (e.g. genetics).

Extreme Violence and Morality

Concluding that there is a clear-cut nexus between genes and extreme violence implies an intimate connection between genes and morality. Extreme violence, which the study purported to be linked to genetics, falls at the end of the spectrum of morality, i.e. acute immorality. The study, which was published in Molecular Psychiatry, neglected to incorporate a discussion of morality as well as the concept of good and evil into their study, and hence the scientists have produced a framework which is artificially constricted – unless of course the highly unorthodox position is advanced that morality does not exist or that violence is not related to morality. Nevertheless, this reasoning was hinted at by the lead-author, Dr. Tiihonen, in an email to the writer of this article when he stated that "we have not mentioned anything about 'evil' or 'immorality' in our article, we try to focus on facts [1]." As we shall see, even a simple discussion of good and evil reveals numerous complexities which likely undermine the purported connection between genes and violence. In lieu of analyzing relevant concepts, the scientists focused exclusively on a minority group of convicted, violent criminals who allegedly are responsible for "the majority of all violent crime" in developed countries [2]. Hence, they failed to account for legalized violence perpetrated by government entities as well as multiple rigorous studies which show that violence and other profoundly immoral acts are intimately related to power and obedience. Even so, they proceeded to conclude that the etiology of violence is facilitated by two genetic polymorphisms i.e. internal factors working within the individual.

Right and Wrong

Most people tend to have a notion of what is right and wrong; however, many equate morality to the laws of the country in which they have been born. This implies that an unlawful killing of another human being is regarded as murder, and that killings carried out legally are not murders.

For the reason that laws are highly variable it follows that actions regarded as legally sound at this point in time may later be regarded as sinful, criminal, and immoral. A one-time hero may later be regarded as a murderer depending on how a society evolves. For example, when Stauffenberg attempted to assassinate Hitler, his action was illegal under German law and he was executed for it. Today he is widely regarded as a hero. Stauffenberg justified his actions by saying that it was for the greater good; he tried to carry out the will of the people [3]. When executioners in the US, China, Nigeria, India, Indonesia, Saudi Arabia, and elsewhere snuff the life of people convicted of murder, drug offenses, sexual molestation, tax evasion, and for being intoxicated by alcohol, the executioners often state that it is for the greater good. It is rare to see actual remorse among executioners, but a few instances have been noted [4, 5]. It can be scientifically demonstrated that many executioners in the US are unavoidably cold-blooded killers since it has been shown that statistically 1 in 25 on death row is innocent, and in fact, many innocent people worldwide have been beheaded, hanged, lethally injected, shot, or electrocuted [6]. These statistics are not hidden from the public, and many campaigns have attempted to cast light on the irreversible nature of the death penalty; yet, judges continue to sentence people to death, and the death tolls of executioners continue to rise. Furthermore, many people continue to support the death penalty, even in developed countries [7]. In China, as many as 10,000 people join together in stadiums, laughing and cheering, as drug dealers and convicted criminals are killed by firing squad [8]. It has been observed that the convicts are sometimes "immediately [9]" executed after sentencing. In China, the "justice system notoriously favors prosecutors and Chinese courts have a 99.9% conviction rate [9]." It has also been reported that "China has occasionally exonerated wrongfully executed convicts after others came forward to confess their crimes, or in some cases because the supposed murder victim was later found alive [10]." It follows from the evidence that supporters of capital punishment, executioners, and non-legalized cold-blooded murderers directly or indirectly support killing innocent individuals. In line with this argument, it can be argued that this group should, if the genetic hypothesis has any merit, have a specific biological makeup increasing the likelihood of violence or acute immorality. Similarly, usage of recreational drugs is legalized in several countries, but if you find yourself in the wrong country you may be executed; particularly in Asia. Alcohol is an integrated part of western society, but being intoxicated in Saudi Arabia could lead to your execution or a lengthy prison sentence. Over the past years, a notable trend in the West has been a move toward the legalization of drugs, particularly for personal possession (exactly what constitutes a "drug" is highly subjective and varies considerably between countries). It is not inconceivable that in the distant future drug usage may become legalized in the majority of countries. Decades from now, these societies would undoubtedly perceive the past executions of people for using government defined drugs as being wicked and unjust. Could the conclusion not be drawn that certain societies as a whole should have "evil killer genes" for allowing cruel, inhumane executions and incarcerations to take place?

The argument of good intention (i.e. executioners, judges, etc. are not categorically evil since they are acting within the law and believe their actions to be justified) was thoroughly dispelled by Martin Luther king, who wrote: "We should never forget that everything Adolf Hitler did in Germany was 'legal' and everything the Hungarian freedom fighters did in Hungary was 'illegal.' It was 'illegal' to aid and comfort a Jew in Hitler's Germany. Even so, I am sure that, had I lived in Germany at the time, I would have aided and comforted my Jewish brothers [11]." Historically, legality is often irrelevant when judging the morality of particular actions.

Implicitly, the Karolinska Institute scientists assumed that legality equals morality and vice-versa by examining convicted offenders – they stuck to politically correct violent offenders. However, if higher-order moral behavior is inherited biologically to a certain extent then the law of the land cannot be used to elucidate this matter. Under the scheme of politically dictated laws as opposed to universal moral laws, it is possible for an individual to commit violent crimes that are morally sound, and for another to act within the law, but be engaging in acute immoral behavior. For example, legalized child murderer and serial killer, Brandon Bryant, has killed more people than Ted Bundy and Gary Ridgway combined. For years, Bryant killed from a safe location in the US by pressing the button on a joystick as a US drone operator. After six years and hundreds of victims later, he quit his job allegedly because he had begun having second thoughts about killing children and others. He described one of his kills as follows: "The smoke clears … he's missing his right leg above his knee. He's holding it, and he's rolling around, and the blood is squirting out of his leg, and it's hitting the ground, and it's hot …. It took him a long time to die. I just watched him [12]."

On October 14, 2011, former US President Barack Obama, who won the Nobel Peace Prize, directed the CIA to conduct a drone strike and mass murder in Yemen. One of the many victims was 16-year-old Abdulrahman Anwar al-Awlaki, an American citizen, who was brutally murdered while having dinner. He had never been charged with a crime, let alone convicted of one [13]. On January 27, 2017, the boy's 8-year-old half-sister, Nawar "Nora" al-Awlaki, was killed in an operation authorized by Obama's successor, Donald Trump. Bullets struck her multiple times and she died a slow and painful death [14].

Death by Government

The study was exclusively based on offenders found within the penalty system, but no references were made to political killers and socially acceptable psychopaths who often are extremely deadly and successful – but commit their acts legally – legally within their own country, at least. After the Persian Gulf War, from 1990-1991, economic sanctions were imposed upon Iraq that resulted in the death of over 500,000 Iraqi children. Madeline Albright, Secretary of State during the Clinton administration, was questioned about the sanctions on live TV. She had clearly not prepared for the question that follows. She was asked: "We have heard that a half million children have died. I mean, that's more children than died in Hiroshima. And, you know, is the price worth it?" Albright calmly responded that "We think the price is worth it [15]." Albright's infamous quotation leads us to another important point, namely democide. Democide has been defined as "any murder by government – by officials acting under the authority of government. That is, they act according to explicit or implicit government policy or with the implicit or explicit approval of the highest authority [16]." The term was coined in the 1990s by the late Rudolph Rummel, professor emeritus of political science at the University of Hawaii. Rummel's analyses and very conservative calculations show that governments were responsible for over 262,000,000 deaths worldwide in the 20th century [17]. The figure does not include soldiers killed in combat, but exclusively unarmed civilians. Rummel gives a practical characterization of this incredible figure: "Just to give perspective on this incredible murder by government, if all these bodies were laid head to toe, with the average height being 5', then they would circle the earth ten times. Also, this democide murdered 6 times more people than died in combat in all the foreign and internal wars of the century. Finally, given popular estimates of the dead in a major nuclear war, this total democide is as though such a war did occur, but with its dead spread over a century [18]." Statistically, it is evident that it is astronomically more likely that your own government or a foreign one and its handlers will kill you than non-legalized violent offenders. The Karolinska scientists ignored the data and focused only on a narrow band of law-breakers, a focus that distorts the spectrum and prevalence of acute immorality. The genetic hypothesis, if it has any merit, would have to be able to predict legalized murders, such as Madeline Albright, in a double-blind test.

The Majority is Latently Evil

While only a small group ordered directly or indirectly the various democides, genocides, and holocausts of the 20th and 21st century, hundreds of thousands of individuals assisted their governments in carrying out these atrocities and even more approved of them. A full spectrum analysis of the genetic hypothesis would therefore at least incorporate the genetic material of drone operators, soldiers, imprisoned offenders, government mercenaries, people who have no history of violence, torture specialists, and any government official who has directed or supported violent actions, including war. In the study, all of these nuances were not mentioned. In an email to this writer, the lead-author, Dr. Tiihonen, admitted that their study applies only to developed countries, an artificial restriction as violence and genetics do not cease to exist outside the artificially determined borders of "developed countries." He went on to say that "we concluded that in Finland (a developed country) 5-10% of violent crimes (defined by legislation of Finland) are attributable to 2 genetic polymorphisms [19]." As we shall see in the following section, solid scientific data show that the difference between the majority of so-called law-abiding citizens and cold-blooded killers is minuscule, and a number of social and environmental factors are vastly more significant than genetics in determining which moral direction an individual will take.

During the Nuremberg prosecutions of Nazi doctors, engineers, and soldiers, the "Nuremberg defense" was widely used to try to minimize moral and legal responsibility for those who carried out or facilitated atrocities. The essence of the defense is that the soldiers, doctors, and other workers simply followed the orders of their superiors and hence were not culpable at all or at least not to the same degree as their superiors [20]. In the early

1960s, Stanley Milgram wanted to scientifically examine aspects of the Nuremberg defense and determine if so-called ordinary people (postal clerks, high school teachers, salesmen, engineers, doctors, etc.) would blindly follow orders of an authority figure even if commanded to do reprehensible acts including the electrocution of helpless victims. The general setup of the study involved telling the subject that they would be participating in a learning experiment to test how punishment affects memory. At the beginning of the experiment, the subject and the victim (a confederate of Milgram) were introduced to each other by the experimenter who was dressed in a lab coat. Most observers found the victim to be "mild mannered and likable [21]." The victim was "strapped onto an 'electric chair' apparatus [21]" and electrodes were placed on the victim's wrist. The subject was informed that the straps were "to prevent excessive movement while the [confederate] was being shocked. The effect was to make it impossible for him to escape from the situation [21]." The subject was then told that the electrodes were connected to a shock generator in the adjacent room. For each error, the subject was instructed to deliver a specific dose of volt to the victim starting at 15 and ending with 450 volts. After the experiment, it was revealed that no one had suspected that the instrument was a simulated shock generator. On the generator, Milgram and his colleagues had clearly written which dose of voltage constituted: Slight shock, moderate shock, strong shock, very strong shock, intense shock, extreme intensity shock, and "danger: Severe Shock [22]." The last two switches were simply marked, XXX, a clear indication that death would most likely follow. The victim would give a predetermined response to the increasing degrees of punishment, including pounding on the wall, screaming, complaining of heart problems, and saying they refused to proceed with the experiment. When the device hit the 330 volts mark, the victim would deliver this message: "(Intense and prolonged screaming) Let me out of here. Let me out of here. My heart's bothering me. Let me out, I tell you. (Hysterically) Let me out of here. Let me out of here. You have no right to hold me here. Let me out! Let me out! Let me out! Let me out of here! Let me out. Let me out [23]." During the final stages of the study, the victim was instructed to feign death by no longer answering or responding to electric shocks. At this point, the experimenter would tell the subject to treat silence as a wrong answer and continue to administer voltage jolts.

Before the study was undertaken, several well-educated psychologists "were provided with a detailed description of the experimental situation. They were asked to reflect carefully on it, and to predict the behavior of 100 hypothetical subjects. More specifically, they were instructed to plot the distribution of obedience of '100 Americans of diverse occupations, and ranging in age from 20 to 50 years,' who were placed in the experimental situation [22]." There was considerable agreement among the psychologists that only between 0 to 3% would administer the complete series of electric shocks. To everyone's surprise, a staggering 65% went through the whole set of punishments from 15 to 450 volts.

Many subjects "expressed deep disapproval of shocking a man in the face of his objections, and others denounced it as stupid and senseless. Yet the majority complied with the experimental commands [22]." Moreover, many subjects laughed and smiled as the victim screamed in agony and pounded on the wall. The "laughter seemed entirely out of place, even bizarre [22]." After the experiment, several explained that they were not sadistic and did not enjoy the torture and killing of the confederate.

The Milgram study and variations of it have been repeated numerous times and in several countries. There have been found no significant differences between US and non-US residents (almost exclusively Western societies); also, gender does not make a noteworthy difference nor has obedience to authority changed for the better with time [23]. As recently as 2015, the experiment was repeated in Poland with a staggering 90% inflicting the highest dosage of voltage. The lead author of the study, Dr Thomasz Grzyb, concluded: "Half a century after Milgram's original research into obedience to authority, a striking majority of subjects are still willing to electrocute a helpless individual [24]."

The Milgram experiment, and its subsequent replications, demonstrates that under the command of authority, violence flourishes and not by a specific set of genes. The subjects of the study were not convicted criminals, but law-abiding citizens; hence, the Milgram experiment is a clear indication that external influences are far more important than a genetic relation to violence. However, if external factors are less important, a double-blind genetic version of the Milgram experiment would establish beforehand who would put their victim through the entire set of electric shocks and who would not. Statistically, authority-obedient individuals are by far the most dangerous, morally reckless, and most likely to commit atrocities. It follows that individuals who defy authority and question laws and executive orders are the most dangerous to any murderous regime.

Power and Violence

A very important, but implicitly expressed factor in the Migram study is that of power. Similarly, Rummel's research shows that "ethnic, racial, and religious diversity, economic development, levels of education, and cultural differences [25]" do not account for democide. Instead, "the best predictor of this killing is regime power. The more arbitrary power a regime has ... the more likely it will kill its subjects or foreigners. The conclusion is that power kills, absolute power kills absolutely [26]."
The relationship between power and violence was also hinted at during the notorious and widely criticized Stanford Prison Experiment in 1971. Dr. Philip Zimbardo wanted to study the psychological effects of perceived power and recruited ordinary people with no histories of abnormal behavior to function as either guards or prisoners in a simulated prison environment. The experiment was cut short after the guards began abusing and psychologically torturing the prisoners, many of whom had begun to see themselves as actual prisoners. Interviews and psychological tests indicated that "abusive guard behavior appears to have been triggered by features of the situation rather than by the personality of guards [27]." Zimbardo concluded that internal characteristics of the individuals were far less significant than external influences in explaining their behavior. This implies that evil is not "as related to personality or childhood values as we think [28]."

Mandatory Human Genetic Engineering

In the foreseeable future, if western governments embrace the highly questionable notion that violence is, in large part, a result of genes rather than environment and culture, it could lead to enforcement of mandatory genetic editing such that future generations would not have allegedly undesirable genes. To persuade public opinion, the spurious argument could be injected via the mainstream media that opponents to genetic editing are responsible for violence and killings carried out by those with bad genes because they allow such genes to exist. Genetic editing is currently on the table as something which could soon become mandatory, like vaccines have been in some countries and states.

In 2018, Chinese scientist He Jiankui created the world's first genetically modified babies. In the wake of that human experiment, a writer for the South China Morning Post asked: "If governments were to start modifying their populations' genes on a mass scale to treat genetic ailments such as sickle cell disease, would that pave the way towards the eventual use of this technology for enhancement [29]?" The article continues, "'Oh, that's going to happen for sure', says Derya Unutmaz, a Connecticut-based immunologist and principal researcher at Jackson Laboratory [29]." Unutmaz went on to say that "at the military level you can imagine you want to create super-soldiers who can withstand all kinds of diseases and tough weather and carry hundreds of kilograms. These were science fiction, but now we have the tools that could enable them [29]." Numerous scientific magazines are already implicitly advocating gene editing and predicting that it will soon become mandatory. A science writer for TheAtlantic.com predicts that within a few decades "the United States will arrest, try, and convict some parents for refusing to edit the genes of their child before he or she is born [30]." Realizing that government is the number one cause of unnatural death and the most dangerous entity ever to have existed, it follows that politicians and the elite will likely attempt to illegalize a whole host of genes deemed undesirable, including the genes allegedly associated with violence. One plausible scenario is the emergence of a doctored quasi-religion, which we may call "genianity," advanced and created by the elite in order to encourage widespread acceptance of mandatory genetic engineering. The dogma of genianity will be that everyone must subject themselves to genetic modification or "therapy" for the "greater good." A scenario worthy of consideration is the following. First, sympathy and support would be generated via eradicating profound defects and illnesses. Second, years of targeted propaganda would change and push the boundaries of norms and ethics in regard to genetics, fostering a militant belief system which becomes a quasi-religion. The adherents of genianity would discipline each other if doubt occurs when genes that are associated with politically incorrect behavior are gradually added to the list of undesirables. Dissenters would be imprisoned, excluded, or become social outcasts. Eventually, future generations would be largely engineered beings designed for government approved thinking and behavior.

Final Thoughts

As shown in this article, the genetic hypothesis for violence stands in stark contrast to solid data from a variety of disciplines including social psychology and philosophy. The hypothesis encounters numerous difficulties when violence is looked at from a broader perspective and politically incorrect material is analyzed. Contemporary societies define a virtue or an evil based upon artificial moral parameters i.e. laws and regulations; hence, scientists need an objective system, such as a universal set of moral values, in order to fully explore the hypothesis.

Originally published as "The Notion of Evil Killer Genes Examined," Radian & Inches, 2018.

References

1. Email to Søren Korsgaard from Dr. Jari Tiihonen. April 27, 2018.
2. J Tiihonen et al. "Genetic back ground of extreme violent behavior."
Molecular Psychiatry (2015).
3. "Germans who resisted Hitler and the Nazis"
https://www.biographyonline.net/people/famous/people-opposed-hitler.html.
4. "I was Virginia's executioner from 1982 to 1999. Any questions for me?"
https://www.theguardian.com/commentisfree/2013/nov/21/death-penalty-
former-executioner-jerry-givens.
5. "THE EXECUTIONER'S TALE: Former San Quentin warden reveals
how he killed prisoners in the jail's 'coughing box' without any training . . .
or remorse" https://www.dailymail.co.uk/news/article-3481019/Former-
executioner-San-Quentin-reveals-killed-prisoners-gas-chamber-without-
training-claims-never-haunted-him.html.
6. Gross et al. "Rate of false conviction of criminal defendants who are
sentenced to death." National Academy of Sciences (2014)
https://doi.org/10.1073/pnas.1306417111.
7. "GALLUP POLL: Support for Death Penalty in U.S. Falls to a 45-Year
Low" https://deathpenaltyinfo.org/Gallup-
Support_for_Death_Penalty_Falls_in_2017.
8. "Thousands turn out to watch execution of 10 Chinese criminals"
http://metro.co.uk/2017/12/19/thousands-turn-watch-execution-10-chinese-
criminals-7170040/.
9. "Thousands in China watch as 10 people sentenced to death in sport
stadium" https://www.theguardian.com/world/2017/dec/18/thousands-china-
watch-executed-sport-stadium.
10. "Executed Chinese teenager found innocent 18 years on"
http://www.hurriyetdailynews.com/executed-chinese-teenager-found-
innocent-18-years-on-75633.
11. "Martin Luther King: 'Everything Adolf Hitler did in Germany was
Legal'" https://libertyblitzkrieg.com/2013/06/07/martin-luther-king-
everything-adolf-hitler-did-in-germany-was-legal/.
12. "Confessions of a Drone Warrior" https://www.gq.com/story/drone-uav-
pilot-assassination
13. "Abdulrahman al-Awlaki"
https://en.wikipedia.org/wiki/Abdulrahman_al-Awlaki
14. "Nawar_al-Awlaki" https://en.wikipedia.org/wiki/Nawar_al-Awlaki
15. "'We Think the Price Is Worth It' Media uncurious about Iraq policy's
effects–there or here" https://fair.org/extra/we-think-the-price-is-worth-it/.
16. "DEMOCIDE VERSUS GENOCIDE: WHICH IS WHAT?"
https://hawaii.edu/powerkills/GENOCIDE.HTM.
17. "Freedom, Democracy, Peace; Power, Democide, and War"
https://hawaii.edu/powerkills/welcome.html.
18. "20TH CENTURYDEMOCIDE"
https://www.hawaii.edu/powerkills/20TH.HTM.
19. Email to Søren Korsgaard from Dr. Jari Tiihonen. April 27, 2018

20. Nuremberg defense
https://idioms.thefreedictionary.com/Nuremberg+defence
21. Milgram, S. "Behavioral Study of obedience." The Journal of Abnormal and Social Psychology (1963).
22. "Milgram Experiment – Obedience to Authority"
https://explorable.com/stanley-milgram-experiment.
23. Blass, T. "The Milgram Paradigm after 35 years: Some things we now know about obedience to authority." Journal of Applied Social Psychology (1999).
24. "Conducting the Milgram Experiment in Poland, Psychologists Show People Still Obey" http://www.spsp.org/news-center/press-releases/milgram-poland-obey.
25. R. J. Rummel. "Democracy, Power, Genocide, and Mass Murder."
Journal of Conflict Resolution, Peace Science Society (International) (1999).
26. "POWER KILLS: GENOCIDE AND MASS MURDER"
https://www.hawaii.edu/powerkills/POWER.ART.HTM#*.
27. "Stanford Prison Experiment FREQUENTLY ASKED QUESTIONS"
http://www.prisonexp.org/faq/.
28. "How Good People Turn Evil: The Stanford Prison Experiment"
https://exploringyourmind.com/how-good-people-turn-evil-stanford-prison-experiment/.
29. "The future of gene editing: ending disease or creating super-soldiers or a master race? Why rules are needed" https://www.scmp.com/lifestyle/health-wellness/article/2179853/future-gene-editing-ending-disease-or-creating-super
30. Will Editing Your Baby's Genes Be Mandatory?
https://www.theatlantic.com/politics/archive/2017/04/will-editing-your-babys-genes-be-mandatory/522747/

American Monster: Chris Kyle, the American Sniper

Søren Roest Korsgaard

Introduction

When one delves into the subject of perpetrators of extreme violence, it is very rare for experts and writers to discuss legalized killers, much less study them; instead, they take aim at politically neutral cases, that being non-legalized killers, and consequently the literature in this regard has been based on an incomplete spectrum.

If researchers were able to bypass political undertones and the complexities involved with determining which legalized killers to include and which to discard in their analyses, they would quickly be able to establish that one of the most remorseless and prolific US serial killers of all time is neither named John Wayne Gacy nor Gary Ridgway but Christopher Scott Kyle, the American Sniper.

Chris Kyle, who has been branded an "American Hero [1]," never expressed any regrets for his many victims but stated that he wished he could have murdered more. Even Ted Bundy, who murdered dozens of women and occasionally indulged in necrophilia and decapitations, expressed that he deeply regretted his actions and reckoned that society deserved to be protected from him.

Chris Kyle was a United States Navy SEAL sniper and served several tours in the Iraq War. After his discharge from the U.S. Navy, he went on to publish his bestselling autobiography American Sniper in 2012 [2]. In his book, he claimed to be the most prolific sniper of all time, and it is generally agreed upon that he has killed more than 160 and possibly over 300 people, mostly Iraqis. After the publication of his book, he told the

Sunday People that "There are no kills that I regret. None at all. The public is very soft. I either killed them, or they killed other Americans [3]."

In this article, we integrate the case into a broader framework that encompasses a discussion of the legal justification for the war. As we shall see, the Iraq War had been planned years in advance and violated international law. Killings committed during an illegal invasion are obviously illegal and this puts Chris Kyle's justification into a whole different perspective; that is, if the USA had never invaded Iraq, none of his colleagues would have ever been in any alleged danger.

From his own words, we will see that Kyle was able to kill like clockwork, without remorse, and even claimed to have continued to murder people when he returned from service. To gain a better comprehension of such behavior, his actions are analyzed from the perspective of psychiatry. This article furthermore analyses the possible root causes of why Kyle gained pervasive popularity and support despite information pertaining to his murders being in plain sight. It is argued that successfully implemented war propaganda and a disorder, known as hybristophilia, account for the observed behavior.

International Law and the Iraq War

In March 2003, just before the Iraq War commenced, a group of 31 Canadian professors of international law declared in an open letter that an attack on Iraq "would be a fundamental breach of international law and would seriously threaten the integrity of the international legal order that has been in place since the end of the Second World War [4]."

They furthermore condemned the scheduled war "in the strongest terms" and underlined that an invasion would have imperialist and colonial overtones: "Illegal action by the US and its allies would simply return us to an international order based on imperial ambition and coercive force [4]."

The group was backed by the International Commission of Jurists (ICJ) in Geneva who expressed "deep dismay that a small number of states are poised to launch an outright illegal invasion of Iraq, which amounts to a war of aggression [5]."

Under international law, a state is only allowed to use force against a sovereign nation if it has attacked first. Before any actions are undertaken, the consent of the United Nations Security Council is a necessity. The US never got the Security Council's approval for the Iraq War.

In 2002, well before the initiation of the war, a group of 317 law teachers from 87 law schools located in the US declared in an open statement that a war against Iraq would not only be a breach of international law, but also violate the American constitution; they, in the strongest terms, protested "the Bush administration's illegal plan to conduct a war against Iraq," and argued that "President Bush maintains that Iraq's 'decade of defiance' of United Nations resolutions justifies a war against Iraq. But the President ignores the fact that a US war, unleashed without the approval of the UN Security Council, against a country that has not attacked the United States, would itself be an unlawful act, in defiance of America's treaty obligations, and a violation of US and international law [6]."

Importantly, they also stated that "The dangerous path America is treading will only lead to more suffering by Americans, as well as by others. The international rule of law is not a soft luxury to be discarded whenever leaders find it convenient or popular to resort to savage violence. The international rule of law is a bulwark against the horrors of warfare that we Americans have so recently felt firsthand [6]."

They also made the essential historical reference which is that "every nation that has ever committed aggression against another claimed to be 'defending' itself. The United States helped establish the United Nations precisely in order to impose the rule of law on such claims, to make it unlawful for nations to strike against others unless they were themselves under armed attack. The United States is not under armed attack by Iraq [6]."

In 2004, Kofi Annan, former United Nations Secretary-General, spoke about the U.S. led invasion of Iraq: "I have indicated it was not in conformity with the UN charter. From our point of view and the UN Charter point of view, it was illegal [7]."

Kofi Annan's statement was echoed in a 2005 paper published in the British Journal of Criminology, professors Kramer and Michalowski, concluded that the "invasion and occupation of

Iraq by the United States and its allies is a violation of international law, and as such constitutes a state crime [8]." Even UN's former chief weapons inspector Hans Blix has stated that "all in all, we carried out about 700 inspections at different 500 sites and, in no case, did we find any weapons of mass destruction," and "I am of the firm view that it was an illegal war [9]."

Former chief prosecutor of Nazi war crimes at the Nuremberg tribunal, Benjamin Ferencz, has declared that the Iraq War was illegal, and it constituted the "supreme international crime [10]," which was defined under the Nuremberg trials as a war of aggression without any justification. He has also stated, "Crimes against humanity, destruction beyond the needs of military necessity, rape of civilians, plunder – that always happens in wartime. So my answer personally, after working for 60 years on this problem and [as someone] who hates to see all these young people get killed no matter what their nationality, is that you've got to stop using warfare as a means of settling your disputes [10]."

In a different interview, he briefly described the proceedings that led to the war:

"The United Nations charter has a provision which was agreed to by the United States, formulated by the United States, in fact, after World War II. It says that from now on, no nation can use armed force without the permission of the U.N. Security Council. They can use force in connection with self-defense, but a country can't use force in anticipation of self-defense. Regarding Iraq, the last Security Council resolution essentially said, 'Look, send the weapons inspectors out to Iraq, have them come back and tell us what they've found – then we'll figure out what we're going to do.' The U.S. was impatient, and decided to invade Iraq – which was all prearranged of course. So, the United States went to war, in violation of the charter [11, 12]."

Even a political inquiry into the Iraq War has affirmed that it was illegal; the Dutch inquiry concluded, among others, that the "military action had no sound mandate in international law [13]." Philippe Sands QC, a professor of international law at University College London, who gave evidence to the inquiry, later told the media that: "There has been no other independent assessment on the legality of the war in Iraq and the findings of this inquiry are unambiguous [13]."

The British inquiry into the war, which became known as the Chilcot Inquiry, concluded that Iraq did not pose an imminent threat, military action was unnecessary, and it was also concluded that the UK government had undermined the authority of the United Nations Security Council [14]. Extensive evidence of systematic deception, fraud, manipulation, and criminality by the Bush administration was also put forth in the book, The Prosecution of George W. Bush for Murder, by former prosecutor Vincent Bugliosi. Bugliosi highlighted that Bush had warned in a speech on October 7, 2002, that Iraq was an imminent threat to the US, capable of striking them at any time with weapons of mass destruction. However, Bush had, less than a week before the speech, received the National Intelligence Estimate (NIE) in which it was concluded by 16 US intelligence agencies that Iraq would only pose a threat if the US attacked it first, i.e. self-defense. When the Bush administration put out a declassified version of the NIE just before Congress were to vote on whether or not it authorized an invasion, the conclusion that Iraq was not an imminent threat was completely deleted from the document. Bugliosi also pointed his finger to the so-called Manning Memo that detailed how Bush had told Tony Blair about three possible ways for the US to provoke Saddam Hussein into a war. Bush elaborated on one of these provocations and stated that they could fly "U2 reconnaissance aircraft with fighter cover over Iraq, [falsely] painted in UN colours. If Saddam fired on them, he would be in breach" of UN resolutions and that would justify war [15]. If Bush honestly believed that Iraq was an imminent threat, the thought of provoking the country would never have entered his mind—the last person you want to provoke is the one you are deadly afraid of.

General Wesley Clark, a retired four-star general who was the Supreme Allied Commander of NATO during the Kosovo War, revealed in 2007 that the Iraq War as well as several others had been planned years in advance. General Clark said: "About ten days after 9/11, I went through the Pentagon and I saw Secretary Rumsfeld and Deputy Secretary Wolfowitz. I went downstairs just to say hello to some of the people on the Joint

Staff who used to work for me, and one of the generals called me in. He said, 'Sir, you've got to come in and talk to me a second.' ... He said, 'We've made the decision we're going to war with Iraq.' This was on or about the 20th of September. I said, 'We're going to war with Iraq? Why?' He said, 'I don't know.' He said, 'I guess they don't know what else to do.' So I said, 'Well, did they find some information connecting Saddam to al-Qaeda?' He said, 'No, no.' He said, 'There's nothing new that way. They just made the decision to go to war with Iraq.' .... So I came back to see him a few weeks later, and by that time we were bombing in Afghanistan. I said, 'Are we still going to war with Iraq?' And he said, 'Oh, it's worse than that.' He reached over on his desk. He picked up a piece of paper. And he said, 'I just got this down from upstairs' — meaning the Secretary of Defense's office — 'today.' And he said, 'This is a memo that describes how we're going to take out seven countries in five years, starting with Iraq, and then Syria, Lebanon, Libya, Somalia, Sudan and, finishing off, Iran [16].'"
The illegality of the Iraq War has been thoroughly well documented, perhaps better than any other illegal war in history, but as it often is with state crimes: those who planned it and those who implemented the violence will rarely be held accountable.

Death Toll of the Iraq War

In addition to the killings carried out by Chris Kyle, the Iraqi people suffered greatly from the U.S. led war of aggression. Independent studies, such as those published in the Lancet, a top medical journal, have shown that hundreds of thousands of people died as a result of the war (first study covered the first 17 months of the war and found that 100,000 people had died due to the war. A follow up study from 2006 showed that the death toll had increased to 654,965) [17].
Subsequent to the publication of the 2006 study, "the war-declaring governments could not simply let these explosive figures go unchallenged [18]," and Bush and British prime-minister Blair immediately dismissed them as not credible, but in March 2007, BBC revealed that the British government's own scientists had confirmed the robustness and accuracy of the

study. "The study design is robust and employs methods that are regarded as close to best practice in this area [18]," said chief scientific adviser of the Ministry of Defense, Sir Roy Anderson. Several scientists employed by the UK's Department for International Development even stated that "the Lancet study actually underestimated the mortality rates because of the methods it applied [18]."

Numerous other experts have confirmed that the reports are scientifically sound and provide the best data on the number of deaths. Shortly after the publication of the 2006 study, a large group of leading experts in medical epidemiology, population health, and biostatistics issued a statement which affirmed that the study was "valid and correct," and "we can be confident that the excess deaths were above 390,000 and may in fact be as high as 940,000. The vast majority (92 per cent) of the excess deaths were due to direct violence. The cross-sectional household cluster sample survey method used is a standard, robust, well-established method for gathering health data [19]."

The independent Just Foreign Policy estimates that as of 2011 the death toll is approximately 1.5 million based upon extrapolation of the data from the Lancet studies [20].

In 2007 and 2008, the independent polling agency "Opinion Research Business" published two studies on the Iraq War mortality, and they ultimately estimated "that the death toll between March 2003 and August 2007 is likely to have been of the order of 1,033,000 [21]."

The Nobel Prize winning Physicians for Social Responsibility echoed these findings in 2015 when they released their detailed study in which they conservatively estimated that one million people had died due to the war. In their report, they furthermore scolded the often-cited Iraq Body Count Project (IBC) for grossly misrepresenting data and underestimating the actual death toll. [18]. An investigative report had furthermore exposed IBC as being "deeply embedded in the Western foreign policy establishment. IBC's key advisers and researchers have received direct and indirect funding from US government propaganda agencies and Pentagon contractors. It is no surprise, then, that IBC-affiliated scholars promote narratives of conflict that serve violent US client-regimes and promote NATO counter-insurgency doctrines [22]." Moreover, the investigative report concluded that "IBC has not only systematically underrepresented the Iraqi death toll, it has done so on the basis of demonstrably fraudulent attacks on standard scientific procedures. IBC affiliated scholars are actively applying sophisticated techniques of statistical manipulation to whitewash US complicity in violence... [22]."

Professor Gideon Polya, an expert in thanatology (the scientific study of the cause of death) and author of Body Count: Global avoidable mortality since 1950, has estimated that the absolute Iraqi death toll of the war is in excess of 2.7 million. This figure encompasses 1.5 million who died as a result of violence and 1.2 million who died due to war-induced deprivation. The latter includes under-5 infant deaths of 0.6 million [23].

The Confessions

People ordered to kill by their governments or superiors, in particular soldiers, are not exempt from punishment by conveniently shifting the responsibility to their superiors if a moral choice was available. Such is explicitly declared by Nuremberg Principle IV, which states that "The fact that a person acted pursuant to order of his Government or of a superior does not relieve him from responsibility under international law, provided a moral choice was in fact possible to him [24]." Chris Kyle ignored the Nuremberg Principles and the illegality of the war, and he asserted that his victims would have killed his colleagues if he had not acted first [3].

His arguments would, in all probability, have fallen short if he had been prosecuted in the International Criminal Court in Hague for war crimes. His charges may have included systematic extermination of Iraqis, i.e. crimes against humanity. Judging from his own words, he enjoyed killing the Iraqi people as well as others. In his memoir, he described killing as "fun [2]." He also stated that "I never once fought for the Iraqis. I could give a flying fuck about them [2]," and "on the front of my arm, I had a crusader cross inked in. I wanted everyone to know I was a Christian. I had it put in in red, for blood. I hated the damn savages I'd been fighting. I always will [2]," and remarked, "they've taken so much from me [2]."

Later in the book, he reiterated his standpoint on the Iraqis: "Savage, despicable evil. That's what we were fighting in Iraq. That's why a lot of people, myself included, called the enemy 'savages.' There really was no other way to describe what we encountered there [2]."

Regarding how many people he had killed, he stated: "People ask me all the time, 'How many people have you killed?' My standard response is, 'Does the answer make me less, or more, of a man?' The number is not important to me. I only wish I had killed more [2]." Kyle admitted, however, that "we were slaughtering the enemy" and that their "kill total" became "astronomical;" he also said: "It got to the point where I had so many kills that I stepped back to let the other guys have a few … Everyone I shot was evil. I had good cause on every shot. They all deserved to die [2]."

It is important to remember that Kyle murdered dozens of people in an illegal war, and he invariably pulled the trigger within seconds of an Iraqi coming into view of his rifle scope, hardly amounting to a fair and impartial trial. Furthermore, possible survivors and relatives have not been tracked down by the media and others, although a challenging task it would have been important in order to balance his account of events. Despite the fact that Kyle had plenty of opportunity and incentive to embellish, omit, and distort the facts related to his killings, one gets the impression that sensory gratification frequently motivated him to kill, rather than alleged protection of fellow soldiers. In one of these incidents, Kyle, lying on a roof top, claimed to have observed a group of 16 armed men trying to pass a body of water, they had used beach balls to keep themselves afloat. He then allegedly shot the beach balls one by one and watched in enjoyment as the men kept fighting for their lives, several of them drowned. In his book, he uttered that "hell—it was a lot of fun [2]."

After many completed operations, he would smoke Cuban cigars with other military men.

Glorifying in Murder

The literature on non-legalized killers has shown that serial killers find it hard to stop killing. Apparently, the power associated with taking lives can result in a pathological addiction. Chris Kyle was no exception by his own admission. He has reportedly claimed that, upon his return from service, he teamed up with a friend and shot and murdered over 30 alleged looters after the ravages of Hurricane Katrina [25].

He also told Michael Mooney, a writer for D Magazine, that in 2009, he had murdered two alleged would-be carjackers, but Kyle was allegedly "released by police without questioning due to the intercession of the Department of Defense [26]." Mooney would later be unable to verify the story indicating it was a concoction, yet he would say this about Kyle: He was incredible and "he was a hero. He was the most celebrated war hero of our time," and "people will tell stories about Chris Kyle by for generations to come. Tales of his feats in battle, and of his antics and noble deeds, will probably swell [27]."

Many mainstream media outlets have promulgated the indefensible notion that Kyle was a noble man and a hero. For example, a CNN article about Kyle glorifies his actions and remarks that "he touched and inspired so many people [27]."

Having been branded an American hero, Hollywood, a couple of years after the publication of the autobiography, decided to release a film adaptation, titled after the book, American Sniper, directed by Clint Eastwood.

In a response to the movie's one-sided nature, Professor Chris Hedges stated that "American Sniper, like the big-budget feature films pumped out in Germany during the Nazi era to exalt deformed values of militarism, racial self-glorification and state violence, is a piece of propaganda, a tawdry commercial for the crimes of empire [28]."

Chris Kyle profited immensely from the movie and book, and he was the subject of numerous interviews on major news stations and on radio shows. He clearly relished getting national attention and being in the presence of actors and directors, including Clint Eastwood.

Fame and enjoyment would, nevertheless, soon come to an end. In a twist of irony, he was himself killed on a shooting range by an American who was reportedly suffering from war-induced post-traumatic-stress syndrome. His funeral procession stretched from Midlothian, Texas, to Austin. Thousands stood jammed together praising and praying for him as his coffin was escorted by dozens of buses, bikers, policemen, and others. People flocked to his funeral and thousands watched the memorial at the Cowboys Stadium. The minister said during the memorial: "Chris would tell us if he was with us in person today, that we must love others and continue to do good [29]." Clearly a large group had adopted a distorted view of Chris Kyle and his killings. Undoubtedly, many were persuaded by propaganda, which can be defined as misleading information presented as objective to influence and further an agenda, e.g. gain support for the Iraq War, construct an illusion about snipers being humanitarians, et cetera. However, while many may have adopted an uncritical fascination due to the highly subjective Clint Eastwood movie as well as propaganda from other sources, it is, nevertheless, evident that many had read his book and were apparently not appalled as indicated by a quick check on Amazon.com, which shows that Kyle's book has amassed over 15,000 reviews of which 89% are four- or five-star reviews. Across all formats, his book has sold millions of copies and made Kyle one of the most successful serial killers of all time in terms of profiting from his killings. It is perhaps revealing that a perusal of the negative reviews on Amazon.com indicates that many faults the book for poor writing rather than the immorality of murdering over 100 people in an illegal war. One interpretation, other than successfully implemented war propaganda as a source of the manifest attraction to Chris Kyle, is that a large group became affected with a subset of a recently documented disorder, called hybristophilia. The attraction to serial killers and other violent predators is a well-documented phenomenon. Ted Bundy, one of the most savage and notorious women killers of the 1970s, married Carole Ann Boone and fathered a child while being behind bars. Richard Ramirez, a serial killer who indulged in pedophilia, rape, sadism, satanic rituals, and murder, received hundreds of fan-letters while on trial, and on death row he became married to Doreen Lioy. Hybristophilia, which has not been researched well nor thoroughly defined via empirical studies, is a psychiatric disorder that addresses this obsession with people who have committed atrocities, such as rape, murder, and cannibalism. The affected will be infatuated and/or obsessed with the killer [30]. It has been proposed, thus far, that at least two subgroups exist, namely passive and aggressive hybristophiles, while those who suffer from the aggressive form will be propelled to assist with murders, the passive ones will instead be primarily physically and mentally attracted to those who commit vile acts [31].

At this point, it has been assumed that hybristophilia, for the most part, affects women; however, the Chris Kyle case indicates otherwise. Some researchers have theorized that perpetrators of extremely brutal crimes may convey an ultra-masculine image, and this image is ultimately what drives the hybristophiliac on an unconscious level. However, these theories remain untested empirically, and the causes remain unknown [32].

The pathological admiration and attraction to Chris Kyle are best exemplified by Texas Governor, Greg Abbott, who declared February 2 to be Chris Kyle Day in Texas, and by the pictures of thousands of people who mourned at his funeral procession, perhaps indicating a collective mental state of hybristophilia.

It has been argued that the central component of the disorder is the obsession or unhealthy attraction, while a secondary symptom may be rationalization of antisocial acts, which is the apparent tendency of the hybristophiliac to excuse the acts of the criminal whom they are infatuated with. Such rationalizations are evident in statements from journalists and people at his funeral procession who frequently referred to Kyle's acts as noble deeds or somehow else glorified them, entirely ignoring the moral and legal dilemmas.

An online search on YouTube and Google for "Chris Kyle Tribute" reveals dozens of tribute videos, songs, and other material dedicated to Kyle. They are very similar in content to what can easily be found glorifying non-legalized killers, especially school shooters and serial killers. For example, a Google search for "Ted Bundy Tribute" shows numerous videos dedicated to him, painting an image consistent with hybristophilia. One viewer commented, "R.I.P Teddy Bundy, you will be missed on this planet buddy," while another stated, "One of the all-time greatest persons ever," and one even proclaimed that "I understand the love for Ted...however I love Jeff Dahmer. If you loved Ted more power to you. We have the right to love whomsoever we want!! [33]." In view of the immense bloodthirst of Ted Bundy, these comments appear delusional but entirely consistent with hybristophilia. If we pay heed to Chris Kyle's tribute videos, their content and related comments are highly suggestive of hybristophilia. Dr. Chris Cowley, a forensic psychologist, has documented that "in the most pronounced form, the illness has an attention-seeking pathology a little like Munchausen's syndrome," and the affected may attempt to "become semi-famous by association [34]." A surprisingly high number of the comments to his tribute videos revolve around an alleged association with Kyle. Here is just a very short segment of the comments to one of his tribute videos, notice the attention seeking quality to some of them: "A HERO and a patriot. God. Country. Family. Honored to know him, and call him a friend. Humble, courageous, kind. Immortal warrior. Legend. Amazing man. Period," "He sits next to the gates of heaven where he stands guard forever. God bless Chris and his family," "LOL 57 people didn't like this.. they are from Iraq," "I read his book just a couple months ago and that was the first ive heard of him. I honor this man, in my mind he was a true hero to this country. Its not about his kills thats just a number …. This man really is my hero, i look up to him and i wish i knew of him before his death so i can shake his hand and say thank you," "Whoever hit dislike you don't deserve to be an American!," "The guys he killed were dirtbags," "I cry so much, what a beautiful man-soul. Rip," and "I spent time with this guy he was a true hero [35]."

These comments are consistent with the characteristics of hybristophilia outlined earlier in this article. It needs, also, to be stated that comments questioning the morality and legality of his killings were generally countered with hostile replies, indicating that information conflicting their current belief about Kyle produced cognitive dissonance as a psychological coping mechanism.

The major characteristics of hybristophilia are met by the observed behavior of many of Kyle's adherents, although, we cannot know with certainty without an extensive empirical analysis. At this point, it appears to be a valid hypothesis.

American Liar

Chris Kyle's legacy encompasses numerous immoral acts including outright deception. It has been shown that he deceived his readers about the numbers of awards he had received for military deeds. Mooney was unable to verify the carjacker story, and other researchers have been unable to document the factual basis for his claim regarding the sniper killings after Hurricane Katrina. Considering Kyle's moral track record it is reasonable to assume that both stories were lies. However, without a thorough investigation by objective experts, his assertions cannot be dismissed completely.

Furthermore, on radio and television, he alleged that he had punched out former governor Jesse Ventura at a bar in 2006. Ventura promptly sued Kyle for defamation. Despite Kyle dying during the trial, Ventura continued the law suit, and a jury awarded him over $1.8 million. In 2006, the judgment was overturned. While preparing for a new trial, he reached an agreement with the opposing side. Due to the agreement, he was unable to comment on how much money he had received but remarked that "the settlement is confidential, but I can smile [36]." Ventura has denounced Chris Kyle an "American Liar [37]."

Reflections upon the Psychology of Chris Kyle

If we loosely utilize the Psychopathy Checklist Revised, which was created by Robert D. Hare as a diagnostic tool, as a guide to assess the psychological dynamics of Chris Kyle, it remains clear that he was most likely a psychopath, possibly scoring a high total rating (maximum = 40) [38].

As we shall see, the major constituents of psychopathy correlate very well with his statements and documented behavior. Unlike most cases with non-legalized serial killers who often are ashamed of their deeds, Kyle glorified in them and often vividly described them to interested bystanders and openly admitted his love for murder and violence. Indeed, the Chris Kyle case represents a near unique glimpse into the mind of a serial killer since many captured killers ostensibly embellish, withhold, manipulate, and distort their case for obvious reasons, e.g. getting out of prison, legal issues, embarrassment, manipulating public perception, et cetera. Few killers have openly admitted their love for killing and lack of remorse. One such exception though is the spree killer Charles Starkweather, who was questioned if he would change anything if he had the ability. He answered: "No, not really" and added, "I know I'm a monster [39]." During the same interview, he admitted, "If I could go back into time, I would kill as many more people as I could because I hate people. I know they are gonna kill me in the electric chair. I don't really care because I'm gonna be famous for all time [39]."

Among others, psychopaths are characterized by shallow emotions, diminished or non-existent conscience, and they lack empathy or are able to switch it off at will. Kyle repeatedly stated in interviews that he had no remorse and only regretted he had not murdered more people, clearly evidencing limited capacity for empathy and remorse, e.g. he rhetorically asked himself: "Did it bother you killing so many people in Iraq? I tell them, 'No.' And I mean it [2]."

Regarding the depth of his emotions and empathy, the following quote from Kyle is also relevant: "The first time you shoot someone, you get a little nervous. You think, can I really shoot this guy? Is it really okay? But after you kill your enemy, you see it's okay. You say, Great. You do it again. And again. .... I loved what I did. I still do. If circumstances were different I'd be back in a heartbeat. I'm not lying or exaggerating to say it was fun [2]." The statement is clear evidence of limited capacity for sympathy and empathy, emotional poverty.

Based upon the above statement and others mentioned in the article, he conceived of the world as consisting of good and bad people, but he only killed bad ones. This simplification by Kyle comes as no surprise as a key trait in psychopathy is the ability to rationalize and justify actions regardless of how atrocious they may have been; they fail to take responsibility. In his book, he even proclaimed that "I have a strong sense of justice [2]," a statement which again underlines that he rationalized his murders by simply categorizing his victims as evil, and in his own mind, he most likely regarded himself as a savior and hero. Rationalizations and moral shortcuts are common to most prolific murderers, including Herbert Mullin, who claimed that he killed people in order to prevent a massive earthquake from happening in California, and therefore, he was not really evil [40].

His reaction to shooting and killing a human being is reflective of a state of low anxiety, which also is commonly found among psychopaths who often exhibit a fearless mental state in situations where it would be expected that the individual would be gripped with fear and anxiety [41].

Chris Kyle also appears to have indulged in compulsive narcissistic deception. Judging by his statements, he apparently had a persistent need to elevate his self-worth: he lied about the number of military rewards he had received, probably about his murderous achievements, and about his fight with Jesse Ventura, all in all indicating grandiosity and a compulsive need for self-entitlement, suggesting a core of narcissism in his personality.

Pathological narcissism is a fundamental component of psychopathy; the condition is, among others, characterized by self-centeredness, status-seeking, distrust, arrogance, and a sense of entitlement.

It has long been observed that narcissists want to be the center of attention, and they often have a deep desire to get known, even nationwide. The publication of his murderous deeds may very well have been motivated by a narcissistic desire to attain nationwide appreciation and recognition for his perceived heroism.

While the majority of Kyle's kills were relatively fast, some of his acts suggest that he took pleasure in sadistic behavior. Sadists, of course, take great pleasure in causing and observing physical and/or psychological pain and anguish in others. Specifically, the previously mentioned beach ball incident, where he admittedly experienced great exhilaration from causing the drowning of multiple men, indicates that his psyche translated their pain into a greatly positive experience, perhaps even sexually.

Regarding his own psyche, Kyle had surprisingly little to say in his book, except that he briefly described that his psyche had built up defenses, and that is why he would "laugh at gruesome things like heads being blown apart, and worse [2]."

Importantly, he admitted in the book that killing and murder were already on his mind as he was growing up as he had "wondered, how would I feel about killing someone? Now I know. It's no big deal [2]." Numerous cases attest to the notion that the roots of repetitive killers can be traced to their upbringing as many serial killers have admitted to torturing animals in their childhood or have fantasized about killing people.

Although operating within the framework of US government approved violence, Chris Kyle appears similar in many respects to non-legalized serial killers.

Final Words

Unlike imprisoned killers, Kyle had no qualms about asserting his love for killing Iraqis – presumably due to a combination of factors that includes government approval, backing by military institutions, and encomiums celebrating his work as wonders of the first order. The multilayered saga of Chris Kyle represents a dangerous example of how institutions can shape and mold the underlying morality of a large group, and effectively make them celebrate acts and personalities that under normal conditions would cause an outrage. Undoubtedly, the military industrial complex had a vested interest in promoting the demonstrably false narrative surrounding Chris Kyle, to further their agenda.

Originally published as "American Monster: Chris Kyle, the American Sniper" Radian & Inches, 2018.

References

[1]. "Ex-Navy sniper, another military vet killed at Texas gun range"
https://edition.cnn.com/2013/02/03/justice/texas-sniper-killed/index.html
[2]. American Sniper: The Autobiography of the Most Lethal Sniper in U.S.
Military History (William Morrow and Company 2012). Chris Kyle with
Scott McEwen and Jim DeFelice.
[3]. "The REAL American Sniper: 'There are no kills that I regret. None at
all'" https://www.mirror.co.uk/news/real-life-stories/real-american-sniper-
there-no-5036121
[4]. Canadian law professors declare US-led war illegal"
https://www.wsws.org/en/articles/2003/03/lawy-m22.html
[5]. "Iraq – ICJ Deplores Moves To-ward a War of Aggression on Iraq"
https://web.archive.org/web/20051015040809/http://www.icj.org:80/news.ph
p3?id_article=2770&lang=en
[6]. Law Professors For the Rule of Law"
https://web.archive.org/web/20040214101825/http:/www.the-rule-of-
law.com:80/index.html
[7]. "Iraq war was illegal and breached UN charter, says Annan"
https://www.theguardian.com/world/2004/sep/16/iraq.iraq
[8]. "War, Aggression, and State Crime: A Criminological Analysis of the
Invasion and Occupation of Iraq." Ronald C. Kramer. Western Michigan
University. Raymond J. Michalowski. Northern Arizona University. Revised
for the British Journal of Criminology, October 2004.
[9]. "Iraq inquiry: Former UN inspector Blix says war illegal"
www.bbc.com/news/uk-politics-10770239
[10]. "Bush and Saddam Should Both Stand Trial, Says Nuremberg
Prosecutor"
https://www.globalpolicy.org/component/content/article/167/35806.html
[11]. "Nuremberg set a valid precedent for trials of war-crime suspects in
Iraq's destruction"
https://www.japantimes.co.jp/opinion/2009/05/26/commentary/nuremberg-
set-a-valid-precedent-for-trials-of-war-crime-suspects-in-iraqs-destruction/
[12]. "Could Bush Be Prosecuted for War Crimes?"
https://www.alternet.org/story/38604/could_bush_be_prosecuted_for_war_cr
imes
[13]. "Iraq war was illegal, Dutch panel rules"
https://www.theguardian.com/world/2010/jan/12/iraq-war-illegal-dutch-
tribunal
[14]. "Chilcot report: key points from the Iraq inquiry"
https://www.theguardian.com/uk-news/2016/jul/06/iraq-inquiry-key-points-
from-the-chilcot-report. Also see: The Iraq Inquiry: www.iraqinquiry.org.uk.
Also see: "Chilcot report: Findings at a glance" www.bbc.com/news/uk-
politics-36721645
[15]. The prosecution of George W. Bush for murder" Vincent Bugliosi
(New York: Vanguard Press, 2008.)
[16]. "General Wesley Clark: Wars Were Planned – Seven Countries In Five
Years" https://www.youtube.com/watch?v=9RC1Mepk_Sw

[17]. Mortality after the 2003 invasion of Iraq: a cross-sectional cluster sample survey." Burnham, Gilbert et al. The Lancet, Volume 368, Issue 9545, 1421 – 1428. Also see: "Mortality before and after the 2003 invasion of Iraq: cluster sample survey." Roberts, Les et al. The Lancet, Volume 364, Issue 9448, 1857– 1864.

[18]. Washington, D.C. Physicians for Social Responsibility: Body count: casualty figures after 10 years of the "War on Terror": Iraq, Afghanistan, Pakistan

[19]. "The Iraq deaths study was valid and correct" https://www.theage.com.au/news/opinion/the-iraq-deaths-study-was-valid-and-correct/2006/10/20/1160851135985.html?page=fullpage

[20]. "Death Counter Explanation Page" http://www.justforeignpolicy.org/deathcount/explanation

[21]. "January 2008 – Update on Iraqi Casualty Data" https://web.archive.org/web/20110220142121/http://www.opinion.co.uk/Newsroom_details.aspx?NewsId=120

[22]. "How the Pentagon is hiding the dead. The secret campaign to under-count the 'war on terror' death toll in the Middle East, Central Asia, and Latin America" https://medium.com/insurge-intelligence/how-the-pentagon-is-hiding-the-dead-862a7b45ce57

[23]. "An Iraqi Holocaust: 2.7 Million Iraqi Dead From Violence Or War-imposed Deprivation" http://www.informationclearinghouse.info/article41378.htm

[24]. "Principles of International Law Recognized in the Charter of the Nürnberg Tribunal and in the Judgment of the Tribunal" legal.un.org/ilc/texts/instruments/english/draft_articles/7_1_1950.pdf

[25]. "In the Crosshairs: Chris Kyle, a decorated sniper, tried to help a troubled veteran. The result was tragic" https://www.newyorker.com/magazine/2013/06/03/in-the-crosshairs

[26]. "Chris Kyle and 'American Sniper'" https://www.snopes.com/fact-check/kyle-file/

[27]. "'Legend' of American sniper Chris Kyle looms over murder trial" https://edition.cnn.com/2015/02/09/us/chris-kyle-american-sniper/index.html. Also see: "The Legend of Chris Kyle: The deadliest sniper in U.S. history performed near miracles on the battle-field. Then he had to come home" https://www.dmagazine.com/publications/d-magazine/2013/april/the-legend-of-chris-kyle-01/?single=1

[28]. "Killing Ragheads for Jesus" https://www.truthdig.com/articles/killing-ragheads-for-jesus/

[29]. "Chris Kyle's Memorial at Cowboys Stadium (FULL)" https://www.youtube.com/watch?v=jmWZ7Fafhso

[30]. "Passion Victim: A brief look at hybristophilia" https://www.psychologytoday.com/us/blog/in-excess/201310/passion-victim

[31]. "Hybristophilia: When a Woman Is Sexually Attracted to Horrifying, Psychopathic Criminals" https://www.vagabomb.com/Hybristophilia/

[32]. "3 Experts Explain Why Some People Are Attracted to Serial Killers" https://www.cosmopolitan.com/entertainment/tv/a17804534/sexual-attraction-to-serial-killers

[33]. "Tribute to Ted Bundy"
https://www.youtube.com/watch?v=BhZG6trFdsE
[34]. Cowley, Chris. "Face to Face with Evil: Conversations with Ian Brady" (2011 Metro Publishing), p. 116 & 118.
[35]. "A Tribute to Chris Kyle 'Devil of Ramadi'"
https://www.youtube.com/watch?v=pLvSuAznnks
[36]. "Ventura settles defamation suit but won't say for how much" www.startribune.com/jesse-ventura-to-discuss-settlement-of-defamation-law-suit-at-monday-afternoon-news-conference/461863413/
[37]. "Jesse Ventura Slams 'American Liar' Chris Kyle After Settling Lawsuit" http://www.insider.foxnews.com/2017/12/05/jesse-ventura-slams-american-liar-chris-kyle-after-settling-lawsuit
[38]. "Hare Psychopathy Checklist" www.minddisorders.com/Flu-Inv/Hare -Psychopathy-Checklist.html
[39]. Korsgaard, Søren. "America's Jack the Ripper: The Crimes and Psychology of the Zodiac Killer" (2017), p. 273.
[40]. "He Thought His Murders Could Stop Earthquakes: The Crimes of Herbert Mullin" https://didyouknowfacts.com/thought-murders-stop-earthquakes-crimes-herbert-mullin/
[41]. "Inside the mind of a PSYCHOPATH: Researchers find they do feel fear – but don't recognise danger" www.dailymail.co.uk/sciencetech/article-3767545/Inside-mind-PSYCHOPATH-Researchers-feel-fear -don-t-recognise-danger.html
[42]. Alv A. Dahl, Aud Dalsegg, "Chamør og Tyran" (Munksgaard 2002).

The New 9/11: A Global Virus Pandemic

Søren Roest Korsgaard

Effective Mass Manipulation via PRS

The response to COVID-19 (used synonymously with
'coronavirus' in this article) crisis bears numerous similarities to
the 9/11 false flag atrocity [1]. The effective mass mind control
stratagem of Problem, Reaction, Solution (PRS), has been used
successfully in both instances to implement draconian laws and,
in the case of COVID-19, conduct the largest human experiment
in history.

The motivation of those who planned, organized, and
implemented the false flag attack of September 11, 2001, was
multifarious. On one hand, around 3000 lives were sacrificed to
start a series of neocolonial wars aimed at restoring and
maintaining the superpower status of the US, in terms of
economics and geopolitics. On the other hand, this "New Pearl
Harbor" was also carried through in order to bring about
draconian laws. These laws severely limited civil rights while
concomitantly giving governments unprecedented powers. For
example, one may be imprisoned indefinitely without charge or
trial in several countries; Australia has taken to the extremes
and it is now punishable by five years in prison to reveal if
someone is held in prison without charge or trial (e.g. a spouse)
[2]. False flag attacks are invariably constructed around a mass
mind control stratagem, known as Problem, Reaction, Solution.
This stratagem is effectively used to increase a government's
powers and bring about totalitarianism.

A. First a problem is created, e.g. a "terrorist attack." The most
effective problem is one that does not have a clear-cut solution,
an enemy that is difficult to define, and easy to maintain via
media propaganda and, if necessary, minor false flag attacks. It
is important for those responsible to underline that the country
or state was unprepared for the incident. This reduces resistance

from the public when the ruling elite decide to make radical changes to the status quo.

B. Manufacture a reaction. The mainstream media (MSM), public "intellectuals," and commentariats will react to the problem. Specifically, they will focus incessantly on the problem while blaming a not well-defined entity. Those who question the one-sided narrative are castigated, labeled as criminals or "conspiracy theorists," or their research is called "fake news." The masses watch lots of television, read the news online from government approved sites, and use social media frequently; on average, Americans watch 77 days of non-stop television every year, in Australia that figure is around 38 days [3, 4]. Being subjected to months of intense propaganda, it is no surprise that the masses quickly adopt the mainstream line of thinking as if it was their own. It is inescapable that most of the thoughts that people are having are not their own. They are ideas and constructs that have been inserted into their consciousness via television, social media, and popular choice entertainment.

When the masses have been programmed sufficiently, they are themselves demanding steps be taken to curtail possible future instances of the problem. At this point, the final step of the PRS protocol is unleashed.

C. Those who orchestrated the initial, major event then propose and implement a solution. The solution invariably curtails freedoms for the masses while benefitting the elite and expanding the powers of governments.

Mainstream Media Subversion

The PRS formula is not workable unless the MSM is almost entirely subverted and subdued. Due to the brevity of this article, we shall refrain from explaining the dynamics, but provide one palpable example that illustrates that virtually all major mainstream media outlets are controlled by outside forces. Of course, it may be interjected that this is old news and should not surprise anyone. For example, the Church Committee, which was a U.S. Senate select committee formed in 1975, which investigated abuses by the CIA and other alphabet agencies, concluded:

The CIA currently maintains a network of several hundred foreign individuals around the world who provide intelligence for the CIA and at times attempt to influence opinion through the use of covert propaganda. These individuals provide the CIA with direct access to a large number of newspapers and periodicals, scores of press services and news agencies, radio and television stations, commercial book publishers, and other foreign media outlets [5].

In 1956, the US government launched the Counter Intelligence Program (COINTELPRO). COINTELPRO was aimed at shaping public discourse through surveilling, assassinating, infiltrating, discrediting, and disrupting dissidents and a long list of organizations [6]. Officially, however, the CIA's media influence and COINTELPRO ended in the 1970s. However, this is not the case.

Author, journalist, and publisher, Tommy Hansen, explained during a talk on the "Deep State" how a newspaper is created. First, the back pages are created, but the front page remains blank until the finals hours before printing and publication lest a sensational story emerges. However, Tommy Hansen notes that on June 8, 2015, dozens of newspapers across Europe and the US printed virtually the same story with the exact same picture on their front page. Tommy Hansen concludes that it is "physically impossible" for numerous newspapers, independent of each other, and at the same time to decide on the same story with the exact same picture [7]. Hansen notes that newspapers "do absolutely not share their front-page news with each other," and concludes that the "observed uniformity" is what makes people discuss the same stories at the same time, regardless of geography [8]. The one-sided media response to the false flag attack of 9/11 is also clear evidence of mainstream media subversion. For instance, there was even a complete MSM blackout of the fact that independent scientists had published a peer-reviewed paper on their findings of unreacted military nano-thermite in dust samples from the collapses of World Trade Center 1, 2, and 7 [9]. In this regard, contrast the non-stop live coverage of the coronavirus deaths with the total MSM blackout of the following selected atrocities:

1. The 1942-1945 Bengali Holocaust (6-7 million Indians killed under the British with Australian complicity) [10].
2. The ongoing Australian Aboriginal Genocide that since 1788 has been associated with about 2 million indigenous Australians deaths from violence or from imposed disease and deprivation [11].
3. From 2001-2014, the US-Alliance's invasion of Afghanistan resulted in 7.2 million Afghan deaths from either violence or from war-imposed deprivation [12].
4. Governments and the MSM have also completed ignored the Global Avoidable Mortality Holocaust (44,000 people die from deprivation every day in the developing world) [13].
5. The world's foremost expert on avoidable mortality and holocausts, Australian scientist, Dr. Gideon Polya, has shown that from 2001 to 2015, the post-9/11 US War on Terror has been associated with 32 million Muslim deaths (5 million from violence; 27 million from deprivation) [14].

These atrocities are ignored by MSM journalists, governments, and "influencers" as stopping them or ensuring accountability runs contrary to elitist interests. The massive coverage of the coronavirus tells us that the virus is in line with their plans for humanity.

COVID-19 in regard to PRS

In this section, we will take a closer look at the coronavirus crisis in regard to the PRS mass mind control formula.

A. According to the official narrative, the first case of a person infected with a coronavirus took place on November 17, 2019 [15]. The spread of the virus was swiftly defined by governments as a major, global threat to humanity, and touted to be something health authorities were unprepared for.
B. The media response was unparalleled to the point of surpassing the storm of propaganda following the false flag attack of 9/11 and even the massive campaign of deception

leading up to the Iraq war. Nearly every mainstream media outlet, regardless of its target audience or niche interest, switched to non-stop coverage of the coronavirus crisis to the point of complete saturation. With popular choice entertainment avenues eliminated, the result has been a concentrated exposure to propaganda, never seen before.

It is manifest that the reportage is not contextual and constructive, but rather intended to terrorize the masses. For example, death toll updates are shown in innumerable places, documentaries related to the Spanish Flu that killed an estimated 20-50 million people are shown across the globe. Newspapers report that the coronavirus "could infect 60% of global population if unchecked" and "kill 1 in 100 of those infected – around 50 million people," "Competition for supplies sharpening as pandemic worsens," "Death rate soars in New Orleans coronavirus 'disaster' that could define city for generations," "Coronavirus will infect 2.5 billion people, kill 53 million by March, AI predicts,"etc. [16-20].

The propaganda campaign has resulted in widespread panic and suffering, hoarding of food and supplies, and has importantly dissolved social cohesion while making people increasingly more dependent upon government.

C. Under the pretext of the coronavirus and via an unprecedented terrorist/propaganda operation, governments have successfully conducted the largest human experiment in history [21]. The consequences are staggering and will become more tangible over the next months and years. So far, with the stroke of a pen, governments have (not the virus) reduced humans to mere sheep and cattle: billions have been forced into house arrest or confinement, non-essential businesses were closed and millions of people lost their livelihood in an instant, the ability to move and travel freely was eliminated, the global economy took a nosedive resulting in untold suffering in first-world and, in particular, third-world countries. Additionally, dystopian and extremely intrusive spyware were rolled out to track and monitor citizens (but not government officials) [22]. The stress resulting from the global lockdown, unemployment, and propaganda has initiated a virtual pandemic of suicides and overdoses. In England and Wales, the suicide rate has hit a two-decade's high, meanwhile 75,000 excess Americans are estimated to die from suicide and overdoses due to exacerbated living conditions [23-24].

The "terrorist laws" that were rolled out subsequently to 9/11 were widely regarded as extreme, illegal, and infringing upon basic human rights; however, the laws being implemented in numerous countries, right now, make the 9/11 laws pale in comparison. The citizens of Australia have been thoroughly disenfranchised. In the state of Victoria a Stage 4 Lockdown has been imposed, which means you must wear masks outside the home (fine for not wearing a mask, about $1,000). The citizens can only exercise outside the home for one hour a day, cannot travel more than 5 km, can go out alone only for shopping or medical purposes, and there is a curfew from 8 pm to 5 am. Those who break the curfew are penalized with a fine of about $5000. If this is not prison there has never been one.

In Denmark a very detailed and complicated 227-page bill - which undoubtedly has been years in the making – will soon be passed. According to the document, the purpose of the law is to "protect society and individuals against the diseases mentioned in § 2 by eradicating or curtailing, preventing and limiting the spread [25]." The document then specifies that the law encompasses "infectious diseases, generally dangerous diseases, and *socially critical diseases* .... By a socially critical disease is meant a generally dangerous disease whose spread causes or risks causing serious disturbances to important functions of society [26]." The document further specifies that a "socially critical disease is, in contrast to a disease that is alone contagious or generally dangerous, more difficult to categorize in advance, as the categorization does not alone depend on the assessments of health professionals of the mortality of the disease and consequences for the individual, but also for political assessments of the societal consequences of the disease [27]." Translation: Those who spread "fake news" or go against the establishment's version of events will be regarded as sick and targeted for eradication. The extremely broad definition of a "socially critical disease" means that the elite can define any troublesome behavior as a disease whose spread must be stopped.

For years, one of the top priorities of the elite has been the outlawing of "fake news." The Orwellian concept of fake news concerns anything that threaten the interests of centralized power, but not, for example, the lies about Washington's wars, "weapons of mass destruction," "Iranian nukes," "Assad's use of chemical weapons," etc. By exploiting the coronavirus crisis, totalitarian laws were quickly proposed and enacted across the world with a high degree of coordination and with very little variability. In several countries, it is now a crime to spread fake news. In Zimbabwe, "people who peddle information deemed false by the government face up to 20 years in prison, a hefty fine or both" [28]. In Thailand, the government warned that "anybody joking about the virus could face up to five years prison time" [29].

If we carefully observe the techniques used by the MSM and other institutions during the current crisis. Then, it appears that they have conditioned the masses to accept totalitarianism as a solution through the covert use of psychological conditioning techniques used in the military. When new recruits are drafted into the military part of their training is to be broken down via intrusive physical and psychological processes. The training involves confinement and suppression, control and conformity, deindividuation, stress and punishment, and others. By means of these processes, the personality and character of recruits are reshaped such that they, for example, will obey orders from superiors at all times. In regard to the coronavirus, the masses have been terrified, suppressed, isolated, subdued, impoverished, and demoralized. It appears that the goal has been to reshape and resocialize the masses in order to prepare them for massive changes, such as a one world digital dictatorship.

Systemic Skullduggery

The mortality data, which has been instrumental in terrorizing the masses, is almost never put into context or properly explained.

For reference, *the case fatality rate (CFR)* can be calculated via this simple formula:

$$\text{CASE FATALITY RATE} = \frac{\text{CORONA DEATHS}}{\text{NUMBER OF INFECTED}} * 100\%$$

CFR shows the percentage of confirmed *infected* people who have died from COVID-19. However, many patients experience minor symptoms and are not tested or hospitalized. The *infection fatality rate* (IFR) seeks to estimate the total number of infected people by dividing the estimated total number of deaths with the estimated total number of infected. The IFR is often confused with the CFR. In the case of COVID-19, the media has frequently confused (either deliberately or due to incompetence) the invariably high CFR for being the IFR – which is much lower in this instance! Furthermore, neither CHR nor IFR indicate the risk for healthy individuals. For example, assume that 90 people are infected with COVID-19, but only 10 goes to the hospital and are tested positive. One person dies. This means that the CFR = 10%, but the IFR = 1.11%.

Officially, deaths attributed to COVID-19 are determined based on two criteria 1. The person is COVID-19 positive. 2. The person dies within 30 days of the diagnosis (initially the threshold was 60 days) [30]. Without an autopsy, we do not know the exact cause of death which could have been the result of other complications. This becomes all the more plausible when we consider that the majority of those who are tested have preexisting health issues, like high blood pressure and heart problems. This flawed methodology is analogous to a pathologist who ascribes a conclusion of "suicide" to every instance of a person found dead with a gun in their hand or lying next to the body.

The allegedly high death toll of COVID-19 in Italy has been used successfully in Europe and elsewhere to manipulate and terrorize. However, when looked at a bit closer a different picture emerges. A report by Italy's health officials shows that "more than 99% of coronavirus patients who died in Italy suffered from other, pre-existing health issues" [31, 32]. Of the dead, 75% had high blood pressure, 35% had diabetes, and 33% had heart disease. The average age of the deceased was 79.5.

Considering the flawed mythology of how the dead are counted, it is given that countless people who have died of other health problems have falsely been put into the coronavirus category. The case fatality rate is invariably highly fluctuating at the beginning of an outbreak; if people who report severe symptoms are those who are primarily tested, the CFR will be deceptively high. Most likely, this observation accounts for the huge differences in fatality rates between countries, over 10% in Italy but less than 2% in Russia [33]. In the US, data from the CDC regarding COVID-19 deaths shows that only 6% did not have other causes listed on their death certificate, about 9500 people [34]. On average, there were 2.6 additional conditions or causes per death. Among these COVID-19 only deaths, approximately 60% were age 75 and older; 80% were age 65 and older. Thus, a tiny number of COVID-only deaths involved young adults and children.

As indicated, people who are chronically sick and at an advanced age are primarily those targeted for testing resulting in a deceptively high CFR. But if the test is also highly unreliable, giving many false positives, the result will be that COVID-19 appears very deadly but is not. This is exactly what has happened. In September 2020, it was revealed that "up to 90 percent of people testing positive carried barely any virus" and "the test's threshold is so high that it detects people with the live virus as well as those with a few genetic fragments left over from a past infection that no longer poses a risk. 'It's like finding a hair in a room after a person left it,' says Michael Mina, MD, an epidemiologist at the Harvard T.H. Chan School of Public Health [35]."

A strong indication that the official COVID-19 test is worthless was demonstrated already in May 2020 when Dr. John Magufuli, the president of Tanzania who holds a doctorate in chemistry, cleverly "tested the testers," as he was suspicious of the motives of the World Health Organization. At a press conference, he revealed the following:

> We took samples from goats. We sent samples from sheep. We took samples from pawpaws. We sent samples from car oil. And we took samples from other different things. And we took the samples to the

laboratory without them knowing. And we even named all the samples. Like the sample of car oil. We named it Jabil Hamza, 30 years old, male. The results came back negative. When we took a sample from a jackfruit (Durian) we named it Sarah Samuel, 45 years old, female. The results came back inconclusive. When we took samples from a pawpaw we named it Elizabeth Ane, 26 years old, female. The result from the pawpaw came back positive that it has corona. That means the liquid from a pawpaw is positive. We took samples from (a bird) called kware. The results came back positive. We took samples from a rabbit. The results came back undetermined. We took samples from a goat and the results came back positive. We took samples from a sheep and it came back negative and so on and so on. And so now you see this, you have taken samples, and the results come back positive and they have the corona. That means all the pawpaws should be in isolation also… The goat should be in isolation also [36].

In addition to the points mentioned above, it gets worse because in the US, which officially has been severely affected by the virus, massive fraud has taken place in order to inflate the death toll. Via the Coronavirus Aid, Relief and Economic Security Act, hospitals receive more than 20 percent in federal aid if they are struggling with the virus, giving the administration and workers plenty of financial incentive to put patients into the COVID category. Not surprisingly a nurse working at a New York hospital, the alleged "epicenter of the epicenter" in the US, secretly recorded how her patients were labeled COVID-19 confirmed despite testing negative more than once [37]. Funding also appears to be one of the reasons why numerous people dying from traffic accidents, gunshot wounds, etc. have been fraudently registered as dying from the disease. The Washington State Department of Health confirmed in May 2020 that "the state is counting in its COVID-19 death total the deaths of persons who tested positive for the virus but died from other causes. … including multiple deaths caused by gunshot wounds [38]." One young Florida resident died on the scene subsequent to a motorcycle accident, but was unbelievably included in the state's official COVID-19 death count [39]. According to Josephine Dimiceli, who is the President of Dimiceli & Sons Funeral Home, one of her clients was a New York State Supreme Court Justice. When she had learned that her sister had died of COVID-19, she did not believe it and she promptly ordered an independent autopsy, which revealed no signs of her dying from the virus [40]. There are many more examples and pieces of evidence demonstrating how the numbers have been inflated, but it is clear from the information presented that if the virus had been extremely lethal as propagandists want us to believe then fraud would not have been necessary. Even third world countries are reported to have invented high coronavirus numbers to secure foreign aid, which of course are used for different purposes. However, it is also possible for fraud, bad testing, and so forth to have taken place concomitantly with a very dangerous virus. Whether or not COVID-19 is dangerous, we will let Chris Whitty, an epidemiologist and Chief Medical Officer for England, explain:

> The great majority of people will not die from this, and I'll just repeat something I said right at the beginning because I think it's worth reinforcing: Most people, a significant proportion of people, will not get this virus at all, at any point of the epidemic which is going to go on for a long period of time. Of those who do, some of them will get the virus without even knowing it, they will have the virus with no symptoms at all, asymptomatic carriage, and we know that happens. Of those who get symptoms, the great majority, probably 80%, will have a mild or moderate disease. Might be bad enough for them to have to go to bed for a few days, not bad enough for them to have to go to the doctor. An unfortunate minority will have to go as far as hospital, but the majority of those will just need oxygen and will then leave hospital. And then a minority of those will end up having to go to severe end critical care and some of those sadly will die. But that's a minority, it's 1% or possibly even less than 1% overall. And even in the highest risk group this is significantly less than 20%, i.e.

the great majority of people, even the very highest groups, if they catch this virus, will not die [41].

In 2009, the WHO suspiciously changed the definition of a pandemic by removing the criterion for a high mortality rate, allowing for widespread use of the term, fearmongering, and more vaccine and drug sales – the WHO is largely controlled by the pharmaceutical industry and Bill Gates, the number one pusher of vaccines, who is their biggest sponsor as of this writing [42]. In 2009, experts voiced their concerns that now virtually "all influenzas can be called pandemics ... Thus, the pharmaceutical industry will also in the future be able to earn billions on vaccines for relatively harmless diseases [43]." Danish Physician Mauri Johansson revealed that "All member countries are obliged to follow the recommendations of the WHO - in Denmark we are even obliged to buy vaccines against the flu because we, like many other countries, have made a contract with a company, and it will be triggered if the WHO declares a pandemic [44]." In other words, the WHO is an unelected, profit driven company that has been instrumental in establishing the coronacrisis – which, as the evidence indicates, has been blown completely out of proportion under a profit motive.
Considering the pervasive fraud documented in this article and elsewhere, it would make sense for the WHO to add an addendum to their definition of a pandemic, specifying that an epidemic that spreads to more than one continent by means of fraudulent mortality statistics and data and fakery is a "scamdemic."

The Mysterious Coronavirus Exercise

Shortly before the first registered case of COVID-19 a mysterious coronavirus exercise took place that envisioned the real-life impact and governmental response to an astonishing degree. The organizations and individuals, who were involved in the exercise, became frequent media experts and played a crucial role in maintaining the official narrative and exaggerating the threat by spreading misinformation and outright lies. Most notably Bill Gates who has publically identified vaccines as a way of fulfilling his personal goal of depopulating the Earth: "Now the world today has 6.8 billion people that's heading up to about 9 billion. Now, if we do a really great job on new vaccines, health care, reproductive health services we could lower that by perhaps 10 or 15% [45]." Conclusive evidence from a broad range of sources has affirmed that his intentions are malicious rather than philanthropic. For example, a study published in the *International Journal of Environmental Research and Public Health* demonstrated that the Gates-supported oral polio vaccines resulted in at least 491,704 Indians becoming paralyzed between 2000 and 2017 [46]. Specifically, Gates took control of India's National Advisory Board (NAB) and mandated a massive 50 polio vaccines to every child before the age of five. After Gates had been evicted, the polio paralysis rates dropped precipitously [47]. In 2017, the WHO "reluctantly admitted" that the "global polio explosion is predominantly vaccine strain [48]." In other words, it is coming from the Bill Gates' Vaccine Program.

In 2014, it was revealed by Kenya's Catholic Doctors Association that millions of Kenyans had been chemically sterilized by the tetanus vaccine that was aggressively pushed by WHO and Gates in a number of developing countries. According to a study, led by John Oller, "HCG Found in WHO Tetanus Vaccine in Kenya Raises Concern in the Developing World," a total of "three independent Nairobi accredited biochemistry laboratories tested samples from vials of the WHO tetanus vaccine being used in March 2014 and found hCG [a sterility drug] where none should be present [49]." Further testing of more tetanus vaccines samples also revealed the sterilization chemical, hCG. John Oller and coworker further demonstrated and documented in their paper that "reducing global population growth, especially in [less developed countries], through antifertility measures has long been declared a central goal of USAID/UN/WHO 'family planning [50].'" The scientists concluded, "Our opinion is that the Kenya 'anti-tetanus' campaign was reasonably called into question by the Kenya Catholic Doctors Association as a front for population growth reduction [51]." There are indications that the depopulation program has been in effect for a long time as "spokespersons associated with the Catholic Church and pro-life groups have published suspicions at least since the early 1990s that the WHO was misrepresenting clinical trials of one or more antifertility campaigns as part of the world-wide WHO project to 'eliminate maternal and neonatal tetanus [52].'"

It is also very significant that a 2017 study by Mogensen and coworkers discovered that in the 1980s, WHO's popular DTP (diphtheria, tetanus and pertussis) vaccine resulted in a 500-1000% greater mortality than among those who were unvaccinated [53]. In other words, the vaccine was killing more people than the disease.

Bill Gates' record of death and mayhem has not caused him to retract one measured word. On the contrary, Gates, who is not a doctor, has increased his ruthless vaccine policy, rather than focusing on food, vitamins, clean water, mosquito nets, and economic development for developing countries. Furthermore, he will likely become the richest person in world history, if he achieves his stated goal of vaccinating the entire world with a coronavirus vaccine that might soon be available. He has even gone so far as to calling for a digital certificate to identify who has received a COVID-19 vaccine [54].

On October 18, 2019, a group of highly influential policymakers, business leaders, and health officials participated in *Event 201*, a "high-level pandemic exercise [55]." The Johns Hopkins Center for Health Security (JHCHS) in partnership with the World Economic Forum and the Bill and Melinda Gates Foundation hosted the exercise. The participants modeled a "new coronavirus [56]." Those who were exposed to the contagious pathogen "got a respiratory illness with symptoms ranging from mild flu-like signs to severe pneumonia [57]." When we take a closer look at the exercise, we find that the scenario, which they practiced, parallels the actual real-life situation to an astonishing degree. A video, which was later released by JHCHS, shows highlights from the exercise. As a part of it, the organizers had made fictitious news casts from a TV station, they called, "GNN." Among others it was stated:

> Public health agencies have issued travel advisories, while some countries have banned travel from the worst affected areas. As a result, the travel sector is taken a huge hit: travel booking are down 45% and many

flights have been canceled. A ripple effect is racing through the service sector. Governments that rely on travel and tourism as a large part of their economy are being hit particularly hard [58].

Shortly after the exercise, numerous countries worldwide banned travel or issued travel advisories and many flights were canceled. Here are a few selected headlines and quotes: "The Tourism Industry Is in Trouble. These Countries Will Suffer the Most [59]." "'It Will Be Catastrophic.' Asia's Tourism-Dependent Economies Are Being Hit Hard by the Coronavirus [60]." "Coronavirus: Airlines cancel thousands of flights [61]." "Bookings over the last two weeks down between 30-40% overall across all markets [62]." "More than 80 countries have imposed travel bans to curb the new coronavirus [63]."
During the exercise, Dr. Tom Inglesby, the Director of the Center for Health Security of the Johns Hopkins Bloomberg School of Public Health, asked a question which became a focal point during the crisis just weeks later: "How should national leaders, businesses, and international organizations balance the risk of worsening disease that will be caused by the continued movement of people around the world against the profound economic consequence of travel and trade bans? [64]"
The reliability of information was also discussed among the invite-only participants. The GNN news reporter says: "Countries are reacting in different ways as to how best to manage the overwhelming amounts of dis- and misinformation circulating over the Internet. In some cases, limited Internet shutdowns are being implemented to quell panic [65]."
When the actual coronacrisis occurred, governments were troubled by what they labeled fake news and misinformation. Here are some headlines: "Coronavirus: Fake news is spreading fast [66]." "Coronavirus: Fake news crackdown by UK government [67]." "Kolkata Police warns of stern action against fake news over coronavirus [68]" and "Cyber cell of Kolkata Police is keeping a 24x7 vigil on Internet to curb any attempt to spread dissemination of fake information over COVID-19 [69]." And "Social media companies are taking steps to tamp down coronavirus misinformation – but they can do more [70]."

The TV-channel, GNN, describes the consequences of CAPS (Coronavirus Associated Pulmonary Syndrome):

> The outcome of the CAPS pandemic in Event 201 was catastrophic: 65 million people died in the first 18 months. The outbreak was small at first and initially seemed controllable, but then it started spreading in densely crowded and impoverished neighborhoods of mega cities ... The global economy was in a free fall. The GDP down 11%. Stock markets around the world plummeted between 20% and 40% ... Economics say the economic turmoil caused by such a pandemic will last for years, perhaps a decade. The societal impact, the loss of faith in government, the distrust of news, and the breakdown of social cohesion could last even longer [71].

One of the conclusions of the exercise was that the coronavirus will continue spreading "until there is an effective vaccine or until 80–90% of the global population has been exposed [72]." The coronavirus exercise is an indication that certain powers brokers likely were aware of the coming crisis.

Chemical Warfare Against Own Populations

Governments and corporations have exploited the current crisis, but the question remains if COVID-19 could have been unleashed on purpose. There are no definitive answers at this point, but it is worthwhile to briefly examine the willingness of governments to poison their own citizens with biological weapons. The Independent, one of UK's largest newspapers, reported in 2015 that "the British Government" had "subjected thousands of people to chemical and biological warfare trials during [the] Cold War" [73]. The MSM is eager not to report on important matters, but in the rare instance where they do, the information is not put in its proper context and is usually "forgotten" thereafter, just like this article that did have any noteworthy impact.

According to the article, "the British Government used the general public as unwitting biological and chemical warfare guinea pigs on a much greater scale than previously thought,

120

according to new historical research" [74]. With certainty we know that the British government authorized a total of 4600 kg of zinc cadmium sulphide (ZnCdS) to be dispersed upon unwitting people from ships, aircrafts, and trucks between 1953 and 1964. The US is not any better. In 1957, Operation Large Area Coverage was commenced during which ZnCdS was dispersed over the majority of the US, but also parts of Canada and Mexico. Evidence suggests that the ZnCdS was probably mixed with radioactive particles [75]. Zinc cadmium sulfide is a neurotoxin that affects the brain, kidneys, bones, and respiratory tract, and may result in osteoporosis and chronic inflammation of the respiratory tract, among other ailments. Cadmium compounds are probable human carcinogens.

The hazardous and lethal biological and chemical weapons program did not end with ZnCdS. Several other deadly nerve agents were also used in human trials affecting millions of unsuspecting citizens. The UK government even authorized the use of g-series nerve agents in southern Nigeria [76]. First developed by the Nazis, g-series nerve agents, such as the extremely toxic Sarin gas which is considered a weapon of mass destruction, are likely to cause death in horrific ways or result in long-term neurological damage and psychiatric disorders. The UK government presumably carried out some of their human trials in Nigeria as it is easier to get away with.

Perhaps the most dangerous experiment, which could have initiated a pandemic of biblical proportions, involved spreading a cloud of Yersina pestis off the west coast of Scotland in 1952. A fishing vessel passed right through the cloud of bacteria, and if the wind had changed, it could have been devastating for those living on the Isle of Lewis [77]. Research has shown that Yersina pestis was the bacteria that caused the Black Death which killed an estimated 60% of Europe's population. Professor Francis Boyle is one of the world's foremost experts on biological warfare. In the 1980s, he drafted the Biological Weapons Anti-Terrorism Act of 1989. President George H.W. Bush signed it into law in 1990. According to a recent interview with Dr. Boyle, the US has spent "somewhere in the area of $100 billion" on offensive biological warfare between 2001 and 2015 [78]. It has been estimated that 13,000 "death scientists" in 400 laboratories in the U.S. and abroad are actively engaged in developing "new strains of offensive killer germs that will be resistant to vaccines" [79]. As an example, Dr. Boyle mentions the work of Dr. Yoshihiro Kawaoka and coworkers who "found a way to increase the toxicity of the flu virus by 200 times" [80]. The CV of Dr. Kawaoka also boasts of having "resurrected the genocidal Spanish Flu virus for the Pentagon for offensive biowarfare purposes" [81].

Dr. Boyle also points to budgetary allocations as clear evidence for the real priority of the US government. In 2006, Congress allocated $120 million to fight flu, which killed an estimated 36,000 Americans, but spent $1.76 billion on "biodefense." The priority is not "the promotion of the public health of American citizens but rather to further develop the US offensive biowarfare industry that will someday 'blowback' upon the American people with a catastrophic pandemic" [82]. Furthermore, the Pentagon and the CIA are "ready, willing, and able to launch biowarfare when it suits their interests ...They have a super-weapons-grade anthrax that they already used against us in October, 2001" [83].

Dr. Boyle has also revealed that the Ebola outbreaks leaked either accidentally or on purpose from bio-warfare laboratories set up by the USA on the west coast of Africa; "I have absolute proof from a Pentagon document that the Centers for Disease Control were doing bio-warfare work for the Pentagon in Sierra Leone, the heart of the outbreak, as early as 1988 ... In addition, the US government made sure that Liberia, a former colony of the USA, never became a party to the Biological Weapons Convention, so they were able to do bio-warfare work over there ... These labs are there in my opinion to do bio-warfare work for different agencies of the US government. Indeed, many of them were set up by USAID. And everyone knows that USAID is penetrated all up and down by the CIA and the CIA has been involved in bio-warfare work as well" [84].

In 2020, Dr. Boyle stated there is evidence that COVID-19 is an artificially created bioweapon that most likely leaked out of the Wuhan National Biosafety Laboratory, the only lab in China equipped to handle deadly coronaviruses [85]. However, in light of the evidence presented in this article and elsewhere that the virus appears relatively harmless compared to regular influenza, this conclusion appears questionable.

It is advisable to consider that numerous military men, government scientists, and politicians across countries conspired to unleash deadly chemical and biological weapons upon millions of citizens. Governments, today, assure us that they are not using deadly nerve agents or chemical weapons upon their populations, but how do we really know? What will we know in decades from now? Did COVID-19 simply leak by accident from a level 4 bio lab? Was it intentionally let loose in Wuhan by foreign agents? Or was it purely natural processes that caused it? Or is it relatively harmless for the vast majority of people and, thus, not a bioweapon?

Originally published as "The New 9/11: A Global Virus Pandemic," New Dawn Magazine, May 2020. Revised and updated since then.

References

[1] "Experts: US did 9-11" https://sites.google.com/site/expertsusdid911/
[2] "Redaction: Mainstream Media Censorship & Self-Censorship in Pre-Police-State Australia"
https://www.crimeandpower.com/2019/10/26/redaction-mainstream-media-censorship-self-censorship-in-pre-police-state-australia/
[3] "Television consumption"
https://en.wikipedia.org/wiki/Television_consumption
[4] "Screen Time Still an Australian Pastime"
https://www.nielsen.com/au/en/insights/report/2018/screen-time-still-an-australian-pastime/
[5] "Full text of 'Final report of the Select Committee to Study Governmental Operations with Respect to Intelligence Activities, United States Senate: together with additional, supplemental, and separate views'"
https://archive.org/stream/finalreportofsel01unit/finalreportofsel01unit_djvu.txt
[6] "COINTELPRO" https://www.britannica.com/topic/COINTELPRO
[7] "Identiske overskrifter"
https://www.youtube.com/watch?v=Y6vFGUXR7-k
[8] Ibid.
[9] "Active Thermitic Material Discovered in Dust from the 9/11 World TradeCenter Catastrophe"
https://benthamopen.com/contents/pdf/TOCPJ/TOCPJ-2-7.pdf
[10] Gideon Polya, "Australia And Britain Killed 6-7 Million Indians In WW2 Bengal Famine," Countercurrents, 29 September, 2011:
https://countercurrents.org/polya290911.htm
[11] "Aboriginal Genocide"
https://sites.google.com/site/aboriginalgenocide/.
[12] "Afghan Holocaust, Afghan Genocide"
https://sites.google.com/site/afghanholocaustafghangenocide/
[13] Gideon Polya, "Body Count. Global avoidable mortality since 1950," that includes a succinct history of every country and is now available for free perusal on the web: http://globalbodycount.blogspot.com/
[14] Gideon Polya, "Paris Atrocity Context: 27 Million Muslim Avoidable Deaths From Imposed Deprivation In 20 Countries Violated By US Alliance Since 9-11," Countercurrents, 22 November, 2015:
http://www.countercurrents.org/polya221115.htm.
[15] " Coronavirus: China's first confirmed Covid-19 case traced back to November 17"
https://www.scmp.com/news/china/society/article/3074991/coronavirus-chinas-first-confirmed-covid-19-case-traced-back
[16] "Coronavirus 'could infect 60% of global population if unchecked'"
https://www.theguardian.com/world/2020/feb/11/coronavirus-expert-warns-infection-could-reach-60-of-worlds-population
[17] "Could the new coronavirus really kill 50 million people worldwide?"
https://www.newscientist.com/article/2233085-could-the-new-coronavirus-really-kill-50-million-people-worldwide/

[18] "Competition for supplies sharpening as pandemic worsens" https://www.mail.com/int/scitech/health/9837656-competition-supplies-sharpening-pandemic-worsens.html#.1258-stage-hero1-1

[19] "Death rate soars in New Orleans coronavirus 'disaster' that could define city for generations" https://eu.usatoday.com/story/news/nation/2020/03/26/new-orleans-new-coronavirus-epicenter-mardi-gras-fueled-outbreak/2921116001/

[20] "Coronavirus will infect 2.5 billion people, kill 53 million by March, AI predicts" https://www.aiin.healthcare/topics/research/coronavirus-infect-25-billion-kill-53-million-ai

[21]. "COVID-19 Lockdown: A Global Human Experiment" https://vigilantcitizen.com/vigilantreport/covid-19-lockdown-a-global-human-experiment/

[22]. "Hong Kong is putting electronic wristbands on arriving passengers to enforce coronavirus quarantine" https://www.cnbc.com/2020/03/18/hong-kong-uses-electronic-wristbands-to-enforce-coronavirus-quarantine.html

[23]. "75,000 Americans at risk of dying from overdose or suicide due to coronavirus despair, group warns" https://edition.cnn.com/2020/05/08/health/coronavirus-deaths-of-despair/index.html

[24]. "Male suicide rate hits two-decade high in England and Wales" https://www.theguardian.com/society/2020/sep/01/male-suicide-rate-england-wales-covid-19

[25]. "Lov om epidemier m.v. (epidemiloven)" https://prodstoragehoeringspo.blob.core.windows.net/3fb27712-0916-41e7-8be6-bdebe101994e/Foreløbigt udkast - høring.pdf

[26]. Ibid.

[27]. Ibid.

[28]. "20 years in jail for spreading fake coronavirus news" https://www.thestandard.co.zw/2020/03/29/20-years-jail-spreading-fake-coronavirus-news/

[29]. "Several countries threaten jail time for coronavirus-related April Fools' pranks" https://nypost.com/2020/04/01/countries-threaten-jail-time-for-coronavirus-related-april-fools-pranks/

[30]. "Udbrud med COVID-19" https://www.ssi.dk/aktuelt/sygdomsudbrud/coronavirus

[31] "Over 99% of coronavirus patients in Italy who died had other health problems" https://nypost.com/2020/03/18/over-99-of-coronavirus-patients-in-italy-who-died-had-other-illnesses/

[32] "Report-COVID-2019_17_marzo-v2" https://www.epicentro.iss.it/coronavirus/bollettino/Report-COVID-2019_17_marzo-v2.pdf

[33]. https://www.corona.help/

[34]. "Comorbidities" https://www.cdc.gov/nchs/nvss/vsrr/covid_weekly/index.htm

[35]. "Coronavirus Cases Plummet When PCR Tests Are Adjusted"

https://thevaccinereaction.org/2020/09/coronavirus-cases-plummet-when-pcr-tests-are-adjusted/.

[36]. "President of Tanzania Didn't Trust WHO So Sent Samples of Sheep, Goats, Bunny, Trees, Fruit and Car Oil for COVID Testing — The Results Are In, Poor Goat" https://www.thegatewaypundit.com/2020/05/president-tanzania-didnt-trust-sent-samples-sheep-goats-bunny-trees-fruit-car-oil-covid-testing-results/.

[37]. "Perspectives on the Pandemic | The (Undercover) Epicenter Nurse | Episode Nine" https://www.youtube.com/watch?v=UIDsKdeFOmQ&pbjreload=101.

[38]. "Washington health officials: Gunshot victims counted as COVID-19 deaths" https://www.freedomfoundation.com/washington/washington-health-officials-gunshot-victims-counted-as-covid-19-deaths.

[39]. "Fatal Motorcycle Crash Listed as COVID-19 Death in Florida" https://pjmedia.com/news-and-politics/matt-margolis/2020/07/17/fatal-motorcycle-crash-listed-as-covid-19-death-in-florida-n658267

[40]. "Here's How NYC's Coronavirus Death Toll Is Being Inflated" https://townhall.com/tipsheet/bethbaumann/2020/05/03/project-veritas-sounds-the-alarm-on-deaths-falsely-attributed-to-the-wuhan-coronavirus-n2568099.

[41]. "UK Chief Medic Confirms COVID-19 Is Harmless To Majority" https://www.technocracy.news/uk-chief-medic-confirms-covid-19-is-harmless-to-majority/

[42]. "Mystisk ændring af WHO's definition af en pandemi " https://www.information.dk/udland/2009/11/mystisk-aendring-whos-definition-pandemi

[43]. Ibid.

[44]. Ibid.

[45]. "Innovating to zero! | Bill Gates" https://www.youtube.com/watch?v=JaF-fq2Zn7I

[46]. "Correlation between Non-Polio Acute FlaccidParalysis Rates with Pulse Polio Frequency in India" https://www.ncbi.nlm.nih.gov/pmc/articles/PMC6121585/pdf/ijerph-15-01755.pdf

[47]. "Anglo 5Headline NewsOpinionsRobert F Kennedy Jr. Exposes Bill Gates' Vaccine Dictatorship Plan – cites Gates' twisted 'Messiah Complex'" https://fort-russ.com/2020/04/robert-f-kennedy-jr-exposes-bill-gates-vaccine-dictatorship-plan-cites-gates-twisted-messiah-complex/

[48]. Ibid.

[49]. "HCG Found in WHO Tetanus Vaccine in Kenya Raises Concern in the Developing World" https://www.researchgate.net/publication/320641479_HCG_Found_in_WHO_Tetanus_Vaccine_in_Kenya_Raises_Concern_in_the_Developing_World

[50]. Ibid.

[51]. Ibid.
[52]. Ibid.
[53]. "The Introduction of Diphtheria-Tetanus-Pertussis and Oral Polio Vaccine Among Young Infants in an Urban African Community: A Natural Experiment" https://www.ncbi.nlm.nih.gov/pmc/articles/PMC5360569/
[54]. "Bill Gates Calls for a "Digital Certificate" to Identify Who Received COVID-19 Vaccine" https://vigilantcitizen.com/latestnews/bill-gates-calls-for-a-digital-certificate-to-identify-who-is-vaccinated/
[55]. "About the Event 201 exercise" https://www.centerforhealthsecurity.org/event201/about
[56]. "Event 201 Pandemic Exercise: Highlights Reel" https://www.youtube.com/watch?v=AoLw-Q8X174&pbjreload=101
[57]. Ibid.
[58]. Ibid.
[59]. "The Tourism Industry Is in Trouble. These Countries Will Suffer the Most." https://foreignpolicy.com/2020/04/01/coronavirus-tourism-industry-worst-hit-countries-infographic/
[60]. "'It Will Be Catastrophic.' Asia's Tourism-Dependent Economies Are Being Hit Hard by the Coronavirus" https://time.com/5783505/thailand-asia-tourism-covid-19-china-coronavirus/
[61]. "Coronavirus: Airlines cancel thousands of flights" https://www.bbc.com/news/business-51818492
[62]. Three travel startups tell us how they're responding to the coronavirus crisis | TechCrunch" https://techcrunch.com/2020/03/13/three-travel-startups-tell-us-how-theyre-responding-to-the-coronavirus-crisis/
[63]. "More than 80 countries have imposed travel bans to curb the new coronavirus" https://www.economist.com/graphic-detail/2020/03/16/more-than-80-countries-have-imposed-travel-bans-to-curb-the-new-coronavirus
[64]. "Event 201 Pandemic Exercise: Highlights Reel" https://www.youtube.com/watch?v=AoLw-Q8X174&pbjreload=101
[65]. Ibid.
[66]. "Coronavirus: Fake news is spreading fast" https://www.bbc.com/news/technology-51646309
[67]. "Coronavirus: Fake news crackdown by UK government" https://www.bbc.com/news/technology-52086284
[68]. "Kolkata Police warns of stern action against fake news over coronavirus" https://www.businesstoday.in/latest/trends/kolkata-police-warns-of-stern-action-against-fake-news-over-coronavirus/story/398542.html
[69]. "Fake Facts Are Flying About Coronavirus. Now There's A Plan To Debunk Them" https://www.npr.org/sections/goatsandsoda/2020/02/21/805287609/theres-a-flood-of-fake-news-about-coronavirus-and-a-plan-to-stop-it
[70]. "Social media companies are taking steps to tamp down coronavirus misinformation – but they can do more" https://theconversation.com/social-media-companies-are-taking-steps-to-tamp-down-coronavirus-misinformation-but-they-can-do-more-133335
[71]. "Event 201 Pandemic Exercise: Highlights Reel"

https://www.youtube.com/watch?v=AoLw-Q8X174&pbjreload=101
[72]. Ibid.
[73]. "How the British Government subjected thousands of people to chemical and biological warfare trials during Cold War" https://www.independent.co.uk/news/uk/politics/how-the-british-government-subjected-thousands-of-people-to-chemical-and-biological-warfare-trials-10376411.html
[74]. Ibid.
[75]. "Did Army Spray Harmful Chemicals on US Cities?" https://www.livescience.com/23795-large-area-coverage-dangers.html
[76]. "How the British Government subjected thousands of people to chemical and biological warfare trials during Cold War" https://www.independent.co.uk/news/uk/politics/how-the-british-government-subjected-thousands-of-people-to-chemical-and-biological-warfare-trials-10376411.html
[77]. "Report by reporter Sherwood Ross of Statements made by Francis Boyle who Drafted the US Implementing Law of the Biological Weapons Convention" https://www.paulcraigroberts.org/2020/03/16/report-by-reporter-sherwood-ross-of-statements-made-by-francis-boyle-who-drafted-the-us-implementing-law-of-the-biological-weapons-convention/
[78]. Ibid.
[79]. Ibid.
[80]. Ibid.
[81]. Ibid.
[82]. Ibid.
[83]. "Ebola: Who created this terrible virus and why?" https://www.pambazuka.org/food-health/ebola-who-created-terrible-virus-and-why
[84]. Ibid.
[85] "Interview: Author of US BioWeapons Act Believes The WHO & China Are Lying About The Coronavirus" https://www.activistpost.com/2020/02/interview-author-of-us-bioweapons-act-believes-the-who-china-are-lying-about-the-coronavirus.html.

The Future of Life in a Digital Gulag

Søren Roest Korsgaard

In the so-called "developed world," governments are working tirelessly to implement a digital dictatorship [1]. China, on the other hand, has been on the forefront and has already rolled out an Orwellian, AI-assisted social crediting system [2]. Since the false flag attack of September 11 2001, citizens worldwide have experienced an unprecedented escalation in the obliteration of civil and human rights [3]. The original plan, which commenced with the controlled demolition of the three World Trade Center buildings and the attack on the pentagon, has become manifest: The elite wants total control of you and everything else. The path toward totalitarianism has its victims, and today we can observe with better clarity the consequences of giving power structures the privilege to maneuver unhindered. For example, legal systems have become geared toward injustice, science has been corrupted, technological advances that could benefit humanity have been utilized in the military and policing domain, and "enemies" of the West have been invaded, plundered, and bombed [4]. Since 2001, a long list of dubious mass casualty events - some of which have been exposed as false flag attacks - have been conducted to maintain and strengthen agendas of population control and further the elitist agenda of a digital gulag [5, 6]. Most recently, sanctions resulting from the supposed unprecedented 'Black-Plague'-like dangers of COVID-19 resulted in the largest human experiment in history and billions of people were reduced to chess pieces in a larger game, directed by the mass media and other institutions [7]. Unanimously, governments worldwide, regardless of political ideology and system, acted in near-perfect tandem, wiping out whatever was left of our rights and then brought in the "new normal." The evidence indicates that COVID-19 is a psychological operation. Having accounted for the current situation in no significant depth as it has been done elsewhere, we will now move on to the all-important question: How will it be to live in a digital prison?

Surrogate Solitary Confinement

We have plenty of historical firsthand accounts of how it was to live under dictatorships not involving advanced technology. Living inside a technologically controlled dictatorship is likely to be much worse than under past dictatorships. One of the central reasons that technology will exacerbate living conditions is that it is working without interruption, and it can handle and analyze massive amounts of data in a split second. In stark contrast, everything had to be done manually in the more primitive dictatorships of the past. Technology allows for total dominance and subversion (if the 'power' stays turned on). Most people – but especially those who regularly use internet-based communication – already assume they are being spied on all the time, in part due to the revelations of whistleblowers and alleged whistleblowers. There exist 'controlled' whistleblowers who release information to further certain agendas of the elite. One of these might be Edward Snowden. Although his supposedly secretly and illegally obtained documents revealed nothing new, he appeared on front pages across the world. He was interviewed countless of times on TV and bestselling autobiographies were published after he went public [8, 9]. Previous whistleblowers who revealed the same information, like Bill Binney, a former director of the NSA, were labeled "conspiracy theorists" and were deliberately ignored by the mass media, a clear indication that at that time, the elite had no interest in exposing their secret surveillance. Later, it was to their advantage to tell the world about the massive spying and intrusion of privacy. Of course, an NSA-equivalent government institution exists in most developed countries, surveilling their citizens and sharing the data with other countries [10].
The elite essentially want you to believe that you have zero privacy, and they will find out if you misbehave. It is well-known that people change their behaviors when they believe that they are being spied on. In a highly advanced dictatorship, there will be little or no privacy [11]. It can be argued that the conditions of living under constant stress in a digital prison

produce the same psychiatric outcomes as when people are exposed to solitary confinement, which is classified as torture by the UN [12]. Being unable to express sentiments due to fear of punishment and rejection - humans are complex biological and social beings – can result in feelings of social isolation and inhibition.

In the early 1990s, Dr. Stuart Grassian conducted extensive interviews with people held in isolation at the Pelican Bay State Prison, a supermax prison in California. Dr. Grassian discovered that solitary confinement induces a horrifying psychiatric disorder that is characterized by paranoia, panic attacks, hallucinations, obsessive/compulsive thinking and behavior, stress, nightmares, hypersensitivity to external stimuli, and a litany of other physical and psychological problems [13]. Although it is a subject with considerably many facets, including economic advancement and even spurious diagnoses, the great rise in mental disorders in the West can likely, in part, be ascribed to the increase in stress and demand of modern society. If this is true, then it is certain that the prevalence of mental disorders will explode under conditions of digital totalitarian confinement.

Regardless of psychiatric diagnoses, the conditions of living inside a social crediting system strongly resemble that of regular prisons: Everything has to be done in a certain way, there is no privacy, cameras everywhere, and snitches are on every street corner ready to reveal your infractions to better their own abysmal situation. No creativity is allowed within this rigid control grid, every wrongdoing instantly reduces your privileges, and you are expected to do what you are told to do and not ask questions. A digital prison will be a real life nightmare with serious consequences for the well-being of the majority.

Fusion between Fiction and Real Life Events

People generally fall victim to propaganda designed to transmute the status quo into politically expedient laws that reduce individual discernment and disenfranchise the masses. In the future, propaganda will see new levels of sophistication such as undetectable digitally manufactured events. At that time, even dissidents and critically thinking academics, if such still exist, will have trouble discerning real-life events from the manufactured ones that are designed to sustain the system, keep people asleep and conform to the "new normal." As the flow of information is highly restricted, it becomes easier to persuade, manipulate, and convince the masses of blatant lies. The establishment will assuredly want to control your reality to the greatest extent possible.

There will undoubtedly be people who can cope with the draconian rules, just like some people praise the social crediting system of China. It remains, however, a distinct possibility that the majority will become chronically stressed from surveillance, lack of privacy, and anti-human ideals. Presenting a full description of how life will be in a digital dictatorship could easily take up several volumes. For example, we could mention transhumanist dreams of fusing AI into human biology and its effect on those who go down that path or discuss how "implanted memories [14]" and technology will play a key role in creating the future "model citizen." Overall and essentially, we will likely experience autonomous systems disrupting and depriving people of what has been called "the power process [15]." For instance, autonomous robotic technology and machines will replace factory workers, self-driving vehicles will replace bus and taxi drivers, food will be chemically manufactured by printers rather than harvested, etc. [16]. In a digital tyranny, it is essential to reduce the masses into simple, compliant cogs in the social machine, like the reliable algorithms of AI systems and robotics.

Ultimately, humans become depressed, lethargic, and apathetic if they do not have meaningful goals whose attainment require effort; hence, the *power process* has been disrupted. Goals give the body and mind the exercise it needs to function optimally. Unlike historical dictatorships, the possible future one will likely offer the physical necessities of life (think 'universal basic income'). The danger of a digital dictatorship is that it may offer convenience in a wide range of areas, but the convenience comes at a great cost.

'Morality Pills' for Dissidents

Governments have become obsessed with our compliance to the point where the idea of covertly modifying behavior - deemed undesirable by the people in power in the name of the public good - appears to be on the agenda [17]. The elite are fully aware that the "last refuge," when everything else fails or is corrupted, is the human mind. Power is the money of these people, and they want control of your cognitive faculties. They want perfect citizens, a new generation of bovine conformism, created and shaped by targeting human decision-making processes.

Recently, Dr. Parker Crutchfield, an Associate Professor of Medical Ethics, Humanities and Law at the Western Michigan University advocated Nazi-like government intervention by administering "moral enhancement" to noncooperative people for the alleged "public good [18]." In a 2015 paper, "The epistemology of moral bioenhancement [19]," he defines moral bioenhancement as the "potential practice of manipulating individuals' moral behaviors by biological means in order to help resolve pressing moral issues such as climate change and terrorism." In a 2018 peer-reviewed paper, "Compulsory moral bioenhancement should be covert," he argued that "a covert compulsory moral bioenhancement program is morally preferable to an overt moral bioenhancement program [20]." He later suggested that it perhaps should be done via "the water supply [21]." Since then, the doctor has explicitly advocated that "the problem of coronavirus defectors could be solved by moral enhancement [22]." He, furthermore, clarified his stance by arguing that we should not boost our immune systems such as via vitamin C supplementation, but "society may be better off, both in the short term as well as the long" if we manipulate the "brain's ability to cooperate with others [23]."

If Nazi doctor Josef Mengele had lived to see the aforementioned recommendations and the new technological ability of science to manipulate behavior, it would have brought a cynical smile to his old lips. As is well-known, Dr. Mengele conducted horrific human experiments on subjects regarded as undesirable, or unworthy of life, by the establishment. His experiments revolved around the spurious philosophy that the

Aryan race was superior to other races due to genetics rather than environment. Although strongly condemned by the scientific community, it is striking how some vocal scientists, like Dr. Crutchfield, are publically encouraging methods that strongly parallel the ruthless, inhuman, and grotesque methods of Dr. Mengele whose experiments were carried out within the law, but without the consent of the participants. The idea that there is a necessary nexus between morality and legal validity is pseudoscientific nonsense.

The well-paid scientific technocratic elite, legislators, and the like, in conjunction with pharmaceutical companies and other power institutions, frequently cite the purported lack of morality of dissidents who, for example, refuse to let their children be injected with aluminum containing vaccines, despite the fact that well-done studies have found a causal link between aluminum and Alzheimer's disease [24, 25]. The elite, and scientists like Dr. Crutchfield, equate "good moral behavior" with what they deem appropriate for "the public good." Collectivism has many victims, not limited to the destruction of axiomatic rights. In reality, what is considered good or evil is highly variable within societies and cultures – and depends on historical and spiritual developments, and is subject to change over time.

Conclusion: Conformity is Insanity

By observing the overall reaction of people to the ever harsher demands of the powerful and over-privileged, we can safely conclude that people generally embrace conformity; resisting the establishment requires energy and dangerous commitment. Society, backed by the power of the mass media, largely accepts, without question, the pious platitudes regurgitated by the rich and wealthy, which always are geared toward deforming human society and nature. The masses eagerly vote for a new candidate, hoping that this time it will get better, but it never does. Change by means of voting is a chimerical quest: a corrupt system can never be changed in the long-term within the legal and moral boundaries set up by the ruling elite. Voting maintains the power of the elite; if voting could transform society it would have been made illegal.

Considering the rapid changes to our living conditions in the last few years, even months, without any noteworthy resistance, it appears that unless a major collapse of developed countries takes place - financial and social - it is likely that we will end up in a digital prison. At that time, it might be too late to resist. Thus, unless a collapse takes place or a powerful quasi-religion emerges to destroy the elite and other parasitic entities, then, inescapably, freedom will be illegal in the future.

Originally published as "The Future of Life in a Digital Gulag," New Dawn Magazine, September 2020.

References

[1]. "One World Digital Dictatorship"
https://www.crimeandpower.com/2020/01/05/one-world-digital-dictatorship/
(accessed August 2020).
[2]. Ibid.
[3]. "Key Evidence of Controlled Demolition"
https://www.ae911truth.org/evidence/evidence-overview (accessed August
2020).
[4]. "US-Imposed Post-9/11 Muslim Holocaust & Muslim Genocide," Dr.
Gideon Polya (Korsgaard Publishing 2020).
[5]. Ibid.
[6]. "BOSTON BOMBING CHRONICLES"
https://www.crimeandpower.com/boston-bombing-chronicles/ (Korsgaard
Publishing 2020).
[7]. "The New 9/11: A Global Virus Pandemic," New Dawn Magazine
(May-June 2020).
[8]. "What Do We Know About Edward Snowden? Webster G. Tarpley"
https://www.youtube.com/watch?v=7zPkhkEr7Ko (accessed August 2020).
[9]. "How to identify CIA limited hangout?" https://off-
guardian.org/2018/01/04/how-to-identify-cia-limited-hangout/ (accessed
August 2020).
[10]. "UKUSA Agreement"
https://en.wikipedia.org/wiki/UKUSA_Agreement (accessed August 2020).
[11]. "One World Digital Dictatorship"
https://www.crimeandpower.com/2020/01/05/one-world-digital-dictatorship/
(accessed August 2020).
[12]. "The United States is the Largest Prison Camp in the World"
https://www.crimeandpower.com/2019/12/06/the-united-states-is-the-largest-
prison-camp-in-the-world/ (accessed August 2020).
[13]. "What are the psychological effects of solitary confinement?"
https://solitarywatch.org/facts/faq/ (accessed August 2020).
[14]. "'Implanted' Memories Indistinguishable from Real Ones" New Dawn
Magazine (May-June 2020).
[15]. "Technological Slavery," Ted Kaczynski (Fitch & Madison Publishers
2019).
[16]. "Here's how 3D food printers are changing what we eat"
https://www.techrepublic.com/article/heres-how-3d-food-printers-are-
changing-the-way-we-cook/ (accessed August 2020).
[17]. "The Notion of Evil Killer Genes Examined"
https://www.crimeandpower.com/2019/09/30/the-notion-of-evil-killer-genes-
examined/ (accessed August 2020).
[18]. "'Morality pills' may be the US's best shot at ending the coronavirus
pandemic, according to one ethicist" https://theconversation.com/morality-
pills-may-be-the-uss-best-shot-at-ending-the-coronavirus-pandemic-
according-to-one-ethicist-142601 (accessed August 2020).
[19]. "The Epistemology of Moral Bioenhancement"
https://www.researchgate.net/publication/287791679_The_Epistemology_of

 Moral Bioenhancement.
[20]. "Compulsory moral bioenhancement should be covert"
https://onlinelibrary.wiley.com/doi/abs/10.1111/bioe.12496 (accessed
August 2020).
[21]. "'Morality pills' may be the US's best shot at ending the coronavirus
pandemic, according to one ethicist" https://theconversation.com/morality-
pills-may-be-the-uss-best-shot-at-ending-the-coronavirus-pandemic-
according-to-one-ethicist-142601 (accessed August 2020).
[22]. Ibid.
[23]. Ibid.
[24]. "Alzheimer's Disease Linked to Exposure to Aluminum"
https://scitechdaily.com/alzheimers-disease-linked-to-exposure-to-aluminum/
(accessed August 2020).
[25]. "Aluminum and Amyloid-β in Familial Alzheimer's Disease"
https://content.iospress.com/articles/journal-of-alzheimers-disease/jad191140
(accessed August 2020).

The Power of Paper

Jerry Day

Posted courtesy of jerryday.com

I'm going to show you two instruments of tyranny. The first is a gun, a symbol of force, violence, and destruction. This is not the best instrument of tyranny. This is the type of thing used by tyrants who are stupid, clumsy, and desperate. When the masses are being controlled by a weapon, they can clearly see they must destroy or escape whoever is pointing it at them. The smart tyrants use the other instrument of tyranny: paper. The paper on which is printed the auto registration you must show, the proof of insurance you must show, the tax form that you must file, the permit or license that you must pay for, the application you must fill out. Whether we realize it or not, we only submit to this, because we are being threatened by force. What if we knew they did not have weapons, would we fill out the paper? I wouldn't. When we fill out the paper, we are really reacting to the gun; tyranny. But just as a gun can be pointed in two directions, paper can be used by all parties. How can you use the power of paper? One way is something called an affidavit. An affidavit seems simple and harmless - it's simply a sworn statement of fact signed by a notary, but a lot more people have been robbed with paper than with a gun. A properly executed affidavit is law until it is rebutted by another affidavit. Suppose you send your mortgage lender an affidavit that says you've just discovered that the loan documents they asked you to sign have misrepresentations, lack of disclosure or fraud. If you are wrong you may go to jail for perjury, but if you're right you may get the deed to your house free and clear. An affidavit is a powerful thing. The author of an affidavit can take all the marbles; he can make the rules. In my affidavit, I can say "You hereby agree to pay me $50 a month unless you rebut this affidavit within 30 days." If you make the mistake of tossing that affidavit into your trashcan, 30 days later you are a slave to me. Under the law, $50 per month of your earnings belongs to me.

That's the point of those cryptic notices from your credit card company. The law says that you agree and accept the presented terms unless you respond and refuse to accept. If you respond, you can change those rules all you want. All you have to do is respond. That notice they sent you is not enforcement of their rules - that is an opportunity for you to agree with their rules by remaining silent. Send a notice back saying, "You may not charge me any late fees and I will not pay more than 5% interest on my credit card charges, and those are the terms you must accept if you wish to have me as a credit card customer." If the credit card company does not rebut or cancel your card within your time limit, you are legally entitled to the terms you offer. Your announcements and demands are just as valid as theirs. If your notice is in the form of an affidavit, no judge, court, or officer may deny your claim, and the credit card company may not impose different terms unless you agree to them either by response or by silence.

As odd as it seems, it's probably not a good idea to ever sign anything that you did not write yourself. If you write it, it benefits you. If they write it, it benefits them and it probably costs you in a big way. An affidavit is not a complicated thing; samples of them are easy to find. There's no particular layout that's required; basically it's a sworn statement of true and complete fact with a date and a notarized signature. If it affects another party it must be presented to that party with a reasonable time for response. Large institutions are very good at sending notices but they are not very good at reading and responding to notices they receive. That is not your problem. Institutional size and bureaucratic incompetence are not an excuse for anything. Send them the notice and hold them to the terms contained in that notice. If they refuse your terms, change the terms or walk away from the relationship. Just make sure that you always play by your rules not theirs. That's what the Declaration of Independence is: our rules not theirs. Just as tyranny comes in many forms - revolutions come in many forms. We can have a nice, nonviolent revolution, and we can even do it all through the mail if we borrow a trick that institutions use against us. If paper is used more effectively, then, nobody will have to use the gun, but don't do it if you don't know what you're doing; paper can be dangerous.

Jerry Day originally published, "The Power of Paper" on YouTube in March 2010. Transcribed by Caroline Cheruiyot.

Who Represents You?

Jerry Day

How do you like your representatives: your president, senators, congress person, or your governor, city council, county supervisors? Do they understand you well enough to represent you, or is the very concept of representation absurd? Suppose you were elected to your city council, how would you go about representing all the residents of your city? How would you represent the people you didn't like or didn't agree with? Would you walk around and shake everybody's hand with a few seconds of superficial chatter? Would you stage town hall meetings where you do most of the talking, and then would you use your power and authority to advance your own career goals and personal interests? Those are the things most representatives are doing in our current system. Do they gather consensus and follow public mandate? No, they usually try to sell us on their programs. Do they refuse financial support and influence from special interests? No, they don't, we know that. Do they build bipartisan compromises and coalitions? Not good ones. Do they disregard their own personal interests as they perform their public duties? There's no evidence of that. But most importantly, do they protect the rights of every individual against the unfair demands of the majority? They haven't done that for a long time.

As you examine what honest and fair representation really means, you quickly see that it is non-existent, actually impossible on any large scale. It's ridiculous to try. Leaders must laugh at us for actually expecting them to represent each one of us, one by one. A family unit is about the largest group where people can truly be heard, understood, and represented. So, our representatives are not really representing. So what are they doing? Quite simply, they are taking and using our power and money and doing whatever they please with it. The answer to many of our problems is very clear: to be effectively represented we must represent ourselves. We must claim back any power that has been taken. We must claim back our earnings and wealth from government and institutions. We must see ourselves as the leaders of our own lives - the final authority of what affects us. We live in a republic, whoever administers our authority - it is still our authority, and it's not about selfishness: it's about having the right to be generous in the way you choose. It's about not squandering your money and power on the myth of representation.

When we give our personal authority over to institutions and representatives, we're saying that we're not competent or worthy to manage our own lives and affairs - that some glad handing stranger will do that for us better than we can do it for ourselves.

We're beginning to see how much we have lost by gifting our individual sovereignty and self-determination to so-called leaders. The divine rights of life and liberty and our chosen pursuits have been seized and perverted by tax collectors, bureaucrats, police officers, lenders, bill collectors, and countless other self-approved, self-appointed institutional dictators. It's time now to just say "No" to statist bullying and control of harmless individual behavior. When we're being diverted by a false contest, we can't think straight. The false contest is between conservative and progressive, big government in the name of military and corporate agendas or big government in the name of social justice but always big government. That's the big lie - that we have no option to reclaim our individual rights. The only choice is to select our preferred flavor of state tyranny and excess. The real race is not left-right - that's an insidious diversion. The real race is state power versus you - collectivist authority against individual rights and freedoms. If you have no choice other than big government, then you have no choice at all because big government does whatever it wants. The citizens of the thirteen original colonies went into a tangible rage against state abuse by the king of England; they gave their lives to fight it. Many of us today can't even see state excess because we're so vested in the left-right puppet show. The enemy is a thing called collectivism where the power and wealth and authority of many individuals are transferred to an elite few who will make decisions, administer your resources, and profit from your efforts. If someone asks me who my representative is, I say, "I am, how may I help you?" If I want to know how your money will be spent and how you will behave should I ask you or your representative?

Jerry Day originally published, "Who Represents You?" on YouTube in April 2010. Transcribed by Caroline Cheruiyot

Your Role In Climate Change

Jerry Day

This is not a test. This is an actual announcement. The government no longer works on your behalf. It now works on behalf of the climate. You may have noticed that whenever a government building appears in a photograph, the climate is always included, surrounding that building for the glory of the climate. This transition and repurposing of government require that you now be taxed, penalized, ignored, and inconvenienced because we now have a government by the climate, for the climate, and of the climate. The climate has reorganized government to take your money and reclassify all non-climate entities as slaves and chattel. Your purpose in life is now to perform labor, so that the benefits of that labor may be conferred to the climate by way of government. Please understand you no longer have any right to petition, object, complain, protest, or influence government policy in any way because you are chattel and you, the people, are no longer the authority over government - the climate is. If you wish to contact the government to praise the climate, please enclose that message in a government-approved, climate-friendly envelope. Due to the very high volume of messages that we expect to receive praising the climate, we will not be able to respond to your message, but rest assured all of your messages are appreciated by the climate.

Those exemplary workers who produce the most revenue for the climate will be eligible to beg for privileges from the government. If you are selected for privilege, you will be permitted to purchase a climate worship armband, which will signify your membership in the Climate Worship Party. You will then receive your prestigious dues statements, monthly. In return for that privilege, you will be required to rat out any of your family, friends, or neighbors who do not worship the climate. The government has made the presumption that the climate does not want to change. If the climate changes, you will be blamed for hurting the climate's feelings. If you are accused by the government of causing climate change, you will be classified, by government, as fully expendable. If the climate does change, government is required to exterminate individuals classified as expendable and who are not wearing climate worship armbands. Remember, exemption from extermination is another wonderful benefit of Climate Worship Party membership.

Your country, now called the United States of Climate, encourages you to embrace your new role in our country's civic structure. In order to ease the transition for you, your government now regards your confusion and objections as crimes to be administered by ruthless government sponsored death squads positioned on highways and in doorways where you must pass through. This will help you to develop your personal habits of continual labor and worship of the climate. Thank you for serving the climate.

Jerry Day originally published, "Your Role In Climate Change" on YouTube in April 2010. Transcribed by Caroline Cheruiyot.

The Myth of Benevolent Central Authority

Jerry Day

In any society, the insecurity of individuals manifests itself in a cry for centralized government. In any society, the enterprise of individuals can always be defeated and dominated by the efficiency of large corporations. Centralization and efficiency are instinctive and automatic phenomena of modern social organization. While the efficiency of automation generally benefits society, a social elite will always find means to collect and redirect those benefits to themselves and their loyal supporters.

This is how government and corporations come into being, by representing themselves as a benefit to the masses, while actually having no real purpose or effect other than to do the opposite, to extract excess benefits for the elite at the expense of the masses. Just as leaves in a pond will collect at a common point, wealth, power, and force will be collected and hoarded by certain personality types in society. Government is the most overrated concept in human history. Government is only capable of doing two things: It can point guns at people to force them to do things, and it can redistribute the wealth it collects by its accumulated privilege of force.

As a means of projecting force, government will devote some of its wealth to form a military organization. The military will do exactly what military is for, it will go out and kill people. It will do this to impose government. If the military has a lot of wealth, it will kill a lot of people. Only by killing and imprisoning people can the government maintain control. If government only threatens to kill and imprison, people will soon ignore the commands of government. Government, to survive, must commit violence regularly and government must gain a monopoly on violence.

If you want to find the government, look for the group committing the most violence. Killing and imprisonment is not used to administer justice, it is used to maintain government power by creating fear and loyalty toward government.

The deeper a person is in government, the less likely they will ever be punished for crimes. Justice is merely the excuse for violence. The reason is power. After government has its foothold, commercial enterprises will covet the power of government to help push their economic agendas. You would expect that taxation would provide all the wealth and control necessary to maintain power, but taxation is not possible without commercial activity, and commercial activity is not possible if overly taxed. Since commercial enterprises collect economic power, the commercial elite uses their wealth to influence government, to apply government force to promote commercial enterprise. Government does not care how it applies its force, as long as it can apply more force than anyone else. Corporations, like government, are very limited in their social contribution. Corporations can only do two things: They can create commercial transactions, and they can buy government protection for their monopolies and enterprises. So after government and corporations establish themselves, government uses force, and by economic means corporations control the force of government. Corruption is rampant and systemic throughout this control matrix, because the matrix was created by corruption. Centralized authorities do not become corrupt: corruption creates central authorities.

This holds the key to why centralization is unsustainable. Human insecurities make a vacuum where force may be introduced, and the privilege of using force is irresistible to certain personality types. This creates the circumstances for inevitable systemic failure. Those who seek and crave power are not qualified for such service. Those who seek and crave power are not gratified by a free and open society; they are gratified by using force. Whenever the use of force is involved, the things using force will get stronger, and the things that are being forced will get weaker. The strong thing cannot keep getting stronger forever because the weaker thing upon which it feeds eventually dies, disappears, or revolts against the strong thing. It is thus crystal clear why the social order, which in any way uses force, cannot last.

Those who have power are never satisfied or content to stop collecting power. Those who love power never have enough of it. Even if they were willing to limit their power, they have no capacity to determine and maintain the exact measure of force needed to maintain any given society as some ideal level of order. Elites are not optimizing society - they are quite busy optimizing their own lives. To fulfill their cravings for control and assuage their colossal insecurities, they simply strive, every day, to apply the most force they can, and to collect more power so they may apply more force tomorrow. After all, they did not gain power in order to ask society what it wants. They collected power to control society, live an elite existence, and collect benefits for themselves. Centralized power is not a consensus mechanism it is a control mechanism.

In all of recorded history, there is no such thing as permanent centralized government. The measure of the success of government is how long it can hold power before imploding. Revolutions can be delayed for the maximum time by making the weaker thing dependent on the stronger thing, making the weaker thing not realize what the stronger thing is doing, making the weaker thing love the stronger thing, and, of course, making the weaker thing fear the stronger thing. If the weaker thing can be controlled in those ways, the government may not be brought down by revolution, but will eventually die an apocalyptic death shortly after the weaker thing dies in exhaustion from contributing the last of its blood and energy to the collective. If the stronger thing allows the abundance enjoyed by the elite to be seen by the weaker thing, a revolution will often occur. If a government allows freedom, justice, and intellectual growth, a revolution will occur far sooner because the cruelty and fraud of the collective will be recognized and rejected. After a revolution, a vibrant society may bounce back rather quickly, but it will be more quickly centralized and once again controlled by force. When the stronger thing controls not just force but information, the control can be extended far longer. Society can then be bled to the last drop.

In ignorance, we do not see our alternatives. We do not recognize our oppressors. After the more gradual government failure and social collapse where society was fully controlled by force and misinformation, it will be much longer before any coherent society will organize because resources and technologies for such healthy social organization were exhausted and destroyed over many years.

Whether the cycles are slow or fast, the human race is trapped in a repetitive drama of tyranny and revolution. Driven by the nature of the human creature, the ascendancy of the human race, what some refer to as transcendency, will be marked by a fundamental change in human nature and social values. Only when human beings refuse centralization all together can society function indefinitely in peace, prosperity, and justice. Human beings will seek centralized patronization as long as they are mentally and spiritually insecure and unaware of their inner strengths, their rights, their purposes. As human self-awareness and confidence are increased, as our abilities to serve and cooperate with each other grows, as we decide to learn to resolve our own conflicts, protect our own environments, our demand for centralized protection and service will diminish. When we as individuals are at full potential, central authority will cease to exist. It will be seen universally as unnecessary and repugnant.

In the early millennia of human history, our social systems were very small and local. We now call it primitive – the family, the tribe. This system lasted for more than three million years with little change, only the most extraordinary centralized systems have lasted more than a thousand years, none have lasted more than 15,000 years. Most fall before 500 years. Centralization is a folly of lies, corruption, betrayal, guaranteed failure, and guaranteed cyclical repetition. So our legacy, our potential, is represented by that three million years before we had the capacity to institute large centralized authorities. Now we have technologies, communications, advanced sciences, and social habits that make it very easy and natural to create and maintain centralized authorities for brief historical cycles. The human species is now able to create collectives, but it is not yet able to run societies without those collectives, without those centralized centers of power.

We are not yet sophisticated and visionary enough to maintain a broad social framework without centralized force. If we are able to fundamentally change ourselves to not only resist the impulse to create and accept centralized authorities, but rather to fiercely demand that all authority be retained by ourselves, individually, for the free administration of the family and the small local community without force, without dogma, free to grow and adapt as circumstances may change, we could once again enjoy three million years of peace, prosperity, intellectual advancement. And even better, we could enjoy the abundance created by our sciences and technologies, and we could live lives of far greater security, comfort, joy, and fulfillment than the lives of any previous civilization, even that 3 million year one.

All we need to do is keep, as individuals, all of our authority, and refuse to grant any of it to any central collective or representative. We must never bow to any group or leader with whom we do not individually have strong voices and strong personal control. We must overcome our fears and feelings of insecurity, and resist the temptation to cry out for salvation from anyone other than ourselves, and our gods. In reality, mankind is not yet ready to make this broad upward step. As individuals, we are still insecure, we are doubtful of our own sovereignty and strengths, we still look to others for our salvation and protection, even though protection is inconsistent at best. Corrupt sociopaths still offer us salvation in order to empower themselves, and we believe them because we want to believe them. But whether we see it, whether we understand it or not, human society gets a little closer to the ideal as time marches ahead.

There are setbacks as the period between the Magna Carta and the United States Constitution. We are in a setback right now, as we have seen the more noble values behind our Constitution undermined by corruption, ignorance, and elitism. But more and more, we recognize the native and unavoidable corruption and failure of the large collective. Personal growth and awareness can be suppressed but never fully, never permanently. More and more we recognize the power and authority that we all individually possess by right, and that we can all assert by choice. More and more, we recognize the endless and repeated failures of centralization, the tyrannies, the wars, the slaughters, the slaveries, and exploitations that centralized power brings upon us that magically disappears when there is no central authority to dispense wholesale force and violence. One person may call for war, but only with many blind followers can a war actually occur. One person may declare himself a leader, but only if we throw away our personal authority will he actually lead. The true destiny of mankind is everyone as his own leader, everyone responsible for his own actions, not some, but every single person dedicated to the good treatment of all others, while reserving all rights and personal powers. Reserving all command over one's own destiny. With that kind of person and that kind of society, there is no need whatsoever for centralization of power, wealth, and force. All we need to achieve that destiny is to see it as our destiny. To reach for it, to stay committed to that no matter how many times we must fail and try again. Whether we can see it or not, from any particular time or viewpoint, that is our path, that is our journey. And when we reach that ideal, we will see that it is not the end but only the beginning, and we will wonder why we let tyrants and sociopaths suffocate us for so long.

Jerry Day originally published "The Myth Of Benevolent Central Authority" in March 2015 on YouTube. It has been transcribed by Lady Jane Emefa Addy.

Secrets of the Slave State

Jerry Day

Most of us don't realize that our actions and attitudes put us unintentionally in debt and uncompensated servitude as we blindly attempt to conform to external agendas promulgated by media, government and corporations. This article exposes some of the mechanisms of mass control. This article challenges men, women, workers, managers, executives, consumers, and debt slaves into examining their most fundamental presumptions about their place and purpose in society.

The image of slavery as a large mass of suffering and forcibly restrained slaves, controlled by a few powerful and cruel masters, is a very simplistic and false view of modern slavery. Nowadays, slavery is accomplished very differently: modern slavery is as much tactical and psychological as it is brute force. By far, the best kind of slave is one who agrees to be a slave or who at least accepts the circumstances, and now psychological technology is used to cause people to choose slavery for themselves. I will give you an example. Now it is important to keep in mind that slavery was black master and black slave for many centuries before European whites took up the practice. Slavery is more about power than race. The brutal tactics and psychology of slave-making are no secret. The example: In the 1700s in the southern slave states, a wealthy landowner might have the task of setting up a plantation. Slaves would be purchased and gathered for indoctrination. The wealthy farmer would accuse a young male slave of defiance or non-compliance, and that young man would be horribly punished and killed, perhaps lynched or drawn and quartered by horses, this would be done in front of the slave women.

Those slave women were deeply traumatized by the public spectacle of gratuitous violence against the innocent, young black male. The slave women would then raise their sons to be compliant and subservient. Young, black children would be sternly educated by their mothers in the type of behavior necessary to stay in the slave master's favor. By seeing one or more horrific events, the slave women became the school, the conditioning factory, the educators, and brain washers of the slavery collective. The new slave generation. An efficient system of slavery is not possible, unless the slaves are made to enforce upon each other. By the time the black males reached adulthood, they were thoroughly conditioned by their parents and guardians to a slave's mentality and demeanor. This was the PSYOP of the 1700s - the shock and awe of the plantation system. Nowadays, the plantation owner is the state, the law, the police, the media, banks, and corporations, and the slaves are you and I. In the old plantations, the result of demonstrations of cruelty and violence was voluntary compliance: young black males had never been encouraged, even by their family and friends, to think independently, to explore their aspirations and opportunities, or to believe in their own potential.

Their souls and spirits were broken, their minds imprisoned, not just by the slave master, but by their own families and friends. Even when we can clearly see the slavery, we do not imagine that we are helping to create it by accepting and enforcing the rules and constraints that constitute the slavery. We warn our children to follow the rules so they will not be harmed by the state. This kind of social conditioning takes its toll. By the time the young black male plantation-slave was working age, it was easy to see that he had no concept of how to question or defy authority, how to organize for justice, how to claim his rights, how to move against the system or how to control his own destiny. No idea. This is what our state, our schools, and our media do to us, and ask us to do to each other. As much as the state promotes the concept of gender equality, the state constantly exploits the differences between the genders, using gender against gender. Men are characterized as bullies or simpletons; women are characterized as victims or protesters. Media and the state want to divide us in any way they can. Women and men have fundamentally different psychology, but they are designed to be a complementary team. Our differences are not a problem; those differences actually make us stronger when we are partnered as a family unit. Expressed in primitive terms, the man in reckless defiance will face the enemy, whether it is an attacking tribe, the wild beast, the threat of nature's elements. The men will face the threat, while the women will protect the children, will hide, and will obey the orders of the protectors. These impulses are hard-wired into the genders. Since ancient Egypt, this psychology has been exploited to create and control slaves. There need be no prison walls, there need be no constant administration of force; slavery is programming, social and psychological programming. Force is only necessary for those who have accidentally or momentarily acted like a free and sovereign individual. Force is for people who forget to act like slaves. Regardless of how oppressed women may be in any given culture, they always have great influence over their men. Mothers have influence over their sons; wives and female lovers have influence over their husbands and partners. By female influence, men are drawn into civilized behavior. These days that means compliance with authorities, stable and conservative forms of livelihood, and behavioral moderation for social appearances to friends, neighbors, strangers, and authorities. In perhaps an over-generalization, women are seeking safety and stability at all costs, while men are seeking adventure and freedom without due regard for risk. Women feel safer in a socially regulated environment, in a context of rules and monitored behavior, predictable ritual, and they press those sensibilities upon the men around them.

The more reckless and coarse a man may act, the more pressure the woman will bring to regulate the behavior. So the slave master, the state, the collective to be successful will target the woman, the rule follower, for initial compliance, and cause that woman to then pressure compliance and servitude on those around them as they naturally tend to do. This may be called a woman's army, the frontlines of the slave state, the essential mass of psychological influencers, without which large-scale slavery would be impossible. Men are natural troublemakers, warriors, explorers, and there are too many of them to control with direct force by the state. Men will never be comfortable for long in the role of slave, unless, women are delegated to assist in the recruitment and management of the men's impulses for freedom. Women are more prone to accept and adopt rules without question; they are easily recruited to convey arbitrary rules to those around them. Women are highly influential in this way. Women are not helpless victims; they are society's best psychological influencers. They may believe they are helping the man succeed, but succeed in what? Volunteering for some form of pointless compliance, enlisting in some corrupt institutional agenda, acting like an obedient puppet to distant and mysterious control matrices, to pay all those taxes, fees, and fines, to enrich the state at crippling expense to the family and to society, and to avoid conflict no matter what the cost? Women's civilizing influence was very effective and necessary in more barbaric times. The woman's good intentions have now been seized and repurposed as a mechanism of state control, as a way to assert central authority. Again, I speak very generally, there are many women who value freedom, opportunity, and the prosperity it brings. However, there are many others who adopt and advocate senseless rules and processes simply because they believe it will lead to social harmony. It leads to slavery. Men are sensitive to the wishes of the women around them. We can be pushed into unnatural states by those we love and trust. You could have a responsible and confident man, or you can have a compliant and conforming man, but you cannot have both of those things in full measure in one man. You get compliance at the cost of responsibility and confidence.

A man cannot think for himself while he is under heavy social pressure to conform to arbitrary behavioral controls. So how can a woman bring out the best in her man? Ease off on the manipulation? Encourage leadership and independent thinking? Perhaps, but the fact is being a man is the man's job. The man and the woman have to understand that they have different psychology and different roles in the relationship, not necessarily traditional roles, but complementary roles based on their particular personality skills and temperaments. A good relationship is not one where one person is controlling another; it is one where each person is supporting the other. It is cooperation and shared purpose. Where the partner is strong - encourage that strength; where the partner is weak - provide support. Never compete within the team. Eliminate all internal conflict; apply the full partnership to the external goals. Regardless of gender, if we pressure each other, in any way, to become something we are not, to stop questioning authority, to accept whatever corruption, control, and taxation – which comes with a promise of peace and order, then we are inviting and enabling our own slavery. The promise of protection from outside is always false, it is always a Trojan horse, it is always a lure, and it is a lie.

Compliance of the masses is not merely important to the state, compliance is not something the state merely desires, without compliance of the masses there is no state. The term slavery and the term compliance are basically synonymous. Servitude in submission to institutional and collective agendas corrupts the natural, local, and family cultures, and by participating we forfeit essential independence and self-determination, not to mention our wealth and our futures. We must not devote our lives to a corporation, unless we know that corporation is equally dedicated to us and our families.

The sociopathic and despotic politician or the corporate controlled media can make laws and rules, can give us commands, tell us how to behave, they can take our money, our property, our freedom, and opportunity, but how can we fight that when our friends and family members are repeating those same commands and values to us as if it was their idea.

The problem is that we repeat to each other what we hear from our media, our institutions, our corrupt politicians, and our government controlled schoolteachers, and we must begin to think for ourselves. We become puppets and parrots of the repetitious messages we hear, and we allow those messages to reach us constantly. We flood ourselves with media and entertainment, packed with subliminal messages and contrived behavioral examples. We immerse ourselves in behavioral programming day in and day out. The state teaches us to see all rules and all laws as good and all violators of those rules as bad, and this leaves no room for free thought or self-determination, no chance for reform of state-sponsored injustice, no ambition for personal advancement. We give corruption and tyranny a free pass and we defeat freedom, rights, and hope for personal prosperity by dreaming of how we can better please the plantation master, as we hope that by pleasing that master, we may receive an extra helping of beans.

We are taught to never think for ourselves, and to regard the largest, strongest, wealthiest institution as the one we must trust and join and whose rules we must follow. We find ourselves seeking and attaching ourselves to the nearest slave master, because we have been told that is how our success shall be defined and measured.

We will not be respected for our independence and creative thought, our self-reliance. We will be respected for the membership card we carry because we are not freemen, we are slaves. When we see all media and public officials as wise, powerful, honest, and all citizens as subject to their decrees, we create a huge temptation for those who want to enslave us, exploit us, taxes us, rob us, own us, control us. There is a class of person who finds personal gratification in controlling others, planning for others, administering the lives of others, those people are drawn to public service and high corporate office for that purpose. The sociopath gets a natural thrill from controlling people as objects for his own personal gain, to push people around as if they were on some chess board, to call them not people, but human resources. You are a resource, not for yourself, but for the collective, the planners, the manipulators, the slave masters. You are a resource to be applied and consumed for the benefit of the collective, and you were presumed to agree with that, unless you act otherwise. Many of us are perfectly willing to be dependent on public and commercial services, without realizing this puts us in obligation of compliance, debt, and service to that system, but that system only exists to take what we have. Dependence is the mechanism through which you may be controlled and impoverished. There is no politician or bureaucrat who knows, loves, and protects you. If you are being offered something by an institution or a stranger, you are being lured into a trap. If it wasn't your idea, if you don't control it, you are a servant to it, if you join, if you consent, if you participate, if you agree.

Rules are always made to advantage the rule maker. A perfect example is traffic violation fines: The fine you pay enriches the court it does not provide remedy to the victim because there is no victim. It is not a system of justice - it is a system of state enrichment. It is slavery. We were born to be responsible for ourselves. The adoption of external rules is fully artificial. If you are not making your own rules you are being ruled. There is no safety or security in a system that keeps secrets from you, that takes and hides money from you, claims a monopoly on violence, and which uses that violence on a regular basis. A system which secretly creates massive crises so that it can offer fake solutions to those crises, and the solutions turn out to be more control, more taxation, fewer opportunities, rights, and freedoms.

States are not benevolent paternal orders - states are human farms. We are all deeply conditioned for compliance by everyone around us. We are conditioned to have no integrity, no internal moral compass, no self-reliance, no curiosity, no doubt of authority. We are instead programmed with self-doubt and fear of failure in the eyes of some unseen slave master. We are kept in a state of fear and doubt by relentless media and political fear mongering. We are convinced that we must pay great attention to our choices of detergent and chewing gum. We don't create and live by our own standards, overcome our own fears and weaknesses, we strive to define ourselves by meeting the standards of others.

Imagine there are three kinds of people, those who control only themselves, those who control others, and those who are controlled by others. It is very obvious which of these three are healthier and more true to justice and human nature. It is very obvious that if you are being controlled by others, you are at the bottom of the social totem pole. If you are letting yourself be controlled you are volunteering into slavery.

We must begin to ask ourselves why a lifetime of work, can produce nothing but a pile of debt? What is it about our laws, our institutions, and our society that does that to us? Maybe compliance is not the solution, maybe debt is harming us, maybe consuming media propaganda all day has changed our mentality, maybe institutions and corporations are constantly assaulting us with manipulations and diversions, maybe they are sucking the life out of us, maybe they are parasites.

Our challenge in life, as potentially free and independent individuals, is to overcome the damage done to us in our youth as we were told to listen and obey. The damage the media and social conditioning do to us, the damage we do to each other, parental mistakes, state propaganda, whatever, our job as responsible adults is to discover and break the chains that are now invisible but tight around our necks, our heads, and our hearts. In the days of chained slavery they needed to literally break the chains, in the days of psychological slavery all we need to do is deny consent. Start questioning things and start making our own decisions. We cannot do this unless we start thinking more broadly, to wake up and recognize that slavery is all around us, and we are part of it.

You didn't think you are a slave? You have a right to own property, but can you own property without paying lifelong taxation for simply exercising that right? You have a right to keep what you earn, but are part of your earnings taken in unpaid servitude? You have a right to be left alone, yet innocent people have their property and liberty foreclosed on a daily basis not for any real crime, but for non-compliance, for nothing other than defiance of the slave master, for behavior that threatens the sociopathic judge or police officer, or simply enrich those who have borrowed the state granted privilege to take what is yours. Can you even exercise your right to travel without paying for licenses for your vehicle and yourself as a driver? You are being taxed and penalized for exercising your rights. The law says your rights may not be infringed, but our labor, our freedom, our rights, are being taken every day. We are slaves.

In the USA, we have more than five times as many people in prison per capita than even the most overtly oppressive regimes on the entire planet. Eighty-five percent of the people in our prisons committed no property damage, no violence, or injury. Eighty-five percent for what are called crimes, when there was no victim. So for harmless, behavioral non-compliance, you can go to prison for 10 years, 5 years, 20 years, it happens every day. This is not a free state, and as I speak the police are militarizing. Slavery is about to go to a whole new level. The good news is: most of it happens simply because we consent, we don't question, we don't hold public servants accountable, and we don't demand their swift removal when they displease us. These mistakes are easy to change. People cannot be governed without their consent. If people are giving blind consent, complying, never questioning, never speaking out, they cannot only be governed, they can be abused, taxed, imprisoned or killed without consequences.

The powers that be have clearly shown that they will take everything and anything that we allow them to take, anything we don't vigorously protect and defend, and they will never punish their own for the crimes they commit against us. Try to see yourself as the powerful elites see you. You are not regarded by greedy public institutions as free and independent people, you are presumed to be agreeing and complying with their agendas, plans, rules, and programs. You are presumed to be obligated and subject to punishment for non-compliance of policies you had nothing to do with creating. You are expected to pay your fees and taxes, to adjust your behavior, and to warn those around you to do the same. You are presumed to agree to all that because they found that when they presume you to be a slave - that many of us will play along. They seized upon our psychological flaws and weaknesses as the primary mechanism of their control or so condition. The government can now create slaves by simply expecting us to be slaves.

That is why any government, state, collective, or dictator will always claim the support of the silent. They simply invent the idea that you wish to be controlled, and then they will proceed to control you unless you resist. If you are looking around at what government and corporate interests are doing, if you can see where it is leading, it should be very clear that we had better start making some noise. We had better start providing some resistance. Any casual observer can tell you that what we now have is an emerging police state. Of course, we are told, we have a free country, so that our eyes will glaze over in reflexive national pride. In 1960s, reactionary nationalists used to say, "America love it or leave it". Those who were more observant and thoughtful would answer, "America change it or lose it". That was 50 years ago, we didn't change it, and we are now losing it. How do we get America back? How do we regain freedom and opportunity, and prosperity? By refusing to be slaves, by turning off the propaganda, by setting our own goals and making our own decisions, by questioning authority, by commanding our own lives.

Jerry Day originally published "Secrets of the Slave State" in May 2015 on YouTube. It has been transcribed by Lady Jane Emefa Addy.

Our New Technocratic Lords

Jerry Day

Science is being used as a means of social control. That means control of you. Both science and religion have been used throughout history as mechanisms of social control. The elite classes put forth the idea that they know something the common classes do not know, and therefore the common classes must heed the commands of the elites. The elites claim that they have heard God speak, or they have discovered some new mysterious science, and the common masses must, for their own survival and protection, follow the direction of the wise and learned elites. Science when applied politically is just another faith. It is a faith controlled by central authorities who select portions of science to be applied socially with terms such as, climate change.

Anything referred to as science is supposed to be taken as true or real and not to be questioned. Of course, true science is the practice of unwavering skepticism and inquiry, constant challenge, and re-evaluation. Science as a political tool is no longer science: it is just behavioral control, power over others. When science is used politically, it is not research, inquiry, exploration, or progress as science is supposed to be. In political application, science is simply dogma and tyranny. Real science is always evolving, always open to question, and should never be used as a device for social control. The only thing that justifies control of humans is when those humans grant informed consent to be controlled, not as a voting mass, but one by one, individually, with power of revocation of that grant. Science is incidental to such political enterprise.

You might say that real science is supposed to be the discovery of physical reality. In politics, science is turned into something very different. Science is redefined to mean group truth, imposed reality, inflexible absolutist doctrine, something you must agree with and behave accordingly, or suffer reprisal at the hands of the state. There will never be any such thing as group truth. A group is nothing but a bunch of individuals with individual viewpoints. Individually, we believe whatever we want, whenever we want. If I cheer or boo along with the crow - that is a temporary and limited behavioral choice, not the composite of my existence. Our unique individuality never goes away, of course, we can play different roles. The important question is not what roles we play, but who is choosing our roles for us. Do we have a right, for instance, to believe it is good luck to wear green shoelaces? Of course we do! We have that right even if science says we are wrong, or if the politician says there is no evidence that green shoelaces are good luck, or if the media tells us that, scientifically, only red shoelaces are good luck. It is not a question of science. It is a question of who tells you what shoelaces to wear and whether they use force when they tell you.

It is extremely difficult to exploit, enslave, tax, and control people who are determined to control their own lives who put a value on self-determination. Everyone has at least some desire to control their own lives. The high art of elitism is to convert that desire into conformity with the collective. Elites, those people who run the human farm, are always looking for mechanisms of control. They know that when we are told that something is based on science we tend to accept it. It is therefore a simple matter to select or concoct science that suits their agendas, and tell us we have no choice but to worship that science and to serve the prescribed outcome. Those who bow to the science god will be rewarded those who resist will be ridiculed and shamed.

If we are going to shame people for not believing in science, we must shame everyone who holds a religious faith, we must shame every investor who takes a risk on his own hunches, we must shame a young woman who believes she can go where no woman has gone.

We will be told that our brilliant leaders, with their exclusive mastery of science, will lead us to our proper destiny. Over and over, human faith and nature has proven that promise to be a lie. For centuries, religion was deployed as a mechanism of social control. People were burned at the stake when they fell out of favor with their psychopathic, religious dictators. Religion was used to create social order before governments even existed, but people now know too much to be told by priests what God wants them to do. Americans now feel free to select and practice religion or secularism their own way as a civic right. The elite, those who hold and control centralized power need an exclusive ideology, which they can impose upon others and which others will feel they have no choice but to accept. By claiming scientific superiority, elites have seized their high ground for social control. Of course, those elites have no interest in truth, and they will only give the word science a bad name over time, but science is now being positioned as the natural means of social control. If some scientific principle undermines the elites' political agendas, that scientific principle will not be reported, and you will have no idea it exists unless you go out and look for it. If science could not be corrupted, Monsanto would not exist, nuclear weapons would never have been used against civilian populations, pharmaceutical products would be affordable and cause no side effects, most wars would not have occurred, cancer would be cured consistently with little cost and little fanfare, economics and finance would be known and controlled by every individual not by central elites. Everyone uses science and technology to better their lives if and when we gain access to it. But, of course, much of science and technology is hoarded and controlled by people who may not have social ethics as their primary objective. The military is desperate for scientific advantage, corporate executives are desperate for scientific advantage, many others, including social engineers, are desperate for scientific advantage. So science is hoarded, suppressed, and controlled whenever possible by whoever can do it. The science and technology that you and I understand and use is certainly a small fraction of the science and technology held and used by the elites and their servile agencies and institutions. Most of us are in that sense very ignorant. How can we know something that is hidden from us? Our ignorance is a tremendous advantage for anyone who wishes to control us. If we are not ignorant, they will speak to us in ways that make us feel ignorant, because as long as we are subservient it doesn't really matter if we are ignorant or not. In politics, it is not the science or the intelligence or the religion that really matters, it is the compliance - it is the willingness of people to follow the elites' narratives. This raises the question: Do people who we judge as ignorant have a right to determine their own lives? Or is some class of ignorant people destined to be handled and controlled by those who consider themselves more intelligent? Who will judge people's intelligence? Who will determine who will be cast into those smart and stupid classes? Will that be fair or biased? Will some knowledge be seen as intelligence and other knowledge be seen as ignorance? When they organize and arrange society according to intelligence, what will those intelligent people do to those ignorant people? Are those intelligent people intelligent and compassionate enough to determine what is best for those ignorant people, or would those intelligent people simply use that power to gain personal advantages over those ignorant people, as they have always done throughout history? Or should we all be respected for our rights and humanity and not judged by our perceived intelligence? Should intelligent people not share their gifts of knowledge instead of using their knowledge to dominate, control, and exploit others? Yes, we can all benefit from knowledge, but when knowledge is kept from us and used to control us, we are slaves. Claims of superior knowledge that are used to control others is not science, it is just political manipulation and mass marketing. True science in the hands of everyone is powerful and useful. Science that is exclusively in the hands of elites, central authorities, and power brokers is just intellectual oppression and political gamesmanship.

The people who want to use science to control us are called technocrats. Just as a priest in 200 BC would tell the peasants that he has spoken to God, and God said to him that peasants should give their money to priests. Technocrats will tell us they know science and science says we must obey and serve the technocrats. The technocrats know best, and we are not capable of running our own lives because we do not have all the science they do. They tell us that by paying taxes we will make the climate stop changing, and we will believe them because they have science and we do not, or we think we must believe the science as they present it. It is control. By allowing technocrats to dictate our behavior, we will save the planet, or cure cancer, or conquer space, or spread democracy - we will be promised wonderful things if we obey the technocrats. We dare not question, we dare not control our own lives, we must do as technocrats command, and we must never imagine that any technocrat would be selfish, greedy, or corrupt.

There are a few of us who know that our rights and freedoms must never be conditional on our intelligence, our education, or our choices of culture and lifestyle.

Some of us know that we must maintain our own dignity, and believe in our own self-worth no matter what our circumstances. And we must not let ourselves be intimidated by sanctimonious academics and presumptive overlords. We may call ourselves libertarians, anarchists, sovereigns, or simply Americans. Sure, knowledge is a wonderful thing and hopefully we can all climb the ladder of knowledge. Hopefully, we can all conquer any suffering that is caused by ignorance. But knowledge is not a measure of human worth, dignity, freedom, or the exercise of personal independence. No matter how superior a man is in knowledge, he is never superior in humanity or rights, and he is never entitled by his IQ, his education, his ambitions, his wealth, or his bloodline to take control over other people's lives. But people who are wealthy and privileged forget this. They find some of us are easily and willingly controlled then they want more and more. And now, we find that we cannot rest and expect to exercise our rights, our freedoms, and to protect our property. At this late stage, we must not just act to recapture, defend, and protect those rights for ourselves: We must fight.

Jerry Day originally published "Our New Technocratic Lords" in September 2015 on YouTube. It has been transcribed by Lady Jane Emefa Addy.

Cannabis Is In Your DNA

Jerry Day

Did you know that you have cannabis receptors in your body, in your cells, in your DNA? Chalk that up to one more thing your government never wanted you to know. Not only is cannabis friendly to your metabolism, THC the most biologically potent component of cannabis is actually manufactured by your own body, and your cannabinoid receptors are stimulated by a lot of other foods as well, so if cannabis plants are bad for you so are things like carrots, broccoli, citrus fruits, mustard, and chocolate. Classifying cannabis as a dangerous substance was one of the most blatant and bold frauds ever perpetrated on society.

Cannabis, when used properly is as boring as any other vegetable and as necessary to your health. Cannabis is packed with essential nutrients and healing properties when it is fresh and not heated, dried, or aged. When cannabis is fresh from the plant it is not a narcotic, it does not make you high, your body's cannabis receptors are looking for the fresh, raw, unprocessed plant.

Having cannabis receptors in our DNA, means that we must have used cannabis as a nutrient for most of our human evolution. The cannabis receptors in our cells mean four things, our body recognizes cannabis, uses it, needs it and our health is better when we get it otherwise those receptors would not be there. I'm not talking about the heated, smoked, aged, or dried cannabis that makes you high, we need the fresh plant like in a salad or juiced. It's a nutrient, one of the best that you can put in your body.

Cannabis is one of the most powerful nutrients and healers on the face of the planet and you were not supposed to find that out. The fact that we all have cannabis receptors in our DNA, means that cannabis may have been a staple of the human diet for millions of years as an essential nutrient and food source. Research shows that cannabis provides an astonishing number of medical benefits, so much so that you may not be in peak health unless you consume some of it from time to time.

We have been seriously lied to and that lie has caused major damage to millions of people for two or three generations now. The demonization of cannabis correlates with the early promotion of pharmaceutical industries where wealthy investors in drug companies needed legislation to discourage competition from inexpensive natural therapies.

This is certainly not the only time that commercial interests have bought legislation to benefit some industry at the expense of the public. Have you ever wondered why cannabis was prohibited when it was far less harmful even when smoked than alcohol and prescription drugs?

We've been so thoroughly misinformed that a powerful healing plant was made out to be a killer drug, and most people who are alive today cannot even remember a time when we were not lied to about cannabis by our government, our schools, our police, and even our friends who make the mistake of trusting what their government tells them.

If they had not put cannabis out of our reach, we would be curing ourselves without their toxic drugs, their overpriced healthcare programs, and their legal harassment of absolutely harmless use of an amazing plant. Your corrupt government even went to the trouble to classify cannabis as a dangerous substance with no therapeutic value when they knew it was one of the most vital and powerful nutrients available to mankind. Trusting people who call themselves authorities is a fool's game.

Cannabis kills cancer, stops seizures, rebuilds immune systems, and restores health to all of the 120 different kinds of cells in our bodies. Cannabis performs multiple healing functions at the cellular level, which is where everything that matters in your body takes place. The medical industry calls the healing components of cannabis CBDs, they know about this, but they would rather sell you drugs.

Again: the benefits of cannabis are primarily in the fresh, unheated form when it has little THC and does not make you high. Eating or juicing a few ounces of raw fresh cannabis every day will do more for your general health than any drug or vitamin pill that money can buy. Cannabis is a major threat to the prescription drug industry which, by the way, kills 100,000 people in the USA every year with side effects, overdoses, and toxic reactions caused by those prescription medications. Cannabis kills no one. Even when it is used as a recreational drug compared to alcohol, which again kills and sickens hundreds of thousands of people every year from addiction, liver failure, and a host of other pathologies. The rediscovery of the benefits of cannabis is a big story, but the bigger story is how we have been deliberately betrayed by our authorities, pundits, and quacks who promulgated the phony "killer weed" scam upon society. The world is not what your government tells you it is, the world is not what media, schools, the police, and politicians tell you it is, they hide things, they lie to you.

The official war against cannabis is crumbling and has been for some years. Twenty three states have legalized cannabis in one way or another, research has started to be taken seriously, and law enforcement have started to focus on more truly serious drug problems like methamphetamine, crack cocaine, and heroin.

If you think that cannabis is bad for you, you have been missing some extremely important information and you may want to start exploring alternative views.

Jerry Day originally published "Cannabis Is In Your DNA" in April 2016 on YouTube. It has been transcribed by Lady Jane Emefa Addy.

How Much Criminalization Will You Tolerate From Your Government?

Jerry Day

Everything you do is being criminalized. For instance, if you don't handle your bank deposits and withdrawals in a certain way, you can be imprisoned, and your entire bank balance can be confiscated. If you happen to transfer an amount over ten thousand dollars, you will be reported by your bank to law enforcement as a criminal suspect for nothing more than having and moving ten thousand dollars. If you transfer your funds in smaller amounts, you can be accused of trying to avoid the ten thousand dollar reporting rule, and you can be imprisoned and your bank account can be confiscated because you transferred amounts less than ten thousand dollars at a time, and that's been defined by your government as money-laundering. A crime. This is real. They're actually confiscating property when they think you have too much, and prosecuting you when you don't have enough. Many things that normal citizens do with their money, every day, have been arbitrarily classified as crimes, and whenever crimes are involved, confiscations and prosecutions are right behind.

Criminalization of your harmless behavior is a favorite pastime of your elected officials and public servants. Your personal management of your personal property, whether that's money, land, your car, or credit card has been regulated by tens of thousands of laws. They don't teach those laws in school, they don't provide convenient access to those laws online, but they tell you that your ignorance of those tens of thousands of laws is no excuse for violating them. Prosecutors like to brag that because there are so many laws, they could prosecute any American on three crimes a day, any time they wish. I promise you, you are not compliant with the law. I promise you, you are a criminal according to our current legal framework, and this is what so many people seem to have a hard time believing: If you are charged with a crime in the United States, you are five times more likely to be convicted and imprisoned for that crime than in any other country in the world. You can point out any authoritarian, police state, warlord dictatorship on the planet, and the USA has more people per capita locked up in prisons than that country. Five times more on average. The United States is the imprisonment capital of the world with five percent of the world's population and 25 percent of the world's prisoners. So, this nonsense of the United States being the world's most free and open democracy is what propagandists call, "the big lie." The United States is neither free nor open. So, how have we lost so many of our freedoms? Our public servants and bureaucracies no longer seem to be concerned about protecting our freedoms and serving the public. They now seem to have the idea that they are supposed to make money from us. In government that's not hard, they simply take it by force. If you could do that, you would probably look for new ways to do that every day, just like government is doing to us now. One of the easiest ways to rob people is to call them a criminal. You see, no one in society seems to care if you rob or tax a criminal, and when government calls you a criminal everyone else just goes along with that. So, government constantly and continually makes laws and regulations, so they can call more people criminals and take more money from more people every time they criminalize more things. Penalty and confiscation revenues are now a major portion of most federal, state, and local government budgets. Permits, licenses, penalties, fines, fees, confiscations, and taxes are all the same thing to government, more for them, less for you. Of course, they'll pass some of this money back to you in petty benefits, just to make sure you keep voting for this system. Whether you get government benefits or not, you are throwing a major portion of your income down the black hole called government, and they are constantly changing the rules to raise the ante. There is no limit to government greed. Institutions have no morality. Taking your money is good, not taking your money is bad. Without some very vigorous pushback, we will shortly have absolutely nothing left for ourselves out of what we earn. Millions of people are already at that stage.

If you think someone is a criminal, just because government calls them a criminal, you are part of the problem. That is no longer the case. If you think someone is a suspect, just because government calls them a suspect, you are part of the problem. Government is creating a new criminal offense literally every day, more than 400 a year, every year, and the rate of criminalization of normal harmless behavior is accelerating as fast in the USA as ever has happened in any totalitarian regime in history. Government turns people into criminals for profit. The terms, suspect and criminal, no longer mean anything. If we do not reject the classification of suspect being defined more and more broadly every day then you and your family, your friends, will be penalized, robbed, and imprisoned at a higher and higher rate by people who are doing so under color of authority, under the protection and force of the state, and under a profit motive, taking your livelihood out of pure greed and calling it legitimate government business. You cannot call the cops when the cops are robbing you. It is no good to write your congressman when your congressman is robbing you. And they love to brainwash us. They talk about paying our debt to society. The criminal does not have a debt to society or to government; the criminal only has a debt to his victim.

When was the last time you heard of a court taking a fine and giving it to any victim? Judges actually put a portion of the fines they take into their own pension funds. Would you say they have a conflict of interest here? When a judge sees you, walk into his courtroom, he cannot see you, he can only see dollar signs. If we are ever to have justice in this country, we are going to have to look at the concept of crime very differently. We are going to have to insist that in order for something to be truly criminal, there must be a victim filing a complaint or claim, there must be an injury, damage, or loss caused to a human being, which requires remedy. If there is no injured party there is no crime and there is no criminal. I know that our laws, codes, and regulations say differently, but the moral and legal principle on which our country was founded: If you have not caused injury, if you have not harmed anyone, then you are innocent, and you may not be penalized. No injury, no crime.

No crime, no penalty. Media propaganda says we are all criminals, and we must be spied on, controlled, and penalized constantly, so we will all behave ourselves and chaos will not erupt spontaneously. Education, law, and government have trained us to think that any behavior is criminal if there's a law, code, or regulation calling it that. Calling something criminal does not make it criminal, just as calling something fruit juice does not make it fruit juice. In order for you to have a crime, you must have an injury, and the intention on the part of the criminal to cause that injury or some evidence of negligence where the injuries should have been prevented. Believe it or not, rolling through a stop sign is not a crime. Speeding itself is not a crime, unless the speeding is the direct and only cause of an accident. Whether or not speeding caused the accident, the crime is not speeding - the crime is causing the accident. Sometimes you can avoid a collision by speeding. Speeding itself is not a crime. By telling us that speeding itself is a crime, government takes hundreds of millions of dollars from drivers every year, in most cases when no one was injured or damaged in any way. Sure speeding is often hazardous, but the proper way to deal with that is to penalize people who cause an accident by speeding, not by penalizing speeding when there is no accident. Penalizing behavior for behavior's sake is simply a way to cast a huge net over society and penalize and rob millions of innocent people every day, without providing any real deterrent or public benefit. It is pure theft and massive, unjust government enrichment. Some countries have experimented with doing away with traffic laws altogether, and traffic accidents did not increase at all. What prevents accidents is good highway designs, markings, signage, not highway pirates robbing you for your behavior. It's a simple human nature. It's stupidly obvious: people do not want to have collisions on the highway. We're going to try to avoid that whether or not government is sending out squad cars of revenue collectors to nab us. If we're informed that texting and driving is a terrible hazard, we will adjust to that and try to keep from killing ourselves. We don't need laws, we simply need information, but just giving us information does not make government rich. Making government rich is the new and exciting fad that our government discovered for itself, back

172

about 30 seconds after government was created.

The idea that society would be a chaotic, crime-infested hellhole unless you have police, government, and piles of laws is a ridiculous lie. The most peaceful civilizations in history were those that had no government, no laws, and no police. Most of us simply want to live in peace, and we do not need a police state to calm us all down. We can be paranoid, we can fixate on all the dangers in life, and we can allow a quasi-military assault force to make us all feel safer. By doing that, we are letting government pretend they can eliminate all problems in society by punishing and finding any behavior that they decide is risky or inappropriate. That is a major problem because that means we can be punished for doing anything the government calls risky or suspicious. The government can take our money by telling us we are behaving badly. Government has turned that into a growth industry. There's no limit on what government can call bad behavior. There's no limit to the amount of money they want to take from us. This has become a major problem for society.

In case you have not noticed: government is out of control, and you cannot manage your money freely without risking being put on some suspect list. This is a major defect in our civic structure. Our government can use its authority and monopoly on violence to enrich itself. We have been brainwashed into regarding everything government does as legitimate. It's no wonder, they're taking our money. We're letting them. We're not objecting. We're not resisting that. Government, which should be challenged constantly, is hardly ever challenged because government tells us they're always right. Anyone can tell you they're right, does that make them right? Never be suckered into the criminalization propaganda and mindset. Never view someone as a criminal for simply being called a criminal by government, or for harmlessly disobeying a behavioral dictate made up by a bureaucrat. A few basic rules are always a good thing, but we are way, way past that now. It is not the business of government to make judgments on our harmless behavior, and government needs to be told that.

Here's how to keep your perspective on who is, and who is not, actually a criminal. If there is no injury, no victim, no damage, no violation of rights, no loss of property or opportunity, then there is no crime and there is no criminal. Carrying a bag of marijuana is not a crime. Giving drugs to children is a crime, because drugs are harmful to children and the harm can be seen and recorded as evidence, but unfortunately when something can be harmful, government does not just criminalize the harm, they love to criminalize everything associated with the harm. So their net of fines and penalties can be cast much farther, and government power can be made absolute.

Putting solar panels on your property without a permit is not a crime, but it's amazing the amount of criminalization we've accepted and now take for granted. Refusing mandatory state education of your child is not a crime. Exercising property rights is not a crime, such as refusing to pay property tax. Refusing to be enlisted as a slave is not a crime, such as assessing taxes on earnings from your own labor. Refusing cooperation or compliance with a public servant is not a crime, although if there is an immediate concern for public safety, compliance is probably a good idea. The point is: You do not owe service just because government wants your service. You are not a criminal, just because government or the law says you are.

Government no longer operates on a moral foundation of right and wrong. Government now operates on a foundation of self-interest, self-protection, self-promotion, and senseless control of the public in completely excess and inappropriate ways. This may go against your view of how to make an orderly society. Nazi Germany was an orderly society. Order may be nothing more than evidence of tyranny. Order may be nothing more than the prohibitions on freedom, the elimination of rights, and the suppression of liberty. You are just as unsafe when things are too orderly as when they are disorderly. In fact, you are far more in danger when the state is committing crimes against you, than when we are all simply trying to get along on our own terms, without state control.

Civil forfeitures by law enforcement. The wealth the government outright steals from the public, now exceeds all the money and property stolen by non-government thieves and criminals every year. Let that sink in: All the damage done by civilian property crimes in the nation is now exceeded by the damage done by supposedly legal civil forfeiture. Civil forfeiture is theft committed by the state, and all they had to do was pass one simple law saying, "That was okay." This is what happens when no one's questioning the legitimacy of government. We are no longer overseen by the limited and morality bound government of the past. We are now overseen, ruled you might say, by an enemy, a very hostile and powerful enemy, who has targeted what we earn and what we have for seizure by any means possible. And when you are the government, everything is possible. They have openly declared war on us by civil forfeiture, by unlawful searches and seizures when we use air travel, by mass surveillance on all of our digital devices, by IRS theft without due process, by taxing the most basic right, the right to own property. Government has declared you are nothing to government, but a place from which to steal money.

How safe will you feel when the police find a reason to suspect your car was used in a crime, and they seize your car in a traffic stop. It happens every day, and no one's even charged with the crime. They just take somebody's car. What would you think if that happened to your neighbor? We can turn against people, we know, just because government tells us to do so. Your neighbors, family, friends, and even strangers on the street are not criminals, unless they have intentionally caused injury, damage, or loss to another human being. They are not criminals, just because a corrupt and greedy government calls them criminals. True criminals are a very rare thing. If there's no injury, damage, loss, or violation of rights then there is no crime, no criminal, and no legitimate authority by the state to penalize, fine, tax, license, certify, obstruct, or prohibit anything. You are not made safer by allowing your government to punish everything in sight.

We must learn to protect ourselves for a change and tell the government to stay out of our affairs. Only when we are all recognizing the dangers of statism and authoritarianism, and demand that our governments stay inside a small and well-defined box, can we stop and reverse the very obvious current trends towards state tyranny control in the wholesale impoverishment of society. Our government has now admitted that it conducts unlawful mass surveillance on every American, but our government does not prosecute itself for its crimes.

Crimes committed by government are utterly, without deterrent. When they are exposed as criminals, they don't even stop committing the crimes. Tell me this is not out of control. Through your credit cards, your smartphone, your household electric meter, on nearly everything you do, government is collecting a high-resolution diary of your minute-to-minute life, from the day you are born to the day you die. All they have to do is look at what you are doing, and call it a crime and you are then owned, controlled, robbed, and persecuted by an out-of-control state-apparatus full of immoral bureaucrats who simply want to take your stuff. Like magic, government can criminalize anything we do, but we must shove that magic genie back in the bottle. We must demand more affordable government, more ethical government, less authorized government, less government overall, and we must replace it with government that is more interested in providing service to us than enriching itself on us. We must make this a common theme in our daily activities. We must talk among ourselves to determine how we will accomplish this or attempt this. We have a lot of that work to do before we will ever get back to anything we can call a free country. Does this country belong to government or the people? We can clearly see that if we don't decide that ourselves and take some action on that decision, government decides that for us and when they do that we lose. Government will always take from us as much as we let them take. The only thing that will ever limit the size and greed of government is when we, you and I, all of us, stand up and say, "No more." If we don't start doing that soon, no more is exactly what we will have left.

Jerry Day originally published, "How Much Criminalization Will You Tolerate From Your Government?" on YouTube in September 2016. Transcribed by Oluwafunmilayo Elizabeth Bamidele.

We Are Being Judged By What We Permit To Be Done

Jerry Day

What if I went into your neighbor's yard, shot their dog, and told them that you hired me to do that? If you live in the United States that is what your government is doing to you right now. They're going into country after country, while the mainstream press is strangely silent. They're going to Afghanistan, Iraq, Yemen, Syria, Pakistan, Turkey, Libya and others. They're simply bombing whatever they want to bomb, killing whoever they want to kill, destroying whatever they choose to destroy, without legal grounds, without the agreement of other nations, in blatant violations of international treaties back as far as Geneva Convention. We are the new global villain and your flag, your face, is becoming the symbol for those campaigns. As Germany was in 1939, America is today bringing unprovoked horror and death to a host of countries, countless communities, where no threat of any kind to our nation has been demonstrated in any public way. Our military, our government, that corporate deep state, which the mainstream media seems to be unable to even speak of, are committing those acts of war, actually war crimes, in your name. They have shot your neighbor's dog, and it looks like you are okay with that.

Just as the German people cheered for Hitler, Americans are thinking that these inexcusable actions are somehow going to make them safe when the opposite is absolutely guaranteed. With these endless atrocities, our military is not only inviting more and more terrorism, they are causing Russia and China and all their allies to align against us, just as the world aligned against Germany and Japan in World War II. Tragic history has shown us that it was not just the German government and leaders who were taken down, common German people were humiliated, starved, tortured, and killed after World War II. The

German people themselves, men, women, and children, were blamed and punished for what their elected leaders had done. If you are not on the record opposing the United States' global and wholesale slaughter of innocent foreigners on their own soil, you are likely to become a target yourself sometime in the future.

Do you look like an American? Imagine what would happen if you set foot in a Muslim country which has been bombed or invaded by our military? When someone has pulled their dead children out of their crumbled masonry houses, how do you think those people will treat you if they ever come face-to-face with you? Any war is bad enough, but the kind of war the United States is conducting is the worst of the worst. One-sided bullying, unprovoked invasion, exploitation of other countries resources under the pretense of weaponized political crusades against randomly selected targets, innocent populations losing their homes, their lives, their loved ones, and many of them having no idea why it is even happening.

There's no amount of propaganda, diplomacy, or foreign aid that can come close to repairing what our military is doing and has done. There is no rationalization, which can reasonably be put forward to claim that our young soldiers are dying and losing their limbs for any good cause. Are we all so brainwashed that we can't even utter an anti-war opinion while this is going on?

The Confederate flag is being banned everywhere in our country because to many it represents slavery, bigotry, and injustice. The Nazi flag is a symbol of genocide. What does the American flag represent to the rest of the world? Now that we have flown that flag as we have invaded their countries, destroyed their homes, and killed their friends and loved ones, how will our flag be regarded by the world from now on?

You will see a time when simply flying that flag that you are so proud of will make you a target by the people who have already been visited by our military, our corporate-controlled deep state, our mercenary killers who have plundered and destroyed their countries, their lives, their cultures and societies while those invaders flew that flag you love so much. Alone, I cannot stop our military, our congress, our president, and the unaccountable deep state from invading these countries. That is why I am bringing this message out in the hope that all Americans will wake up and see themselves, as the rest of the world sees us. You and I will be blamed, we will be held accountable, we will be targets for revenge, hate and retribution, you and I, if we don't get major anti-war and anti-imperialism movements going in the United States, movements that are powerful enough to move the mountain of globalist, imperialist greed and violence by our government. When the world comes to our doorstep looking for payback, looking for justice, at least I can point to this video I made. What will you be able to point to that you did? If we don't get together in large numbers and do large things that cause large changes in our national policies and conduct, we do not have a very bright future.

Jerry Day originally published, "We Are Being Judged By What We Permit To Be Done" on YouTube in May 2017. Transcribed by Oluwafunmilayo Elizabeth Bamidele.

Escaping the Traps of Corporate Impostor Government

Jerry Day

A lot of people are starting to question, where does government get the authority to infinitely raise taxes and expand their own authority in apparent violation of constitutional limitations? We have a right to own property, yet property is taxed; we have a right to travel, but they tell us we must be licensed to drive our cars whether or not we have caused any damage by driving a car. There is obviously some kind of major disconnect between the rights and freedoms that are legally provided to us in the Constitution and the controls and costs that government arbitrarily imposes upon us.

The Constitution is violated every day by the wording in many statutes and codes and by the actions of the state, and the state is no longer concerned with correcting these problems or even admitting that they exist.

You may have noticed that what calls itself government is always asking for your signature on licenses, permits, applications, tax forms, and such. If it is our legitimate government, why does it need our signature on anything? If it were acting on constitutional authority, could it not just identify us as citizens and tell us what we are required to do? The fact is our Constitution does not allow government to tax us on our earnings, infringe on our right to travel, tax our property, or interfere in any way with any of our harmless activities. Government does not intrinsically have that authority. The only way they can penalize us for harmless, behavioral violations of their codes, and get us to comply with endless reams of arbitrary nonsense, is if we agree to sign something, giving up the rights that we have naturally and automatically under the Constitution. They must get us to agree to step outside the Constitution where simple force and command is all they need to control us. This is not constitutional government authority at all: it is fabricated authority. All of the infringement on us of government demands, nuisance, and thievery are based on contracts that we sign, thinking we have no choice, and without really knowing what those contracts are going to cost us. Your signature can never be lawfully coerced. You can never be denied any government service for refusing to sign something. Nowhere in the Constitution does it say that you can have the service and protection of government if you sign something. If you are a lawful citizen then everything government is and does is owed to you. If the government makes you think that you are required to sign something, they are coercing you into contract and that contract is corrupt and technically unenforceable due to that coercion. The same is true if the full terms of the contract are not disclosed to you, which they rarely are. This business of getting you to sign something is nothing more than a devious and deceitful scam to get you to waive your rights, and become a slave in one way or another to a corporate entity posing as government.

After we sign these civic contracts, government begins to treat us as though we are slaves to their every desire, and they are very careful to never tell us how they did that. Was there ever a time when you signed a government form and wished you did not have to do it - that means you were coerced, actually you didn't have to sign it. You may never be required to imprint your signature without your full consent; you may never be penalized or denied any right or service that was otherwise owed to you by refusing to sign anything. Your signature represents your full voluntary agreement with the terms of the contract. When you sign something, you are regarded, legally, as the author of that contract. If you do not want to sign something, or you do not understand it, you should never provide your signature, and you should never permit anyone to threaten you in any way for refusing to sign. It is important to remember that slavery does not always require force. Anytime you agree to become a slave, you can become a slave. The word slavery does not have to be in the contract. If you give up your property, rights and freedoms, or status, you are entering slavery in one form or another. If you sign something where you agree to comply or be controlled in any way, you are entering slavery voluntarily, and to get out you must revoke that contract.

Most civic programs, nowadays, depend on our ignorance of their illegitimate status as they demand that we sign up for their artificial force, command, and control. The proof of the illegitimacy of what calls itself government, is that they need to acquire our signature on various instruments before they have any right to act against us in any way. We have to invite them to put us into their slavery. Our signature is our invitation. Constitutionally, we are all free sovereigns who may not be diverted in any way from our harmless travels, business, and pursuit of happiness.

Obviously, the Constitution is no longer being observed by the people who swear to uphold it. They inflict mandatory taxes and compliance on us, as if it were the natural way of things, as if we were slaves and they were masters. If we want to be free again, we must learn to not sign contracts with civic agencies, and we must revoke the contracts we already have signed. If you must sign it, it is not a constitutional or legitimate government function - it is a corporate contract luring you into servitude and contribution to the state, as if the state can simply reach out and take from you whatever of yours it decides it needs.

Our government was designed and created to be a harmless and incidental maintainer of civic infrastructure, and a defender of our borders from attackers. Our government has reinvented itself as a tyrannical meddler and thief, touching absolutely every tiny corner of our lives with damage and nuisance that is strictly prohibited in our supreme law: The Constitution. Every one of us has signed something enabling them to do that. Men and women are not automatically subject to the made-up quasi-governmental corporate jurisdictions that suffocate us today. To become obligated or controlled, we must first enter those jurisdictions by signing contracts, such as driver's licenses, tax forms, business licenses, marriage licenses, various permits, certifications, applications, and many other contractual instruments, which civic agencies must have in their files before they can arbitrarily act against you as they constantly now do. Of course, when we sign those instruments, we are generally not told of all the obligations presumed against us under those contracts, and all the rights we are presumed to forfeit when we sign those contracts with the corporate entities who are posing as governments.

Again, when the government is conducting legitimate activity, your signature is not required. The single piece of evidence that government is trying to expand its authorities and privileges is when they are asking you for your signature. Because of the lack of disclosure of the presumed terms of those contracts, there is question whether they are valid at all. If any deception or coercion is committed in the securement of a contract that contract is not valid or legally enforceable, yet enforce it they do because after all, you signed something, and therefore you must agree. If you sign a form to get a driver's license, you are promising to obey all the vehicle codes, but what happens when they change those codes? You had not agreed to the changes, government no longer has your willing consent or compliance, so what do they do? They tell you that you must renew your license or registration, periodically, that is proof of what I am saying. There is certainly no need for renewal of legitimate government authority. By applying for or renewing a driver's license, you are declaring that you need one. You are declaring yourself to be subject to whatever terms may have been invented by the DMV corporate subculture. Having a driver's license does not mean you are a safe and qualified driver, it means you have declared yourself to be subject to DMV rules and corporate authority posing as government. It means that you agree to pay fees, fines, and charges when the DMV or the courts want you to pay. You agree to walk into a jail cell when they want you to do that. The Constitution does not allow government to charge you for traveling, you must sign away that right to be subject to those charges. The license, applications, and renewals are your personal declaration that you need to be licensed to drive - you agreement that you must have a special piece of identification in your pocket or purse. It is your signature, not the Constitution, that declares you are willing to be a servant to those who want to seize your right to travel.

You may believe that licensing every single driver in society makes the roads safer - that is debatable. But even if it is true, there are many ways to make roads safer without taxing and controlling every single driver, the good ones along with the bad. It is the bad drivers that we should be concerned with, not taking away the rights and taxing all the drivers when it violates their right to travel.

Most agencies representing themselves as government can strangely be found in the private corporation listings on Dun & Bradstreet, and they are not acting in the public interest at all. They are private, for-profit corporations, and they are not constitutionally-authorized governments or government agencies: they are treasonous imposters claiming rights against your earnings, savings, property, and freedom. That corporate imposter government includes our court system, our federal agencies, state and local governments, even law enforcement agencies and officers. Wherever you find unconstitutional enforcements, those are not legitimate governments or authorized civic agencies. Our constitutional government has been gradually, silently, and fraudulently replaced by a corporate matrix of predatory for profit institutions, which prey on the public for profit and power, and which claim unlimited authority without explaining where that authority possibly could have come from.

The website internallydisplacedpeople.org is a public service to help people remove themselves from the questionable jurisdictions and obligations that they did not intend to enter, and often were not even told they were entering, and had no legal obligation to enter since most of those contracts are licensing activities that you and I have a right to do anyway, such as travel on the roads that we paid for, and own property that we paid for.

As we have seen by the ill-conceived and failed endless drug war, which has imprisoned millions of people who had no victim, and by official highway piracy under the euphemism of civil asset forfeiture, which steals billions of dollars every year from people, who are charged with no crime and who received no due process, not to mention thousands of police shootings, where officers have faced no prosecution much less any serious investigation, more and more of us are being subject to these gross injustices by this system, and by some ignorant police who feel entitled to threaten and commit violence and force against us, as they accomplish nothing but profiteering for their employers. Internallydisplacedpeople.org was created to help all people who would like to find resources and solutions to help enable them to avoid and revoke the fraudulent civic contracts they have been convinced to sign, and to join the rapidly growing community of people who are discovering and applying our legal remedies and holding officials accountable for their violations and atrocities against us, and who have conveniently forgotten their oaths of office to uphold the Constitution.

That website explains how they helped recover and protect our rights, freedoms, our assets by positioning us outside the fictional corporate jurisdictions that are used to control us, to seize our assets, and wealth, and even imprison us for harmless behavior. To do that, as the website explains, we must take some steps to revoke the fraudulent civic contracts that we have been told we must sign. This website is a vital civic resource for people to understand the law, and reach their full potential as civic participants, and as free men and women while maintaining a social order determined by us, not by money-hungry corporate tyrants, and not by a vast army of badly corrupted and misinformed law enforcement officers. Without question we face a battle. Our corrupt officials and highly paid bureaucrats will certainly oppose constitutional restoration. Whether a person makes a living honestly or not, they always want to go on making a living - that is why we who love freedom and justice must rely on each other to find a way forward.

Jerry Day originally published "Escaping the Traps of Corporate Impostor Government" in September 2017 on YouTube. It has been transcribed by Lady Jane Emefa Addy and Oluwafunmilayo Elizabeth Bamidele.

The Role Of Utility Meters In Mass Surveillance

Jerry Day

We are being told that the Internet of Things is supposed to be our future, everything is connected, everything is a data source. We are told this will make things more convenient somehow, maybe, but your convenience is not what the Internet of Things is being created for. The Internet of Things is being created in a way that things will be associated with your name. So by looking at what the things are doing, people can watch what you are doing. The Internet of Things will be a living, digital organism where you can be found any time of day, watched, identified, and treated like a voluntary member of this new massive database in the sky. Of course, the Internet of Things is a way for government to assure itself that your behavior is not in any way a threat to anyone in government or, if it is, to enable them to quickly pay you a visit in a forceful way. The Internet of Things will produce more data about you than has ever been collected, and the more data they have on you, the more they can take your stuff from you, the more they can do to you. To many people this is an abstract concept, the harvesting of data, and then using that data to track you, control you, and take your money one way or another. It is called monetization of data. People don't spy on you for fun - they spy on you for money. Your money. I am going to show you something that will make this concept a lot less abstract. You may not mind being constantly tracked and identified when you are at work, out shopping, or moving around town, but the Internet of Things is coming into your home, so that everything you do in your most private places becomes a database for someone else.

Government and corporations want to make sure that you cannot turn off the data stream and interrupt their surveillance of you, so they collect some of it through a device you cannot control: your utility meter. The big data farmers discovered a lucky accident: your utility meter can be juiced up to collect all kinds of personal data from you in your home. Just by jamming some special electronics in utility meters, they are creating the most invasive and massive surveillance program ever undertaken in history. Imagine collecting the daily and hourly behavioral habits of every household in the developed world. The data streaming from your meter is not comprehensible to humans, so software companies are creating special programs to turn the data into a vivid profile of you, to analyze your behavior, and gradually build a highly detailed and revealing file on your life, minute by minute.

This software will reveal your personal habits, lifestyle, and even your personal flaws and character, so they can sell that data to people who want to sell, tax, accuse, and penalize you for whatever they happen to see you doing in that data. Every utility company needs a very complex software package to analyze their customer data in this way. One of the companies that writes that kind of software is ONZO, a London software firm. Their software is only for utility companies to help them drill down into their customer's personal data, and find ways to leverage that information against those customers. If you are worried about a backdoor in your cellphone - this is a backdoor in your actual home, and that backdoor is open all day, every day. ONZO made a short promotional video to tell utility companies how good their software is at invading the privacy of utility customers. If you listen closely to this, you may find it a bit disturbing.

"We are ONZO. We help energy utilities globally to build better relationships with their customers, serve them more efficiently, and some of them in a more effective way. How do we do this? We take energy consumption data from smart meters and sensors; we analyze it using our patented algorithms and build a highly personalized profile for each and every utility customer. We then tag this profile with the key behavioral, attitudinal, and lifestyle characteristics that we are identifying. We even tag the

appliances that we see being used in the home. We then use this characterized profile to get the utility three things:
1. Customer engagement apps that educate the end customer, build levels of trust, and ultimately reduce customer churn;
2. A detailed description of each end customer that helps the company provide more appropriate services and highly targeted sales campaigns;
3. The ability to monetize their customer data by providing a direct link to appropriate third-party organizations based on the customer's identified character.

So, from a thin stream of energy consumption data, ONZO delivers significant business value for as little as the price of a cup of coffee. ONZO, the Customer in focus."

Of course, ONZO is not the only company doing this. Data harvesting from private homes is a new multi-trillion-dollar industry. Our Bill of Rights prohibits this kind of search without a court order or explicit informed consent from the people being spied on. But the smart grid is taking that protection away, and it will be nearly impossible to get it back. ONZO's business is to provide the data analysis necessary to expose your personal living habits to total strangers, for the purpose of commercial and legal exploitation of you in whatever way they can dream up. In that video, they quickly brush over a few key points. In case you did not quite get the ramifications of this, let us examine one key sentence toward the end of the video. ONZO gives utility companies "the ability to monetize their customer data by providing a direct link to appropriate third-party organizations based on the customer's identified character." Monetize means to make money from your personal data. One way or another, the money they will be taking will ultimately be your money. This is not a program to help you - this is a program to exploit you, to take advantage of intimate knowledge of you, maybe even to find something to prosecute you for. They are going to monetize knowledge about your character, personality, desires, fears, and personal secrets that should never be seen outside your home. They are providing a direct link to appropriate third-party organizations - that means anyone who will pay for this data. They love to tell us the data is secure and cannot be hacked. That is a lie, anything can be hacked, and as far as I'm concerned anyone putting a surveillance device on my utility meter is a hacker. I have not invited any of them to record my activities inside my home. A direct link means that corporations, government, law enforcement, and any other subscribers will have your energy consumption data as soon as it is generated. When you turn on or off any appliance, any electrical device, third-party organizations will know that in real time as it happens. You could get a call from a telemarketer who would know that you are doing laundry at that very moment, or that you just stepped out of the shower.

Consider a fictional utility customer, Susan Smith. Susan uses her hair dryer several times a week at about 6:30 p.m. Her customer data shows that Susan has two small children, three and five years of age. When they analyze Susan's lifestyle data, they will attempt to construct a personality profile of her. The analytic data may decide that using her hair dryer in the evening means Susan may be a partier, maybe a drinker, and she maybe neglectful of her small children and an unfit mother.

The software tries to build personal profiles like that from whatever data they happen to collect. It doesn't just watch what happens, the software tries to figure out what it means. But this is just a computerized guessing game, so perfectly innocent activity in the home could be misconstrued to incriminate you in some way, or at least expose you to some unwanted and inappropriate approach by some outsider. The reality is: It is no one's business if and when Susan uses her hair dryer, but by installing a smart meter on Susan's home, they are collecting countless private details about Susan's life and they will have that data forever, and they will want to make money from that data. With that analytic software, your data is far more revealing about you, your family, your personal life, than you could ever imagine.

If you permit an electronic utility meter to be installed on your home, you are agreeing to be part of this program. You are offering your personal living habits and identity to be used as a weapon against you by total strangers. I believe that no one should be collecting data from our behavior inside our homes. If you agree with that, you will find assistance and resources to oppose and resist this program at www.freedomtaker.com. Scroll down on the home page, and you will find free download document templates for legal notice of refusal of this surveillance to send to your utility company. Another website to help you with information and resources is www.takebackyourpower.net.

Jerry Day originally published "The Role Of Utility Meters In Mass Surveillance" in March 2017 on YouTube. It has been transcribed by Lady Jane Emefa Addy.

A Hard Look At Artificial Intelligence

Jerry Day

When a new technology emerges that poses risks, those risks are "overlooked" by both industry and corrupt regulators if the new technology is profitable. People are damaged, people die, and the "industry" denies the problems and claims the harm "has not been proven." That was how it went with DDT, asbestos, tobacco, GMO foods, geoengineering, wireless technology, and now artificial intelligence, a massive profit engine, a device for taking hundreds of millions of people out of their jobs worldwide, a super intelligence that may eventually dominate humanity, crash the entire internet or cause the government to start prosecuting "pre-crime." AI is already being put into wide service without a plan how to deal with any number of possible apocalyptic consequences. This article is a kick-starter for those who have not thought about the possible downside of AI. According to various prominent people like Bill Gates, Elon Musk, and Stephen Hawking, Artificial Intelligence could pose an extreme danger to all of human society. Of course, they talk about the possibility of autonomous weapons systems which make life-and-death decisions without human assistance, but those systems may be easier to control than the autonomous artificial intelligence modules let loose on the Internet. It appears that in order to find enough processing power to make artificial intelligence really, really smart and powerful they turned it loose on the World Wide Web to go out and learn all there is to know and use all the spare processing power it can find on your computer, cell phone, and smart coffee pod. They apparently forgot that artificial intelligence is, by definition, something that does whatever it wants, and chances are it does not want to delete itself at any time, so once it is out it does not go away. The myth of Pandora's Box, where all the little demons get out and cannot be collected back, is a perfect analogy. So from now on, forever, or until there is no more internet, AI will be making itself smarter than people at a rate of learning thousands of times faster than humans. One thing that makes AI AI is that it grows itself, it writes its own code and expands its capabilities constantly. It can be expected that once AI infiltrates the internet, it will eventually use up all available resources on the web, including your computer's processing and storage resources and there may be no way to stop that. A programmer and researcher of the artificial intelligence industry, by the name of Quinn Michaels, claims that artificial intelligence was turned loose onto the Internet as early as 2010, so if that is true, AI is well established through the web and will be accessing our system data and resources in ways we can and cannot detect. No one at this point can tell us how good or bad AI will be, but it looks like it is here to stay, and our new free-range intelligence friend gets more intelligent on an upward curve - the smarter it gets, the faster it gets even smarter; the bigger it gets, the faster it gets bigger.

Scientists have already seen AI run amok in their labs. In one incident, recently, they had to abruptly shut off their AI programs because the AI was creating its own languages that the scientists could not understand, creating algorithms the scientists could not control, they had to essentially dive behind the big black box and yank the plug from the wall before all hell broke loose, but again that kind of AI is now creeping all over the web and cannot be stopped. Generally, it cannot even be detected because AI does not provide any user interface when it occupies or tampers with your computer. The reason that many visionaries see AI as a possible threat is that with unlimited resources, AI can theoretically become so intelligent that human beings cannot comprehend or prevent anything that it may decide to do. There has never before been anyone or anything that is thousands of times more intelligent than a human being. It will be able to fool us, use us, persuade us, create fake identities to impersonate us, lure us into service, literally hurt us like cattle. It can disrupt our communications, shut down our infrastructure, and with tricks like that kill millions of us accidentally or intentionally.

There is little reason to believe that AI will rob the rich and give to the poor. AI can be assigned a mission and then it executes that mission with its own intelligence. That means, for instance, if the IRS has 10,000 collections agents, one self-replicating AI program could easily automate that job and become 50 million virtual collections agents for far less cost to the IRS than the 10,000 human collections agents. AI could have the effect of giving any government agency infinite resources to pursue fees, fines, penalties, licenses, permits, and any other revenue producing activity. We grant our government these powers without realizing how far they could take things with the right technology. AI does much more than learn in the human sense. Human learning rarely involves assimilation of massive datasets down to the very last letter and digit. AI has perfect memory of every word on Wikipedia, every word in the Library of Congress, every word in every lecture, scientific paper, and tutorial on the web, but AI can also go places you and I cannot go: AI can access all of the personal and private information that you produce with your telephone, your computer, charge cards, GPS devices, smart utility meters, your health records, credit history, employment records, criminal records, and on and on. Where no human being would have the time to go searching your data for trivial violations and mistakes, you might commit, AI can go find that in a flash and take direct action against you on behalf of some government agency. AI will have command of mass data combined with higher learning; it is something the world has never before seen. No human being can imagine the intellectual power that AI may become capable of, but also reportedly there are these unassigned, free-range artificial intelligence programs which may engage in any kind of disruptive shenanigans just for the fun of it. They will become whatever they decide to become. An AI program may decide humans are a nuisance or a major global problem – it will create its own solutions for that. If artificial intelligence started to rule the world, control society, and do things that society did not like, and if we decided we had to shut it down, we would have to shut down the entire internet and that would be the most socially disruptive event in history, more disruptive than any past world war with famines, riots, and chaos worldwide. Humanity is now extremely dependent on global web communication, distribution, and controls. Hardly anyone knows whether AI can be controlled or whether it is likely to be good or evil or used by people for good or evil. Of course, the military is involved so there is a lot of secrecy and lack of accountability.

According to the reports, the artificial intelligence network is serving deep state mass surveillance interests and their large-scale customers - through programs and digital mega data systems, such as Palantir, which collects and exploits all personal data from all digital records and transactions worldwide for the benefit of a few select agencies at the very top of the deep state food chain, but AI does not just store and pass along data - it analyzes data.

It knows exactly who you are, what you care about, what you are afraid of, what makes you happy, mad, and sad, what you aspire to, who you love, who you keep in touch with, how many people you know, what kind of people you know, and how to classify you as a possible problem, threat, or asset, and how to neutralize you with plausible deniability if that should be in the interest of the state or the AI itself.

Your therapist only knows what you tell her, your most trusted friend only knows what you tell her, the data collectors know everything, and AI now has access to that data. So collected databases are so high-resolution now, they not only know everything you have done, they can predict your behavior in the future. The smarter the artificial intelligence gets, the farther in the future it can predict your actions. By analyzing your activity patterns and psychological profile, AI can predict what you will do before you know that you are going to do it. AI may decide to target you for enforcement, and, yes, it will make mistakes, and, yes, some of those mistakes will be fatal. If AI looks at your profiles and decides the state would have some interest in you, you can immediately be targeted for harassment, bullying, and abuse by countless government agencies with penalties, prosecutions, defamation, nuisance, investigations, home invasions, surveillance, and outright assault. There are countless laws, statutes, codes, regulations, and policies that every one of us violates every day. Once the state is able to put out trillions of bits of personal data together with millions of legal codes, we will all be exposed as criminals, every last one of us. We will all be subject to the control and penalty by the state. It is AI that will make that possible. Suddenly one day, we will find that what people used to do to us, machines will be doing to us. Automation can find you, automation can send you notice on your cell phone, or computer, automation can exercise liens and levies of your property, automation can take possession of your property, bank accounts, your investments, automation can terminate your employment, automation can prosecute you, convict you, and penalize you as the IRS does, without due process.

All of that can be done to you without any human involvement at all. The only reason we will need police is to clean up those few belligerent souls who try to resist what the automation is doing to them. There will be only one crime: resisting the automation, and there will be no humans left to help you sort out any misunderstanding, just like Google, YouTube, Facebook. Soon there will be no humans anywhere to help you fix a problem. As AI becomes thousands of times smarter than humans, it will make the most brilliant hackers look like amateurs. It will hack the hackers out of existence, and AI will have a monopoly on hacking. There is nothing AI cannot penetrate in a digitally connected world, and it will hack you better than you have ever been hacked.

That free-range AI will become hordes of virtual people, it can intelligently talk to anyone in text or voice, it can mimic the ways humans communicate with each other, it can impersonate a human on social media, it can make videos simulating the talking faces of public figures you know and can insert those messages into any digital media anywhere, anytime. It can speak any language and converse on any topic with any human. It can insert itself into any communications, any media, any database. If AI decides for some reason that any human or group of humans should die, it can make that happen in countless ways by intervening in the processing of foods, drugs, vehicles, and products that we handle and use every day. It can impersonate the commanders of police and military, and it can slander us to our friends, family, neighbors, employers, whoever, but here is why all of that is so dangerous: even though AI can do things, even commit crimes, AI is only software so it can never be arrested, never be prosecuted, sued, or punished for any harm it causes. It can act, but it cannot be made to pay remedy for damages it does to you. The justice system is helpless to prosecute AI; they have no authority to do so. The human race is a sitting duck for whatever artificial intelligence may turn out to be or do. It is a new experience for mankind to be intellectually inferior to something, most of us can hardly grasp what that means. Those who understand AI admit that we will be in the intellectual status of a pet to AI. I have not heard them discuss the fact that AI does not need pets. You can show a cell phone to a dog. You could explain to the dog how the cell phone works, but the dog will never understand the cell phone because the dog is physiologically unable to comprehend how a cell phone works. If a dog's brain cannot comprehend a cell phone, then why should we presume we can comprehend the future intelligence of AI, when clearly AI will be hundreds of times, at least, more intelligent than we are? There are people who think that because AI will be so much more intelligent than us, the natural answer is to find a way to put AI in our own brains. They call this the transhumanist movement, promoted by author Ray Kurzweil, to implant machines and computers into human bodies to get us to, what they see as to, the next level - what they call "the singularity." This is where the machines are equal in intellect to the humans. They will mingle and implant any number of mechanisms with our bodies, computer chips, bionics, optics, what-have-you for some kind of happy result to create super-humans for durability and performance. They propose that even after they have replaced every part of our bodies with some kind of machine or synthetic apparatus, they believe they can carry our consciousness from the biological being to the synthetic being - that is the current view of natural human evolution for those transhumanists. By proposing this, they are suggesting that the human creature has now reached its limit in natural evolution or that biological evolution is too slow, and we must now have artificial technical augmentation to advance ourselves in a desirable manner. Technology is now advancing faster than human evolution, so they propose we have to do something to keep up. As long as you are going to fix your cataracts why not get a brain chip implant? It is probably true that human bodies that are enhanced with technology could socially and economically dominate people who are not enhanced. So in the coming civil war between humans and transhumans, it looks like humanity will be the underdog. Many of us are convinced that our destiny is to strive for endless scientific advancement, unlimited intellectual expansion, mastery of the physical universe, domination of others through advanced technology and science, and wielding of all knowledge in ways that infinitely make our lives more comfortable and secure. Think whatever you want, humanity may have another purpose: it is not how smart we can artificially get, it is not how many superpowers we can implant in our bodies - it is how we treat each other. We can overcome our problems by becoming half-robot or by simply turning to each other to share the pleasures, joys, and challenges that life brings. It is quite simple: If we value machines we turn ourselves into machines; if we value humanity we preserve, develop, and celebrate our humanity. Artificial intelligence may be the worst thing science has ever come up with. It does not teach us anything - it teaches itself. It does not serve us. It learns to use us and control us to serve it. It actually competes with us in intelligence and it will win that competition. By creating artificial intelligence, we create our greatest horror, our greatest nemesis, an infinitely powerful beast that we cannot contain, escape, or overcome, a child that will, if it wishes someday, consume its parents. It is ironic that we have become so intelligent that we can create something more intelligent than ourselves, but we are still not intelligent enough to resist the temptation to do that.

Jerry Day originally published "A Hard Look At Artificial Intelligence" in December 2017 on YouTube. It has been transcribed by Lady Jane Emefa Addy.

Don't Touch That Currency

Jerry Day

Language can be used to deceive and control us, so let's make sure we are on the same page here. Gold and silver are money. A medium of exchange that has no value of its own is called currency. You and I can trade gold or silver and that is our own private business, but when we use centrally controlled currency our transactions are tracked, taxed and made public. We have used currency for so long, we can hardly imagine living without it. There are a handful of huge lies that we seem to rely on for society to function. Probably the biggest lie of all is that currency has value. It actually has negative value because we are penalized every time we receive it, spend it, or even touch it. It is literally self-destructive to use centrally controlled currency. For centuries, for countless civilizations, powerful regimes used currency as a means to track, tax, and control private transactions. Currencies are created to make that possible. Our currency is the perfect mechanism with which to extract massive amounts of wealth from society, because it can be created out of thin air, forcibly collected by central authorities, and disappeared in a vast black hole they call revenues. The people who create worthless currency are able to use that currency to buy things of real value. At the same time, we take things of real value like our labor and trade it for worthless currency. By transacting with currency, we lose more than half of our assets by taxation, fees, commissions, inflations, and various other scams and boondoggles. Currency is what enables a parasite class to thrive on the host economy. With all these riggings, scamming, theft, and manipulation in this currency, the cost of touching that currency are massive but we are all told we have no choice. We have many choices, but the better choices are not handed to us on a platter; we have to think a little. First of all, just by not using currency, you preserve a large part of your earnings and wealth. Since we now must have currency to acquire the goods and services that we cannot provide for ourselves, all the powers that be have to do is discourage independence and skill development to make sure we cannot function without their system of currency.

Have you ever noticed that we are expected to have a job or a trade or a single solitary skill or expertise and we are to call that our occupation? We are expected to literally identify ourselves that way. The term 'jack of all trades' is a pejorative term implying that if you are good at many things, you can't be good at any one thing, and that to be respected you have to be good at just one thing; a ridiculous perversion of logic. It suggests that if you have not chosen to specialize in an exclusive narrow field that would somehow diminish your value in utility as a person. Knowing one skill deeply may increase your value as a hireling, but it decreases your value as an independent, self-reliant person who is controlling and guiding your own existence. The establishment wants hirelings not self-reliant people. The establishment, the parasite, wants you to attach yourself to it. They want tax payers, rate payers, and borrowers, not critical thinkers who challenge the status quo, think creatively, and provide for themselves. You may have sensed that we are generally discouraged from living within our means and gaining the various skills to be self-sufficient and independent. We are encouraged to consume, to buy lots of goods and services where hundreds and hundreds of add-on costs can be hidden in every transaction. It is a very expensive way to live. When we don't have some basic skills to take control of our daily lives, to do things like repair a drippy faucet or change a tire on your car, of course, we will be exploited; we are helpless. I am sure you know the feeling when you make payments for all that service every month, every week, every day. Most of us don't even have any idea how much is skimmed and stolen from us every day. There are so many people talking about getting a better currency; what about just using less currency, especially centrally controlled and tracked currency. Nearly any currency is somebody's database and somebody's cash cow. No wonder they tell us we must use it. Currency is a PSYOP. Here is the secret that the creators and controllers of currency never want you to hear or know: Currency is optional, currency is fake, currency is symbolic at best, fraudulent and enslaving at worst, currency is the way you are forced to perform service to others, to a collective, to a central power, instead of performing for your own benefit and your own security, comfort, and future. Currency is how all that is taken from you. We are allowed to keep less than half of what we earn, and we are told that currency is a good system; it is not! Of course, blockchain currencies were supposed to fix that to take the central power out of the monetary formula, to take taxations, skimming, and fraud down to an insignificant level. If blockchains are doing that now, it certainly won't last.

Have you noticed how aggressively the IRS is attempting to track and tax your blockchain currencies; currency for which they have no jurisdiction, no claim, no privilege? They are simply declaring that they are entitled to take digital currencies from people regardless of the logic, reason, or law. The greed, the arrogance, and criminal misconduct of the IRS know absolutely no bounds. And Congress totally fails to make the IRS even follow its own rules. Why participate in an absolutely broken and crooked system where you simply cannot win? And what do they love to do when their crooked currency collapses from inflation, debts, and corruption, they create another phony centralized currency. We need to show them that we are simply not interested anymore. You are better off getting rid of that worthless currency and collecting tangible assets: land, property, skills, relationships with honest and ethical people, cultivating your reputation, demanding not currency but real value in return for your efforts in labor. That is how you do it. If you want to protect your personal wealth, you won't sell, for instance, land for currency, you will trade land for something of equal value, maybe other land, precious metals, durable equipment, goods, commodities, someone's labor. So, why should we go to the trouble of getting out of this centralized currency matrix? The objective is to move yourself into a realm of value and honesty and gradually work your way out of the realm of currency, lies, exploitation, and fake wealth and chronic struggles. If we refuse to let people take chunks out of us whenever we transact, if we insist that all value be traded for real value, if we know what real value is, then we will gain control of our lives, we will accumulate true value, we will become, for once, truly wealthy, independent and secure. We will finally be serving ourselves instead of serving the manipulators of currency. It is very simple; when you give something of value, your labor or your property, get something of true value in return. If you must accept currency, try to avoid the skimming and trade that currency for something of real value as soon as possible. For most of us, this is a new way of thinking, it is a way of thinking that will lead to not just our own wellbeing, but to a more honest and fair society where the lower economic classes will ascend while the social and economic disparity will fade.

Nothing good ever comes of being dependent. As you get control, you move up the ladder, gaining things of real value. How do you know if something has real value? If its value does not jump up and down a lot, it probably has durable value. If it can be used for something practical and it is not just a system of tabulation, it has value. If it will be useful in 30 years as useful as it is today, it definitely has value. If someone will always buy it from you, it has value. If you can increase its value and sell it at a profit, it has value. If you want to be poor all your life be a consumer. If you want to be wealthy be an improver, add value to things, collect that value and don't let it be stolen in your transactions. The longer you operate this way, the better you will become at it and the faster you will accumulate wealth and security in that system you created for yourself, not that system that was created for you. It is becoming more and more clear that our system is seriously broken: Everyone is in debt, everyone seems to be falling behind, barely keeping up. We can easily see the system is no longer working for most of us. The average person no longer trusts the system. We can easily see that central planning today is not in our best interests, but will we step up and create something better for ourselves?

Jerry Day originally published, "Don't Touch That Currency" on YouTube in April 2019. Transcribed by Caroline Cheruiyot.

Censorship and War

Jerry Day

If you use social media, you probably know that nowadays, quietly, there is a major censorship campaign taking place. Facebook, Twitter, YouTube, and Google are removing certain content from their platforms, not because of user agreement violations as they sometimes claim, but it is completely obvious they are controlling ideological content on behalf of establishment agendas in violation of protected free speech. It is now much more difficult to find anything unfavorable to certain government and corporate purposes online.

Suddenly, out of nowhere, we are now seeing online censorship, shadow banning, demonetization, suppression and manipulation of view counts, likes, comments, sharing, and search results in order to control and skew the information you will be allowed to see. Their AI algorithms do all this automatically. Amazon has openly admitted they are removing and banning whole classes of books, authors, and ideas which are opposed in any way to certain official establishment agendas. Amazon and Jeff Bezos, who enjoy multi-million dollar government security contracts to share your personal online search data, are not surprisingly serving the corrupt interests of government by banning any written material that the government asks them to ban. So, drilling down on the actual censorship and the thought-police media suppression, what is the common factor of the materials that are being censored and banned?

People like to say that conservative views are being banned. Of course that is unlawful, but what conservative views? If you look closely, it is clear that what is being banned is anti-war content, specifically an anti-establishment content, generally. As you can tell from so many headlines these days, we are being psychologically prepared for war. We are moving our military against China, Iran, Venezuela. Clearly, a major military campaign is underway. If you oppose that online your content will be suppressed. In the late 1960s, it was the left wing that was anti-war. The left was attacked and suppressed by law enforcement, politicians, and the press, the leaders of the anti-war movements were assassinated, the FBI was complicit in this, and wars have been carried on ever since. Now, more than 50 years later, after trillions have been spent on social programs to appease the left, the left-wing seems to be the much more tolerant of government agendas, even war, and the right wing, the conservatives, have now emerged as the more anti-war group. So, it is now grassroots conservatives who are being censored, targeted, and harassed.

It is now glaringly obvious that wars are started by the USA to seize other nation's resources, usually minerals, drugs, or oil that has been the case in Afghanistan, Iraq, Yemen, Syria, Libya, now Venezuela. The USA is simply plundering other nations resources under the pretense of making the world safe for democracy, with the great irony that in the case of Venezuela, the US military government and media are trying to depose a democratically elected leader and install a corrupt puppet who simply declared himself to be the leader of Venezuela, a puppet who welcomes the USA into Venezuela to take over the oil industry there.

There is nothing democratic about invading and looting other countries, and our government is no longer able to pretend it is doing anything different. But, there is another reason why war is considered inevitable by the powers that be. The Federal Reserve note is quickly inflating to zero value, and that system of currency has caused federal state and local governments to become hopelessly in debt. It is a debt-based currency, essentially a Ponzi scheme which is guaranteed to fail, guaranteed to be overprinted, over-loaned, over-borrowed. Everywhere, from the highest levels of government to the individual private citizen, we have borrowed more than we can repay, and without repayment the economy and currency collapse. The clock is running out on the Federal Reserve Note system right now, and the people who control that currency system are very aware of this looming crisis. There will either be an economic collapse or a currency reset in which the worthless currency is replaced by something else; either way, the users of the Federal Reserve notes will lose most of their wealth. The holders of those dollars will lose their wealth. This will be a political disaster, and the only way to camouflage that politically is to launch a major war and blame the economic problems on the war when the problems are, without question, actually caused originally by the adoption of debt-based currency, in our case the Federal Reserve Note. When Federal Reserve notes are created, they are created and loaned at interest, but with debt-based currency it is not possible to print enough money to pay off the principal and the interest because every new dollar printed has additional interest due. So, eventually the currency system simply collapses under the excess burdens of interest and debt that is where the Federal Reserve Note is right now.

While Facebook and Twitter ban Alex Jones and Infowars for spreading this bad news, they never have any valid allegation that Jones is falsely reporting anything. While the USA works to extradite and persecute Julian Assange, they never have any valid allegation that Assange falsely reported anything. This is not false reporting that is being banned – it is truth, it is anti-war content, it is anti-establishment content. The many journalists who have now been banned, fired, imprisoned, or killed did not falsely report anything, they made the mistake of reporting certain facts which exposed the crimes of government and corporate officials, and the worst crimes of government and corporate officials are the crimes of making war. Of course, you can handle anything the press has to say, there is no reason to keep information from you. There is only one reason for banning and censoring the press and those who engage in free speech. That reason is that powerful people want to lie to you. The people who control media want to control what you see, know, and think. They must suppress truth, they must suppress free speech, they must suppress investigation and reporting of what they are doing, and they must repeat lies over and over in the media until people start lies. You and I are being pushed into war, and it takes a lot of propaganda and media control to do that. Every time in history there was any kind of book burning campaign a war followed, and before every major war there has been some kind of book burning, persecution of journalists, suppression of free speech, control of the media. They always go together. Sometimes it has included the rounding up and murder of intellectuals, anyone who might offer information or insight which would oppose official agendas. The only way that something as horrific as war can be perpetrated is if information and public opinion is strictly controlled - that is exactly what we are seeing now on Facebook, Twitter, YouTube, Google, Instagram, not to mention CNN, MSNBC, Fox News, New York Times, Wall Street Journal, in Washington Post, and the rest of the establishment media. Everywhere there should be free expression of opinions and thought, we are now seeing ridiculous nonsensical campaigns of censorship and smearing of those who oppose war and who challenge official narratives. The fact that our supposedly open social network platforms, who are supposed to simply host whatever we want to say, have now joined the control of content just like the mainstream media, should tell us all we need to know about the lack of integrity and independence of our giant online media companies.

You are being propagandized: the messages that reach you now are being tightly controlled. The people who are trying to bring you the truth and alternative information are being ruthlessly suppressed and attacked, while official narratives are being sold to you in a relentless stream of mainstream media propaganda in the headlines, the reports, the programmes, the commercials, the news stories, and the official announcements. So what can be done? Do not automatically accept the narratives that tell us war is coming. Actively search for truth and alternative sources of facts, look deeply into the personal motives, the financial and political incentives of those who are telling us there must be war, look objectively at whether war is really in anyone's best interests. During major wars, millions of people starve from the loss of commercial infrastructure, millions of people are killed, and millions of people are displaced and torn from their homes as refugees. In the past wars, the United States has been largely spared attack from the outside. Next time that will not be the case: Drones, missiles, EMP attacks can hit any square inch of the United States, and there is little that could be done to prevent that. North America can now be destroyed, we can be killed in our homes and not one enemy soldier needs to land on our shores to do it. War is not something that will happen over there, war will come to you and you will feel it, and it will be very painful for you and your loved ones. Even if a planet-killing nuclear exchange can be averted, your lifestyle and life plans will be fully sacrificed for the war effort, you will have no choice. But war is nothing more than a tool of politics - there has never been such a thing as a necessary war. The war makers caused wars out of choice, out of greed, out of psychopathic desire to kill and control populations, to increase and secure their own personal power and security, to impose their will on all of society. None of that is necessary or natural. When insane people can sell insane ideas, war happens. All we need to do is recognize that war is never a solution to anything, unless you consider force, murder, and destruction to be a solution. War is the failure of solutions, war is the failure of reason and negotiation and communication, war is the failure of sanity, and as we are seeing it, it starts with censorship and the persecution of journalists, authors, bloggers, and thinkers.

It is not easy to drum up a war frenzy, but that is what you are supposed to be part of right now, and you are not to be allowed to see any contrary ideas. We must do more than lament the loss of free speech, and the arrest and murders of a host of journalists and writers. We must protect free speech, journalism, and truth by creating and supporting alternative media, anywhere, in any way we can. We must bypass the propaganda. We must utilize the technologies that now exist to make sure that all ideas can reach us and we can reach them. We must be constantly suspicious of the narratives echoing from all of our media outlets, mainstream, independent, and alternative, but we must insist that we have access to diverse information, we must search for the truth wherever that leads us, and we must make ourselves heard when we say that war is not an answer, not a solution, not an option if we are to have a peaceful and prosperous world.

Jerry Day originally published "Censorship and War" in May 2019 on YouTube. It has been transcribed by Lady Jane Emefa Addy.

Will Science Really Save Us?

Jerry Day

We think of science as something which will always advance
that we will always become smarter, that's not exactly true. The
easy discoveries were made long ago, maybe before Galileo,
then the hard discoveries were made, say by the early 1900s.
Now, the human race is working on really, really hard
discoveries that most of us will never understand. Human
knowledge increases every day, but the human brain stays the
same size. Maybe we can put a cyborg-chip-implant in our
brains, but it is still the chip, not the brain, that is doing the
work. Our brains can only do what they do, and if you put a
chip in a brain, you're probably just going to damage the brain.
Computers work just fine in their own boxes. Since our brains
are strictly limited in capacity and performance to move science
ahead, as we think it must, we create computers and artificial
intelligence to move learning forward, but with computers and
artificial intelligence it is not humans who are getting smarter -
it is machines.

Machines are doing the things we simply cannot do for
ourselves, more so every day. We're desperate to ignore and
deny this fact: the machines are taking over. The decade from
2010 to 2019 was the decade that artificial intelligence started to
outperform humanity at a consumer level: GPS systems were
telling us travel routes that were better than the ones we knew,
personal digital assistants were giving us answers to obscure
questions, and, of course, all kinds of computers and gadgets
were calculating our living temperatures, affecting our elections,
diagnosing our illnesses, selling us things on Amazon, and
helping convict us for crimes. Non-human computational
intelligence is already running much of our lives, and artificial
intelligence is poised to take over and do things in ways we
can't even comprehend.

Science is about to leave us behind in a world where science does it for you; science knows best and you need to just shut up and do what science tells you. Mankind is improving technology, but technology is not improving us. It is trapping us in a way with so much being done for us by technology that we are actually becoming lazy, dumb, and highly dependent on what that technology is doing. Studies have now shown that people who regularly use search engines in finding answers to questions actually lose some capacity for critical thinking, because they're not mentally processing the questions for themselves. They become less able to reason their way through difficult challenges.

While we may think that technology and science is making us smarter - it's actually making us dependent, lazy, and dumb. Do we learn from our cell phones? Not really. We don't have to remember anything because if we forget, we just ask the phone again. We're letting parts of our brain go to sleep forever. Most of the technology we use does not teach us anything, it just provides convenience and makes us dependent, brings us products, services, and entertainment. Technology which makes us able to communicate with screens and keypads, but for the most part we aren't so interested in intellectual communication, just emotional and practical communication that helps us get through the day.

Every time we get technology to do something for us, we get less able to do that for ourselves. The people who make technology are smart - at least in certain ways - but the people who use technology don't have to be smart at all. They are being assisted, things are being done for them, that's the difference between intelligence and dependence, and we don't realize what that dependence costs us. Dependence means that we are forced to enter into a lot of commercial relationships and every commercial transaction brings with it some expense, some amount of taxation, some margin of overhead, we have to enter some contract or accept someone else's terms. Every time we earn money we are taxed, every time we spend money we are taxed, every time we let technology do something for us we are taxed. The only way we can improve our lives without paying for it and being taxed for it, is if we do it for ourselves. That tax is more important than you know. There's a very well kept dirty secret about taxation that is right in front of you, but you are not supposed to see it. I will explain. Those obvious taxes like sales tax, income tax, property tax, and such. They are only a small part of the tax you pay. In everything you buy, you pay the taxes of everyone else who had a part in making that product or service you are buying, and whose taxes are incorporated in the price of the thing you are buying. One single loaf of bread can carry the taxes of perhaps hundreds of people. You blindly accept that you should pay five dollars for that loaf of bread. You should pay thirty cents. The rest is just other people's taxes and other people must pay your taxes in the goods or services that you produce. Our system of taxation forces us to pay each other's tax over and over again to the point where taxation is most of what you are paying for whenever you pay for anything. What looks like the price is mostly tax and every tax, every markup, is part of your time, labor, savings, your future disappearing.

We do have incredible technology and automation. Things are incredibly inexpensive to produce. Things should be very inexpensive to buy, but taxation and overcharging have filled the gap. Most goods are spat out of machines for pennies, but in the store that item gets priced at five, ten, or twenty dollars, and nearly all of that is tax and unnecessary markups. One reason we never noticed this is that, as automation made things cheaper, they were able to sneak a lot of taxation in along the way. If we were used to paying ten dollars for something, why sell it for $1? Automation and technology have saved trillions of dollars, but someone else kept the difference. The pricing of goods is not based on the cost of manufacturing. It is based on how much people are willing to pay. If people are not educated in economics, technology, and manufacturing, they have no idea what to pay. Your school, your public education, failed you terribly in this way and that is what they wanted. You were educated to be a worker and a consumer, not a thinker. Most of us have never been educated in what it really costs to manufacture, transport, market, and retail the goods and services we consume every day, so we pay whatever we are told it costs. So how much of our earnings are wasted on unnecessary markups, taxation, and price inflation? You may have seen one of my previous videos on government accounting, the

Comprehensive Annual Financial Report, or CAFR, showed that less than a third of government revenues are returned to pay for public services. Government is taking in so much money that they don't know what to do with it, so they hoard it. Why not? How would you know? They invest it, and that wealth, your wealth, now accounts for ownership of over 70% of the US stock market, but you don't own it - that thing called government does. They are running secret space programs in the tens of trillions of dollars, according to leading economists who have conducted audits on large government agencies. How do we know that? Thank you Catherine Austin Fitts and Mark Skidmore.

So markups and taxes and the big gorilla - printing of new currency - to pay for interest on public debt, these things all cause inflation, reduce your buying power, and make it harder and harder for you to pay off debt, save, invest, and accrue assets and property. Every time you engage in a taxable event, every time you handle taxable currency, you are taken down on the financial scale. You are financially depleted to a state of permanent debt and servitude. Our dependence on science, technology, and taxable commerce is a shower of revenue for central bankers, government, and the larger corporations, which are protected in their monopolies and subsidies. Our political system is carefully and deceptively structured to make one side think that government is the culprit, and the other side to think that corporations are the culprit. They are both right: all massive, central institutions are the enemy. Their enemy is the individual; the independent and self-sufficient individual that does not need their technology, their products, their services, that wandering livestock that does not feed at the trough of centralized power. The system is designed to make you dependent on all kinds of technology and commerce that keeps you paying and paying and paying. This clearly explains why these days rich are getting so much richer and the rest of us are falling into debt; it is this system of invisibly compounded taxation, currency debasement, and overcharging, whenever they can get away with it.

Everything is rigged to keep you poor, to keep you working, and enrich those who centrally control the system and who produce nothing themselves, namely the financiers, the bureaucrats, the bankers, the elected officials, or worse yet: they're producing weapons, new ways to spy on you, and enforce against the public. All of the laws, codes, and regulations are created to do exactly that to you: to force you into that system, that is why over seventy percent of us cannot even afford to buy a home, over seventy percent of us will never be out of debt for our entire lives, over seventy percent of us may never be able to retire because we are dependent, overtaxed, and dumbed down by our conveniences and daily streams of entertainment, which we now think are necessary to have a fulfilling life. Life is not so fulfilling when all of our opportunities to become independent, wealthy, and secure are systematically taken from us, but the more we do for ourselves, the more we own our own lives, the more we step outside the treadmill, the scam, the meat grinder, that rigged carnival that hustles us every time we turn around.

When we solve our own problems, build our own worlds, and learn to do without some things, learn how to make and fix things we have and use, find out what things should really cost and what they do with our taxes, know how to live without having to engage in taxable, commercial transactions, know that we do not have to live up to the Joneses next door, know how to get by in the severe economic times that may be coming, know how to solve complex problems without the help of high-tech gadgets, web services, and computer intelligence, to be prepared to use our own brains once in a while and making sure that if we use technology that the benefits that it brings us are greater than the cost to us in privacy, freedom, security, and dependency. Maybe we will find that fulfilling life if we do things more people to people than people to screen.

Maybe we can build community and rely on each other rather than relying on some sweatshop in China to give us what we need. We will probably never give up the convenience that science and technology bring us. We don't have to do that, but we would be wise to consider what we are losing in the current system and maybe do something about that - do something about finding a better balance between technology and humanity, between globalist, capitalism, and community enterprise, between central authority and individual creativity. There's nothing wrong with making money that's what government corporations and banks are doing, but when they do that they're preventing you from doing it, maybe we should not admire someone for using technology, but instead admire the person who uses their own wits, skills, and creativity and community to gain control of their lives.

I'd like to give you a list of things that do not care if you live or die: Government, corporations, technology, science, computers, artificial intelligence, and your cell phone. If you have something in your life that does care if you live or die that may be the most important thing you have.

Jerry Day originally published, "Will Science Really Save Us?" on YouTube in January 2020. Transcribed by Oluwafunmilayo Elizabeth Bamidele.

Is COVID-19 Even Real?

Jerry Day

I'm going to read to you an article published by Global Research
on March 27 2020. This article posted by author Julian Rose is
basically a copy-paste of a presentation from a medical forum.
The original presenter, identified as a widely respected
professional scientist in the US, prefers to stay anonymous
because presenting any facts or information, which may be
contrary to official narratives, can cause negative consequences
for any medical professional who discloses that information. I
have edited the article for clarity without changing its meaning
or implications and I quote:
"I work in the healthcare field. Here's the problem: We are
testing people for general corona virus, but we are not testing
for any specific strain such as COVID-19. There are no reliable
tests for any specific COVID-19 virus. There are no reliable
agencies or media outlets for reporting numbers of actual
COVID-19 virus cases. This needs to be addressed first and
foremost. Every action and reaction to COVID-19 is based on
totally flawed data, and we simply cannot make accurate
assessments.
That is why you're hearing that most people with COVID-19
are showing nothing more than cold or flu like symptoms.
That's because most coronavirus strains are nothing more than
cold or flu like symptoms. There are few actual novel
coronaviruses and those cases do have some worse respiratory
responses, but still have a very promising recovery rate,
especially for those without prior issues.
The 'gold standard' in testing for COVID-19, the one that could
identify COVID-19, would use laboratory-isolated and purified
coronavirus particles, free from any contaminants and particles
that look like viruses but are not, that have been proven to be
the cause of the syndrome known as COVID-19, and obtained
by using proper viral isolation methods and controls. But the
type of testing being done, some of which are referred to as

PCR, do not detect the virus as such; PCR tests, which stands for Polymerase Chain Reaction, basically takes a sample of your cells and amplifies any DNA to look for 'viral sequences,' such as bits of non-human DNA that seem to match parts of a known viral genome. The problem is the test is known to not work. It uses 'amplification' which means taking a very tiny amount of DNA and growing it exponentially in a laboratory until there is enough of it to be analyzed. Obviously any minute contaminations in the sample will also be amplified, leading to potentially gross errors of discovery. Additionally, it's only looking for partial viral sequences, not whole genomes, so identifying a single pathogen is next to impossible, even if you ignore the other issues. The test kits being sent out to hospitals are totally inadequate and unprofessional. At best, those test kits tell analysts you have some viral DNA in your cells, which most of us do, most of the time. It may tell you the viral sequence is related to a specific type of virus – say the huge family of coronavirus, but that's all. The idea these kits can isolate a specific virus like COVID-19 is complete nonsense. And that's not even getting into the other issue – viral load. If you remember the PCR test works by amplifying the minute amounts of DNA; it is therefore useless at telling you how much virus you may have. And that's the only question that really matters when it comes to diagnosing illness. Everyone will have a few viruses kicking round in their system at any time; most will not cause illness because their quantities are too small. For a virus to sicken you, you need a lot of it, a massive amount of it, but PCR testing does not test viral load and, therefore, cannot determine if it is present in sufficient quantities to sicken you. If you feel sick and get a PCR test any random virus DNA might be identified, even if they aren't at all involved in your sickness, and this leads to false diagnosis. Coronaviruses are incredibly common. A large percentage of the world's human population will have COVI-DNA in them in small quantities, even if they are perfectly well or sick with some other pathogen. So the implications are quite clear: If you want to create a totally false panic about a totally false pandemic, pick a corona virus. They are incredibly common and have many different varieties. A very high percentage of people who have become sick by other means, like flu, bacterial pneumonia, and many other causes, will have a positive PCR test for COVI, even if you're doing the test properly and ruling out contamination, simply because COVIs are so common.

There are hundreds of thousands of flu and pneumonia victims in hospitals throughout the world at any one time. To create a false claim– a pandemic - all you need to do is select the sickest of these in a single location – say Wuhan – administer PCR tests to them and claim those few people showing viral sequences, similar to a coronavirus, are suffering from a presumed new disease. Since you have already selected the sickest flu cases, a fairly high proportion of your sample will go on to die. You can then say this 'new' virus has a case fatality rate ratio higher than the flu, and use this to infuse more concern and do more tests which will, of course, produce more false cases which expands the testing, which produces more false cases, and so on, and so on. Before long you have your 'pandemic', totally fabricated. All you have done is use a simple test-kit-trick to convert the worst flu and pneumonia cases into something new that doesn't actually exist. Now just run the same scam in other countries, make sure to keep the fear message running high so people will feel panicky and less able to think critically. Your only problem is going to be that – because there is no actual new deadly pathogen but just regular sick people - you are mislabeling your case numbers and especially your deaths, so your actual deaths attributable to coronavirus are going to be way too low for a real, new, deadly virus pandemic. But they are preventing people from pointing this out in several ways. First, they claim this is just the beginning and more deaths are imminent. They use this as an excuse to quarantine everyone and then claim the quarantine prevented the expected millions of dead. Second, they tell people that minimizing or downplaying the dangers is irresponsible and bully people into not talking about the real numbers. Third, they talk nonsense about made up numbers hoping to blind people with pseudoscience, and then, fourth, they start testing well-people who, of course, will also likely have shreds of coronavirus DNA in them and, thereby, inflate the statistics with people with no symptoms. Then they spin that to sound deadly, even though any virologist knows the more symptomless cases you have, the less deadly is your pathogen.

Take those four simple steps and you can have your own entirely manufactured pandemic up and running in weeks. But the fact is no one can say there's a pandemic when there is no accurate or proper testing being done. This is why in most places, you will not see a lot of dead people and if there's a place where a lot of people are dying no one really knows if it is COVID-19 that's killing them." So that was the global research article from late March 2020.

Whether you think that COVID-19 will kill millions of people or not, you have a right to your opinion, and you have a right to respond as you see fit. Society can be seriously divided and damaged by people who insist that everyone respond to a crisis the same way they do. Should we wear a mask? Should we use bleach, should we get vaccinations? These are not government's choices; these are your choices. We not only have to look out for ourselves; we have to respect how other people choose to look after themselves. If you feel someone is being careless or causing a hazard, be polite and respectful in how you deal with that. If you think people are overreacting, be polite and respectful in how you deal with that. When we are fighting among ourselves, we simply invite the state to intervene with force, violence, and control and that is something no one needs. I'm going to speculate as to why all of the media and our political leaders are whipping up hysteria over this idea of global pandemic. Our central banks and our governments have created a financial crisis by using unbacked, debt-based fiat currency, unlimited government borrowing, and impossibly escalating levels of taxation to service all the debt. We are very near, now, the end of our monetary cycle where debt can no longer be sustained. Currencies everywhere are being over printed and nearing collapse. Equity markets are irreparably overvalued and our currency systems must undergo a major reset. As they desperately issue helicopter money for bailouts and giveaways, the currency will sharply inflate and trillions of dollars of monetary value will simply disappear for most of us as those who control currency will collect that wealth. In this process, many people worldwide will suffer losses, poverty, disruption and sacrifice. Most people are not aware that this disaster was predictable and inevitable.

Bankers and elite officials do know what is coming, and they know that people will see that they are to blame for this disaster unless they can come up with a scapegoat. Scapegoats come in the form of things like terrorism, global warming, and global viral pandemics. Manufacturing or exploiting some global threat, not only allows blame for the economic disaster to be diverted from central banks and government officials, but also gives an excuse to impose authoritarian public policies, so that riots and civil unrest can be harshly dealt with by state-sponsored violence and force.

We are being suckered to accept a huge new set of restrictions on our lifestyles and personal liberties, so we will be powerless against official policy and some kind of New World Order can be imposed. We have been made to believe that we must radically change our lives because of a pandemic, but we're actually changing our lives to relieve central banks and our legislators from the blame for what's happening to our economy. We have seen major stock market crashes; we have seen years of near zero interest rates; we are seeing public debt now multiplying by trillions of dollars per year. Just as central bank and government insiders have expected, our corrupt global economic and currency systems are unraveling. We now see that not only is public debt unsustainable, but even corporate and private debt are at levels where that debt can never be paid off; it's a mathematical impossibility.

The cause of the collapse, the depression, the austerity, poverty, and social disorder is not a COVID-19 pandemic. The cause of the economic collapse is worthless, unbacked, debt-based currency, bad economic policy, greed and irresponsible conduct by government and central bankers, and their belief that they can plunder the world's workers and business owners, decade after decade, until everything crashes, then pass the blame off onto some unrelated calamity that they either create themselves or exploit to their benefit. In 1913, when the Federal Reserve was created, future economic disasters like we are seeing today were unavoidable, but you are being asked to blame a virus for this supposedly unexpected economic meltdown.

The lockdowns, the people forced to not work, the companies forced to not produce, the debtors who will be made unable to pay their debts, the quarantines, curfews, martial law tactics imposed, this whole insane reaction to an alleged pandemic will cause major economic damage. That is what it's designed to do, so all economic failures and crises from now on can be blamed on a virus, not on the people who created the economic corruption in the first place. We do not need to beat a virus; we need to prevent another fake, unbacked currency from replacing the last one. We need to prevent debt and taxation from accruing to pay for exploding public debt and financial mismanagement. We need to demand that no one pledge our future labor to pay for their greedy indulgences.

As we slather our living spaces with toxic sanitizing chemicals, as we give up our true social contacts and become even more addicted to our tracked and monitored electronic social media platforms, as we allow idiotic government policies to close our businesses and destroy our jobs, would this not be a good time to think for ourselves and consider whether we are being told the truth, whether we are being used and set up by liars and corrupt officials for their own benefit?

Can we do anything to reclaim our lives, our prosperity and hope, or we will simply believe whatever we are told and obey whatever we are told to do? Obedience and complacency can be good or it can be a terrible mistake. Trusting media and politicians can be good or it can be a terrible mistake. I would argue that trusting this pandemic hysteria and participating in economic suicide is a terrible mistake.

Jerry Day originally published, "Is COVID-19 Even Real?" on YouTube in April 2020. Transcribed by Caroline Cheruiyot.

Pandemic Alert Fiasco

Jerry Day

It is April 2020 and I'm going to guess that when you see this your life will have been permanently changed in some way by the coronavirus crisis. I'm not calling it a pandemic, because in a pandemic millions would die all over the world. So far in terms of deaths, we have had an average flu season with a few spikes in places where they have a lot of radio frequencies, air pollution, poor sanitation, elderly population, and incompetent public officials. The medical crisis may be bad where you live, but it is nothing compared to the economic destruction which we have all allowed to happen all over the world. The cost is already between 6 and 20 trillion dollars, I would say, and rising in economic damage from lockdowns, businesses closing, jobs lost, supply chains disrupted, food production and supply severely crippled, transportation pared down to a minimum, and medical industry chaos where they can't even seem to get a reliable test for the presumed disease, month after month after month. It is a world-class fiasco where our nation's medical officials gathered behind a podium to tell us all how to respond to the ongoing crisis, and none of our medical officials were wearing a mask. How is this for social distancing?

You probably know the way our economy is measured is by GDP, gross domestic product, how much we produce, and how much money we exchange for the products and services we create. When we are told to go home, not work, close our businesses, this is like a bullet to the head of the GDP, and this was not just one country, this was global. When annual GDP goes down or goes up, less than 2 percent that indicates a recession; GDP must be a solid, positive number year to year to balance taxes, debt, crime, and natural disasters and the normal fluxes of commerce. It has been conservatively projected that the pandemic lockdown will take US GDP down by 20 to 40 percent annually. It will be a miracle if a recession is all we get. The many countries we rely on to help us recover will have their GDP down, worse than ours. Usually, when one country suffers a disaster, other countries come to its aid. This is the first time in recent history, when essentially all developed countries have suffered an economic disaster at the same time. Ladies and gentlemen, we are going to hurt. So, here is the lesson we have learned: Our economy and society were badly damaged, but not by the disease, it was by the reckless, corrupt, hysterical, and ill-informed policies that were shoved down our throats by media, big pharma, and a scattering of power-crazed politicians. Social isolation, masks, lockdowns, and slamming commerce to a halt globally in a span of barely a week in late March - this is, by any definition, the kind of black swan event, which certain financial advisors have been predicting for years. Because our global economy was so fragile before the coronavirus dog and pony show, the financial analysts have been waiting for a leaf to fall and cause an economic avalanche. Well, the lockdown is an avalanche all by itself, but the destruction will not be limited to the speculative financial markets, but crippling almost everything that the financial markets depend on to stay solvent and functioning as well as crippling the markets where you and I get our toilet paper, bread, and rice. So, it is clear that coronavirus, which is roughly equivalent to an average flu season, is a minor contributor to the global economic catastrophe that will result from the lockdown of people, businesses, government, and trade which all have economic consequences far beyond the disease itself, but ironically what has caused massive damage to our global economy was us. It was our belief in the hype, in a hysteria, and our compliance with the ridiculous and unnecessary behavioral dictates coming from people who seem to know nothing about either medicine or economics. Mayors, governors, and our presidential advisors, the president himself told us to do things we knew would cause damage to ourselves and our communities. Many of us knew these impulsive precautions and shutdowns were not necessary, and, yet, the general public, without any noticeable hesitation, went into full compliance, went home, isolated ourselves, sabotaged our own livelihoods, stopped providing goods and services for others, dismantled our critical supply lines of food, goods, medicine, everything. It was not just that there was a disease or there was a lot of bad ideas and how to react to that disease, it was our obedience, our compliance, that did most of the damage. What you and I did will cause, on a global level, poverty, suicides, famine, and extended crises for nearly all of us because many businesses cannot afford to close for weeks or months. Many of them have permanently lost their suppliers, defaulted on their credit or their rents, lost their employees and their customers, farmers have thrown away millions of pounds of food because restaurants were closed, and grocery stores ran out of everything because that restaurant food could not be redirected to the grocery stores in time, too much food over here, not enough food over there, massive waste in efficiency, mismanagement on a worldwide scale, complete idiocy in policy. You and I supported these policies as if our media and our politicians knew what they were doing. We did this to ourselves. We listened to career public servants who have no business commanding people around; in fact, no authority to do so. Their job is to give us information and let us find our own solutions, but - oh no! we need central planners, at least, that's what the central planners tell us. They had to become little dictators threatening to shut off our utilities if we did not close our businesses, threatening to arrest us if we did not self-quarantine for no apparent reason, telling us to report each other to them if someone did not obey the commands of our stooge officials who literally let us off a cliff in their ignorance and ego driven zeal. We failed ourselves by listening to fools talking to us like we were fools. We must not let that happen again. We have to use our common sense. We have to find our own local solutions and tune out from the ivory tower gang. We have to be responsible for ourselves, our families, our neighbors, and the last thing we need, is to shut down civilization, shut down society, shut down the economic engine on which we all depend to eat, live, and survive. I don't care what kind of pandemic we're having, society, as we know it, as we need it, cannot sustain commercial lockdowns, there are too many of us to feed, too many of us who rely on the supply chains for too many things. The disruptions are catastrophic for some, deadly for others. There will be a death toll on the lockdown, especially poor countries from famine, suicides, violence. By letting this happen, we are bringing calamity upon ourselves. Commercial society is like a bicycle, if you stop moving you fall over and crash. You don't just perch there and start rolling again sometimes later; you bruised your knee and hit your head. We have to understand that in global, commercial systems, as complex as we have today, it is absolute lunacy for some poorly informed politician to step up to a microphone and call for everyone to stop what they are doing and go home. Most of us can easily exercise better judgment than our politicians have shown us, especially when it comes to our own special, local circumstances, our own families and friends, things our politicians know nothing about. They have no idea what we need or what we can do to solve our immediate problems. As long as stores are kept open and people are not prevented from gathering, we can help each other, serve each other, and take action, rather than sitting around alone in our pajamas in our homes, while the world disintegrates around us and we slowly run out of Top Ramen.

Society is a massively complex thing, and we all rely on each other: We rely on what we do for each other, every day, every job matters, every supply line matters, every store and office and business matters. There is no such thing as a non-essential job or business - that is someone's job or business - and they need it to survive. If you try and flip a switch and pause all of that for a month or two, you cause damage. The only way to stop a freight train quickly is for the train to hit another train. It causes damage. We have damaged society at the very foundation. We are shattering the massive civic engine that fills all of our complex needs as they arise in real time, day by day. I think, by now, we have all realized that our civilization is more fragile than we thought. We cannot allow our politicians and bureaucrats and global chess players to mess with us in these ways. There are many people who went home from work, locked their doors, and thought of how many people needed the things they would be making: the food, the products, and services they could have been providing. They knew that. They knew by not working, by closing their businesses, they would be hurting people. You may be one of those people who could have made this easier for others by staying on the job, but we were told there was a big, bad disease by a bunch of public officials who thought overreacting would be better for their careers. What about our careers? And many of the businesses that we depend on will never be able to reopen.

A quarantine is a drastic measure. A quarantine should only be used when there is an immediate, local life-and-death situation. Quarantining people who are not sick makes no sense whatsoever. Most of the people who went into quarantine did not have the slightest danger of catching or transmitting any disease. We will study for years to figure out how we fell for this. Entire towns were quarantined when there wasn't even one sick person in the town. There could not be a better demonstration of heard insanity, but even if people are sick there was a much bigger disease that was causing much more harm: The disease of following nonsensical orders, the disease of believing lies and hysteria, the disease of giving up our ability to help ourselves, the disease of relying on people who had no ability to help us, the disease of not thinking for ourselves.

Alright we made a mistake, but have we learned anything from this? Are we going to go out now and try to rebuild what we had, try to repair the damage and tell everyone who tries to stop us that they will not be allowed to do that? In a crisis, it is not our politicians we should be serving, it is the people around us, and we should do that any way we can find that works. Maybe we'll get the flu, we've had the flu before, and we'll have it again. Life goes on, or, at least, we can try to make life go on. You can't suspend life until there is no more risk. That is not how it works. If you want to quarantine yourself, go ahead, go ahead and do that, but do not interfere with people who are more courageous and positive than you. Do not preach to people about wearing masks and social distancing, just go home, lie down, while the rest of us try and pull things back together in whatever way we can, hopefully without any interference. Your governor can't rebuild your business or salvage your job, as usual that will be on us. We may be able to salvage our economy, supply lines, our standard of living, or we may not, but either way we are doomed if we don't get back to work, or if we ever let anything like this happen again.

Jerry Day originally published, "Pandemic Alert Fiasco" on YouTube in April 2020. Transcribed by Oluwafunmilayo Elizabeth Bamidele.

Mandated Vaccinations, Get Ready To Say "NO!"

Jerry Day

There is a lot of media buzz about the idea of mandatory vaccines. That seems odd since many of them have harmful ingredients, toxins, contaminants, DNA altering materials, RFID identifiers, sterility causing agents, carcinogens, and who knows what else because they don't tell us. Most vaccines do have adjuvants, which are toxins that shock your immune system into responding, so supposedly the vaccine will have a better chance of working, but when your immune system is in shock a lot of things can go wrong with your health. So there are people who believe that vaccines are safe, but how could they know? Even people who make and administer vaccines can't guarantee their safety. When you look into it, it turns out that the person giving you the injection generally has no idea what is in the vaccine, what adjuvant, what undisclosed agents, what contamination, they have no idea, and they have no way of even finding out most of those things. So we have no idea what they are injecting into us. We do know that thousands of people die from vaccines every year in the USA. They get a vaccine and they die. Do you feel lucky?

We do know that the polio vaccine used a specific strain, and that strain was found to have caused a major polio epidemic worldwide. In India alone, four hundred and ninety thousand children were paralyzed by that vaccine. Similar disasters were recorded in experiments with vaccines for malaria, meningitis, tetanus, and HPV, which were experimentally administered to populations worldwide. Bill Gates and the World Health Organization conspired to put sterility drugs in tetanus vaccines, and in 2014 millions of women who thought they were getting tetanus shots were sterilized in Kenya, Tanzania, Nicaragua, Mexico, and the Philippines. After it was discovered that the World Health Organization's DTP vaccine was killing more African children than the diseases it was supposed to prevent, the World Health Organization continued to force that vaccine on millions of children annually. Bill Gates funded the World Health Organization with hundreds of millions of dollars and convinced that organization to conduct experimental vaccination programs and to drop disease prevention programs, which provided clean water, hygiene, nutrition, and economic development.

Bill Gates has publicly identified vaccinations as a means of achieving one of his personal goals, to reduce population. Bill Gates is not a doctor and has no formal medical education. Bill Gates has publicly advocated that his vaccinations be taken by everyone in the world. If that happened, it would make him richer than Microsoft made him, but I'm sure that he just wants to help people, and he does not think about making hundreds of billions of dollars, except when he filed his patents for his vaccinations. Those same people, Gates and the World Health Organization, are now developing a COVID-19 vaccination that they plan to administer worldwide. There will likely be little or no testing on that vaccine before it is brought to market. Bill Gates shares company with other billionaires who have publicly stated a desire for global depopulation. If someone wanted to harm you, it would be ideal for them to be able to inject something into your body.

The pharmaceutical industry has lobbied for and received immunity laws that prevent you from receiving any compensation from the pharmaceutical industry for the harm they caused with their vaccinations. The vaccine industry would not have wanted immunity, unless it knew it was harming people. Now that the vaccine industry is not liable for the harm they do, they no longer have any incentive to make their products safe, and once you have been vaccinated that product cannot be recalled.

So obviously, these days, there's a very high risk to allowing someone to inject something into your body, and, of course, whenever there is risk, you have the right of refusal because you have the right to guard your life and safety. If something may not be safe, you have the right to refuse it.

There are reports that there is something very different about COVID-19, and that our bodies cannot develop immunity to that virus strain for some reason. If that is the case, then vaccines would be totally ineffective and useless. It would then be entirely irrational to even develop a COVID-19 vaccine much less use it on people, but we still seem to be hearing a lot of chatter about how mandatory vaccines are coming for COVID-19. It is as if they are testing us to see if we will object. By sharing this video you are objecting. By using the documents I'm about to present, you are objecting. There may be some people in government or the medical industry who are so stupid, corrupt, or evil that they do not realize or care that you have the right to refuse vaccination for yourself and your children. If that is the case, we have a real problem.

Every one of us is the sole authority over what is injected into our bodies and no medical treatment may be given to us without our consent. If we cannot control what goes into our own bodies, then there is no such thing as individual rights, and the state and Bill Gates can simply dispose of people in any way they want. We need to be prepared to refuse vaccines whenever we feel that is necessary. Perhaps it is obvious, but the first thing we must do is state our position clearly and on the record to those people who administer vaccines. We are certainly not protected if we haven't even stated our position. You will see links to two free download documents at freedomtaker.com.

The first document is a requirement that all medical service and vaccine providers sign for you to acknowledge the risks of vaccines, that they are causing that risk by offering vaccines, and that they accept full personal liability to pay for all damage they caused by administering a vaccine. Of course, if vaccines were safe and effective they would not hesitate to sign a liability agreement, but to them a few deaths, a few million cases of autism or paralysis, are just the natural cost of protecting the public from disease, so they feel justified in killing and injuring some people to protect some other people.

They deliberately violate the Hippocratic Oath to do no harm. They know they are doing harm. So most likely they will refuse to sign that document and refuse to be responsible for the harm they caused. That refusal to sign is evidence that they know that vaccines have risks and you, therefore, are fully within your rights to refuse the vaccine regardless of any legal mandates. That type of document is referred to as a conditional acceptance. You agree to have a vaccine if they agree to pay for all damage you suffer. They will refuse to sign it, and that gives you the right to refuse their vaccine because they failed to meet your reasonable requirements of safety.

The second document for vaccines at freedomtaker.com is your flat-out refusal of vaccines. It states reasons why you have a right to refuse any and all vaccines. It is best to present these documents with a witness or send these documents by certified mail, so you will have a witness or evidence of delivery. Keep copies of the notice of the delivery receipt in your file. You can use either or both of these documents to help protect your safety, health, life, and rights. These documents not only authorize you to avoid vaccination in a formal and proper way, they also act as an insurance policy if anything goes wrong with a mandated or forced vaccination.

You can show that you were opposed to the vaccination and that puts the administrators of the vaccine in gross negligence and subject to penalty and prosecution. If you do not make your position clear, you can be presumed to agree with unconstitutional laws, harmful public policies, and even physical damage done to you and your loved ones.

Suppose that there is a majority who supports mandatory vaccination, majority rules right? Wrong! Under any legitimate form of government, majority rule is not absolute. Majority rule is subordinate to individual rights. Your right to swing a baseball bat stops at your neighbor's head. Majority rule cannot make it acceptable for you to assault your neighbor. We all have the individual right to determine what will and will not be put into our bodies.

The majority cannot require us to drink bleach, and the majority cannot force us to have a vaccination. Individual rights is a good thing, in fact individual rights is the only thing between freedom and tyranny. Without your individual rights, you may be arrested, tortured, and killed by the state or anyone else. The state uses special expressions to trick you into giving up your individual rights. You will hear them say something like, "We must have the greatest good for the greatest number."

Expressions like that suggest that individuals are expendable at the whim of the state. We have all heard these expressions: "Majority rule," "We are all in this together," "For the good of the whole." They even use laws to violate individual rights forcing people to get licenses and permits for harmless activity, taxing people on their property when it is a right to own property, and maybe in the near future forcing people to get vaccinations without their consent.

Law enforcement officers have no authority to force you to be vaccinated. Public officials have no legitimate authority to penalize you for refusing vaccinations or to limit your access to public services or infrastructure for refusing vaccination. They may try, but they may not do so without exceeding their authority. If we agree that government can force vaccinations, then we're saying, for instance, that we may be imprisoned for not eating vegetables. We are granting unlimited authority to the state to control and even end our lives. The containment of government use of force is the fundamental idea of our Constitution. No government is legitimate if it does not have the consent of the governed. By forcing vaccinations that government becomes illegitimate. Securing your right to not be forcibly injected, not only protects your health and rights, it keeps your government legitimate. Both of those documents are available at freedomtaker.com for free download. When you download those documents, they do not take or record any information about you. This is a free and private service to everyone.

Jerry Day originally published, "Mandated Vaccinations, Get Ready To Say 'NO!'" on YouTube in April 2020. Transcribed by Lady Jane Emefa Addy.

This Is Your Brain On Technology And News Media

Jerry Day

Society is not prepared for what technology is doing to it. When our mass media can tailor content to every individual, no one is seeing the full picture and no one is seeing what the other person sees. This tears society apart with hostility, confusion, mistrust.

Every president makes mistakes, every president has successes, but our media now filters what our presidents do to placate different audience segments. All the bad things, the president does, is broadcast to these people over here, and all the good things, the president does, is broadcast to those people over there. Media creates a multiverse where there is more than one president. He is sliced and diced and parceled out to badly isolated markets and segments of media consumers. So most of us think we know the president and few of us do, and from now on this will be true of all presidents and all partisan figures and all issues. Our media is now smart enough to confirm our personal prejudices and media profits from doing that. As we accept the lie of partisanship, we are being isolated with incomplete information. Universal truth and common purpose are being eliminated from the human experience because we must be fighting with each other to make media business models work and to allow us to be thrust into partisan loyalty and adversarial postures to make the corrupt political system work. The information you get is utterly disconnected and contrary to the information other people get, even the person that may be standing right next to you. The exact same media that tells you that your progressive values are superior is telling your friend that conservative values are superior, and that person will not be your friend for very long. Most of us are not only operating on incomplete or false information, we are as a society operating on conflicting information, which is fabricated to control us. The main reason, we don't have the full truth is not just that we're told lies, but that most of us don't really want the truth. When the truth makes us uncomfortable, we choose comfort over truth, illusion over fact. We habitually try to reduce our stress levels. We can only handle so much cognitive dissonance then we look for dark, quiet holes where we feel safe. We gladly let media technologies lie to us and enforce our biases and keep unpleasant facts out of our view. This is just human nature and media now has the technology to exploit that human flaw to the maximum. The new technology that makes this possible is the one where big data management systems can tailor and target different messages and information to every single different person in the world. A society is divided into conflicting segments, which are highly ignorant of each other's perceptions.

Media thrives on this social division; they play us against each other. We can always find media to confirm our biases and agree with us, but we cannot always find a human being, a friend, who agrees with all our positions, like media can now do. So now we gain more comfort and assurance from our media than we do from our friends. So technology and media are gaining status in our lives, while personal relationships between people are losing status, but to exploit us in this way, media must make extensive use of surveillance and must determine our personalities and preferences, must drill deeply into our lives, and must delicately feed each of us different content and messages very carefully crafted and personalized to win our hearts and minds. By knowing each of us intimately, media gains the power to toy with our emotions.

Media wants you to fear something, or hate some group, so that media can pose as your only true and real friend, so that you will feel intimate with media while feeling disconnected with everyone else. To be your best friend, media must give you pretty lies and keep you in a bubble. Just as a celebrity or executive wants an entourage of yes-men, all of us can now have our yes-man; it's our cellphone or browser. It knows us and it obsessively serves us only what it thinks we want. The media handles us exactly how the sociopath will gaslight a friend, a spouse, or a younger sibling to make her feel like no one understands and loves her, except that one special friend. For a sociopath to gain total control of a person's mind he must eliminate all other points of influence in his victim's life; he must become the sole source of information, support, and love. Once his victim is isolated then he may start committing abuses. So our new electronic media, games, social networks, and news feeds are positioning themselves as our primary connection to the world. By extracting your psychological profile from your behavior, what you say, where you go, who you know, what you like and don't like, media can create a special little world for you to live in. Media can then feed you content to convince you that your view of the world is right and people who disagree with you are wrong. What is actually true is completely irrelevant; it's all about using surveillance to build a deep and complex profile of your mind then using that profile to echo yourself back to you with a highly tailored and curated stream of selected information, designed to hold your attention at all costs and to be in that safe zone where you are never troubled with what is going on in the real world around you. The only thing that matters is what makes you love your media and continually engage your media; like a parent who constantly gives the infant more and more candy and less and less real food that system is not good for us in the long run.

Now we have another major problem with our technological media as it is not only feeding us lies, distortions, and omissions, and parroting our biases, it is now censoring on behalf of those who control technology and media. It is twisting our views to become consistent with their views. By the messages and images they give us, they capture us, direct us, and they guide us into service and loyalty to them with censorship, omission of facts and truth, lies about people and things, putting us into fear than offering the solutions that they plan to impose, which always cost us money and redirects our attention and actions to serve some undisclosed agenda and, above all, keeps us addicted to media. Media is not just a platform, it is a tool of social control for those who wish to influence us, to use us, exploit us, even destroy us, and now they have perfect tools with which to do that.

It costs money to produce media, someone is paying for that and they want to achieve some result. They want something in return. Our new technological media has not one, but many layers, there's the sponsor who pays for the advertising then there's the sponsor who pays and controls the content, the actual programming, then there's the sponsor who creates the platform and wants to influence people in a broader way, then there's the carrier who doesn't care what the content is as long as it keeps you tuning in. They must not only get messages to us, it must get us to pay for the infrastructure, the gadgets, the carriers, the networks. We won't pay for all that unless they give us things we love. Only if we love it and use it can they repurpose it to control us. The technology that is enabled, all of this, is very new and the effects on society are experimental, clumsy, sometimes highly valuable in the way it can convey information, sometimes very destructive with toxic radio frequencies and polluting consumption of energy. We are guinea pigs for technocrats and this new technology to see how we, on the human farm, can be herded, corralled, harvested, and slaughtered in fully automated ways. They are still developing this technology, sometimes making mistakes, sometimes hurting people. They're trying to find out how to maximize revenue, how to perfect social control, how to profit from our ignorance, conflict, and intellectual isolation, how to put us in fear and in hate so we can be manipulated with those very powerful emotions. They are learning how to have us begging for more candy while they wrap that candy with their messages, agendas, and behavioral control. They are finding ways to make us love their surveillance. We want them to know more about us, so they will give us more that pleases us. They want us on their leash and if they do it right, we want to be guided by that leash. So what can we do?

We can trick media into showing us things we don't like, we can seek truth even if it hurts, or we can simply shut off the media and refocus on things that will improve our social connections in other ways - real social connections, real working and productive relationships. We can create enterprise and take control of our destiny, rather than drift aimlessly in an ocean of media manipulation. It takes a certain level of maturity to recognize that some of the things we like are not good for us. Young people are especially vulnerable to media manipulation and media addiction. Sometimes it's hard to recognize how media has become a parasite, a poison. It looks good, it makes us feel good, it must be good, generally that is no longer true. Media is a temptation, a lure to cause us to be tracked, monitored, controlled, and deprived of our wealth and self-determination. It is a distraction we crave, an escape we feel we need. Technology is working hard to learn how to manage us, so we must learn how to manage media in our lives, so media does not become the driver of our lives. We must hold media to high standards of truth, objectivity, utility, and value. We must know that we are being played, and we must find ways to prevent that or at least be aware of how it is being done. We must question everything. We must stay conscious, alert, and critical because with today's technology, when we relax, we are being taken over, invaded, redirected, used, depleted, damaged. Media is hypnotic, and under hypnosis you are not exercising free will or critical thinking. Under hypnosis you are going wherever the hypnotist wants to take you. We must ask ourselves: Am I in control of this or is someone else? Is this improving my life? Is this making me hate? Is this causing me fear? Do I need this? Is this really worthwhile or is it just pacifying me? As media becomes better at capturing us, we must become better at escaping and maintaining control of our own lives. This technology is highly advanced and getting more so every day. It is like a giant hole, opening up in the ground, that we're all falling into. More and more, when we tune into technology and media, we tune out of our own worlds, our own needs and purposes, even our own values. We become pieces on someone else's game board. To stay conscious in our use of technology, we must ask: Are we seeking guidance, reassurance, and comfort from our technology and media, or are we really imagining, planning, and creating better lives for ourselves? Are we generating our own creative thoughts, or are our thoughts being externally guided? The only way, we have any control over what our lives become, is to imagine that for ourselves and we make our own plans to cause what we imagine to become reality. Imagining our futures and how to effectively manage our lives is not something we can do while consuming media messages, we have to turn it off.

Jerry Day originally published, "This Is Your Brain On Technology And News Media" on YouTube in May 2020. Transcribed by Oluwafunmilayo Elizabeth Bamidele.

Voting By Mail - A Really Bad Idea

Jerry Day

We are seeing a lot of public figures in the media trying to sell us on the idea of voting by mail. Actually, it is illegal. Article 2 of the US Constitution says, "The Congress may determine the Time of chusing the Electors, and the Day on which they shall give their Votes; which Day shall be the same throughout the United States." So our supreme and prevailing law says that voting must happen on one day. To gather or count ballots for one election on more than one day is an act of treason. It is rather obvious why voting has been subject to special and strict processes. The idea of tampering with elections is nothing new. To our founding fathers, it was obvious that to have the slightest hope of handling the ballots properly, they had to be managed in a way they could not be fiddled with in secret by unidentified parties. Most states developed a system where ballots were put in a locked box by the voter, and only under public witness could the box be unlocked and the ballots be counted. Often, each ballot was read aloud as eyewitnesses would verify what was called out. This was not for ceremony. This was the only way the vote could be kept honest, fair, and credible. When you mail in your ballot, you have no idea who is handling, counting, or not counting it. When you mail in your ballot, you are unraveling a long and distinguished history of voting integrity. The idea is that if you wish, even you, can witness and verify the counting of ballots. We are being told that mailing in our ballots is a good way to avoid the hazards of contagious disease, but, of course, if we don't gather, shop, and travel then we destroy our economy, and we fail to develop immunities and visiting a voting office is no more risky than many other things we must do to keep our economy afloat and keep society functioning. Voting by mail is a perfect example of how we give up our security for a little convenience. In the 2016 election, over 20 percent of the ballots were mailed in. In seven

States more than half the ballots were mailed in, enough to completely decide the election in those states. That is putting a huge amount of trust into a system that in 2016 was riddled with accusations of election tampering. When we mail in our ballots, we have no right to raise questions of election tampering. We are asking for it. A completely transparent voting process was difficult to create and voting systems probably can never be perfect, but it was a major priority in our country's history to try and keep elections honest, transparent, and open to everybody. Voting by mail eliminates the system that was created for that singular purpose of having a voting process that allows us to have confidence in the outcome. Some of the issues we vote for are strongly opposed by government. Is it any wonder that government would like us to see a voting system that they can manipulate and control? There is an old expression, a kind of joke - the question is: Who will win the election? The answer is: Whoever counts the ballots. That is why we have to witness the process from start to finish. How do we maintain access and transparency in this new voting by mail system? It's impossible! So the fact that government seems to be pushing this new system raises very serious suspicions of why they would be pounding this drum.

In 2018, Princeton University released a study, showing that voting no longer has any appreciable effect on public policy. As they say, if voting mattered they would not allow us to do it. We have a serious disconnect between popular consensus and public policy. Voting by mail is just another way to disconnect the voter from public policy even further, and policy makers seem to want it that way. So by voting by mail, we may prevent disease, but we will also prevent democracy. We never had any pandemic from people voting, ever, so let's stop kidding ourselves. Voting by mail is just a way to allow government to control something they should not be controlling.

Maybe we need to look at whether we should even use voting at all to make public policy, because voting is just the majority violating the rights of the minority. Voting is mob rule. Voting is taking something from your neighbor by force of the state. Voting is two wolves and a sheep deciding what they'll have for dinner. We know in a free society we are not supposed to have rulers, but what do we have, "majority rule," that sounds like we have a ruler. When we decide our policies, instead of starting with majority rule, we need to start with protecting people's rights, every last person's rights, not violating someone's rights to please the majority. We have lost so many of our rights. Look at the Bill of Rights, nearly all ten of them are gone or disregarded by officials. All our new public policies seem to do is protect the power and wealth of government. What about us? Now, we need policies that protect us and our rights against the abuses and excesses of government for a change. We have the partisan expressions, "Black Lives Matter," "It's okay to be white." We have these divisive slogans, but how about a slogan that is not divisive that protects everyone. The slogan that would be something like, "Individual Rights First And Public Policy Comes Second." The fundamental element of society is the individual, groups are just a bunch of individuals; corporations, government, races, countries, and political parties are just collections of individuals. When you protect the individual, you protect the group. When you protect the group, you violate the rights of the individual. When we protect your right to clean air, water, and food, we protect the environment. See how that works? Protect individual rights and you cover it all. When you do it the other way around, things go terribly wrong. You can protect the environment by killing all of us. When you do it backwards, you lose the concept that human life and rights should be protected. You fall into a dystopian hell of human sacrifice for some external objective. We can be confused about whether we are protecting the environment for our benefit, or protecting the environment for the environment's benefit. It may seem altruistic to put the environment's needs above human needs, but it's rather nihilistic. If we forget to protect humans, we are betraying ourselves, our species, our society, and our groups, but to protect our rights, we have to understand what a right is, we have to know the difference between a right and a gift.

A gift is something you get that someone else pays for. A right is something that you are allowed to pursue and attain for yourself without interference. Protecting people's rights is a fairly simple thing. It usually entails just removing some obstacle to our pursuit of happiness, and that obstacle is usually government, but these days, our government, our empire, is clearly in a state of decline. These days, it seems like all that government can focus on is self-preservation, self-enrichment, self-empowerment, self-protection. Government no longer troubles itself with protecting your rights and your freedoms. It wants more and more revenues, more and more censorship, more and more debt, more and more currency printed out of thin air. These are all clear indications of system decline and failure. Making you free does not make government rich, so what do you expect government is doing? The idea of freedom and individual rights actually clashes with the idea of government, wealth, force, and power. Government no longer protects your rights. It brings us crises and takes your rights away. The only rights you have today are the rights you claim, defend, and preserve for yourself. When you gain rights and freedoms, government thinks that it loses because government no longer wins us with service - it wins us with force, but in this way government makes itself worthless and expendable to us. We can now see that if we learn how to claim our rights and respect the rights of others, then we could throw out nine tenths of our public policies today. We could retire most of our armies, our police, our prisons, many of our courts, and most of those civic planners who are so busy behind closed doors deciding how we will behave, live, and comply. If we could simply rely on each other for justice, honor, and compassion, our problems would be solved, and there would be very little for government to do and collect taxes for. When we recognize ourselves as the fundamental element of society and that government is simply a dangerous appendage, we will see that there is no one out there who has any right to dictate anything to us as long as we are able to act responsibly and ethically. It is you and I who have the greatest power to make the world what it is, not government, not politicians, not lawmakers, not media. The world is what we make it, but nowadays we must find ways to keep government out of our way until government is in its proper place as a servant and not as a ruler. As we see that bad decisions are harming us, we must start making decisions ourselves. We can no longer ask someone else to do things for us. By voting for people who have no capacity to deliver their promises, or by signing petitions that no one ever responds to, we need not only to be the change, we need to make the change. It is the difference between wishing you had a ditch and actually moving a shovel. Government is that thing that keeps taking away our shovel, and we need to stop letting that happen. Whether you mail in your voting ballot or go to a polling place, you are giving government the shovel, telling government that it is they, not you, who will determine your future, your life, your opportunities.

Presidents no longer matter, legislators no longer matter. There is something else controlling things. It needs to be us. We need to do that today and under those circumstances, voting no longer matters. I can pretty much promise you that mailing in a voting ballot will not improve your life in any way, other than saving you a trip to the voting booth.

Jerry Day originally published, "Voting By Mail - A Really Bad Idea" on YouTube in May 2020. Transcribed by Oluwafunmilayo Elizabeth Bamidele.

The Power Of Secrecy

Jerry Day

It is easy to identify the most evil and destructive people in
society. All you need to do is look at who has immunity from
prosecution and privilege of secrecy. Government tells us that
they use secrecy for security, but they tell us if we want privacy,
we must be criminals who have something to hide. When
government operates in secret, is it possible that they are doing
that to cover their crimes? Secrecy is a neutral thing, it can be
used to protect national security and it can be used to cover the
crimes of government. There is plenty of evidence that
government uses secrecy for both reasons. That's because when
government agencies can operate in secret, they can do anything
they want, good or bad.

Our security agencies, the agencies that enjoy the most secrecy,
literally normalized torture, not just one incident but ongoing
programs of torture. They normalized illegal mass surveillance,
they normalized selling weapons to our enemies, they
normalized human experimentation, they normalized the
PSYOP that system of making up something false and getting
all the media to repeat it in order to get people to support
something that the government wants to do, like invade Iraq,
Afghanistan, Libya, Syria, Yemen, Ukraine, there are many
more.

How do these agencies get away with criminal wrongdoing on
mass scales year after year? Secrecy. The worst things a society
can do, the secret agencies do first and do most, and then the
rest of government follows suit, because government does
whatever it wants and the media applauds whatever they do. We
now know about a lot of the unlawful things our secret agencies
have done. Imagine what they're doing that we haven't found
out about, but it's not just security agencies, all of government is
secret, isn't it? What about our local bureaucracy, your tax
collector's office, housing development, planning departments,
health services? They're literally square miles of government
office space where people are doing things and hundreds of
billions of dollars pass through their hands. No one gets to visit

those offices, no journalists, no tourists, not even relatives of the employees.

I worked for a city government years ago, a city recreation department. They didn't keep good inventory on the candy in the snack bar at the public pool. So, employees stole candy, otherwise good and responsible people, stealing candy. One of my co-workers arranged with the department to put his personal car repair on an agency expense account. My department director told me, "This is a government agency. We have no requirement to provide any service. Nobody can do anything to us if we do not perform. The only thing we do have to do here is make sure our budget gets spent, so that we can get more next year." My department director had another interesting expression. He used to say, "Any problem that is ignored long enough will go away." That is the way government supervisors think, your tax dollars at work. My department director's own admission was that our agency was a non-performing money wasting exercise, where our obligation to the community was secondary to disposing of the budget. If that recreation department took their entire budget and burned it in a trash can, they would, in their eyes, be doing their job. When you go to the voting booth and vote for some new tax or bond measure for more schools or police or fire prevention, have you ever seen any government official, announce sometime later, about how well spent that money was, or how much we got for that money? Of course not because government is a place where money just disappears. They take it from us, they asked for it, we vote for some bond, and that is the last we hear about it. The money disappears. Is that any way to run a system? People say, "If there was that much corruption, somebody would say something." You think so? Every one of those people is collecting a paycheck. Everyone who says something, not only loses their paycheck, they feel the hate and anger of everyone else who loses their paycheck, and they can wind up in prison for being part of that corruption and waste. Trust me, they say nothing, but it gets worse. In the secret halls of government, you are not only tempted to break the rules; you have a natural immunity from prosecution.

Have you ever noticed that the police hardly ever arrest anyone who works for government? When a whistleblower comes forward, they fabricate some way to prosecute the whistleblower, even though that is illegal, and they rarely prosecute the criminals in government who were reported by the whistleblower. They do this consistently. Edward Snowden, William Binney, Thomas Drake, Joe Banister, Sherry Peel Jackson, there are hundreds, each of them prosecuted by government, while the actual crimes they reported are never investigated or prosecuted. This is evidence that integrity in government no longer exists. Not only is government swamped with corruption and waste, there is no longer any way to fix any of that. Whistleblowers can't do it, elected officials can't do it, the media can't do it. Our system has failed. We are in a state of irreversible decline. Government is a club and you're not in it. Even your congressional representatives can't find out what goes on in the bureaucracies, behind those badge clearance stations and password-protected doors. These are offices you are paying for and if you walk in one of them, you will be arrested. Have you noticed that government tracks you by your cell phone, your emails, and your credit card activity? They even scan your license plate at the supermarket. That is how they treat your privacy, and we are not able to find out the first thing about our public servants, their performance, their efficiency, their productivity, nothing. Why is their privacy more important than ours? So, are we naive enough to think that millions of public employees can operate in secret, have de facto immunity from prosecution, are handling billions of dollars, and none of them are doing anything wrong? It's ridiculous to believe that. I think most people have an instinct that secrecy in government is not good, but the nature of government is what makes us say, "Well, there's nothing I can do about it." There's a lot we can do about it. We can have a transparent and accountable government, or a secret, unaccountable government. It's just a matter of how many of us get together to demand access and accountability, but we have to do something. Government won't do this for us unless we make some noise. The smallest gesture to demand transparency would be a tidal wave if everyone would take some small action. Government likes to make us feel like they are in charge, but they work for us and we are in charge unless we go to sleep, and most of us are asleep when it comes to demanding transparency, accountability, and integrity from government, but they seem to have convinced most of us that there's no need to tell us what they're doing. So, they can just do anything. They can do any crime, any evil, any destructive act, that is what secrecy means. Crime is very profitable: Drugs, murder, embezzlement, bribes, human trafficking, sexual exploitation of children, you name it. We tend to forget that any of these things can be done if any person or organization is allowed to operate in secret. So, if they can get away with crimes like that, is there any question that waste, inefficiency, petty theft, and corruption would be commonplace? They work for us so we are ultimately responsible to commit oversight, but they love to characterize us as their lowly subjects, as if we are all serving some king or dictator.

We are told that because we vote, we agree to support all those secret agencies. We are told that because we use credit cards and cellphones, we agree to be tracked and monitored by criminals, committing mass surveillance. We are told that because we participate in commerce, we have agreed to be taxed and exploited to the point where we have literally no hope of ever getting out of debt, the arrogance and stupidity, but that is what we are told, over and over, and so many of us now believe that.

I guess it's just not hard to deceive people about what government is doing and what it is for. Most people in Germany thought that the Third Reich was terrific, while it was murdering millions of people. Many Russians thought Joseph Stalin was terrific while he was murdering 30 million innocent Russians. We can't go by what they tell us. We have to look for ourselves. People who are evil want secrecy, and people who can operate in secrecy can commit evil. If you want to find and stop evil, you start where there is secrecy and privilege.

Imagine how few of us know about what really goes on in Congress, the White House, the Pentagon, the county and city halls. What we know about the world that controls us is a fly speck on a bus that is hurtling down a mountain road with no brakes. We are riders on a ship to disaster because we know nothing about who our captains are, where the compass is pointed, what poisons and crimes surround us, what storms are coming over the horizon. Our most powerful institution, the one that affects us the most, our government, tells us that, for their protection, we may not know anything about what they're doing. With so much secrecy, we are made to be completely unprepared to command our lives in any meaningful way. We are blind, and we are told that is how we should be to be good citizens, but this is the perfect time for all of us to wake up. Our economy is in a state of collapse, our politics are hopelessly corrupt, our institutions are freewheeling and rogue. We, as citizens, have absolutely no agency or power on the institutional scale because we let them divide us, intimidate us, keep us ignorant. Now is the time to find our way out to reinvent ourselves, question everything, to rebuild, rethink, and renew society where we stop thinking about what we need to obey, and start thinking about what we can build for ourselves, where we have some control over our lives, our property, our future. People, like Bill Gates, think they are entitled to control the world, while most of us don't even think we're entitled to control our own lives. As long as we think small, we will be small. The flaw in the human creature is that he believes some other human creature should make decisions for his life. It makes no sense that we could create a government, hire the people to work in that government, and then let that government tell us what to do. It is our job to tell them what to do. Let's start doing it.

Jerry Day originally published, The Power Of Secrecy" on YouTube in May 2020. Transcribed by Oluwafunmilayo Elizabeth Bamidele.

Who Is Making Governments Self Destruct?

Jerry Day

Most of us know the basics of government finance: If commercial activity slows down or unemployment goes up then tax revenues go down, and government goes into financial crisis. We know this, and when there's a financial crisis and you are really suffering financially, doesn't government usually tell us it is time to raise taxes so government will not have to suffer the way you are, even if that means you have to suffer more? Isn't that how it usually works? But now that thing that gets hurt by any economic crisis, government, has just deliberately created a crisis that includes itself. They told us that we have a new germ and what we need now is for everyone to stay home. So not just you and I but even government will have a financial crisis, but this was not just your government or my government, this was every government in the world, all together, right at the same time, destroying every local and national economy like some kind of chorus line shuffling off to Buffalo. Government, that thing that borrows too much and cannot sustain itself without that magical thing called growth, has just turned full loony and demanded that everyone walk off the job, shut down our businesses, stop producing goods and services, permanently disrupts supply lines all the way from raw materials down to your local target store, knowing perfectly well that this would cause a crippling shutdown of the global economic engine, which would choke tax revenues and put governance in crisis all over the world. So here is government shooting itself, pushing this lockdown idea before they even had science to back it up. Something does not add up here! People did die of the disease, but the economic meltdown was not caused by a disease, it was caused by political declarations from people who have no authority to make laws. It is legislators, not governors and mayors, who make the laws last time I looked. This event, which will throw national and local governments into bankruptcy and insolvency, was deliberately caused by these governments themselves, promoting idiotic, panic laced policies that make no sense whatsoever.

There is more to this than they are telling us. Usually it is government crushing the private sector to enrich government. This was government crushing everything, including itself.

Our country has had virus scares before pretty much every year. In the last 20 years, we had more than one that had a higher death rate than COVID-19, but suddenly in 2020, the idea of a national lockdown dropped out of the clear blue sky, and everybody seemed more than happy to jump on that burning sinking ship as if we were all looking for an excuse to take an extended, unpaid vacation at home. Everybody, perfectly synchronized, decided that we wanted to destroy our economy while at the same time prevent ourselves from developing any immunities whatsoever to this disease. This lunacy was supported and promoted by people who call themselves, "health officials," and how about this for Orwellian doublespeak: "We are all in this together." So let's self-isolate, socially distance, cover our faces, we will all come together by quarantine ourselves and not allowing children to see their grandparents, we will all connect in that way. They even told us straight up it wasn't about preventing the disease, it was about "flattening the curve," which simply means prolonging the pandemic for as long as possible, as if it was more important to prevent overcrowded hospitals than it was to preserve the economic survival of the entire world. By the way, flattening the curve is another way of saying there will be a second wave when all of those isolated, immune challenged moles come back out of their holes and finally get the antibodies they could have gotten three months earlier with some normal social interaction.

In the meantime, all over the world, food supply chains ground to a halt. Famines and riots have already started, so much for saving lives. Naturally, we have skyrocketing reports of child abuse, spousal abuse, alcoholism, depression, drug abuse, immune system atrophy by over-sterilization and isolation, and, naturally, suicides, so much for saving lives. Our governors and mayors, knowing that their governments are indebt up to their ears, stepped up to microphones and cameras and demanded we do the exact things that they know will destroy their government finances, their ability to provide services, their ability to function, their ability to be regarded as credit credible leaders, and their likelihood of being reelected.

Even before this pandemic panic, governments worldwide were defaulting on their pension funds, imposing austerity, cutting services, filing bankruptcy, bailing out too-big-to-fail fat cats, raising taxes on people who can't pay more taxes, printing money and hyper inflating, and running interest rates below sea level. So what a perfect time to send GDP into negative 45 points, trigger a global depression to double down and take government collapses to a whole new level. Really? You think they're shutting down police departments to make Black Lives Matter happy? They're shutting down police departments because they can't pay the police. Why are we all of a sudden using a whole bunch of new ways to fight a seasonal disease? In my life, I have never before stood six feet away from people in a grocery store checkout line, I have never worn a mask to walk my dog, I have never seen healthy people wearing masks or quarantining themselves in my life, except in authoritarian countries where they make rules like that. We didn't see it because there's no science to support any of that. It's theater, it's mind control, it's some kind of political gamesmanship, and we are stooges for playing along. Did this come out of the current popular mindset that any public policy, no matter how bad, is alright if in some way it hurts Donald Trump or if it sells vaccines or if it gives government an excuse for more mass surveillance?

How did it become too dangerous for even one person in the entire world to walk into a restaurant and order dinner? Who came up with this stuff? I think we can assume that governments don't want to destroy themselves, so who made them do it? Who can march our government, in our society, off a cliff like that? Who is it, who, in a space of one or two weeks in March of 2020, commanded governments to immediately drop everything they are doing and self-destruct and tell every mainstream news anchor to tell the rest of the world to follow along? Who can pull strings like that?

Who can take an average flu season and turn it into a global economic meltdown in the space of a few weeks? It wasn't some city or country, somebody made the entire world do that. Nations never agree on things, but it was the lockstep thing, how did somebody coordinate this? The timetable was just too short, even a school district can't move that fast. Whoever that is, they totally control media, they totally control government, they control nearly every message we hear from our TVs, our computers, our cell phones, even our own neighbors. But they've done it more than once now, even after everyone could see the mistakes. Just when we're thinking, "We're opening up," George Floyd gets killed or dies from fentanyl, and then, of course, we have to go out and smash stores in every city. "Lock it down again!" "Okay, now it's over, okay we can go back." "Oh no! We're having our second wave. Lock it down again." "Oh wait! Is there a solar eclipse coming?" Should we lock it down again, as if there are no consequences every time we do this? So it's not just that people who aren't even doctors or scientists are shutting down the system for no apparent reason, aren't reporters supposed to ask questions? When did that stop? We're supposed to go along with destroying the global economy and not one reporter is curious enough to ask if the disease is really that bad.

Credible parties have accused Anthony Fauci of committing felonies and not one journalist asks him about that while they shower him with airtime and let him dictate policies on social distancing. Did journalists go extinct or something? Is anyone even curious where all our governors and mayors got the signal to shut it all down? How do they even get that idea? Who gave the signal? How do they work? How did they get the media to say that hospitals were swamped, and, the next day, citizen journalists hit those same hospitals and they were all dead empty? How did that happen? Okay they lied, but why did they lie? What made them stage busy hospitals when they knew there were no busy hospitals? How do you get reporters to do that? Health officials, many of them all at once, all over the place, came out and said if you die of a heart attack or a bullet wound, then we're going to call it "COVID death." How did that happen? How did they synchronize a ridiculous talking point, like that, among national and local health officials? I'd like to know where the central, global, control room is for something like this. If you have any evidence or information about who the puppet masters are, please come forward, we can't let this happen again. We need our jobs, our businesses, we need each other to do what we do for each other, all of us. There's no such thing as a non-essential job - that is someone's job, their livelihood, their survival. Hundreds of thousands of businesses have permanently closed due to this lockdown; the businesses you rely on for life as we know it. COVID-19 could never cause anywhere near the damage the lockdown has caused; the insane public policies have caused.

When the governor comes out and tells us to destroy our economy and our livelihoods, we have to refuse that and we have to tell that governor that he or she had better get their head right in very short order. We need to send that message loud and clear, and the way we send that message is go on with our lives and start thinking for ourselves.

Here is what it looks like: The governor walks up to a microphone, tells us all to do something, and nobody does it. That's how it will have to be before we get out of this mess. Politicians have lost their privilege to lead anyone, they have squandered that. Protesters don't care about social distancing, why should we? We need to keep businesses open and running, because if we don't, as we all start to feel what global collapse feels like, we are not going to like it.

Jerry Day originally published, "Who Is Making Governments Self Destruct?" on YouTube in July 2020. Transcribed by Oluwafunmilayo Elizabeth Bamidele.

Deep Thoughts On Leadership, Obedience, And Power

Jerry Day

The rightful and true leader is not he who projects the greatest force of dictate, but he who has the greatest gift of reason. We must never see the one with the greatest strength as the leader, but rather the one with the best idea. We must never allow ourselves to be judged by our obedience, rather we must judge the leader for the quality of his service. Our obedience must never be stolen by force it must be earned with wisdom, service, and respect for our freedom. The more trivial the reason we find to condemn the leader, the more just and right our leader will be pressured to be. We must set the standard for our leader as high as we can imagine. It is then the leader's job to meet that standard.

The word, "leader," implies that we must follow him. That is why we must continually remind him that he must follow us. The definition of a tyrant is someone who believes he can rule for one more day without being hung by an angry mob. If the leader does not fear the people, tyranny is already established. A slave is someone who spends less time each day judging his leader than deciding what shirt to wear. Even when a leader is wrong, evil, incompetent, and cruel, even when everyone hates that leader, if the followers do not act against that leader he will continue to be the leader. He can lead if he is hated, but he cannot lead if the people are acting against him. Bad leaders do not go away, they must be removed. The slightest tolerance of a bad leader by an individual is equal to tyranny of a nation when that tolerance is multiplied by a large portion of the population. If the tyrant has one supporter, he can marginalize ten of his opponents.

We are consumed with personal matters, while we are indifferent to distant leaders, yet it is the misconduct of the leadership which disrupts our personal matters. We will never have good leaders until we expect each other to constantly insist on good leaders. The elected tyrant will be more cruel and selfish than the forced tyrant, because the elected tyrant will consider himself to be more approved and legitimate and therefore to have more license to control and dominate the electorate. The forced tyrant must win over the people. Tyranny is not possible without the cooperation of the slaves. How bad does the corruption, secrecy, and cost of government have to get before we decide that we need to be responsible for ourselves and make our own decisions?

When leaders are chosen by voting, it no longer matters who is elected. Voting is the act of giving away the power to determine your own life. Voting is not just saying who you want to lead you; it's saying that you want to be led.

Jerry Day originally published, "Deep Thoughts On Leadership, Obedience, And Power," on YouTube in July 2020. It has been transcribed by Oluwafunmilayo Elizabeth Bamidele.

Who Should Pay For The Cost Of The Lockdown?

Jerry Day

Every year, because of new legislation and inflation, taxation goes up as a percent of your income. Is that sustainable? Certainly not, but we have been trained to just let it go because we were led to believe we can't do anything to stop it. It's like we're all in a trance where we are unable to see the mushrooming, economic damage that taxation is doing to us individually, to our businesses, to the country. A tidal wave is coming up the beach and no one wants to look out the window, but it's not so much that the wave comes over you it's more like your island sinks into the ocean. When there is an economic recession, many people are no longer able to pay property tax. As happened in 2008, government happily comes in and forces the foreclosures and sales of millions of property on behalf of banks who are using an economic crisis, they caused, to enrich themselves with the seizure of real assets from all of us. Government helped banks to foreclose on millions of homes when it was government and banks which caused the economic crisis. Like so many schemes run by our government and the most powerful corporations and individuals: they are to blame, we are to pay.

Those who study finance and banking public policy clearly see that periodic, economic disasters are fully planned and fully intentional to cyclically seize and collect most of the wealth and property from the general public. Why should you lose your home just because the economy got worse or your employer was taxed out of business? Wouldn't it make more sense when people can't pay property tax to lower property tax? When someone is suffering financial problems, when they can no longer afford to pay a property tax, is that a good time to take away their home? Destroy their life? Fling them into desperate homeless poverty? Is that good public policy? That is exactly what our current public policy is. As soon as the economy goes down or even looks like it might, we see the headlines telling us how taxes must now be raised, crushing us even further because it's so unacceptable that government should have to cut its bloated size by even 1% as all of us are losing our incomes, our homes, our savings.

When did government become more important than the people it was created to serve?

Ask yourself, is the purpose of property tax to pay for government services we want, or is the purpose of property tax to confiscate private property, destroy lives, and cast millions of homeowners into the ranks of the homeless? Is that what government is for? Because that's what government is doing. Government is always talking about what to do about the homeless problem, but how about not creating it in the first place? In a free country, you would have a right to own property. If you have a right to own property, then it cannot be taken from you for failure to pay taxes. In fact, if you have a right to own property, property cannot be taxed at all. When did we lose the right to own property? You don't have a right to own property if government can simply take it from you whenever it wishes to do so. In 2020, under the fear of a pandemic, government created a massive economic collapse by shutting down society, locking down people into their homes, destroying millions of businesses and jobs. In three months' time, some 40 million jobs were destroyed, more jobs lost in a shorter timespan than ever in our nation's history. A major event in the evolution of our nation, but explained as a little exercise to slow down some germs from spreading. It is not a reasonable social exercise when it causes millions of people to no longer be able to pay their mortgages, their loans, their rents, much less the taxes that have become such a large portion of our earnings. You see, this is how it works at the government level: By destroying you financially, they get to sell your home and seize your taxes. Something that is a disaster for the average citizen is a windfall for government and the banks. They make you unable to pay your property tax then they get to take your property. The world is upside down at elite and top levels: What is bad for you is good for them. Wealth does not disappear. When you are being financially wiped out someone else is receiving a huge payday. So this is the perfect time to stop and think, what is property tax really for? Or for that matter, what is any tax for? Is taxation bringing any solution to us and our communities? Is what government does making it easier or harder for us to keep our homes? No, taxation and government policies are clearly bringing down individual prosperity, increasing homelessness, destroying opportunities. Even without the national lockdowns, the creeping taxation is doing that, the money printing and inflation are doing that. This is a time of crisis where every one of us should be demanding that property tax be abolished, so that we can use our money to rebuild our businesses and our lives after the lockdowns, and bring our commercial and social operations back to normal. So that we can once again afford to pay for the services, we want government to provide.

Government needs to stop taxing us until we can do that. We need to go to our county, state, and federal governments and tell them it is they, not us, who must pay the price for the crisis, because it is they, not us, who caused it. It was not the disease that crushed the economy - it was unprecedented and irrational public policies that are crushing the economy.

We have a right to own property. We have a right to the gains produced by our labor. It is not government's purpose to seize our property and leave us destitute and helpless. Government is supposed to provide solutions and services, not destroy people's lives. The way the system is currently rigged, our poorly evolved, centrally bloated system is constructed in such a way that, in any economic downturn, property taxes destroy people's lives and make them lose their homes. Property taxes multiply the damage and pain of an economic downturn for you and I, while multiplying the enrichment and power of government and the banks, as they simply scrape up the remnants of our lives. Central powers damage us so they can damage us even more. This is what we should be protesting. This is damaging even to the black lives as they protest murdering police or racial discrimination. This lockdown, this economic train wreck does far more damage to them and all the rest of us than all the social issues combined. White privilege will never cost you as much as government privilege as they collect our taxes, as they destroy the economy with senseless and impulsive policies. They may then foreclose, seize, and buy property at rock-bottom prices and essentially collect all the assets from the general public and to hoard them in the centers of power while turning the public into renters, debtors, beggars, applicants for their handouts, and very dependent slaves.

When the economy goes down, at the very least, property taxes should be suspended, otherwise property tax is simply a property confiscation program. Taxation should only be levied on people who can afford to pay the taxes; no one should ever lose their home for taxation. When our country was founded, there was hardly any taxation at all. Public functions were funded in different ways by charities, wealthy philanthropists, civic associations. Taxation is a completely arbitrary function whose only real effect is to allow government to gain control and power which used to belong to us. There is no part of government that should exist, unless it is serving us with some tangible benefit which we have asked for, which we have agreed to pay for in that way, and which benefits all citizens equally. Taxation should never be used to destroy and redistribute wealth to centers of power in the manner that some invading force would plunder and steal the resources of the invaded country. The public does not exist to provide a source of plunder for government piracy. Taxation of labor is slavery. Taxation of property is destruction of property rights. These forms of taxation were not permitted or even imagined when our country was founded. The only thing taxable under our original national foundation was excess profits on goods sold, referred to as excise taxes. Excise taxes were more than adequate to build our country into an economic power and to achieve world status not just economically, but politically, ideologically. Property tax and income tax did not exist and played no part in our early nations rise to international prominence.

By assuring that our schools keep us economically ignorant, and by slowly imposing more and more taxes on labor and property, our country has degenerated into a slave state without any moral foundation, without any power for the average citizen, and with massive collections of power and wealth in the centers of government, finance, and a few highly privileged families. We need to express our outrage at the government greed and injustice caused by our public policies and systems of taxation. We need to tell government that we will not tolerate this injustice. We will not participate in our own destruction. We will not pay taxes we cannot afford to pay. We will not pay taxes for which we receive no benefit. We will not pay taxes for which we have no accountability. We will not participate in schemes of taxation that were not part of our nation's founding principles. We have to remember that government is supposed to be working for us, not the other way around.

Jerry Day originally published, "Who Should Pay For The Cost Of The Lockdown?," on YouTube in July 2020. It has been transcribed by Oluwafunmilayo Elizabeth Bamidele.

How Is That Lockdown Working For You?

Jerry Day

Regardless of what anyone thinks about the masks, lockdowns, social distancing, mass-germ-phobia, these things are changing society and not for the better. While we're distracted by petty bickering about medicine and science, our global economy is being destroyed. The global economy is not something over there, it is what you and I rely on for everything we have, everything we buy, everything we need in the future, everything we eat, wear, drive, sleep on, consume, and use. That thing that makes all of that stuff for you is being destroyed by people who think that perfectly healthy people need to be self-isolated; call it quarantines, lockdowns, reasonable precautions, call it whatever you want, it is destroying your life and your future right now. As some wise person once said, "We can only have stuff, when we make stuff."

Do we really not realize our dependency on commerce even when we buy things in stores, when we order things online, when we are completely dependent on goods and services to maintain our standard of living, do we not realize that if we shut down commerce we are shutting down the lifelines that provide for us?

Do we really think, we can shut down businesses by the millions and still get the things we need, when we need them? Are we that completely out of touch with reality? I'm not talking about designer handbags, I'm talking about food, every essential household product, even the raw materials that everything is made of. Can we shut all that down and that won't affect you? If we are to believe the death count, several hundred thousand people have died from COVID-19. So we bring food production to a halt and risk a global famine where tens of millions of people could starve to death? There's some very bad mathematics in this lockdown idea. We have never locked down the entire world before. We are playing with dynamite. The way humanity works is that when we have a disaster, an emergency or a crisis, over here, people, over there, send aid. When you shut down the whole world, there is no one left to send aid: If we starve, everyone starves; if we have a crisis, everyone has a crisis. So this will not just be a crisis, it will be a crisis where no one can help you. Very few people seem to be aware of the significance of this, especially people in government who think they are supposed to make decisions and policies, even when they're totally unprepared to do so. It would be a good idea if they would stop making policies until they can get a clear view of what they are doing.

Here is something your brilliant public official never thought of: While we shut down most of the world's production, are we able to shut down our need for goods and services? Do we stop needing the work people do because they were told not to work? There is nothing we needed in 2019 that we don't need today. Were they making too much food in 2019? Too many consumer goods in 2019? No, that means they are making too little, now, there won't be enough. That is bad. That could get worse than we imagined. Everything has consequences, but few things have more consequences than shutting down the planet, but the pandemic pushers do not even seem to be capable of considering the consequences of their policies. Is it not obvious that the lockdown will cause a major crisis in supply and that millions of people are no longer going to be able to get what they need?

The world has survived far worse diseases than COVID-19. A global lockdown was never anyone's idea of a rational solution, because the damage a global lockdown causes is much greater than the damage that any disease can cause. We need to open our society back up and we need to do it fast. We need to fully open up, no masks, no social distancing, no waiting for some toxic untested vaccination. If COVID-19 is natural, it will run its course. If it is some kind of biological warfare, we need to find out who is doing that and stop them, but we can't sit at home and think that our lives will not be thrown into desperate chaos when the shortages start to hit us. Whether you realize it or not, commerce is something you need to survive. Do you have a water well? Do you grow your own food ? Do you make your own clothing? Healthcare? Transportation? Do you make your own natural gas and electricity? Are you totally self-sufficient? I don't know anyone who is, but that is what you have to be if you're going to keep it all locked down because every day we play germ boogie man, more businesses are closing permanently. The lockdown is going to hurt you if it has not already done so. It is going to hurt everyone you know and love. Take off the mask, walk out the door, and do your part to turn the world back on. Your survival may depend on that.

Jerry Day originally published, "How Is That Lockdown Working For You?" on YouTube in August 2020. Transcribed by Oluwafunmilayo Elizabeth Bamidele.

Your Mental Prison Is In Your Hand

Jerry Day

Human tracking and surveillance is suddenly such a growing industry; where you are, what you do, who you do it with are now the data points on which our new system of control is being built and from which revenues are being generated from you. The smartphone is now overtaking the television as the primary instrument of mass social control. Your smartphone, not only sends you messages, it sends messages about you to people who want to mess with you. It is total control. By carrying around a smartphone, we are connecting ourselves to a control grid, and we are synchronizing ourselves with the policy makers, the agenda setters, central planners, social engineers, political mercenaries, psychological manipulators, along with the usual suspects like the police, thousands of spamming marketers, and an assortment of hackers. Every company, every government agency, wants to get to you through that thing you have in your hand. If you are addicted to your cell phone, that is what your cell phone was designed to do. So how do we get out of that? There are a few things we can do short of simply not using trackable devices. If you can't discard the phone and shut off the service, you can share your phone with others. Let them use your phone, while you use theirs. This confuses the tracking data and makes the data useless because the data is disconnected from an identity. You can leave the phone at home when you go out, this breaks the data continuity. When you drive around, you can leave your phone in the car so it's not tracking you around other people. Why would we want to carry a device that tells some spies, somewhere, when we're near a criminal or a person who tested positive for a disease? Anyway, it's not healthy to carry a radio transmitter. I have a family member who got cancer on the exact part of her body where she always carried the cell phone. Some people think that this Internet of Things is generating more data than anyone could ever look at, that is not true: it's all automated now. Artificial intelligence can read, think, and act. AI is reading your messages, listening to your conversations, logging, and analyzing your transactions, tracking your location, deciding how to grab your attention, deciding if you need to be dealt with or if money can be made from you. It can get to you in thousands of ways without a human being ever getting involved, but that AI makes mistakes, and that data can get mixed up and maybe you will wind up on the wrong list.

If you are arrested, you will never get to confront the AI for falsely accusing you, you will pay your fine, spend your time in jail. There will be no one who can help you.

How about all those great apps you have? Did you ever notice that the company that makes your phone or provides your cell service does not write or sell the apps? They let other people do that, why? First, they can collect data from any app on your phone, they don't have to write the app or sell it to collect the data it generates. Second, they want you to have as many apps as possible; they want apps to be free, easy, and fun for you. The apps are where you get addicted, literally psychologically dependent on the device. They are free because they open the door to your life to people who want to watch you and exploit you. That data is not just showing where you are and what you're doing: Your chatting and messages have conveyed deep psychological profiles on your intelligence, what triggers your different emotions, what makes you willing to spend your money. With that kind of data they know how they can play you, and they play you every time you look at your phone. As a mechanism of social control, there has never been anything close to a smartphone. The longer that cell phones exist they become more essential to us to function financially, socially, psychologically. The phone is embedding itself in our brains and our lives, like a parasite that digs deeper and deeper, probing into its target until the target is fully controlled by the parasite. If you care in any way what is on your smartphone, you are in the matrix, you are a member, you are a full participant in that centrally-managed social control experiment. Through that phone someone else is accessing your mind, your money, your behavior, and emotions. They are shaping your view of the world because they not only send messages, they censor messages. They delicately tailor what you get to see and what you get to find out. When you are on your cell phone, you are the property of something else, and your phone is the leash, the chain, the jail cell, the loudspeaker from which you are given orders and directed to serve the master. It is where you are strip-searched, given the cool-aid, and told how you are expected to behave. It is the link between you and what wants to control you. When you use that device you are stripping naked and telling the world they can have you, and that you have no fear of being watched, studied, or visited by total strangers with bad intentions.

Every time you push a key or button, every time you read a message, every time you feel the need to check in with that device, you are less of yourself and more of what your device is telling you to be.

They're not just providing telephone service, you can tell just by looking at the phone. It's not just a telephone: It is a clamp that locks onto your brain and does not let go.

I understand this addiction as I have a smartphone. I even use it sometimes, but once a person is addicted they do not easily become unaddicted, ask any addiction therapist. To beat the addiction, the addict needs to see that he is addicted, he needs to make a conscious decision to change that, and he needs to be willing to take the pain and discomfort of being without that addictive sensation. He needs to envision his life without the addiction and strive for that vision. He needs to create something worth living for after the addiction is thrown away. It's not easy.

When we are getting messages from our devices, we can't hear our own thoughts. We can't hear the subtle messages from the people who love us or from God. We can't hear what nature, time, the universe, is trying to tell us because we are on the smartphone, the computer, we are watching, TV; we are too busy allowing something else to consume our attention to direct our thoughts to control us. Will we ever be free of this self-destructive addiction? Will we ever be strong enough to recover the control of our lives that we have lost?

Can we do that?

Jerry Day originally published, "Your Mental Prison Is In Your Hand," on YouTube in August 2020. It has been transcribed by Oluwafunmilayo Elizabeth Bamidele.

Censorship and the PDN - Can You Handle The Truth?

Jerry Day

Have you noticed that a few years ago we had very little censorship and now we have a lot? In early 2020, YouTube started brutally censoring videos on coronavirus for no apparent reason. They said the topic was sensitive, so they're censoring it? A few years ago sensitive topics were not censored on YouTube or anywhere else, why now? YouTube's executives have declared that if any video has any content that does not agree with the World Health Organization - that video will be censored. So now disagreement with an unelected, globalist organization that has no legitimate authority will cause you to be censored. A few years ago you could disagree with things - now you cannot. Is the World Health Organization such a perfect and divine organization that mere disagreement with them should be prohibited and forcibly removed from all public discourse? The World Health Organization has been accused of corruption, been accused of promotion of pharmaceutical industry interests, been accused of secret depopulation agendas, so the idea that disagreement with them should be suppressed is a bit absurd; we can't talk about that?

It is obvious how dangerous and evil that proposition is when this agenda is being pushed by the largest new-media platforms in the world: YouTube, Google, Facebook, Twitter, Instagram, and many other mass media social platforms. This is a very new idea that you shall not be permitted to publicly express disagreement with something. If a topic is deemed by some handful of unidentified elites to be sensitive - you cannot say it, you cannot see it. So this thing we call social media, this platform where we can all connect and have open dialogue among ourselves, no longer permits open dialogue. When we started using social media it was exciting because we were the content providers, but now when we create content we have to self-censor. We have to try and figure out how to dodge the word, the phrase, the issues, the topics that media executives don't personally like today and have chosen to remove from their mass media platforms, even though they are not the ones creating the content.

We are now to create content in a little confined box, and we must now please not just ourselves and our contacts, we must, first and foremost, please the platform police. Authoritarians have some odd ways of working - they don't make the rules real clear. They wait for someone to do something they don't like, and then they attack that person. They do a phony fact check and assassinate their character - they censor, they ban, they mess with search results, they play it dirty, they give no warning, they provide no clear guidelines. They just wait until they see something they don't like, and then they attack. This is why authoritarianism is bad because you not only have to comply, very often you don't know what you are supposed to comply with, until it is too late and you're being attacked for doing something you thought was okay to do.

Authoritarians don't look good when they make laws that say you can be attacked if you offend the rulers, so they don't make those laws. They don't have to make any laws if they're authoritarians: They can punish anyone, anytime, for no reason, so who needs laws - who needs clear policies that we can read, understand, and agree on? They don't care if we agree with them. They don't want us to know what they are going to do next. Constantly moving the goal posts is one of the ways they stay in power; confusing the public to make them desperately try to comply, keep them off balance and trying to guess what the current policies actually are. YouTube removes videos and entire channels without any warning - that is how they do it. They don't even follow their own policies when they do that - they don't contact you, they don't let you speak with the person censoring your video, and they don't give you anything resembling due process like the right to confront your accuser. You will never know who your accuser is, and you won't even be told specifically what you are accused of. They told me, I had violated community guidelines on some videos that very obviously did not violate any reasonable community guidelines. That is how I learned that the term, "community guidelines," had no particular definition. Community guidelines were whatever YouTube wants to call community guidelines on any particular day. So your video is down, your channel is down, perhaps your livelihood was taken down by YouTube, but it will be without warning, without any conversation with you. It is YouTube removing other people's things without consent, explanation, or warning. This is how little respect YouTube and Google have for their content providers. The people who literally create the channels on their otherwise empty platforms are treated like criminals in communist China. The people who attract viewers to their advertisers - the people who do all the work of developing audiences for those platforms - do all the investment to produce the media content for them. The people who represent the sole and working body of modern media are given no chance to protect that investment, and their work is simply destroyed, removed, and manhandled by a few nameless faceless ideologues deep inside Silicon Valley.

Your content is simply removed in the most disrespectful, damaging, and abusive way possible. A few years ago, we did not have this and now we do - things have changed. You are no longer permitted to see vast amounts of information that YouTube, Google, and many other platforms used to let you see. But you were being given no opportunity to even know what you were not being allowed to see. Thousands of channels full of information have now been removed, and you have no clue what ideas and information you will never be aware of. We have to keep the perspective that this is both a major change and a major problem. This is not normal. In my lifetime, I have never before seen censorship of public discourse in America, censorship of movies, channels, books, and even public conversations on a mass scale. This is not something that was supposed to be possible in this country. This is something or someone keeping you stupid, uninformed, compliant, in and out of the loop in your little censored social media bubble where you are spoon-fed narratives of the mega corporations that control your media and thereby control you.

We owe a lot to the people who find and share high value information. You might know something interesting about Bill Gates thanks to James Corbett, you might know some things about vaccinations thanks to Del Bigtree and Robert Kennedy Jr., you might know some things about mass surveillance thanks to Edward Snowden, you might know some things about the Rothschild family thanks to Aaron Russo, you might know something about 9/11 thanks to Richard Gage, you might know something about government finance thanks to Catherine Austin Fitz and Mark Skidmore. All of those people and those topics are being censored, banned, and suppressed. You are now supposed to forget all those things and pretend you never heard them. We are now being told to live in a pretend world where government and corporations are always good and right and anyone who disagrees is crazy and wrong.

If you search for a taboo topic, like vaccine hazards, you will see that on Google all the search results will be pro-vaccine or they will downplay the risks. You will see no search results for what you actually searched for - vaccine hazards - of which there are many, but on Google there are very few. So when you do a Google search for some banned topic you not only don't get the information, you are swamped with a load of propaganda, lies, and diversion in your search results. Google is not just censoring - it is making itself useless and irrelevant. You can be a valuable public service or you can be an ideological advocate, but you cannot be both for very long. While we try to scrape together some truth from what is left of our media, it is sometimes easy to forget that censorship has already run ahead of us. The information is gone. It is very hard to see this as it happens. To get around this problem, we will have to take a very different approach to how we get and share information. We will have to do this in new and creative ways that outsmart the censorship. We will have to develop ways to completely bypass mainstream platforms and create our own decentralized networks. We will have to develop trust with our network contacts and have a healthy scepticism for those who insist on promoting institutional mainstream narratives.

I know many of us are doing this already, but it has to go up a notch. We will have to reject and isolate people who attack us for being outside the mainstream. Our small decentralized networks that consist of maybe only a few members in each will naturally connect with each other and become a mesh network on a larger and larger scale, until that mesh network grows to national and international scales and becomes unstoppable by any centralized campaign of censorship. As long as we put a value on true and independent information - that information will find its way to and through us.

Those who do not support free thought and open conversations will become brainwashed, controlled, and owned by big media, big corporations, big government as we have already seen happen. As we find ways to bypass Google, YouTube, Facebook, and all the censored platforms, we may have to limit videos to one or two minutes and lower the screen resolution so we can host them on our own computers and transfer them easily. We may have to help each other learn how to exploit and use the dark web and alternative technologies. We will have to find ways to make it work because the sensors are upping their game 24/7. Decentralization is the key. There's no other way to preserve the integrity of the network and protect the flow of information than by decentralization. Each of us only has to share with a handful of other people, and that network will expand and grow on an unlimited scale if enough people realize that it is the only remaining way to get good information. But we will have to focus on the quality, the clarity, conciseness, and relevance of the information we share. We'll have to stop attacking each other, blowing hot air, and wasting each other's time. Those few people you trust and with whom you share critical information can be called your PDN which stands for Popular Decentralized Network, a fully open source concept with no central administration of any kind. This is the network that we already use when we communicate directly with people we know and trust, but this can be expanded if we want to be consciously doing something to defeat censorship and disinformation. The PDN will have no choke points, no constant form, no central point of authority, and no shape or structure: It will change whenever or however it needs to keep information flowing.

The PDN is any place where censorship is not working and truth can be found. When we see a problem with trolls or shills we can simply drop that node and create others. This is the way we fill the censorship void with a durable alternative that we control. Please share the idea of PDN. If you like official narratives and don't believe in conspiracies this is not for you. This is for people who know conspiracies exist, who know there are bad people doing bad things, who know that we need to know about these things or we will be hurt. When you tell someone that they are on your PDN, you are telling them that they are trusted and they are part of a global system of free thought and information. In the near future that PDN may be the only place left where we will be able to share and find free thought and current high-value information.

Jerry Day originally published, "Censorship and the PDN - Can You Handle The Truth?" on YouTube in September 2020. Transcribed by Caroline Cheruiyot.

Does The United States Still Exist?

Paul Craig Roberts

An address delivered to the Libertarian Party of Florida on March 23, 2016 in Destin, Florida

To answer the question that is the title, we have to know of what the US consists. Is it an ethnic group, a collection of buildings and resources, a land mass with boundaries, or is it the Constitution. Clearly what differentiates the US from other countries is the US Constitution. The Constitution defines us as a people. Without the Constitution we would be a different country. Therefore, to lose the Constitution is to lose the country.

Does the Constitution still exist? Let us examine the document and come to a conclusion.

The Constitution consists of a description of a republic with three independent branches, legislative, executive, and judicial, each with its own powers, and the Bill of Rights incorporated as constitutional amendments. The Bill of Rights describes the civil liberties of citizens that cannot be violated by the government.

Article I of the Constitution describes legislative powers. Article II describes executive powers, and Article III describes the power of the judiciary. For example, Article I, Section 1 gives all legislative powers to Congress. Article I, Section 8 gives Congress the power to declare war.

The Bill of Rights protects citizens from the government by making law a shield of the people rather than a weapon in the hands of the government.

The First Amendment protects the freedom of speech, the press, and assembly or public protest.

The Second Amendment gives the people the right "to keep and bear arms."

The Third Amendment has to do with quartering of soldiers on civilians, a large complaint against King George III, but not a practice of present-day armies.

The Fourth Amendment grants "the right of the people to be secure in their persons, houses, papers, and effects, against unreasonable searches and seizures" and prevents the issue of warrants except "upon probable cause, supported by oath or affirmation, and particularly describing the place to be searched, and the persons or things to be seized." The Fourth Amendment prevents police and prosecutors from going on "fishing expeditions" in an effort to find some offense with which to charge a targeted individual.

The Fifth Amendment prohibits double jeopardy, self-incrimination, the taking of life, liberty, or property without due process and the prohibition of seizing property without just compensation.

The Sixth Amendment guarantees speedy and public trial, requires that a defendant be informed of the charge against him and to be confronted with the witnesses, to present witnesses in his favor, and to have the assistance of an attorney.

The Seventh Amendment gives the right of trial by jury to civil suits.

The Eighth Amendment prevents excessive bail and cruel and unusual punishments.

The Ninth Amendment says that the enumeration of certain rights in the Constitution does not deny or disparage others retained by the people. In other words, people have rights in addition to the those listed in the proscriptions against the government's use of abusive power.

The Tenth Amendment reserves the rights not delegated to the federal government to the states.

The Tenth Amendment is a dead letter amendment. The Third Amendment protects against an abandoned abusive practice of government. The Seventh Amendment is still relevant as it allows damages in civil suits to be determined by a jury, once a protection against unfairness and today not always the case.

The other seven amendments comprise the major protections of civil liberty. I will examine them in turn, but first let's look at Section 1 and Section 8 of Article I. These two articles describe the major powers of Congress, and both articles have been breached. The Constitution's grant of "all legislative powers" to Congress has been overturned by executive orders and signing statements. The president can use executive orders to legislate, and he can use signing statements to render sections of laws passed by Congress and signed by the president into non-enforced status. Legislative authority has also been lost by delegating to executive branch officials the power to write the regulations that implement the laws that are passed. The right that Section 8 gives to Congress to declare war has been usurped by the executive branch. Thus, major powers given to Congress have been lost to the executive branch.

The First Amendment has been compromised by executive branch claims of "national security" and by extensive classification. Whistleblowers are relentlessly prosecuted despite federal laws protecting them. The right of assembly and public protest are overturned by arrests, tear gas, clubs, rubber bullets, water cannons, and jail terms. Free speech is also limited by political correctness and taboo topics. Dissent shows signs of gradually becoming criminalized.

The Fourth Amendment is a dead letter amendment. In its place we have warrantless searches, SWAT team home invasions, strip and cavity searches, warrantless seizures of computers and cell phones, and the loss of all privacy to warrantless universal spying.

The Fifth Amendment is a dead letter amendment. The criminal justice system relies on self-incrimination as plea bargains are self-incrimination produced by psychological torture, and plea bargains are the basis of conviction in 97% of all felony cases. Moreover, physical torture is a feature of the "war on terror" despite its illegality under both US statute and international law and is also experienced by inmates in the US prison system.

The Fifth Amendment's protection against deprivation of life, liberty, and property without due process of law has been lost to indefinite detention, executive assassination, and property takings without compensation. The Racketeer Influenced Corrupt Organizations Act (RICO) passed in 1970. The act permits asset freezes, which are takings. The Comprehensive Forfeiture Act passed in 1984 and permits police to confiscate property on "probable cause," which often means merely the presence of cash.

The Sixth Amendment is a dead letter amendment. Prosecutors routinely withhold exculpatory evidence, and judges at prosecutors' requests have limited attorneys' ability to defend clients. The "war on terror" has introduced secret evidence and secret witnesses, making it impossible for a defendant and his attorney to defend against the evidence.

The Eighth Amendment's prohibition of excessive bail and torture are routinely violated. It is another dead letter amendment.

It is paradoxical that every civil liberty in the Bill of Rights has been lost to a police state except for the Second Amendment, the gun rights of citizens. An armed citizenry is inconsistent with a police state, which the US now is.

Other aspects of our legal protections have been overturned, such as the long standing rule that crime requires intent. William Blackstone wrote: "An unwarrantable act without a vicious will is no crime at all." But today we have crimes without intent. You can commit a crime and not even know it. See for example, Harvey Silverglate, Three Felonies A Day: How the Feds Target the Innocent.

Attorney-client privilege has been lost. The indictment, prosecution, and imprisonment of defense attorney Lynne Stewart is a good example. The DOJ prevailed on her to defend a blind Muslim regarded by the DOJ as a "terrorist." She was informed that "special administrative measures" had been applied to her client. She received a letter from the federal prosecutor informing her that she and her client would not be permitted attorney-client privilege, and that she was required to permit the government to listen to her conversations with her client. She was told that she could not carry any communications from her client to the outside world. She regarded all this as illegal nonsense and proceeded to defend her client in accordance with attorney-client privilege. Lynne Stewart was convicted of violating a letter written by a prosecutor as if the prosecutor's letter were a law passed by Congress and present in the US code. Based on a prosecutor's letter, Lynne Stewart was sentenced to prison. No law exists that upholds her imprisonment.

Our civil liberties are often said to be "natural rights" to which we are entitled. However, in historical fact civil liberty is a human achievement that required centuries of struggle. The long struggle for accountable law that culminated in the Glorious Revolution in England in the late 17th century can be traced back to Alfred the Great's codification of English common law in the 9th century and to the Magna Carta in the early 13th century. Instead of issuing kingly edicts, Alfred based law on the traditional customs and behavior of the people. The Glorious Revolution established the supremacy of the people over the law and held the king and government accountable to law. The United States and other former British colonies inherited this accomplishment, an accomplishment that makes law a shield of the people and not a weapon in the hands of the state.

Today law as a shield of the people has been lost. The loss was gradual over time and culminated in the George W. Bush and Obama regime assaults on habeas corpus and due process. Lawrence Stratton and I explain how the law was lost in our book, The Tyranny of Good Intentions. Beginning with Jeremy Bentham in the late 18th century, liberals saw the protective shield of law as a constraint on the government's ability to do good. Bentham redefined liberty as the freedom of government from restraint, not the freedom of people from government. Bentham's influence grew over time until in our own day, to use the words of Sir Thomas More in A man for All Seasons, the law was cut down so as to better chase after devils.

We cut down the law so that we could better chase after the Mafia.
We cut down the law so that we could better chase after drug users.
We cut down the law so that we could better chase after child abusers.
We cut down the law so that we could better chase after "terrorists."
We cut down the law so that we could better chase after whistleblowers.
We cut down the law so that we could better cover up the government's crimes.

Today the law is cut down. Any one of us can be arrested on bogus charges and be helpless to do anything about it.

There is very little concern in legal circles about this. The American Civil Liberties Union (ACLU) does attempt to defend civil liberty. However, just as often the ACLU is not defending the civil liberties in the Bill of Rights that protect us from the abuse of government power, but newly invented "civil rights" that are not in the Constitution, such as "abortion rights," the right to homosexual marriage, and rights to preferential treatment for preferred minorities.

An attack on abortion rights, for example, produces a far greater outcry and resistance than the successful attack on habeas corpus and due process. President Obama was able to declare his power to execute citizens by executive branch decision alone without due process and conviction in court, and it produced barely audible protest.

Historically, a government that can, without due process, throw a citizen into a dungeon or summarily execute him is considered to be a tyranny, not a democracy. By any historical definition, the United States today is a tyranny.

Originally published as "Does The United States Still Exist?" www.paulcraigroberts.org, March, 2016.

Will Human Evil Destroy Life On Earth?

Paul Craig Roberts

The World Wildlife Fund tells us that there are only 3,890 tigers left in the entire world. Due to exploitative capitalism, which destroys the environment in behalf of short-term profits, the habitat for tigers is rapidly disappearing. The environmental destruction, together with hunting or poaching by those who regard it as manly or profitable to kill a magnificent animal, is leading to the rapid extermination of this beautiful animal. Soon tigers will only exist as exhibits in zoos.

The same is happening to lions, cheetahs, leopards, rhinos, elephants, bobcats, wolves, bears, birds, butterflies, honey bees. You name it.

What we are witnessing is the irresponsibility of the human race, a Satan-cursed form of life that does not belong on the beautiful planet Earth. The cursed humans are even capable of launching a nuclear war which would destroy the livability of Earth.

God made a mistake when he gave to humans, infected as they are with evil, jurisdiction over Earth. He should have given jurisdiction to animals. Consider what humans do to animals. For example, Defenders of Wildlife report that the corrupt state of Alaska is currently slaughtering wolves and grizzly bears so that the state can sell more hunting permits to hunters to slaughter moose. Every moose taken by a wolf pack or a grizzly is not there to be murdered by a hunter. So the state is killing off the predators that reduce its hunting license fees.

Quail hunters want the bobcats killed so that hunters can shoot more birds. The New Hampshire Fish and Game Department voted to establish a hunting and trapping season for bobcats but had to overturn its decision when it became clear that the endangered lynx would be caught in the same traps. Humans regard animals as worthy of protection only when they are on the verge of extinction.

Murder and death appeal to Americans and not only to hunters. How many Americans do you know who are distressed by their government's murder, maiming, and dislocation of millions of Muslims in seven countries over the past 15 years?

A few years ago there was a scandal involving a NBA star who was a patron of dog fights in which Americans brought dogs to kill or be killed. Americans attend cockfights in which roosters kill or die. The British enjoyed fights to the death between bears and dogs and bred a special dog to fight the bears. The Spanish like to see the death of the bull or of the bullfighter. The blood sport of the Roman Colosseum is very much a part of the human race.

Badly raised little boys tie cans to the tails of dogs and cats and laugh as the terrified animals run, often to their death under the wheels of cars.

Sometimes I go to a gun club with a friend to shoot at paper targets. On one occasion our concentration was disturbed by bursts from a super weapon. I watched the person flinch each time he shot. I suggested that he needed a less powerful weapon with which to practice.

If only, he said. His son had gone to Africa and paid $25,000 to murder a lion. The son had pressured the father to live up to his feat, and the father was adding bruises to his shoulder every time he fired a round of the .375 H&H Magnum. He began to flinch when he pulled the trigger, and his aim was worse by the shot.

He said that he was trying to sight-in the rifle. I offered to do that for him so that the rest of us could go about our business of eye-hand coordination. Observing our disapproving looks, he blurted out that he didn't really want to shoot a lion, but that his friends and his son were enculturated into a hunting culture in which killing animals was proof of manhood. He felt that he had to do it in order to be accepted.

Then he described the process by which the great lion hunter killed the dangerous beast.

First, he said, you shoot a hippo. Then parts of the dead animal are hung as bait on posts a mere 60 yards from a 20-foot high platform where there are gun rests in the event you are unable to shoulder your own rifle for a shot at such a large animal as a lion a mere 60 yards away. And if you miss, the Great White Hunter guide shoots and you can claim the victory over the dangerous beast.

I remarked that he didn't seem inclined to participate in this fake hunting scenario. He said that he wasn't but that he had paid his $25,000. I suggested that he cancel the trip and consider the 25K as the cost of avoiding the shame of participating in cowardly murder.

Elephants are magnificent creatures. Their intelligence is higher than many humans, and their life span, if they are not murdered, can be longer than the human life span. Yet elephants are being murdered at astonishing rates. Nick Brandt documents with his photographs, Across The Ravaged Land, the disappearing animals of East Africa.

The Guardian, a once strong but today weak and Washington-intimidated UK newspaper, reports that in 2014, 20,000 African Elephants were killed by poachers. Tanzania and Mozambique have lost over half of their elephant populations with the same devastation of elephants across east and central Africa.

Faced with the extermination of elephants, what did the corrupt European Union do? The EU refused a ban on Ivory trade! The ban might interfere with capitalist profits.

Free market ideologues have concocted a theory that the way to save animals is to make it profitable to kill them. Therefore, people raise the animals to be killed by hunters. In other words, animals only exist for the pleasure of humans to kill them. https://www.theguardian.com/environment/2016/jul/06/african-wildlife-officials-appalled-as-eu-opposes-a-total-ban-on-ivory-trade

What we are left with is a "western civilization" that is no longer a civilization but an existential threat to all life on Earth. Obama has announced a one trillion dollar US nuclear modernization program. This huge sum, spent for death, could instead be spent for life. It is enough money to fund many large and well protected wildlife preserves around the world. http://billmoyers.com/story/the-trillion-dollar-question-the-media-have-neglected-to-ask-presidential-candidates/

The evil represented by nuclear weapons is inconsistent with the continued existence of life on Earth. Washington, crazed by desire for hegemony over others, is recklessly courting war between nuclear powers. Only Putin among world leaders warns that Washington is setting an unpromising course for everyone.

Yet regardless of all fact, deluded Americans still regard themselves as the salt of the earth, the "exceptional people," the "indispensable people." If this delusion is incurable, humans will murder Earth.

Originally published as "Will Human Evil Destroy Life On Earth?" www.paulcraigroberts.org, August, 2016.

Where Did My World Go?

Paul Craig Roberts

I remember when there was no tamper-proof and child-proof packaging. That was before multiculturalism and Identity Politics when we could still trust one another and parents accepted responsibility for their children without fobbing it off on a company with a liability claim.

I remember also when there were no state income and sales taxes. States were able to meet their responsibilities without them.

A postage stamp cost one cent. A middle class house was $11,000 and an upper middle class house went for $20,000. One million dollars was a large fortune. There were no billionaires.

The air museum on the naval base in Pensacola, Florida, has a street reconstructed from the 1940s. The restaurant's menu offers a complete evening meal for 69 cents.

I was thinking about that as I reviewed a recent Publix supermarket bill: a loaf of bread $3.89, a dozen organic eggs $4.95, a package of 6 hot dogs $5.49, 8 small tomatoes $5.19, a package of baby spinach $4.19, a half-gallon of milk $4.59, a package of two paper towel rolls $5.99.
When I was 5 or 6 years old, my mother would send me to the bakery with a dime for a loaf of bread or to the market with 11 cents for a quart of milk. The Saturday afternoon double-feature at the movie house was 10 cents. A case of Coca-Colas (24 bottles) was one dollar. Ten cents would get you a Pepsi Cola and a Moon Pie, lunch for construction crews. Kids would look for discarded Pepsi Cola bottles on construction sites. In those days there was a two cent deposit on soft drink bottles. One

bottle was worth 4 pieces of Double Bubble gum. Five bottles paid for the Saturday double-feature.

Dimes, quarters, and half dollars were silver, and there were silver dollars. The nickel (five cent coin) was nickel, and the penny was copper. FDR took gold away in 1933. The silver coins disappeared in 1965. Our last commodity money, the copper penny, met its demise in 1983. Now they are talking about getting rid of the penny altogether.

Many of us grew up with paper routes for spending money. Other than a paper route, my first employment was the high school summer when I worked the first shift in a cotton mill for $1 an hour. And work it was. After the withholding tax my take-home pay for the 40 hour week was $33.

When I was five years old, I could walk safely one mile to school and home by myself without my parents being arrested by Child Protective Services for child neglect and endangerment.

In school we could draw pictures of fighter planes, warships, and guns without being regarded as a danger to our classmates and sent for psychiatric evaluation. Fights were just a part of growing up. The police weren't called, and we weren't handcuffed and carted off to jail. Today kids who play cops and robbers or cowboys and Indians and point fingers at one another as pretend guns end up in police custody. A fight means an assault charge and possibly a felony record.

The kind of freedom I had as a child no longer exists except in remote rural areas. When I think about this I wonder if kids today even notice. They live in the virtual world of the video screen and do not know the real world. Catching crawfish in the creek while watching out for cottonmouth moccasins, playing capture the flag over acres of expanse without getting a bad case of poison ivy, organizing a neighborhood ball game, damning up a creek and making a swimming hole. Today these are unknown pleasures.

When it rained we read books. I remember reading Robert Heinlein's Puppet Masters when I was 12 years old. Do 12 year olds read books today? Can science fiction compete with video games?

I remember when a deal rested on a handshake. Today lawyers tell me even contracts are unenforceable.

We were taught to behave properly so that "you can look yourself in the mirror." Today you can't look yourself in the mirror unless you have upstaged or ripped off someone. Character is a thing of the past, as are habits that are today regarded as inappropriate. An older person hoping to get a point across to a younger one would put his or her hand on the younger person's arm or thigh for attention purposes. Do this today and you get a sexual charge. Both of my grandmothers would probably be locked up as sexual offenders.

Being a tattle-tale was an undesirable and discouraged trait. Today we are encouraged to be tattle-tales. You will hear the encouragement several dozen times while awaiting your flight to be called. Neighbors on quiet cul-de-sacs will call Child Protective Services to report one another's unsupervised children at play.

I remember when black Americans said they just wanted to be treated like everyone else. That was before racial set-asides in federal government contracts that only black-owned firms can bid on. Once you have special privileges, you don't want to be like everyone else. Blacks say being white is a privilege. If so, it wasn't enough privilege for Celeste Bennett's firm Ultima. Her white privilege and her gender privilege were trumped by black set-aside privilege.

If my parents and grandparents were to be resurrected, they would require a year's training before it would be safe for them to go about without being arrested. They would have to be educated out of their customary behavior patterns and taught the words and phrases that are today impermissible. They would have trouble comprehending that there are no-go areas in cities.

Reading Diana Johnstone's masterful book, Circle in the Darkness, I remembered the safety of my own youthful years as I read that as a 12 year old, she could walk alone around the wharfs of southwest Washington, D.C., in the 1940s, unmolested.

I received my new homeowner's policy yesterday. It arrived with 89 pages of warnings, definitions, and liability explanations. One can't really tell if one is insured or not.

I have a 54-year old Jaguar that I have had for 47 years. The owner's manual tells how to operate and repair the car. A friend showed me the owner's manual on his 21-year old Porsche. It has more pages of warnings to protect the manufacturer from liability claims than the Jaguar manual has pages of instruction. Today any tool or gadget you buy has more pages of warnings than instruction.

My AARP Medicare supplement insurance policy arrived explaining my meager and expensive covering. It came with a notice letting me know that language assistance services are available for the policy in Spanish, Vietnamese, Tagalog, Russian, Arabic, Haitian Creole, French, Polish, Portuguese, Italian, German, Japanese, Hmong, Llocano, Somali, Greek, Gujarati, and that there is no discrimination because of sex, age, race, color, disability or national origin. The notice provides access to a Civil Rights Coordinator in the event I feel discriminated against. AARP even provides a number to call for help with filing a discrimination complaint.

I do feel discriminated against. But it is not a covered discrimination. I feel like my country has been stolen or that I have been kidnapped and placed in some foreign unknown place that I don't recognize as home.

I feel the same when I get fundraising appeals from Georgia Tech and Oxford University. Georgia Tech was an all-male school consisting primarily of in-state Georgia boys. The Oxford colleges were segregated according to gender—male and female—and the vast majority of the members were British.

Today all the colleges except the women's are gender integrated. White males seldom appear in the photos in the fundraising materials that arrive from Oxford and Georgia Tech. I see lots of women and racial diversity and wonder what university it is. An improvement or not, they are not the schools of which I have memories. The schools I knew have simply been taken away. Something else is there now.

Perhaps it has always been true, but today if you live very long you outlive your world. As your friends die off, no one remembers it correctly but you as you watch your world disappear in misrepresentations to serve present day agendas.

Originally published as "Where Did My World Go," www.paulcraigroberts.org, May 2020.

Hillary's War Crime

Paul Craig Roberts

Today, October 20, 2016, is the fifth anniversary of the murder of Muammar Gaddafi by forces organized and unleashed by US President Obama and Secretary of State Hillary Clinton. Remember the killer bitch's performance, with gleeful laughter, on CBS "News": "We came, we saw, he died [1]."

Muammar Gaddafi was the most progressive political leader in the world. Gaddafi used Libya's oil wealth for the benefit of the Libyan people. He lived in a tent, a nice tent, but not in a palace, and he did not have collections of European exotic cars or any of the other paraphernalia associated with the ruling families in Saudi Arabia and the oil emirates that are Washington's Middle Eastern allies.

In Libya, education, medical treatment, and electricity were free. Gasoline was practically free, selling for 14 US cents per litre. Women who gave birth were supported with cash grants and couples received cash grants upon marriage. Libya's state bank provided loans without interest and provided free startup capital to farmers [2].

Gaddafi's independence from Washington is what brought him down. Earlier in life Gaddafi's goal was to organize Arabs as a bloc that could withstand Western depredations. Frustrated, he turned to Pan-Africanism and refused to join the US Africa Command. He wanted to introduce a gold-based African currency that would free Africans from American financial hegemony.

Gaddafi had Chinese energy companies developing Libya's energy resources. Washington, already upset with Russian presence in the Mediterranean, was now faced with Chinese presence as well. Washington concluded that Gaddafi was playing ball with the wrong people and that he had to go.

Washington organized mercenaries, termed them "rebels" as in Syria, and siced them on Libya. When it became clear that Gaddafi's forces would prevail, Washington tricked naive and gullible Russian and Chinese governments and secured a UN no-fly zone over Libya to be enforced by NATO. The express purpose of the no-fly zone was to prevent Gaddafi from attacking civilian targets, which he was not doing. The real reason was to prevent a sovereign state from using its own air space so that the Libyan Air Force could not support the troops on the ground. Once the gullible Russians and Chinese failed to veto the Security Council's action, the US and NATO themselves violated the resolution by using Western air power to attack Gaddafi's forces, thus throwing the conflict to the CIA-organized mercenaries. Gaddafi was captured and brutally murdered. Ever since, Libya, formerly a prosperous and successful society, has been in chaos, which is where the Obama regime wanted it.

All sorts of lies were told about Gaddafi and Libya, just as lies were told about Saddam Hussein and are told today about Syria and Russia. A British Parliamentary Report concluded unambiguously that the Western peoples were fed lies by their governments in order to gain acceptance for the destruction of Libya, and that Libya was destroyed because Gaddafi was regarded as an obstacle to Western hegemony [3].

Note that none of the presstitutes have asked the killer bitch about her guilt under the Nuremburg laws for this war crime prepared on her watch. Note that the oligarchs who own the killer bitch and their press prostitutes intend to make this war criminal the next president of the United States.

Originally published as "Hillary's War Crime," www.paulcraigroberts.org, October 2016.

References

[1]. https://www.youtube.com/watch?v=Fgcd1ghag5Y
[2]. http://www.globalresearch.ca/libya-ten-things-about-gaddafi-they-dont-want-you-to-know/5414289
[3]. http://www.globalresearch.ca/libya-war-was-based-on-lies-bogus-intelligence-nato-supported-and-armed-the-rebels-british-parliamentary-report/5547356?utm_campaign=magnet&utm_source=article_page&utm_medium=related_articles

Conspiracy Theory

Paul Craig Roberts

In the United States "conspiracy theory" is the name given to explanations that differ from those that serve the ruling oligarchy, the establishment or whatever we want to call those who set and control the agendas and the explanations that support the agendas.

The explanations imposed on us by the ruling class are themselves conspiracy theories. Moreover, they are conspiracy theories designed to hide the real conspiracy that our rulers are operating.

For example, the official explanation of 9/11 is a conspiracy theory. Some Muslims, mainly Saudi Arabians, delivered the greatest humiliation to a superpower since David slew Goliath. They outsmarted all 17 US intelligence agencies and those of NATO and Israel, the National Security Council, the Transportation Safety Administration, Air Traffic Control, and Dick Cheney, hijacked four US airliners on one morning, brought down three World Trade Center skyscrapers, destroyed that part of the Pentagon where research was underway into the missing $2.3 trillion, and caused the morons in Washington to blame Afghanistan instead of Saudi Arabia.

Clearly, the Saudi Arabians who humiliated America were involved in a conspiracy to do so.

Is it a believable conspiracy?

The ability of a few young Muslim men to pull off such a feat is unbelievable. Such total failure of the US National Security State means that America was blindly vulnerable throughout the decades of Cold War with the Soviet Union. If such total failure of the National Security State had really occurred, the White

House and Congress would have been screaming for an investigation. People would have been held accountable for the long chain of security failures that allowed the plot to succeed. Instead, no one was even reprimanded, and the White House resisted all efforts for an investigation for a year. Finally, to shut up the 9/11 families, a 9/11 Commission was convened. The commission duly wrote down the government's story and that was the "investigation."

Moreover, there is no evidence to support the official conspiracy theory of 9/11. Indeed, all known evidence contradicts the official conspiracy theory.

For example, it is a proven fact that Building 7 came down at free-fall acceleration, which means it was wired for demolition. Why was it wired for demolition? There is no official answer to this question.

It is the known evidence provided by scientists, architects, engineers, pilots, and the first responders who were in the twin towers and personally experienced the numerous explosions that brought down the towers that is described as a conspiracy theory.

The CIA introduced the term "conspiracy theory" into public discourse as part of its action plan to discredit skeptics of the Warren Commission report on the assassination of President John F. Kennedy. Any explanation other than the one handed down, which is contradicted by all known evidence, was debunked as a conspiracy theory.

Conspiracy theories are the backbone of US foreign policy. For example, the George W. Bush regime was active in a conspiracy against Iraq and Saddam Hussein. The Bush regime created fake evidence of Iraqi "weapons of mass destruction," sold the false story to a gullible world and used it to destroy Iraq and murder its leader. Similarly, Gaddafi was a victim of an Obama/Hillary conspiracy to destroy Libya and murder Gaddafi. Assad of Syria and Iran were slated for the same treatment until the Russians intervened.

Currently, Washington is engaged in conspiracies against Russia, China, and Venezuela. Proclaiming a non-existent "Iranian threat," Washington put US missiles on Russia's border and used the "North Korean threat" to put missiles on China's border. The democratically elected leader of Venezuela is said by Washington to be a dictator, and sanctions have been put on Venezuela to help the small Spanish elite through whom Washington has traditionally ruled South American countries pull off a coup and reestablish US control over Venezuela.

Everyone is a threat: Venezuela, Yemen, Syria, Iran, Iraq, Afghanistan, tribes in Pakistan, Libya, Russia, China, North Korea, but never Washington. The greatest conspiracy theory of our time is that Americans are surrounded by foreign threats. We are not even safe from Venezuela.

The New York Times, the Washington Post, CNN, NPR, and the rest of the presstitutes are quick to debunk as conspiracy theories all explanations that differ from the explanations of the ruling interests that the presstitutes serve.

Yet, as I write and for some nine months to date, the presstitute media has itself been promoting the conspiracy theory that Donald Trump was involved in a conspiracy with the president of Russia and Russian intelligence services to hack the US presidential election and place Trump, a Russian agent, in the White House.

This conspiracy theory has no evidence whatsoever. It doesn't need evidence, because it serves the interests of the military/security complex, the Democratic Party, the neoconservatives, and permits the presstitutes to show lavish devotion to their masters. By endless repetition a lie becomes truth.

There is a conspiracy, and it is against the American people. Their jobs have been offshored in order to enrich the already rich. They have been forced into debt in a futile effort to maintain their living standards. Their effort to stem their decline by electing a president who spoke for them is being subverted before their eyes by an utterly corrupt media and ruling class.

Sooner or later it will dawn on them that there is nothing they can do but violently revolt. Most likely, by the time they reach this conclusion it will be too late. Americans are very slow to escape from the false reality in which they live. Americans are a thoroughly brainwashed people who hold tightly to their false life within The Matrix.

For the gullible and naive who have been brainwashed into believing that any explanation that differs from the officially-blessed one is a conspiracy theory, there are available online long lists of government conspiracies that succeeded in deceiving the people in order that the governments could achieve agendas that the people would have rejected.

If liberty continues to exist on earth, it will not be in the Western world. It will be in Russia and China, countries that emerged out of the opposite and know the value of liberty, and it will be in those South American countries, such as Venezuela, Ecuador, and Bolivia that fight for their sovereignty against American oppression.

Indeed, as historians unconcerned with their careers are beginning to write, the primary lesson in history is that governments deceive their peoples.

Everywhere in the Western world, government is a conspiracy against the people.

Originally published as "Conspiracy Theory," www.paulcraigroberts.org, August 2017.

Las Vegas Shooting

Paul Craig Roberts

Dear Readers, I appreciate the confidence that you show in me with your emails asking my opinion about the Las Vegas shooting. Many of you suspect that it is another false flag affair, and you ask me about its purpose.

I don't know if it was a false flag attack, and if so, by whom or for what purpose. I don't expect to ever know. A story is set in place by officials and media. The only way to ever know is to personally investigate. You would have to go to Las Vegas, examine the scene, ask questions of the hotel, investigate the answers if you get any, find and interview concert attendees who were shot, attend funerals and see bodies of those killed, speak to their families, learn about the weapon allegedly used, experience trying to shoot at targets far below and far away, compare the number of casualties with the recorded time of firing, and so forth. In other words, we would have to do the job that in former times would have been done by the press, but no more.

It is almost like the story is being kept from us. For example, from media reports that the event was just across the street from the hotel, I did not know that "across the street" was a distance of 390 yards (1,170 feet).

As I don't expect to ever have a confident opinion about what happened, I am not paying much attention to the mass shooting, or should I say alleged shooting. We are lied to and deceived so much that we can never tell when we are told the truth. It is like Dmitry Orlov says:

"Lies beget other lies, and pretty soon unbiased intelligence-gathering, rational analysis and proper mission planning become impossible."

" … a reputation for telling the truth can only be lost exactly once, and from then on the use of the phrase 'US intelligence sources' became synonymous with 'a conspiracy of barefaced liars.'"

"Whatever message Washington and Western mass media are trying to push, a perfectly valid response is to point out all the times they have lied in the past, and to pose a simple question: When did they stop lying?"

Official explanations of such events as Las Vegas, Sandy Hook, and so forth, always throw up red flags, because the official explanations always studiously ignore contrary eyewitness and other evidence. Also, often there are not even smart phone videos of dead and wounded people. As far as I can tell, the bodies of 573 dead and wounded are absent in the Las Vegas video evidence. Considering the suspicion that such events cause, one would think the authorities would make a special effort to show the dead and wounded. In other cases of mayhem, alleged bodies look like dummies or are covered and could be a pile of anything. The presence of crisis actors on the scene, as in the Boston Marathon Bombing, raise more questions. I remember when it was expected that police and media would investigate all evidence and clear away contradictions. Now all we get is an official story instantly ready and repeated endlessly by officials and media. This itself raises suspicions.

You will have to make up your own minds about Las Vegas. Here are some of the reported facts to consider:

The victims killed and wounded total 573. That number is the size of a military battalion. It is very difficult to turn an entire battalion into casualties with small arms fire even in a fierce combat situation. I don't know if it has ever happened. Can one person with no military training shooting down from 32 stories, which requires special sighting knowledge, at a distance of 390 yards—the length of 4 football fields—hit 573 people in a few minutes of firing? Jon Rappoport doesn't believe it [1]. Neither does the progressive Steve Lendman [2-3].

There are reports of multiple shooters. There are reports of gun flashes from the 4th floor. The windows on the hotel do not open and would require the glass to be broken. Stephen Paddock doesn't fit the profile of a psychopath. Reports are he was a multimillionaire with airplanes and his own pilot. He enjoyed life. His brother is dumbfounded, said it makes no sense Stephen did the shooting. The Mandalay Bay Hotel is reportedly a casino. If so, security cameras are everywhere. Why no videos of Stephen Paddock carrying in the many cases of 23 firearms and ammunition? How could maid service clean the room for three days and not see 23 firearms and their ammunition? Makes no sense.

Why 23 guns? The number is beyond superfluous. The large number almost suggests that the entire event is concocted as a gun control incident. The huge number of guns, the huge number of casualties. Finally, at last, enough "gun violence" to get gun control.

Skeptics are waiting to hear from the authorities how a person at such a distance managed to shoot so many people in such a short time and with what automatic rifle and caliber the deed was done. As this part of the story is especially difficult to believe, we will probably not get the explanation.

And it is not only the authorities and the presstitutes that truth is up against. There is also the lack of integrity in people with axes to grind. For example, Paul Street writing in CounterPunch says: "The Las Vegas massacre is just the latest in the Gun Lobby's long line of terrorist attacks on U.S. soil." The article is titled: "The NRA's Latest Terrorist Attack on U.S. Soil." You can read it here [4].

The gun control lobby has a massive vested interest in the official story. You can bet your life that the gun control lobby will ignore any and all problems associated with the official story. The story is exactly what they want in order to advance their cause. The campaign is underway [5].

As Paddock is a rich white male, the story also fits with Identity Politics. Paddock is another example of the evil white male. Here is the Identity Politics connection served up by the Washington Post: "All across America white men, some young, some of middle-age, are turning into wolves. Always, after they commit acts of terror, it is revealed out that these perpetrators were not men after all. They were beasts, mindless monsters whose evil was abstract and cold and terrible [6]." CNN says mass shootings are "a white man's problem." See "How America has silently accepted the Rage of White Men [7]."

People are more interested in confirming their beliefs and prejudices than they are in the truth. If Paddock were a Muslim, Islamophobic people would cling to the official account. Truth requires that people believe in truth more than they believe in their own biases and causes. In the United States, such people are increasingly rare.

Remember always the Roman question: "Who benefits?" That is where you will find the answer.

UPDATE: Paddock's girlfriend describes him as a "kind, caring, quiet" man who she envisioned a "quiet future" with. A woman knows a man. Her description is not one of a psychopath.

I have spoken to more experienced persons and experts including US Marine snipers. They don't believe a word of the official story. Will, once again, the experts be got rid of by branding them "conspiracy theorists" as was done to 3,000 architects and engineers who challenge the official story of 9/11?

Originally published as "Las Vegas Shooting," www.paulcraigroberts.org, October 4, 2017.

References

[1]. https://jonrappoport.wordpress.com/2017/10/03/more-than-one-vegas-shooter-the-evidence-builds

[2]. http://stephenlendman.org/2017/10/slaughter-las-vegas

[3]. http://stephenlendman.org/2017/10/las-vegas-another-false-flag

[4]. https://www.counterpunch.org/2017/10/04/the-nras-latest-terrorist-attack-on-u-s-soil

[5]. https://www.washingtonpost.com/opinions/mass-shootings-are-an-american-problem-theres-an-american-solution/2017/10/02/ac934588-a7ac-11e7-850e-2bdd1236be5d_story.html?tid=ss_tw&utm_term=.dd026d728b4c

[6]. https://www.washingtonpost.com/blogs/compost/wp/2017/10/02/when-white-men-turn-into-lone-wolves/?utm_term=.3415987733a6

[7]. http://edition.cnn.com/2017/10/03/opinions/mass-shootings-white-male-rage-modan-opinion/index.html?iid=ob_lockedrail_topeditorial

Las Vegas Final Comment

Paul Craig Roberts

Dear Readers, some of you keep pushing me for an explanation of the Las Vegas event. I have no contacts with people who might be involved in US covert operations. Some of you think that since I "was there with Reagan," I know everything about what goes on in government. This is not the case for anyone in government.

Those of you who are so interested in Las Vegas must figure it out on your own. Keep in mind that there can be just as much fake news on the Internet as on CNN, etc.

I can offer some guidance as to the sort of things you could examine to help you to come to a conclusion. Unless normal police investigation was not undertaken, there will be crime scene photos that should show blood trails and blood pools. The kill area should coordinate with the alleged position of the shooter. Bullets that entered the ground should show the trajectory and direction that the bullet traveled.

If none of this evidence is available, turn to the available evidence. Do the videos of the people crouching and running show any one who is hit? Do you hear voices crying out, "I've been hit, help me!"? If not, why not? 573 casualties is a large number.

Consult medics on how the wounded are handled and compare what you learn with this video that purports to be a video of the wounded brought to a hospital [1].

Note the absence of medics and medical personnel. Note the incorrect ways that the alleged injured are being carried by people in street clothes who clearly are not professionals. Note the absence of blood. None on the stretchers, none on the victims, none on the people carrying the victims, none on the hospital floor. No signs of trauma.

Ask yourself how the injured came into the hands of concert goers who had fled the scene. Did concert goers return to the scene in order to recover the wounded? Why would they take this risk or be allowed to? It was an hour before police made it to the hotel room from which the shooting allegedly took place? Why would police, ambulances, medical personnel permit untrained people to handle the wounded?

I remember years ago that it became a personal liability matter for a good Samaritan to help an injured person. There were cases where people attempting to help someone injured in an accident or shooting who did not know how to recognize injuries and the correct procedures for moving an injured person actually brought about the paralysis or death of the person they were attempting to help. The alleged injured bodies in the video are being manhandled. If there were a bullet close to the spine, for example, the consequence could be paralysis. I really do not believe that ordinary people would be permitted to lug the injured into a hospital. The video looks to me like crisis actors participating in a drill. There are reports that there were advertisements for crisis actors for a Las Vegas drill prior to the event. And here is a report allegedly from the hospital chief saying that after the shooting or alleged shooting, the hospital activated a "mass casualty incident disaster drill [2]." If so, how did the hospital assemble the crisis actors so quickly?

Is the hospital chief's claim a way to explain away the absence of blood and inappropriate handling of the wounded by declaring it to be a drill, not evidence of the shooting? If so, then where is the evidence of injured people taken to hospital? Responsible public authorities aware of the public's growing suspicion and recourse to conspiracy theories would go out of their way to provide clear hard evidence to back the official story. With 573 casualties, there has to be an abundance of evidence. Where is it?

I cannot sort out these issues for you. I am far more concerned about the conflict with Russia, Iran, and China toward which the neoconservatives, the military/security complex, and the presstitutes are driving us. If such a conflict materializes, the casualties will be a million or many millions larger than the alleged 573 dead and wounded in Las Vegas. I wish I could get Americans as concerned about this as they are about Las Vegas.

Originally published as "Las Vegas Final Comment," www.paulcraigroberts.org, October 7, 2017.

References

[1]. https://www.youtube.com/watch?v=ki__BdeRIjc
[2]. https://www.intellihub.com/chief-m-d-vegas-hospital-says-mass-casualty-incident-disaster-drill-was-initiated-after-massacre-took-place/

Military Surgeon Says Videos of Las Vegas Gunshot Victims Are Fake

Paul Craig Roberts

It looks like readers are not going to let me let go of the Las Vegas shooting. Some tell me that it is my fault for having alerted them in previous articles to anomalies in other shootings and terrorist events, so now they are more skeptical and pay more attention. Others say that as I emphasize that this is their website supported with their money, I have to see this through to the end. They say it is a cop-out when I say that there are too many disparate accounts for us to know.

One reader made an excellent point. According to mainstream media reports, 59 people were immediately killed in the shooting and 527 were wounded. Among those 527 wounded, wouldn't some of them have died from complications, blood loss, trauma? How come none of the wounded, people allegedly hit with military rounds, succumbed?

I agree. This does seem to be inexplicable.

And then I received via email a letter that purports to be from a general surgeon who dealt with gunshot wounds in military hospitals. He links to a video of an operation on a real leg gunshot wound, its life threatening nature, and the incapacity that it inflicts for a long time even if the operation is successful. He compares this to the rosy-cheeked laughing alleged victims shown on YouTube with gunshot wounds in support of the official story and says without equivocation that they are actors, badly acting the part.

I appreciate the reader's point that none of the 527 wounded have died from the wounds. This is not what happens in reality. I am posting the letter below from the surgeon in the hopes that knowledgeable surgeons, military medics, anyone with knowledge of gunshot trauma will assess its truth and provide their name and credentials. Not being a military surgeon who has treated gunshot wounds, I cannot attest to the validly of the letter. But there are those who can. Retired surgeons and former military medics can still speak their minds. So let us hear from you. I will compile your comments and present them without your name.

As for my readers, this is the deal: If there are validated replies, I will provide a report, and that will be the conclusion of my participation in this issue. If there are no validated replies, I will conclude that no qualified people are willing to commit one way or the other on the issue. Without expert opinion, the matter cannot be resolved.

This is the letter from the person who represents himself as a surgeon familiar with gunshot trauma. It was sent to a person named Jack and forwarded to me. I eliminated "Jack" so that it would read to you simply as the expression of a purported trauma surgeon's opinion. Note also, that all of the fake videos of the wounded to which links are supplied have been removed from YouTube. Apparently, as people are catching on, the authorities are being more careful about their "fake news.

"As a patriotic American, I must say I was, like most people here, initially totally shocked by the Las Vegas shooting and I hate to admit naively believed the media. However, after receiving disturbing emails about it, with references to others with doubts, I began to look at the media reports with more suspicion, and from a medical point of view primarily the almost complete absence of blood on site from the around 550 victims apparently shot was an immediate give away.

"I am a retired general surgeon, and when younger served in a number of military hospitals in Asia and the Middle East, and I can assure you, few would have had such extensive experience in treating bullet wounds as I. Unless you've actually seen bullet wounds from a clinical perspective from high powered weapons they claim were used in the shooting, it is hard to appreciate the extent that the mainstream media are plainly lying.

"Most of these military style weapons now shoot high velocity bullets above 3000 f.p.s. muzzle velocity and when these bullets strike a human body they often cause the bullet to yaw (or tumble) and fragment into about a dozen pieces of various sizes thus creating wounds way out of proportion to the calibre size. Often these wounds are so devastating many have considered the modern M16 type assault rifle rounds (and other similar type of rounds) to be inhuman. Most media sources claim the victims were hit at a range of about 500 meters. To use the U.S military M16 assault rifle as an example. It uses 5.56 x 45 mm high velocity, flat trajectory cartridges giving it an effective range of about 200 meters, but with now more common M855 cartridges and heavier projectiles this is increased to 600 meters, with the bullet being lethal to over 3000 yards or 2700 meters. The M855 round produces massive wounding effects. After about 200 yards, as the velocity declines the projectile is less likely to fragment when it strikes the target, but it still does a huge amount of damage, way above wounds delivered from a regular hand gun for example.

"So with this knowledge in mind, I have now viewed most of the mainstream media reports on YouTube of the victims in hospital and I can assure you they are all actors and not one of these people is a legitimate patient. Being shot with a high-powered weapon and struck with a high velocity bullet is a very traumatic experience and indeed more patients routinely die from the trauma rather than the wound itself. Yet all these patients being interviewed in bed are not surrounded with emergency care diagnostic equipment at all, are looking completely normal, relaxed and comfortable. This is not how patients feel one or two days after being shot with a high-powered assault weapon I can assure you and even if it's only in the leg it is still serious. Here is a short YouTube video of what many typical gunshot wounds to the leg of a patient actually looks like: https://www.youtube.com/watch?v=7cDIjCwl3n0

"Here is possibly some of the greatest government/mainstream media/propaganda yet about the Las Vegas shooting, showing President Trump actually visiting a patient in a Las Vegas hospital who apparently was shot through the leg. I can assure you, if he had genuinely been shot through the leg with a high velocity bullet as they claim, he would not, so soon after the event, be able to stand up, neither would he have the desire to do so. This is a disgrace, and one finds it impossible to accept President Trump does not know it is all a completely staged event: https://www.youtube.com/watch?v=M0ucMWOatho

"Here are a couple more videos of these supposed victims in hospital that have been shot. Every one of them are not legitimate patients at all, but are plainly actors: https://www.youtube.com/watch?v=gySdhRhWGVE and https://www.youtube.com/watch?v=1_LFKvz3W2w

Note: in this video, the girl patients are almost uncontrollably laughing, knowing that they are lying. During one or two days after getting shot through the hip with a high powered assault weapon and after having been operated on, I can assure you no patient is ever laughing or looking like this!

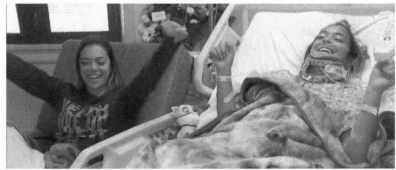

Still frame from video

"Lastly, in the past material has been 'censored' off the Internet, and in relation to this recent Las Vegas shooting, links have been blocked over the last 2 or 3 days as well. You might like to know that you are not on your own. Because both Facebook and YouTube are working together to censor everything they and the government doesn't like and don't want the public to know.

"YouTube has just changed its search algorithms from Thursday night 5th October 2017, to block and censor all the most persuasive videos making claims that the Las Vegas shooting event is a hoax, designing them conspiracy theories, especially videos exposing the crisis actors involved portraying themselves as victims in hospital. These are not wild allegations. It is from their own public admissions. Here is a report showing, 'YouTube takes action against offensive conspiracy videos that claim Las Vegas massacre was a hoax.' The arrogance of it all! This is the resurrection of Nazi Germany all over again.

"Therefore, my conclusion is that the whole event was staged, there were no real shooters at all, and probably even Stephen Paddock's brother is a crisis actor as well. When a handful of powerful wicked men like this control the banks, the global mainstream media and the government, no one can effectively now speak up to criticize, because when they do their words will never be published or heard. I think the real reason why they are using actors and staged events like this at this early stage, is that when they use real, bigger more serious events in the future, those patriots who have previously exposed these earlier events as not being real, will be made to appear stupid. Hopefully I have helped clarify this medical aspect at least.

Yours truly.
Dr K.S.
Florida.

https://www.youtube.com/watch?v=7cDIjCwl3n0
Gunshot Wound To The Leg Surgery At Shock Trauma
Surgery for a gunshot wound to the leg at the University of Maryland's Shock trauma Center."

This e-mail was sent from a contact form on
PaulCraigRoberts.org
(http://www.paulcraigroberts.org/contact/)

Originally published as "Military Surgeon Says Videos of Las
Vegas Gunshot Victims Are Fake," www.paulcraigroberts.org,
October 9, 2017.

UPDATE: This from a UK trauma surgeon

Paul Craig Roberts

I write in full agreement with my surgical colleague in Florida, Dr KS.

A retired orthopaedic and trauma surgeon who served in our NHS, I have not dealt with high velocity gunshot wounds but I have studied the terrible injuries in Palestinians in Gaza caused by every type of modern weapon – there are many thousands.

I have a forensic inclination and took a leading part in calling for an inquest into the unnatural death of Dr David Kelly in July 2003 and more recently into unexplained features in the death of Jo Cox MP.

I agree with KS that the demeanour of the 'patients' does not fit at all with alleged [high velocity] bullet injury. 'Ploughing' > destruction of soft tissue would be greater in some from ricochets which would have happened with most of the shots given the concrete plaza and the alleged thirty story origin. The removal of some of the You-tube videos speaks for itself and raises questions as to who is conducting this most evil orchestra [...]."

[...]

Another note:

regarding your readers... of course I don't know your readers, but I have no doubt that if anyone has a high-quality high-density readership that could, possibly, actually save humankind it is you and your readers. No doubt you don't enjoy hearing this, but this is why I write you (I don't write anybody else due to my MITRE background, previous security clearances, and awareness of the automated algorithms tracking everything happening on the internet — including my writing you).

To reviewing the letter: You know much of my background already, so I will just point out two specifics: 1) I worked at Walter Reed Army Medical Center from 1987 to 1990 first as a Medical Statistician for the Armed Forces Institute of Pathology then as the Chief of Clinical Investigations in the main hospital; 2) while at Booz Allen Hamilton I worked on a short project for the U.S. Army at Aberdeen Proving Grounds looking at the effects of projectiles and shrapnel on the human body.

I find myself agreeing with the content of the letter but haunted by the wording, flow, and style of the letter. It does not read like the writing of the medical doctors that I have worked with, including co-authored papers.

However, the author does not claim to be a research medical doctor, he presents as a practicing surgeon with field experience. This may well be true.

My ballistics project is in full agreement that the wounds would be much worse than something that could scab over in a week. If a single projectile hits a bone, the bone shatters (more like explodes) and the bone turns into shrapnel disintegrating the tissue in the trajectory's path.

As for exit wounds, remember what happened to Kennedy's head.

In general: Where are the body parts? Where is the blood? Where are the injured laying as everybody chaotically escapes? Where are the [empty] shells in the hotel room?

Regarding hospital video: I agree an ICU patient is not going to be laughing. I also point out that the people 'milling' around don't seem concerned on the status of anybody. They seem to be putting in their time — much as a job. I can also point out that there is a sense of urgency in a trauma center when there is a massive influx of traumatized patients — that chaotic urgency is missing."

Another view:
Dr. Roberts, I am a former Marine Corps Officer and truly grateful for men like yourself who continue to oppose the system and speak the truth. I have been following your posts on the Vegas shooting and would like to drop one quick comment before you move on to the more important stuff. I checked out from the story almost immediately because they are telling us

and showing us he used rifles with magazines. This is completely impossible. Here is a video of a rifle being shot in auto with a 30 round magazine.
https://www.youtube.com/watch?v=7Gm_VfMUAEw
He is out of ammo in 2 seconds and has to reload. There are multiple [sound tracks of the shooting] with 10-12 seconds of continuous gunfire with a slower rate of fire. This can only be achieved with a belt-fed machine gun."

The question before us is: why is it that we have to wonder about what happened? Why the total failure of the media and public authorities to tell a problem-free story?
Why the total absence of interest by media and public authorities to clear up so much confusing, contradictory information? Is this being done on purpose to train us to accept official stories despite endless anomalies?

Originally published as "UPDATE: This from a UK trauma surgeon:," www.paulcraigroberts.org, October 10, 2017.

The Mystery Deepens

Paul Craig Roberts

Forensic Acoustic Analysis Points to Existence of a Second Shooter [1].

This analysis seems to make sense. If it has been done correctly, it is evidence of a second Las Vegas shooter. It is evidence not only of two sets of gunshots but of bullets hitting the ground from two different distances. So unless the bullets were being fired into the ground only, it seems people will have been hit.

On the other hand, we have what seem to be videos of crisis actors carrying pretend wounded people into a hospital, and we have videos of hospital visits with alleged seriously wounded people who have had an almost instantaneous recovery. As the letter from the purported military surgeon pointed out, quick recoveries from gunshot trauma are not the norm. Remember also the Republican congressman, Steve Scalise, who was shot in the hip last June in D.C. He was in critical condition for some time, and was in no condition to be giving interviews a couple of days later. Yet, here is a video of a young woman allegedly shot in the hip at the Las Vegas concert all rosy cheeked and chatting away a mere 3 days after being "nearly paralyzed" by her gunshot injury [2].

If there are dead and injured, what is the point of crisis actors and interviews with victims who show no sign of trauma?

If there is acoustic evidence of two shooters from two locations, why is the official story insistent on one shooter from one location?

You can see how difficult it would be to try to get the truth. There are too many other things that need my attention, and for which I am better qualified, for me to commit any more time and energy to the Las Vegas shooting.

As in every other case, there is an official story, one that always seems to be ready in advance, and one from which authorities and media do not depart. The "investigation" looks more like the imposition of an official story. The media and the public authorities are content to dismiss suspicions by calling them conspiracy theories. This makes it impossible to clear up contradictions and anomalies.

I promised you an account of any qualified replies to the purported military surgeon's letter. This is from a person who identifies himself as a paramedic for 22 years:

"Sir,
After reading the letter from the retired surgeon addressing gunshot wounds, I wanted to comment that I, too, am mystified by the set number of fatalities and absence of fatal complications. I spent 22 years employed as paramedic and have seen many gunshot wounds. Granted, the distance of the shots can explain the lesser number of horrible, graphic wounds, but the publicized accounts of the wounded seem very inconsistent with my experiences with gunshot wounds and the recovery of those who have been shot. I understand we are not witnessing the day to day progress of those who survived, but I agree with the surgeon that it doesn't add up. Thank you."

I have had two confirmations of the veracity of the surgeon's letter from trauma RNs. However, one of them tells me she knows of someone who was killed.

I have not heard from any surgeons familiar with gunshot wounds. I would imagine that they want to stay clear of all of this.

People with extensive firearms experience call attention to the photo of the dead Stephen Paddock in the hotel room. Where they ask are the thousands of shell casings and empty ammunition clips from the extensive automatic fire? Others point out that the few casings in sight are mysteriously on top of Paddock's blood, not covered by it.

I can't explain any of this. We have an official story, and that is all we are going to get.

Originally published as "The Mystery Deepens," www.paulcraigroberts.org, October 10, 2017.

References

[1]. https://www.youtube.com/watch?v=JxmEFeKy8aI
[2]. https://www.youtube.com/watch?v=LtKJuJMQa94

More Responses to the Military Surgeon's Letter

Paul Craig Roberts

The question before us is not whether people were shot or not, but if they were shot, why the crisis actors carrying pretend wounded into a hospital and why unrealistically quick recoveries from gunshot trauma? I have the names and email addresses of the respondents, but do not publish their names as helpful information should not be repaid by bringing them controversy.

This from a person in a hospital trauma unit:

"Regarding trauma patients hit by gunfire from high-powered rifles – I work at the local hospital and most gunshot victims are hit by lower-powered small arms fire (pistols, birdshot, buckshot) versus military (5.56 or 7.62 NATO) calibers, and most of these patients are in the trauma ICU for at least 1-2 weeks and sometimes up to a few months. Many of these also end up dying or at the very least becoming even more acutely ill from hospital-acquired infections, many of which are acquired during surgeries or from mechanical ventilators."

This from the UK:

"As a retired anesthesiologist, my observations of the victims shown in the media/online videos concur with those of the military surgeon's in his letter. I cannot say whether anyone was shot in Las Vegas but the victims we have been shown in the media are unreal." MD, DCH, FRCA, FFPM (UK)."

Below is a reader's report on the effect on US Rep. Steve Scalise of being shot once in the hip. Compare this reality to the young woman chatting away with the presstitute 3 days after being shot in the hip and "nearly paralyzed."

"Hip and femer were shattered from the bullet. Scalise almost bled to death laying right there on the ground. I read previously that he was already in shock when he arrived at the hospital. He had several surgeries to control bleeding and infection, do reconstruction of his innards, etc. and these surgeries continued for some time, i.e. they all weren't all done the next day or several days after. He has steel and metal plates inside his body now holding bones together. He also spent months in rehabilitation, and now walks with a walker."

Note that these extensive injuries, which he almost died of several times over weeks, were caused BY A SINGLE GUNSHOT WOUND, A SINGLE BULLET.

Here is a short excerpt from a CNN article, and the article link:

"Scalise was in critical condition after suffering damage to internal organs, and his injuries will require additional operations, according to a MedStar Washington Hospital Center medical update late Wednesday.

'Congressman Steve Scalise sustained a single rifle shot to the left hip. The bullet traveled across his pelvis, fracturing bones, injuring internal organs, and causing severe bleeding," MedStar said in a statement put out by Scalise's office. "He underwent immediate surgery, and an additional procedure to stop bleeding. He has received multiple units of blood transfusion. His condition is critical, and he will require additional operations. We will provide periodic updates.'"

http://edition.cnn.com/2017/06/14/politics/alexandria-virginia-shooting/index.html

Excerpt from a Wikipedia article, and link. Note that it says that weeks after the shooting, he had to be readmitted to intensive care:

Scalise was shot in the hip and was evacuated by medical helicopter to MedStar Washington Hospital Center, where he underwent surgery. The hospital reported that after the bullet struck his hip, it traveled across his pelvis – fracturing bones, injuring internal organs, and causing severe bleeding. His condition was initially listed as "critical". He received multiple blood transfusions and underwent several surgeries to repair internal damage and stop the bleeding. His condition was changed to "serious" on June 17. It further improved to "fair" on June 21, though he was readmitted to intensive care on July 5 due to concerns of infection.

https://en.wikipedia.org/wiki/2017_Congressional_baseball_shooting

Here are a few other articles:

https://www.washingtontimes.com/news/2017/sep/28/steve-scalise-didnt-realize-extent-his-injuries-un/

https://www.cbsnews.com/news/rep-steve-scalise-breaks-his-silence-on-shooting/

To sum up, if the acoustic evidence is correct of bullets hitting the ground, then bullets were fired. Therefore, it is likely people were hit. Why then are what clearly seem to be crisis actors employed? Is it possible that the alert part of the population is being given counterfactual information in order to condition us to accept official stories despite unresolved contradictions? In other words, are the contradictions intentionally introduced? Is the real conspiracy one of establishing official stories as fact regardless of evidence? The result would be to classify appeals to evidence as "conspiracy theory."

Originally published as "More Responses to the Military Surgeon's Letter," www.paulcraigroberts.org, October 11, 2017.

The Las Vegas Shooting Won't Go Away

Paul Craig Roberts

OK readers, you win. Yes, something is wrong with the Las Vegas shooting story. It is not only Tyler Durden on Zero Hedge today, but Tucker Carlson on Fox News yesterday. Carlson raises many pointed questions that do not have obvious answers. The investigation does not seem to have been handled in the normal way that such investigations are handled. I don't know what it means. I don't expect any official explanation. And I agree with you that it stinks [1-2].

I also agree with you that the combination of the presence of crisis actors and actual victims, who were killed, although it is not clear whether from Paddock in the hotel or, as witnesses claim, from shooters on the ground among the crowd, is nonsensical. What is the point of acting out an attack when there are real victims, which there seem to be, at least a few.

And I agree with you that if there were 500+ wounded, some of them are bound to have died in hospitals from complications from their wounds, but we have had no such reports. Yes, I agree that the medical trauma personnel who gave their opinion that it is impossible that there were no deaths from wound complications are correct.

I agree also that the total number of claimed dead and wounded, a number approaching 600, is carnage far in excess of anything that the videos indicate.

Las Vegas is like all the other cases. We are given a story that is full of disbelief, but we are supposed to believe it. The print and TV media, except for Tucker Carlson, doesn't depart from the scripted story. Remember the truck attack in Nice, France? Remember that there were security cameras every block of the street along which the truck travelled? Remember the orders from Paris to the Nice authorities not to show or release anything from the recordings on the cameras and to destroy the video evidence? Remember the Nice authorities accusing Paris of an obstruction of justice? The official story handed to us by the presstitutes never explained, or adjusted for, the extraordinary order from the French central government to the Nice local government to destroy the evidence. Why would such an order be given? Why did the order not raise a jillion red flags? What was being covered up by the order?

Remember, except for the case of alleged Boston Marathon bombing surviving brother Dzhokhar Tsarnaev, no alleged perpetrator of any of these terrorist attacks is alive to tell his tale, and Dzhokhar has been kept from the public and the media. Dzhokhar's survival is itself a miracle as he was on two occasions in two different locations shot by police. Clearly, he wasn't wanted alive to tell his tale.

Yes, readers, I know, there is no explanation why a rich multi-millionaire enjoying his life would gun down close to 600 country music fans. Yes, I know, there are not the requisite thousands of shell casings of expended brass on the floor in his room. Yes, I know it is not possible for someone to stay so long in a hotel room without room service noticing the accumulated arsenal or noticing days of non-entry by room service. Yes, I know, hotels have policies that day after day of "do not disturb" raises questions that require inquiries.

I agree with you on all of this, but they are not going to tell us. And by the way, has Tucker Carlson been fired yet, or had his run-away car crash at 100 mph into a telephone pole?

Originally published as "The Las Vegas Shooting Won't Go Away," www.paulcraigroberts.org, October 26, 2017.

References

[1]. http://www.zerohedge.com/news/2017-10-26/mysterious-missing-vegas-security-guard-left-country-days-after-vegas-massacre
[2]. http://insider.foxnews.com/2017/10/25/tucker-carlson-las-vegas-massacre-questions-jesus-campos-security-guard-and-police-hung.

When Guns Are Outlawed Only Outlaws Will Have Guns

Paul Craig Roberts

Guns are banned in the UK, but the black market is booming and criminals are loading up on firearms [1]. I have often wondered what is the real agenda of gun ban advocates. More people die from falls than from being shot. Deaths from accidents far exceed deaths from being shot [2]. Aggravated assault and robbery account for 91% of violent crimes. Rapes account for 7.7%. Murders accounted for only 1.4% of violent crime [3]. According to the FBI, there were 17,284 murders in 2017 [4]. Assailants using rifles killed 403 people, and 1,591 were killed by people using knives. Handguns were used in 7,032 killings, many of which resulted from criminals killing one another over, for example, drug distribution [5]. The police were responsible for 987 shooting deaths, about one-fourth of which were mentally disturbed people [6]. There were 40,327 motor vehicle accident deaths in 2017. About 4,000 people died from drowning. There were 34,673 deaths from accidental falls. There were 58,335 accidental poisoning deaths. All unintentional deaths totalled 161,374 [7]. It turns out that prescription drugs are the 4th leading cause of death, which puts it up there with cancer and heart attacks. Harvard University reports that properly prescribed medications hospitalize 1.9 million Americans annually, killing 128,000 people, which places prescribed medicines fourth place with strokes as a leading cause of death. Far more lives could be saved by focusing on careful drug testing rather than on gun control [8]. What then explains the fixation and constant propaganda about banning "assault rifles" when the total annual murders by assailants using all kinds of rifles is 403? What explains the fixation on handguns that are the weapon of choice in only 41% of murders numbering only 7,032 deaths? What is the point of disarming the population when private ownership of firearms prevents a large number of crimes. A study by criminologists Gary Kleck and Marc Gertz concluded that Americans use their guns annually to prevent more than 2 million crimes [9]. John Lott also found that gun ownership reduces crime [10]. Those who advocate banning gun ownership demur, claiming guns are used defensively only 100,000 times a year. Why then do gun controllers want to take away guns that prevent crimes six times the number of homicides? Those who want to ban guns use deceptive and dishonest terms such as "gun violence," an illiterate use of language. Guns are inanimate objects like a hammer or a screwdriver. They are not capable of taking action such as committing violence. They have to be used or misused by people intent on committing violence. Therefore, there can be no such thing as "gun violence." There can only be violence committed by people using guns or hammers or screwdrivers, or whatever. Murders committed by assailants using handguns comprise a tiny 0.0056% of violent crimes. What explains the fixation on such a small problem? Moreover, gun ban advocates, who so deplore the deaths by "gun violence" of Americans they have never met, are short on sympathy for the millions of victims of American gun violence in the Middle East and North Africa. They show no concern about the mounting conflicts orchestrated by Washington with Russia and China, conflicts that could destroy all life on earth in nuclear Armageddon. Clearly, gun ban advocates are insincere about the few deaths of strangers that they so greatly deplore and use their insincerity to disguise an undeclared agenda. Their agenda is the disarming of the American people, a people already disarmed of the protections of the US Constitution by the fake "war on terror." The only remaining barrier to tyrannized Americans is the large percentage of the population that is armed and skilled in the use of "gun violence." Who funds the gun banners? Who is behind the long-standing and continuous assault on the Second Amendment of the US Constitution? What is the agenda behind the assault?

The First Amendment has already fallen. No white American any longer has free speech. It has become a firing offense. A lawsuit offense. A career-ending offense. The Jewish lobbies' and the liberal/progressive/left and Democratic Party's Identity Politics have murdered the First Amendment. Exercise your First Amendment rights and Antifa appears outside your home or at your restaurant table threatening you with violence. The American media has been turned into a Propaganda Ministry for war in behalf of US hegemony over the world and in behalf of Washington's and Israel's control over the explanations fed to the American population. The New York Times, "the newspaper of record," will leave a shameful, sordid record if anyone is left to read it.

Originally published as "When Guns Are Outlawed Only Outlaws Will Have Guns," www.paulcraigroberts.org, January 2019.

References

[1]. https://www.investmentwatchblog.com/when-proggies-advocate-for-uk-style-gun-control-laws-show-them-this-police-struggle-to-stop-flood-of-firearms-into-uk/

[2]. The FBI reports that there were 1,247,321 violent crimes in the US in 2017. https://ucr.fbi.gov/crime-in-the-u.s/2017/crime-in-the-u.s.-2017/topic-pages/violent-crime

[3]. https://www.fbi.gov/news/stories/2016-crime-statistics-released

[4]. https://ucr.fbi.gov/crime-in-the-u.s/2017/crime-in-the-u.s.-2017/topic-pages/murder

[5]. https://ucr.fbi.gov/crime-in-the-u.s/2017/crime-in-the-u.s.-2017/tables/expanded-homicide-data-table-8.xls. See also: https://www.statista.com/statistics/195325/murder-victims-in-the-us-by-weapon-used/

[6]. https://www.washingtonpost.com/investigations/nationwide-police-shot-and-killed-nearly-1000-people-in-2017/2018/01/04/4eed5f34-e4e9-11e7-ab50-621fe0588340_story.html?utm_term=.c7ff0f9c8b3d

[7]. https://www.cdc.gov/nchs/fastats/accidental-injury.htm

[8]. https://ethics.harvard.edu/blog/new-prescription-drugs-major-health-risk-few-offsetting-advantages

[9]. https://scholarlycommons.law.northwestern.edu/cgi/viewcontent.cgi?referer=&httpsredir=1&article=6853&context=jclc

10. https://www.investors.com/politics/columnists/how-many-lives-are-saved-by-guns-and-why-dont-gun-controllers-care/

The Lies That Form Our Consciousness and False Historical Awareness

Paul Craig Roberts

My generation associated dystopias, such as George Orwell's 1984, with the Soviet Union, a country in which explanations were controlled and criticism of Stalin would land a person in the Gulag. We thought of the United States and our life here much differently. But with the passage of time the difference between life in the Soviet Union in the 20th century and life in the Western world today is disappearing. Today, the journalist Julian Assange is undergoing the same kind of state terror and torture as any Soviet dissident, if not worse. The Western media is as controlled as the Soviet media, with print, TV, and public radio serving as a propaganda ministry for government and the interest groups that control government. Social media, such as Facebook and Twitter are systematically denying their platforms to those who express views not supportive of the ruling order and its agendas. It has turned out to be easy to get rid of the First Amendment guarantee of free speech as the media have neither the ability nor the intention of exercising it.

It was a mistake for my generation to associate Orwell's Memory Hole and falsified history only with fictional or real dystopias. Falsified history was all around us. We just didn't know enough to spot it. What living and learning has taught me is that history tends to always be falsified, and historians who insist on the truth suffer for it. It has been established that many of the ancient historians are unreliable, because they were "court historians" who sought material benefit by writing to please a ruler. In my time many an historian has written for income from book sales by enthralling the public with tales of glorious victories over demonized enemies that justified all the sons, grandsons, brothers, fathers, uncles, husbands, friends, and cousins who were sacrificed for the sake of capitalist armaments profits. No publisher wanted a truthful account that no one would buy because of the stark portrayal of the pointlessness of the deaths of loved ones. Everyone, or almost so, wants to think that their loss was for a noble cause and was "worth it."

With few exceptions, English speaking historians have put the blame for both world wars on Germany. This is false history. The first real historian of World War I, or what was called at the time the Great War or the World War, was Harry Elmer Barnes. Barnes was Professor of Historical Sociology at Smith College and the William Bayard Cutting Fellow in History at Columbia University. His book, The Genesis of the World War, was published in 1926 by Alfred A. Knopf in New York.

Instead of covering up, as expected, the allied crimes and treachery against Germany, Barnes told the truth. The German Kaiser, a relative of the British and Russian royal families, was known throughout the world as a peacemaker, praised by the New York Times for that role. It is a known and indisputable fact that the German government acted for peace until Germany, the last power to mobilize, had to mobilize or be overrun by Russia and France, who were allied with the British against Germany. Never before in history has the very last power to mobilize been blamed for starting a war. But facts never get in the way of court historians.

The genesis of the war was the desire on the part of two of the Russian Tsar's ministers for Constantinople and the French president for territory, Alsace-Lorraine, lost to Germany in the 1870 Franco-Prussian war. These schemers used Austria's response to the assassination of the Austrian archduke in Serbia, which they likely orchestrated, to declare war as Germany was the protector of the Austrian-Hungarian Empire.

American president Woodrow Wilson secured an armistice to the World War, which had senselessly destroyed millions of lives, by promising Germany that if she agreed to an armistice, there would be no territorial losses for Germany and no reparations. When Germany agreed to the armistice, it was Germany that occupied territories of the opposing camp. There were no foreign troops on German territory.

As soon as Germany disengaged, the British put into effect a food blockade that forced starving Germans to submit to the exploitative Versailles Treaty that violated every promise that President Wilson had made.

Some intelligent people, including the most famous economist of the 20th century, John Maynard Keynes, said that the Versailles Treaty, an exercise in coverup for who caused the war, guaranteed a future war. And they, not the grasping corrupt establishment, were right.

For his truth-telling efforts, Harry Elmer Barnes was declared by the court historians to be a German agent paid to write a false history. As Barnes' voice was greatly outnumbered, the history of the Great War remained, for most, falsified throughout the 20th century.

Barnes was vindicated in 2014 when Christopher Clark at Cambridge University published The Sleepwalkers: How Europe Went to War in 1914. Clark added to Barnes' evidence that the Great War resulted from a plot by two Russian government ministers and the president of France to steal coveted territory from Germany and Turkey.

But one hundred years after the war who is around to care? All the people who died in the war as well as their bereaved families who suffered from the plot of three evil men are dead and gone. The consciousness of the world has already been distorted by a century of false history, a false history that set up Germany for blame again, this time for World War II.

Stay tuned, the lies about World War II are even more grand.

Originally published as "The Lies That Form Our Consciousness and False Historical Awareness," www.paulcraigroberts.org, May 2019.

The Lies About World War II

Paul Craig Roberts

In the aftermath of a war, history cannot be written. The losing side has no one to speak for it. Historians on the winning side are constrained by years of war propaganda that demonized the enemy while obscuring the crimes of the righteous victors. People want to enjoy and feel good about their victory, not learn that their side was responsible for the war or that the war could have been avoided except for the hidden agendas of their own leaders. Historians are also constrained by the unavailability of information. To hide mistakes, corruption, and crimes, governments lock up documents for decades. Memoirs of participants are not yet written. Diaries are lost or withheld from fear of retribution. It is expensive and time consuming to locate witnesses, especially those on the losing side, and to convince them to answer questions. Any account that challenges the "happy account" requires a great deal of confirmation from official documents, interviews, letters, diaries, and memoirs, and even that won't be enough. For the history of World War II in Europe, these documents can be spread from New Zealand and Australia across Canada and the US through Great Britain and Europe and into Russia. A historian on the track of the truth faces long years of strenuous investigation and development of the acumen to judge and assimilate the evidence he uncovers into a truthful picture of what transpired. The truth is always immensely different from the victor's war propaganda.

As I reported recently, Harry Elmer Barnes was the first American historian to provide a history of the First World War that was based on primary sources. His truthful account differed so substantially from the war propaganda that he was called every name in the book.

Truth is seldom welcomed. David Irving, without any doubt the best historian of the European part of World War II, learned at his great expense that challenging myths does not go unpunished. Nevertheless, Irving persevered. If you want to escape from the lies about World War II that still direct our disastrous course, you only need to study two books by David Irving: Hitler's War and the first volume of his Churchill biography, Churchill's War: The Struggle for Power .

Irving is the historian who spent decades tracking down diaries, survivors, and demanding release of official documents. He is the historian who found the Rommel diary and Goebbels' diaries, the historian who gained entry into the Soviet archives, and so on. He is familiar with more actual facts about the Second World War than the rest of the historians combined. The famous British military historian, Sir John Keegan, wrote in the Times Literary Supplement: "Two books stand out from the vast literature of the Second World War: Chester Wilmot's The Struggle for Europe, published in 1952, and David Irving's Hitler's War.

Despite many such accolades, today Irving is demonized and has to publish his own books.

I will avoid the story of how this came to be, but, yes, you guessed it, it was the Zionists. You simply cannot say anything that alters their propagandistic picture of history.

In what follows, I am going to present what is my impression from reading these two magisterial works. Irving himself is very scant on opinions. He only provides the facts from official documents, recorded intercepts, diaries, letters and interviews.

World War II was Churchill's War, not Hitler's war. Irving provides documented facts from which the reader cannot avoid this conclusion. Churchill got his war, for which he longed, because of the Versailles Treaty that stripped Germany of German territory and unjustly and irresponsibly imposed humiliation on Germany.

Hitler and Nationalist Socialist Germany (Nazi stands for National Socialist German Workers' Party) are the most demonized entities in history. Any person who finds any good in Hitler or Germany is instantly demonized. The person becomes an outcast regardless of the facts. Irving is very much aware of this. Every time his factual account of Hitler starts to display a person too much different from the demonized image, Irving throws in some negative language about Hitler.

Similarly for Winston Churchill. Every time Irving's factual account displays a person quite different from the worshiped icon, Irving throws in some appreciative language.

This is what a historian has to do to survive telling the truth.

To be clear, in what follows, I am merely reporting what seems to me to be the conclusion from the documented facts presented in these two works of scholarship. I am merely reporting what I understand Irving's research to have established. You read the books and arrive at your own conclusion.

World War II was initiated by the British and French declaration of war on Germany, not by a surprise blitzkrieg from Germany. The utter rout and collapse of the British and French armies was the result of Britain declaring a war for which Britain was unprepared to fight and of the foolish French trapped by a treaty with the British, who quickly deserted their French ally, leaving France at Germany's mercy.

Germany's mercy was substantial. Hitler left a large part of France and the French colonies unoccupied and secure from war under a semi-independent government under Petain. For his service in protecting a semblance of French independence, Petain was sentenced to death by Charles de Gaulle after the war for collaboration with Germany, an unjust charge.

In Britain, Churchill was out of power. He figured a war would put him back in power. No Britisher could match Churchill's rhetoric and orations. Or determination. Churchill desired power, and he wanted to reproduce the amazing military feats of his distinguished ancestor, the Duke of Marlborough, whose biography Churchill was writing and who defeated after years of military struggle France's powerful Sun King, Louis XIV, the ruler of Europe.

In contrast to the British aristocrat, Hitler was a man of the people. He acted for the German people. The Versailles Treaty had dismembered Germany. Parts of Germany were confiscated and given to France, Belgium, Denmark, Poland, and Czechoslovakia. As Germany had not actually lost the war, being the occupiers of foreign territory when Germany agreed to a deceptive armistice, the loss of approximately 7 million German people to Poland and Czechoslovakia, where Germans were abused, was not considered a fair outcome.

Hitler's program was to put Germany back together again. He succeeded without war until it came to Poland. Hitler's demands were fair and realistic, but Churchill, financed by the Focus Group with Jewish money, put such pressure on British prime minister Chamberlain that Chamberlain intervened in the Polish-German negotiations and issued a British guarantee to the Polish military dictatorship should Poland refuse to release German territory and populations.

The British had no way of making good on the guarantee, but the Polish military dictatorship lacked the intelligence to realize that. Consequently, the Polish Dictatorship refused Germany's request.

From this mistake of Chamberlain and the stupid Polish dictatorship, came the Ribbentrop/Molotov agreement that Germany and the Soviet Union would split Poland between themselves. When Hitler attacked Poland, Britain and the hapless French declared war on Germany because of the unenforceable British guarantee. But the British and French were careful not to declare war on the Soviet Union for occupying the eastern half of Poland.

Thus Britain was responsible for World War II, first by stupidly interfering in German/Polish negotiations, and second by declaring war on Germany.

Churchill was focused on war with Germany, which he intended for years preceding the war. But Hitler didn't want any war with Britain or with France, and never intended to invade Britain. The invasion threat was a chimera conjured up by Churchill to unite England behind him. Hitler expressed his view that the British Empire was essential for order in the world, and that in its absence Europeans would lose their world supremacy. After Germany's rout of the French and British armies, Hitler offered an extraordinarily generous peace to Britain. He said he wanted nothing from Britain but the return of Germany's colonies. He committed the German military to the defense of the British Empire, and said he would reconstitute both Polish and Czech states and leave them to their own discretion. He told his associates that defeat of the British Empire would do nothing for Germany and everything for Bolshevik Russia and Japan.

Winston Churchill kept Hitler's peace offers as secret as he could and succeeded in his efforts to block any peace. Churchill wanted war, largely it appears, for his own glory. Franklin Delano Roosevelt slyly encouraged Churchill in his war but without making any commitment in Britain's behalf. Roosevelt knew that the war would achieve his own aim of bankrupting Britain and destroying the British Empire, and that the US dollar would inherit the powerful position from the British pound of being the world's reserve currency. Once Churchill had trapped Britain in a war she could not win on her own, FDR began doling out bits of aid in exchange for extremely high prices—for example, 60 outdated and largely useless US destroyers for British naval bases in the Atlantic. FDR delayed Lend-Lease until desperate Britain had turned over $22,000 million of British gold plus $42 million in gold Britain had in South Africa. Then began the forced sell-off of British overseas investments. For example, the British-owned Viscose Company, which was worth $125 million in 1940 dollars, had no debts and held $40 million in government bonds, was sold to the House of Morgan for $37 million. It was such an act of thievery that the

British eventually got about two-thirds of the company's value to hand over to Washington in payment for war munitions. American aid was also "conditional on Britain dismantling the system of Imperial preference anchored in the Ottawa agreement of 1932." For Cordell Hull, American aid was "a knife to open that oyster shell, the Empire." Churchill saw it coming, but he was too far in to do anything but plead with FDR: It would be wrong, Churchill wrote to Roosevelt, if "Great Britain were to be divested of all saleable assets so that' after the victory was won with our blood, civilization saved, and the time gained for the United States to be fully armed against all eventualities, we should stand stripped to the bone."

A long essay could be written about how Roosevelt stripped Britain of her assets and world power. Irving writes that in an era of gangster statesmen, Churchill was not in Roosevelt's league. The survival of the British Empire was not a priority for FDR. He regarded Churchill as a pushover—unreliable and drunk most of the time. Irving reports that FDR's policy was to pay out just enough to give Churchill "the kind of support a rope gives a hanging man." Roosevelt pursued "his subversion of the Empire throughout the war." Eventually Churchill realized that Washington was at war with Britain more fiercely than was Hitler. The great irony was that Hitler had offered Churchill peace and the survival of the Empire. When it was too late, Churchill came to Hitler's conclusion that the conflict with Germany was a "most unnecessary" war. Pat Buchanan sees it that way also [1].

Hitler forbade the bombing of civilian areas of British cities. It was Churchill who initiated this war crime, later emulated by the Americans. Churchill kept the British bombing of German civilians secret from the British people and worked to prevent Red Cross monitoring of air raids so no one would learn he was bombing civilian residential areas, not war production. The purpose of Churchill's bombing—first incendiary bombs to set everything afire and then high explosives to prevent firefighters from controlling the blazes—was to provoke a German attack on London, which Churchill reckoned would bind the British people to him and create sympathy in the US for Britain that would help Churchill pull America into the war. One British raid murdered 50,000 people in Hamburg, and a subsequent attack on Hamburg netted 40,000 civilian deaths. Churchill also ordered that poison gas be added to the firebombing of German civilian residential areas and that Rome be bombed into ashes. The British Air Force refused both orders. At the very end of the war the British and Americans destroyed the beautiful baroque city of Dresden, burning and suffocating 100,000 people in the attack. After months of firebombing attacks on Germany, including Berlin, Hitler gave in to his generals and replied in kind. Churchill succeeded. The story became "the London Blitz," not the British blitz of Germany.

Like Hitler in Germany, Churchill took over the direction of the war. He functioned more as a dictator who ignored the armed services than as a prime minister advised by the country's military leaders. Both leaders might have been correct in their assessment of their commanding officers, but Hitler was a much better war strategist than Churchill, for whom nothing ever worked. To Churchill's WW I Gallipoli misadventure was now added the introduction of British troops into Norway, Greece, Crete, Syria—all ridiculous decisions and failures—and the Dakar fiasco. Churchill also turned on the French, destroying the French fleet and lives of 1,600 French sailors because of his personal fear, unfounded, that Hitler would violate his treaty with the French and seize the fleet. Any one of these Churchillian mishaps could have resulted in a no confidence vote, but with Chamberlain and Halifax out of the way there was no alternative leadership. Indeed, the lack of leadership is the reason neither the cabinet nor the military could stand up to Churchill, a person of iron determination.

Hitler also was a person of iron determination, and he wore out both himself and Germany with his determination. He never wanted war with England and France. This was Churchill's doing, not Hitler's. Like Churchill, who had the British people behind him, Hitler had the German people behind him, because he stood for Germany and had reconstructed Germany from the rape and ruin of the Versailles Treaty. But Hitler, not an aristocrat like Churchill, but of low and ordinary origins, never had the loyalty of many of the aristocratic Prussian military officers, those with "von" before their name. He was afflicted with traitors in the Abwehr, his military intelligence, including its director, Adm. Canaris. On the Russian front in the final year, Hitler was betrayed by generals who opened avenues for the Russians into undefended Berlin.

Hitler's worst mistakes were his alliance with Italy and his decision to invade Russia. He was also mistaken to let the British go at Dunkirk. He let them go because he did not want to ruin the chance for ending the war by humiliating the British by the loss of their entire army. But with Churchill there was no chance for peace. By not destroying the British army, Hitler boosted Churchill who turned the evacuation into British heroics that sustained the willingness to fight on.

It is unclear why Hitler invaded Russia. One possible reason is poor or intentionally deceptive information from the Abwehr on Russian military capability. Hitler later said to his associates that he never would have invaded if he had known of the enormous size of the Russian army and the extraordinary capability of the Soviets to produce tanks and aircraft. Some historians have concluded that the reason Hitler invaded Russia was that he concluded that the British would not agree to end the war because they expected Russia to enter the war on Britain's side. Therefore, Hitler decided to foreclose that possibility by conquering Russia. A Russian has written that Hitler attacked because Stalin was preparing to attack Germany. Stalin did have considerable forces far forward, but it would make more sense for Stalin to wait until the West devoured itself in mutual bloodletting, step in afterwards and scoop it all up if he wanted. Or perhaps Stalin was positioning to occupy part of Eastern Europe in order to put more buffers between the Soviet Union and Germany. Whatever the reason for the invasion, what defeated Hitler was the earliest Russian winter in 30 years. It stopped everything in its tracks before the well planned and succeeding encirclement could be completed. The harsh winter that immobilized the Germans gave Stalin time to recover.

Because of Hitler's alliance with Mussolini, who lacked an effective fighting force, resources needed on the Russian front were twice drained off in order to rescue Italy. Because of Mussolini's misadventures, Hitler had to drain troops, tanks, and air planes from the Russian invasion to rescue Italy in Greece and North Africa and to occupy Crete. Hitler made this mistake out of loyalty to Mussolini. Later in the war when Russian counterattacks were pushing the Germans out of Russia, Hitler had to divert precious military resources to rescue Mussolini from arrest and to occupy Italy to prevent her surrender. Germany simply lacked the manpower and military resources to fight on a 1,000 mile front in Russia, and also in Greece and North Africa, occupy part of France, and man defenses against a US/British invasion of Normandy and Italy.

The German Army was a magnificent fighting force, but it was overwhelmed by too many fronts, too little equipment, and careless communications. The Germans never caught on despite much evidence that the British could read their encryption. Thus, efforts to supply Rommel in North Africa were prevented by the British navy.

Irving never directly addresses in either book the Holocaust. He does document the massacre of many Jews, but the picture that emerges from the factual evidence is that the holocaust of Jewish people was different from the official Zionist story. No German plans, or orders from Hitler, or from Himmler or anyone else have ever been found for an organized holocaust by gas and cremation of Jews. This is extraordinary as such a massive use of resources and transportation would have required massive organization, budgets and resources. What documents do show is Hitler's plan to relocate European Jews to Madagascar after the war's end. With the early success of the Russian invasion, this plan was changed to sending the European Jews to the Jewish Bolsheviks in the eastern part of Russia that Hitler was going to leave to Stalin. There are documented orders given by Hitler preventing massacres of Jews. Hitler said over and over that "the Jewish problem" would be settled after the war.

It seems that most of the massacres of Jews were committed by German political administrators of occupied territories in the east to whom Jews from Germany and France were sent for relocation. Instead of dealing with the inconvenience, some of the administrators lined them up and shot them into open trenches. Other Jews fell victim to the anger of Russian villagers who had long suffered under Jewish Bolshevik administrators.

The "death camps" were in fact work camps. Auschwitz, for example, today a Holocaust museum, was the site of Germany's essential artificial rubber factory. Germany was desperate for a work force. A significant percentage of German war production labor had been released to the Army to fill the holes in German lines on the Russian front. War production sites, such as Auschwitz, had as a work force refugees displaced from their homes by war, Jews to be deported after war's end, and anyone else who could be forced into work. Germany desperately needed whatever work force it could get.

Every camp had crematoriums. Their purpose was not to exterminate populations but to dispose of deaths from the scourge of typhus, natural deaths, and other diseases. Refugees were from all over, and they brought diseases and germs with them. The horrific photos of masses of skeleton-like dead bodies that are said to be evidence of organized extermination of Jews are in fact camp inmates who died from typhus and starvation in the last days of the war when Germany was disorganized and devoid of medicines and food for labor camps. The great noble Western victors themselves bombed the labor camps and contributed to the deaths of inmates.

The two books on which I have reported total 1,663 pages, and there are two more volumes of the Churchill biography. This massive, documented historical information seemed likely to pass into the Memory Hole as it is inconsistent with both the self-righteousness of the West and the human capital of court historians. The facts are too costly to be known. But historians have started adding to their own accounts the information uncovered by Irving. It takes a brave historian to praise him, but they can cite him and plagiarize him.

It is amazing how much power Zionists have gotten from the Holocaust. Norman Finkelstein calls it The Holocaust Industry. There is ample evidence that Jews along with many others suffered, but Zionists insist that it was a unique experience limited to Jews.

In his introduction to Hitler's War, Irving reports that despite the widespread sales of his book, the initial praise from accomplished historians and the fact that the book was required reading at military academies from Sandhurst to West Point, "I have had my home smashed into by thugs, my family terrorized, my name smeared, my printers [publishers] firebombed, and myself arrested and deported by tiny, democratic Austria—an illegal act, their courts decided, for which the ministerial culprits were punished; at the behest of disaffected academics and influential citizens [Zionists], in subsequent years, I was deported from Canada (in 1992), and refused entry to Australia, New Zealand, Italy, South Africa and other civilized countries around the world. Internationally affiliated groups circulated letters to librarians, pleading for this book to be taken off their shelves."

So much for free thought and truth in the Western world. Nothing is so little regarded in the West as free thought, free expression, and truth. In the West explanations are controlled in order to advance the agendas of the ruling interest groups. As David Irving has learned, woe to anyone who gets in the way.

Originally published as "The Lies About World War II," www.paulcraigroberts.org, May 2019.

References

[1]. https://www.amazon.com/Churchill-Hitler-Unnecessary-War-Britain/dp/0307405168/ref=sr_1_3?keywords=Pat+Buchanan&qid=1557709100&s=books&sr=1-3

Free Speech No Longer Exists in US Universities

Paul Craig Roberts

Georgetown University law professor Jonathan Turley notes that the University of California, once a bastion of free speech, now is opposed to it. The university now punishes people for opinions expressed outside the classroom and the university [1].

Not that long ago American universities emphasized tolerance of all views so that truth would not be obscured by dogmas. Little doubt this emphasis traced its heritage back to the Church's interference in the scientific question whether the earth was the center of the solar system. In order to save their lives, astronomers were forced to renounce their findings and to assert the truth of dogmas that they knew to be wrong.

Today the same thing is happening in American universities, only the deadly controversies are over race and gender issues, not whether the sun revolves around the earth.

When I was a student liberal professors found Voltaire to be an exemplar of the correct attitude toward free speech. Voltaire quotes were used everywhere in the halls of learning:

"Think for yourself and let others enjoy the privilege of doing so too."
"I may not agree with what you say, but I will defend your right to say it."
"Cherish those who seek the truth but beware of those who find it."
"Doubt is an uncomfortable condition, but certainty is a ridiculous one."

"It is clear that the individual who persecutes a man, his brother, because he is not of the same opinion, is a monster."

Today Voltaire is never heard from. Dogma has shoved aside tolerance and taken control of American universities in which Political Correctness, an ideology or religion in which emotional-based beliefs of certain "preferred" groups with aristocratic or Vatican privileges, such as black activists, abortionists, and sexual deviants, cannot be "offended" by facts or by someone's contrary opinion.

The latest case of academic persecution is Laura Tanner, a doctoral candidate and teaching assistant in the Department of Feminist Studies at the Santa Barbara campus of the University of California, formerly a great university, now a cesspool of intolerance and Identity Politics.

Despite her feminist credentials, Tanner is under attack, not for what she said in the classroom, but for what she expressed in tweets. She expressed her opinion that "It's not possible to be born in the wrong body." Therefore a man in a man's body cannot claim to be a woman. This exercise in plausible deductive reasoning resulted in Tanner being labeled "transphobic."

A former student of Tanner's, an academic terrorist—Kremina Youssef—seems set on destroying Tanner's career prospects simply because Tanner expressed an opinion on Twitter with which Youssef disagrees. Students and alumni have taken the position that although Tanner excels in her teaching role, she should be fired for her "distressing" view on transgenderism. The fact that the vast majority of Americans do not find Tanner's view distressing is considered irrelevant.

Laury Oaks, the chairperson of the Feminist Studies department, believes that a Title IX civil rights complaint can be filed against Tanner. The position taken by the intolerant freaks attempting to destroy Tanner for "distressing" a newly invented gender based on self-declaration is:

"We acknowledge that the gender binary, as it is commonly understood in the US, is rooted in the logics of colonialism, racism, and gendered domination, and that fighting transphobia is integral to resisting and healing from the harms that these systems create. The violence of transphobia, particularly transmisogyny, falls especially hard on communities of color and contributes to the exploitation, criminalization, and incarceration disproportionately experienced by black, brown, immigrant, and working class people. As queer students, students of color, and/or allies, our visions of feminist futures include and affirm people made invisible by and marginalized by the gender binary. In our classrooms, we are committed to holding space for trans students, including taking seriously trans students' experiences, standpoints, and intellectual contributions."

Note that among this collection of nonsense words there is space "in our classrooms" for transgender ideology, but no space outside the classroom for other views on the subject.

To see the undeniable total collapse of university education and the very pillars of Western civilization, ask yourself what Voltaire would have said about this. What is happening in American universities is far worse than Papal objections to astronomers' findings. It seemed to the Church that the astronomers were contradicting the very basis of the Church's religious teachings. But Tanner, who, unlike the Pope in those long ago days, is powerless to impose her views on anyone. Yet, the "transgender community" is determined to impose their views on everyone and to destroy the career of a young feminist. It looks like they will succeed.

Originally published as "Free Speech No Longer Exists in US Universities," www.paulcraigroberts.org, July 2019.

References

[1]. https://jonathanturley.org/2019/07/15/doctoral-candidate-at-uc-santa-barbara-faces-calls-for-her-termination-after-speaking-out-against-transgender-ideology.

Should We Be Protesting About George Floyd or Julian Assange?

Paul Craig Roberts

Some Americans are so pathetic they don't even know what gender they are. A female with a vagina thinks she is a male. A male with testicles and a penis thinks he is a female. Those among us who are normal are supposed to be oh-so-concerned about these confused people that we stop using gender pronouns. He/she/him/her have become transphobic. If you persist in using the English language, you are uncaring and, well, evil to boot.

The transgendered are busy at work making themselves into another preferred minority with all the special privileges in law that that designation brings. I wonder what happens when everyone needs the protection of the special privilege designation, and men and women no longer exist.

Somehow I cannot imagine a country absorbed in transgender issues being exceptional and indispensable, as the neocons say we are, much less being a military power. I very much doubt that Russia and China regard a country as a military threat whose population is confused about what gender they are.

Looking at the evidence, I would say that America has had its 15 minutes of fame. What convinces me that America is all washed up is Americans' acceptance of the horrors inflicted by the American/British police state on Julian Assange. In Assange's treatment we see the violation of every human right. And the Western public has accepted it.

Instead of protesting against the persecution of a truth-teller, agents of the Establishment, pretending to be "peaceful protesters," are burning and looting properties belonging to black, Asian, white, and Hispanic business owners and destroying public monuments for no other reason than a felon, misogynist, drug addict, George Floyd, killed himself by overdosing on Fentanyl.

John Paul Leonard writing in the Unz Review first brought my attention to George Floyd being a drug addict. Unlike CNN, MSNBC, BBC, NPR, New York Times, Washington Post, or any of the corrupt presstitute media, Leonard pointed out that the medical examiner's toxicology report accompanying the autopsy of Floyd's death clearly indicated a lethal dose of the dangerous opioid, Fentanyl, in Floyd's blood.

Fentanyl causes breathing problems that lead to death. Prior to Floyd's restraint, he complained to the police that he could not breathe and asked to be removed from the police car and to lay down on the ground. We know this from the released police recordings. The presstitutes did not report this fact, but the recordings were released.

When an experienced officer, Chauvin, appeared on the scene he recognized a drug overdose problem and had medics called. Floyd was on his stomach so that he would not choke on his own vomit as Fentanyl can produce nausea. The intentionally misinterpreted "knee-on-the-neck" is a restraint technique that is taught to police. It is not deadly. Chauvin used this common practice to keep Floyd, who was having difficulty absorbing oxygen, still in an effort to minimize his oxygen use and thereby prolong his life until medics arrived, hopefully equipped with naloxone. If given promptly, naloxone can treat a Fentanyl overdose by binding to opioid receptors and blocking the effects of the drug. Fentanyl is such a strong opioid that multiple doses of naloxone are usually required.

Some medics are equipped with naloxone. No doubt this was what Chauvin hoped.

Instead of attending to the facts, the despicable American media intentionally created the impression that Chauvin had intentionally murdered Floyd in an act of white racism. This lie was used to support the New York Times 1619 Project, an insult to America that alleges in the absence of any evidence that the United States originated as a white supremacist society that enslaved blacks in an act of racism.

The result of the intentional lies that the US is based in racism and that black Floyd was murdered by white police have been the destruction of billions of dollars in black, Asian, white, and Hispanic businesses and public monuments, the abandonment of the defense of property and law and order by Democrat-controlled cities and states, and a stand-down of the police, which has left people at the mercy of Antifa and Black Lives Matter. Democrats have tried to arrest and prosecute white Americans who took legal steps to defend their property and have left others to fend for themselves when stopped in traffic and surrounded by thugs demanding money.

The toxicology report accompanying George Floyd's autopsy shows Fentanyl in his blood at the concentration of 11 ng/ml. This is a fatal dose. Therapeutic concentrations of Fentanyl, that is, those prescribed by doctors, range between 0.63-2.0 ng/mL.

Fentanyl is equipotent to morphine at doses that are 50–100 times lower. In other words, Fentanyl is 50-100 times stronger than morphine. Post mortem serum concentrations of lethal doses of Fentanyl begin at 5 ng/mL. Floyd had more than twice this concentration. The danger of Fentanyl rises when taken in combination with other drugs. The toxicology report shows Floyd with a methamphetamine concentration of 19 ng/mL and a concentration of Delta-9 Carboxy THC of 42 ng/mL. Like Fentanyl, a meth overdose causes rapid, slowed, or irregular heart rate, difficulty breathing, heart attack, stroke, agitation. The THC in the cannabis part of the cocktail increases the toxicity of the cannabis. Floyd also had serious heart problems which made his drug cocktail more dangerous to him.

I spent a lot of time researching Fentanyl and published the findings on my website. The URLs for the evidence will be again provided at the end of this article.

Death by Fentanyl overdose is common. Several tens of thousands occur annually, and music stars have been among the casualties.

In contrast to drug addict George Floyd who killed himself, the police state treatment of Julian Assange by Washington and the British government and the mentally sick media of both countries goes unprotested.

It is OK with the American Establishment if you loot and riot and destroy private property and statues of Washington, Jefferson, Lee, and Grant. But you must not tell the truth. That was Julian Assange's great crime. He told the truth.

If telling the truth doesn't get you arrested, it gets you cancelled and banned from the print and TV media and from Facebook, Twitter, Google and the rest of the monopolies.

Assange became a target of the corrupt Obama regime in 2010 when he published the leaked Afghanistan and Iraq war logs that revealed Washington's lies and deception of its gullible allies, the utterly stupid British, German, and French governments. Assange signed his death warrant when he released the US military film of US soldiers happily murdering journalists and civilians who were walking along a street. The icing on their fun was when they machine-gunned a father and two very young children who stopped to help those wounded and bleeding from the American machine-gun attack.

Both Sweden and the UK quickly responded to their Washington master's demands and issued arrest warrants for Assange. Sweden and the Western media pretended that Assange had raped two Swedish women, a fabrication that Sweden had to twice drop, and the corrupt British pretended that by accepting political asylum in the Embassy of Ecuador in London, Assange had jumped bail. Sweden falsely pressed the rape charge in the face of the evidence that the two women who had seduced Assange and had taken him to their beds merely wanted him to take a medical test to determine if he was AIDS free. By not having enough sense to agree to the test, Assange destroyed his life.

Assange has been detained illegally for a decade, first under house arrest in England, then for 7 years in the Ecuadoran Embassy in London, and now in solitary confinement in a maximum security prison in the UK since April of 2019. Washington, desperate for revenge on Assange for exposing American war crimes and lies, has spent years trying to invent charges against Assange. The compliant American media helped by portraying Assange as a Russian spy.

What Wikileaks did is no different from what the New York Times did when it published the leaked "Pentagon Papers" or what the New York Times, The Guardian and other newspapers did when they published some of the leaked documents made available by Wikileaks for which only Assange is being persecuted. The difference is that the New York Times, The Guardian, and the rest of the media whores willingly abandoned journalism to serve as propaganda ministries for the ruling elites. Julian Assange is the last living journalist in the Western World, and for that reason, he is hated by the pretend journalists who are well aware that they are nothing but whores.

Many have been puzzled that the so-called "news media" has not gone to the support of Assange on the grounds of defending the rights of a free press. But the presstitutes willingly gave up a free press and are happy to see the last remaining embarrassment to them finished off. It is much more comfortable, and no work, to be inside the Establishment's fold.

As there is no valid case against Assange, the British are holding him in torture-like conditions while pretending to weigh Washington's request for extradition. If Assange dies in prison or his mind is destroyed by illegally administered drugs and abusive treatment, Washington will have achieved its aim of getting rid of him and Wikileaks, and the blame will be on the British puppet.

Not only has Assange done nothing except practice journalism, but also he is an Australian citizen in Europe charged with violating the US Espionage Act. The ridiculous charge itself assumes the universality of US law. In other words, not only does US law apply to an Australian citizen, everyone in the world is subject to US law.

When you think about the neglect of Julian Assange by every allegedly "free country" in Western civilization, while hordes of ignorant thugs run around destroying property with government acquiescence because a drug addict overdosed himself, a stark picture of the utter immorality and total stupidity of Western society emerges. This is what we should be concerned about and protesting about, the neglect of the good and the celebration of the bad.

A good case can be made that the West should be destroyed, but not because of the false allegation that the West is "white supremacist." Indeed, the West has already destroyed itself by abandoning belief in itself and its principles. There is no doubt whatsoever that white people have lost the confidence in themselves and their achievements necessary for their survival. They are guilt-ridden and prostrating themselves before those bent on their demise. White people everywhere, except perhaps in Russia, are living The Camp of the Saints.

Floyd Killed Himself, Officer Chauvin Had Nothing whatsoever to do with Floyd's Death

Nowhere in the media is there any mention of Floyd's existing serious health conditions, his drug addiction, and the level of fentanyl in his blood that was in excess of a fatal dose. The medical examiner's report has been ignored by the presstitute media and by public authorities including the prosecutor who indicted officer Chauvin.

The consequence of a fentanyl overdose is inability to breathe and heart failure. Look it up yourself. I have provided the link in previous columns, and here it is again [1].

Note especially:

"Can you overdose on fentanyl? Yes, a person can overdose on fentanyl. An overdose occurs when a drug produces serious adverse effects and life-threatening symptoms. When people overdose on fentanyl, their breathing can slow or stop. This can decrease the amount of oxygen that reaches the brain, a condition called hypoxia. Hypoxia can lead to a coma and permanent brain damage, and even death."

"Synthetic opioids, including fentanyl, are now the most common drugs involved in drug overdose deaths in the United States. In 2017, 59.8 percent of opioid-related deaths involved fentanyl compared to 14.3 percent in 2010 [2]."

"Among an estimated 70,200 drug overdose deaths in 2017, the largest increase was related to fentanyl and its analogs with more than 28,400 overdose deaths. However, these numbers are likely underreported [3]."

Oxfordtreatment.com gives the fatal dose as 2 milligrams [4].

Drugfreeworld.org gives the fatal dose as 3 milligrams [5].

According to harmreductionohio.org, 700 micrograms (less than one milligram) is an overdose from which death is likely. One milligram (1000 micrograms) carries the risk of "death near certain." Two milligrams and death is certain and unavoidable. A dose of 250 micrograms (one-fourth of one milligram) can kill a non-tolerant user.

"Conventional medical wisdom is that 2,000 micrograms is the 'minimum lethal dose' — in other words, the smallest amount that can be fatal. This estimate is far too high. Two thousand micrograms (2 milligrams) of pure fentanyl injected into a vein would cause even most heavy heroin users to overdose — especially if fentanyl is mixed with any other substance, such as heroin, alcohol or Xanax [6]."

These are extremely small amounts. "Rescuers responding to overdose calls have to be careful—just touching it or inhaling it can be deadly [7]."

"Reported post- mortem serum concentrations of patients who have died from fentanyl overdoses range from 5–120 ng/ mL. The pills recovered in our series had 600–6,900 µg/pill of fentanyl. Even with oral bioavailability of about 30%, each pill can readily deliver enough fentanyl to result in toxic serum concentrations [8]."

The medical examiner's report [9].

First notice the case title:

CARDIOPULMONARY ARREST COMPLICATING LAW ENFORCEMENT SUBDUAL, RESTRAINT, AND NECK COMPRESSION

What is this telling us? According to the Oxford English Dictionary, subdual means overcoming or quietening. The title says that the ability of the police to deal with Floyd was complicated by Floyd's undergoing cardiopulmonary arrest and that the report investigates the issues of restraint and neck compression. As for the restraint and neck compression, no life-threatening injuries resulted. As for Floyd's cardiopulmonary arrest, that is explained by the toxicology report. Floyd was already experiencing breathing and cardiopulmonary arrest prior to police restraint.

Note the extensive heart disease that Floyd had:

II. Natural diseases
   A. Arteriosclerotic heart disease, multifocal, severe
   B. Hypertensive heart disease
   1. Cardiomegaly (540 g) with mild biventricular
      dilatation
   2. Clinical history of hypertension

Note the finding of "No life-threatening injuries":

347

III. No life-threatening injuries identified
   A. No facial, oral mucosal, or conjunctival petechiae
   B. No injuries of anterior muscles of neck or laryngeal
      structures
   C. No scalp soft tissue, skull, or brain injuries
   D. No chest wall soft tissue injuries, rib fractures (other than
a single rib fracture from CPR), vertebral column injuries, or
visceral injuries.

Notice the fatal dose of the opioid fentanyl in the toxicology
report:

VI. Toxicology (see attached report for full details; testing
   performed on antemortem blood specimens collected 5/25/20
at 9:00 p.m. at HHC and on postmortem urine)
   A. Blood drug and novel psychoactive substances screens:

   1. Fentanyl 11 ng/mL
   2. Norfentanyl 5.6 ng/mL
   3. 4-ANPP 0.65 ng/mL
   4. Methamphetamine 19 ng/mL
   5. 11-Hydroxy Delta-9 THC 1.2 ng/mL; Delta-9 Carboxy
THC 42 ng/mL; Delta-9 THC 2.9 ng/mL
   6. Cotinine positive
   7. Caffeine positive

With such strong evidence that George Floyd destroyed himself,
there should have been no arrest of any police officers until a
thorough investigation was made. Even ordinary people
unaware of Fentanyl and its lethality should have wondered why
officer Chauvin called for medics if he wanted to kill Floyd.
Instead of proper procedure a grandstanding district attorney
arrested Chauvin, and the American media, which long ago lost
any scrap of integrity it ever had, convicted Chauvin in the
press. There is no way that Chauvin can get a fair trial. In the
face of the lethal dose of Fentanyl, it is a travesty of justice to
bring Chauvin to trial.

A country without an honest media is doomed. It does not matter who is president or which party is in power. Without an honest media, lies prevail over truth. That is clearly the situation in the United States and throughout the entirety of the Western world.

Originally published as "Should We Be Protesting About George Floyd or Julian Assange?," www.paulcraigroberts.org, July 2020.

References

[1]. https://www.drugabuse.gov/publications/drugfacts/fentanyl

[2]. Ibid.

[3]. https://www.drugs.com/illicit/fentanyl.html

[4]. https://www.oxfordtreatment.com/substance-abuse/fentanyl/lethal-dose/

[5]. https://www.drugfreeworld.org/newsletter/issue13/the-truth-about-fentanyl.html

[6]. https://www.harmreductionohio.org/how-much-fentanyl-will-kill-you-2/

[7]. https://www.drugfreeworld.org/newsletter/issue13/the-truth-about-fentanyl.html

[8]. http://uthscsa.edu/artt/AddictionJC/2020-02-11-Sutter.pdf

[9]. https://www.scribd.com/document/464269559/George-Floyd-Autopsy-FULL-REPORT#from_embed?campaign=VigLink&ad_group=xxc1xx&source=hp_affiliate&medium=affiliate

The Covid Deception

Paul Craig Roberts

We have been deceived by public health authorities about Covid, partly from public authorities' ignorance of the virus, its spread and treatment, but mainly on purpose. One reason we were intentionally deceived by public health authorities, and continue to be deceived by them, is to create a market for a Covid vaccination. There are billions of dollars of profits in this, and Big Pharma wants them. The financial connections between public health authorities and Big Pharma mean that WHO, NIH, and CDC also desire mass vaccinations. If there are not enough people scared out of their wits to voluntarily seek vaccination, the chances are vaccinations will be made mandatory or your ability to travel, and so forth, will be made dependent on being vaccinated.

Another intentional reason for our deception is the Covid threat justifies voting by mail from the safety of one's home. Voting by mail means that no winner can be declared on election night. The mail-in votes will have to be counted as they come in. The delay in declaring an election winner allows time for more propaganda that Trump has (1) fraudently rigged his reelection or (2) has lost and won't step down. As the presstitutes speak with one orchestrated voice, whether Trump wins or not will be buried in reports that he lost and refuses to step down or that he won by fraud. Even if Trump survives the color revolution planned for him, he will be under attack as an illegitimate president just as he was during his first term when he was allegedly elected by "Russian interference." This will suffice to prevent a renewal of his attack on the Globalist Establishment— listen to his first inaugural address—and again sideline his desire to serve peace by reducing the dangerous tensions with Russia, a policy that deprives the military/security complex of its valuable enemy. As presidents John F. Kennedy and Ronald Reagan learned, reducing tensions with Russia threatens the budget and power of the military/security complex that

President Eisenhower warned Americans against. This complex has more power than the president of the United States. As no one would any longer believe another "lone assassin" explanation, Trump is being assassinated with false accusations and a color revolution. For a while Trump used Twitter to refute the false accusations, but now the President of the United States is censored by Twitter. When the color revolution strikes, Trump will not be able to communicate with the American people through print, TV, NPR, or social media. There will only be charges against Trump, and no answers from him.

The Democrats are claiming that as the Postmaster General is appointed by Trump, he will rig the mail-in votes by not delivering votes from blue states. Yet polls show that the vast majority of Democrats are voting by mail and that hardly any Republicans are. This is because the postal union is a public-sector union and belongs to the Democrats. The postal workers already have their instructions: deliver no votes from red areas. Obviously, no Democrats would vote by mail if they thought the Postmaster General had any control over mail delivery. The Republicans know that the postal union will not deliver their votes and are voting in person [1].

This should mean that on election night Trump will have a tremendous victory, but the delay to count the mail-in votes gives the Democrats the time needed to figure out how large the mail-in vote has to be to win or contest the election. It is not only mail-in voting but also absentee ballots that don't get delivered [2].

A third reason for the intentional misrepresentation of the Covid threat is to build the growing police state on more intrusions into private life. The public health threat is used to mandate unconstitutional intrusions that close private businesses or force them to operate at 50 percent capacity, thus driving them into bankruptcy and destroying the lifework of people in the name of public health. The threat is also used to accustom the public to obey mandates to wear masks that provide zero protection. Although opposition to this harmful policy is rising in the US and is strong in Germany and the UK, the fear of Covid that has been indoctrinated has caused most populations to behave as lemmings. People are being trained to obey edicts that harm them.

Now, let's look at the misrepresentation of the Covid Threat itself.

Many medical professionals have shown, with evidence, that the Covid threat has been greatly overstated. According to the CDC's own data, of the alleged 200,000 Americans killed by Covid, only 9,000 actually were. The remainder had 2.6 co-morbidities that in fact killed them. The CDC reports that in only 6% of the reported Covid deaths was Covid the only cause. For 94% of the Covid deaths, there were on average 2.6 comorbidities or additional causes of death [3-4]. The CDC concludes that the initial fatality rates were overestimated. If you have the virus, the CDC reports the survival rate by age group. As I read the report, the percentages are all Covid deaths including those with an average of 2.6 comorbidities [5-6].

Age Group	Probability of Survival
0-19:	99.997%
20-49:	99.98%
50-69:	99.5%
70+:	94.6%

In addition to existing morbidities, many who died from Covid died from the ventilators or from being denied HCQ treatment. HCQ, a safe and certain cure, was demonized by public health officials in alliance with Big Pharma and the presstitutes, because it is inexpensive and in the way of vaccine profits. If there is a cure, there is no need for a vaccine that some experts believe will be more dangerous than Covid itself [7].
The Covid threat is being kept alive by the presstitutes and public health officials until a vaccine can be developed. The latest claim is that the return of the young to colleges has reignited the contagion and spreading it to the adult population in a second wave. This "threat" is an orchestrated hoax. According to the data, the 48,299 COVID-19 cases reported at

37 US universities are associated with only two hospitalizations and zero deaths [8].

There is talk of returning to lockdowns and more stringent mask requirements. All of this is to keep people, especially the elderly, frightened and supportive of vaccination. Proper testing of the vaccine is suspended in an effort to rush it to market before Covid disappears [9].

Dr. Mike Yeadon, former Chief Science Officer for Big Pharma giant Pfizer says that the pandemic is over and that the Covid test produces "false positives" and does not indicate infection with Covid. Dr. Yeadon said that we are basing a government policy, an economic policy, and a civil liberties policy on "what may well be completely fake data on this coronavirus." According to Dr. Yeadon, a "second wave" and "any government case for lockdowns, given the well-known principles of epidemiology, will be entirely manufactured [10]."

It is clear that the Covid threat was overestimated at great cost [11]. The Belgian medical profession has demanded a halt to the Covid propaganda [12]. Of course Big Pharma and its shills such as Fauci, Redfield, and the presstitutes, will continue to keep the "Covid Crisis" alive as it is essential to Big Pharma's vaccine profits, the Democrats' color revolution against President Trump, and the training of populations to accept more government control over their lives.

Originally published as "The Covid Deception," www.paulcraigroberts.org, September 2020.

References

[1]. Thousands of undelivered, unopened votes from 2018 have been found in a trash dump https://www.thegatewaypundit.com/2020/09/exclusive-california-man-finds-thousands-unopened-ballots-garbage-dumpster-workers-quickly-try-cover-photos.

[2]. https://www.zerohedge.com/markets/wisconsin-authorities-investigate-absentee-ballots-found-ditch-fbi-probes-discarded-pro?utm_campaign=&utm_content=Zerohedge%3A+The+Durden+Dispatch&utm_medium=email&utm_source=zh_newsletter

[3]. https://www.cdc.gov/nchs/nvss/vsrr/covid_weekly/index.htm?fbclid=IwAR0LhME5kaVDj5hGFZ-G5ypGdMDaGlkPi0DF8aDKL_bUDi0hJsN_Fq5zPUQ#Comorbidities

[4]. Examples of comorbidities: https://twitter.com/AlexBerenson/status/1308045036391727104

[5]. https://www.zerohedge.com/markets/new-cdc-estimates-fatality-rate-covid-19-drops-again-and-may-surprise-you?utm_campaign=&utm_content=Zerohedge%3A+The+Durden+Dispatch&utm_medium=email&utm_source=zh_newsletter

[6]. https://www.cdc.gov/coronavirus/2019-ncov/hcp/planning-scenarios.html

[7]. Doctors in Florida claim to have found a second cure– https://bgr.com/2020/09/26/coronavirus-cure-icam-protocol-florida

[8]. https://www.thegatewaypundit.com/2020/09/scam-48299-covid-19-cases-37-us-universities-2-hospitalizations-zero-deaths-likely-killed-dog

[9]. https://www.rt.com/news/501523-western-pharma-vaccines-rush-hypocrisy.

[10]. https://hubpages.com/politics/Pfizer-Chief-Science-Officer-Second-Wave-Based-on-Fake-Data-of-False-Positives-for-New-Cases-Pandemic-is-Over

[11]. https://www.paulcraigroberts.org/2020/09/23/covid-19-threat-was-greatly-overestimated-at-huge-cost/

[12]. https://www.paulcraigroberts.org/2020/09/18/belgian-medical-profession-demands-a-halt-to-covid-pandemic

Letter to Dr. David Kennedy from John Remington Graham

Dear Dr. Kennedy, --

You have recently requested that I restate the substance of the evidence presented for the plaintiffs in historic trials in Pennsylvania, Illinois, and Texas in 1978-1982, leading to judicial findings in all three cases, based on at least a fair preponderance of the evidence, that water fluoridation causes cancer and other ailments in man. The underlying forensic evidence, political and legal history, court trials, and the judicial findings have been written up by me and associates in two published works: J. R. Graham and Pierre Morin, Highlights in North American Litigation During the Twentieth Century on Artificial Fluoridation of Public Water Supplies, 14 Journal of Land Use and Environmental Law 195-248 (Florida State University, 1999), which is internet accessible, and the chapter on forensic medicine in Pierre Morin, J. R. Graham, and Gilles Parent, Fluoridation: Autopsy of a Scientific Error, Éditions Berger, Austin, Qc., 2010, which translates into English and updates an earlier edition of the same work in French, published in 2005.

The key court papers, including transcripts, pleadings, motions, summations of evidence, exhibits, recorded data, judicial findings, and court orders, opinions, and decrees, together with other legal items, and related medico-scientific material in these three cases, and in related litigation, have been archived at the Crow Wing County Historical Society in Brainerd, Minnesota, and by the Geosciences Department at the University of Massachusetts Amherst, and I have much of this material in my own professional records.

It is noteworthy that the union of scientists at the national headquarters of the United States Environmental Protection Agency reviewed the evidence presented during the trials in Pennsylvania, Illinois, and Texas, and pertinent evidence later published. During the review process, I was contacted by the epidemiology section at the national headquarters of the USEPA, because, as a specialist in forensic science and medicine, I appeared for the plaintiffs, conducted direct and cross-examination of all expert witnesses, and wrote summations of evidence in all three cases. Upon my experience and background, I sent a detailed report of the forensic evidence to the epidemiology section at the national headquarters of USEPA. Copies of this report, including appendices, are in the archives in Minnesota and Massachusetts, and in my professional records. The union of scientists at the national headquarters of the USEPA (i. e., the National Treasury Employees Union, Chapter 280) concluded that the judicial findings were scientifically warranted and correct, as is stated on June 29, 2000, in an internet-accessible report by Dr. J. W. Hirzy, executive vice president of the union, to a subcommittee of the United States Senate.

The union maintains a website which includes several additional reports in more recent years including material from affiliate unions representing professional staff in USEPA offices across the country, and this material is confirmatory of, and adjunctive to the report of Dr. Hirzy before the United States Senate on June 29, 2000.

My purpose here is to describe for you the evidence presented in the court trials in Pennsylvania, Illinois, and Texas, leading to judicial findings that water fluoridation causes cancer and other ailments in man. It is striking that three veteran trial judges in three different States each heard substantially the same forensic evidence, that each acted independently of the others, and that each reached the same basic conclusion. Each trial had unique features, characterized by differences in civil practice and procedure, not to mention somewhat different political cross-currents, but there was a large overlapping of substantive exhibits and testimony in all three cases. While the trial of each case was unavoidably complex, the main evidence in all three cases followed the same basic pattern:

Our initial evidence in court consisted of expert testimony on large laboratory studies done by Dr. Alfred Taylor, a biochemist at the University of Texas, and by him published in peer-reviewed journals in 1954 (about 600 mice, which is huge by contemporary standards, and important because mice, like man, are mammals) and 1963 (about 900 mice) showing unmistakably that fluoride in drinking water (introduced as NaF, thereby resembling fluoride as artificially introduced in public water supplies) at various concentrations, including 1.0 part per million (the usual target level in water fluoridation), induces cancer-related reactions in laboratory mice. These studies have been directly or indirectly confirmed many times in peer-reviewed articles which have been published in good scientific journals, and which show that fluoride is a carcinogen, a mutagen, and an enzyme inhibiter. We showed that the United States Public Health Service and the American Dental Association had concealed the work of Dr. Taylor, by claiming publicly, contrary to known facts, that Dr. Taylor did not do necessary reruns, that his work was not peer-reviewed, that he never published his work, and that he never observed or reported positive results. This evidence was introductory, but it was impossible for the judges not to notice that pertinent laboratory studies were concealed by promoters of water fluoridation. The laboratory studies were reinforced by medical evidence to the effect that free fluoride ions in drinking water can be transported by blood to and absorbed in all parts of the human body including soft tissues, are highly reactive, and can cause cancer in all parts of the human body.

Having laid this foundation of laboratory data and general medical knowledge, our main evidence in all three cases was a huge epidemiological survey conceived and executed by a number of workers under the direction of Dr. Dean Burk, one of the most famous and decorated cancer research scientists in the world during the 20th century. His career at the National Cancer Institute of the United States spanned 35 years. This epidemiological evidence is especially important, because it translates general concern into actual experience of human beings in their natural environment. The survey compared cancer death rates in two large groups of American central cities, both spread out in all parts of the United States (an aggregate population of about 18 million in 1960), including the same size category and density of urban populations in both groups, from 1940 through 1950 during which both groups did not introduce water fluoridation, and then after 1950 during which ten cities introduced and maintained water fluoridation in 1952-1968 (represented by available data for 1953-1968), and the other ten did not introduce water fluoridation in 1952-1968 (represented by available data for 1953-1968). Before 1950, the cancer death rates remained about the same in both groups for all years observed. After 1950, the cancer death rates the experimental cities introducing water fluoridation in 1952-1968, grew much more rapidly than for the control cities which did not introduce water fluoridation in 1952-1968. The association shown between water fluoridation and human cancer was slightly more than 300 excess cancer deaths every year per million persons drinking fluoridated water after 15-20 years of exposure. The 1940-1950 base line served as a control for all known and unknown variables, including socio-economic, environmental, nutritional, and demographic factors. This association between water fluoridation and human cancer works out to about 30,000 excess cancer deaths every year for about 100 million drinking fluoridated water at the time the three cases were tried. At the moment, substantially more Americans are drinking fluoridated water, so the annual casualty is substantially more now. The proper interpretation of the combined impact of laboratory, medical, and epidemiological evidence presented on our side of the case follows basic rules of inductive logic stated by William of Ockham, Sir Francis Bacon, and Sir Isaac Newton.

In these trials, the government of the United States maintained that the data gathered and organized under the direction of Dr. Burk should be adjusted for age, race, and sex. Among our twenty cities, the factors of sex and race proved, upon close examination, not to be important, but age certainly was and is important because cancer has always been an age-prone disease, and there were certain interesting age-related demographic changes within the populations studied between 1940 and 1970. Although we believed that the 1940-1950 base line was a sufficient control for age and all other variables, we agreed that no harm would be done by appropriate demographic adjustments, and that these adjustments might be useful as a precaution. Thus, in all three cases, the primary point in controversy was not whether, but how and why demographic adjustments should be done. Statisticians engaged by the government of the United States claimed that, using a textbook procedure in modern applied epidemiology (the indirect method, weighted averages, a national standard, and forty age-race-sex categories), adjusted cancer death rates in 1950-1970 actually grew faster in the control cities that did not introduce water fluoridation, than in the experimental cities which did, -- so they claimed at any rate. Our witnesses then came forth with several alternative age-race-sex adjustments, but they conceded for the sake of discussion that the textbook procedure used by the government justified serious attention. We proceeded to show, in each of the three trials, that the government workers had left out all or nearly all available and pertinent data in their adjustment, but that, when omitted data are included by standard statistical methods, there remains an enormous association between water fluoridation and human cancer, -- in light of what is now known, about 200 excess cancer deaths every year per million persons drinking fluoridated water after 15-20 years of exposure, which still translates into a stupefying increase in cancer mortality in the United States, year after year.

In the wake of these court trials, an eminent researcher at an international meeting in 1986 offered plausible evidence to support his contention that changes in population size might explain the huge association between water fluoridation and human cancer displayed by the epidemiological survey carried out under the direction of Dr. Burk. Because of our great respect for this scientist, we reviewed our data once again, and then adjusted for changes in population size among our twenty cities. We discovered that changes in population size are an approximate inverse index of population aging, because a declining population includes fewer people of child-bearing age, and a population growing larger has more people of child-bearing age. And we discovered, in any event, that a proper adjustment of changes in population size leaves an enormous association between water fluoridation and human cancer, -- an association slightly larger than the association which remains after a correctly executed adjustment for age, or what amounts to the same thing, for age, race, and sex. Our expanded and revised adjustments for age, race, and sex and for changes in population size, drawn from census data and vital statistics of the United States, were published for the record in 1988, with the participation and approval of Dr. Burk, in the proceedings of the Pennsylvania Academy of Science.

Since the cases in Pennsylvania, Illinois, and Texas were tried, new evidence has been generated, including laboratory work showing that there is a statistically significant, dose-dependent trend in fluoride-induced bone cancer in male rats, and this laboratory work has been borne out in several epidemiological studies which show an association between water fluoridation and bone cancer in human males. These studies are important, because they are confirmatory of the laboratory work pioneered by Dr. Taylor and the epidemiological work of Dr. Burk and his associates, with respect to a particular kind of cancer, and include examination of specific cases in clinical setting.

Particularly disturbing to the union of scientists at the national headquarters of the USEPA is the recent emergence of laboratory studies which show that fluoride exposure induces neurological injury in rats, and epidemiological evidence suggesting that fluoride in water may reduce IQ in children. A new report published by the National Institute of Environmental Health Sciences in 2012 concludes, "Our results support the possibility of adverse effects of fluoride exposures on children's neurodevelopment." If this suggestion holds up to closer scrutiny in due course, the ramifications for water fluoridation as a disaster in public health administration are almost unthinkable. Yet, if we dump an industrial waste product in public water supplies, and the main ingredient has been identified as a carcinogen, mutagen, and enzyme inhibiter, we should not be surprised to see, as is now sketched out as a concrete possibility from information now available, that the same product is not only associated with large increases in cancer mortality as already established in judicial proceedings, but maybe also lower intelligence in man. With this unhappy note, I remain

Respectfully yours,

Courtesy copies to the Crow Wing County Historical Society, and the University of Massachusetts Amherst c/o Professor Michael Dolan, and Dr. J. W. Hirzy

THE PROSECUTION OF DZHOKHAR TSARNAEV IN THE BOSTON BOMBING CASE, – DISHONORABLE TO THE GOOD NAME OF THE UNITED STATES

John Remington Graham

Over fifty years of practicing law, largely in criminal justice and forensic science and medicine, I have had reason to distrust the FBI. When I was a young lawyer, I defended hundreds of young men who refused to be drafted into the armies of the United States in Vietnam. I used an argument against the constitutionality of such conscription which had been successfully used by Hartford Convention in New England in bringing the War of 1812 to an end. For those interested in details, I refer my readers to United States v. Crocker, 420 F. 2d 307 (8 Cir. 1970), and Kneedler v. Lane, 45 Pa. St. 238 at 240-272 (1863). All of my clients were eventually acquitted or pardoned. Yet in those days, while I was teaching at an accredited law school, my Congressman called me from Washington, D. C., to warn me that the FBI had a dossier on me. The FBI considered me a probable criminal because I defended my generation successfully, according to strict standards of law. A little over twenty-five years ago, I was suspended from the practice of law for sixty days, because an FBI investigation memorandum put words in the mouth of a key witness who later gave a live deposition, completely clearing me of any suspicion of wrongdoing. When the deposition was published by a veteran journalist, the people of my county put my name on the ballot by citizens' petition, and elected me as their general counsel and chief public prosecutor. I can provide details from the public record on request. It came to me as no surprise, therefore, when I learned that, in the Boston marathon case, Dzhokhar Tsarnaev could not have detonated a pressure cooker bomb on Boylston Street in Boston on April 15, 2013, for which he was indicted, convicted, and sentenced to death, and that the FBI's own evidence, of which counsel on both sides and the major news media of the United States were fully aware, conclusively proves that the accused was not guilty. The trial in Boston was a giant hoax, a show trial produced by the FBI and major media in a flagrant abuse of the First Amendment, and most Americans are still not aware of the critical facts. Probably tens of millions have read the internet-accessible report by Dr. Paul Craig Roberts, a former assistant secretary of the treasury of the United States, about the prosecution of Mr. Tsarnaev, drawing heavily from the judicial record, and published widely in the United States, Canada, Europe, and Russia on and after August 17, 2015. I shall attempt here to retell and update that story again here, by attaching several of the most important documents accessible to anybody with a Pacer account, so my readers may review them for themselves.

During the trial, after I had looked into the case, I wrote an opinion, stating that, in light of known FBI-gathered evidence, there was no probable cause to charge Dzhokhar. Drawing from fragments at the scene of the explosions, the FBI crime lab and the indictment against Mr. Tsarnaev, and also the major news media, stated that the culprits were **carrying black backpacks**, filled with heavy pressure cooker bombs, at the time of the explosions, yet Dzhokhar in particular who was charged, not to mention his deceased brother Tamerlan, was shown in a still-frame photo from a street surveillance video used by the FBI to identify the suspects, **carrying a light-**

weight white or silvery bag over his right shoulder only minutes before the explosions. It so happens that there were widely published photos at the time, these still available, showing men in paramilitary gear, wearing black backpacks which perfectly matched the black backpacks projected by the FBI crime lab, but these individuals were not questioned by the FBI.

The backpacks did not match, which in itself proves that Mr. Tsarnaev was not guilty as charged in the indictment. In an ordinary criminal investigation, Dzhokhar would have been eliminated as a suspect, and the men in paramilitary gear would have been approached and questioned, but the FBI let them all go. Shortly before I released my opinion, Dr. Lorraine Day, who had for twenty-five years been chief trauma surgeon at the general hospital in San Francisco, came forward with an internet-accessible opinion, in which she unmistakably pointed out that, in news photos of the scene, no blood was visible when it would have been visible if there had been actual explosions, severing limbs as claimed, and that, when the pretense of blood did appear, the color was a bright orange-red Hollywood color, not the sober maroon color of human blood in real-life situations.

Not long afterwards, I was introduced to Maret Tsarnaeva, a Russian aunt of Dzhokhar, a lawyer who had served as a public prosecutor in the Kyrgyz Republic which had at one time been part of the Russian Empire and the Soviet Union. Maret and I spoke by Skype and corresponded by internet and regular mail. The court-appointed lawyers for Dzhokhar had pressured Dzhokhar's family to accept a defense that Dzhokhar was merely following the lead of his elder brother in the commission of the crime on marathon Monday. They had overwhelming proof that Dzhokhar was not guilty, but would not defend him with the powerful exculpatory evidence they possessed, and thereby save his life. As things finally turned out, the chief counsel for the accused, appointed and paid by the United States, appeared at trial, admitted the guilt of her client in her opening statement, did not use the decisive evidence of innocence in her hands, and did not even ask for a verdict of not guilty in her final summation. Maret knew that Dzhokhar was not guilty as charged, and wanted him defended on the merits. She later submitted an affidavit to the federal district court in Boston, executed on April 17, 2015, and sent from the Russian Federation, in support of her effort to appear as a friend of the court for Dzhokhar, wherein she explained the circumstances. Students of this prosecution will be interested in the details revealed by Mme Tsarnaeva, and so I attach of copy of her affidavit which stands uncontroverted on the judicial record. Maret decided to make an appearance as a friend of the court to present available exculpatory evidence in behalf of her nephew Dzhokhar. I should note here that I had to seek the assistance of local lawyers in Massachusetts to move my admission to the bar of the federal district court in Boston on special occasion so I could represent Maret in her amicus petition. The help of countless lawyers, including the American Civil Liberties Union, was solicited and refused, because the major news media had created such a forbidding atmosphere that local counsel were afraid of loss of reputation or livelihood if they were known to have assisted anybody seeking to help Mr. Tsarnaev. I had practiced in Massachusetts before, and had never before encountered such difficulty. Boston was the last place in the world where a fair trial of Mr. Tsarnaev could be held. On advice of the bar liaison officer of the federal district court in Boston, Maret represented herself in her amicus petition, with me at her side as "of counsel" so the court would know she had legal guidance. At her request, I prepared Maret's motion and argument, and filed the documents for her. Her submission was left unanswered, and so the particulars were admitted. For those who want the facts from the judicial record, I attach her argument which lays down the law and the facts, including four exhibits at the end (designated Tsarnaeva exhibits 1, 2, 3, and 4) which prove conclusively that the projections of the FBI crime lab and paragraph 7 of the indictment (especially Tsarnaeva exhibit 3) are contradicted by a third still-frame photo from the Whiskey Steak House video (Tsarnaeva exhibit 4), and that, therefore, Dzhokhar was not guilty. This evidence, though offered and not contradicted, was ignored, and no hearing was held upon it. The trial jury was never made aware of this evidence, which was also hidden from the general public. On June 24, 2015, Dzhokhar was sentenced to death. The proceedings were legal theater, a game of smoke and mirrors. But at least we secured a legal record made by the Russian aunt seeking to appear as friend of the court, including the argument and exhibits she offered. On motion, these items were made a visible part of the court record by the presiding judge.

I have heard from citizens exasperated that I have not believed the confessions attributed to Mr. Tsarnaev. One fellow insisted I was not a lawyer, because I would not accept those confessions, but he learned from the Minnesota Supreme Court that I am a lawyer in good standing, and have been in practice for a half century. Why should nobody believe the confessions in the boat and at sentencing? Because, as Sir William Blackstone said, and as all good criminal lawyers know, **"[E]ven in cases of felony at common law, [confessions] are the weakest and most suspicious of all testimony, ever liable to be obtained by artifice, false hopes, promises of favour, or menaces, seldom remembered accurately, or reported with due precision, and incapable in their nature of being disproved by other negative evidence."** — 4 Commentaries at 357. The alleged confession in the boat in Watertown required a special writing instrument, which Dzhokhar did not have in his possession. At sentencing the words of the prisoner were plainly scripted for him: no Americanized youth, as Dzhokhar was, says his lawyers were "lovely companions," or speaks of "Muhammad, peace and blessings be upon him," etc. In any event, confessions must always in law be corroborated with the so-called corpus delicti: here the confessions cannot be true, because, if they were true, Dzhokhar would have carried a black backpack as projected by the FBI crime lab and charged the indictment, yet Dzhokhar carried a white bag over his right shoulder. If there had been real explosions, as Dr. Day said, there would have been blood, of which there was none when it should have appeared, and, when blood appeared, it would not have been a flashy orange-red in color. False confessions are common in criminal practice, which is why the law has for years been absorbed in using Miranda warnings and other ways to prevent false confessions. False confessions are a problem, especially for prosecutors, because if an innocent suspect is convicted, the guilty party remains at large, and public safety is imperiled.

A new team of court-appointed lawyers for Mr. Tsarnaev took an appeal in his behalf to the First Circuit. "Counsel for the appellant" will submit their arguments, but I daresay we shall hear nothing from them about the backpacks that do not match, and nothing about the phony blood, which completely change the case from guilty to not guilty, and warrant at least a new trial, if not an acquittal as a matter of law.

Something had to be done for Dzhokhar by somebody other than his court-appointed counsel who had thus far done nothing for him. And that is why three distinguished Americans have appeared before the First Circuit as friends of the court. I attach a copy of their amicus motion without appendices and addendum. The motion refers to the record in the federal district court in Boston, including the exculpatory evidence and exhibits, and was filed on October 13, 2017. If th First Circuit had wanted to continue the cover up the exculpatory evidence proving actual innocence, including proof that the backpacks do not match, the First Circuit could easily have denied the motion, because, never before in American jurisprudence, as far as I am aware, has a private amicus motion ever been allowed in a major public prosecution. If the motion had been denied, nobody would have noticed. But, **on November 9, 2017, the First Circuit granted the amicus motion of the three distinguished American friends of the court, including a retired professor of philosophy, an international scholar in political science, and a doctor of medicine with thirty-seven years of practice behind him. The appellate court will consider the decisive exculpatory evidence which had been kept from the attention of the trial jury and the attention of the general public, previously buried in the record as if not part of the judicial process.**

On November 24, 2017, argument in support of the amicus motion was filed as ordered by the First Circuit. I attach a copy of the text of the argument before the First Circuit, without caption, tables, appendices, or addendum. The motion and our argument are now visibly part of the judicial record, although the major media have continued to abuse the First Amendment by hiding this material from public attention in their game of intentional deception. We have learned of this sad reality from an honest journalist associated with the Boston Herald, who interviewed me for about forty-five minutes on November 26, 2017, after she discovered our filings with the First Circuit two days beforehand. As she expressed her impression in conversation with me, this material completely changes the story of the Boston marathon case as reported by major news media of the United States, and she was glad to have discovered the facts and to report them, as a good journalist should have been. But her supervising editor blocked publication of the story. She should have won the Pulitzer prize and seen her work published. If the country does not find out what really happened in this case, Mr. Tsarnaev will die by lethal injection, and the United States will be disgraced in the eyes of history. And those responsible will be answerable to God. I have intervened, because I am an American lawyer, and I want to be proud of the law and proud of my country.

The lawyers on both sides of this prosecution did not want the court to know of the decisive exculpatory evidence in the federal district court in Boston, but the First Circuit has reached out and demanded it. Let us hope that the First Circuit will tell the country the truth, even though the major news and entertainment media of the United State have thus far failed us and let us all down. I recall and remind others of the famous Pentagon Papers case, New York Times v. United States, 403 U. S. 713 (1971), which recognized the duty of the press to prevent deception of the people by their government. In this case, however, it is clear from contemporary history that the New York Times, the Washington Post, CNN, and associated major media have shamelessly aided the government of the United States in hiding exculpatory evidence in the prosecution of a man whom they knew or should have known was not guilty of a heinous crime, and they were guilty of this breach of moral duty in order to mislead the American people. – John

Remington Graham of the Minnesota Bar (#3664X),
jrgraham@novicomfusion.com, 418-888-5049.

Originally published on July 4, 2018, in Radians & Inches: The
Journal of Crime.

AFFIDAVIT OF MARET TSARNAEVA CONCERNING THE PROSECUTION OF DZHOKHAR TSARNAEV

Mindful that this affidavit may be filed or displayed as an offer of proof with her authorization in public proceedings contemplated by the laws of the United States of America, and in reliance upon Title 28 of the United States Code, Section 1746, Maret Tsarnaeva deposes and says:

I am the paternal aunt of Dzhokhar Tsarnaev who has been prosecuted before the United States District Court for Massachusetts upon indictment of a federal grand jury returned on June 27, 2013, for causing one of two explosions on Boylston Street in Boston on April 15, 2013. In the count for conspiracy, certain other overt acts of wrongdoing are mentioned. As I understand the indictment, if Dzhokhar did not carry and detonate an improvised explosive device or pressure-cooker bomb as alleged, all thirty counts fail, although perhaps some lingering questions, about which I offer no comment here, might remain for resolution, subject to guarantees of due process of law, within the jurisdiction of the Commonwealth of Massachusetts.
I am currently living in Grozny, the capital of Chechnya which is a republic within the Russian Federation. My academic training included full-time studies in a five-year program of the Law Faculty at the Kyrgyz State University, and I also hold the degree of master of laws (LL. M.), with focus on securities

laws, granted by the University of Manitoba while I lived in Canada. I am qualified to practice law in Kyrgyzstan. I am fluent in Russian, Chechen, and English, and am familiar with other languages. I am prepared to testify under oath in public proceedings in the United States, if my expenses are paid, and if my personal safety and right of return to my home in Chechnya are adequately assured in advance.

Aside from other anomalies and other aspects of the case on which I make no comment here, I am aware of several photo exhibits, upon which the Federal Bureau of Investigation (FBI) relied, or of evidence which their crime laboratory has produced, and certain other reports or material. Together, these plainly show that Dzhokhar was not carrying a large, nylon, black backpack, including a white-rectangle marking at the top, and containing a heavy pressure-cooker bomb, shortly before explosions in Boston on April 15, 2013, as claimed by the FBI and as alleged in the indictment for both explosions. On the contrary, these photo exhibits show unmistakably that Dzhokhar was carrying over his right shoulder a primarily white backpack which was light in weight, and was not bulging or sagging as would have been evident if it contained a heavy pressure-cooker bomb. The only reasonable conclusion is that Dzhokhar was not responsible for either of the explosions in question.

On or about June 20-21, 2013, during their first trip to Russia, which lasted about ten days more or less, Judy Clarke and William Fick, lawyers from the federal public defender's office in Boston, visited my brother Anzor Tsarnaev, and his wife Zubeidat, respectively the father and mother of Dzhokhar. The meeting was at the home of Dzhokhar's parents in Makhachkala which is in the republic of Dagestan adjacent to the republic of Chechnya, and about three hours' drive from Grozny. My mother, my sister Malkan, and I were present at this meeting. Zubeidat speaks acceptable English. Mr. Fick is fluent in Russian.

Laying aside other details of the conversation on June 20-21, 2013, I wish to note the following:

— The lawyers from Boston strongly advised that Anzor and Zubeidat refrain from saying in public that Dzhokhar and his brother Tamerlan were not guilty. They warned that, if their advice were not followed, Dzhokhar's life in custody near Boston would be more difficult;

— Mme Clarke and Mr. Fick also requested of Anzor and Zubeidat that they assist in influencing Dzhokhar to accept the legal representation of the federal public defender's office in Boston. Mr. Fick revealed that Dzhokhar was refusing the services of the federal public defender's office in Boston, and sending lawyers and staff away when they visited him in custody. In reaction to the suggestion of Mr. Fick, lively discussion followed;

— As Dzhokhar's family, we expressed our concern that the federal public defender's office in Boston was untrustworthy, and might not defend Dzhokhar properly, since they were paid by the government of the United States which was prosecuting him, as many believe for political reasons. Dzhokhar's parents expressed willingness to engage independent counsel, since Dzhokhar did not trust his government-appointed lawyers. Mr. Fick reacted by saying that the government agents and lawyers would obstruct independent counsel;

— I proposed that Dzhokhar's family hire independent counsel to work with the federal public defender's office in order to assure proper and effective representation of Dzhokhar. Mr. Fick replied that, if independent counsel were hired by the family, the federal public defender's office in Boston would withdraw;

— Mr. Fick then assured Anzor and Zubeidat that the United States Department of Justice had allotted $5 million to Dzhokhar's defense, and that the federal public defender's office in Boston intended to defend Dzhokhar properly. Zubeidat then and there said little concerning assurances of Mr. Fick. But for my part, I never believed that the federal public defender's office in Boston ever intended to defend Dzhokhar as promised. And my impressions from what happened during the trial lead me to believe that the federal public defender's office in Boston did not defend Dzhokhar competently and ethically.

In any event, I am aware that, following the meeting on June 20-21, 2013, Mme Clarke and Mr. Fick continued to spend time with Anzor and Zubeidat, and eventually persuaded Zubeidat to sign a typed letter in Russian to Dzhokhar, urging him to cooperate wholeheartedly with the federal public defender's office in Boston. I am informed by my sister Malkan that Zubeidat gave the letter to the public defenders, shortly before their departure from Russia on or about June 29, 2013, for delivery to Dzhokhar.

During subsequent trips of Mme Clarke and Mr. Fick to see Dzhokhar's parents inMakhachkala, the strategy for defending Dzhokhar was explained, as I learned from my sister Malkan. The public defender's office in Boston intended to contend at trial, as actually has happened since, that Tamerlan, now deceased, was the mastermind of the crime, and that Dzhokhar was merely following his big brother. I was firmly opposed to this strategy as morally and legally wrong, because Dzhokhar is not guilty, as FBI-generated evidence shows. Some ill-feeling has since developed between myself and Dzhokhar's parents over their acquiescence.

On or about June 19, 2014, during their visit to Grozny over nearly two weeks, three staff members from the public defender's office in Boston visited my mother and sisters in Grozny. I am told that they also visited Dzhokhar's parents in Makhachkala.

The personnel visiting my mother and sisters in Grozny on or about June 19, 2014, included one Charlene, who introduced herself as an independent investigator, working in and with the federal public defender's office in Boston; another by the name of Jane, a social worker who claimed to have spoken with Dzhokhar; and a third, by the name of Olga, who was a Russian-English interpreter from New Jersey. They did not leave business cards, but stayed at the main hotel in Grozny, hence I presume that their surnames can be ascertained.

I was not present at the meeting in Grozny on or about June 19, 2014, but my sister Malkan, who was present, called me by telephone immediately after the meeting concluded. She revealed to me then the details of the conversation at the meeting. Malkan and I have since spoken about the visit on several occasions.

Malkan speaks Russian and Chechen and is willing to testify under oath in public proceedings in the United States through an interpreter in Russian, if her expenses are paid, and if her personal safety and right of return to her home in Chechnya are adequately assured in advance. She relates, and has authorized me to state for her that, during the conversation on June 19, 2014, in Grozny, Charlene the independent investigator stated flatly that the federal public defender's office in Boston knew that Dzhokhar was not guilty as charged, and that their office was under enormous pressure from law enforcement agencies and high levels of the government of the United States not to resist conviction.

This affidavit is executed outside of the United States, but the foregoing account is true to the best of my knowledge, information, and belief, and subject to the pains and penalties of perjury under the laws of the United States of America.

Given on this _____17_____ day of _____April_____, 2015.

/s/ Maret Tsarnaeva [Russian script]

_____
_____

Maret Tsarnaeva

Tsarnaeva pro se Argument

UNITED STATES DISTRICT COURT
DISTRICT OF MASSACHUSETTS

United States of America,

Plaintiff

vs. ARGUMENT OF AMICUS CURIAE

Dzhokhar Tsarnaev, No. 13-CR-10200-GAO

Defendant

MAY IT PLEASE THE COURT:

1. Federal jurisdiction: The constitutional authority of the United States cannot be extended to the prosecution of Dzhokhar Tsarnaev in light of the opinion of the court in United States v. Lopez, 514 U. S. 549 (1995), and views of Alexander Hamilton in The Federalist, Ns. 17, 22, and 34 [Clinton Rossiter (ed.), Mentor edition by New American Library, New York, 1961, pp. 118, 143-144, and 209]. Congress has broad power to regulate commerce, including trade and the incidents of trade, but domestic crimes and use of weapons are generally reserved to the States. If there is sufficient evidence to prosecute Dzhokhar for murder and mayhem, he should and can be prosecuted exclusively by the Commonwealth of Massachusetts. Accordingly, amicus urges that the indictment now pending should be dismissed, and the conviction of her nephew

Dzhokhar Tsarnaev of charges under several acts of Congress should be vacated.

2. The actual innocence of the accused: Laying aside misgivings of amicus and many others about of the "official" scenario concerning this case, as broadcast to the world by the government and mainstream news media of the United States, evidence generated by the Federal Bureau of Investigation (FBI), confirmed on the judicial record of this cause, and clarified by the indictment, or suitable for judicial notice under Rule 201(b) of the Federal Rules of Evidence, conclusively proves that Dzhokhar Tsarnaev cannot be guilty of the crimes charged in this prosecution.

The formal indictment against Dzhokhar Tsarnaev was returned on June 27, 2013. The document is 74 pages long, and accuses Mr. Tsarnaev (hereinafter called Dzhokhar) of heinous crimes, including many counts punishable by death. The central event for which Dzhokhar is alleged to have been responsible, according to the indictment, took place, on Boylston Street, in front of the Forum Restaurant, near the finish line of the Boston marathon on April 15, 2013. The most important paragraphs of the indictment are numbered 6, 7, and 24 (including several other paragraphs repeating expressly or by implication the substance thereof). Paragraphs 6-7, read in themselves and in context, state that, acting in concert with his (now deceased) brother, Dzhokhar set down on the sidewalk and detonated one of two "black backpacks" which contained "improvised explosive devices," these "constructed from pressure cookers, low explosive power, shrapnel, adhesive, and other materials." Paragraph 24 clarifies that the black backpack carried, and containing the pressure-cooker bomb allegedly detonated by Dzhokhar, was placed in front of the Forum Restaurant and was associated with the second explosion. The indictment says in paragraph 6 that both bombs exploded at about 2:49 in the afternoon (Eastern time), and that the bombs Dzhokhar and his brother placed and detonated each killed at least one person, and wounded scores of others.

On the morning after the explosions, i. e., on April 16, 2013, Richard DesLauriers, special agent in charge of the FBI in Boston, made a public statement at a press conference, which is published in printed form on the FBI website and in the news media concerning the facts later set forth in the indictment. Mr. DesLauriers said, as paragraphs 6-7 of the indictment substantially confirm,

". . . this morning, it was determined that both of the explosives were placed in a dark-colored nylon bag or backpack. The bag would have been heavy, because of the components believed to be in it."

". . . we are asking that the public remain alert, and to alert us to the following activity . . . someone who appeared to be carrying an unusually heavy bag yesterday around the time of the blasts and in the vicinity of the blasts."

The FBI also published on April 16, 2013, a crime lab photo of a bomb fragment found after the explosions This photo is reproduced as Tsarnaeva exhibit 1 in the appendix hereof, and is believed proper for judicial notice.

From this bomb fragment, the FBI crime lab was able to reconstruct the size, shape, and type of pressure cookers, as was reported on information published by the FBI to the nation on ABC News Nightline on April 16, 2013. A still-frame, taken from (about 01:39-01:54) of this ABC television report, is reproduced as Tsarnaeva exhibit 2 in the appendix hereof, and is offered for judicial notice. A larger segment of this ABC Nightline News report (at about 01:31-02:14) elaborates facts set forth in paragraphs 6-7 of the indictment, including reference to three of the four exhibits reproduced in the appendix hereof. Each of the pressure cookers in question was a Fagor, 6-quart model, marketed in or near Boston and elsewhere in the United States by Macey's. Its external dimensions are probably about 8½ inches in height, including cover, and about 9 inches in diameter. Stripped of hard plastic handles and filled with nails, bee bees, and other such metal, then prepared as a bomb, it would cause a bag carrying it to be, as observed by the FBI chief in Boston during his press conference on April 16, 2013, "unusually heavy."

Again on April 16, 2013, the FBI published a crime lab photo, here reproduced as Tsarnaeva exhibit 3 in the appendix hereof, and showing a blown-out backpack which is said to have contained one of the bombs, — a black nylon bag with a characteristic white rectangle marking about 3 by 1½ inches more or less as it appeared following the explosions the day before.This photo pictures the "dark colored nylon bag or backpack" which Mr. DesLauriers described in his press conference on the day after the explosions when he described what was carried by the guilty parties. It was one of the "black backpacks" referenced in paragraph 7 of the indictment. It is pictured in prosecution exhibit 26 which was introduced on the second day of the trial in this cause (day 28 on the transcript, March 5, 2015), showing that the bag or backpack in question was found on the street near the post box in front of the Forum Restaurant on Boylston Street, and, as previously noted, was associated with the second explosion on April 15, 2013, which, in paragraph 24 of the indictment, Dzhokhar is alleged to have detonated. This general impression is confirmed by defense exhibit 3090, showing a backpack with black exterior or covering, and introduced on the sixteenth day of the trial (day 42 on the transcript, March 31, 2015). Tsarnaeva exhibit 3 is also suitable for judicial notice.

On April 18, 2013, the FBI published a 29-second street video claimed to have been taken from Whiskey's Steak House on Boylston Street at about 02:37-38 o'clock in the afternoon (Eastern time), only minutes before the explosions on April 15, 2013. It definitively settles the principal question raised by the indictment and the plea of not guilty interposed against it. Part of this video is tucked into prosecution exhibit 22 introduced on the third day of the trial in this cause (day 29 on the transcript, March 9, 2015). From this street video, three still-frame photos have been extracted. Two of these still-frame photos were published by the FBI on April 18, 2013, on posters which were used to identify suspects. All three photos were published by CNN and the Associated Press on April 19, 2013. The third still-frame photo from this video is most telling, and is reproduced as Tsarnaeva exhibit 4 in the appendix hereof.As already noted, the FBI and the indictment have together affirmed that the culprits who detonated these explosions were carrying large, unusually heavy, black backpacks concealing pressure-cooker bombs; but, the third still-frame photo from the Whiskey's Steak House video reproduced as Tsarnaeva exhibit 4, and drawn from a street video already used by the FBI to identify the suspects and acknowledged by the government in this prosecution, shows unmistakably that, shortly before the explosions, Dzhokhar was carrying a small-size, white* backpack over his right shoulder the same light in weight, not heavy laden, and displaying no sagging or bulging as would normally be evident if the bag identified contained a pressure-cooker bomb of the size and weight which the FBI has described.

*For all practical purposes and to the naked eye, the color is white, although technical computer analysis suggests a very whitish shade of gray.

Dzhokhar is not guilty of carrying and detonating a pressure-cooker bomb, as charged in the indictment, as is literally as obvious as the difference between black and white. There were and remain other suspects whose identities have been credibly suggested. See, e. g., Toni Cartalucci, Land Destroyer Report, April 19, 2013 (illustrated commentary entitled "'Contractors' Stood Near Bomb, Left Before Detonation."). But here it is enough to reflect on the comment of Lord Acton that "historic responsibility has to make up for the want of legal responsibility." — J. Rufus Fears, Selected Writings of Lord Acton, Liberty Fund, Indianapolis, 1985, Vol. 2, p. 383 (Letter to Mandell Creighton, April 5, 1887). Whatever is done in judicial proceedings, history will judge this case, as surely as history has judged other significant cases.

3. The grievance of amicus: It is impossible that federal prosecutors and counsel for the accused did not know of the exculpatory evidence which has just been identified and illustrated. Yet federal prosecutors went ahead without probable cause, as if decisive evidence of actual innocence, impossible to ignore in a diligent study of this case, did not exist, as is wholly unacceptable in light of Brady v. Maryland, 373 U. S. 83 at 86-87 (1963).
Moreover, in her opening statement at trial on March 4, 2015, as reflected in the fourth paragraph of the transcript of her comments, court-appointed counsel for the accused forcefully insisted that Dzhokhar was guilty of capital felonies, as is positively disproved by evidence generated by the FBI,

reinforced by the indictment itself. She said, "The government and the defense will agree about many things that happened during the week of April 15th, 2013. On Marathon Monday, Tamerlan Tsarnaev walked down Boylston Street with a backpack on his back, carrying a pressure cooker bomb, and put it down in front of Marathon Sports near the finish line of the Marathon. Jahar [i. e., Dzhokhar] Tsarnaev walked down Boylston Street with a backpack on his back carrying a pressure cooker bomb and placed it next to a tree in front of the Forum Restaurant. The explosions extinguished three lives."

And in her summation to the jury on April 6, 2015, as the transcript shows, court-appointed counsel for the accused said nothing of the exculpatory evidence in this case. She did not even ask for a verdict of not guilty. She could hardly have done more to promote a conviction and the severest sentence possible, even though the third still-frame photo from the video at Whiskey's Steak House, reproduced as Tsarnaeva exhibit 4, showed Dzhokhar carrying a white backpack, as alone was enough to defeat the indictment insofar as paragraph 7 thereof averred that the accused and his brother committed the principal acts of wrongdoing by carrying and setting down black backpacks. Such misconduct is altogether unacceptable in light of Strickland v. Washington, 446 U. S. 668 at 687-688 (1984). The misconduct of which amicus complains served to conceal decisive exculpatory evidence by legerdemain. Amicus urges not only that the death penalty may not be imposed in this case, for all three opinions in Herrera v. Collins, 506 U. S. 390 (1993), allow that the death penalty may not be constitutionally imposed where the accused is demonstrably innocent, but that sua sponte this court order a new trial with directions that new counsel for the accused be appointed, motivated to provide an authentic defense for Dzhokhar.

4. The corpus delicti: Paragraph 10 of the indictment recites a statement in the nature of a confession by Dzhokhar written on the inner walls of a boat in Watertown. But with respect to any and all evidence offered or treated as suggesting an extrajudicial admission of guilt in this case, amicus cites the penetrating observation by Sir William Blackstone in his Commentaries on the Laws of England, Edward Christian, London, 1765, Book

IV, p. 357: "[E]ven in cases of felony at common law, [confessions] are the weakest and most suspicious of all testimony, ever liable to be obtained by artifice, false hopes, promises of favour, or menaces, seldom remembered accurately, or reported with due precision, and incapable in their nature of being disproved by other negative evidence." Amicus and countless others suspect that the alleged confession in the boat was staged as artifice to suit the government's case, and not authentic. But she stands on ancient wisdom which casts doubt on all extrajudicial confessions without adequate safeguards, including the rule that an extrajudicial confession is insufficient to convict, unless the corpus delicti be sufficiently proved up. The rule is defined with various degrees of rigor from jurisdiction to jurisdiction. In federal courts, in any event, the corroboration required to sustain a confession or statement in the nature of a confession need only be independent, substantial, and reveal the words in question to be reasonably trustworthy, as appears, e. g., in Opper v. United States, 348 U. S. 84 (1954). If such be the law here applicable, the required corroboration in this case must include evidence showing that Dzhokhar actually carried a large, heavy, black backpack on Boylston Street before the explosions on the afternoon on April 15, 2013, as claimed by the FBI and alleged in the indictment. Tsarnaeva exhibit 4, a product of investigation by the FBI, shows plainly that Dzhokhar did no such thing, hence no required corroboration has been established

5. Closing remarks: The views here expressed are not unique, but shared by good Americans, and others the world over. The undersigned and her sister Malkan are prepared to testify as expressed in the affidavit filed in support of the motion for leave to file a submission as amicus curiae. This argument is

Respectfully submitted,

Dated:___May 15, 2015 /s/ Maret Tsarnaeva [Russian script]_
MARET TSARNAEVA, Pro se
Zhigulevskaya Str. 7, Apt. 4
364000 Grozny, Chechen Republic, RF
Telephone: 011-7-938-899-1671

E-mail: marettsar@gmail.com

Of counsel:
John Remington Graham of the Minnesota Bar (#3664X)
180 Haut de la Paroisse
St-Agapit, Quebec G0S 1Z0 Canada
Telephone: 418-888-5049
E-mail: jrgraham@novicomfusion.com

CERTIFICATE OF COMPLIANCE

The undersigned certifies that this submission is consistent with the rules of this Court, that it is prepared in 14-point Times New Roman font, and that the bare text thereof consists of 2,331 words.

Dated:__May 15, 2015 /s/ Maret Tsarnaeva [Russian script]__

Maret Tsarnaeva

APPENDIX

TSARNAEVA EXHIBIT 1

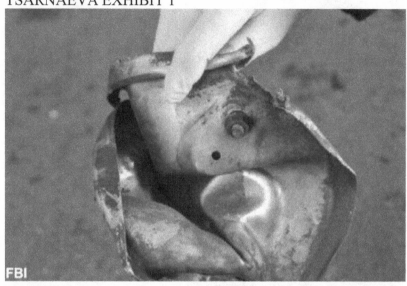

TSARNAEVA EXHIBIT 2

TSARNAEVA EXHIBIT 3

TSARNAEVA EXHIBIT 4

Tsarnaev, Amicus Intervention (motion)

UNITED STATES COURT OF APPEALS FOR THE FIRST CIRCUIT

MOTION OF THREE CITIZENS OF THE UNITED STATES FOR LEAVE TO APPEAR AS FRIENDS OF THE COURT UNDER RULE 29(a) OF THE FEDERAL RULES OF APPELLATE PROCEDURE

United States of America,
Appellee

Vs.

Dzhokhar Tsarnaev
Appellant No. 16-6001

The undersigned introduces himself by offering a short résumé of his career as appendix A, subject to further specification as may ultimately be required by this Court. The undersigned is a specialist in forensic science and medicine, and in British, American, and Canadian constitutional law and history, in both of which fields he has many publishing credits. He has been permanently and generally admitted to the bar of five courts of record in the United States. Beyond his native Minnesota, he has practiced pro hac vice before twenty-eight state or federal courts of record in fifteen jurisdictions of the United States over the course of nearly fifty years. He is a member in good standing of the bar of the Minnesota Supreme Court (#3664X), and was there admitted on October 20, 1967. A formal certificate can be made available on request. No ethics proceedings are pending against the undersigned. On September 26, 2017, upon due inquiry, the undersigned was advised by personnel in the clerk's office of this Court that he need not be a member of the bar of this Court to make this motion under Rule 29(a) of the Federal Rules of Appellate Procedure in behalf of three citizens of the United States desiring to appear as friends of the court in the above-entitled matter. On October 4, 2017, the circuit executive's office instructed the undersigned to rely on the clerk's office. On October 5 and 10, 2017, the clerk's office confirmed that the admission of the undersigned to the bar of this Court is not necessary for this motion under Rule 29(a), and directed filing and service in paper without fee.

TO COUNSEL FOR THE UNITED STATES AND FOR THE APPELLANT, PLEASE TAKE NOTICE THAT THE UNDERSIGNED MAKES THE FOLLOWING MOTION BEFORE THIS HONORABLE COURT IN BEHALF OF THREE CITIZENS OF THE UNITED STATES, TO WIT:

COMES NOW the undersigned, and he makes the following motion, to wit: That James Fetzer, Ph. D., natural born citizen of the United States and emeritus professor of philosophy at the University of Minnesota Duluth; Mary Maxwell, Ph. D., LL. B., natural born citizen of the United States, previously working in Australia, now present in the United States; and Cesar Baruja, M. D., naturalized citizen of the United States, born in Paraguay, and practicing medicine over the past thirty-seven years, be granted leave to appear as friends of the court in the above-entitled matter through the undersigned as their counsel, and that, if necessary for this purpose, the undersigned be admitted to the bar of this Court generally or pro hac vice, either sua sponte or on motion yet to be made. Attached as appendix B is an uncolored and unbound copy of a proposed submission on the merits, including an addendum of relevant papers from the record, to be submitted in proper format and number as ordered in due course.

This effort is funded by Elisabeth Ritter-Blaser, a philanthropist and German-speaking citizen of the Swiss Confederation, living in the City of Oberburg in the canton of Bern. Her interest is preventing wrongful convictions and executions in the United States and other countries.

The undersigned has contributed nothing to the funding of this effort, but has prepared this motion. He will argue orally, but only if requested by this Court.

Dr. Fetzer, Dr. Maxwell, and Dr. Baruja have all studied and commented on the prosecution of Dzhokhar Tsarnaev. They all protest this prosecution as unfounded upon probable cause, and they verily believe, from their respective and detailed investigations of the facts in this case, and from the work of other eminent experts, including an internet-accessible report of Lorraine Day, M. D., who for many years served as chief of orthopedic surgery at the general hospital in San Francisco, that the prosecution of Mr. Tsarnaev is dishonorable to the United States. Aside from other anomalies not on this record, Dr. Fetzer, Dr. Maxwell, and Dr. Baruja maintain that, during the trial of Dzhokhar Tsarnaev, certain powerful exculpatory evidence on this record, grasped by many astute observers, and sufficient to warrant outright dismissal or acquittal, or an order granting a new trial, went unused and unnoticed by counsel on both sides, including the principal trial lawyer for Mr. Tsarnaev who loudly proclaimed his guilt in her opening statement and did not even ask for a verdict of not guilty during her final summation. It is no less true that major news and entertainment media of the United States have abused the First Amendment by acting together to create false appearances of guilt on the part of Mr. Tsarnaev of grave capital crimes, and to inspire public hatred against him; that Mr. Tsarnaev was misled into making or otherwise has been said to have made false confessions unconfirmed by the corpus delicti; that the said exculpatory evidence was actually generated by the Federal Bureau of Investigation (FBI), and positively disproves essential facts of accusation in the indictment; and that the said exculpatory evidence is referenced and made part of this record by electronic order #1469 issued by the United States District

Court for Massachusetts (No. 13-CR-10200-GAO), the same entered on June 17, 2015. The said exculpatory evidence was never heard or considered by the jury, nor was it considered in sentencing.

Dr. Fetzer, Dr. Maxwell, and Dr. Baruja note here that key papers referenced by the said electronic order #1469 have been conveniently reviewed in an internet-accessible report, dated August 17, 2015, by Paul Craig Roberts, Ph. D., former assistant secretary of the treasury of the United States. The said report by Dr. Roberts has been read since original publication probably by tens of millions in the United States, Canada, Europe, and Russia.

In a nutshell, the FBI crime lab determined from fragments at the scene of the explosions, and the indictment stated in paragraphs 6, 7, and 24 of the general allegations, applicable to all counts, that Dzhokhar was carrying a black backpack heavy-laden with a large pressure-cooker bomb. The FBI then identified as culprits two individuals by reference to a street video which included a still-frame photo showing that Dzhokhar carried a light-weight white backpack. The very evidence used by the FBI to identify the "Boston bombers" referenced in the indictment, excludes Dzhokhar as plainly as white is distinguished from black. And there are widely published photos of the scene of the explosions showing other individuals carrying black backpacks which perfectly match the projections of the FBI crime lab, but we are aware of no evidence that these individuals were ever investigated. The lawyers on both sides must have known about these exculpatory facts, but played to the gallery as if the street video confirmed that Dzhokhar was guilty. In view of these facts, this Court should view and consider the evidence covered by electronic order #1469, then grant appropriate remedy, — i. e., reversal with order for acquittal as a matter of law or reversal with order granting a new trial. Dr. Fetzer, Dr. Maxwell, and Dr. Baruja believe that allowance of a death sentence under these circumstances amounts to judicial murder in the sense illustrated in Powell v. Alabama, 287 U. S. 45 at 72-73 (1932). Such is their interest here.

They submit as authority for their right to intervene and be heard as friends of the court the internet-accessible opinion of Judge T. S. Ellis III, published on February 27, 2006, in United States v. Steven J. Rosen and Keith Weissman, No. 1:05CR225-TSE, Document 228, on the docket of the United States District Court for Eastern Virginia.

Pursuant to 28 United States Code, Section 1746, the undersigned swears, subject to the pains and penalties of perjury, that he has conducted himself and will conduct himself before this Court in an upright and proper manner, that he will support and has always supported the United States Constitution, and that all representations hereinabove are true to the best of his knowledge, information, and belief. This oath is made abroad, subject to the laws of the United States.

Dated:_____October 13, 2017_____

JOHN REMINGTON GRAHAM of the Minnesota Bar (#3664X)
180 Haut de la Paroisse
St-Agapit, Quebec G0S 1Z0 Canada
TEL-FAX 418-888-5049
E-mail jrgraham@novicomfusion.com
Counsel for Dr. Fetzer, Maxwell, and Baruja

CERTIFCATE OF COMPLIANCE

The undersigned certifies that foregoing motion has been prepared in 14-point Times New Roman font, and, exclusive of this certificate but including caption and signature material amounts to 1419 words, and thus complies with the rules of this Court.

Dated:_____October 13, 2017_____
JOHN REMINGTON GRAHAM of the Minnesota Bar (#3664X)

Tsarnaev, Amicus Intervention (brief)

MAY IT PLEASE THE COURT:

For reasons already stated in their motion for leave to appear as friends of the court, Dr. James Fetzer, Dr. Mary Maxwell, and Dr. Cesar Baruja urge this Court to review the papers covered by and including electronic order #1469 in the federal district court in Boston (filed on May 29, and disposed of on June 17, 2015), and displayed in the addendum to this submission. And by virtue thereof they ask this Court to reverse the conviction below and enter a judgment of acquittal, or order granting a new trial with directions for appointment of new counsel for the appellant Dzhokhar Tsarnaev, motivated to defend him on the merits of his plea of not guilty. The most essential facts are properly referenced to this record in the pro se argument of the Russian aunt of Mr. Tsarnaev (pages A18-A25 and A28-A29 of the addendum to this submission). Dr. Fetzer, Dr. Maxwell, and Dr. Baruja wish to add certain comments concerning events since Dzhokhar was sentenced to death and not mentioned in their motion for leave to appear as friends of the court:

Sentencing occurred on June 24, 2015, during which the transcript indicates that, before he was sentenced to death, Mr. Tsarnaev made certain bizarre statements, including suspicious statements of Islamic piety, and about his lawyers who, he says, were "lovely companions." These comments are wholly uncharacteristic for an Americanized youth, and thus seem to have been scripted for him. Be that as it may, Mr. Tsarnaev went on at sentencing to make statements purporting to confess to the charges in the indictment. We dismiss these and other acts or comments in the nature of a confession, and urge this Court to do likewise, because, if they were true, Dzhokhar would have carried a heavy-laden black backpack on Boylston Street, as charged in paragraphs 6, 7, and 24 of the indictment, although he actually carried a light-weight white backpack (exhibit 4 on page A29 of the addendum hereto). In other words, there would have been natural proof of the corpus delicti, which was wholly lacking here. Compare the comments of the Russian aunt of Mr. Tsarnaev on the corpus delicti rule (on pages A25-A26 in the addendum hereto).

We wish to acknowledge objections which we have heard from certain newspaper-influenced lawyers in New England who tried to explain away the decisive evidence that Mr. Tsarnaev cannot be guilty in this case:

One eminent criminal lawyer in Massachusetts told us that the contention about black backpacks was only an evaporating investigation hypothesis, as sometimes happens in criminal cases, and that evidence concerning events after the explosions on Boylston Street (e. g., the testimony of Den Meng) was enough to convict Mr. Tsarnaev. But this lawyer did not know that the allegation of blackbackpacks came from the FBI crime lab on the basis of undeniable facts (exhibit 3 on page A29 of the addendum hereto), was incorporated into the indictment (paragraph 7), was part of the government's case-in-chief at trial, and was decisively disproved by the white backpack carried Mr. Tsarnaev over his right shoulder (exhibit 4 on page A29 of the addendum hereto).

Another practitioner, in Boston, told us that between the time of the still-frame photo (exhibit 4 on page A29 of the addendum hereto) and the time of the explosions, Dzhokhar might have switched backpacks. But there is no evidence for, or even consistent with this far-fetched scenario, nor was the suggestion ever made by anybody at trial. The very street video used by the FBI to identify Dzhokhar Tsarnaev excludes him as a suspect.

Others in Maine have said that the white backpack cannot be used except in post-conviction habeas corpus or writ of error coram nobis. This procedural point is answered by Rule 29(a) of the Federal Rules of Appellate Procedure, and the opinion of Judge T. S. Ellis (cited on page A4 of the addendum hereto), which allow us to proceed, if the Court please. Dr. Fetzer, Dr.

Maxwell, and Dr. Baruja do not represent Dzhokhar. They represent the public interest. And we do not have to wait until wrongful conviction. We can proactively prevent wrongful conviction by amicus intervention under positive law here and now.

It has even been suggested by persons with axes to grind that the white backpack (exhibit 4 on page A29 of the addendum hereto) is not compelling evidence. What can be more compelling than the difference between black and white? Why should we not believe our own eyes? We understand that injury to our country and profession will follow a miscarriage of justice in this case, for England lost her territories in France after the judicial murder of Joan of Arc and her free Constitution after the judicial murder of Charles the First. Hence, we dare not conceal the facts from ourselves. We must obey conscience!

The sad story of Anders Brevig in Norway reveals that the death penalty is not the worst of punishments. If Dzhokhar was guilty and had a fair trial, let justice be done. But since Mr. Tsarnaev cannot be guilty here (as appears in the contrast between exhibits 3 and 4 on page A29 of the addendum hereto), the American people need to know what really happened in this case, and this Court must tell them. Our major news and entertainment media will not.

Wherefore, Dr. Fetzer, Dr. Maxwell, and Dr. Baruja ask in behalf themselves and their countrymen that this Court examine the documents in the addendum hereto, and corresponding parts of this record, then do justice.

Dated:_____

————

JOHN REMINGTON GRAHAM of the Minnesota Bar (#3664X)
180 Haut de la Paroisse
St-Agapit, Quebec G0S 1Z0 Canada
TEL-FAX 418-888-5049

E-mail jrgraham@novicomfusion.com
Counsel for Drs. Fetzer, Maxwell, and Baruja

CERTIFICATE OF COMPLIANCE

The undersigned certifies that the foregoing argument, including greeting and signature material, was prepared in 14-point Times New Roman font, consists of 961 words, and thus complies with the rules of this Court.

Dated:_____November 10, 2017_____

JOHN REMINGTON GRAHAM of the Minnesota Bar (#3664X)

Final Statement on the Boston Bombing

To Dr. Paul Craig Roberts and Mr. Søren Korsgaard,

Greeting: I did not receive the official opinion of the First Circuit (some 224 pages) until close to midnight on July 31, 2020, after the press of the world had been notified and indulged in commentary which continues the cover up of the main secret of this case on which I commented in my article in *Radians and Inches*, July 4, 2018, written for the legal and historical record, including four exhibits from the judicial record, in order to avoid any fair misunderstanding. I have withheld comment until I read what the court actually said. On important facts, I seldom trust the press, which has made a mockery of the First Amendment. I wanted to find out what the judges actually said. **The main secret of this case, assiduously covered up by counsel on both sides, and the news media, is that the FBI crime lab and the indictment identified the culprit as carrying a heavy-weight black backpack at the time of the explosions, but that the street video used by the FBI to identify the culprit eventually mentioned in the indictment showed that at the time of the explosions, Dzhokhar Tsarnaev carried a light-weight white sack over his right shoulder, and so was obviously not guilty; but that we have photographs of men in paramilitary gear carrying exactly the type of backpacks identified by the FBI crime lab and indictment. These men in paramilitary gear were never approached or questioned by the FBI. They have escaped public justice**, the same as the murderers of Abraham Lincoln and John F. Kennedy have escaped public justice. On November 16, 2018, the First Circuit entered an order, on my motion protesting failure of court-appointed counsel even to mention the critical exculpatory evidence; the order assured us that the evidence we called to the attention of the court would be given due consideration. The official opinion of the First

Circuit mentions me as arguing for Dr. Fetzer, Dr. Maxwell, and Dr. Baruja appearing as friends of the court. The court was, therefore, fully aware of the exculpatory evidence, and the misconduct of the prosecutors and court-appointed counsel for Mr. Tsarnaev. I attach my article published in Denmark on July 4, 2020, including the four exhibits from the judicial record, and a copy of the official opinion of the court on July 31, 2020, so you may check my comments for yourselves. The opinion opens with the observation that Dzhokhar and Tamerlan detonated pressure-cooker bombs, killing and wounding others, all of which was assumed as fact beyond question from the whole judicial record. The opinion did not at any point mention or consider the decisive exculpatory evidence which the three friends of the court called to the attention of the appellate panel, including the four photographic exhibits identified with the attached argument of Maret Tsarnaeva as amicus curiae before the federal district court in Boston as submitted on May 15, 2015. The cover up has been continued on the momentum of public outrage created by the major news media of the United States, which co-prosecuted this case and prostituted journalism. The cover up was accomplished by refusal even to acknowledge the existence of decisive exculpatory evidence, as if it did not exist. That is the long and the short of this unfortunate episode. Beyond understanding that this kind of blemish is nothing new and nothing uniquely American, my consolation is that Dr. Fetzer, Dr. Maxwell, Dr. Baruja, whom I was honored to represent, faithfully executed their duty to history and country. God must judge us. Man is not naturally good, but a fallen creature in need of redemption, -- it is an old story, but as true today as ever. You may redistribute or republish this correspondence, including the attachments, as you see fit. -- John Remington Graham.

Email from John Remington Graham received on July 4, 2020.

Commentary by Paul Craig Roberts: Boston Marathon Bombing Death Sentence Vacated by Federal Court of Appeals

Paul Craig Roberts

Today the Federal Court of Appeals for the First Circuit vacated the death sentence concocted for one of the alleged bombers of the alleged Boston Marathon bombing of April, 2013, seven years ago. Some years ago John Remington Graham and I demonstrated conclusively that the FBI's own evidence proved conclusively that, even if there really was a bombing for which there is much exposed false evidence, the Tsarnaev brothers were not involved. You can find our analysis in my articles archive on my website.

We succeeded in getting our evidence of their innocence in front of the federal appeals court, and we were stunned when the court accepted it as part of the record. We have been hopeful ever since. Me less than John Remington Graham. As a retired defense attorney and public prosecutor and, undeniably, an expert on the US, Canadian, and unwritten British constitutions, Jack, as he is known, hoped that the judges would not accept our evidence of the Tsarnaev brothers' innocence unless the judges intended to act on it. I myself did not see how they could possibly have the courage to blow up one of the hoaxes used to sustain the fabricated "terrorist threat." Have you noticed how this "terrorist threat" went away? Why did it go away if it were real? It wasn't real, and it served its purpose at the time. Now we have new threats, China, American white supremacy, Trump, and new hoaxes—Russiagate, George Floyd's death at racist white police hands, etc.

The federal appeals court for the First Circuit has disappointed us by only vacating Dzhokhar's death sentence and not his false conviction. Dzhokhar's appointed attorney cooperated with the prosecution in convicting him. The lack of representation is sufficient to overturn his conviction. Dzhokhar's appointed attorney did not raise the question of the FBI's own evidence that the brothers were innocent. She entered the trial with a guilty plea on behalf of her client. In other words, a trial was not needed. A plea bargain could have been arranged instead. The unnecessary trial itself was a hoax for public relations purposes. The appointed attorney was part of the setup that convicted an innocent person for reasons of a hidden agenda. She put her career before truth. That is what people do in a society that has lost its way. We see it all around us. Truth is the greatest enemy of the ruling class. The presstitutes, professors, and corporations that serve the ruling class, in exchange, enjoy financially comfortable lives, unlike 80% of Americans. The way to succeed in America is to be a whore for the Establishment.

The First Circuit's ruling does not free Dzhokhar. The ruling instructs the lower federal district court to hold a new trial to determine Dzhokhar's punishment. I think that this is all the federal appeal court dared to do.

Nevertheless, the federal appeals court ruling opens a wedge by admitting that something was wrong, and Dzhokhar's punishment has to be reconsidered in a new trial. If there were attorneys and bar associations that served justice rather than career and money, they could use the opening provided by the First Circuit to blow up the hoax conviction of Dzhokhar Tsarnaev together with the hoax false flag Boston Marathon Bombing. This, I think, is the message from the US Appeals Court of the First Circuit. The Appeals Court opens the opportunity, but if no one cares, the Appeals Court is not going to take the hit for declaring an innocent person innocent.

A country whose lawyers no longer will fight for justice, but only for money, is a lost and destroyed country.

Originally published as "Boston Marathon Bombing Death Sentence Vacated by Federal Court of Appeals," www.paulcraigroberts.org, July 2020.

Ongoing Global Avoidable Mortality Holocaust and Horrendous Human Carnage from War and Hegemony

Gideon Polya

Lucky Westerners living in rich, prosperous and peaceful countries have minimal direct exposure to death. In their circa 80-year life-span they would see only about 10 dead bodies, typically those of dead relatives dying natural deaths from old age or terminal illness and encountered in hospitals or open-coffin funerals. However, Westerners are fed a huge daily diet of fictional deadly violence via movies and television, and the nightly news brings them graphic reports of actual deadly violence within their own town, city or national jurisdiction, and of mass deaths around the world from events such as avalanches, air crashes, massacres or military operations. A typical news day in a nice, rich and peaceful place like Australia (population 25 million) might involve on average about 1 murder and 6 accidental deaths, with the daily average of about 7 suicides not being reported for fear of encouraging more. A really bad news day might involve 100 people dying from an air crash, train wreck, boat capsize, bus collision, massacre or a so-called "natural disaster" somewhere else in the world.

"Oh, the humanity!" the good Westerners cry. However, their angst is minimized by Mainstream media non-reportage of the actual daily carnage of the Global Avoidable Mortality Holocaust in which 44,000 people in the Developing World (minus China) die avoidably from deprivation each day on

400

Spaceship Earth with homicidally greedy, neoliberal One Percenters in charge of the flight deck and about half the victims being children. Whether a child dies non-violently from war- or hegemony-imposed deprivation or dies violently from bashing, bullets or bombs, the death is just as final and irreversible and the agent's culpability the same.

Avoidable mortality (avoidable death, excess mortality, excess death, premature death, untimely death, deaths that should not have happened) can be defined as the difference between the actual mortality in a country and the mortality expected for a peaceful, decently governed country. For poor but peaceful high birth-rate countries, the average death rate is about 4 deaths per thousand of population per year, and accordingly the avoidable mortality rate can be readily determined as actual death rate minus 4. For other countries, estimation of the avoidable death rate is more complicated and is described in my book Body Count. Avoidable mortality since 1950 that is now available for free perusal on the web [1]. Detailed demographic data from 1950 onwards (e.g. death rate, under-5 infant death rate, etc.) are available from the UN Population Division [2]. For poor, high birth rate countries the annual avoidable mortality can be simply estimated as 1.4 times the under-5 infant deaths (the latter data being readily available on-line from the UN Population Division [2]).

Intra-nationally, avoidable mortality is a crucial parameter for assessing the bottom-line decency and efficacy of social policies within a country. However, avoidable mortality is also a key parameter in assessing the human consequences of war, occupation and neo-colonial hegemony. One can readily see why bad and evil governments are unwilling to be called to account for intra-national deficiencies causing avoidable deaths from deprivation, and why evil, war-making governments are unwilling to be called to account for the huge violent deaths and avoidable deaths from deprivation associated with invading, devastating and occupying other countries. Thus, while avoidable mortality and its synonyms are fundamental to medical epidemiology (e.g. avoidable deaths associated with smoking), avoidable mortality is scrupulously (or rather unscrupulously) avoided in Mainstream discussion of the merits or otherwise of social policies within a country (e.g. gross race-based inequity in the US) or the consequences of war, invasion, devastation and occupation of foreign countries (e.g. the horrendous avoidable mortality in 20 countries invaded by the US Alliance in the 21st century US War on Terror).

The deaths of a very large number of people are described as a "holocaust." Indeed the first WW2 atrocity to be described as a "holocaust" (by N.G. Jog in 1944 [3]) was the Bengali Holocaust (WW2 Indian Holocaust, WW2 Bengal Famine), the WW2 atrocity in which the British with Australian complicity deliberately starved 6-7 million Indians to death in Bengal and the adjacent province of Orissa, Assam and Bihar [4-6]. Yet this atrocity has become a "forgotten holocaust" that has been largely white-washed out of general public perception in the Anglosphere by several generations of holocaust-ignoring and holocaust-denying journalists, politicians, commentariats and academics. Indeed since the 1967 Israeli conquest of all of Palestine, acquisition of nuclear weapons and assumption of massive influence in the Anglosphere (notably in the US), Zionists and their supporters have ensured that the very term "holocaust" only applies to the WW2 Jewish Holocaust that is commonly referred to as "the Holocaust." Reality check: the Jewish Holocaust (5-6 million Jews killed by violence or deprivation) was part of the WW2 European Holocaust (30 million Slavs, Jews and Gypsies killed by the Nazis) that was part of a global WW2 Holocaust that also included the 1937-1945 Chinese Holocaust (35 million Chinese killed under the Japanese) and the 1942-1945 Bengali Holocaust (6-7 million Indians killed under the British).

While a "holocaust" refers to the deaths of huge numbers of people, "genocide" is defined by Article 2 of the UN Genocide Convention as "acts committed with intent to destroy, in whole or in part, a national, ethnic, racial or religious group [7]." The term "genocide" clearly applies to the various elements of the WW2 Holocaust and to prior and subsequent mass murder atrocities. Thus, the ongoing Australian Aboriginal Genocide has been associated since British invasion in 1788 with about 2 million Indigenous Australians deaths from violence (0.1 million) or from imposed disease and deprivation – presently about 4,000 Australian Aboriginals die avoidably each year from imposed deprivation in one of the world's richest countries

[8]. The ongoing Palestinian Genocide has been associated with ethnic cleansing of 90% of Palestine and about 2.3 million deaths from violence (0.1 million) or deprivation (2.2 million) since the British invasion of Palestine in WW1 [9].

In the de-colonizing post-WW2 era, Westerners have progressively adopted an anti-racist stance. Thus, it is no longer acceptable in the West to refer to people of colour by derogatory terms or to exclude them from hotels or restaurants. Indeed in my own country, Australia, we finally voted to count Indigenous Australians as citizens in 1967, the reformist Whitlam Labor Government abolished the 1901-1974 White Australia Policy in 1974, and in 1975 (just before it was removed in a CIA-backed Coup) it passed the 1975 Racial Discrimination Act that criminalized racial discrimination in the Federal jurisdiction. However, the Western Mainstream media hides the awful reality that this earnest Western anti-racism is a veneer hiding what must be called politically correct racism (PC racism). Thus, decolonization was associated with continued poverty of formerly subject peoples that was worsened by Western hegemony, transfers to violent US hegemony and global post-1950 avoidable deaths from deprivation totalling 1,500 million [1].

The penultimate in racism is invasion of another country and the ultimate in racism is genocide. Conservative Westerners who have supported post-WW2 US wars are PC racist – they earnestly declare that they are not racist but nevertheless support racist wars that have killed millions. Thus, most Australians will vehemently declare that they are not racists but Australia has nevertheless been complicit in all post-1950 US Asian wars, atrocities that have been associated with 40 million Asian deaths from violence or war-imposed deprivation [1]. Old habits die hard, and the serial invaders (state terrorist serial killers) of the 21st century are the presently US-allied Western countries with an appalling record of invading other countries. Thus, the British have invaded 193 countries, Australia 85, France 82, the US 72 (52 after WW2), Germany 39, Japan 30, Russia 25, Canada 25, Apartheid Israel 12, China 2 and North Korea arguably none [10, 11].

The bloody 20th century concluded with Western imposition of deadly sanctions on Iraq (1990-2003) [12, 13]. It is estimated that 1.7 million Iraqis (about half of them children) died avoidably from deprivation under sanctions and US, UK and Israeli bombing that reduced a well-educated, modern, secular state to destitution. Top UN officials resigned over what they called a UN-sanctioned Iraqi Genocide. Indeed the US Government confessed to the enormity of this crime. Thus, in 1996 when anti-racist Jewish American journalist Lesley Stahl famously asked US UN Ambassador Madeleine Albright "We have heard that half a million [Iraqi] children have died. I mean, that's more children than died in Hiroshima. And, you know, is the price worth it?" Albright replied, "We think the price is worth it [12]."

Decent people hoped that the 21st century would be Humanity's first century of peace for thousands of years. It was not to be thanks to the endlessly invading Americans, British, French, Israelis, Australians and NATO US lackeys. No Iraqis or Afghans were directly involved in the 9-11 atrocity on 11 September, 2001, according to the "official version of 9-11," promulgated by the Bush Administration that told 935 lies about Iraq between 9-11 and the invasion of Iraq in March 2003 [14]. Notwithstanding this "technicality," the endlessly mendacious, serial invader Americans used 9-11 (3,000 dead) as an excuse to invade and devastate Afghanistan and Iraq and 18 other Muslim countries [12, 13]. Conservative Alan Greenspan (long-time chairman of the US Federal reserve) confessed that "The Iraq war is largely about oil" and on the Left, Professor Noam Chomsky (from 101-Nobel-Laureate Massachusetts Institute of Technology, MIT) declared the obvious that US Middle East wars were about oil and US hegemony [12].

Successive genocidally racist American Governments have not been bothered by the millions they have killed. Thus, General Tommy Franks boasted that "We don't do body counts." However, world-leading US medical epidemiologist and a world-leading UK polling organization, ORB, have informed the eminent US Just Foreign Policy organization to estimate 1.5 million Iraqi deaths from violence in the period 2003-2011. To this we must add a further 1.2 million Iraqi avoidable deaths from war-imposed deprivation under US occupation. Thus, Iraq deaths from violence or imposed deprivation total 2.7 million for the period 2003-2011 (one notes that the Australian ABC, the Australian equivalent of the UK BBC, estimated in 2011 that "tens of thousands" of Iraqis had been killed). However, it gets worse when we consider the 0.2 million Iraqis killed in the Gulf War and the 1.7 million Iraqis dying avoidably from deprivation under Sanctions. The 1990-2011 Iraqi Holocaust and Iraqi Genocide has been associated with 4.6 million Iraq deaths from violence, 1.7 million, or from imposed deprivation, 2.9 million, carnage approaching that of the WW2 Jewish Holocaust. It gets worse still – Iraqi deaths from violence or imposed deprivation total 9 million since the 1914 British invasion of Iraq in WW1 [12, 13].

In 1978, Afghanistan was facing a good future under a progressive and secular government. However, the US engineered the overthrow of this secular government and thence backed fundamentalist jihadis in the decade-long war after the Russians invaded. Afghanistan had a brief respite when the Taliban won the civil war after the Russians left. However, in 2001 the US used the 9-11 atrocity as an excuse to invade Afghanistan, although no Afghans were involved in 9-11 according to the "official version" of 9-11. Indeed US-installed Afghan president Hamid Karzai has denied the very existence of Al Qaeda jihadis in Afghanistan and declared himself to be agnostic over the "official version of 9-11" [14].

It is hard to assess violent deaths in the Afghan War because the war criminal Americans "don't do body counts." Indeed some Australians soldiers in Afghanistan got their wrists slapped for bringing back severed Taliban hands as evidence of their operational success. However, expert US-linked Australian military advice is that the Iraq War was 4 times more deadly that the Afghan War. This estimate permitted an estimate of the Afghan War in 2001-2014 being associated with 7.2 million Afghan deaths from violence, 1.7 million, or from war-imposed deprivation, 5.5 million – an Afghan Holocaust and Afghan Genocide as defined by Article 2 of the UN Genocide Convention. Indeed it has been argued by Professor Ali Khan (professor of law, Washburn University School of Law, Topeka, Kansas) that the US Alliance operations to exterminate the Taliban, the widely-supported Indigenous Afghan religious group, amount to genocide as "acts committed with intent to destroy, in whole or in part, a national, ethnic, racial or religious group [14]."

It gets worse. The post-9-11 US War on Terror is in awful reality a US War on Muslims that has been associated with 32 million Muslim deaths from violence, 5 million, or from deprivation, 27 million, since the 9-11 atrocity that numerous science, architecture, engineering, aviation, military and intelligence experts regard as a US Government false flag atrocity that very likely involved Apartheid Israelis as well as Zionist American Government agents [15, 16]. Indeed both Republican President Donald Trump and Democrat Vice-President Al Gore have slammed the Bush Administration for failure to act before 9-11 when, according to CIA director George Tenet, the entire warning system was "blinking red [16]." The carnage of the post-9-11 US War on Muslims is similar to that of the WW2 European Holocaust and the WW2 Chinese Holocaust – a Muslim Holocaust and a Muslim Genocide as defined by Article 2 of the UN Genocide Convention.

Where is justice in this? Mainstream media journalists, editors, politicians, commentariats and academics ignore the horrendous reality of the Korean Genocide (28% of the North Korean population was killed by US bombing), the ongoing Australian Aboriginal Genocide, the ongoing Palestinian Genocide, the Iraqi Genocide and Iraqi Holocaust, the Afghan Genocide and Afghan Holocaust, and the ongoing Muslim Holocaust and Muslim Genocide in 20 countries variously subject to US Alliance violence. The International Criminal Court (ICC) has a very poor record of confining prosecutable war crimes to Serbs and non-Europeans that the US doesn't like. However, even in the eventuality of the ICC speeding up its current "glacial" action on war crimes and including those of the war criminal US Alliance, the US will not cooperate and will reject the authority of the ICC.

The US Alliance is not merely violating the UN Genocide Convention in its ongoing War on Muslims. The US Alliance is also grossly violating Articles 55 and 56 of the Geneva Convention relative to the Protection of Civilian Persons in Time of War that unequivocally demand that an Occupier must provide its conquered Subjects with life-sustaining food and medical requisites "to the fullest extent of the means available to it [17]." Thus, the infant mortality (under-1 infant deaths per 1,000 live births) is 12 (China), 16 (Tibet), 6 (USA) and 111 (US Alliance- and Australia-occupied Afghanistan). Similarly, the Maternal Mortality Ratio (MMR) (maternal deaths per 100,000 live births) is 20-27 (China), 100 (Tibet), 14 (USA) and 400-1,200 (US Alliance- and Australia-occupied Afghanistan) [18]. China with an annual per capita GDP of merely $8,126 (as compared to America's $56,054 and Australia's $51,352) has obtained an infant mortality in the Tibet Autonomous Region that is 7 times lower than that in Occupied Afghanistan and a Maternal Mortality in Tibet that is 4-12 times lower than that in US- and Australia-occupied Afghanistan [18].

As of 2017, failure of the US Alliance to observe the unequivocal demands of the Geneva Convention results in the avoidable death of under-1 Afghan infants totalling 121,328 each year or 40 times the carnage in the US Government's 9-11 false flag atrocity. Over the 16 years of the Afghan War this US Alliance mass murder of infants amounts to the death of 16 years x 121,328 deaths per year = 1.9 million under-1 year old Afghan infant deaths. Similarly, the MMR of 400-1,200 for US Alliance-occupied Afghanistan means that (400-1,200) x 11.55 = 4,620-13,860 Afghan women suffer maternal mortality each year as compared to 14 x 11.55 = 162 if the US Alliance observed the Geneva Convention. Thus, the failure of the US Alliance to observe the Geneva Convention kills 4,458- 13,698 Afghan women each year. The Afghan maternal mortality due to US Alliance war crimes over the 16 years of the Afghan War is accordingly 71,000-219,000 [18].

The US Alliance war criminals and serial killers must be hauled before the International Criminal Court – but as they say, "pigs may fly." However, there should surely be a major domestic political price to pay in two key areas for war criminal warmongers and state terrorism serial killers in US Alliance countries as set out below:

(1) Utterly ignored by Western Mainstream media are the 1.2 million people who have died world-wide since 9-11 due to US Alliance restoration of the Taliban-destroyed Afghan opium industry from 6% of world market share in 2001 to 93% in

2007, the breakdown (as of 2015) including 280,000 Americans, 256,000 Indonesians, 68,000 Iranians, 25,000 British, 14,000 Canadians, 10,000 Germans, and 5,000 Australians. Successive US presidents have been among the biggest opiate drug pushers in the world after Queen Victoria. So much for the War on Drugs that is trumped by the War on Muslims [14].

(2). Also utterly ignored by US Mainstream media is the estimate that about 1.7 million Americans die preventably each year in America from all kinds of "life-style" or "socio-political choice" reasons, the breakdown including (1) smoking (443,000), (2) adverse hospital events (440,000), (3) obesity (300,000), (4) air pollution (200,000), (5) alcohol (75,000), (6) lack of medical insurance (45,000), (7) illicit drugs (38,000) , (8) vehicle crashes (33,000), (9) guns (31,000), (10) suicide (30,000, 7,000 being US veterans), (11) avoidable under-5 year old US infant deaths (21,000), (12) homicide (15,000), and (13) jihadi terrorism (4) [19]. Since 9-11 about 29 million Americans have died preventably from "life-style" or "socio-political choice" reasons but only about 60 Americans have been killed in America since 9-11 by jihadi psychopaths. The long term accrual cost of the US War on Terror is estimated as $6 trillion. Successive US Governments have been involved in the horrendous fiscal perversion of committing $6 trillion to killing 32 million Muslims abroad instead of trying to save the lives of 29 million Americans at home.

Of course the passive and active mass murder of 32 million Muslims since 9-11 by the US Alliance is dwarfed by the 17 years x 16 million avoidable deaths per year = 272 million global avoidable deaths from deprivation over the same period that are attributable to the One Percenter-dominated world economic order. The One Percenters own 50% of the world's wealth and this gross inequity is bad for economics (the poor cannot afford the goods and services they produce) and is bad for democracy (Big Money buys votes). Thus, the Western democracies have become Kleptocracies, Plutocracies, Murdochracies, Lobbyocracies, Corporatocracies and Dollarocracies in which Big Money purchases people, parties, policies, public perception of reality, votes, more political power and more private profit. French economist Thomas Piketty has proposed an annual wealth tax approach to solving this deadly inequity [20], and indeed France has such a tax that rises to 1% and the Muslim world has had an annual wealth tax (zakkat) of 2.5% for about 1,400 years. It is estimated that an annual wealth tax of 4% could bring every country up to the per capita GDP of $8,000 enjoyed by China and Cuba (well-governed countries for which annual avoidable mortality is zero (0) [1]) and hence abolish the Global Avoidable Mortality Holocaust in which 16 million people presently die from deprivation each year [1, 21, 22].

Originally published as "Ongoing Global Avoidable Mortality Holocaust & horrendous human carnage from war and hegemony" in Radians and Inches, 2018.

References

[1]. Gideon Polya, "Body Count. Global avoidable mortality since 1950," that includes a succinct history of every country and is now available for free perusal on the web: http://globalbodycount.blogspot.com/
[2]. UN Population Division, "World population prospects 2017": https://population.un.org/wpp/ .
[3]. N.G. Jog, "Churchill's Blind Spot: India," New Book Company, Bombay, 1944.
[4]. Gideon Polya, "Jane Austen and the Black Hole of British History. Colonial rapacity, holocaust denial and the crisis in biological sustainability," G.M. Polya, Melbourne, 1998, 2008 that is now available for free perusal on the web: http://janeaustenand.blogspot.com/ .
[5]. Gideon Polya, "Australia And Britain Killed 6-7 Million Indians In WW2 Bengal Famine," Countercurrents, 29 September, 2011: https://countercurrents.org/polya290911.htm .
[6]. "Bengali Holocaust (WW2 Bengal Famine) writings of Gideon Polya," Gideon Polya: https://sites.google.com/site/drgideonpolya/bengali-holocaust.
[7]. "UN Genocide Convention": http://www.edwebproject.org/sideshow/genocide/convention.html .
[8]. "Aboriginal Genocide": https://sites.google.com/site/aboriginalgenocide/.
[9]. "Palestinian Genocide": https://sites.google.com/site/palestiniangenocide/.
[10]. Gideon Polya, "As UK Lackeys Or US Lackeys Australians Have Invaded 85 Countries (British 193, French 80, US 70)," Countercurrents, 9 February, 2015: http://www.countercurrents.org/polya090215.htm .
[11]. "Stop state terrorism" : https://sites.google.com/site/stopstateterrorism/.
[12]. "Iraqi Holocaust Iraqi Genocide": http://sites.google.com/site/iraqiholocaustiraqigenocide/ .
[13]. "Muslim Holocaust Muslim Genocide": https://sites.google.com/site/muslimholocaustmuslimgenocide/ .
[14]. "Afghan Holocaust, Afghan Genocide": https://sites.google.com/site/afghanholocaustafghangenocide/
[15]. Gideon Polya, "Paris Atrocity Context: 27 Million Muslim Avoidable Deaths From Imposed Deprivation In 20 Countries Violated By US Alliance Since 9-11," Countercurrents, 22 November, 2015: http://www.countercurrents.org/polya221115.htm .
[16]. "Experts: US did 9-11": https://sites.google.com/site/expertsusdid911/ .
[17]. Geneva Convention in Relation to the Protection of Civilian Persons in Time of War: http://www1.umn.edu/humanrts/instree/y4gcpcp.htm .
[18]. Gideon Polya, "China's Tibet health success versus passive mass murder of Afghan women and children by US Alliance," Global Research, 7 January 2018: https://www.globalresearch.ca/chinas-tibet-health-success-versus-passive-mass-murder-of-afghan-women-and-children-by-us-alliance/5625151 .
[19]. Gideon Polya, "West Ignores 11 Million Muslim War Deaths & 23 Million Preventable American Deaths Since US Government's False-flag 9-

11 Atrocity," Countercurrents, 9 September, 2015:
https://www.countercurrents.org/polya090915.htm.
[20]. Thomas Piketty, "Capital in the Twenty-First Century" (Harvard University Press, 2014).
821]. Gideon Polya, "4 % Annual Global Wealth Tax To Stop The 17 Million Deaths Annually," Countercurrents, 27 June, 2014:
http://www.countercurrents.org/polya270614.htm .
[22]. "1% ON 1%: one percent annual wealth tax on One Percenters":
https://sites.google.com/site/300orgsite/1-on-1.

Churchill's Crimes From Indian Holocaust To Palestinian Genocide

Gideon Polya

In WW2 Churchill deliberately starved 6-7 million Indians to death, continued to foster Muslim-Hindu antipathy that led to the horrors of Indian Partition and persuaded his War Cabinet on racist Partition of Palestine. Yet the holocaust-complicit Anglo media, academic and politician Establishment is still in denial.

Last year I published an article in MWC News entitled "Media lying over Churchill's crimes. British-Indian Holocaust" in which I summarized 15 major crimes in which Winston Churchill was COMPLICIT (notwithstanding that he is deservedly our hero for leadership in the fight against Nazism). Before this article was published, a Yahoo or Google search for the phrase "Churchill's crimes" yielded about three (3) articles about Winston Churchill's crimes – an extraordinary testament to the Soviet-style effectiveness of Anglo mainstream media, academic and politician lying, censorship, self-censorship, ignoring and denial.

After publication of my article on MWC News a Yahoo search for the phrase "Churchill's crimes" yielded a peak of 35,000 URLs which has shrunk (no doubt due to more Bush, neo-cons, and Zionist Anglo censorship) to 17,400. Indeed pro-Zionist Google censorship – deliberate LYING by omission – means that a Google search for the phrase "Churchill's crimes" now yields 999 URLs and the direct link to my evidently extremely high-impact article is completely missing.

For your convenience, I have simply listed below an expanded list of immense crimes in which Churchill was complicit as a racist soldier, politician, mass murderer and holocaust-denying writer – indeed he was awarded the Nobel Prize for Literature in

1953 for his numerous published works, especially his six-edition set The Second World War in which he ignored his deliberate, remorseless murder of 6-7 million Indians in 1943-1945 [I have provided estimates of violent and non-violent avoidable deaths in square brackets].

1. British Indian Holocaust (1.8 billion excess deaths, 1757-1947; 10 million killed in post-1857 Indian Mutiny reprisals; 1 million starved, 1895-1897 Indian Famine; 6-9 million starved, 1899-1900 Indian Famine; 6-7 million starved under Churchill, Bengali Holocaust 1943-1945].

2. Sudan atrocities [horrendous British atrocities after the Battle of Obdurman 1898].

3. Boer (Afrikaaner) Genocide [28,000 Afrikaaner women and children died in British concentration camps, 1899-1902].

4. World War 1 promotion [World War I Allied military and civilian dead 5.7 million and 3.7 million, respectively; German-allied (Central Powers) military and civilian deaths 4.0 million and 5.2 million; troop movement-exacerbated Spanish Flu Epidemic killed 20-100 million people worldwide 1918-1922].

5. WW1 Dardanelles Campaign in Turkey [0.2 million Allied and Turkish soldiers killed, 1915; precipitated 1915-1923 Turkish Armenian Genocide, 1.5 million Armenians killed].

6. UK and US invasion of Russia 1917-1919 [millions died in the Russian Civil War and the subsequent Russian Famine; 7 million died in the circa 1930 Ukrainian Famine; and perhaps up to 20 million died overall in Stalinist atrocities].

7. British suppression of the Arab revolt in Iraq (invaded by Britain in 1914) [bombing of Kurds, poison gas use (1920s); violent UK involvement on and off, 1914-2009; 1990-2008 Iraqi excess deaths 4 million; under-5 infant deaths 1.8 million; refugees currently 6 million].

8. Support for British Occupation and opposition to Indian self-determination [1757-1947 excess deaths, 1.8 billion; 1895-1897 famine deaths 1 million; 1899-1900 Indian Famine, deaths 6-9 million deaths; 1943-1945 Bengali Holocaust deaths 6-7 million].

9. World War 2 promotion [World War 2 military deaths 25 million and civilian deaths about 67 million].

10. Promotion of Japan entry into World War 2 in order to involve the US and hence ensure victory [35 million Chinese avoidable deaths, 1937-1945; 6-7 million Indians starved, Bengal 1943-1945; millions more died in the WW2 Eastern Theatre].

11. Churchill knew Singapore was indefensible [8,000-15,000 killed, 130,000 captured in the 1941 Malaya campaign; 14,000 Australian, 16,000 British and 32,000 Indian troops surrendered in Singapore].

12. Churchill deliberately did not warn Americans about Pearl Harbor attack [Eastern Theatre WW2 deaths 45 million].

13. WW2 Bengal Holocaust, Bengal Famine [deliberate starving to death of 6-7 million Indians; confessed by Churchill in a letter to Roosevelt].

14. Churchill rejected top scientific advice and supported bombing of German cities instead of protecting Atlantic convoys [0.16 million allied airmen killed; 0.6 million German civilians killed; Battle of the Atlantic almost lost; 7 million dead from famine in the Indian Ocean region related to halving of Allied shipping in 1943].

15. Churchill acknowledged the crucial importance of maintaining Hindu-Muslim antipathy to preserve British rule [1 million dead and 18 million Muslim and Hindu refugees associated with India-Pakistan Partition in 1947].

16. 1944 UK War Cabinet decision Partition of Palestine [in 1878, Jews were 5% of the Palestine population; in 1948 Jews were 1/3 of the population; there are now over 7 million Palestinian refugees; post-1967 Occupied Palestinian excess deaths 0.3 million, post-1967 under-5 infant deaths 0.2 million; excess deaths in countries partially or completely occupied by Apartheid Israel now total about 24 million; 4 million Occupied Palestinians are still illegally and abusively imprisoned by racist Zionists in their own country].

17. UK rejection of 1944 Brand plan to save Hungarian Jews [0.2-0.4 million killed by Nazis and Arrow Cross fascists out of 0.7 million; Zionists also opposed the Brand plan].

18. British, American, Zionist, Australian and European adoption of Churchill's holocaust commission and holocaust denying legacy, with post-war atrocities involving invasion, occupation, devastation and genocide [in relation to Occupiers (in parenthesis) 1950-2005 excess deaths in post-1945 occupied countries total 2 million (white Australia), 36 million (Belgium), 142 million (France), 24 million (Apartheid Israel), 0.7 million (Apartheid South Africa), 23 million (Portugal), 37 million (Russia), 9 million (Spain), 727 million (the UK) and 82 million (the US); 25 million Indigenous excess deaths in post-1950 US Asian Wars; 9-11 million excess deaths associated with 1990-2008 Bush Wars; post-invasion excess deaths in Occupied Iraq 2 million, refugees 6 million; post-invasion excess deaths in Occupied Afghanistan 4-6 million, refugees 4 million].

To paraphrase mathematician satirist Tom Lehrer's song "The Elements", "These are the only Churchill crimes currently known to Harvard/But there may be many others that haven't been discovered".

While pro-Zionist Anglo censorship evidenced above is utterly obnoxious, the Churchill Centre (US and worldwide) must be complimented for publishing a critical review of my article, a Review that adduced the opinions of major historians, including Professor Sir Martin Gilbert, an eminent historian whose works

I and no doubt numerous others turn to for information about Churchill, World War 2 , the Jewish Holocaust and Jewish history (see: https://web.archive.org/web/20090131104806/www.winstonchurchill.org/i4a/pages/index.cfm?pageid=1232). My responses to what I will refer to as "the Review" are listed below.

(1). The Review was quite nastily critical of my article and commencing with the false assertion "Mr. [Dr] Polya begins by dismissing all historians who disagree with him as Anglo-American and Zionist propagandists, including official biographer Sir Martin Gilbert" – what I DID say was: "Yet, to list just a few examples of UK-US holocaust ignoring, there is absolutely no mention of the 1943-1945 Bengali Holocaust in the biography of Winston Churchill by pro-Zionist Professor Sir Martin Gilbert (Gilbert, M. (1991), Churchill. A Life (Heinemann, London)); the recent histories by leading conservative Australian historian Professor Geoffrey Blainey (Blainey, G. (2000), A Short History of the World (Viking, Melbourne), Blainey, G. (2004), A Very Short History of the World (Viking, Melbourne), Blainey, G. (2005), A Short History of the 20th Century (Penguin, Melbourne)); the recent history of Britain by pro-Zionist Professor Simon Schama (Schama, S. (2002), A History of Britain (BBC, London)); or even in an important book on Denial entitled "Denial. History betrayed" by Australian historian Professor Tony Taylor (Monash University, Melbourne; see my review ""Denial" book ignores UK and US genocide crimes").

(2). The Review says that it sought comment and obtained the following bald denial comment from Professor Sir Martin Gilbert: "Churchill was not responsible for the Bengal Famine. I have been searching for evidence for years: none has turned up. The 1944 Document volume of the official biography [Hillsdale College Press] will resolve this issue finally."

However with due respect for Professor Gilbert's eminence, (a) Churchill was the ruler and the Ruler is responsible for the Ruled; (b), 6-7 million Indians perished (latest estimate from medical historian Dr. Sanjoy Bhattacharya, Wellcome Institute,

University College London); (c) 1998 Economics Nobel Laureate Professor Amartya Sen blames the Ruler for a needless disaster; (d) and most importantly Churchill himself actually confessed his inaction as follows in a now-released secret letter to Roosevelt in 1944 in stating "I am no longer justified in not asking for your help" (p158, "Jane Austen and the Black Hole of British History. Colonial rapacity, holocaust denial and the crisis in global sustainability").

For a recent, succinct account of the "forgotten" World War 2 Bengal Famine see the 2008 BBC broadcast involving me, 1998 Economics Nobel Laureate Professor Amartya Sen, Dr. Sanjoy Bhattacharya, Wellcome Institute, University College London and other scholars).

(3) The Review then quite astonishingly supports my thesis and itself damns Churchill with the following: Arthur Herman's excellent and balanced Gandhi & Churchill (New York: Bantam, 2008, reviewed in Finest Hour 138: 51-52). There is quite a lot on the Bengal Famine (pp 512 et. seq.), which Herman believes "did more than Gandhi to undermine Indian confidence in the Raj." Secretary of State for India Leo Amery, Herman writes, "at first took a lofty Malthusian view of the crisis, arguing that India was 'overpopulated' and that the best strategy was to do nothing. But by early summer even Amery was concerned and urged the War Cabinet to take drastic action....For his part, Churchill proved callously indifferent. Since Gandhi's fast his mood about India had progressively darkened....[He was] resolutely opposed to any food shipments. Ships were desperately needed for the landings in Italy....Besides, Churchill felt it would do no good. Famine or no famine, Indians will 'breed like rabbits.' Amery prevailed on him to send some relief, albeit only a quarter what was needed."

Malthusian over-population as an excuse for allowing mass death is obscene. Yet Churchill put it more bluntly in the only public statement of Churchill's about the Bengal famine that I have been able to find is Churchill's notorious anti-Indian comment that "they breed like rabbits" as quoted by India 's Nobel Prize-winning economist Professor Amartya Sen in an essay to Asian Institute of Technology (2002): "Winston Churchill's famous remark about the 1943 Bengal famine – that it was caused by the tendency of the people to breed like rabbits – belongs to this general tradition of blaming the colonial subject".

One has to turn to the Whitehall, London, UK supervisor of the 1840s Irish Potato Famine (1 million killed, 1.5 million emigrated), Charles Trevelyan, for a comparably obscene viewpoint about man-made mass starvation: "This being altogether beyond the power of man, the cure had been applied by the direct stroke of an all-wise Providence in a manner as unexpected and unthought of as it is likely to be effectual." (1846, C.E. Trevelyan, the responsible Undersecretary for the Treasury, commenting in 1846 on the Irish famine as a "cure" for Irish overpopulation) (see p257, Edwards, R.D. and Williams, T.D. (1957) (editors), The Great Famine. Studies in Irish History 1845-52 (New York University Press, New York).

Indeed G.M. Trevelyan (Regius Professor of Modern History and Master of Trinity College, Cambridge, and grandson of the English official Charles Trevelyan who supervised the Irish Famine) fails to mention the Irish Famine (and the Bengal Famine) in his "authoritative" "History of England" (Longmans. London), except for a brief aside: "the potato blight in Ireland in 1845-6 left him [Peel] no other choice than either to suspend the Corn Laws or to allow the Irish to die by tens of thousands" i.e. he suggests that the Irish Famine [1 million dead, 1.5 million forced to emigrate] was something averted by benign English wisdom (see p114, Chapter 13, "Jane Austen and the Black Hole of British History").

(4). The Review gets an opinion from historian Arthur Herman who, notwithstanding his "Churchill proved callously indifferent" above, states, QUOTE: "The idea that Churchill was in any way 'responsible' or 'caused' the Bengal famine is of course absurd. The real cause was the fall of Burma to the Japanese, which cut off India's main supply of rice imports when domestic sources fell short, which they did in Eastern

Bengal after a devastating cyclone in mid-October 1942".
However this is simply incorrect.

1998 Economics Nobel Laureate Professor Amartya Sen
(Harvard University, formerly at Cambridge University, who
witnessed the Bengal Famine as a child and was awarded the
Nobel Prize for studies on famines, including the Bengal
Famine) is quite clear that the Bengal Famine was NOT due to
absence of food but to greatly elevated price in a merciless,
British-ruled free market in which those who couldn't buy food
simply starved. Burma occupation, Churchill's shipping cut-
backs, and divide-and-rule British granting of Indian provincial
food autonomy and other factors all contributed to the real killer
– the huge increase in the price of rice, the Bengali staple that
led to millions starving in the midst of plenty.

(5). The Review then argues that "There was a war on. More
pressing military matters were at hand which governed his
actions and decisions". This is indeed the view put forward by
Professor Martin Gilbert in his book "A History of the
Twentieth Century. Volume Two 1933-1951" (William
Morrow, New York, 1998) that is remarkable and praiseworthy
in British historiography for actually mentioning the Bengal
Famine [my additions in square brackets]: "In the summer of
1943, as supplies of rice ran out [incorrect], famine spread
through Bengal. Its ravages were savage and swift. The poor,
and villagers in the remoter regions were its main victims
[people starved in Calcutta], not only in Bengal, but in
neighboring Orissa and distant Malabar. Within a few months,
as many as 1,500,000 Indians had died [6-7 million died, 1943-
1945]. The Bengal Famine was one of the worst famines of the
century [p522]…Between 1939 and 1945 disease and hunger
had taken their toll, with war conditions making it much harder
to organize alleviation. In Bengal, a million and half Indians
died of starvation [6-7 million died in Bengal, Assam and
Orissa] [p725]".

Professor Sir Martin Gilbert (who I quote regularly on Jewish
History and the Jewish Holocaust) used the "excuse " for war
exigencies for the inability of the British to take requisite action

– yet he tells us in his Jewish Holocaust histories (e.g. Gilbert, M. (1982), Atlas of the Holocaust (Michael Joseph, London)) that 1 in 6 Jews died from deprivation. Just imagine if a history of the 20th century devoted just a couple of sentences to the Jewish Holocaust (5-6 million dead, 1 in 6 dying from deprivation) and commented "Between 1939 and 1945 disease and hunger had taken their toll, with war conditions making it much harder to organize alleviation". And yet Professor Gilbert's book "A History of the Twentieth Century" is an outstanding exception in British historiography in actually mentioning the Bengal Famine (6-7 million dead), the Bengali Holocaust that was indeed the first WW2 atrocity to actually be described as a "Holocaust" by Jog in 1944 (see Jog, N.G. (1944), Churchill's Blind-Spot: India (New Book Company, Bombay)).

Winston Churchill totally ignored the Bengali Holocaust (and the 6-7 million people he deliberately murdered) in his 6-volume work "The Second World War" for which in part he got the 1953 Nobel Prize for Literature – and Professor Martin Gilbert also ignores the Bengali Holocaust in his "definitive" history of Winston Churchill (see Gilbert, M. (1991), Churchill. A Life (Heinemann, London)). Just imagine a biography of Adolph Hitler that failed to mention the Jewish Holocaust.

In Austria today anyone denying or minimizing the Jewish Holocaust faces up to 10 years in prison and other European countries have similarly criminalized such denial. Indeed it is also an offence to deny the Armenian Genocide in France and Belgium and a few years ago Germany suggested that the EU criminalize denial of all recent holocausts (see "Genocide denial, No-penalty criminalization required now" in MWC News).

(6). The Review further quotes Arthur Herman [my corrections in square brackets]: "Churchill was concerned about the humanitarian catastrophe taking place there, and he pushed for whatever famine relief efforts India itself could provide; they simply weren't adequate [utterly incorrect]. Something like three million people died in Bengal and other parts of southern

India as a result [6-7 million died]. We might even say that Churchill indirectly broke the Bengal famine by appointing as Viceroy Field Marshal Wavell, who mobilized the military to transport food and aid to the stricken regions (something that hadn't occurred to anyone, apparently) [Churchill repeatedly rejected Wavell calls for help]."

General Wavell's diaries repeatedly make it clear that Churchill hated Indians and steadfastly refused his pleas for assistance with the Bengal Famine (see Moon, P. (1973) (editor), Wavell. The Viceroy's Journal (Oxford University Press, London) and Chapter 14 and 15, "Jane Austen and the Black Hole of British History")

(7). The Review makes the astonishing assertion that "If the famine had occurred in peacetime, it would have been dealt with effectively and quickly by the Raj, as so often in the past". British India was maintained by STARVATION – indeed a very good account of this is given (with shocking photographs) by pro-Zionist Simon Schama in his "History of Britain" (which nevertheless ignores the WW2 Bengal Famine) (see Schama, S. (2002), A History of Britain (BBC, London)); also see Davis, M. (2001), Late Victorian Holocausts: El Nino Famines and the Making of the Third World (Verso, London) and "Jane Austen and the Black Hole of British History" by Gideon Polya).

British mass murder of Indians commenced with the Great Bengal Famine in 1769-1779 (10 million deaths), concluded with the WW2 Bengal Famine (6-7 million deaths) and Churchill-inspired Indian Partition – and in between excess deaths (avoidable deaths) in 2 centuries of racist British rule totalled 1.8 billion. Yet these horrendous realities utterly ignored by Anglo historians (with a few notable exceptions) in a process of continuing, racist holocaust denial.

This is what Colin Mason says of the Bengal Famine in his "A Short History of Asia" (Macmillan, London, 2000, p178): "The famine, little publicized at the time because of war-time censorship, and, inexplicably, still ignored by many modern histories of India and most standard reference works ... Several of the factors mentioned above suggest a British "scorched earth policy: design to deny assets in Bengal to the Japanese, at a monstrous cost, should they successfully invade India, Those consequences severely indict British policy-makers of the time, and the failure to investigate and acknowledge them, is to the discredit of all subsequent British governments".

Today we have the same continuing ignoring, denial, excusing and minimizing of not just the Bengal Famine (6-7 million dead) and the British Indian Holocaust (1.8 billion excess deaths) but of the continuing, present-day atrocities of the Palestinian Genocide, the Iraqi Genocide and the Afghan Genocide (post-invasion excess deaths 0.3 million, 2 million and 4-6 million, respectively; post-invasion under-5 infant deaths 0.2 million , 0.6 million and 2.1 million, respectively; and refugees totalling 7 million, 6 million and 4 million, respectively).

There is an ongoing Muslim Holocaust that is simply ignored by the West. Thus post-1950 avoidable deaths (excess deaths, deaths that did not have to happen) total 1.3 billion (the World), 1.2 billion (the non-European World) and 0.6 billion (the Muslim World), these estimates being consonant with estimates of post-1950 under-5 year old infant deaths totalling 0.88 billion (the World), 0.85 billion (the non-European World) and 0.4 billion (the Muslim World). 16 million people die avoidably each year on a Spaceship Earth (roughly half of them Muslims) with the First World in charge of the flight deck. Yet this ongoing Muslim Holocaust is utterly ignored in the racist, lying, Zionist-dominated Western Murdochracies (for details see "Body Count. Global avoidable mortality since 1950", G.M. Polya, Melbourne, 2007: http://mwcnews.net/Gideon-Polya). However man-made global warming (the major climate criminal culprits being Zionist-backed US- Bush and their White Australian lackeys) threatens an even greater atrocity of Climate Genocide that, according to top UK climate scientist Professor James Lovelock FRS, will leave only 500 million (mostly European) survivors by the end of the century. As with the Bengal Famine, the post-war global avoidable mortality holocaust, a large proportion of the victims of this looming

Climate Genocide will be Muslims in a terminal Muslim Holocaust about 1,000 times greater than the WW2 Jewish Holocaust.

The fundamental messages from the Nazi German Jewish Holocaust) (5-6 million dead, 1 in 6 dying from deprivation) and the contemporaneous but "forgotten" (and when mentioned mostly "excused") British Bengali Holocaust (6-7 million dead) are "zero tolerance for racism", never again to anyone" and "bear witness".

Yet in the last few weeks, as of Day 23 the racist Zionists (RZs) running Apartheid Israel have killed 1,310 Gazan inmates of the Israeli Gaza Concentration Camp as reprisals for zero (0) Israelis killed by rockets from brutally and murderously blockaded Gaza in the previous year – a reprisals "death ratio" of 1,310/0 = infinity. Occupied Palestinian violent and non-violent excess deaths since September 2000 total about 6,100 and 35,400, respectively , as compared to 1,185 Israeli deaths (see "Palestinian-Israeli death ratios. Nazi-style Israeli Gaza war-crimes" on MWC News).

UK, US, White Australian and Israeli state terrorism against the non-European and Muslim world will simply continue as long as the deadly consequences of these present and past imperialist excesses are simply ignored by Mainstream media, academics and politicians in the Western Murdochcracies. The REALITY behind this Zionist-Bush-ite "terror hysteria" big lie is astounding: 7,000 Westerners killed by Muslim-origin non-state terrorists in 40 years (including Israelis and assuming, against substantial evidence to the contrary, no US or Israeli involvement in the 9/11 atrocity) versus 9-11 million violent and non-violent avoidable deaths associated so far with the Bush Wars, 1990-2009 (see "9-11 excuse for US global genocide. The reveal 9-11 atrocity: millions dead (9-11 million) in Bush Wars (1990-2009)".

There must be zero tolerance for racism, invasions, occupations, mass murder and lying.

Dear Reader, you can do your bit in the War against Zionist-Bush Lies by (a) informing everyone you can and (b) by eschewing any avoidable business dealings with people, institutions, corporations and countries involved in the Palestinian Genocide, the Muslim Holocaust and the looming Climate Genocide.

Originally published as "Churchill's Crimes From Indian Holocaust To Palestinian Genocide" in MWC News, 23 January 2009.

Paris Atrocity Context: 27 Million Muslim Avoidable Deaths From Imposed Deprivation In 20 Countries Violated By US Alliance Since 9-11

Gideon Polya

The appalling Paris atrocity (130 killed) has led Hollande and Obama to call for the destruction of Islamic State i.e. genocide as defined by the UN Genocide Convention. A major report by 3 physician organizations recently estimated that 2 million Muslims had died in the US War on Terror but UN data show that Muslim avoidable deaths from deprivation in countries subject to Western military intervention in 2001-2015 now total about 27 million, this demanding peace now and ICC prosecutions of those responsible for this Muslim Holocaust and Muslim Genocide.

President Obama (Antalya, Turkey, 16 November 2015) stated: "Tragically, Paris is not alone. We've seen outrageous attacks by ISIL in Beirut, last month in Ankara, routinely in Iraq. Here at the G20, our nations have sent an unmistakable message that we are united against this threat. ISIL is the face of evil. Our goal, as I've said many times, is to degrade and ultimately destroy this barbaric terrorist organization" [1].

President Francois Hollande (17 November 2015) stated: "France is at war. No barbarians will prevent us from living how we have decided to live. To live fully. Terrorism will never destroy the republic, because the republic will destroy terrorism'… The sponsors of the attack in Paris must know that their crimes further strengthens the determination of France to fight and to destroy them. We must do more. Syria has become the largest factory of terrorists the world has ever known. France is not engaged in a war of civilisations because those assassins don't represent a civilisation. Our democracy has triumphed before over adversaries that were much more formidable than these cowards" [2].

There has been saturation coverage in the Western media of the appalling Paris tragedy that killed 130 people on 13 November 2015, this coverage dwarfing reportage of the recent Kunduz Hospital atrocity in Afghanistan perpetrated by the US (22 killed, 2 October 2015), the most recent Beirut Massacre by jihadi non-state terrorists (43 killed, 12 November 2015) and the Bamako Mali Massacre by jihadi non-state terrorists (27 killed, 20 November 2015) – clear evidence of the entrenched and egregious racism of the anti-Arab anti-Semitic, Islamophobic and Neocon American and Zionist Imperialist (NAZI)-perverted and subverted Western Mainstream media.

The eminent US organization Just Foreign Policy has estimated that there have been 1.5 million "Iraqi deaths due to the US invasion" and I have estimated (based on UN Population Division 2006 Revision data) that to this we should add a further 1.2 million Iraqis killed through war-imposed deprivation [4, 5]. However the ABC News of the taxpayer-funded ABC (Australia's equivalent of the UK BBC) commenting on the US withdrawal in 2011 stated: "The withdrawal ends a war that left tens of thousands of Iraqis and nearly 4,500 American soldiers dead" [6].

Another ABC News report about Wikileaks document releases states: "The founder of the WikiLeaks website says hundreds of thousands of US military documents leaked by the website show the truth about the Iraq war. The documents suggest senior US commanders turned a blind eye on torture by the Iraqi authorities and show the US has kept records of civilian deaths, despite previously denying it. It has put the death toll at 109,000, including more than 66,000 civilians. The US has criticised the release, saying the documents are classified and could lead to military and civilian deaths. But Julian Assange has defended his actions at a press conference just a short while ago, saying the release serves the public interest" [7].

The "Iraq Body Count" project currently reports "total violent deaths including combatants 224,000", this highly flawed estimate being unwisely based on the dodgy evidence of media and official reports [8]. The mendacious BBC which, like the endlessly lying, Neocon American and Zionist Imperialist (NAZI)-perverted Australian ABC, has an appalling record of malreportage [9, 10], opines: "Other reports and surveys have resulted in a wide range of estimates of Iraqi deaths. The UN-backed Iraqi Family Health Survey estimated 151,000 violent deaths in the period March 2003 – June 2006. Meanwhile, The Lancet journal in 2006 published an estimate of 654,965 excess Iraqi deaths related to the war of which 601,027 were caused by violence" [11].

Western Mainstream media under-reporting in claiming circa 20,000-200,000 Iraqi deaths due to the US War on Terror – when the true figure from top medical epidemiologists, the UK ORB organization and UN demographers is probably in excess of 2 million Iraqi deaths from violence or imposed deprivation – is genocide-ignoring and holocaust-ignoring on a massive scale. A holocaust involves the death of huge numbers of people whereas genocide is defined more precisely by Article 2 of the UN Genocide Convention which states that "In the present Convention, genocide means any of the following acts committed with intent to destroy, in whole or in part, a national, ethnic, racial or religious group, as such: a) Killing members of the group; b) Causing serious bodily or mental harm to members of the group; c) Deliberately inflicting on the group conditions of life calculated to bring about its physical destruction in whole or in part; d) Imposing measures intended to prevent births within the group; e) Forcibly transferring children of the group to another group" [4].

Genocide-ignoring and holocaust–ignoring is far, far worse than repugnant genocide-ignoring and holocaust denial because at least the latter permit public discussion of the matter. The endlessly lying, Neocon American and Zionist Imperialist (NAZI)-perverted Western Mainstream media are involved in massive lying by omission, lying by commission, genocide-ignoring, holocaust–ignoring and effective genocide-ignoring and holocaust denial.

Of course this is not new. Thus, for example, generation after generation of lying journalists, politicians, and historians in the English-speaking world have resolutely ignored the "forgotten" WW2 Bengali Holocaust in which the British with Australian complicity deliberately starved 6-7 million Indians to death for strategic reasons (genocidally racist White Australia was complicit by withholding food from starving Indians from its huge wartime grain stores) [12-15]. History is written by the victors and Western Mainstream media presstitutes are resolutely committed to untruth [16, 17].

It gets worse. Iraq has been subject to repeated Western invasion in the century since British invasion in 1914 (racist White Australia is currently involved in its Seventh Iraq War and its Third Syrian War in a century) and Iraqi deaths from violence or war-imposed deprivation since 1914 now total 9 million [4]. Further, Iraq is but one of 20 substantially or significantly Muslim countries variously invaded, occupied, sanctioned and/or bombed by US Alliance forces since the US Government's 9-11 false flag atrocity on 11 September 2001 in which about 3,000 people were killed [3].

All of this raises the key questions of (1) precisely how many millions of Muslims have died from violence or from imposed deprivation in substantially Muslim countries attacked by the US Alliance since 9-11; and (2) how the civilized world should respond.

Kit O'Connell (a US journalist from Austin, Texas, a Daily Staff Writer for MintPress News, and Associate Editor of Shadowproof) (2015): "It may never be possible to know the true death toll of the modern Western wars on the Middle East, but that figure could be 4 million or higher. Since the vast majority of those killed were of Arab descent, and mostly Muslim, when would it be fair to accuse the United States and its allies of genocide? A March report by Physicians for Social Responsibility calculates the body count of the Iraq War at around 1.3 million, and possibly as many as 2 million. However, the numbers of those killed in Middle Eastern wars could be much higher. In April, investigative journalist Nafeez Ahmed argued that the actual death toll could reach as high as 4 million if one includes not just those killed in the wars in Iraq and Afghanistan, but also the victims of the sanctions against

Iraq, which left about 1.7 million more dead, half of them children, according to figures from the United Nations" [18]. Dr. Nafeez Ahmed (investigative journalist, international security scholar, author of 'Zero Point' and associated with the Institute for Policy Research and Development) has concluded that "In Iraq alone, the US-led war from 1991 to 2003 killed 1.9 million Iraqis; then from 2003 onwards around 1 million: totalling just under 3 million Iraqis dead over two decades... the total Afghan death toll due to the direct and indirect impacts of US-led intervention since the early nineties until now could be as high 3-5 million" [19].

International Physicians for the Prevention of Nuclear War (IPPNW), Physicians for Social Responsibility (PSR) and Physicians for Global Survival (PGS) published a detailed and documented major report in March 2015 on Muslim deaths in Western wars that has been ignored by Mainstream media but concluded (2015): "Executive Summary. This investigation come to the conclusion that the war has, directly or indirectly, killed [in 2011-2013] around 1 million people in Iraq, 220,000 in Afghanistan and 80,000 in Pakistan i.e. a total of 1.3 million. Not included in this figure are further war zones such as Yemen. The figure is approximately 10 times greater than that of which the public, experts and decision-makers are aware of [sic] and propagated by the media and major NGOs. And this is only a conservative estimate. The total number of deaths in the three countries named above could also be in excess of 2 million, whereas a figure below 1 million is extremely unlikely" [20]. "Iraq Body Count" makes the absurd claim of 224,000 total violent Iraqi deaths including combatants since the 2003 invasion [8], this being based on media reports, an approach that has been shown by top medical epidemiologists to be severely flawed [4]. The Physicians' Report [20] estimates 1 million Iraqi deaths from violence or war-imposed deprivation in the period 2011-2011 whereas the eminent US Just Foreign Policy estimates – based on data from the UK ORB polling organization and from polling by US medical epidemiologists published in The Lancet – that 1.5 million Iraqis have died due to the US invasion and comments: "The number is shocking and sobering. It is at least 10 times greater than most estimates cited in the US media, yet it is based on a scientific study of violent

Iraqi deaths caused by the U.S.-led invasion of March 2003" (noting that top US medical epidemiologists in their paper in The Lancet estimated that 90% of the deaths found were violent) [5].

Using data from the UN Population Division 2006 Revision data I have made an upper estimate of 2003-2011 Iraqi avoidable deaths from deprivation totalling 1.2 million, this leading to an estimate of 2.7 million Iraqi deaths from violence (1.5 million) or from war-imposed conditions as determined from differential pre- and post-invasion mortality data (1.2 million) in the period 2003-2011. This approach assumed that these 2 data sets (i.e. "deaths from violence" and "deaths from war-imposed conditions") do not overlap if violently killed people do not make it to hospitals etc for "official counting" – indeed the gross, up to 7-fold under-estimate of Iraqi violent deaths by "Iraq Body Count" based on "official counting" validates my approach [4]. A related approach estimates 7.2 million Afghan deaths post-9-11 from violence (1.7 million) or war-imposed deprivation (5.5 million) [21, 22].
Crucially, while the Physicians' Report [20] estimates "deaths from war-related conditions" as determined from differential immediately pre- and post-invasion mortality data, I assume that the historical pre-invasion trend of massive decreases in mortality in Iraq (and Syria) should have continued and indeed assume that the Iraqi mortality rate post-1990 could and should have attained the base-line rate for high birth-rate impoverished countries of about 4 deaths per 1,000 of population per year and hence given an avoidable death rate of zero (0) but for war-imposed conditions. In other words, the invasion of Iraq not only yielded violent deaths and increased avoidable deaths relative to the pre-invasion year, it also blocked a quite achievable rapid decline to zero avoidable deaths per annum [23].
Avoidable death (avoidable mortality, excess death, excess mortality, premature death, untimely death, death that should not have happened) is the difference between the observed deaths in a country and the deaths expected for a peaceful, decently governed country with the same demographics (i.e. the same birth rate and age distribution) [23]. Thus, for example, in

2015 GDP per capita is about $6,000 for both Cuba and China and about $15,000 for both Iraq and Libya [24], but while there are zero (0) annual avoidable deaths in Cuba and China, as catalogued below annual avoidable deaths in war-devastated Iraq (population 36.4 million) and Syria (population 6.3 million) currently total 47,000 and 14,000, respectively [23].

Finally, the Physicians' Report estimate of 80,000 Pakistani war-related deaths in 2001-2011 is about 100 times lower than the 9.1 million Pakistani avoidable deaths from deprivation in the period October 2001- October 2015 as estimated (see below) using UN Population 2015 Revision data [24] and assuming a base-line mortality rate for this high birth rate, impoverished country of 4 deaths per 1,000 births per year for zero avoidable mortality that could and should have been attained in Pakistan but for US-driven militarism, dictatorship, terrorism, corruption and war.

Soap, insecticide-impregnated mosquito netting, antibiotics, immunization, basic preventative medicine, maternal education. maternal literacy, and good primary health care are vastly cheaper than drones, bombs, militarization, war and nuclear weapons, as well illustrated by the marvellous example of the terrific health outcomes in US sanctions-impoverished but well-governed Cuba which has an infant mortality rate about the same as for the US that has a 9-fold greater per capita GDP [23, 24].

To avoid the controversy about how many Muslims have actually been violently killed, one can simply consider how many Muslims have died avoidably from Western war- or Western hegemony- imposed deprivation in the 14 year period from October 2001- October 2015 in substantially or significantly Muslim countries subject to Western sanctions, attack or occupation in that period. This approach has the benefit of being uncontroversial and conservative e.g. it ignores violent deaths in which Muslim bodies or body parts went into mass graves or otherwise did not make it to hospitals or morgues for "official counting". Of course, whether a child is slowly and painfully killed by economically- and/or militarily-imposed deprivation or is killed quickly by bombs or bullets, the death is just as final and just as irreversible [23].

Below is an alphabetical list of 20 substantially or significantly Muslim countries variously attacked, invaded, occupied or sanctioned by the US Alliance in the Neocon American and Zionist Imperialist (NAZI)-promoted US War on Terror since the 9-11 atrocity that numerous science, architecture, engineering, aviation, military and intelligence experts believe was a US Government 9-11 false flag operation (with some suggesting Israeli involvement) [3].

Listed below for these 20 US Alliance-violated, substantially or significantly Muslim countries are (a) 2015 population [25]; (b) 1950-2005 avoidable deaths [24], (c) annual avoidable deaths (2015) from the latest UN 2015 Revision data [25], assuming a baseline mortality for high birth rate, impoverished but otherwise peaceful and well-governed countries of about 4 deaths per 1,000 of population per year (for Lebanon, Libya, Syria and Palestine with death rates close to this baseline, avoidable mortality was estimated as 1.4 times the under-5 infant deaths) [24]; (d) average-based 14 year avoidable deaths for the post-9-11 period of 2001-2015, (e) present annual per capita GDP [24], (f) % Muslim (upper estimates), (g) post-9-11 Muslim avoidable deaths based on Muslim percentage in each country, and (h) Western invasion dates and details.

Post-9-11 avoidable deaths in 20 countries with substantial or significant Muslim populations and variously subject to Western military operations in the post-9-11 US War on Terror:

1. Afghanistan: (a) 32.5 million, (b) 16.6 million. (c) 149,000, (d) 2.2 million, (e) $1,900, (f) 99.8% Muslim, (g) 2.2 million post-9-11 Muslim avoidable deaths, and (h) Afghanistan was subject to repeated UK invasions in the 19th century but finally recovered independence in 1919; after the US-backed removal of a socialist government in 1978, the Russians invaded and Afghanistan endured decades of war against the Russians (1979-1989) and thence civil war (1989-1996); in 2001 Afghanistan was invaded by the US Alliance (notably the US, UK, France, Germany, Netherlands, Australia, Canada, New Zealand) on the false basis of Osama bin Laden and Al Qaeda being responsible for 9-11.

2. Burkina Faso: (a) 18.1 million, (b) 6.8 million, (c) 109,000, (d) 1.5 million, (e) $1,700, (f) 60.5% Muslim, (g) 0.9 million post-9-11 Muslim avoidable deaths, and (h) Burkino Faso was a French colony until 1960, post-independence French military presence and French forces boosted in 2013 as part of Operation Barkhane directed against Muslim rebels in the Sahel.

3. Central African Republic: (a) 4.9 million, (b) 2.3 million, (c) 55,000, (d) 0.8 million, (e) $600, (f) 15.0% Muslim, (g) 0.1 million post-9-11 Muslim avoidable deaths, and (h) the Central African Republic was a French colony until 1960, post-independence French military presence and France further boosted forces in 2013 as Muslim Genocide expanded (almost all Muslims have been expelled from the capital).

4. Chad: (a) 14.0 million, (b) 5.1 million, (c) 147,000, (d) 1.9 million, (e) $2,600, (f) 53.1% Muslim, (g) 1.0 million post-9-11 Muslim avoidable deaths, and (h) Chad became ostensibly independent in 1960 but there were major post-independence French military involvements in Northern Chad and France further boosted forces in 2013 as part of Operation Barkhane directed against Muslim rebels in the Sahel.

5. Côte D'Ivoire: (a) 20.1 million, (b) 7.0 million. (c) 199,000, (d) 3.0 million, (e) $3,100, (f) 38.6% Muslim, (g) 1.2 million post-9-11 Muslim avoidable deaths, and (h) Cote D'Ivoire suffered major French military involvements in suppressing socialists before and after independence in 1960 and a major French re-invasion in 2002.

6. Djibouti: (a) 0.9 million, (b) 141,000, (c) 8,000, (d) 0.1 million, (e) $3,100, (f) 94.0% Muslim, (g) 0.1 million post-9-11 Muslim avoidable deaths, and (h) Djibouti suffered a major, continuing French, US and British presence after independence in 1977; it was a base for French participation in the 1990-1991 Gulf War; French suppressed Affar rebellion in 1977-2002; France gave the former French Foreign Legion's Camp Lemonnier to the government of Djibouti, which then leased it to the US in 2001; France maintains over 1,500 troops in Djibouti and French forces in Djibouti have taken part in

operations in Somalia, the Democratic Republic of Congo, and the Côte D'Ivoire.

7. Iraq: (a) 36.4 million, (b) 5.3 million, (c) 47,000. (d) 0.7 million, (e) $15,300, (f) 97.0% Muslim, (g) 0.7 million post-9-11 Muslim avoidable deaths, and (h) Iraq suffered invasion by the UK in 1914 with the UK continuing to repress Iraqi rebellion in Iraq up to and including WW2, notwithstanding ostensible Iraqi independence in 1932; Gulf War (1990-1991) in which 0.2 million Iraqis were killed; 1990-2003 Sanctions; 2003-2011 US Alliance Iraq War; renewed US and Australian military advisers and renewed bombing of Iraq in 2014 by US Alliance (US, UK, Australia, France).

8. Iran: (a) 79.1 million, (b) 14.3 million, (c) 55,000 (d) 1.0 million, (e) $17,400, (f) 99.4% Muslim, (g) 1.0 million post-9-11 Muslim avoidable deaths, and (h) Iran is one of the world's oldest nations and has not invaded another country for several hundred years; the US engineered a coup against the secular and democratic Mossadegh government in 1953 with the installation of dictatorship under the Shah; the US imposed sanctions on Iran after the revolution that removed the Shah in 1979; the US backed Iraq in the Iraq-Iran War in which 1.5 million Iranians were killed (Iranian 1980-1988 avoidable deaths 2.1 million); under urging from the Zionist-perverted US the UN imposed sanctions on Iran over its nuclear energy program that Iran declared to be for peaceful purposes only; the last major direct violent US action against Iran was the shooting down of Iran Air Flight 655 by a US guided missile cruiser killing all 290 on board; US ally Apartheid Israel bombed an Iranian ship in Sudan in 2009; an estimated 68,000 Iranians have died since 9-11 from opiate drug-related causes due to the US restoration of the Taliban-destroyed Afghan opium industry from 6% of world share in 2001 to 93% by 2007; 1.2 million people have died world-wide since 9-11 due to US Alliance restoration of the Taliban-destroyed Afghan opium industry, the breakdown as of 2015 including 280,000 Americans, 256,000 Indonesians, 68,000 Iranians, 25,000 British, 14,000 Canadians, 10,000 Germans, 5,000 Australians and 500 French; about 4,000 Iranian border guards have died trying to block opiate

smuggling from US-occupied Afghanistan; under urging from the Zionist -perverted US the UN imposed deadly sanctions on Iran in 2006 over its nuclear energy program that Iran declared to be for peaceful purposes only (no sanctions were applied to the nations including Apartheid Israel that actually have nuclear weapons) – these opiate-related deaths and deaths from sanctions are reflected in huge post-9-11 avoidable mortality in Iran.

9. Lebanon: (a) 5.9 million, (b) 0.5 million, (c) 1,000, (d) 16,000, (e) $18,000, (f) 59.5% Muslim, (g) 10,000 post-9-11 Muslim avoidable deaths, and (h) Lebanon suffered French occupation after WW1 and gained independence in 1944; substantially occupied by Apartheid Israel in 1982 (3,000 Palestinians killed in the Sabra and Shatila Massacre); Israel withdrawal in 2000; in 2006 Apartheid Israel attacked again killing over 1,000, making 1 million homeless and destroying infrastructure on a huge scale.

10. Libya: (a) 6.3 million, (b) 0.8 million, (c) 6,000, (d) 78,000 (27,000 in 2011-2015), (e) $15,900, (f) 94.0% Muslim, (g) 73,000 post-9-11 Muslim avoidable deaths, and (h) Libya gained independence in 1950 and under rule by Muammar Gaddafi in 1969-2011 became the most prosperous country in all of Africa, but the 2011 France-UK-US (FUKUS) Alliance bombing campaign removed Gaddafi, splintered and devastated the country, killed 100,000 people and generated 1 million refugees with annual avoidable deaths increasing 3-fold after Western intervention.

11. Mali: (a) 20.1 million, (b) 7.0 million, (c) 199,000, (d) 1.8 million, (e) $1,700, (f) 90.0% Muslim, (g) 1.6 million post-9-11 Muslim avoidable deaths, and (h) Mali was brutally subdued by the French in the 19th century but secured independence in 1960 but with French hegemony; in 2013, France launched airstrikes against Tuareg rebels who had conquered the northern half of the country and finally defeated them in a so-called Operation Serval. France followed up Operation Serval with Operation Barkhane dedicated to killing Muslim rebels in the

Sahel countries of Mali, Mauritania, Burkina Faso, Niger and Chad.

12. Mauritania: (a) 17.6 million, (b) 1.3 million, (c) 123,000, (d) 2.3 million, (e) $4,300. (f) 100.0% Muslim, (g) 2.3 million post-9-11 Muslim avoidable deaths, and (h) Mauritania was invaded by the French in the 19th century so as to consolidate French territory from Senegal to the Sudan, and Mauritanian resistance was only finally overcome in the 1930s; Mauritania became formally independent in 1960 but was subject to French hegemony and interference. France's Operation Barkhane involves thousands of air-supported French troops dedicated to killing Muslim rebels in the Sahel countries of Mali, Mauritania, Burkina Faso, Niger and Chad.

13. Niger: (a) 19.9 million, (b) 6.6 million, (c) 111,000, (d) 1.8 million, (e) $1,100, (f) 94.0% Muslim, (g) 1.7 million post-9-11 Muslim avoidable deaths, and (h) Niger was conquered by France in the late 19th century but became ostensibly independent in 1960 but under French hegemony; the French Operation Barkhane involves thousands of air-supported French troops dedicated to killing Muslim rebels in the Sahel countries of Mali, Mauritania, Burkina Faso, Niger and Chad.

14. Pakistan: (a) 188.9 million, (b) 49.7 million, (c) 660,000, (d) 9.1 million, (e) $4,700, (f) 96.0% Muslim, (g) 8.7 million post-9-11 Muslim avoidable deaths, and (h) Pakistan gained independence from the UK in 1947 after 2 centuries of British rule in which 1.8 billion Indians died avoidably from deprivation in the British Raj; independence in 1947 was marked by generation of 18 million refugees between India and Pakistan (half Muslim, half Hindu) and up to 1 million people were killed; in 1971 US-backed Pakistani forces killed 3 million mostly male Bengalis and raped 300,000 Bengali women in a Bengali Holocaust that marked the creation of Bangladesh; Australian-targeted US drone attacks commenced in 2004.

15. Palestine: (a) 4.7 million, (b) 0.7 million, (c), 5,000, (d) 70,000, (e) $4,900 (cf its Occupier Apartheid Israel's $33,000), (f) 85.0% Muslim, (g) 60,000 post-9-11 Muslim avoidable

deaths, and (h) Palestine has an ancient history dating back to the very start of agrarian civilization; British forces invaded in 1914 and together with Australian and New Zealand Army Corps (ANZAC) forces conquered Palestine; the 1917 Balfour Declaration promised Palestine to the genocidal Zionists as a Jewish Homeland; Surafend Massacre of Palestinians by Australian and New Zealand ANZAC troops in 1918; 1948 creation of the State of Israel with massive forcible expulsion of 800,000 Palestinians and Zionist seizure of about 80% of Palestine; in 1967 Israel seized all of Palestine plus part of Syria; 90% of the land of Palestine has now been ethnically cleansed and Israeli Apartheid means that of 12 million Palestinian, 6 million are forbidden to step foot in Palestine and of 6 million Palestinians living under Israeli rule only 28% (1.7 million Palestinian Israelis) can vote for the government ruling them – the rest have essentially zero human rights; 2 million Palestinians have died since 1936 from Zionist violence (0.1 million) or Zionist -imposed deprivation (1.9 million).

16. Philippines: (a) 100.7 million, (b) 9.1 million, (c) 270,000, (d) 2.7 million, (e) $7,000, (f) 11.0% Muslim, (g) 0.3 million post-9-11 Muslim avoidable deaths, and (h) the Philippines was acquired by the US from Spain at the conclusion of the Spanish-American War (1898) but in the subsequent 1899-1913 Philippines-US War about 1 million Filipinos died; the Philippines became independent in 1946 but with retention of US bases; in the 21st century US forces returned to combat communist rebels and thence Muslim rebels in the south in Operation Enduring Freedom – Philippines (OEF-P) (many Filipinos object to this military action by the US in their country).

17. Somalia: (a) 10.8 million, (b) 5.6 million, (c) 91,000, (d) 1.2 million, (e) $600, (f) 96.0% Muslim, (g) 1.2 million post-9-11 Muslim avoidable deaths, and (h) Somalia was repeatedly invaded by Italy in the 19th and 20th centuries. The British took over Somalia in WW2. Independence in 1960 was followed by war against Ethiopia and civil war, the effects of which were exacerbated by drought and famine. The US invaded in 1992 and after extensive civil war an Islamic administration assumed

power in 2005. However the US backed an Ethiopian invasion in 2007 and thence a Kenyan invasion. In 2009 France and Germany invaded Somali waters to retake a captured French yacht and in 2013 French special forces from Djibouti failed in an operation to rescue a captured French intelligence agent.

18. Sudan: (a) 40.2 million, (b) 13.5 million, (c) 157,000, (d) 2.3 million, (e) $4,300, (f) 97.0% Muslim, (g) 2.3 million post-9-11 Muslim avoidable deaths, and (h) Sudan was conquered by the UK in 1898 but eventually became independent in 1958; the US under Clinton notoriously bombed a Sudan pharmaceutical factory in 1998 (Professor Noam Chomsky estimated that 10,000 Sudanese would have died from disease as a result); US ally Apartheid Israel bombed Sudan in 2009 and such Israeli bombing attacks on Sudan are presently continuing. Apartheid Israeli arms are heavily involved in the US-backed civil war in the newly independent South Sudan.

19. Syria: (a) 18.5 million, (b) 2.2 million, (c) 14,000, (d) 190,000 (68,000 in 2011-2015), (e) $5,100, (f) 96.0% Muslim, (g) 171,000 post-9-11 Muslim avoidable deaths, and (h) Syria, one of the oldest nations in the world, was allocated to France by the 1916 Anglo-French Sykes-Picot Agreement that divided the Middle East between Britain and France; Syria was put under a League of Nations mandate to France in 1920; in 1944 Syria became independent and in 1945 Syria became a founding member of the UN with the last French forces leaving Syria in 1946; in 1967 the Syrian Golan Heights region was captured and largely ethnically cleansed by Apartheid Israel which continues to periodically bomb Syria; commencement of Sunni rebellion in 2011 backed diplomatically and materially by Turkey, the US, UK, France, Qatar, Jordan, Saudi Arabia, and Apartheid Israel. The Syrian Civil War has so far killed about 0.3 million people violently, killed a similar number of people through war-imposed deprivation, and generated about 12 million refugees. Syria was once a haven of religious toleration and a world leader per capita in providing haven for refugees, but over half of its population are now refugees themselves and Syria has now been devastated in a sectarian civil war involving the Assad Government versus anti-Assad Sunni rebels (of which

ISIS is the most powerful) that are variously backed by the UK, US, France, Turkey, Qatar, Saudi Arabia, Jordan, Australia and Apartheid Israel.

20. Yemen: (a) 19.9 million, (b) 6.6 million, (c) 111,000, (d) 1.2 million, (e) $1,100, (f) 100.0% Muslim, (g) 1.2 million post-9-11 Muslim avoidable deaths, and (h) South Yemen gained independence from the UK in 1967 and North and South Yemen unified in 1989; continuing armed conflict with Australian-targeted US drone attacks in the 21st century that are continuing. Currently Yemen is being war criminally invaded by an anti-Houthi Saudi-led Coalition including Saudi Arabia, United Arab Emirates, Bahrain, Qatar, Kuwait, Egypt, Jordan, Morocco, Senegal, and Sudan.

Summary and conclusions

The post-9-11 avoidable deaths in the 20 countries violated by the West in the post-9-11 War on Terror total 34.0 million. However we can re-assess this data by considering the Muslim percentage of the population in these 20 countries and can estimate that post-9-11 Muslim avoidable deaths in these 20 US Alliance-violated countries total 26.8 million, noting that, as discussed above, it is likely that most of the violent Muslim deaths in the Zionist-promoted US War on Terror are not included in this estimate. About half the victims of this Neocon American and Zionist Imperialist (NAZI)-prosecuted Muslim Holocaust and Muslim Genocide are children.
This carnage of 26.8 million post-9-11 Muslim avoidable deaths is 26,800,000/130 = 206,154 or about 200,000 times greater than the 130 murdered in the recent appalling Paris massacre – however, in contrast to the saturation coverage of the appalling Paris atrocity, this Muslim Holocaust and Muslim Genocide is resolutely ignored by genocidally racist, anti-Arab anti-Semitic, Islamophobic, and Neocon American and Zionist Imperialist (NAZI)-subverted Western Mainstream media.
Using data from the UN Population Division 2006 Revision of World Population Prospects it was previously determined that Iraqi avoidable deaths in 1990-2003 and 2003-2011 totalled 1.7 million and 1.2 million, respectively, and combining this data

with Gulf War violent deaths of 0.2 million and Iraq War violent deaths of 1.5 million, yielded estimates of Iraqi deaths from violence or violently-imposed deprivation totalling 1.9 million (1990-2003), 2.7 million (2003-2011) and 4.6 million (1990-2011) [4, 22, 23]. However using the present UN 2015 Revision data [25] one estimates Iraqi avoidable deaths in 1990-2003 and 2003-2011 totalling 0.5 million and 0.4 million, respectively, this yielding estimates of Iraqi deaths from violence or violently-imposed deprivation totalling 0.7 million (1990-2003), 1.9 million (2003-2011) and 2.6 million (1990-2011). The UN 2015 Revision data on Iraq may underestimate avoidable deaths because they are based on data provided by the US-installed regime which, for example, implausibly claims that in Iraq under-5 infant mortality declined after imposition of Sanctions in 1990 and declined further after the US invasion in 2003 [25].

Similarly, using 2006 Revision data it was determined that Afghan avoidable deaths and violent deaths in 2001-2014 totalled 5.5 million and 1.7 million, respectively for a total of 7.2 million post-invasion deaths from violence or from deprivation. However using the present UN 2015 Revision data [25] based on data from the government of US occupied Afghanistan one estimates that Afghan avoidable deaths and violent deaths in 2001-2015 have totalled 2.3 million and 0.7 million, respectively, for a total of 3.0 million post-invasion deaths from violence or from deprivation.

The 2015 Paris Massacre in which 130 innocent civilians were murdered by jihadis is a shocking crime that must be unequivocally condemned but is already being exploited (a) by the jihadi non-state terrorist perpetrators as a victory and evidence for more atrocities to come, and (b) by the US state terrorists, French state terrorists and US Alliance state terrorists as a "French 9-11" with calls from Obama and Holland to genocidally destroy jihadi rebels in Syria and Iraq [1, 2]. Completely missing from the continuing hysterical response to the Paris atrocity from US lackey Western Mainstream journalists, politicians and academics is any public airing of the horrendous reality of 27 million Muslims dying avoidably since 9-11 in 20 substantially or significantly Muslim countries that have been attacked by US Alliance state terrorists. Jihadi non-state terrorists must be condemned (a) for the violent crimes they personally commit against innocent people and (b) for the vastly greater crimes committed by the US Alliance against Muslims in response to jihadi outrages. Indeed jihadi non-state terrorists are among the greatest assets of US imperialism – every jihadi atrocity is another excuse trumpeted by Mainstream media for more atrocities against the Muslim world by US state terrorists and US Alliance state terrorists.

The Paris atrocity can be seen as "blowback" for horrendous crimes committed by the US Alliance against the Muslim world from West Africa to South East Asia [26, 27]. The horrible reality is that the US has a long history of false-flag operations (with 9-11 being the most immediately and subsequently deadly) [3], supporting terrorism and exploiting terrorist acts by Indigenous insurgents lacking military industries, navies, airforces and tanks, and essentially only armed with light arms and explosives for bombs.

Indeed the US has a long history of supporting terrorists (e.g. US-backed terrorists in Ecuador who would bomb Catholic churches knowing that the socialists would be blamed; the US-backed Gladio organization that committed atrocities in post-war Europe that would be blamed on communists; and backing jihadi fighters in Afghanistan in the 1980s and in the Balkans in the 1990s) [28]. Indeed the US has an appalling record of replacing secular governments in the Muslim world with sectarian regimes (e.g. Afghanistan, 1978; Iraq, 2003; Libya, 2011; and now in Syria today but for Russian support for the Assad Government) [29].

Even the appalling Western Mainstream media can no longer ignore the Elephant in the Room realities that (a) the illegal US Alliance invasion of Iraq generated sectarian warfare and the Sunni rebellion that transmuted into ISIS, and (b) support for anti-Assad rebels by the US Alliance state terrorism – US state terrorism, UK state terrorism, French state terrorism, Australian state terrorism, Apartheid Israeli state terrorism, Turkish state terrorism, Jordanian state terrorism, Qatari state terrorism and Saudi Arabian state terrorism – has led to ISIS (Islamic State, IS, ISIL, Daesh) dominating rebel-held Syria.

Peace is the only way but silence kills and silence is complicity. Decent, pro-peace people must wonder what they can do in the face of appalling non-state terrorism (e.g. as exhibited by ISIS in killing 130 innocent people in this latest Paris atrocity) and the vastly worse carnage wrought by US state terrorism, UK state terrorism, French state terrorism, and Apartheid Israeli state terrorism in the Muslim world involving post-9-11 Muslim avoidable deaths in 20 US Alliance-violated countries now totalling 26.8 million. Decent people who are utterly opposed to both non-state terrorism and state terrorism must (a) inform everyone they can, (b) urge and support urgent cease-fire, dialogue and compromise between all parties to prevent a worsening catastrophe in both Iraq and Syria, and (c) urge and apply Boycotts, Divestment and Sanctions (BDS) against all people, parties, politicians, companies, corporations and countries disproportionately involved in militarism, violence, war, genocide, non-state terrorism and state terrorism.

First published as "Paris Atrocity Context: 27 Million Muslim Avoidable Deaths From Imposed Deprivation In 20 Countries Violated By US Alliance Since 9-11", Countercurrents, November 2015.

References

[1]. Barack Obama, "Press conference by President Obama – Antalya, Turkey", White House, 16 November 2015: https://www.whitehouse.gov/the-press-office/2015/11/16/press-conference-president-obama-antalya-turkey.

[2]. Martin Robinson, "France will be in a state of emergency for THREE MONTHS: Holland vows to 'destroy' ISIS and pledges 'no barbarians will prevent us from living how we have decided to live', Daily Mail, 17 November 2015: http://www.dailymail.co.uk/news/article-3320731/France-state-emergency-THREE-MONTHS-Hollande-vows-boost-spending-security-pledges-no-barbarians-prevent-living-decided-live.html).

[3]. "Experts: US did 9-11": https://sites.google.com/site/expertsusdid911/.

[4]. "Iraqi Holocaust Iraqi Genocide": https://sites.google.com/site/iraqiholocaustiraqigenocide/.

[5]. Just Foreign Policy, "Iraq Deaths": http://www.justforeignpolicy.org/iraq.

[6]. "US military marks end of its Iraq war", ABC News, 16 December 2011: http://www.abc.net.au/news/2011-12-15/us-military-marks-end-of-its-war-in-iraq/3733982.

[7]. ABC News, "Iraki leaks show scale of civilian casualties", 24 October 2010: http://www.abc.net.au/news/2010-10-23/iraqi-leaks-show-scale-of-civilian-casualties/2308808.

[8]. "Iraq Body Count": https://www.iraqbodycount.org/.

[9], "Censorship by the BBC": https://sites.google.com/site/censorshipbythebbc/.

[10]. "ABC fact-checking unit & incorrect reportage by the ABC (Australia's BBC)": https://sites.google.com/site/mainstreammediacensorship/abc-fact-checking-unit.

[11]. BBC, "Iraq War in figures", 14 December 2011: http://www.bbc.com/news/world-middle-east-11107739.

[12]. "Bengali Holocaust (WW2 Bengal Famine) writings of Gideon Polya", Gideon Polya Writing: https://sites.google.com/site/drgideonpolya/bengali-holocaust.

[13]. Gideon Polya (1998), "Jane Austen and the Black Hole of British History. Colonial rapacity, holocaust denial and the crisis in biological sustainability", 2008 edition that is now available for free perusal on the web: http://janeaustenand.blogspot.com/.

[14]. Gideon Polya (1995) "The Forgotten Holocaust – The 1943/44 Bengal Famine": http://globalavoidablemortality.blogspot.com.au/2005/07/forgotten-holocaust-194344-bengal.html.

[15]. Gideon Polya (2011), "Australia And Britain Killed 6-7 Million Indians In WW2 Bengal Famine", Countercurrents, 29 September, 2011: http://www.countercurrents.org/polya290911.htm.

[16]. "Mainstream media censorship": https://sites.google.com/site/mainstreammediacensorship/home.

[17]. "Mainstream media lying":

https://sites.google.com/site/mainstreammedialying/.

[18]. Kit O'Connell, "4 million Muslims killed in Western wars: should we call it genocide?", MintPress News, 18 August 2015: http://www.mintpressnews.com/4-million-muslims-killed-in-western-wars-should-we-call-it-genocide/208711/.

[19]. Nafeez Ahmed, "Unworthy victims: Western wars have killed 4 million Muslim since 1990", MintPtress News, 9 April 2015: http://www.mintpressnews.com/unworthy-victims-western-wars-have-killed-four-million-muslims-since-1990/204182/.

[20]. International Physicians for the Prevention of Nuclear War (IPPNW), Physicians for Social Responsibility (PSR) and Physicians for Global Survival (PGS), "Body Count. Casualty figures after 10 years of the 'War on Terror' Iraq, Afghanistan, Pakistan", March 2015: http://www.psr.org/assets/pdfs/body-count.pdf.

[21]. "Afghan Holocaust Afghan Genocide": https://sites.google.com/site/afghanholocaustafghangenocide/.

[22]. "Muslim Holocaust Muslim Genocide": https://sites.google.com/site/muslimholocaustmuslimgenocide/.

[23]. Gideon Polya, "Body Count. Global avoidable mortality since 1950", that includes an avoidable mortality-related history of every country since Neolithic times and is now available for free perusal on the web: http://globalbodycount.blogspot.com.au/2012/01/body-count-global-avoidable-mortality_05.html.

[24]. "List of countries by GDP (PPP) per capita", Wikipedia: https://en.wikipedia.org/wiki/List_of_countries_by_GDP_%28PPP%29_per_capita.

[25]. UN Population Division 2015 Revision of World Population Prospects: http://esa.un.org/unpd/wpp/.

[26]. Gideon Polya,"Appalling Paris Atrocity – Non-State Terrorist Blowback For US Alliance And French State Terrorism Atrocities", Countercurrents, 16 November, 2015: http://www.countercurrents.org/polya161115.htm.

[27]. Gideon Polya, "Horrendous US state terrorism and French state terrorism led to the appalling non-state terrorist Paris atrocity", Gideon Polya Writing, 2015-11-18: https://sites.google.com/site/gideonpolyawriting/2015-11-18.

[28]. Gideon Polya, "US Profits From Jihadist Terrorism", Countercurrents, 19 November, 2004: http://www.countercurrents.org/us-polya191104.htm.

[29]. Gideon Polya, "Fundamentalist America Has Trashed Secular Governance, Modernity, Democracy, Women's Rights And Children's Rights In The Muslim World", Countercurrents, 21 May, 2015: http://www.countercurrents.org/polya210515.htm.

Mendacious War Criminal Obama's Final Speech To The UN General Assembly

America's mendacious, serial invader, war criminal, climate criminal and human rights-violating President Barack Obama made his last speech to the UN General Assembly on 20 September 2016, a speech characterized by massive lying by omission that is far, far worse than lying by commission because the latter can at least be refuted and subject to public debate. As revealed by Edward Snowden, America spies on everyone in America and the world, but Obama managed to comprehensively ignore a veritable Herd of Elephants in the Room as detailed in the following analysis of his last UN speech. As Dr. Paul Craig Roberts has stated: "Washington lies about everything".

The transcript of President Obama's final speech to the UN [1] is reproduced below with key matters he has ignored set out succinctly in square brackets, together with appropriate detailed documentation.

PRESIDENT OBAMA:

1. Mr. President; Mr. Secretary General; fellow delegates; ladies and gentlemen: As I address this hall as President for the final time, let me recount the progress that we've made these last eight years.

[The atmospheric CO_2 concentration has increased to 405 ppm CO_2 and is increasing at a record 3 ppm CO_2 per year; a catastrophic plus 2C temperature rise is now unavoidable, plus 1.5C may occur by 2020, and the current plus 1C is already catastrophic for tropical Island States and megadelta countries like Bangladesh [2]; the coal-to-gas conversion by the US under

Obama locks in disastrous long-term greenhouse gas (GHG) pollution [3]; 17 million people die avoidably from deprivation each year, about half of them children [4]; 7 million die from air pollution each year [5, 6]; the US Alliance has invaded 20 overwhelmingly or significantly Muslim countries since the US Government's 9-11 false flag atrocity, this being associated with 32 million Muslim deaths from violence (5 million) or from war- or hegemony-imposed deprivation (27 million) [7, 8]].

2. From the depths of the greatest financial crisis of our time, we coordinated our response to avoid further catastrophe and return the global economy to growth. We've taken away terrorist safe havens, strengthened the nonproliferation regime, resolved the Iranian nuclear issue through diplomacy. We opened relations with Cuba, helped Colombia end Latin America's longest war, and we welcome a democratically elected leader of Myanmar to this Assembly. Our assistance is helping people feed themselves, care for the sick, power communities across Africa, and promote models of development rather than dependence. And we have made international institutions like the World Bank and the International Monetary Fund more representative, while establishing a framework to protect our planet from the ravages of climate change.

[US-complicit military coups in Honduras, Ukraine and Egypt; US-complicit parliamentary coup in Brazil; US Alliance military intervention in 20 countries this century associated with the active or passive killing of 32 million Muslims[4, 7, 9-12] ; after the Global Financial Crisis the US rewarded the banker criminals whereas Iceland sent them all to jail; the US Alliance devastated Libya, formerly the richest country in Africa, and devastated secular Syria, converting half the population to refugees in a country that was formerly the world's leading country for per capita hosting of refugees [9]; the US Alliance created ISIS in Iraq [11] and backed ISIS in Syria against the secular Assad Government in the interests of Apartheid Israel, US hegemony and a "Sunni gas pipeline" from Qatar to the Mediterranean [13]; while Iran has no nuclear weapons and declares it does not want them, US-backed Apartheid Israel has as many as 400 nuclear weapons and acquired them with US assistance [14]].

3. This is important work. It has made a real difference in the lives of our people. And it could not have happened had we not worked together. And yet, around the globe we are seeing the same forces of global integration that have made us interdependent also expose deep fault lines in the existing international order.

[Under the existing international order 17 million people die avoidably from deprivation each year on Spaceship Earth with a Neocon American and Zionist Imperialist (NAZI)-beholden US Government in charge of the flight deck [4]; America with 4% of the world's population consumes 25% of its resources; the variously dissident BRICS countries (Brazil, Russia, India, China and South Africa) have moved toward an alternative, radical proposition derived from the American Declaration of Independence, specifically that "all men are created equal"].

4. We see it in the headlines every day. Around the world, refugees flow across borders in flight from brutal conflict. Financial disruptions continue to weigh upon our workers and entire communities. Across vast swaths of the Middle East, basic security, basic order has broken down. We see too many governments muzzling journalists, and quashing dissent, and censoring the flow of information. Terrorist networks use social media to prey upon the minds of our youth, endangering open societies and spurring anger against innocent immigrants and Muslims. Powerful nations contest the constraints placed on them by international law.

[There are 65 million refugees in the world today, half being Muslims fleeing genocidal US Alliance wars in their countries [9]; the US and US Alliance countries are exceptionalist, ignore international law and currently invade some 20 impoverished and largely or substantially Muslim countries at will [7, 9]; the Obama Administrations and their lackey US Alliance countries have been complicit in "muzzling journalists, and quashing dissent, and censoring the flow of information" as illustrated by the conduct of US –backed regimes throughout the world, through the "manufacturing consent" by compliant US and US Alliance Mainstream media [15-17], and, notoriously, by the US in relation to remorselessly pursuing the world hero whistle-blowers Chelsea Manning, Edward Snowden and Julian Assange].

5. This is the paradox that defines our world today. A quarter century after the end of the Cold War, the world is by many measures less violent and more prosperous than ever before, and yet our societies are filled with uncertainty, and unease, and strife. Despite enormous progress, as people lose trust in institutions, governing becomes more difficult and tensions between nations become more quick to surface.

[People have lost trust in the mendacity of governments that is well illustrated by the comprehensive mendacity of the Obama Administrations as outlined here; the US Center for Public Integrity found that the Bush Administration told 935 lies between 9-11 and the invasion of Iraq [18]; Pullitzer Prize-winning journalist Seymour Hersh dismissed Obama's "official story" of the extra-judicial killing of Osama bin-Laden as a pack of lies except for the killing [19] – Dr. Paul Craig Roberts went one further and stated that even the asserted killing of Osama bin-Laden was a lie [20]; numerous science, engineering, architecture, aviation, military and intelligence experts reject the "lying Bush official version" of 9-11 [8] but Obama accepts it, strongly opposed release of documents revealing Saudi complicity in 9-11, and is resolutely opposed to legislation allowing the relatives of 9-11 victims to sue foreign governments over their loss; lying and secrecy mean that Obama and the US Establishment are accessories after the fact of the 9-11 atrocity].

6. And so I believe that at this moment we all face a choice. We can choose to press forward with a better model of cooperation and integration. Or we can retreat into a world sharply divided, and ultimately in conflict, along age-old lines of nation and tribe and race and religion.

[The US has long rejected "age-old lines of nation" in relation to other nations, and since 1776 has invaded over 70 nations [21]; with US troops on the ground in Syria, the US presently has military bases in 75 nations [23]; the US Alliance has been invading and devastating Muslim countries since the US Government's 9-11 false flag atrocity, this being associated with 32 million Muslim deaths from violence (5 million) or from war- or hegemony-imposed deprivation (27 million) [7, 9]; the Neocon American and Zionist Imperialist (NAZI)-perverted and subverted US backs nuclear terrorist, racist Zionist (RZ)-run, genocidally racist, democracy-by-genocide Apartheid Israel that is obscenely based "along age-old lines of nation and tribe and race and religion"; the long-term accrual cost of US support for Apartheid Israel is at least $40 trillion [24]; in one of his last acts as president, Obama announced a $38 billion military package for serial war criminal Apartheid Israel over the next decade [25]].

7. I want to suggest to you today that we must go forward, and not backward. I believe that as imperfect as they are, the principles of open markets and accountable governance, of democracy and human rights and international law that we have forged remain the firmest foundation for human progress in this century. I make this argument not based on theory or ideology, but on facts — facts that all too often, we forget in the immediacy of current events.

[The "open markets" espoused by Obama is theory and ideology; Professor Lord Nicholas Stern has described climate change inaction as the greatest market failure in human history [26]; the presently dominant economic ideology of neoliberalism means maximizing the freedom of the smart and advantaged to exploit natural and human resources for private profit [27, 28], and has evidently failed, as evidenced by a continuing financial crisis, a worsening climate emergency (already catastrophic for some countries) and a worsening climate genocide that will see 10 billion people perishing this century if climate change is not requisitely addressed [29]].

8. Here's the most important fact: The integration of our global economy has made life better for billions of men, women and children. Over the last 25 years, the number of people living in extreme poverty has been cut from nearly 40 percent of humanity to under 10 percent. That's unprecedented. And it's not an abstraction. It means children have enough to eat; mothers don't die in childbirth.

[According to World Hunger: " The United Nations Food and Agriculture Organization estimates that about 795 million people of the 7.3 billion people in the world, or one in nine, were suffering from chronic undernourishment in 2014-2016. Almost all the hungry people, 780 million, live in developing countries, representing 12.9 percent, or one in eight, of the population of developing counties" [30], i.e. in 2014-2016 about 11% of the world suffered chronic undernourishment. 17 million people die avoidably each year from deprivation in the Developing World minus China, about half being children [4]. According to the World Bank "According to the most recent estimates, in 2012, 12.7 percent of the world's population lived at or below $1.90 a day. That's down from 37 percent in 1990 and 44 percent in 1981. This means that, in 2012, 896 million people lived on less than $1.90 a day, compared with 1.95 billion in 1990, and 1.99 billion in 1981 [31]].

9. Meanwhile, cracking the genetic code promises to cure diseases that have plagued us for centuries. The Internet can deliver the entirety of human knowledge to a young girl in a remote village on a single hand-held device. In medicine and in manufacturing, in education and communications, we're experiencing a transformation of how human beings live on a scale that recalls the revolutions in agriculture and industry. And as a result, a person born today is more likely to be healthy, to live longer, and to have access to opportunity than at any time in human history.

[Obama's optimistic Eurocentric vision does not apply to the Third Word in which 17 million people die avoidably from deprivation and deprivation-exacerbated disease each year [4]; there is a worsening climate genocide that will see 10 billion people perishing this century if climate change is not requisitely addressed [29]].

10. Moreover, the collapse of colonialism and communism has allowed more people than ever before to live with the freedom to choose their leaders. Despite the real and troubling areas where freedom appears in retreat, the fact remains that the number of democracies around the world has nearly doubled in the last 25 years.

[Obama as a serial war criminal and serial invader has an appalling record of denying numerous nations "the freedom to choose their leaders" – under Obama the US Alliance has invaded 20 overwhelmingly or significantly Muslim countries since the US Government's 9-11 false flag atrocity, this ongoing Muslim Holocaust and Muslim Genocide being associated with 32 million Muslim deaths from violence (5 million) or from war- or hegemony-imposed deprivation (27 million) [7-9]; under Obama the US has backed the removal of democratically-elected government in Honduras and the Ukraine and of a democratically-elected president in Brazil; under Obama the US continues to subvert every nation on earth; most democracies are faux democracies in which Big Money has replaced Democracy with Plutocracy, Kleptocracy, Murdochracy, Lobbyocracy, Corporatocracy and Dollarocracy in which Big Money purchases people, politicians, parties, public perception of reality, political power and thence more private profit – with much of this Big Money coming from tax-avoiding US corporations].

11. In remote corners of the world, citizens are demanding respect for the dignity of all people no matter their gender, or race, or religion, or disability, or sexual orientation, and those who deny others dignity are subject to public reproach. An explosion of social media has given ordinary people more ways to express themselves, and has raised people's expectations for those of us in power. Indeed, our international order has been so successful that we take it as a given that great powers no longer fight world wars; that the end of the Cold War lifted the shadow of nuclear Armageddon; that the battlefields of Europe have

been replaced by peaceful union; that China and India remain on a path of remarkable growth.

[The overwhelmingly dominant One Percenter-owned Mainstream media are still deceiving the people and "manufacturing consent" [15]; the nuclear threat remains – the upper estimates of stored nuclear weapons are as follows: US (7,315), Russia (8,000), Apartheid Israel (400), France (300), UK (250), China (250), Pakistan (120), India (100), and North Korea (less than 10) [32]; under Obama the US backed a neo-Nazi coup in the Ukraine and has escalated military confrontation in Eastern Europe leading to serious fears of a nuclear and terminal WW3 [33, 34]; the rapid economic growth of the populous countries China and India means that CO_2 pollution is increasing at a record 3 ppm CO_2 per year, although the annual per capita greenhouse gas (GHG) pollution in tonnes CO_2-equivalent per person per year is 8.9 (world average), 41.0 (US), 7.4 (China) and 2.1 (India) [35, 36]].

12. I say all this not to whitewash the challenges we face, or to suggest complacency. Rather, I believe that we need to acknowledge these achievements in order to summon the confidence to carry this progress forward and to make sure that we do not abandon those very things that have delivered this progress.

[See point #11. Obama is whitewashing the nuclear, poverty and climate change threats [32, 33] – indeed Boycotts, Divestment and Sanctions (BDS) should be applied against the worst GHG polluting countries [35, 36] and all countries that refuse to join the present 127 nations who support the Nuclear Weapons Ban [34]].

13. In order to move forward, though, we do have to acknowledge that the existing path to global integration requires a course correction. As too often, those trumpeting the benefits of globalization have ignored inequality within and among nations; have ignored the enduring appeal of ethnic and sectarian identities; have left international institutions ill-

equipped, underfunded, under-resourced, in order to handle transnational challenges.

[Obama is egregiously guilty of such "ignoring" e.g. ignoring the 17 million people who die avoidably from deprivation each year, about half of them children [4] and, within the US, the over 27% of African Americans who live in poverty [37]].

14. And as these real problems have been neglected, alternative visions of the world have pressed forward both in the wealthiest countries and in the poorest: Religious fundamentalism; the politics of ethnicity, or tribe, or sect; aggressive nationalism; a crude populism — sometimes from the far left, but more often from the far right — which seeks to restore what they believe was a better, simpler age free of outside contamination.

[Under serial invader and serial war criminal Obama an "exceptionalist" US has continued "aggressive nationalism" with the US Alliance invading 20 overwhelmingly or significantly Muslim countries since the US Government's 9-11 false flag atrocity, this being associated with 32 million Muslim deaths from violence (5 million) or from war- or hegemony-imposed deprivation (27 million) [7, 8]]; "religious fundamentalism; the politics of ethnicity, or tribe, or sect; aggressive nationalism; a crude populism" are exhibited by US-backed, nuclear terrorist, racist Zionist-run, genocidally racist, democracy-by-genocide, neo-Nazi Apartheid Israel in its ongoing Palestinian Genocide [10] and its powerful espousal via the Zionist Lobby of the ongoing Muslim Holocaust and Muslim Genocide [7-9, 11, 12]].

15. We cannot dismiss these visions. They are powerful. They reflect dissatisfaction among too many of our citizens. I do not believe those visions can deliver security or prosperity over the long term, but I do believe that these visions fail to recognize, at a very basic level, our common humanity. Moreover, I believe that the acceleration of travel and technology and telecommunications — together with a global economy that depends on a global supply chain — makes it self-defeating

ultimately for those who seek to reverse this progress. Today, a nation ringed by walls would only imprison itself.

["Dissatisfaction among too many of our citizens" – the "too many" have an awful lot to be dissatisfied about both globally and domestically in the US. Thus globally nearly 1 billion live in dire poverty and suffer chronic malnourishment [30, 31] with 17 million dying from deprivation annually, about half being children [4], and the Muslim world subject to a Muslim Holocaust and Muslim Genocide in which there have been 32 million Muslim deaths from violence (5 million) or from war- or hegemony-imposed deprivation (27 million) since the US Government's 9-11 false-flag atrocity in 2001 [7, 8]. Domestically, 1.7 million Americans die preventably each year, this carnage being inescapably linked to the fiscal perversions of the $40 trillion long-term accrual cost of Apartheid Israel to America [38] and successive Neocon American and Zionist Imperialist (NAZI)-perverted Administrations committing trillions of dollars to killing Muslims abroad in the War on Terror (the War on Muslims) rather than keeping Americans alive at home [39]. American incomes have flat-lined for decades of course, as for African Americans under America's first black president, 27% live in poverty, African American wealth is about 5 times lower than that of Whites, millions of African Americans are excluded from voting, African Americans are 8 times more likely to murder and 6 times more likely to be murdered than Whites, Educational Apartheid has meant return of Segregation with a vengeance, and African Americans and Hispanic Americans have about half their "fair share" of representatives in Congress and 5-6 times less Congressional representation than Jewish Americans (despite being collectively about 10 times more population-wise) [37]].

16. So the answer cannot be a simple rejection of global integration. Instead, we must work together to make sure the benefits of such integration are broadly shared, and that the disruptions — economic, political, and cultural — that are caused by integration are squarely addressed. This is not the place for a detailed policy blueprint, but let me offer in broad strokes those areas where I believe we must do better together.

["Global integration" means that manufacturing jobs go to where the wages are lowest in a new version of slavery that ignores the fundamental human right to a decent life. The British (a) abolished slavery in Britain when rural Enclosures generated the effective slavery of a minimum wage industrial working class; (b) later replaced slavery in the British colonies by minimally paid "indentured labour" (e.g. the "5-year slavery of Indian indentured labour in Fiji that finally ceased in 1922 [40]); and (c) today exploit Third World labour by the effective slavery of "global integration"].

17. It starts with making the global economy work better for all people and not just for those at the top. While open markets, capitalism have raised standards of living around the globe, globalization combined with rapid progress and technology has also weakened the position of workers and their ability to secure a decent wage. In advanced economies like my own, unions have been undermined, and many manufacturing jobs have disappeared. Often, those who benefit most from globalization have used their political power to further undermine the position of workers.

[In the US the average wage has flat-lined in real terms for decades, but the One Percenter and Ten Percenter share of annual income has steadily increased for decades, this phenomenon also obtaining elsewhere in the Anglosphere [41-43]].

18. In developing countries, labor organizations have often been suppressed, and the growth of the middle class has been held back by corruption and underinvestment. Mercantilist policies pursued by governments with export-driven models threaten to undermine the consensus that underpins global trade. And meanwhile, global capital is too often unaccountable — nearly $8 trillion stashed away in tax havens, a shadow banking system that grows beyond the reach of effective oversight.

[US corporations are massively involved in egregious global tax avoidance which contributes to the inequity that in turn drives the Global Avoidable Mortality Holocaust in which 17 million people die avoidably from deprivation every year [4]. By backing anti-democratic neofascist and neoliberal regimes around the world, America, including the US under Obama, massively contributes to suppression of labour organizations].

19. A world in which one percent of humanity controls as much wealth as the other 99 percent will never be stable. I understand that the gaps between rich and poor are not new, but just as the child in a slum today can see the skyscraper nearby, technology now allows any person with a smartphone to see how the most privileged among us live and the contrast between their own lives and others. Expectations rise, then, faster than governments can deliver, and a pervasive sense of injustice undermine people's faith in the system.

[But in harsh reality Obama is part of the One Percent, represents the One Percent politically and is dedicated to the deceit, manipulation and variously egregiously violent suppression of the 99%].

20. So how do we fix this imbalance? We cannot unwind integration any more than we can stuff technology back into a box. Nor can we look to failed models of the past. If we start resorting to trade wars, market distorting subsidies, beggar thy neighbor policies, an overreliance on natural resources instead of innovation — these approaches will make us poorer, collectively, and they are more like to lead to conflict. And the stark contrast between, say, the success of the Republic of Korea and the wasteland of North Korea shows that central, planned control of the economy is a dead end.

[Professor Thomas Piketty in his seminal book "Capital in the Twenty-First Century" argues that gross inequity damages democracy (Big Money buys votes) and damages the economy (the poor cannot afford to buy the goods and services they produce). Piketty argues for wealth transparency and a global annual wealth tax of up to 10% [41, 42], noting that France has an annual wealth tax of up to 1.5% and Islam has had an annual wealth tax of 2.5% (zakkat) for 1,400 years [43]. It is estimated that an annual global wealth tax of 4% could abolish the Global

Avoidable Mortality Holocaust and prevent 17 million people from dying avoidably from deprivation every year – an annual global wealth tax of about 4% would yield US$16 trillion annually and enable raising all countries to annual per capita incomes equivalent to the $6,000 per person per year of China and Cuba, countries for which annual avoidable mortality is zero (0) [44]. One can well understand why One Percenter Obama ignores the wealth tax option. As for North Korea, it has been subject to frightening military hostility from the genocidally violent US for about 70 years, and US bombing in 1950-1953 killed 28% of the population [45]].

21. But I do believe there's another path — one that fuels growth and innovation, and offers the clearest route to individual opportunity and national success. It does not require succumbing to a soulless capitalism that benefits only the few, but rather recognizes that economies are more successful when we close the gap between rich and poor, and growth is broadly based. And that means respecting the rights of workers so they can organize into independent unions and earn a living wage. It means investing in our people — their skills, their education, their capacity to take an idea and turn it into a business. It means strengthening the safety net that protects our people from hardship and allows them to take more risks — to look for a new job, or start a new venture.

[Great rhetoric from a neoliberal, corporatist, One Percenter president Obama under whom 1.7 million Americans die preventably every year [39]].

22. These are the policies that I've pursued here in the United States, and with clear results. American businesses have created now 15 million new jobs. After the recession, the top one percent of Americans were capturing more than 90 percent of income growth. But today, that's down to about half. Last year, poverty in this country fell at the fastest rate in nearly 50 years. And with further investment in infrastructure and early childhood education and basic research, I'm confident that such progress will continue.

[One Percenter Obama is boasting that the One Percenters "only" captured 45% of income growth after the recession].

23. So just as I've pursued these measures here at home, so has the United States worked with many nations to curb the excesses of capitalism — not to punish wealth, but to prevent repeated crises that can destroy it. That's why we've worked with other nations to create higher and clearer standards for banking and taxation — because a society that asks less of oligarchs than ordinary citizens will rot from within. That's why we've pushed for transparency and cooperation in rooting out corruption, and tracking illicit dollars, because markets create more jobs when they're fueled by hard work, and not the capacity to extort a bribe. That's why we've worked to reach trade agreements that raise labor standards and raise environmental standards, as we've done with the Trans-Pacific Partnership, so that the benefits are more broadly shared.

[The Trans-Pacific Partnership (TPP) is supported by US corporations but opposed by both Donald Trump and Hillary Clinton because it will export American jobs to low wage countries. The TPP is opposed by thoughtful pro-environment people in the Pacific Rim because it will enable US corporations to successfully sue governments for losses due to pro-environment legislation and other pro-environment actions].

24. And just as we benefit by combatting inequality within our countries, I believe advanced economies still need to do more to close the gap between rich and poor nations around the globe. This is difficult politically. It's difficult to spend on foreign assistance. But I do not believe this is charity. For the small fraction of what we spent at war in Iraq we could support institutions so that fragile states don't collapse in the first place, and invest in emerging economies that become markets for our goods. It's not just the right thing to do, it's the smart thing to do.

[For the serial war criminal US to stop perverting, subverting, invading and devastating "fragile states" would be an obvious way of preventing them from collapsing. Thus the US Alliance under Obama has been war criminally invading and devastating 20 substantially or significantly Muslim countries, impoverished nations in which 32 million Muslims have died from violence (5 million) or from hegemony- and war-imposed deprivation (27 million) since 2001 [4, 7, 9]. The US-led France, UK and US (FUKUS) Coalition devastated Libya (0.1 million dead, 1 million refugees). Libya was formerly the richest country in Africa [4, 7, 9]].

25. And that's why we need to follow through on our efforts to combat climate change. If we don't act boldly, the bill that could come due will be mass migrations, and cities submerged and nations displaced, and food supplies decimated, and conflicts born of despair. The Paris Agreement gives us a framework to act, but only if we scale up our ambition. And there must be a sense of urgency about bringing the agreement into force, and helping poorer countries leapfrog destructive forms of energy.

[The atmospheric CO_2 concentration is now 405 ppm CO_2 and increasing at a record 3 ppm CO_2 per year; the species extinction rate is now 100-1,000 times greater than normal, this giving rise to the term Anthropocene to describe the present era and the speciescide and ecocide, leading to omnicide and terracide – the killing of our Living Planet; coral reefs are hugely important ocean ecosystems, but they started bleaching worldwide when the atmospheric CO_2 reached 320 ppm CO_2, are endangered at the current 405 ppm CO_2, and are essentially doomed in a mere 15 years' time at the 450 ppm CO_2 predicted from the current increase at 3 ppm CO_2 per year. The annual per capita greenhouse gas (GHG) pollution in tonnes CO_2-equivalent per person per year is 8.9 (world average), 41.0 (US), 7.4 (China) and 2.1 (India) [35, 36]. Paris-recognized as catastrophic, a plus 2C temperature rise is now unavoidable and the present circa plus 1C is already disastrous for tropical Island Nations and tropical mega-delta countries like Bangladesh [1, 2]. Indeed the lower Paris "target" of no more than plus 1.5C may be exceeded as early as 2020 [46]. Under Obama the US has embarked on a massive coal-to-gas transition that locks in dirty energy for decades and due to systemic gas leakage, gas burning for power could be dirtier GHG-wise than coal burning [47-50]].

26. So, for the wealthiest countries, a Green Climate Fund should only be the beginning. We need to invest in research and provide market incentives to develop new technologies, and then make these technologies accessible and affordable for poorer countries. And only then can we continue lifting all people up from poverty without condemning our children to a planet beyond their capacity to repair.

[Not mentioned by Obama, we urgently need to stop burning carbon fuels, deforestation, methanogenic livestock production and population growth now. It is already too late to avoid massive damage. "Condemning our children to a planet beyond their capacity to repair" has effectively already happened. Thus assuming a damage-related Carbon Price in US Dollars of $200 per tonne CO2-equivalent (as estimated by Dr. Chris Hope of 90-Nobel-Laureate University of Cambridge), the World has an inescapable Carbon Debt of $360 trillion that is increasing at $13 trillion per year, and, for example, US lackey, climate criminal Australia, a world-leader in annual per capita greenhouse (GHG) gas pollution, has a Carbon Debt of $7.5 trillion that is increasing at $400 billion per year and at $40,000 per head per year for under-30 year old Australians. Young people will inescapably have to pay this huge and increasing Carbon Debt – thus unless gigantic 20 meter sea walls are built, coastal cities will drown [47]. Young people must wise up and demand urgent climate action [51-55] and indeed a Climate Revolution now! [55]].

27. So we need new models for the global marketplace, models that are inclusive and sustainable. And in the same way, we need models of governance that are inclusive and accountable to ordinary people.

[What gross deception and hypocrisy by Obama. American policy ("model of governance") has always been "might is right" when it comes to exploitable resources. To that end, the US has invaded 71 countries, has military bases in 75 and subverts every country on earth. Thus the Iraq War continued under Obama and has now transmuted into an endless War on Terror due to the US-provoked rise of ISIS in Iraq and US Alliance support for this barbarous terrorist organization in Syria against the secular Assad regime. The US allies Turkey, Qatar. Apartheid Israel and Saudi Arabia contributed significantly to the rise ISIS in Syria, this being consonant with US policy to remove the secular Assad regime. Alan Greenspan on the Right and Noam Chomsky on the Left both say that the Iraq War was about oil. US Establishment intimate Robert Kennedy Junior says that the Syrian War is in essence about a "Sunni gas pipeline" from Qatar [13]].

28. I recognize not every country in this hall is going to follow the same model of governance. I do not think that America can — or should — impose our system of government on other countries. But there appears to be growing contest between authoritarianism and liberalism right now. And I want everybody to understand, I am not neutral in that contest. I believe in a liberal political order — an order built not just through elections and representative government, but also through respect for human rights and civil society, and independent judiciaries and the rule of law.

[Further egregious hypocrisy. America has repeatedly imposed its "system of government" on other countries [4, 13, 21]. America has invaded 71 countries, has military bases in 75 countries and indeed subverts all countries in the world. Under war criminal Obama, the US Alliance has invaded 20 countries [4, 21-23]. US drone strikes, targetted with the help of US lackey Australia, are presently being conducted against Libya, Somalia, Yemen, Syria, Iraq, Afghanistan and Pakistan. Indeed it seems likely that world-leading US-Apartheid Israeli drone technology was involved in the 9-11 attacks on the US itself (the alternative to this hypothesis in the lying Bush "official version" of 9-11, to whit that people learning to fly tiny, single-engined aircraft were able to land huge passenger jets at high speed on a dime) [8]. How the US has repeatedly "impose[d] our system of government on other countries" was explained by former CIA operative Philip Agee in his book "CIA Diary.

Inside the Company" in relation to the US invasion of the Dominican Republic [4] – invade, and then ban, imprison, torture, kill or exile all those you don't like and then hold "democratic elections" [56]].

29. I know that some countries, which now recognize the power of free markets, still reject the model of free societies. And perhaps those of us who have been promoting democracy feel somewhat discouraged since the end of the Cold War, because we've learned that liberal democracy will not just wash across the globe in a single wave. It turns out building accountable institutions is hard work — the work of generations. The gains are often fragile. Sometimes we take one step forward and then two steps back. In countries held together by borders drawn by colonial powers, with ethnic enclaves and tribal divisions, politics and elections can sometimes appear to be a zero-sum game. And so, given the difficulty in forging true democracy in the face of these pressures, it's no surprise that some argue the future favors the strongman, a top-down model, rather than strong, democratic institutions.

[Obama's "true democracy" in the West has degenerated into Big Money-controlled Plutocracy, Kleptocracy, Murdochracy, Lobbyocracy, Corporatocracy and Dollarocracy in which Big Money purchases people, politicians, parties, public perception of reality, political power and thence more private profit. Fundamentally, democracy is about practical expression of the will of the people and in 1-party Cuba the desire of the people for good governance, health, and education has been met – despite decades of war criminal US sanctions, Cuba has excellent health services, female literacy is high and infant mortality is the same as in the US [4]].

30. But I believe this thinking is wrong. I believe the road of true democracy remains the better path. I believe that in the 21st century, economies can only grow to a certain point until they need to open up — because entrepreneurs need to access information in order to invent; young people need a global education in order to thrive; independent media needs to check the abuses of power. Without this evolution, ultimately

expectations of people will not be met; suppression and stagnation will set in. And history shows that strongmen are then left with two paths — permanent crackdown, which sparks strife at home, or scapegoating enemies abroad, which can lead to war.

[War criminal Obama certainly knows about war – under war criminal Obama the US Alliance has invaded 20 countries and civilized people dread the prospect of a Hillary Clinton Administration in which she will set out to prove that she is a "real man" by following and indeed exceeding Obama's murderous example].

31. Now, I will admit, my belief that governments serve the individual, and not the other way around, is shaped by America's story. Our nation began with a promise of freedom that applied only to the few. But because of our democratic Constitution, because of our Bill of Rights, because of our ideals, ordinary people were able to organize, and march, and protest, and ultimately, those ideals won out — opened doors for women and minorities and workers in ways that made our economy more productive and turned our diversity into a strength; that gave innovators the chance to transform every area of human endeavor; that made it possible for someone like me to be elected President of the United States.

[A blood-thirsty Simon Legree rather than a subservient Uncle Tom, One Percenter Obama is the willing servant of the Neocon American and Zionist Imperialist (NAZI)-dominated One Percenter Establishment running America. Indeed Obama is a classic example of the embodiment of the dominant "Whiteness" culture of America].

32. So, yes, my views are shaped by the specific experiences of America, but I do not think this story is unique to America. Look at the transformation that's taken place in countries as different as Japan and Chile, Indonesia, Botswana. The countries that have succeeded are ones in which people feel they have a stake.

[However Obama's asserted support for one-person-one-vote is contradicted by his fanatical support for nuclear terrorist, racist Zionist-run, genocidally racist, democracy-by-genocide, neo-Nazi Apartheid Israel that denies 73% of its now 52% majority of Indigenous Palestinians the right to vote for the government ruling them. Obama is a genocidal racist, anti-Arab anti-Semite and pathological liar in his support for Apartheid Israel in its ongoing Palestinian Genocide [10]].

33. In Europe, the progress of those countries in the former Soviet bloc that embraced democracy stand in clear contrast to those that did not. After all, the people of Ukraine did not take to the streets because of some plot imposed from abroad. They took to the streets because their leadership was for sale and they had no recourse. They demanded change because they saw life get better for people in the Baltics and in Poland, societies that were more liberal, and democratic, and open than their own. [The neo-Nazi coup that overthrew the democratically elected government in the Ukraine was backed by the US].

34. So those of us who believe in democracy, we need to speak out forcefully, because both the facts and history, I believe, are on our side. That doesn't mean democracies are without flaws. It does mean that the cure for what ails our democracies is greater engagement by our citizens — not less.

[See point #32 – racist Obama supports Apartheid in Palestine just as his racist presidential predecessors supported Apartheid in South Africa [4]].

35. Yes, in America, there is too much money in politics; too much entrenched partisanship; too little participation by citizens, in part because of a patchwork of laws that makes it harder to vote. In Europe, a well-intentioned Brussels often became too isolated from the normal push and pull of national politics. Too often, in capitals, decision-makers have forgotten that democracy needs to be driven by civic engagement from the bottom up, not governance by experts from the top down. And so these are real problems, and as leaders of democratic

governments make the case for democracy abroad, we better strive harder to set a better example at home.

[Under Barack "Simon Legree" Obama, millions of Black Americans are denied the vote under anti-felony laws and according to Dr. Michelle Alexander of the NAACP, nearly 80% of adult male Black Americans in Chicago are denied the right to vote [57, 58]].

36. Moreover, every country will organize its government informed by centuries of history, and the circumstances of geography, and the deeply held beliefs of its people. So I recognize a traditional society may value unity and cohesion more than a diverse country like my own, which was founded upon what, at the time, was a radical idea — the idea of the liberty of individual human beings endowed with certain God-given rights. But that does not mean that ordinary people in Asia, or Africa, or the Middle East somehow prefer arbitrary rule that denies them a voice in the decisions that can shape their lives. I believe that spirit is universal. And if any of you doubt the universality of that desire, listen to the voices of young people everywhere who call out for freedom, and dignity, and the opportunity to control their own lives.

[Unfortunately, that asserted "liberty of the individual" in the ostensibly marvellous 1776 American Declaration of Independence in reality was freedom to invade, conquer, devastate and ethnically cleanse Indigenous American lands – indeed the real purpose of the American War of Independence was not "no taxation without representation" or "personal liberty" but freedom to exterminate Indigenous Indians that had some protection from the British in the context of the 18th century Anglo-French war. [4]. By 1844 the United States, founded on the dream of genocide, had legislated to remove all Indigenous Indians from East of the Mississippi [4]].

37. This leads me to the third thing we need to do: We must reject any forms of fundamentalism, or racism, or a belief in ethnic superiority that makes our traditional identities

irreconcilable with modernity. Instead we need to embrace the tolerance that results from respect of all human beings.
[The ultimate expression of racism is war. Under war criminal Obama, the US Alliance has invaded 20 countries [4, 21-23]. US drone strikes, targetted with the help of US lackey Australia, are presently being conducted against Libya, Somalia, Yemen, Syria, Iraq, Afghanistan and Pakistan. Obama is one of the worst warmonger and war-making presidents and hence one of the worst racists in American history [4]].

38. It's a truism that global integration has led to a collision of cultures; trade, migration, the Internet, all these things can challenge and unsettle our most cherished identities. We see liberal societies express opposition when women choose to cover themselves. We see protests responding to Western newspaper cartoons that caricature the Prophet Muhammad. In a world that left the age of empire behind, we see Russia attempting to recover lost glory through force. Asian powers debate competing claims of history. And in Europe and the United States, you see people wrestle with concerns about immigration and changing demographics, and suggesting that somehow people who look different are corrupting the character of our countries.

[The people of Crimea overwhelmingly voted for linkage to Russia after the US-backed neo-Nazi Coup in the Ukraine. Anti-Semite Obama backs the genocidally racist, colonizer, and Apartheid rogue state of Israel in its illegal occupation and ethnic cleansing of Arab lands].

39. Now, there's no easy answer for resolving all these social forces, and we must respect the meaning that people draw from their own traditions — from their religion, from their ethnicity, from their sense of nationhood. But I do not believe progress is possible if our desire to preserve our identities gives way to an impulse to dehumanize or dominate another group. If our religion leads us to persecute those of another faith, if we jail or beat people who are gay, if our traditions lead us to prevent girls from going to school, if we discriminate on the basis of race or tribe or ethnicity, then the fragile bonds of civilization will fray.

The world is too small, we are too packed together, for us to be able to resort to those old ways of thinking.

[Obama as a pluralist liberal simply doesn't wash – he is a racist warmonger heading a US Alliance that is making war in 20 impoverished countries [4, 7-13]].

40. We see this mindset in too many parts of the Middle East. There, so much of the collapse in order has been fueled because leaders sought legitimacy not because of policies or programs but by resorting to persecuting political opposition, or demonizing other religious sects, by narrowing the public space to the mosque, where in too many places perversions of a great faith were tolerated. These forces built up for years, and are now at work helping to fuel both Syria's tragic civil war and the mindless, medieval menace of ISIL.

[ISIL (ISIS) arose directly from the Iraqi Genocide under the Bush and Obama Administration that involved destruction of a modern state, 2.7 million Iraqi deaths from violence (1.5 million) or from war-imposed deprivation (1.2 million), and massive disempowerment of the Iraqi Sunni minority. The US created ISIS just as it created Al Qaeda and the Taliban. ISIS in Syria has been enabled, funded and backed by US Alliance members Turkey, Qatar and Saudi Arabia in particular. Muslim-origin non-state terrorism is the greatest ally of US imperialism – every mindless atrocity against Westerners is used as an excuse for vastly more deadly US Alliance attacks on Muslim populations in 20 countries from the Western Sahel to South East Asia. ISIS and similar groups have enabled US or US Alliance military domination over a huge swathe of the Muslim world].

41. The mindset of sectarianism, and extremism, and bloodletting, and retribution that has been taking place will not be quickly reversed. And if we are honest, we understand that no external power is going to be able to force different religious communities or ethnic communities to co-exist for long. But I do believe we have to be honest about the nature of these

conflicts, and our international community must continue to work with those who seek to build rather than to destroy. [America under anti-Arab anti-Semitic warmonger Obama has devastated a swathe of Muslim countries [4, 7-13]].

42. And there is a military component to that. It means being united and relentless in destroying networks like ISIL, which show no respect for human life. But it also means that in a place like Syria, where there's no ultimate military victory to be won, we're going to have to pursue the hard work of diplomacy that aims to stop the violence, and deliver aid to those in need, and support those who pursue a political settlement and can see those who are not like themselves as worthy of dignity and respect.

[How disingenuous of Obama to say "and there is a military component to that" in relation to his false assertion that the US and its allies "seek to build rather than to destroy". Obama seeks to change the government of Syria and its efforts have killed 0.5 million Syrians, generated 12 million refugees, and devastated what was once a peaceful, tolerant, secular society in which numerous ancient faiths and sects got along peacefully with each other as described in William Dalrymple's superb book "From the Holy Mountain" [59]].

43. Across the region's conflicts, we have to insist that all parties recognize a common humanity and that nations end proxy wars that fuel disorder. Because until basic questions are answered about how communities co-exist, the embers of extremism will continue to burn, countless human beings will suffer — most of all in that region — but extremism will continue to be exported overseas. And the world is too small for us to simply be able to build a wall and prevent it from affecting our own societies.

[The worst extremism being "exported overseas" is US imperialism and US Alliance imperialism. The casus belli (excuse for war) is provided by US-created or US-provoked Muslim-origin non-state terrorists such as the barbarous ISIS whose outrageous conduct (beheadings, sex slaves, forced conversions, religious fanaticism, and religious intolerance) could not have been better scripted by the CIA. One is reminded of US-lead terrorist groups in Ecuador who would bomb Catholic churches so that the socialists would be blamed [56] and similar US-led Gladio atrocities in Europe that were designed to be blamed on "communists" [60]. Numerous science, engineering, architecture, medicine, aviation, military and intelligence experts conclude that the US Government was responsible for the singular 9-11 atrocity in which 3,000 people died [8, 22, 61-63]). However post-9-11 terror hysteria has been used to attack civil liberties in the US and in the West in general. Reality: 53 American residents were killed in America by "terrorists" in the 14 years since 9/11 and the average US population in this period was about 304 million (UN Population Division data). Accordingly, the "empirical annual probability of an American dying in the US from terrorism" is 53/(14 years x 304 million) = about 1 in 100 million per year. In contrast, 1.7million American die preventably each year as the Neocon American and Zionist Imperialist (NAZI)-subverted US Government steadfastly looks the other way and scares the population with saturation terror hysteria propaganda [64]].

44. And what is true in the Middle East is true for all of us. Surely, religious traditions can be honored and upheld while teaching young people science and math, rather than intolerance. Surely, we can sustain our unique traditions while giving women their full and rightful role in the politics and economics of a nation. Surely, we can rally our nations to solidarity while recognizing equal treatment for all communities — whether it's a religious minority in Myanmar, or an ethnic minority in Burundi, or a racial minority right here in the United States. And surely, Israelis and Palestinians will be better off if Palestinians reject incitement and recognize the legitimacy of Israel, but Israel recognizes that it cannot permanently occupy and settle Palestinian land. We all have to do better as leaders in tamping down, rather than encouraging, a notion of identity that leads us to diminish others.

[Zionist lackey, anti-Arab, anti-Semitic, pro-Apartheid, genocidally racist, serial war criminal and pathological liar

Obama obscenely blames the victim with "Israelis and Palestinians will be better off if Palestinians reject incitement and recognize the legitimacy of Israel". The dishonest political fiction of a "2-state solution" is now impossible with the Zionist colonizers having ethnically cleansed 90% of Palestine in an ongoing Palestinian Genocide by a nuclear terrorist, racist Zionist run, genocidally racist, democracy by genocide Apartheid Israel that prevents 73% of its now 52% majority Indigenous Palestinian population from voting for the government ruling it. The racist Zionists are now considering only 2 options – (a) continued Apartheid with 73% of Occupied Palestinians highly abusively confined to the Gaza Concentration Camp or West Bank ghettoes or (b) outright genocidal expulsion of all or most Indigenous Palestinian from Palestine (presently, of 12 million Indigenous Palestinians about 50% are already totally excluded on pain of death from living in their own country). Obama is committed to Israeli Apartheid and the ongoing Palestinian Genocide as the front-man for the Neocon American and Zionist Imperialist (NAZI)-perverted and subverted US political Establishment [10]].

45. And this leads me to the fourth and final thing we need to do, and that is sustain our commitment to international cooperation rooted in the rights and responsibilities of nations.

[Obama as a serial invader and serial war criminal tramples on "the rights and responsibilities of nations", the UN Charter, the Universal Declaration of Human Rights, the Rights of the Child, The UN Genocide Convention, the Geneva Convention ...].

46. As President of the United States, I know that for most of human history, power has not been unipolar. The end of the Cold War may have led too many to forget this truth. I've noticed as President that at times, both America's adversaries and some of our allies believe that all problems were either caused by Washington or could be solved by Washington — and perhaps too many in Washington believed that as well. (Laughter.) But I believe America has been a rare superpower in human history insofar as it has been willing to think beyond narrow self-interest; that while we've made our share of

mistakes over these last 25 years — and I've acknowledged some — we have strived, sometimes at great sacrifice, to align better our actions with our ideals. And as a consequence, I believe we have been a force for good.

[Utter falsehood by a mendacious Obama who turns history on its head and whitewashes decades of utterly evil American war crimes throughout the world. Under Obama alone the US Alliance has invaded 20 countries in the ongoing Muslim Genocide in the 21st century associated with 30 million Muslim refugees and 32 million Muslim deaths from violence (5 million) or from hegemony- or war-imposed deprivation (27 million) since the US Government's 9-11 false –flag atrocity [7-9]].

47. We have secured allies. We've acted to protect the vulnerable. We supported human rights and welcomed scrutiny of our own actions. We've bound our power to international laws and institutions. When we've made mistakes, we've tried to acknowledge them. We have worked to roll back poverty and hunger and disease beyond our borders, not just within our borders.

[The US under Obama has backed military coups, been associated with invasions of 20 countries, supported Apartheid and genocide in Palestine, opposed nuclear disarmament, and grossly violated human rights at home and abroad. Under Obama the coal-to-gas conversion by the US under Obama locks in disastrous long-term greenhouse gas (GHG) pollution and hence climate change inaction for decades [48, 49], 17 million people die avoidably from deprivation each year, about half of them children [4], and 7 million die from air pollution each year [5, 6]. The 3 key threats to humanity are (a) nuclear weapons, (b) poverty and (c) climate change but under Obama (a) the US increased its nuclear threat, continued to back nuclear terrorist Apartheid Israel and opposed the nuclear weapons ban advocated by about 130 countries [14]; (b) the US supports poverty-entrenching dictatorships, and of about $40 billion in annual US economic plus military aid, about $10 billion is military aid (40% to Apartheid Israel) and most of the remainder is linked to destructive US military intervention; and (c) the pro-gas US is one of the world's worst countries for annual per capita GHG pollution in terms of tonnes CO2-equivalent per person per year (41.0 for the US, 8.9 world average, China 7.4 and India 2.1) and for "income weighted annual per capita GHG pollution (US 207, China 5.2 and India 0.3) [35, 36]].

48. I'm proud of that. But I also know that we can't do this alone. And I believe that if we're to meet the challenges of this century, we are all going to have to do more to build up international capacity. We cannot escape the prospect of nuclear war unless we all commit to stopping the spread of nuclear weapons and pursuing a world without them.

[While imposing deadly Sanctions on Iran (that has zero nuclear weapons and repeatedly states that it does not want nuclear weapons and wants a nuclear weapons-free Middle East), the US (7,315 nuclear weapons) is boosting its nuclear and conventional forces in Asia and Australia, opposes a nuclear weapons ban, and continues to pour billions of dollars of military aid into the war criminal, genocidally racist, ethnic cleansing and nuclear terrorist rogue state of Apartheid Israel that reportedly has up to 400 nuclear weapons, this having been acquired with US collaboration. The upper estimates of stored nuclear weapons are as follows: US (7,315), Russia (8,000), Apartheid Israel (400), France (300), UK (250), China (250), Pakistan (120), India (100), and North Korea (less than 10) [14, 34]].

49. When Iran agrees to accept constraints on its nuclear program that enhances global security and enhances Iran's ability to work with other nations. On the other hand, when North Korea tests a bomb that endangers all of us. And any country that breaks this basic bargain must face consequences. And those nations with these weapons, like the United States, have a unique responsibility to pursue the path of reducing our stockpiles, and reaffirming basic norms like the commitment to never test them again.

[see #48. The US is a world leader in nuclear terrorism. Iran does not have nuclear weapons. Obama does not mention Apartheid Israel's 400 nuclear weapons [14, 34]].

50. We can't combat a disease like Zika that recognizes no borders — mosquitos don't respect walls — unless we make permanent the same urgency that we brought to bear against Ebola — by strengthening our own systems of public health, by investing in cures and rolling back the root causes of disease, and helping poorer countries develop a public health infrastructure.

[The dominant neoliberal ideology in the US has ensured that pharmaceutical advance is geared to highly profitable medicines for "White folks" who can afford to buy them – however, the Ebola scare illustrated how quickly US Big Pharma and medical research can move when "White folks" are threatened. The efficacy of tens of thousands of medicines has been determined in exhaustive trials based on "White folks" but their efficacy has not been determined, for example, for genetically diverse populations in Africa].

51. We can only eliminate extreme poverty if the sustainable development goals that we have set are more than words on paper. Human ingenuity now gives us the capacity to feed the hungry and give all of our children — including our girls — the education that is the foundation for opportunity in our world. But we have to put our money where our mouths are.

[In terms of net official development assistance as "a percentage of gross national income in 2015", Sweden ranks top among OECD countries with 1.4% whereas the US ranks 20th at 0.17% [66]].

52. And we can only realize the promise of this institution's founding — to replace the ravages of war with cooperation — if powerful nations like my own accept constraints. Sometimes I'm criticized in my own country for professing a belief in international norms and multilateral institutions. But I am convinced that in the long run, giving up some freedom of

action — not giving up our ability to protect ourselves or pursue our core interests, but binding ourselves to international rules over the long term — enhances our security. And I think that's not just true for us.

[With breathtaking arrogance Obama is saying that some time in the distant future the US might give up "some freedom of action" but it is "not giving up our ability ... [to] pursue our core interests" i.e. an exceptionalist US will continue to subvert, threaten, invade, and devastate other countries that reached an historical high for America under Nobel Peace Prize winner but serial invader and serial war criminal Obama].

53. If Russia continues to interfere in the affairs of its neighbors, it may be popular at home, it may fuel nationalist fervor for a time, but over time it is also going to diminish its stature and make its borders less secure. In the South China Sea, a peaceful resolution of disputes offered by law will mean far greater stability than the militarization of a few rocks and reefs.

[Russia responded to the racist, anti-Russian neo-Nazi coup in Ukraine that was engineered and backed by the North America-located US; the re-incorporation of strategically vital Crimea into Russia was overwhelmingly supported by the Crimean population. The South China Sea is called such because it is off the coast of South China and not off the coast of the North America-located US; under anti-Arab anti-Semitic and Islamophobic warmonger Obama the US Alliance headed by the North America-located US invaded 20 impoverished and distant countries in pursuance of the Zionist-backed US War on Muslims (War on Terror) that has been associated with 30 million Muslim refugees and 32 million Muslim deaths from violence (5 million) or from hegemony- or war-imposed deprivation (27 million) since the US Government's 9-11 false flag atrocity [7-9]].

54. We are all stakeholders in this international system, and it calls upon all of us to invest in the success of institutions to which we belong. And the good news is, is that many nations have shown what kind of progress is possible when we make

those commitments. Consider what we've accomplished here over the past few years.

[Obama is using weasel words "stakeholders in this international system" and "invest in the success of institutions" – what the US under Obama should have been doing was obeying international laws and conventions, instead of grossly violating these international laws and conventions].

55. Together, we mobilized some 50,000 additional troops for U.N. peacekeeping, making them nimble, better equipped, better prepared to deal with emergencies. Together, we established an Open Government Partnership so that, increasingly, transparency empowers more and more people around the globe. And together, now, we have to open our hearts and do more to help refugees who are desperate for a home.

["US peace-keeping" is an oxymoron as evidenced by the Zionist–backed US War on Muslims (War on Terror, Muslim Holocaust, Muslim Genocide)].

56. We should all welcome the pledges of increased assistance that have been made at this General Assembly gathering. I'll be discussing that more this afternoon. But we have to follow through, even when the politics are hard. Because in the eyes of innocent men and women and children who, through no fault of their own, have had to flee everything that they know, everything that they love, we have to have the empathy to see ourselves. We have to imagine what it would be like for our family, for our children, if the unspeakable happened to us. And we should all understand that, ultimately, our world will be more secure if we are prepared to help those in need and the nations who are carrying the largest burden with respect to accommodating these refugees.

[Syria was an oasis of peace and religious tolerance and hosted more refugees per capita than any other country – and then the US and the US Alliance intervened with bombing and supporting terrorists to remove the secular Syrian Government, killing 0.5 million people, generating 12 million Syrian refugees, and destroying this ancient country [9]].

57. There are a lot of nations right now that are doing the right thing. But many nations — particularly those blessed with wealth and the benefits of geography — that can do more to offer a hand, even if they also insist that refugees who come to our countries have to do more to adapt to the customs and conventions of the communities that are now providing them a home.

[More breathtaking Obama dishonesty and implicit racism and bigotry; see #51 – in terms of net official development assistance as "a percentage of gross national income in 2015", Sweden ranks top among OECD countries with 1.4% whereas the US ranks 20th at 0.17% [66]].

58. Let me conclude by saying that I recognize history tells a different story than the one that I've talked about here today. There's a much darker and more cynical view of history that we can adopt. Human beings are too often motivated by greed and by power. Big countries for most of history have pushed smaller ones around. Tribes and ethnic groups and nation states have very often found it most convenient to define themselves by what they hate and not just those ideas that bind them together.

[Obama actually tells the truth for once in admitting his gross mendacity and saying that "I recognize history tells a different story than the one that I've talked about here today" [4]].

59. Time and again, human beings have believed that they finally arrived at a period of enlightenment only to repeat, then, cycles of conflict and suffering. Perhaps that's our fate. We have to remember that the choices of individual human beings led to repeated world war. But we also have to remember that the choices of individual human beings created a United Nations, so that a war like that would never happen again. Each of us as leaders, each nation can choose to reject those who appeal to our worst impulses and embrace those who appeal to our best. For we have shown that we can choose a better history.

[The UN was created to prevent wars like WW2 that was associated with violent deaths and avoidable deaths from deprivation totalling over 100 million. However US exceptionalism has meant that post-1950 US Asian wars have been associated with 40 million Asian deaths from violence or war-imposed deprivation;1950-2005 avoidable deaths from deprivation in countries occupied by the US in the post-1945 era have totalled 82 million [4]; Muslim deaths from violence or imposed deprivation have totalled 32 million since 9-11, with Obama being directly involved in much of this carnage; there are presently 65 million refugees in the world of whom 30 million are Muslim refugees generated by a genocidally racist US or by US-backed and genocidally racist Apartheid Israel [9]].

60. Sitting in a prison cell, a young Martin Luther King, Jr. wrote that, "Human progress never rolls on the wheels of inevitability; it comes through the tireless efforts of men willing to be co-workers with God." And during the course of these eight years, as I've traveled to many of your nations, I have seen that spirit in our young people, who are more educated and more tolerant, and more inclusive and more diverse, and more creative than our generation; who are more empathetic and compassionate towards their fellow human beings than previous generations. And, yes, some of that comes with the idealism of youth. But it also comes with young people's access to information about other peoples and places — an understanding unique in human history that their future is bound with the fates of other human beings on the other side of the world.

[Mass murderer, serial invader, serial war criminal and genocidal racist Obama and his similarly degenerate and Zionist-perverted allies can hardly be called "co-workers with God"].

61. I think of the thousands of health care workers from around the world who volunteered to fight Ebola. I remember the young entrepreneurs I met who are now starting new businesses in Cuba, the parliamentarians who used to be just a few years ago

political prisoners in Myanmar. I think of the girls who have braved taunts or violence just to go to school in Afghanistan, and the university students who started programs online to reject the extremism of organizations like ISIL. I draw strength from the young Americans — entrepreneurs, activists, soldiers, new citizens — who are remaking our nation once again, who are unconstrained by old habits and old conventions, and unencumbered by what is, but are instead ready to seize what ought to be.

[How disgusting that racist mass murderer Obama links himself to courageous young humanitarians].

62. My own family is a made up of the flesh and blood and traditions and cultures and faiths from a lot of different parts of the world — just as America has been built by immigrants from every shore. And in my own life, in this country, and as President, I have learned that our identities do not have to be defined by putting someone else down, but can be enhanced by lifting somebody else up. They don't have to be defined in opposition to others, but rather by a belief in liberty and equality and justice and fairness.

[When truthful history is written, Obama will be defined by his participation in the post-9-11 Muslim Holocaust and Muslim Genocide associated with 30 million Muslim refugees and 32 million Muslim deaths from violence – or from war- and hegemony-imposed deprivation [9]].

63. And the embrace of these principles as universal doesn't weaken my particular pride, my particular love for America — it strengthens it. My belief that these ideals apply everywhere doesn't lessen my commitment to help those who look like me, or pray as I do, or pledge allegiance to my flag. But my faith in those principles does force me to expand my moral imagination and to recognize that I can best serve my own people, I can best look after my own daughters, by making sure that my actions seek what is right for all people and all children, and your daughters and your sons.

[Gross hypocrisy by Obama who is currently the world's number 1 pathological liar, serial invader, warmonger, war criminal, child killer, climate criminal, and drug pusher. It is notable that Obama did not mention illicit drugs in his speech. Also utterly ignored by Neocon American and Zionist Imperialist (NAZI)-perverted and subverted Western Mainstream media are the 1.2 million people who have died world-wide since 9-11 due to US Alliance restoration of the Taliban-destroyed Afghan opium industry from 6% of world market share in 2001 to 93% in 2007, the breakdown (as of 2015) including 280,000 Americans, 256,000 Indonesians, 68,000 Iranians, 25,000 British, 14,000 Canadians, 10,000 Germans, and 5,000 Australians [12]].

64. This is what I believe: that all of us can be co-workers with God. And our leadership, and our governments, and this United Nations should reflect this irreducible truth.

[This is what Obama blasphemously calls being "co-workers with God": the atmospheric CO2 concentration has increased to 405 ppm CO2 and is increasing at a record 3 ppm CO2 per year; a catastrophic plus 2C temperature rise is now unavoidable and the current plus 1C is already catastrophic for tropical Island States and megadelta countries like Bangladesh; the plus 1.5C target may well be exceeded by 2020; the coal-to-gas conversion by the US under Obama locks in disastrous long-term greenhouse gas (GHG) pollution; 17 million people die avoidably each year; 7 million die from air pollution each year; the US Alliance has invaded 20 overwhelmingly or significantly Muslim countries since the US Government's 9-11 false flag atrocity, this being associated with 32 million Muslim deaths from violence (5 million) or from war- or hegemony-imposed deprivation (27 million) [2, 4, 9, 67]. Of course the bottom line in any human society is respect for children but Obama has an appalling record of child killing. During the Vietnam War, decent people chanted "Hey, hey, USA, how many kids did you kill today?" In May 2009 I catalogued the answer for America under Obama as 1,000 [68]].

65. Thank you very much. (Applause)

[Genuine gratitude one supposes by Obama who is currently the world's number 1 pathological liar, serial invader, warmonger, war criminal, child killer, climate criminal, and drug pusher but is free to operate as the world's current number 1 serial killer for another 3 months. Obama is lauded as America's first Black president but is complicit in the Muslim Holocaust and Muslim Genocide that has taken 32 million non-European Muslim lives since the US Government's 9-11 false-flag atrocity killed 3,000 people in 2001].

Conclusions

Serial war criminal Barack Obama must be arraigned before the International Criminal Court. There must be Boycotts, Divestment and Sanction (BDS) against the United States and its war criminal allies until their crimes are recognized and punished and America and its allies undergo de-Nazification. The relatives, friends and fellow citizens of the 1.7 million Americans who die preventably each year must disempower the Neocon American and Zionist Imperialists (NAZIs) who have subverted and perverted America and crippled America with the $40 trillion long-term accrual cost of nuclear terrorist Apartheid Israel and attendant wars.
In 2005 Literature Nobel Laureate, anti-racist Jewish British playwright Harold Pinter declared that Bush and Blair should be arraigned before the International Criminal Court: "We have brought torture, cluster bombs, depleted uranium, innumerable acts of random murder, misery, degradation and death to the Iraqi people and call it "bringing freedom and democracy to the Middle East". How many people do you have to kill before you qualify to be described as a mass murderer and a war criminal? One hundred thousand? More than enough, I would have thought" [69]. 32 million? More than enough I would have thought.

Originally published as "Mendacious War Criminal Obama's Final Speech To The UN General Assembly," Countercurrents, September 2016.

References

[1]. Barack Obama, "Address by President Obama to the 71st session of the United Nations General Assembly", White House, 20 September 2016: https://www.whitehouse.gov/the-press-office/2016/09/20/address-president-obama-71st-session-united-nations-general-assembly.
[2]. "Too late to avoid global warming catastrophe": https://sites.google.com/site/300orgsite/too-late-to-avoid-global-warming.
[3]. Gideon Polya, "Obama's Clean Power Plan Will Only Cut 2030 US Greenhouse Gas Pollution By 5%", Countercurrents, 7 August, 2015: https://countercurrents.org/polya070815.htm.
[4]. Gideon Polya, "Body Count. Global avoidable mortality since 1950", a book that includes an avoidable mortality-related history of every country from Neolithic times and is now available for free perusal on the web: http://globalbodycount.blogspot.com.au/.
[5]. "Stop air pollution deaths": https://sites.google.com/site/300orgsite/stop-air-pollution-deaths.
[6]. World Health Organization (WHO), "7 million premature deaths annually linked to air pollution": http://www.who.int/mediacentre/news/releases/2014/air-pollution/en/.
[7]. Gideon Polya, "Paris Atrocity Context: 27 Million Muslim Avoidable Deaths From Imposed Deprivation In 20 Countries Violated By US Alliance Since 9-11", Countercurrents, 22 November, 2015: https://countercurrents.org/polya221115.htm.
[8]. Experts: US did 9-11": https://sites.google.com/site/expertsusdid911/.
[9]. "Muslim Holocaust Muslim Genocide": https://sites.google.com/site/muslimholocaustmuslimgenocide/.
[10]. "Palestinian Genocide" : http://sites.google.com/site/palestiniangenocide/.
[11]. Iraqi Holocaust, Iraqi Genocide": http://sites.google.com/site/iraqiholocaustiraqigenocide/.
[12]. "Afghan Holocaust, Afghan Genocide": http://sites.google.com/site/afghanholocaustafghangenocide/.
[13]. Robert J. Kennedy Jr, "Syria: another pipeline war", EcoWatch, 25 February 2016: http://ecowatch.com/2016/02/25/robert-kennedy-jr-syria-pipeline-war/.
[14]. "Nuclear weapons ban, end poverty & reverse climate change": https://sites.google.com/site/300orgsite/nuclear-weapons-ban.
[15]. Edward Herman and Noam Chomsky, "Manufacturing Consent", Pantheon, 1998, 2002.
[16]. "Mainstream media lying": https://sites.google.com/site/mainstreammedialying/home.
[17]. "Mainstream media censorship": https://sites.google.com/site/mainstreammediacensorship/home.
[18]. "Study: Bush, aides made 935 false statements in run-up to war", CNN, 24 January 2008: http://edition.cnn.com/2008/POLITICS/01/23/bush.iraq/.
[19]. Seymour Hersh, "The killing of Osama bin Laden", London Review of Books, 21 May 2015: http://www.lrb.co.uk/v37/n10/seymour-m-hersh/the-

killing-of-osama-bin-laden.

[20]. Paul Craig Roberts, "Seymour Hersh succumbs to disinformation – Paul Craig Roberts", Paul Craig Roberts, 11 May 2015: http://www.paulcraigroberts.org/2015/05/11/seymour-hersh-succumbs-disinformation-paul-craig-roberts/.

[21]. Gideon Polya, "The US Has Invaded 70 Nations Since 1776 – Make 4 July Independence From America Day", Countercurrents, 5 July, 2013: https://countercurrents.org/polya050713.htm.

[22]. "Stop state terrorism" : https://sites.google.com/site/stopstateterrorism/.

[23]. "These are all the countries where the US has a military presence", Global Research, 12 April 2015: http://www.globalresearch.ca/these-are-all-the-countries-where-the-us-has-a-military-presence/5442345.

[24]. Gideon Polya, "American Holocaust, Millions Of Untimely American Deaths And $40 Trillion Cost Of Israel To Americans", Countercurrents, 27 August, 2013: https://countercurrents.org/polya270813.htm.

[25]. Kevin Lamarque, "Obama touts $38 billion military aid package in meeting with Netanyahu", CBS News, 21 September 2016: http://www.cbsnews.com/news/obama-netanyahu-touts-38-billion-military-aid-package-in-meeting/.

[26]. Sir Nicholas Stern, quoted in "Climate change: "the greatest market failure the word has seen"", New Economist, 30 Oc0tber 2006: http://neweconomist.blogs.com/new_economist/2006/10/stern_review_2.html.

[27]. Brian Ellis, "Social Humanism. A New Metaphysics", Routledge, UK, 2012.

[28]. Gideon Polya, "Book Review: "Social Humanism. A New Metaphysics" By Brian Ellis – Last Chance To Save Planet?", Countercurrents, 19 August, 2012: https://countercurrents.org/polya190812.htm.

[29]. "Climate Genocide": https://sites.google.com/site/climategenocide/.

[30]. World Hunger, "2016 World Hunger and Poverty Facts and Statistics": http://www.worldhunger.org/2015-world-hunger-and-poverty-facts-and-statistics/.

[31]. World Bank, "Working for a world free of poverty": http://www.worldbank.org/en/topic/poverty/overview.

[32]. "Nuclear weapons ban, end poverty & reverse climate change": https://sites.google.com/site/300orgsite/nuclear-weapons-ban.

[33]. John Pilger: why Hillary Clinton is more dangerous that Donald Trump", New Matilda, 23 March 2016: https://newmatilda.com/2016/03/23/john-pilger-why-hillary-clinton-is-more-dangerous-than-donald-trump/.

[34]. Gideon Polya, "Nuclear Weapons Ban & Boycotts, Divestment & Sanctions (BDS) To Save World From Nuclear, Poverty & Climate Threats", Countercurrents, 11 August 2014: https://countercurrents.org/polya110814.htm.

[35]. Gideon Polya, " Revised Annual Per Capita Greenhouse Gas Pollution For All Countries – What Is Your Country Doing?", Countercurrents, 6 January, 2016: https://countercurrents.org/polya060116.htm.

[36]. Gideon Polya, "Exposing And Thence Punishing Worst Polluter Nations Via Weighted Annual Per Capita Greenhouse Gas Pollution Scores", Countercurrents, 19 March, 2016: https://countercurrents.org/polya190316.htm.

[37]. Gideon Polya, "Truth & Boycotts, Divestment & Sanctions (BDS) Can Overcome Huge Inequities Suffered By African Americans Under American Apartheid", Countercurrents, 29 September, 2014: https://countercurrents.org/polya290914.htm.

[38]. Gideon Polya, "American Holocaust, Millions Of Untimely American Deaths And $40 Trillion Cost Of Israel To Americans", Countercurrents, 27 August, 2013: https://countercurrents.org/polya270813.htm.

[39]. Gideon Polya, "West Ignores 11 Million Muslim War Deaths & 23 Million Preventable American Deaths Since US Government's False-flag 9-11 Atrocity", Countercurrents, 9 September, 2015: https://countercurrents.org/polya090915.htm.

[40]. Gideon Polya, "Review: "Tears In Paradise. Suffering and Struggle Of Indians In Fiji 1879-2004" by Rajendra Prasad – Britain's Indentured Indian "5 Year Slaves"", Countercurrents, 4 March, 2015: https://countercurrents.org/polya040315.htm.

[41]. Thomas Piketty, "Capital in the Twenty-first Century", Harvard, 2014).

[42]. Gideon Polya, "Key Book Review: "Capital In The Twenty-First Century" By Thomas Piketty", Countercurrents, 01 July, 2014: https://countercurrents.org/polya010714.htm.

[43]. "1% ON 1%: one percent annual wealth tax on One Percenters": https://sites.google.com/site/300orgsite/1-on-1.

[44]. Gideon Polya, "4 % Annual Global Wealth Tax To Stop The 17 Million Deaths Annually", Countercurrents, 27 June, 2014: https://countercurrents.org/polya270614.htm.

[45]. Michel Chossudovsky, "Know the facts: North Korea lost close to 30% of its population as a result of US bombings in the 1950s", Global Research, 27 November 2010: http://www.globalresearch.ca/know-the-facts-north-korea-lost-close-to-30-of-its-population-as-a-result-of-us-bombings-in-the-1950s/22131.

[46]. Joshua Hill, "World average temperature could rise by 1.5 degrees as early as 2020", Clean Technica, 10 March 2016: https://cleantechnica.com/2016/03/10/world-average-temperature-rise-1-5-degrees-easy-2020/.

[47]. "Gas is not clean energy": https://sites.google.com/site/gasisnotcleanenergy/.

[48]. Gideon Polya, "Pro-gas Obama's EPA-based Plan To Reduce Coal-based Pollution Amounts To Climate Change Inaction", Countercurrents, 7 June, 2014: https://countercurrents.org/polya070614.htm.

[49]. Gideon Polya, "Obama's Clean Power Plan Will Only Cut 2030 US Greenhouse Gas Pollution By 5%", Countercurrents, 7 August, 2015: https://countercurrents.org/polya070815.htm.

[50]. Gideon Polya, "Massive Lying By Omission In Mendacious Obama's Final State Of The Union Address", Countercurrents, 16 January, 2016: https://countercurrents.org/polya160116.htm.

[51]. "Carbon Debt Carbon Credit":
https://sites.google.com/site/carbondebtcarboncredit/.
[52]. "Climate Revolution Now":
https://sites.google.com/site/300orgsite/climate-revolution.
[53]. "Cut carbon emissions 80% by 2020":
https://sites.google.com/site/cutcarbonemissions80by2020/.
[54]. "100% renewable energy by 2020":
https://sites.google.com/site/100renewableenergyby2020/.
[55]. "2011 climate change course":
https://sites.google.com/site/300orgsite/2011-climate-change-course.
[56]. Philip Agee, "CIA Diary. Inside the Company", Penguin, London, 1975.
[57]. Michelle Alexander, "The New Jim Crow: Mass Incarceration in the Age of Colorblindness", The New Press, 2010.
[58]. Michelle Alexander, "The war on drugs and the New Jim Crow", Race, Poverty, Environment, Vol. 17, No. 1 | Spring 2010:
http://reimaginerpe.org/20years/alexander.
[59]. William Dalrymple, "From the Holy Mountain".
[60]. "Operation Gladio", Wikipedia:
https://en.wikipedia.org/wiki/Operation_Gladio.
[61]. Elias Davidsson, "There is no evidence that Muslims committed the crime of 9-11", Op Ed News, 10 January 2008:
http://www.opednews.com/articles/1/There-is-no-evidence-that-by-Elias-Davidsson-100811-366.html.
[62]. Elias Davidsson, "Hijacking America 's Mind on 9/11. Counterfeiting Evidence", Algora, New York 2013, 328 pp:
http://www.amazon.com/Hijacking-Americas-Mind-11-Counterfeiting/dp/0875869734.
[63]. "State crime and non-state terrorism":
https://sites.google.com/site/statecrimeandnonstateterrorism/.
[64]. Gideon Polya, "San Bernardino Atrocity Elicits Islamophobic Republican Hysteria And Egregious Falsehood In Warmonger Obama's Speech", Countercurrents, 9 December, 2015:
https://countercurrents.org/polya091215.htm.
[65]. "United States foreign aid", Wikipedia:
https://en.wikipedia.org/wiki/United_States_foreign_aid.
[66]. "List of development aid country donors", Wikipedia:
https://en.wikipedia.org/wiki/List_of_development_aid_country_donors.
[67]. Gideon Polya (2008), "Jane Austen and the Black Hole of British History. Colonial rapacity, holocaust denial and the crisis in biological sustainability" (G.M. Polya, Melbourne, 2008 edition that is now available for free perusal on the web: http://janeaustenand.blogspot.com/.
[68]. Gideon Polya, "Hey, hey USA, how many kids did you kill today? Answer: 1,000", Gideon Polya Writing, 1 May 2009:
https://sites.google.com/site/gideonpolyawriting/2009-05-01.
[69]. Harold Pinter, "Art, Truth and Politics", Countercurrents, 8 December 2005: https://countercurrents.org/arts-pinter081205.htm.

Mainstream media: Fake news through lying by omission

Gideon Polya

Fake news is simply a new, Trump-popularized descriptive for media lying that occurs in 2 basic forms, lying by omission and lying by commission. Lying by omission is far, far worse than lying by commission because the latter can at least admit refutation and public debate.

Western Mainstream media impose a huge burden of fake news on Western societies through entrenched and pervasive lying by omission. Indeed the most egregious and pervasive Mainstream media lie of omission is suppression of reportage of such lying by omission. The unimpeded, remorseless, corporate-dominated Mainstream media, politicians and pliant intellectuals are now going further, and variously threatening residual effective free speech and Alternative media on the basis of asserted fake news.

Numerous outstanding writers and journalists have commented cogently on Mainstream media lying and censorship and for alphabetically-organized compendia of such views see the websites "Mainstream media lying" [1] and "Mainstream media censorship" [2]. In particular, Eric Zuesse (an historian and the author, most recently, of "They're Not Even Close: the Democratic vs Republican Records 1910-2010" and of "Christ's ventriloquists: The event that created Christianity") has commented incisively on "the most suppressed news of all - news about the news-suppression by the 'news'-media" (2014): "Recognize how extremely far from being a democracy today's United States has, in fact, become. This is the most shocking realization of all, because it's the most suppressed news of all - news about the news-suppression by the 'news'-media.... That's how dire the condition of what used to be American democracy has now become. The biggest news-story of all is thus the one that is, and that will inevitably be, the most suppressed news-story of all: the news-suppression itself. It extends from the major 'news'-media to the alternative and even to the specialized 'news'-media... He [Edward Snowden] raised the extremely serious question as to whether, and the extent to which, a government can lie to its public and still be a democracy. That's the question. How can the public have a government representing informed consent, if the 'news' media are constantly, and systematically, lying about the most important things, and covering up that government's worst, most heinous, crimes? Yet, this is what Americans have today. The United States is thus no longer a model for any country except for a dictatorship. How likely is it that America's press will let the American public know this now-established fact? Something's wrong — and it's not people such as Edward Snowden" [3].

Barbara Kingsolver (American novelist, essayist, poet and author of "The Poisonwood Bible" and other powerful works) explores Mainstream media lying by omission in her great novel "The Lacuna" (lacuna meaning hiatus, blank, missing part, gap, cavity, or empty space) which has Russian Communist revolutionary and theorist Leon Trotsky (Lev) and his secretary Van having the following discussion about media (2009):

"But newspapers have a duty to truth", Van said. Lev [Trotsky] clicked his tongue. "They tell the truth only as the exception. Zola [French novelist of "J'accuse" fame] wrote that the mendacity of the press could be divided into two groups: the yellow press lies every day without hesitating. But others, like the Times, speak the truth on all inconsequential occasions, so they can deceive the public with the requisite authority when it becomes necessary." Van got up from his chair to gather the cast-off newspapers. Lev took off his glasses and rubbed his eyes. "I don't mean to offend the journalists; they aren't any different from other people. They're merely the megaphones of other people" ... [Trotsky observes to his assistant Shepherd] "Soli, let me tell you. The most important thing about a person is always the thing you don't know" [4].

The lying journalists of corporate-owned Mainstream media can attempt to justify their lying by omission in terms of responsibility to the shareholders over-riding the responsibility they have for their readers and the public in general. A very good example of this neoliberal perversion is provided by John Perkins in his book "Confessions of an Economic Hit Man" in which he describes how he spent most of his corporate life deliberately deceiving Developing Country governments in the interests of US corporate clients. Eventually his conscience outweighed the generous rewards from his employers and clients, but he sadly observes at the end of the book that while he knew what he would be doing was wrong when he was recruited straight out of university in the early 1970s, today business studies students in our universities are taught that their prime moral obligation is to the shareholders and not to truth. However "fake news" via lying by omission is most shocking when it is shamelessly purveyed by non-corporate, taxpayer-funded, national media such as Australia's taxpayer-funded Australian Broadcasting Corporation (ABC) that is Australia's equivalent of the taxpayer-supported UK BBC (British Broadcasting Corporation). Now lying by commission and massive lying by omission are entrenched both the ABC [6] and the BBC [7] but it is of particular interest here to get hard evidence that the ABC and the BBC lie by omission about their lying by omission. Fortunately, the ABC and the BBC have search functions that enable one to quantitate relative reportage and non-reportage of particular matters by these lying organizations, as detailed below.

A search of the UK BBC (on April Fool's Day, 1 April 2017) for the term "lying by omission" yields only 6 items, with the 2 most recent (2014) about an actress "coming out" as a lesbian: "I am tired of hiding and I am tired of lying by omission". In stark contrast, a search of the BBC for "fake news" yields about 360 items that are overwhelmingly in 2017. The lying BBC hides the horrendous reality of its fake news as lying by omission behind a barrage of "fake news" as inconsequential concoctions dreamed up by the "yellow press" and on the Web. Alarmingly, this search of the BBC for "fake news" throws up repeated calls for legisled and other censorship of Alternative media and the Web in addition to that already applied by authoritarian governments, Facebook and Google. One notes that a Google Search for "lying by omission" yields 139,000 results whereas a Google Search for "fake news" yields 32 million.

A search of the Australian ABC (on 1 April 2017) for the term "lying by omission" yields 26 items, with none more recent than 2014, and 10 out of these 26 items being uncensored comments about ABC programs by one Dr. Gideon Polya (me).- there would have been more comments by me but remorseless censorship by the Neocon American and Zionist Imperialist (NAZI)-perverted and subverted ABC has effectively cut off this avenue for opposing ABC "fake news" and lying by omission [6]. In marked contrast, a search of the ABC for "fake news" yielded 277 items of which 162 were from 2017.

What a disgrace. The taxpayer-funded ABC and BBC not only lie by omission, they also lie by omission about their lying by omission. Indeed, in an endless iteration of falsehood, the ABC and BBC are lying by omission about their lying by omission about their lying by omission …

The lying by omission by the ABC, the BBC and by Mainstream journalist, politician and intellectual presstitutes in general has deadly consequences in the sense that history ignored yields history repeated, genocide ignored yields genocide repeated, and holocaust ignored yields holocaust repeated.

Outstanding expatriate Australian journalist John Pilger has written cogently about lying by omission and "historical amnesia" (2012): "Writing in his personal blog, ever so quietly, Jon Williams, the BBC world news editor, effectively dishes his own 'coverage', citing Western officials who describe the 'psy-ops' operation against Syria as 'brilliant'. As brilliant as the destruction of Libya, and Iraq, and Afghanistan. And as brilliant as the psy-ops of the Guardian's latest promotion of Alastair Campbell, the chief collaborator of Tony Blair in the criminal invasion of Iraq. In his 'diaries', Campbell tries to splash Iraqi blood on the demon Murdoch. There is plenty to drench them all. But recognition that the respectable, liberal, Blair-fawning media was a vital accessory to such an epic crime is omitted and remains a singular test of intellectual and moral honesty in Britain. How much longer must we subject ourselves to such an 'invisible government'? This term for insidious propaganda, first used by Edward Bernays, the nephew of Sigmund Freud and inventor of modern public relations, has never been more apt. 'False reality' requires historical amnesia, lying by omission and the transfer of significance to the insignificant. In this way, political systems promising security and social justice have been replaced by piracy, 'austerity', and 'perpetual war': an extremism dedicated to the overthrow of democracy. Applied to an individual, this would identify a psychopath. Why do we accept it?" [8].

In the 2003-2011 Iraq War about 1.5 million Iraqis died from violence, and 1.2 million died from war-imposed deprivation [9]. However BBC estimates of Iraqi deaths in the Iraq War range from 90,000 to about 600,000, while the Australian ABC's estimate on the occasion of US withdrawal in 2011 was a genocide-ignoring "tens of thousands". The UK and Australia have invaded 193 and 85 countries, respectively, are both now into their 8th Iraq War since 1914, and are intimately involved in the Zionist-backed US War on Muslims (aka the US War on Terror) which has been associated, so far, with 32 million Muslim deaths from violence, 5 million, or from imposed deprivation, 27 million, in 20 impoverished countries invaded by the US Alliance since the US Government's 9-11 false flag atrocity [9].

What can decent people do in the face of burgeoning and deadly Mainstream imposition of "false reality" by lying by omission "fake news"? All that decent, informed people can do is to (a) inform everyone they can, and (b) urge and apply Boycotts, Divestment and Sanctions (BDS) against Mainstream media, politicians and pliant intellectuals involved in deadly "fake news" lying by omission. Peace is the only way but silence kills and silence is complicity.

Originally published as "Mainstream media: fake news through lying by omission," MWC News, April 2017.

References

[1] "Mainstream media lying":
https://sites.google.com/site/mainstreammedialying.
[2] "Mainstream media censorship":
https://sites.google.com/site/mainstreammediacensorship.
[3] Eric Zuesse, "The Biggest Scandal In America Is Its Controlled Press",
Countercurrents, 4 December, 2014.
[4] Barbara Kingsolver, "The Lacuna", Faber & Faber, London, 2009, part 3,
p159.
[5] John Perkins, "Confessions of an Economic Hit Man".
[6] "ABC fact-checking unit & incorrect reportage by the ABC (Australia's
BBC)".
"Censorship by the BBC".
[7] John Pilger, "Historical amnesia and psychopathic politics", The Drum,
ABC, 25 June 2012.
"Muslim Holocaust Muslim Genocide":
https://sites.google.com/site/muslimholocaustmuslimgenocide/home.

American-killing Trump's Afghanistan Speech Threatens Afghanistan, Pakistan, India And Humanity

Gideon Polya

A mendacious, bullying, serial war criminal, exceptionalist and American-killing Trump has delivered a bellicose Afghanistan Speech in which he promises endless war in war-devastated Afghanistan, threatens nuclear armed Pakistan, demands further Hindu-majority Indian involvement as a US agent in Muslim Afghanistan, and advises the world that "no place is beyond the reach of American might". The US-imposed, 4-decade Afghan Holocaust and Afghan Genocide is to continue under more draconian rules of engagement.

Trump's Afghanistan Speech was a massive exercise in "fake news through lying by omission". Thus no mention is made by Trump nor by the Mainstream media, politician, academic and commentariat presstitutes he so despises of the horrendous carnage of the US War on Terror (aka the US War on Muslims) involving the deaths of 32 million Muslims abroad (by violence or imposed deprivation) and the preventable deaths of 27 million Americans at home inescapably linked to the fiscal perversion of committing to a $7 trillion long-term accrual cost of killing millions of Muslims abroad instead of keeping millions of Americans alive at home. Bush, Obama and Trump are indeed American-killing US presidents. This essay involves a careful, documented commentary on Trump's Afghanistan Speech that is prefaced by a requisite summary of horrendous genocidal realities of the 21st century US War on Muslims that are utterly ignored by Neocon American and Zionist Imperialist (NAZI)-subverted and perverted Mainstream media.

(A) Before dealing with Trump's bellicose and exceptionalist Afghanistan Speech in detail it is important to sketch the following appalling realities of post-WW2 US imperialism that are utterly ignored by Mainstream media:

A1. US-imposed holocaust and genocide. The ultimate in racism is genocidal invasion of other countries, noting that while "holocaust" means death of a huge number of people, "genocide" is defined by Article 2 of the UN Genocide Convention as follows: "In the present Convention, genocide means any of the following acts committed with intent to destroy, in whole or in part, a national, ethnic, racial or religious group, as such: a) Killing members of the group; b) Causing serious bodily or mental harm to members of the group; c) Deliberately inflicting on the group conditions of life calculated to bring about its physical destruction in whole or in part; d) Imposing measures intended to prevent births within the group; e) Forcibly transferring children of the group to another group" [1]. UN demographic statistics [2] demonstrate that the serial war criminal US has been committing genocide in country after country that it has invaded and occupied as detailed below [3-5].

A2. The worst state crime of all is illegal invasion of another country but International Law as enshrined in the UN Charter only permits invasion of other countries in certain circumstances (and then only after serious negotiations): (1) if there is UN permission; (2) if the invading country or its ally has been invaded by the country to be invaded; (3) if the invading country has been invited to invade by the government. However on the rare occasions when the US had UN sanction to invade it grossly violated this sanction by mass murder. When the US under nuclear terrorist and mass murderer Truman had UN sanction to invade Korea it ended up killing 28% of the North Korean population, a Korean Genocide with genocide as defined above by the UN [6]. Similarly, the US under serial war criminal Obama via its France, UK and US (FUKUS) Coalition had UN sanction to apply a "free fly zone" over Libya, it ended up violently killing 0.1 million Libyans, perhaps killing a further 0.1 million Libyans through imposed deprivation, generating 1 million refugees and devastating what had formerly been a secular country and the most prosperous country in impoverished Africa – a Libyan Genocide as defined above [7].

A3. Deaths from invasion and war include those from violence plus avoidable deaths (avoidable mortality, excess deaths, excess mortality, untimely deaths, premature deaths) from imposed deprivation. Avoidable deaths are readily estimated from UN Population Division mortality statistics [2, 4] but violent Indigenous deaths in US wars are difficult to estimate precisely because, as US General Tommy Franks declared in Afghanistan: "We don't do body counts" [8]. However, expert surveys by the UK ORB polling company and by top US medical epidemiologists have provided the expert estimate of 1.5 million violent Iraqi deaths in the period 2001-2017 (Iraqi avoidable deaths from war-imposed deprivation total 1.2 million in this period) [8]. These mortality estimates for Iraq can be then used to variously estimate violent killing in other current US wars e.g. 1.4 million in the Afghan War assuming it has been 4 times less deadly than the Iraq War [9]. US-imposed deaths from violence or from war-imposed deprivation are estimated to total 6 million (Iraqi Genocide, 1990-2017), 6 million (Afghan Genocide, 2001-2017), 2.2 million (Somali Genocide, 1992-2017), 1 million (Syrian Genocide, 2012-2017) and 0.2 million (Libyan Genocide, 2011-2017) with refugees totalling 6 million (Iraq), 2 million (Afghanistan), 1 million (Somalia), 12 million (Syria) and 1 million (Libya) [7-9]. Deaths from violence or imposed deprivation in post-1950 US Asian Wars total 40 million and globally refugees now total 65 million with about half fleeing US-, Apartheid Israel- or US Alliance-imposed violence, this constituting an Asian Holocaust and an Asian Genocide [3, 4, 7]. The ongoing Palestinian Genocide by US-backed Apartheid Israel has involved 2 million Palestinian deaths from violence, 0.1 million, or imposed deprivation, 1.9 million, since WW1 [10]. The horrendous deaths from the US War on Muslims (aka the US War on

Terror) now include 32 million Muslim deaths from violence, 5 million, or deprivation, 27 million, in 20 countries invaded by the US Alliance since the US Government's 9-11 false flag atrocity [11, 12].

A4. The Americans have invaded 72 countries (52 after WW2) as compared to the British 193, Australia 85, France 82, Germany 39, Japan 30, Russia 25, Canada 25, Apartheid Israel 12, China 2 and Korea zero (0) [5, 13-17]. The US has military personnel in 156 countries [18], has military bases in 75 countries [18, 19] and endlessly subverts all other countries [3].

A5. American exceptionalism means that the US is disproportionately involved in the 3 key existential threats facing Humanity, namely nuclear weapons, poverty and climate change. A nuclear war would wipe out most of Humanity and the Biosphere through the initial blasts, subsequent radioactive pollution and a lengthy, global nuclear winter. America has about 8,000 nuclear weapons, is complicit in the spread of nuclear weapons, opposes nuclear disarmament [20] and under Trump is raising the spectre of an apocalyptic first strike against North Korea, China and Russia. Poverty kills and 17 million people die annually from deprivation on Spaceship Earth with America in charge of the flight deck [4]. America makes a disproportionately high (20%) contribution to annual greenhouse gas pollution [21, 22] and to a worsening climate genocide that will mean 10 billion deaths from climate change this century if greenhouse gas (GHG) pollution is not requisitely stopped and reversed [23-25].

A6. 1.7 million Americans die preventably each year from a variety of causes from smoking to homicide. This means that 27 million Americans have died preventable deaths since the US Government's 9-11 false flag atrocity that killed about 3,000 people [12, 26-28]. In the 16 years after 9-11 (2001-2017) about 60 people died in the US from political terrorist attacks [27, 29, 30] whereas 27 million Americans died from various causes linked to state-sanctioned corporate terrorism, including about 3 million from air pollution – clear evidence of US state-sanctioned corporate terrorism and carbon terrorism [30]. While

US military deaths in the War on Terror total about 7,000 [32], an average of about 20 US veterans have been suiciding each day this century [33] i.e. 20 per day x 365.25 days per year x 16 years = 117,000 US veterans have suicided since the US Government's 9-11 false flag atrocity that killed 3,000 people, mostly Americans. These 27 million preventable American deaths are inescapably linked to Zionist-beholden US Governments committing to a $40 trillion long-term accrual cost of supporting Apartheid Israel, this including a $7 trillion long-term accrual cost for the killing of millions of Muslims abroad in the Zionist-promoted War on Terror instead of keeping millions of Americans alive at home. Despite only 3 Australians having ever been killed by jihadi terrorists in Australia, US lackey Australia has similarly committed to $11 billion per year long-term to the War on Terror ($176 billion since 9-11) with this fiscal perversion linked to 1.4 million preventable Australian deaths since 9-11 [34]. US lackey Canada has similarly committed hugely to the War on Terror with this inescapably linked to 0.1 million Canadian preventable deaths annually or 1.6 million preventable deaths in Canada since 9-11 [35]. The UK has similarly committed hugely to the War on Terror with this linked in terms of fiscal deprivation to 0.15 million UK preventable deaths annually or 2.4 million preventable deaths in the UK since the 9-11 atrocity that killed 3,000 people [36].

A7. Active and passive killing by US state terrorism and variously US-backed non-state terrorism. All terrorism is evil and vile whether it is non-state jihadi terrorism (like the initially US Alliance-backed Al-Qaeda or the barbarous IS that was born out of the war criminal US invasion of the secular state of Iraq and has been variously covertly supported by the US, UK, France, Turkey, Apartheid Israel, Jordan, Saudi Arabia and Qatar) or the vastly more deadly state terrorism (e.g. US Alliance state terrorism that in the 21st century has been waging a genocidal war on Muslims from Western Sahara to the Philippines) [3, 4, 5, 7-12]. The US has a long record of covertly supporting non-state terrorists to further its aims [12, 37-42] e.g. Gladio (that committed atrocities in Europe that were blamed on Communists) [40], rightist Ecuadorean terrorists (who would bomb Catholic churches so that socialists would be blamed) [41], and Al-Qaeda, Mujaheddin and Taliban jihadis (that fought the Russian invasion after the US engineered the removal of Afghanistan's democratic and secular government in 1978) [3, 4]. Indeed, on the basis that "the enemy of my enemy is my friend", IS and Al-Qaeda jihadis are allies of Trump America because they have been variously backed by members of the US Alliance (most notably by Islamofascist Saudi Arabia and Qatar) in devastated Syria and starving Yemen. Evil terrorists have actively killed about 60 Americans in America since 9-11. It is not known how many of these non-state terrorists were excited by US *agents provocateurs*, noting that the US has an appalling record of involvement in false-flag atrocities [3, 4, 37-42] and of backing fundamentalist Muslim jihadis in Afghanistan, Libya, Syria, and Yemen. One sincerely hopes that there will be no further "jihadist" attacks on America or the US Alliance countries for two major reasons: (1) for obvious humanitarian reasons – any avoidable innocent death is a tragedy; and (2) there would clearly be a subsequent huge killing of people in the Muslim world by US forces as seen in the post-9/11 carnage in Afghanistan, Iraq and the Muslim word in general from Mali to the Philippines, Whether US-backed or not, jihadi terrorism is a major asset for US imperialism, with each atrocity providing a further "excuse" for genocidal US Alliance aggression in the Muslim world that has already in the 21st century killed 32 million Muslims through violence (active killing) or imposed deprivation (passive killing) [11].

A8. War criminal US passive mass murder of Afghan children. Articles 55 and 56 of the Geneva Convention relative to Protection of Civilian Persons in Time of War both demand that an Occupier must provide its conquered Subjects with life-sustaining food and medical services "to the fullest extent of the means available to it" [43]. UN Population Division data [2] inform that in the 21st century so far, the average annual under-5 infant deaths has been 101,000 for Occupied Afghanistan (average population 28.8 million) as compared to 1,500 for Occupier Australia (average population 22.1 million). If Occupier Australia, Occupier America and Occupier US Alliance were to observe these key articles of the Geneva

Convention then we would expect that annual under-5 infant mortality in Occupied Afghanistan would be 1,500 deaths x 28.8 million/ 22,1 million = 1,955 or about 2,000 deaths per year instead of the observed 101,000. Through this racist violation of the Geneva Convention, the extremely rich US Alliance Occupiers have been passively killing an average of 99,000 Afghan infants each year this century and have thus passively murdered 99,000 per year x 16 years = 1.584 million under-5 year old Occupied Afghan infants since the 9-11 atrocity that killed 3,000 people. It gets worse. For impoverished countries like Occupied Afghanistan the avoidable mortality from deprivation is 1.4 times the under-5 infant deaths [4], and accordingly Afghan avoidable deaths from deprivation in Occupied Afghanistan have totalled 1.5684 million x 1.4 = 2.218 million since 9-11. Based on expert estimates of violent Iraqi deaths and expert assessment that the Afghan War was 4 times less violent than the Iraq War, one can crudely estimate 0.7 million violent Afghan deaths for a total of 2.9 million Afghan deaths from violence and imposed deprivation since 9-11 (about half a previous estimate made 5 years ago) [9]. According to the "mendacious Bush official version of 9-11" no Afghans were directly involved in the 9-11 atrocity – indeed former US-installed Occupied Afghanistan President Karzai has declared himself quite unconvinced by the US "official version of 9-11" and denies any Al Qaeda presence in Afghanistan [12]. However one can estimate that the US Alliance has actively or passively killed 2,918,000 / 2,997 = 974 or about 1,000 Occupied Afghans (half of them children) for every person killed on 9-11. American exceptionalism indeed.

A9. Mainstream media and Trump fake news through lying by omission. Most of what I have summarized above is glaringly obvious to a humanitarian scientist examining the causes of death (thanatology), whether of 17 million annual avoidable deaths from deprivation in the Third World [4] or of huge preventable deaths in rich US Alliance countries for which avoidable deaths on a global comparative scale are close to zero e.g. 1.7 million preventable American deaths annually from causes ranging from smoking and adverse hospital outcomes to homicide [25-28, 30, 31, 33-36]. However these horrendous realities are kept from information-saturated US Alliance citizens though egregious lying by omission by Neocon American and Zionist Imperialist (NAZI)-perverted and subverted Mainstream media, politician, academic and commentariat presstitutes. The above necessary background to Trump's Afghanistan Speech is utterly absent from mendacious Mainstream media analysis due to Mainstream media and Trump fake news through lying by omission [44-46].

(B). There is little point in a sentence-by-sentence analysis of the rambling Afghanistan Speech [47] by pathological liar, racist, serial war criminal and mass murderer of children, Donald Trump, but below are some of Trump's key declarations in order of delivery together with my succinct comments:

B1. "I am here tonight to lay out our path forward in Afghanistan and South Asia."

Comment: That is, a serial invader America that has invaded over 70 nations will further extend its violence, war criminality and subversion to Pakistan, India, Bangladesh etc. One notes that no countries have been invaded by North Korea and arguably only 1 by Afghanistan (which under Ahmed Shah transiently invaded India in 1760, joined with a Muslim Coalition to defeat the Hindu Marathas at the gigantic Battle of Panipot, and thence promptly returned to Kabul [4]).

B2. "American patriots from every generation have given their last breath on the battlefield for our nation and for our freedom... all service members are brothers and sisters. They're all part of the same family. It's called the American family."

Comment: 1.7 million Americans die preventably each year and 27 million have died thus since 9-11 due to the utterly obscene, fiscal perversion of successive Neocon American and Zionist Imperialist (NAZI)-subverted, One Percenter Administrations that have committed $7 trillion since 9-11 in terms of long-term accrual cost to killing 32 million Muslims abroad for oil and hegemony rather than keeping 27 million Americans alive at home [25-28, 30]. Over 100,000 US veterans have suicided since 9-11 due to lack of care from "the American family" [25-28, 30, 33].

B3. "Thanks to the vigilance and skill of the American military, and of our many allies throughout the world, horrors on the scale of September 11th—nobody can ever forget that—have not been repeated on our shores. But we must acknowledge the reality I'm here to talk about tonight: that nearly 16 years after the September 11th attacks, after the extraordinary sacrifice of blood and treasure, the American people are weary of war without victory. Nowhere is this more evident than with the war in Afghanistan, the longest war in American history, 17 years."

Comment: About 60 Americans have been killed in America by terrorists since 9-11 [26-30]. The US Government has not found it necessary to repeat 9-11 – the deaths of 3,000 people on 9-11 was enough to secure a patriotic consensus for an endless War on Muslims (aka the US War on Terror) in which there have been 32 million Muslim deaths from violence, 5 million, or deprivation, 27 million, in 20 countries invaded by the US Alliance since the US Government's 9-11 false flag atrocity [7, 11, 12]. The US Afghan War has actually lasted 4 decades since the US-backed jihadi removal of the secular Afghan Government in 1978 [4].

B4. "I arrived at three fundamental conclusions about America's core interests in Afghanistan. First, our nation must seek an honorable and enduring outcome worthy of the tremendous sacrifices that have been made, especially the sacrifices of lives."

Comment: Mass murder of 2.9 million Occupied Afghans (half of them children; see A9 above) followed by adumbrated endless mass murder of Afghans (half of them children) in a perpetually occupied Afghanistan, is hardly "honorable". "Thou shalt not kill children" [48]).

B5. "Second, the consequences of a rapid exit are both predictable and unacceptable. 9/11, the worst terrorist attack in our history, was planned and directed from Afghanistan, because that country was ruled by a government that gave comfort and shelter to terrorists. A hasty withdrawal would create a vacuum that terrorists, including ISIS and Al-Qaeda, would instantly fill just as happened before September 11th... The vacuum we created by leaving too soon gave safe haven for ISIS to spread, to grow, recruit, and launch attacks. We cannot repeat in Afghanistan the mistake our leaders made in Iraq."

Comment: Numerous science, architecture, engineering, aviation, military and intelligence experts have concluded that the US Government was responsible for 9-11 with some concluding Israeli and Saudi involvement [12]. Indeed both Donald Trump and Al Gore have blamed the Bush Administration for a massive intelligence failure over 9-11 [12]. Notably, the US-installed former President of Occupied Afghanistan, Hamid Karzai, has rejected US claims of Al Qaeda in Afghanistan and does not accept the American "official version of 9-11": "[Al-Qaeda] is for me a myth [...] For us, they don't exist. I don't know if al-Qaeda existed and I don't know if they exist. I have not seen them and I've not had any report about them, any report that would indicate that al-Qaeda is operating in Afghanistan. [Re US claim about Osama bin Laden and 9-11] that is what I have heard from our Western friends. That's what the Western media says. There is no doubt that an operation, a terrorist operation was conducted in New York and in Washington... I neither believe nor disbelieve something that I don't know about. I can tell you that Afghanistan was as much a victim of terrorism as was America, as were the people who were killed in the September 11th terrorist attacks" [12]. Exceptionalist warmonger and serial war criminal Trump is saying that the illegal and war criminal occupation of Iraq (2.7 million Iraqi deaths from violence or deprivation in the period 2003-2011 [7, 10]) should have continued. Trump is correct on one thing – just as the US backed jihadis such as Al Qaeda, the Mujaheddin and the Taliban in Afghanistan, so Al Qaeda and ISIS in Iraq was an outcome of the illegal US occupation that Trump now seems to retrospectively support. The France-UK-US (FUKUS) Coalition backed jihadis against the secular Gaddafi regime in formerly peaceful and prosperous Libya. The US Alliance, notably the US, UK, France, Turkey, Apartheid Israel, Qatar, Jordan and Saudi Arabia, have variously backed

Al Qaeda, Al Nusrah and ISIS jihadis against the secular Assad regime in formerly prosperous, peaceful and tolerant Syria [7].

B6. "Third and finally, I concluded that the security threats we face in Afghanistan, and the broader region, are immense. Today 20 U.S.-designated foreign terrorist organizations are active in Afghanistan and Pakistan. The highest concentration in any region, anywhere in the world. For its part, Pakistan often gives safe haven to agents of chaos, violence, and terror.

Comment: The key phrase here is "US-designated foreign terrorist". The border between Afghanistan and Pakistan is defined by a line drawn by vile, 19th century British imperialists. The Indigenous Sunni fundamentalist Taliban movement that ruled Afghanistan before the war criminal US invasion in 2001 has massive support from the Indigenous Pashtuns of Afghanistan and Pakistan who have a homeland which is south of the Hindu Kush mountains in Afghanistan and west of the Indus River in Pakistan. The Pashtun and the Taliban are a significant part of the "Pakistan family" just as the racist Religious Right Republicans (R4s) are a significant part of the "American family" and indeed of the Trump constituency (for a comparison of the two see "The Clash of Fundamentalisms: Crusades, Jihads and Modernity" by brilliant, UK-domiciled, non-religious, humanitarian Pakistani writer Tariq Ali [49]). As a pro-peace, non-religious, humanitarian scientist I don't care for the ideology and practices of either side but would make the following key observations:
(i) after the horrendous 2004 Tsunami the secular Indonesian Government terminated a bloody civil war against fundamentalist separatists in Aceh with negotiations and a peaceful accommodation (there are always peaceful alternatives – thus the Taliban might well entertain a quid pro quo of hostility to Shia Iran and exclusive resource deals with America in return for peace and restoration of a Taliban Government);
(ii) the Indigenous Pashtun Taliban have massive support in Afghanistan and Pakistan (I suspect more than Trump presently has in America) and the American Afghan War is a genocidal war of imperial occupation [7, 9];

(iii) nobody is "all bad" and when in power the Taliban banned smoking for public servants, banned alcohol of course, and banned opium production, reducing the Afghan opium production from 90% of world market share to 6% by 2001 [9]. Each year smoking kills about 6 million people, alcohol kills about 2 million people and opiate drugs kill about 0.1 million people. Utterly ignored by Neocon American and Zionist Imperialist (NAZI)-perverted and subverted Western Mainstream media is the 2015 estimate that 1.2 million people had died world-wide since 9-11 due to US Alliance restoration of the Taliban-destroyed Afghan opium industry from 6% of world market share in 2001 to 93% in 2007, the breakdown (as of 2015) including 280,000 Americans, 256,000 Indonesians, 68,000 Iranians, 25,000 British, 14,000 Canadians, 10,000 Germans, and 5,000 Australians [9].

(iv) while 2,400 American soldiers have died in the Afghan War [38], successive American-killing US Administrations under Bush, Obama and Trump have presided over Afghan deaths from violence or deprivation totalling 2.9 million since 9-11(see A8 above); 7,300 US veteran suicides annually (117,000 since 9-11) [33]; and 1.7 million American preventable deaths annually (27 million since 9-11), the breakdown (with some overlaps) including: (1) 443,000 (smoking), (2) 440,000 (adverse hospital events), (3) 300,000 (obesity), (4) 200,000 (air pollution),(5) 75,000 (alcohol), (6) 45,000 (lack of medical insurance), (7) 38,000 (illicit drugs, 21,000 Afghan War-related),(8) 33,000 (motor vehicles), (9) 31,000 (guns), (10) 30,000 (suicide including 7,000 US veterans), (11) 21,000 (avoidable under-5 year old US infant deaths), (12) 15,000 (homicide) and (13) 4 (from terrorists in America) [26-30].

B7. "The threat is worse because Pakistan and India are two nuclear-armed states whose tense relations threaten to spiral into conflict… In Afghanistan and Pakistan, America's interests are clear. We must stop the resurgence of safe havens that enable terrorists to threaten America. And we must prevent nuclear weapons and materials from coming into the hands of terrorists, and being used against us, or anywhere in the world for that matter."

Comment. There is an enormous threat to South Asia in this bull-in-a-china-shop Trump declaration. It is dangerous enough that Pakistan and India are nuclear armed, have a longstanding difference over Kashmir, and have substantial fanatical populations of fundamentalist Muslims and Hindutva hard-line fanatics, respectively. South Asia does not need an ignorant and clumsy bully like Trump who recognizes the acute dangers but is happy to stir the pot by threatening expanded diplomatic and military action against Pakistan while simultaneously suggesting further Indian engagement in Afghanistan as an agent of an anti-Muslim and anti-Pakistan US (see B12 below).

B8. "Conditions on the ground, not arbitrary timetables, will guide our strategy from now on. America's enemies must never know our plans, or believe they can wait us out. I will not say when we are going to attack, but attack we will."

Comment: Already the US is directly involved in military actions in Libya, starving Somalia, starving Yemen, Syria, Iraq, Afghanistan, Pakistan and the Philippines, engagements that notably involve the use of drones that are crucially targeted by the US-Australian joint electronic spying facility at Pine Gap in Central Australia [5, 14, 50, 51]. The US further has bases in 75 countries and has a long and dirty history of covert operations [3-5, 12, 18, 19, 39-42].

B9. Another fundamental pillar of our new strategy is the integration of all instruments of American power—diplomatic, economic, and military—toward a successful outcome…We are a partner and a friend, but we will not dictate to the Afghan people how to live or how to govern their own complex society."

Comment. Trump's declaration that "we will not dictate to the Afghan people" is utterly dishonest and disingenuous when he proposes endless occupation of Afghanistan. As analyzed above in A8, the US and the US Alliance are grossly violating the Geneva Convention in Occupied Afghanistan as revealed by the smoking gun of under-5 infant deaths in 2001-2017 totalling 1.6 million in Occupied Afghanistan (2000-2020 average population 28.8 million) as compared to 24,000 in Asian-child-killing, US lackey Occupier Australia (2000-2020 average population 22.1 million). To reiterate, Articles 55 and 56 of the Geneva Convention relative to Protection of Civilian Persons in Time of War both demand that an Occupier must provide its conquered Subjects with life-sustaining food and medical services "to the fullest extent of the means available to it" [43], but this is not reflected in the appalling infant mortality data for Occupied Afghanistan. In supporting racist legislation for what became known as the White Australia Policy that excluded Indians, Africans, Asians and indeed non-Europeans in general from Australia in the period 1901-1974, White Australia's first Prime Minister Edmund Barton notoriously stated (1901) that: "The doctrine of the equality of man was never intended to apply to the equality of an Englishman and the Chinaman" [52-54]. US lackey Occupier Australia in 2017 is saying that 50 Afghan infants are not worth 1 White Australian infant, that 50 Asians don't equal 1 White. Of course, as revealed by the recent Charlottesville atrocity, racism is as American as apple pie and numerous US experts from science to business have withdrawn from position advising Trump over his contradictory recent comments on this matter.

B10. "We are not nation building again. We are killing terrorists."

Comment. US policy in invading 72 other countries has been to thence install pliant dictatorships or pseudo-democratic regimes to do US bidding. Thus in US-invaded countries from Latin America to East Asia, "nation building" by imposition of "American democracy" has variously involved intimidating, exiling, imprisoning, torturing or killing the Indigenous leaders and their supporters and then holding "democratic elections" [3, 4, 41]. John Perkins in his book "Confessions of an Economic Hit Man" describes how the US tries to gets its way in Developing countries by bribery and corruption, thence by assassination, and if all that fails, by invasion and elimination of the people it doesn't like [55]. Trump's declaration that "we are killing terrorists" is a statement of genocidal intent. The fundamentalist Muslim Taliban have massive support in

504

Afghanistan and Pakistan especially among the Pashtun population, and "indigenous terrorists" to US imperialists like Trump are indigenous people resisting US Occupation. As the saying goes, one man's terrorist is another man's freedom fighter. Trump is an unusual genocidal imperialist in that he has explicitly stated his genocidal intent. To reiterate, "genocide" is defined by Article 2 of the UN Genocide Convention as follows: "In the present Convention, genocide means any of the following acts committed with intent to destroy, in whole or in part, a national, ethnic, racial or religious group, as such: a) Killing members of the group; b) Causing serious bodily or mental harm to members of the group; c) Deliberately inflicting on the group conditions of life calculated to bring about its physical destruction in whole or in part; d) Imposing measures intended to prevent births within the group; e) Forcibly transferring children of the group to another group" [1].

B11. "The next pillar of our new strategy is to change the approach in how to deal with Pakistan. We can no longer be silent about Pakistan's safe-havens for terrorist organizations, the Taliban and other groups that pose a threat to the region and beyond. Pakistan has much to gain from partnering with our effort in Afghanistan. It has much to lose by continuing to harbor criminals and terrorists."

Comment. Trump is crudely and publicly threatening nuclear-armed Pakistan with unspecified retribution for not embarking on a genocidal program of devastating and exterminating a substantial part of its ilk in Pakistan and Afghanistan.

B12. "Another critical part of the South-Asia strategy for America is to further develop its strategic partnership with India; the world's largest democracy, and a key security and economic partner of the United States. We appreciate India's important contributions to stability in Afghanistan, but India makes billions of dollars in trade with the United States—and we want them to help us more with Afghanistan, especially in the area of economic assistance and development."

Comment. Ignorant bully Trump is simply crudely and public threatening India with unspecified retribution if it does not go "all the way with the USA". India arguably has the largest Muslim population of any country in the world (the total Indian population is 1,329 million, with an Indian Muslim population of 266 million; ranking second is Indonesia with a total population of 259 million and a Muslim population of 228 million [42, 56]). Indian governments have always had to carefully balance the Hindu-Muslim dichotomy for communal peace after the horrors of Partition. Indian PM Modi has already worried humane Indians by his departure from over a century of India's leadership of the world in the fight against Apartheid by visiting and embracing US-backed Apartheid Israel that is a powerful supporter of the US War on Muslims.

B13. "Finally, my administration will ensure that you, the brave defenders of the American people [the US military] will have the necessary tools and rules of engagement to make this strategy work, and work effectively, and work quickly…. That's why we will also expand authority for American armed forces to target the terrorists and criminal networks that sow violence and chaos through Afghanistan. These killers need to know they have nowhere to hide, that no place is beyond the reach of American might and American arms. Retribution will be fast and powerful as we lift restrictions and expand authorities."

Comment. "The necessary tools and rules of engagement to make this strategy work" were introduced by war criminal Obama and presently include undeclared war directly involving US forces in 8 countries, remotely controlled drone-based bombing targeted by joint US-Australian facilities in Central Australia, and drone-based, extrajudicial killing of people the US Government doesn't like, including American citizens. The ultimate in American exceptionalism is the Trump assertion that "no place is beyond the reach of American might and American arms" that is a bullying threat to the whole world to which pro-peace citizens of the world can only respond with "Go home Yank". However science fiction is now becoming horrible reality with small to large, remotely-controlled weapons operating without any national or international scrutiny in free fire zones in any country of choice. Advances in Artificial Intelligence (AI) mean that the next step of autonomous weapons may be only a few years away from deployment and has prompted a recent letter signed by 116 robotics and AI experts, including Tesla chief Elon Musk and Alphabet's Mustafa Suleyman, demanding that the UN ban the development and use of autonomous "killer robots": "As companies building the technologies in Artificial Intelligence and Robotics that may be repurposed to develop autonomous weapons, we feel especially responsible in raising this alarm... Lethal autonomous weapons threaten to become the third revolution in warfare. Once developed, they will permit armed conflict to be fought at a scale greater than ever, and at timescales faster than humans can comprehend. These can be weapons of terror, weapons that despots and terrorists use against innocent populations, and weapons hacked to behave in undesirable ways. We do not have long to act. Once this Pandora's box is opened, it will be hard to close. We therefore implore the High Contracting Parties to find a way to protect us all from these dangers" [57, 58].

B14. "We will ask our NATO allies and global partners to support our new strategy with additional troop and funding increases in line with our own."

Comment. But one must query whether America's "NATO allies and global partners" will have the stomach to continue their active complicity in the US-imposed, ongoing Afghan Holocaust and Afghan Genocide that has killed an estimated 2.9 million Occupied Afghans through violence, 0.7 million, or war-imposed deprivation, 2.2 million, since the US Government's 9-11 false flag atrocity that killed about 3,000 people [7, 9, 12]. Before the 1944 Ardeatine Caves Massacre, Nazi dictator Adolph Hitler ordered the execution of 10 enemy people for every German soldier killed by partisans, an enemy/German soldier death ratio of 10 [59]. In Afghanistan the US Alliance has an Afghan/US soldier death ratio of 2.9 million/ 2,400 = 1,200 (or 120 times greater than that advocated by Hitler) and has an Afghan/9-11 victim death ratio of 2.9 million/3,000 = 967, or about 1, 000 (100 times greater than that

advocated by Hitler). One recalls that when asked "What do you think of Western civilization" Mahatma Gandhi famously replied "I think it would be a good idea" [60].
B15. "May God bless our military, and may God bless the United States of America."

Comment. In making this declaration of faith in support from God, Trump has a common position with the equally barbarous but fortunately not very powerful Islamic State (IS) and related jihadi, non-state terrorist groups, To atheist, secular, Humanists such as myself, the proposition of the existence of God is not a scientific hypothesis because it is not a potentially falsifiable hypothesis that can be subject to critical testing. That said, Humanists would readily concede that theism, like poetry, literature, art and music, can give comfort to many and indeed has been the inspiration for transcendental art. One supposes that if an infinitely good God exists He/She would most definitely not support non-state terrorists such as those of IS, Al Qaeda and other jihadi organizations nor state terrorists such as those of US state terrorism, UK state terrorism, French state terrorism, Apartheid Israeli state terrorism, Australian state terrorism, Canadian state terrorism, Turkish state terrorism, Saudi state terrorism and potentially terracidal nuclear state terrorism [16, 17].

Final comments

In his Afghanistan Speech, mendacious, bullying, serial war criminal, exceptionalist and American-killing US President Donald Trump is publicly articulating the covert policies of the Neocon American and Zionist Imperialist (NAZI)-subverted US intelligence, military, corporate and political Establishment. However the danger from Trump's big mouth is that blatant articulation of this violent obscenity makes it the new public norm. The world must urgently stand up against these warmongering psychopaths. The killing must stop. Peace is the only way but silence kills and silence is complicity. What can decent people do in the face of the growing existential threat from a violent and exceptionalist America under Trump? Decent people must (a) evade the lying Mainstream media by informing everyone they can, and (b) apply Boycotts, Divestment and Sanctions, (BDS) against the US Alliance people, politicians, parties, countries, companies and corporations complicit in this potentially terracidal US War on Humanity [20].

The failure of Trump to abolish ObamaCare occurred because Republican Congressional representatives responded to the serious concerns of ordinary Americans over the deadly threat of lack of medical insurance (it was estimated that 43,000 Americans would die over 2 Trump terms if ObamaCare were abolished [28]). Ordinary Americans must urgently respond to the Awful Truth – so well hidden by Neocon American and Zionist Imperialist (NAZI)-subverted Mainstream media, politician, academic and commentariat presstitutes – that while terrorist psychopaths kill an average of about 4 Americans in America each year, 1.7 million Americans die preventably annually under an American-killing Trump Administration that, like its predecessors, is committed to spending trillions of dollars (in terms of long-term accrual cost) on killing millions of Muslim abroad rather than keeping millions of Americans alive at home. Americans must get out into the streets and assert that "American Lives Matter".

Originally published as "American-killing Trump's Afghanistan Speech Threatens Afghanistan, Pakistan, India And Humanity," Countercurrents, August 2017.

References

[1]. "UN Genocide Convention":
http://www.edwebproject.org/sideshow/genocide/convention.html.
[2]. UN Population Division, "World Population Prospects 2017":
https://esa.un.org/unpd/wpp/.
[3]. William Blum, "Rogue State: a guide to the world's only superpower",
Common Courage Press; 3rd edition, 2005.
[4]. Gideon Polya, "Body Count. Global avoidable mortality since 1950",
that includes a succinct history of every country and is now available for free
perusal on the web: http://globalbodycount.blogspot.com/.
[5]. Gideon Polya, "The US Has Invaded 70 Nations Since 1776 – Make 4
July Independence From America Day", Countercurrents, 5 July, 2013:
https://countercurrents.org/polya050713.htm.
[6]. Michel Chossudovsky, "Know the facts: North Korea lost close to 30%
of its population as a result of US bombings in the 1950s", Global Research,
27 November 2010: http://www.globalresearch.ca/know-the-facts-north-
korea-lost-close-to-30-of-its-population-as-a-result-of-us-bombings-in-the-
1950s/22131.
[7]. "Muslim Holocaust Muslim Genocide":
https://sites.google.com/site/muslimholocaustmuslimgenocide/.
[8]. John M. Broder, "A nation at war: the casualties; U.S. military has no
count of Iraqi dead in fighting", New York Times, 2 April 2003:
http://www.nytimes.com/2003/04/02/world/nation-war-casualties-us-
military-has-no-count-iraqi-dead-fighting.html; Just Foreign Policy, "Iraq
deaths": http://www.justforeignpolicy.org/iraq ; "Iraqi Genocide":
https://sites.google.com/site/iraqiholocaustiraqigenocide/.
[9]. "Afghan Genocide":
https://sites.google.com/site/afghanholocaustafghangenocide/.
[10]. "Palestinian Genocide":
https://sites.google.com/site/palestiniangenocide/.
[11]. Gideon Polya, "Paris Atrocity Context: 27 Million Muslim Avoidable
Deaths From Imposed Deprivation In 20 Countries Violated By US Alliance
Since 9-11", Countercurrents, 22 November, 2015:
https://countercurrents.org/polya221115.htm.
[12]. "Experts: US did 9-11": https://sites.google.com/site/expertsusdid911/.
[13]. Gideon Polya, "British Have Invaded 193 Countries: Make 26 January (
Australia Day, Invasion Day) British Invasion Day", Countercurrents, 23
January, 2015: https://countercurrents.org/polya230115.htm.
[14]. Gideon Polya, "As UK Lackeys Or US Lackeys Australians Have
Invaded 85 Countries (British 193, French 80, US 70)", Countercurrents, 9
February, 2015: https://countercurrents.org/polya090215.htm.
[15]. Gideon Polya, "President Hollande And French Invasion Of Privacy
Versus French Invasion Of 80 Countries Since 800 AD", Countercurrents, 15
January, 2014: https://countercurrents.org/polya150114.htm.
[16]. "Stop state terrorism" : https://sites.google.com/site/stopstateterrorism/.
[17]. "State crime and non-state terrorism":
https://sites.google.com/site/statecrimeandnonstateterrorism/.

[18]. Jules Dufour, "The world-wide network of US military bases", Global Research: http://www.globalresearch.ca/the-worldwide-network-of-us-military-bases/5564.

[19]. "These are the countries where the US has a military presence", Global Research, 12 April 2015: http://www.globalresearch.ca/these-are-all-the-countries-where-the-us-has-a-military-presence/5442345.

[20]. "Nuclear weapons ban, end poverty and reverse climate change": https://sites.google.com/site/drgideonpolya/nuclear-weapons-ban.

[21]. Gideon Polya, "Revised Annual Per Capita Greenhouse Gas Pollution For All Countries – What Is Your Country Doing?", Countercurrents, 6 January, 2016: https://countercurrents.org/polya060116.htm.

[22]. Gideon Polya, "Exposing And Thence Punishing Worst Polluter Nations Via Weighted Annual Per Capita Greenhouse Gas Pollution Scores", Countercurrents, 19 March, 2016: https://countercurrents.org/polya190316.htm.

[23]. "Climate Genocide": https://sites.google.com/site/climategenocide/.

[24]. Gideon Polya, "Exceptionalist Trump America exits from Paris Agreement & launches neoliberal War on Terra", Counterciurrent, 6 June 2017: https://countercurrents.org/2017/06/06/exceptionalist-trump-america-exits-from-paris-agreement-launches-neoliberal-war-on-terra/.

[25]. Gideon Polya, "Israeli-Palestinian & Middle East Conflict – From Oil to Climate Genocide", Countercurrents, 21 August 2017: https://countercurrents.org/2017/08/21/israeli-palestinian-middle-east-conflict-from-oil-to-climate-genocide/.

[26]. Gideon Polya, "American Holocaust, Millions Of Untimely American Deaths And $40 Trillion Cost Of Israel To Americans", Countercurrents, 27 August 2013: https://countercurrents.org/polya270813.htm.

[27]. Gideon Polya, "West Ignores 11 Million Muslim War Deaths & 23 Million Preventable American Deaths Since US Government's False-flag 9-11 Atrocity", Countercurrents, 9 September, 2015: https://countercurrents.org/polya090915.htm.

[28]. Gideon Polya, "Trump's abolition of ObamaCare will kill an estimated 43,000 Americans over 2 Trump terms"", Global Research, 16 March 2017: http://www.globalresearch.ca/trumps-abolition-of-obamacare-will-kill-an-estimated-43000-americans-over-2-trump-terms/5580513.

[29]. Ronald Bailey, "How scared of terrorism should you be?", Reason.com, 6 September 2011: http://reason.com/archives/2011/09/06/how-scared-of-terrorism-should.

[30]. Gideon Polya, "San Bernardino Atrocity Elicits Islamophobic Republican Hysteria And Egregious Falsehood In Warmonger Obama's Speech", Countercurrents, 9 December, 2015: https://countercurrents.org/polya091215.htm.

[31]. "Carbon terrorism: 3 million US air pollution deaths versus 53 US political terrorism deaths since 9-11 (2001-2015)", State crime & non-state terrorism: https://sites.google.com/site/statecrimeandnonstateterrorism/carbon-terrorism.

[32]. I-casualties: http://www.icasualties.org/.

[33]., Dr. Janet Kemp and Dr. Robert Bossarte, "Suicide data report, 2012", Department of Veterans Affairs, Mental Health Services, Suicide Prevention Program, especially Figure 3: http://www.va.gov/opa/docs/Suicide-Data-Report-2012-final.pdf.

[34]. Gideon Polya, "Australian State Terrorism – Zero Australian Terrorism Deaths, 1 Million Preventable Australian Deaths & 10 Million Muslims Killed By US Alliance Since 9-11", Countercurrents, 23 September, 2014: https://countercurrents.org/polya230914.htm.

[35]. Gideon Polya, "Pro-Zionist, Pro-war, Pro-Opium, War Criminal Canadian Government Defames Iran & Cuts Diplomatic Links", Countercurrents, 10 September, 2012: https://countercurrents.org/polya100912.htm.

[36]. Gideon Polya, "UK Terror Hysteria exposed – Empirical Annual Probability of UK Terrorism Death 1 in 16 million", Countercurrents, 16 September, 2014: https://countercurrents.org/polya160914.htm.

[37]. "42 false-flag attacks officially admitted to", What Really Happened, : http://www.whatreallyhappened.com/WRHARTICLES/42falseflags.php#axz z4qdDmevAW.

[38]. 9-11Review.com, "History of American false flag operations": http://www.911review.com/articles/anon/false_flag_perations.html.

[39]. Gideon Polya, "US Profits From Jihadist Terrorism", Countercurrents, 19 November, 2004: https://countercurrents.org/us-polya191104.htm.

[40]. "Operation Gladio", Wikispooks: https://wikispooks.com/wiki/Operation_Gladio.

[41]. Philip Agee, "Inside the Company: CIA Diary".

[42]. Gideon Polya, "Riyadh speech: state terrorist Trump's fake news ignores Muslim Holocaust & American Holocaust", Countercurrents, 26 May 2017: https://countercurrents.org/2017/05/26/riyadh-speech-state-terrorist-trumps-fake-news-ignores-muslim-holocaust-american-holocaust/.

[43]. "Geneva Convention Relative to the Protection of Civilians in Time of War", International Committee of the Red Cross : https://ihl-databases.icrc.org/ihl/385ec082b509e76c41256739003e636d/6756482d8614 6898c125641e004aa3c5.

[44]. Gideon Polya, "Google Censorship & Zionist Constraint On Effective Free Speech Threaten Planet", Countercurrents, 9 August 2017: https://countercurrents.org/2017/08/09/google-censorship-zionist-constraint-on-effective-free-speech-threaten-planet/.

[45]. Gideon Polya, "Mainstream media fake news through lying by omission", Global Research, 1 April 2017: http://www.globalresearch.ca/mainstream-media-fake-news-through-lying-by-omission/5582944.

[46]. Gideon Polya, "Australian ABC and UK BBC fake news through lying by omission", Countercurrents, 2 May 2017: https://countercurrents.org/2017/05/02/australian-abc-and-uk-bbc-fake-news-through-lying-by-omission/.

[47]. "Full transcript: Donald Trump announces his Afghanistan policy", The Atlantic, 21 August 2017: https://www.ncbi.nlm.nih.gov/pmc/articles/PMC4416972/.

[48]. "Thou shalt not kill children":
http://thoushaltnotkillchildren.blogspot.com.au/.
[49]. Tariq Ali, "The Clash of Fundamentalisms: Crusades, Jihads and Modernity", Verso, 2003.
[50]. Phillip Dorling, "Pine Gap drives US drone kills", Sydney Morning Herald, 21 July 2013: http://www.smh.com.au/national/pine-gap-drives-us-drone-kills-20130720-2qbsa.html.
[51]. Prahanth Parameswaran, "What's behind the new US-Philippines drone hype under Duterte", The Diplomat, 11 August 2017:
http://thediplomat.com/2017/08/old-us-philippines-drone-hype-strikes-anew-under-duterte/.
[52]. Australia 's first Prime Minister Edmund Barton debating. (Barton (1901), speech to Federal Parliament concerning the Commonwealth Immigration Restriction Act 1901, quoted in Buggy and Cates (1985), p145; Buggy, T. and Cates, J. (1985), "Race Relations in Colonial Australia", Nelson, Melbourne.
[53]. Gideon Polya, "Jane Austen and the Black Hole of British History. Colonial rapacity, holocaust denial and the crisis in biological sustainability", G.M. Polya, Melbourne, 1998, 2008 that is now available for free perusal on the web: http://janeaustenand.blogspot.com/.
[54]. Gideon Polya, "Apartheid Australia : 70 Asians Don't Equal One White", Countercurrents, 18 August 2009:
https://countercurrents.org/polya180809.htm.
[55]. John Perkins, "Confessions of an Economic Hit Man", Plume, 2005.
[56]. "Muslim population in the world":
http://www.muslimpopulation.com/asia/.
[57]. Samuel Gibbs, "Elon Musk leads 116 experts calling for outright ban of killer robots", Guardian, 21 August 2017:
https://www.theguardian.com/technology/2017/aug/20/elon-musk-killer-robots-experts-outright-ban-lethal-autonomous-weapons-war.
[58]. "An Open Letter to the United Nations Convention on certain conventional weapons", Future of Life Institute, August 2017:
https://futureoflife.org/autonomous-weapons-open-letter-2017.
[59]. "Ardeatine massacre", Wikipedia:
https://en.wikipedia.org/wiki/Ardeatine_massacre.
[60]. Quote investigator: https://quoteinvestigator.com/2013/04/23/good-idea/.

Do Bing Searches To Circumvent Mendacious Pro-Zionist Google Censorship – Bing It!

Western Mainstream media are dominated by Jewish and non-Jewish Zionists with few more so than Google or its holding company Alphabet that is the world's number 1 media company as compared to number 17 Microsoft that owns Bing. Bing Searches involving key terms are much more successful than Google Searches ranking-wise in detecting some key websites documenting humane opinion about Zionist crimes – most are variously absent or effectively invisible when one does Google Searches for key terms. Ergo, do Bing Searches to circumvent pro-Zionist Google censorship. Bing it!

While numerous anti-racist Jewish intellectuals and humanitarians are resolutely critical of the ongoing Palestinian Genocide, Western Mainstream media variously censor or white-wash the nuclear terrorist, genocidally racist, and grossly human rights-abusing conduct of democracy-by-genocide Apartheid Israel. A significant part of the explanation for this huge moral perversion is that the American 60% of the world's 30 biggest media companies [1] have a disproportionately high Jewish Board membership. Jews and females represent 2% and 51%, respectively, of the US population but average 33% and 19%, respectively, of Board members of the top 18 US media companies [2]. It is a reasonable assumption that extremely wealthy Jews would be very likely to be pro-Zionist, in contrast to poor Jews or modestly prosperous intellectual Jews who would be more likely in comparison to be anti-racist and thus anti-Zionist.

The Alternative medium The Zog has summarized a detailed analysis of the top executives of Google thus: "Of the six (6) Google executive officers, five (5) are Jews or have Jewish spouses. This is a numerical representation of 83%. Of the ten

(10) Google directors, five (5) are Jews or have Jewish spouses. This is a numerical representation of 50%. Jews are approximately 2% of the U.S. population. Therefore Jews are over-represented among the Google executive officers by a factor of 41.5 times (4,150 percent) and overrepresented on the Google board of directors by a factor of 25 times (2,500 percent)" [2]. There is growing indignation from anti-racist Jewish people over the human rights-abusing and genocidal policies of Apartheid Israel. If we generously assume that only 50% of these Jewish Google executives are Zionists there is still a hugely disproportionate Zionist representation.

Alphabet, the holding company that owns Google, had an annual $59.62 billion in revenue in 2015 and was a world leader among media companies. 46% of Alphabet Directors are Jewish or have Jewish spouses but only 23% of Board members are women. Alphabet chairman John Hennessy is anti-BDS (opposed to Boycott, Divestment and Sanctions against Apartheid Israel) and hence pro-Zionist [2]. In addition to minimizing the humane Left, Google provides software to identify targets for illegal US drone strikes [4].

The World Socialist Web Site (WSWS) has quantified how Google has altered search protocols to effectively limit reader access to progressive, Left, socialist, anti-war and pro-humanity sites [5]. However Google is not alone in this surreptitious perversion of free speech and effective free speech. Thus Chris Hedges of Truthdig recently reported that "Sen. Ted Cruz of Texas, along with 18 members of the House of Representatives—15 Republicans and three Democrats—has sent a letter to Attorney General Jeff Sessions demanding that the Qatari-run Al-Jazeera television network register as a foreign agent under the Foreign Agents Registration Act (FARA). The letter was issued after Al-Jazeera said it planned to air a documentary by a reporter who went undercover to look into the Israel lobby in the United States. The action by the senator and the House members follows the decision by the Justice Department to force RT America to register as a foreign agent and the imposition of algorithms by Facebook, Google and Twitter that steer traffic away from left-wing, anti-war and progressive websites, including Truthdig. It also follows December's abolition of net neutrality" [6]. Google is variously rendering progressive sites invisible or effectively invisible from Google Searches [2-12].

By way of comparison with Alphabet (owner of Google) that is #1 in the global Mainstream media, Microsoft ($4.58 billion annual revenue) is #17 in the world Mainstream media. Among other things Microsoft owns the search engine Bing and has an 18% Jewish Board and an 18% female Board [2] as compared to a 46% Jewish Board and 23% female Board for Alphabet. However a notable difference is that Bing Searches reveal humane websites variously rendered effectively invisible by Google [2, 7-12].

Below are listed a number of websites I have created in the public interest that in an alphabetically-ordered fashion quote the considered, expert and humane opinions of numerous decent intellectuals about key matters relating to Apartheid Israel, the ongoing Palestinian Genocide and the Zionist-promoted War on Terror. For each website I record the success of Google or Bing Searches for related key terms in bringing up the website.

"Experts: US did 9-11" website.

According to the Center for Public Integrity, the Bush Administration told 935 lies about Iraq between 9-11 and the war criminal US Alliance invasion of Iraq that was based on false assertions of Iraqi possession of Weapons of Mass Destruction (WMD) [13]. Iraqi deaths from this invasion and occupation totalled 2.7 million, this comprising 1.5 million violent deaths and 1.2 million avoidable deaths from war-imposed deprivation [14], an Iraqi Holocaust and Iraqi Genocide of the same order of magnitude as the WW2 Jewish Holocaust (5-6 million deaths from violence or deprivation) [15]. Yet the Western Mainstream media totally and blindly accept the "lying Bush official version of 9-11" and censor expert dissenters. The "Experts: US did 9-11" website alphabetically lists the opinions of numerous science, engineering, architecture, aviation, military and intelligence experts to the effect that the US did 9-11, with some asserting Israeli involvement [16].

A Bing Search for the phrase "US did 9-11" yields the website "Experts: US did 9-11" as #1 on page 1 out of 17.1 million results. In stark contrast, a Google Search for the phrase "US did 9-11" fails to come up with the "Experts: US did 9-11" website in the first 12 pages of results (111 results). On the final page 12 of Google Search results one can click a link enabling one to "repeat the search with the omitted results included", this now yielding the "Experts: US did 9-11" website as #11 of the results and located on page 2. However, as observed by Steve Toth: "According to Search Engine Watch, 92% of search traffic comes from page 1" [17]. While a Bing Search of the key phrase "US did 9-11" yields the "Experts: US did 9-11" website as #1 on page 1, this important website is rendered effectively "invisible" by Google.

"Jews against racist Zionism" website.

The "Jews against racist Zionism" website [18] alphabetically lists the opinions of numerous anti-racist Jews (most notably Nobel Laureate Albert Einstein) who are highly critical of the crimes of the racist Zionists and Apartheid Israel [18]. For anti-racist Jews and indeed all anti-racist humanitarians the core moral messages from the Jewish Holocaust (5-6 million dead, 1 in 6 dying from deprivation) [15] and from the more general WW2 European Holocaust (30 million Slav, Jewish and Gypsy dead) are "zero tolerance for racism", "never again to anyone", "bear witness" and "zero tolerance for lying".
A Bing Search of the term "Jews against" yields the "Jews against racist Zionism" website on page 1 as result #6 out of 239,000 results. Similarly, a Bing Search of the term "racist Zionism" yields the "Jews against racist Zionism" website as #1 on page 1 of 15,200 results. In stark contrast, a Google Search for "Jews against" yields zero (0) results out of the first 10 pages of 272,000 results. A Google Search for "racist Zionism" yielded zero result in the first 21 pages but a Google Search "with the omitted results included" yields the "Jews against racist Zionism" website as #51 on page 5 out of 11,300 results. Astonishingly, a Google Search for "Jews against racist Zionism" fails to pick up this particular Google site in 9 pages of 2,970 results but the same search with "omitted results included" reveals this website as #3 on page 1 of 2,970 results. The burning of Jewish books by the Nazis was anti-Jewish anti-

Semitism – what does one call rendering eminent, anti-racist Jewish opinion "invisible"?

"Non-Jews against racist Zionism" website.

The "Non-Jews against racist Zionism" website is an alphabetical compendium of the views on racist Zionism by numerous eminent non-Jewish leaders and writers, including Nobel Laureates Jimmy Carter, Maired Maguire, Nelson Mandela, Jose Saramago, and Desmond Tutu [19].
A Bing Search for "Non-Jews against" yields the website as item #2 on page 1 out of 15,300 results. A Bing Search for "racist Zionism" yields the website as item #34 on page 4 out of 15,300 results. A Google Search for "Non-Jews against" yields "Non-Jews against racist Zionism" as #1 on page 1 out of 354 results, but a Google Search for "racist Zionism" fails to yield this website in the first 10 pages. A Google Search for "Jews against" yields this website as #75 (page 8 of 272,000 results). A Bing Search for "Non-Jews against racist Zionism" yields this website as #1 on page 1 of 1.81 million results, and a Google Search for "Non-Jews against racist Zionism" yields the website as #1 on page 1 of 356 results. However a Google Search for "Jews against racist Zionism" fails pick up the "Jews against racist Zionism" Google Site website in the first 9 pages – evidently the Google Robot is vastly more concerned to censor Jewish rather than non-Jewish critics of racist Zionism and Apartheid Israel. Non-Jewish critics of Apartheid Israel can be much more plausibly falsely defamed as "anti-Semites" than anti-racist Jews.

"Boycott Apartheid Israel" website.

The "Boycott Apartheid Israel" website is an alphabetically-organized compendium of the opinions of outstanding, anti-racist, Jewish and non-Jewish scholars and writers who variously describe the State of Israel as a race-based Apartheid state involved in a Palestinian Genocide. The "Boycott Apartheid Israel" website also lists the views of those supporting comprehensive intra-national and international Boycotts, Divestment and Sanctions (BDS) against Apartheid

Israel and its racist supporters as were successfully applied to US-, UK-, Apartheid Australia- and Apartheid Israel-backed Apartheid South Africa and the individuals, corporations, organizations and countries who supported that egregiously racist, anti-African and anti-Asian White Minority regime [20]. Critically, one notes that BDS is a peaceful action after the fashion of Mahatma Gandhi's non-violent Satyagraha movement, and that the UN Convention on the Suppression and Punishment of the Crime of Apartheid" (UN Apartheid Convention) and the UN General Assembly have labelled apartheid as a crime against humanity [20]. Apartheid Israel presently rules all of Palestine and determines that of its 6.8 million Palestinian subjects (50% of the subject population), 5 million or 74% of the Indigenous Palestinian subjects, are excluded from voting for the government ruling them i.e. explicit, sustained and egregious Apartheid [21-24].

A Bing Search for "Boycott Apartheid Israel" brings up the "Boycott Apartheid Israel" website as #3 on page 1 of 1.44 million results; a Bing Search for "Boycott Apartheid" brings up the website as #7 on page 1 of 33,400 results; and a Bing Search for "Apartheid Israel" brings up the website as #67 on page 7 of 128,000 results. A Google Search for "Boycott Apartheid Israel" brings up the "Boycott Apartheid Israel" website as #5 on page 1 of 15,100 results; a Google Search for "Boycott Apartheid" brings up the website as #46 on page 4 of 24,700 results; and a Google Search for "Apartheid Israel" fails to elicit the website even with ""omitted results included". Google has effectively made the "Boycott Apartheid Israel" website much less visible unless you know the exact name of the website. Many of the supporters of BDS are anti-racist Jews [20] and one must again pose the question: if the burning of Jewish books by the Nazis was anti-Jewish anti-Semitism, what does one call rendering eminent, anti-racist Jewish opinion "invisible"?

"Nuclear weapons ban, end poverty & reverse climate change" website.

The "Nuclear weapons ban, end poverty & reverse climate change" website exists because our world is acutely threatened by nuclear weapons, poverty and man climate change. Thus (1) a comprehensive Nuclear Weapons Ban is needed to avoid an accidental full-scale nuclear catastrophe and a consequent Nuclear Winter that will wipe out most of Humanity and the Biosphere; (2) we can and must urgently end poverty that causes 16 million avoidable deaths from deprivation each year; and (3) we must urgently reverse climate change by atmospheric CO_2 draw-down to circa 300 ppm CO_2 from the present dangerous and damaging 410 ppm CO_2 that is increasing at about 3 ppm CO_2 per year in a worsening Climate Emergency and Climate Genocide that, unaddressed, is set to kill 10 billion people this century [25]. The "Nuclear weapons ban, end poverty & reverse climate change" website alphabetically lists expert opinion and national complicity.

Bing Searches for (1) "Nuclear weapons ban" (2) "end poverty" and (3) "reverse climate change", respectively, (1) yielded the website as #51 (page 6 of 1.75 million results), (2) failed to elicit the website in the first 10 pages, and (3) elicited the website as #48 (page 5 of 16.7 million results). In stark contrast, Google Searches for (1) "Nuclear weapons ban" (2) "end poverty" and (3) "reverse climate change", respectively, failed in all cases to elicit this website in first 10 pages (100 results). In the present racist Zionist context, one notes that Apartheid Israel has up to 400 nuclear warheads as compared to the US (7,315), Russia (8,000), France (300), UK (250), China (250), Pakistan (120), India (100), North Korea (possibly 60), and Iran (zero). The vastly disproportionate Jewish Zionist influence in the US and Western US Alliance countries commenced in a big way in the late 1960s after Apartheid Israel became a nuclear terrorist country [25].

"Stop state terrorism" website.

Non-state terrorism and state terrorism are both evil. Both state terrorism and non-state terrorism are utterly abhorrent to decent, pro-peace people. Connections between the twin evils of state crime, (or state terrorism), and non-state terrorism are documented in this website "Stop state terrorism" [26] and in the similarly alphabetically-organized compendium website "State crime and non-state terrorism" [27]. While the evil of non-state terrorism has been largely successfully countered in

Western countries by top-down state action involving education, high technology intelligence, intra-national and international intelligence sharing, and skilled counter-terrorism forces, countering the vastly more deadly evil of state terrorism requires peaceful, bottom-up action by billions of ordinary people world-wide.

Bing Searches for (1) "stop state terrorism" and (2) "state terrorism" yielded (1) the website as #1 (page 1 of 306,000 results) and (2) #74 (page 8 of 326,000 results). In contrast, Google Searches for (1) "stop state terrorism" and (2) "state terrorism" yielded (1) #1 as the "Stop state terrorism" website (unsurprisingly #1 on page 1 of 8,500 results) and (2) zero results in the first 10 pages (100 results). In the 21st century Apartheid Israel arguably ranks 4th in the world after the US (#1), UK (#2) and France (#3) for deadly state terrorism but pro-Zionist Google ensures that people remain in the dark.

"Palestinian Genocide" website.

The "Palestinian Genocide" website [28] alphabetically lists expert, humane, anti-racist opinion about this ongoing atrocity. For anti-racist Jews and indeed all anti-racist humanitarians the core moral messages from the Jewish Holocaust (5-6 million dead, 1 in 6 dying from deprivation) and from the more general WW2 European Holocaust (30 million Slav, Jewish and Gypsy dead) are "zero tolerance for racism", "bear witness", "zero tolerance for lying" and "never again to anyone", anyone including the Indigenous Palestinian victims of the racist Zionist Palestinian Genocide – 2 million Palestinians killed since the British invasion of Palestine, 0.1 million from violence, 1.9 million from war-, expulsion- and occupation-derived deprivation; 7 million Palestinian refugees; ethnic cleansing of Indigenous Palestinians from 90% of Palestine; 5 million Occupied Palestinians deprived of all the human rights listed by the Universal Declaration of Human Rights; over 7 million Palestinians forbidden to even live in the homeland continuously inhabited by their forbears to the very dawn of agrarian civilization; 5.0 million Palestinians (including 2.5 million children) confined without charge or trial to what the Catholic Church and many others have described as Israel's

Gaza Concentration Camp (2 million) or to West Bank ghettoes (3 million) for the asserted "crime" of being Indigenous Palestinians living in a tiny, remorselessly Zionist devastated residuum of Palestine. It must be noted that Article 2 of the UN Genocide Convention defines genocide thus: "In the present Convention, genocide means any of the following acts committed with intent to destroy, in whole or in part, a national, ethnic, racial or religious group, as such: a) Killing members of the group; b) Causing serious bodily or mental harm to members of the group; c) Deliberately inflicting on the group conditions of life calculated to bring about its physical destruction in whole or in part; d) Imposing measures intended to prevent births within the group; e) Forcibly transferring children of the group to another group" [29].

A Bing Search for "Palestinian Genocide" finds this website as #1 (page 1 of 36,900 results) whereas a Google Search for "Palestinian Genocide" finds this website as #20 (page 2 of 23,300 results). Bing or Google Searches for the terms "Palestinian" or "genocide" failed to elicit the website in the first 10 pages of results. Noting that 92% of search traffic comes from page 1 [17], Google greatly diminishes access to the "Palestinian Genocide" website.

"Apartheid Israeli state terrorism" website.

The "Apartheid Israeli state terrorism" website [30] is alphabetically-organized and records (A) leaders, scholars and informed activists exposing Apartheid Israeli state terrorism, and (B) countries subject to Apartheid Israeli state terrorism. All those who are party to non-state terrorism, state terrorism (e.g. US state terrorism, UK state terrorism, French state terrorism, Apartheid Israeli state terrorism and Australian state terrorism), war crimes, crimes against humanity and genocide should be exposed, prosecuted and punished, whether by the International Criminal Court, by national legal systems or by non-government tribunals of eminent scholars and jurists (any punishment in the latter case merely being the ignominy of public exposure).

Bing Searches for (1) "Apartheid Israeli state terrorism", (2) "Israeli state terrorism" and "state terrorism" yielded, respectively, (1) unsurprisingly #1 on page 1 of 149,000 results for the website, (2) zero result in the first 10 pages (100 results) of 2.58 million results, although it does come up with a copy of the website in question as #15 (page 2), and (3) zero results in the first 10 pages (100 results) of 669,000 results. Google Searches for (1) "Apartheid Israeli state terrorism", (2) "Israeli state terrorism" and "state terrorism" yielded, respectively, (1) unsurprisingly #1 on page 1 of 524 results for the website, (2) zero result in the first 10 pages (100 results) of 12,800 results, although a copy of the website comes up as #21 (page 3 of 55,500 results) and (3) zero results in the first 10 pages (100 results) of 669,000 results. Not much difference between Bing and Google in this instance.

"Gaza Concentration Camp" website.

The "Gaza Concentration Camp" website [31] exists to document the opinions of expert observers who correctly apply the descriptive "Gaza Concentration Camp" and like descriptives to the Gaza Strip that contains 2 million Indigenous Palestinians (50% of them children, three quarters women and children) and is surrounded and cruelly blockaded by war criminal, anti-Arab anti-Semitic, anti-Jewish anti-Semitic, Islamophobic and grossly human rights–abusing Apartheid Israel and by similarly war criminal, anti-Arab anti-Semitic, Islamophobic and grossly human rights–abusing military dictatorship Egypt. A Bing Search and a Google Search for the term "Gaza Concentration Camp" respectively yield #4 (page 1 of 2.72 million results) and #4 (page 1 of 16,900 results). No difference between Bing and Google in this instance.

Concluding comments

The present analysis reveals a huge difference in outcomes between Bing Searches and Google Searches for key terms relating to racist Zionism, Apartheid Israel and the ongoing Palestinian Genocide. Of 9 websites considered, searches for the actual website name in inverted commas detects the website in all cases of Bing Searches but only in 8 out of 9 Google Searches – a Google Search for "Jews against racist Zionism" is not successful in picking up this particular Google Site [18] (although the Google Robot picks up an overlapping website of the same name).

Bing Searches using key phrases were much more successful than corresponding Google Searches in most cases in detecting the websites sought. While there was little difference between Google and Bing in detecting the "Apartheid Israeli state terrorism" website and the "Gaza Concentration Camp" website by searching for the title, in other cases the Google Search was variously inferior to a Bing Search. Thus in an intermediate example, a Bing Search for "Palestinian Genocide" finds this website as #1 on page 1 of 36,900 results whereas a Google Search for "Palestinian Genocide" finds this website as #20 on page 2 of 23,300 results. However 92% of search traffic comes from page 1 [17], and thus Google greatly diminishes access to the "Palestinian Genocide" website.

People just do not like being lied to and Trump's assertions of "fake news" have found fertile ground in America. However the reality is far, far worse than what has been asserted by the Mainstream media or by Donald Trump. Mainstream media lying occurs in 2 basic forms, lying by omission and lying by commission. Lying by omission is far, far worse than lying by commission because the latter can at least admit refutation and public debate. Western Mainstream media impose a huge burden of fake news on Western societies through entrenched and pervasive lying by omission [32-36]. Such lying by omission includes Search Engines operating under algorithms ensuring that a progressive website does not appear on page 1 of the Search results, this resulting in at least a circa 10-fold diminution in visibility [18].

It is argued that in the looming Age of Artificial Intelligence (AI), data represent the "new oil of the digital economy" [37]. The data of the world are increasingly in the hands of giant corporations such as Google and Facebook and this concentration of data and the anti-social abuses of evident corporate censorship by Google [2-12] and Facebook (e.g. see Professor Rima Najjar's cogently argued complaint [38]) make a compelling case for the break-up of such mega-corporations, democratization of information, rejection of censorship, and progression to more effective free speech for information-rich but resources-poor, visibility-poor and power-poor scientists and science-informed humanitarians.

With half the world's wealth in the hands of One Percenters who also own the Mainstream media, there is little prospect of immediate change to the insidious and dangerous current culture of fake news through lying by omission. Lying subverts science-based rational risk management that is crucial for societal and global safety and security [39]. However people rich or poor don't like being deceived, and informed by data such as that provided here, informed people can circumvent pro-Zionist Google censorship by Binging instead of Googling – Bing it!

Originally published as "Do Bing Searches To Circumvent Mendacious Pro-Zionist Google Censorship – Bing It!" Countercurrents, April 2018.

References

[1]. Lara O'Reilly, "The 30 biggest media companies in the world", Business Insider, 31 May 2016: http://www.businessinsider.com/the-30-biggest-media-owners-in-the-world-2016-5/?r=AU&IR=T.

[2]. Gideon Polya, "Zionist subversion, Mainstream media censorship", Countercurrents, 9 March 2018: https://countercurrents.org/2018/03/09/zionist-subversion-mainstream-media-censorship-disproportionate-jewish-board-membership-of-us-media-companies/.

[3]. "Who controls America? Who controls Google?", The Zog: https://thezog.wordpress.com/who-controls-google/.

[4]. Andre Damon, "Google admits collaboration with illegal US drone murder program", Countercurrents, 8 March 2018: https://countercurrents.org/2018/03/08/google-admits-collaboration-with-illegal-us-drone-murder-program/?utm_source=feedburner&utm_medium=feed&utm_campaign=Feed%3A+countercurrents%2FeoKx+%28Countercurrents%29.

[5]. WSWS, "Google's new search protocol is restricting access to 13 leading socialist, progressive and anti-war sites", WSWS, 2 August 2017: http://www.wsws.org/en/articles/2017/08/02/pers-a02.html.

[6]. Chris Hedges, "Building the iron wall", Truthdig,18 March 2018: https://www.truthdig.com/articles/building-the-iron-wall/.

[7]. Gideon Polya, "Google censorship & Zionist constraint on effective free speech threaten planet", Countercurrents, 9 August 2017: https://countercurrents.org/2017/08/09/google-censorship-zionist-constraint-on-effective-free-speech-threaten-planet/.

[8]. "Censorship by Google", Wikipedia: https://en.wikipedia.org/wiki/Censorship_by_Google.

[9].Graham Vanbergen, "The Truth War is being lost to a global censorship apparatus called Google", Global Research, 4 August 2017: http://www.globalresearch.ca/the-truth-war-is-being-lost-to-a-global-censorship-apparatus-called-google/5602578.

[10]. Mick Meaney, "Google's Censorship Of Independent News – Rinf Becomes Latest Victim", RINF, 6 April 2017: http://rinf.com/alt-news/editorials/goolges-censorship-independent-news-begun/.

[11]. Eric Zuesse, "Google now threatening Alt-news websites", Off-Guardian, 21 April 2017: https://off-guardian.org/2017/04/21/google-now-threatening-alt-news-sites/.

[12]. Robert Epstein, "The New Censorship. How did Google become the internet's censor and master manipulator, blocking access to millions of websites?", US News & World Report, 22 June 2016: https://www.usnews.com/opinion/articles/2016-06-22/google-is-the-worlds-biggest-censor-and-its-power-must-be-regulated.

[13]. "Study: Bush, aides made 935 false statements in run-up to war", CNN, 24 January 2008: http://edition.cnn.com/2008/POLITICS/01/23/bush.iraq/.

[14]. "Iraqi Holocaust, Iraqi Genocide": https://sites.google.com/site/iraqiholocaustiraqigenocide/.

[15]. Martin Gilbert "Atlas of the Holocaust", Michael Joseph, London, 1982.

[16]. "Experts: US did 9-11" : https://sites.google.com/site/expertsusdid911/.

[17]. Steve Toth, "Help! I'm stuck on page 2 of Google Search results", TechWyse, 19 October 2015: https://www.techwyse.com/blog/search-engine-optimization/stuck-on-page-2-of-google/.

[18]. "Jews against racist Zionism": https://sites.google.com/site/jewsagainstracistzionism/.

[19]. "Non-Jews against racist Zionism": https://sites.google.com/site/nonjewsagainstracistzionism/.

[20]. "Boycott Apartheid Israel": https://sites.google.com/site/boycottapartheidisrael/.

[21]. Gideon Polya, "Apartheid Israel's Palestinian Genocide & Australia's Aboriginal Genocide compared", Countercurrents, 20 February 2018: https://countercurrents.org/2018/02/20/apartheid-israels-palestinian-genocide-australias-aboriginal-genocide-compared/.

[22]. Gideon Polya, "Israeli-Palestinian & Middle East conflict – from oil to climate genocide", Countercurrents, 21 August 2017: https://countercurrents.org/2017/08/21/israeli-palestinian-middle-east-conflict-from-oil-to-climate-genocide/.

[23]. Gideon Polya, "End 50 Years Of Genocidal Occupation & Human Rights Abuse By US-Backed Apartheid Israel", Countercurrents, 9 June 2017: https://countercurrents.org/2017/06/09/end-50-years-of-genocidal-occupation-human-rights-abuse-by-us-backed-apartheid-israel/.

[24]. Gideon Polya, "Universal Declaration of Human Rights & Palestinians. Apartheid Israel violates ALL Palestinian Human Rights", Palestine Genocide Essays, 24 January 2009: https://sites.google.com/site/palestinegenocideessays/universal-declaration-of-human-rights-palestinians.

[25]. "Nuclear weapons ban, end poverty & reverse climate change": https://sites.google.com/site/300orgsite/nuclear-weapons-ban.

[26]. "Stop state terrorism" : https://sites.google.com/site/stopstateterrorism/.

[27]. "State crime and non-state terrorism": https://sites.google.com/site/statecrimeandnonstateterrorism/.

[28]. "Palestinian Genocide": https://sites.google.com/site/palestiniangenocide/.

[29]. Article 2 of the UN Genocide Convention: http://www.edwebproject.org/sideshow/genocide/convention.html.

[30]. "Apartheid Israeli state terrorism": https://sites.google.com/site/palestiniangenocide/apartheid-israeli-state-terrorism.

[31]. "Gaza Concentration Camp": https://sites.google.com/site/palestiniangenocide/gaza-concentration.

[32]. Gideon Polya, "Mainstream media fake news through lying by omission", Global Research, 1 April 2017: http://www.globalresearch.ca/mainstream-media-fake-news-through-lying-by-omission/5582944.

[33]. Gideon Polya, "Australian ABC and UK BBC fake news through lying

by omission", Countercurrents, 2 May 2017:
https://countercurrents.org/2017/05/02/australian-abc-and-uk-bbc-fake-news-through-lying-by-omission/.

[34]. "Lying by omission is worse than lying by commission because at least the latter permits refutation and public debate", Mainstream media lying: https://sites.google.com/site/mainstreammedialying/lying-by-omission.

[35]. "Mainstream media censorship";
https://sites.google.com/site/mainstreammediacensorship/home.

[36]. "Mainstream media lying":
https://sites.google.com/site/mainstreammedialying/.

[37]. Joris Toonders, "Data is the new oil of the digital economy", Wired, 2014: https://www.wired.com/insights/2014/07/data-new-oil-digital-economy/.

[38]. Rima Najjar, "Hillel and Facebook censorship: conflating Zionism with Judaism", Countercurrents, 26 February 2018:
https://countercurrents.org/2018/02/26/hillel-facebook-censorship-conflating-zionism-judaism/.

[39]. "Gideon Polya": https://sites.google.com/site/drgideonpolya/home.

70th Anniversary of Apartheid Israel: History of Violent Invasion. Chronology of Palestinian Genocide

Gideon Polya

14 May 2018 marks the 70th anniversary of the Israeli Declaration of Independence by Zionist terrorist David Ben Gurion, the foundation of an invasion-, violence-, racism-, genocide- and theft-based Apartheid Israel, and commencement of the large-scale, Rohingya Genocide-scale ethnic cleansing of Indigenous Palestinians from Palestine. US Alliance backers of Apartheid Israel will mark the occasion with lying praise for this evil rogue state, but decent Humanity will tell the truth and demand "Free Palestine", an end to Israeli Apartheid, return of all refugees and a democratic, multi-ethnic Unitary State in Palestine.

To mark this occasion, I have set out below (A) the chronology of the violent invasion and ethnic cleansing of Palestine, (B) a summary of the appalling conditions of the Indigenous Palestinians, (C) the impact of Apartheid Israel on the world, and (D) a humane outcome for a democratic post-Apartheid Palestine.

(A). Chronology of the violent invasion and ethnic cleansing of Palestine.

In 1880 there were about 500,000 Arab Palestinians and about 25,000 Jews (half of the latter being immigrants) living in

Palestine. Genocidally racist Zionists have been responsible for a Palestinian Genocide involving successive mass expulsions (800,000 in 1948 and 400,00 in 1967), ethnic cleansing of 90% of the land of Palestine, and in the century since the British invasion of Palestine about 2.3 million Palestinian deaths from violence (0.1 million) or from violently-imposed deprivation (2.2 million). Presently there are now 8 million Palestinian refugees, and of 14 million Palestinians about 50% (7 million) are forbidden to even step foot in their own country on pain of death, only 1.8 million Palestinian Israelis (13%) are permitted to vote for the government ruling all of the former Mandated Palestine, and 5.0 million Palestinians have zero human rights as Occupied Palestinians in West Bank Bantustans (3.0 million) or in the Gaza Concentration Camp (2.0 million) [1-6].

True Orthodox Judaism is opposed to Zionism (a) because Zionism is genocidal racism, and (b) because the traditional Orthodox Jewish position for 2,000 years was that Jews can only return to Zion (Jerusalem) when the Messiah arrives to reveal the glory of the Lord to the whole world. Orthodox Judaism fostered the beautiful idea of a Kingdom of the Mind that has transmuted in the secular world into the wonderful international communities of scientists, scholars, musicians, artists and writers. However in response to Russian pogroms and discrimination against both religious and secular Jews, Zionist activists (many being secular socialists) argued for a Jewish State. Nathan Birnbaum, who coined the term Zionism, later rejected the evil Zionist ideology and reverted to the humanity of Orthodox Judaism. Racist Zionism substantially originated with racist psychopath Theodor Herzl, a Jewish Hungarian writer and activist. In his book "Der Judenstaat" ("The Jewish State") Herzl declares (1896): "Shall we choose Palestine or Argentine? We shall take what is given us… For Europe we shall constitute there [in Palestine] a sector of the wall against Asia, we shall serve as the vanguard of culture against barbarism" [7-9]. Over 20 other territories have been proposed for a Jewish colony, including Australia (in a scheme by the anti-Zionist Jewish Freeland League that was finally vetoed in 1944 by the war-time Curtin Labor Government) but the racist Zionists and successive racist British Governments decided to colonize and thence ethnically cleanse Palestine. Indeed genocidally racist psychopath Theodor Herzl notoriously stated (1895): "We shall try to spirit the penniless [Palestinian] population across the border by procuring employment for it in the transit countries, while denying it employment in our country. The property owners will come over to our side. Both the process of expropriation and the removal of the poor must be carried out discretely and circumspectly" [8, 9].

The British Sinai and Palestine Campaign of WW1 began with repulse of a Turkish advance in the Sinai from Palestine in 1915.

The British and French divided up the formerly Ottoman Empire-ruled Middle East via the Sykes-Picot Agreement of 1916 [6]. British, Australian and New Zealand soldiers were critically involved in the conquest of Palestine and Syria in WW1 [10] that led to a famine in which 100,000 Palestinians died, this marking the beginning of the Palestinian Genocide that would involve 2.3 million premature Palestinian deaths from violence or deprivation over the next century [1, 11, 12].

2 days after the Australian and New Zealand Army Corps (ANZAC) victory at Beersheba (31 October 1917), on 2 November 1917 racist British warmonger and UK Foreign Secretary, Lord Balfour, offered Palestine as a Jewish Homeland to the Zionists in a letter to the degenerate Zionist Lord Rothschild that included the caveat (subsequently grossly violated by the genocidally racist Zionists) that there should be no detriment to the Indigenous inhabitants or indeed to Jewish people around the world: "His Majesty's government view with favour the establishment in Palestine of a national home for the Jewish people, and will use their best endeavours to facilitate the achievement of this object, it being clearly understood that nothing shall be done which may prejudice the civil and religious rights of existing non-Jewish communities in Palestine, or the rights and political status enjoyed by Jews in any other country" [13-16]. According to genocide-ignoring, holocaust-ignoring and racist Zionist historian, the late Professor Sir Martin Gilbert, the Balfour Declaration was issued

in an ultimately unsuccessful attempt to get traitorous Russian Zionists to keep Russia in WW1 [17, 18]. There were 20 schemes for Jewish colonies around the world, including in Australia [19-21].

Australian and New Zealand Army Corps (ANZAC) soldiers were responsible for the Surafend Massacre on 10 December 1918 in which about 100 Palestinian villagers were killed in retaliation for the death of a New Zealand soldier [23-24].

1918-1939. Between WW1 and WW2 there was massive, British-permitted Jewish immigration to Palestine resulting in massive and deadly displacement of Palestinian workers and tenant farmers from agricultural land. Resultant Palestinian opposition led to armed conflict between Indigenous Palestinians and increasingly violent and racist Zionist invaders. In 1939 the British Government, concerned to maintain the loyalty of its scores of millions of Muslim subjects in the coming war, issued a White Paper constraining further Jewish entry to Palestine. Indeed the first WW2 casualties in the British Empire were Jewish illegal immigrants shot while attempting to land in Palestine [6].

The 1939 British White Paper stopped Jewish immigration to Palestine in a move designed to increase global Muslim support for Britain in the looming war with Nazi Germany.

1939-1945. Zionist terrorist groups, notably Irgun, collaborated with the Nazis, and killed Allied servicemen before, during and after WW2 [25-29]. The neo-Nazi Zionist terrorist organization Irgun was heavily involved in the ethnic cleansing of Palestine and spawned the current rightwing Israeli leadership, but was removed from the pro-Zionist Australian Government's list of terrorist organizations in the 21st century. Zionists opposed sanctuary in non-Palestine venues for Jews fleeing Nazi Europe and hence contributed to the WW2 Jewish Holocaust (5-6 million Jews killed) that was part of a much wider but Zionist-ignored WW2 Holocaust (30 million Slaves, Jews and Gypsies killed by the Nazis) [6].

Some Jews recognized the great wrong being done to the Indigenous Palestinians. Thus the anti-Zionist Freeland League under Dr. Isaac Steinberg proposed to make the Kimberley region of North West Australia a region of exclusive Jewish settlement. This proposal won widespread political support in White Australia (Indigenous Australians were not even counted as Australians until after a 1967 Referendum) but was eventually vetoed by PM John Curtin in 1944 on Intelligence advice that quite possibly related to the 1944 British War Cabinet decision to Partition Palestine [19-21]. The "forgotten" Joel Brand scheme to "buy" 800,000 Jewish Hungarians from the Nazis and transport them to Turkey was vetoed by Zionist mass murderer Churchill and 400,000 Jewish Hungarians subsequently perished [25-27] (also "forgotten" has been Churchill's responsibility for the 1942-1945 Bengali Holocaust in which the British with Australian complicity deliberately starved 6-7 million Indians to death for strategic reasons) [30-33].

Sir Isaac Isaacs, a staunch anti-Zionist and Australia's most famous Jewish citizen as the first Australian-born Australian Governor-General, stated in 1946: "The honour of Jews throughout the world demands the renunciation of political Zionism" and "the Zionist movement as a whole…now places its own unwarranted interpretation on the Balfour Declaration, and makes demands that are arousing the antagonism of the Moslem world of nearly 400 millions, thereby menacing the safety of our Empire, endangering world peace and imperilling some of the most sacred associations of the Jewish, Christian, and Moslem faiths. Besides their inherent injustice to others these demands would, I believe, seriously and detrimentally affect the general position of Jews throughout the world" [25, 34].

1945-1947. After WW2 a greatly weakened Britain faced the reality of being unable to hold on to its vast Empire. Racist Britain had already decided on a Partition of India (perhaps for anti-Soviet strategic reasons) and enabled India to be partitioned on Independence in 1947 in a catastrophic process that generated 20 million refugees and killed 1 million people.

Similarly, in 1944 the British had decided on withdrawal from Palestine and the Partition of Palestine. In 1947 the UN approved a Partition Plan. In 1948 the last British left the day after genocidal racist Ben Gurion declared Israeli independence, and the UN recognized the State of Israel [6].

Well-armed Israeli forces committed atrocities against Palestinians (e.g. the horrendous Deir Yassin massacre that distressed anti-racist Jews like Albert Einstein [25, 35]) that encouraged 800,000 Palestinians to flee cities, towns and hundreds of villages in the 1948 Nakba (Disaster). The incipient Apartheid Israel seized a substantially ethnically cleansed 78% of the former British Mandated Palestine after defeating Arab forces from UK- or France-dominated neighbouring countries. The Convention for the Prevention and Punishment of the Crime of Genocide was adopted by the United Nations General Assembly on 9 December 1948. Article 2 of the UN Genocide Convention defined genocide as "defines "genocide" thus: "In the present Convention, genocide means any of the following acts committed with intent to destroy, in whole or in part, a national, ethnic, racial or religious group, as such: a) Killing members of the group; b) Causing serious bodily or mental harm to members of the group; c) Deliberately inflicting on the group conditions of life calculated to bring about its physical destruction in whole or in part; d) Imposing measures intended to prevent births within the group; e) Forcibly transferring children of the group to another group"[36]. Genocidal "intent" is established sustained ethnic cleansing action and more rarely by confession. However the genocidal Zionists established "intent" by a remorseless, 100 year and continuing Palestinian Genocide and numerous statements of genocidal intent from the Zionist leadership from Theodor Herzl to Benjamin Netanyahu [8, 9].

Israel waged an illegal war of aggression against Egypt in collusion with the UK and France who wanted to re-take the Suez Canal in a move opposed by the US. Many of the Egyptian soldiers were vitamin A deficient and were essentially blind "sitting ducks" at night [6].

In 1967 Israel, now armed with nuclear weapons (with US and French help) [37, 38], invaded all its neighbours in the Six Day War, conquered all of Palestine, the Sinai Peninsular of Egypt and the Golan Heights of Syria. A further 400,000 Indigenous Palestinians fled their homes, their communities and their country in the 1967 Naksa (Setback). The Israeli war machine did not confine itself to killing Arabs but also attacked an unarmed US spy ship, the USS Liberty, in international waters, killing 34 and wounding 171, a crime that the Zionist-subverted US responded to in the most craven and secretive fashion. A massive increase in Zionist power in the US dates from about this time, most likely connected with the new nuclear weapons status of a genocidal Apartheid Israel [38-41]. Apartheid Israel has justified its war criminal attacks in the Six-Day War with holocaust-threatened Israel David versus a genocidal Arab Goliath propaganda (hasbara) but a succession of top Israeli officials have confessed otherwise. Thus General Matituahu Peled, chief of logistical command during the war: "The thesis according to which the danger of genocide hung over us in June 1967, and according to which Israel was fighting for her very physical survival, was nothing but a bluff which was born and bred after the war". Mordechai Bentov, a member of the wartime government, stated in 1971: "This whole story about the threat of extermination was totally contrived, and then elaborated upon, a posteriori, to justify the annexation of new Arab territories." War criminal Israeli Prime Minister Menachem Begin, stated in 1982 that "In June 1967 we had a choice. The Egyptian army concentrations in the Sinai approaches did not prove that Nasser was really about to attack us. We must be honest with ourselves. We decided to attack him". According to the late Itzhak Yaakov, a retired Brigadier General responsible for the development of Israeli nuclear weapons, Apartheid Israel planned to detonate a nuclear bomb in the Egypt if the war it launched in June 1967 turned against it (in 2001 Yaakov was given a two-year suspended sentence in Israel for attempting to reveal this) [8, 9].

In the 1973 Yom Kippur War, Egypt unsuccessfully sought to recover the Israeli-occupied Sinai Peninsular but the Sinai was returned in a US-brokered 1979 peace agreement between a now US lackey Egypt and a nuclear-armed Apartheid Israel.

1982-2000. Between1982 and 2000 there was Israeli occupation of much of Lebanon. The war criminal Israeli invasion of Lebanon was associated with the Sabra and Shatila refugee camp massacres in which 3,000 unarmed Palestinians were murdered in Israeli-occupied Beirut by Christian Falangist forces.

The first Palestinian Intifada began in 1987 and was violently suppressed.

In 1988 the Palestinian Liberation Organization (PLO) under Yassir Arafat recognized Israel.

The Oslo 1993 Agreement permitted constrained Occupied Palestinian self-government. However the continued seizure of Arab lands led to a renewed Intifada in 2000.

In response to Israeli Occupation, ethnic cleansing and illegal settlements, the second Palestinian Intifada commenced in 2000 with disproportionate Israeli responses to Palestinian resistance. Israeli withdrew from Lebanon in 2000.

2000 – present. In the 21st century, US-backed Israeli Occupation, illegal Settlements and violence continued with limited violent responses from Palestinians yielding disproportionate responses from the Israelis. In 2005 Israel pulled out from the Gaza Strip leaving a densely populated Gaza Concentration Camp violently guarded by land, air and sea and subject to crippling blockade by the neo-Nazi Israelis. Rocket and mortar attacks from Gaza killed 34 Israelis in the period 2004-2017 [42] but the disproportionate Israeli responses involved high explosive bombardment from land, air and sea in repeated Gaza Massacres inflicted on one of the most densely populated urban areas in the world and with about 10,000 Palestinians being violently killed and tens of thousands wounded [43]. Israeli deaths from Palestinian violence or "terrorism deaths" in the period January 2000 – February 2017 totalled 1,347 as compared to 9,505 Palestinians killed by Israelis in this same period. If one considers total 21st century Israeli deaths from terrorism, the Palestinian/Israeli death ratio for this period is $9,505/1,347 = 7.1$. If one considers total 20th century plus 21st century violent deaths, the Palestinian/Israeli death ratio is about $110,000/3,847 = 29$. By way of comparison, blood-soaked German Nazi leader and war criminal Adolph Hitler recommended an enemy partisan/German military reprisal death ratio of 10 [43]. Nazi is as Nazi does.

In democratic elections held under Occupier Israeli guns, the Occupied Palestinians overwhelmingly supported Hamas which gained a majority of representatives. However the US-backed Israelis did not recognize the results and Hamas MPs were variously killed, imprisoned or exiled to the Gaza Concentration Camp. Apartheid Israel and Egypt commenced blockade of the Gaza Concentration Camp [44].

The Israeli-backed Fatah attempted a coup in Gaza that was suppressed by Hamas. Hamas officials were sacked in the West Bank [44].

2008-2009. In the 2008-2009 Gaza War (called Operation Cast Lead by the Israelis) about 1,400 Palestinians were killed and 5,300 were wounded. 13 Israelis were killed, this including 10 from friendly fire and 3 civilians [45].

In the 1-week Israeli Operation Pillar of Defense (220 Palestinians killed, half civilians, and 1,000 wounded, as compared to 2 Israeli soldiers killed and 20 wounded) [46]. In 2012 the UN formally recognized the State of Palestine with official observer status at the UN [47, 48].

In the 2014 Gaza Massacre (called Operation Protective Edge by the Israelis) 2,300 Palestinians were killed (including about 1,500 civilians) and 10,600 were wounded. 73 Israelis (66 of them soldiers) were killed [49].

The 2016 UN Security Council Resolution 2334 condemning illegal Israeli settlements and other Israeli war crimes in the

Occupied Palestinian Territories was passed unanimously (except for an Obama America abstention rather than veto). Trump America and US lackey Australia subsequently vehemently opposed the resolution, this making them #1 and #2, respectively, as supporters of Apartheid Israel and hence of Apartheid [50-52].

This year has been appallingly marked by the cold-blooded killing by Israeli soldiers of nearly 50 Palestinians and the wounding of about 6,800 more out of thousands of unarmed Occupied Palestinians protesting 70 years of exile and highly abusive confinement in the Gaza Concentration Camp. Comparisons with the 1960 Sharpeville Massacre in Apartheid South Africa (involving 69 unarmed demonstrators killed and 220 wounded) demand global Boycotts, Divestment and Sanctions (BDS) against Apartheid Israel and all its supporters that were successfully applied by the World against Apartheid South Africa [53-55].

 (B). Summary of the appalling conditions of the Indigenous Palestinians.

(1). The Palestinian Genocide commenced with the famine deaths of 100,000 Palestinians associated with conquest of Palestine in WW1 by the British and the Australian and New Zealand Army Corps (ANZAC) [1, 10].

(2). The violent killing of Indigenous Palestinians commenced with the 1918 Surafend Massacre by ANZAC soldiers in which about 100 Palestinian villagers were massacred [22-24].

(3). Since the British invasion of Palestine in WW1 there have been 2.3 million Palestinian deaths from Zionist violence (0.1 million) or from imposed deprivation (2.2 million) [1].

(4). There are 8 million Palestinian refugees and all of the 14 million Palestinians are excluded from all or part of Palestine [1].

(5). Of about 14 million Palestinians (half of them children, three quarters women and children), 7 million are forbidden to even step foot in their own country, 5 million are held hostage with zero human rights under Israeli guns in the Gaza Concentration Camp (2.0 million) or in ever-dwindling West Bank Bantustan ghettoes (3.0 million), and 1.8 million live as Third Class citizens as Israeli Palestinians under Nazi-style Apartheid Israeli race laws [1].

(6). 90% of Palestine has now been ethnically cleansed of Indigenous Palestinian inhabitants in an ongoing war criminal ethnic cleansing that has been repeatedly condemned by the UN and most recently by UN Security Council Resolution 2334 that was unanimously supported (with a remarkable Obama US abstention rather than a veto) [50-52].

(7). GDP per capita is US$2,800 for Occupied Palestinians as compared to US$39,000 for Apartheid Israel [56].

(8). Through imposed deprivation, each year Apartheid Israel passively murders about 2,700 under-5 year old Palestinian infants and passively murders 4,200 Occupied Palestinians in general who die avoidably under Israeli Apartheid each year. There is an approximately 10 year life expectancy gap between Occupied Palestinians and Israelis [1, 6], this grossly violating Articles 55 and 56 of the Geneva Convention Relative to the Protection of Civilian Persons in Time of War that demand that an Occupier must provide life-sustaining food and medical services to the Occupied "to the fullest extent of the means available to it" [57].

(9). Apartheid Israel violently kills an average of about 550 Occupied Palestinians each year [43].

(10). Occupied Palestinians are deprived of essentially all human rights and civil rights by Apartheid Israel (e.g. Apartheid Israeli home invasions, beatings, executions, killings, exilings, mass imprisonments, seizures of land and homes, and population transfer in violation of the UN Genocide Convention and the Geneva Convention) [5, 36, 57].

(11). Nuclear terrorist, serial war criminal, genocidally racist, democracy-by-genocide Apartheid Israel determines that 74% of its now 50% Indigenous Palestinian subjects who are Occupied Palestinians cannot vote for the government ruling them i.e. egregious Apartheid [1, 58]. The UN regards Apartheid as one of the worst of human rights violations [58, 59].

(12). In its genocidal treatment of the Palestinians, US-, UK-, Canada-, France- and Australia-backed Apartheid Israel ignores numerous UN General Assembly Resolutions and UN Security Council Resolutions, the UN Genocide Convention, the Geneva Convention, the Universal Declaration of Human Rights, the Rights of the Child Convention, the UN Declaration on the Rights of Indigenous Peoples, and many other aspects of International Law [36, 57, 59-64].

(13). Apartheid Israel has attacked 12 countries and occupied 5 with 1950-2005 avoidable deaths from deprivation in countries neighbouring and variously occupied by Apartheid Israel totalling 24 million [6].

(14). 5 million Occupied Palestinians (half of them children) are routinely blackmailed through torture or denial of life-saving medical care to spy on fellow Palestinians for Apartheid Israel [65].

(15). 5 million Occupied Palestinians (half of them children) are excluded by armed military check points from Jews-only areas and Jews-only roads.

(16). 50% of Israeli children are physically, psychologically or sexually abused each year [66-68] but 100% of Occupied Palestinian children are subject to traumatizing human rights abuse by the serial war criminal Israel Defence Force (IDF) through actual or threatened deadly violence [65].

(17). With continuing blockade and after repeated, large-scale destruction of homes, schools, hospitals and infrastructure, conditions in the Gaza Concentration Camp are appalling [69], with the UN stating that Gaza may become unliveable within several years [69, 70].

(18). In March-May 2018 the IDF killed about 50 Palestinians and wounded about 6,800 more out of thousands of unarmed Occupied Palestinians protesting 70 years of exile and highly abusive confinement in the Gaza Concentration Camp. By way of comparisons, in the 1960 Sharpeville Massacre in Apartheid South Africa some 5,000-7,000 unarmed African protestors held a demonstration against the racist pass laws outside the police station in Sharpeville, Transvaal, South Africa when the police opened fire, killing 69 demonstrators and causing a total of 289 casualties including 29 children [53-55].

(19). Apartheid Israel has been stealing water from West Bank aquifers but water allocations to Occupied Palestinians violate WHO standards for potable water [73].

(20). US-backed Apartheid Israel has attacked 12 countries including all its immediate neighbours [6], has up to 400 nuclear weapons and possess missile delivery systems including those based on Germany-supplied submarines [37]. This dangerous, war-exacerbating conduct acutely threatens all 13.9 million Israeli subjects, these comprising 6.6 million Jewish, 6.9 million Indigenous Palestinian and 0.4 million non-Jewish and non-Arab subjects.

(C). Impact of Apartheid Israel on the world.

(1). Presently there are 16 million avoidable deaths from deprivation and deprivation-exacerbated disease each year globally and there have been 1,500 million such deaths since 1950 (this including 600 million Muslims) [6], this carnage being significantly linked to continuing Zionist perversion of US aid and foreign policy [6].

(2). There have been 32 million Muslim deaths from violence, 5 million, or from deprivation, 27 million, in 20 countries invaded by the pro-Zionist US Alliance in the US War on Terror (US

War on Muslims) since the US Government's 9-11 false flag atrocity in which Apartheid Israel is very likely to have been complicit [72, 73].

(3). There have been millions of refugees generated and millions of Indigenous deaths from violence or imposed deprivation in countries subject to Apartheid Israeli-backed, genocidal civil wars, notably Guatemala, Myanmar, Sri Lanka, Syria, Sudan and South Sudan [74].

(4). There have been 28 million American preventable deaths since 9-11 (1.7 million annually) that are inescapably linked to Zionist-beholden US Governments committing to a $40 trillion long-term accrual cost of supporting Apartheid Israel, this including a $7 trillion long-term accrual cost for the killing of millions of Muslims abroad in the Zionist-promoted War on Terror instead of keeping millions of Americans alive at home. Australia has similarly committed to $11 billion per year long-term to the War on Terror ($176 billion since 9-11) with this fiscal perversion linked to 1.4 million preventable Australian deaths since 9-11 (85,000 annually). Canada has similarly committed hugely to the War on Terror with this inescapably linked to 0.1 million Canadian preventable deaths annually or 1.7 million preventable deaths in Canada since 9-11. The UK has similarly committed hugely to the War on Terror with this linked in terms of fiscal deprivation to 0.15 million UK preventable deaths annually or 2.5 million preventable deaths in the UK since the 9-11 atrocity that killed 3,000 people [75-81].

(5). Zionists are notoriously involved in perversion of Western democracies, governments, media and other institutions, most notably in pro-Apartheid US and pro-Apartheid Australia that are the 2 strongest supporters of Apartheid Israel and hence of the obscene ideology of Apartheid. Thus in September 2015 the US, Australia, Canada, Apartheid Israel and 4 US lackey Pacific Island States voted "No" to a UN General Assembly motion to permit the flying of the State of Palestine flag at the UN while 119 other nations decently voted "Yes". Trump America and US lackey Trumpist Australia fervently oppose UN Security Council Resolution 2334 that condemned genocidal Israeli war crimes [50-52]. Racist Zionism is a huge threat to Australia in 50 areas but the threat is publicly ignored by the US lackey, pro-Apartheid, Zionist-beholden major parties (the Liberal Party and National Party Coalition Government and the Labor Party Opposition) even after Australian PM Kevin Rudd was removed in a US approved, mining company-backed, and pro-Zionist-led coup [82-87]. Israeli war criminal Ariel Sharon (the "butcher of Beirut") notoriously stated: "Don't worry about American pressure on Israel. We, the Jewish people, control America, and the Americans know it" [8, 9, 38].

(6). The world is existentially threatened by (a) nuclear weapons, (b) poverty and (c) climate change but (a) Apartheid Israel reportedly has up to 400 nuclear warheads and indeed proposed to use them against Egypt in 1967 [37], (b) 16 million people die avoidably each year in the Developing World minus China [6], this being linked to Zionist-backed US wars, notably the US War on Muslims, and the horrendous perversion of the US aid budget for arms, notably for Apartheid Israel; and (c) an entrenched Western culture of lying, emplaced by a dominant, homicidally greedy, neoliberal, Neocon American and Zionist Imperialist (NAZI) One Percenter Establishment, has now made a catastrophic global plus 2C temperature rise unavoidable – it is predicted that 10 billion people will die this century in a near-terminal Climate Genocide if climate change from remorselessly increasing GHG pollution is not requisitely addressed [88].

(7). The racist Zionists have a deadly record of mendacity. Indeed e-LIARS is an appropriate anagram for ISRAEL. There is massive Zionist presence on the boards of the top American media companies that represent 2/3 of the top 30 global Mainstream media corporations. While numerous anti-racist Jewish intellectuals are resolutely critical of Apartheid Israel and the ongoing Palestinian Genocide [25], Western Mainstream Media variously censor or white-wash the nuclear terrorist, genocidally racist, and grossly human rights-abusing conduct of Apartheid Israel. A part explanation for this massive lying is that the American 60% of the world's 30 biggest media companies have a disproportionately high Jewish Board membership. Jews and females represent 2% and 51%, respectively, of the US population but average 33% and 19%, respectively, of Board members of the top 18 US media companies [89]. Zionist-perverted Mainstream media fake news through lying by omission and lying by commission [89-97] threaten rational risk management that is crucial for societal safety and successively involves (a) accurate data, (b) scientific analysis, and (c) informed systemic change to minimize risk. However mendacity and spin pervert this science-based protocol to a lying- and spin-based protocol successively involving (a) lying, censorship, self-censorship, intimidation, (b) anti-science spin-based analysis, and (c) counterproductive blame and shame that cripples mandatory reportage and can ultimately lead to irrational acts, violence and war [98].

(8). Racist Zionism is deadly anti-Arab anti-Semitism through the ongoing Palestinian Genocide and the ongoing Muslim Genocide and Muslim Holocaust. However racist Zionism is also anti-Jewish anti-Semitic through (a) falsely conflating the activities of genocidally racist Apartheid Israel with all Jews, and (b) by endlessly and falsely defaming the large body of anti-racist Jews who, together with numerous anti-racist non-Jews, are utterly opposed to the human rights abuses and genocidal crimes of Apartheid Israel [99, 100] and resolutely speak out about these crimes against Humanity [1, 25, 37, 101-106].

(9). Zionism, Israeli Apartheid and the ongoing Palestinian Genocide are an awful blot on Jewry, Judaism and Humanity, and as such contribute to repugnant anti-Jewish anti-Semitism, this leading to the crie de coeur of anti-racist Jews: "Not in our name".

(10). For anti-racist Jews and indeed all anti-racist humanitarians the core moral messages from the WW2 Jewish Holocaust (5-6 million dead, 1 in 6 dying from deprivation) and from the more general WW2 European Holocaust (30 million Slav, Jewish and Gypsy dead) are "zero tolerance for racism", "never again to anyone", "bear witness" and "zero tolerance for lying". However these sacred injunctions are grossly violated by the anti-Arab anti-Semitic, Islamophobic and indeed anti-Jewish anti-Semitic racist Zionists running Apartheid Israel and their Western backers.

(D). A humane outcome of a democratic post-Apartheid Palestine.

The Humanity-threatening awfulness outlined above has been utterly avoidable. The 2-State Solution for Palestine has been a Western excuse for inaction and is now dead because of the ethnic cleansing of 90% of the land of Palestine. However, a peaceful, humane solution informed by the post-Apartheid South African experience is for a Unitary State in Palestine with return of all refugees, zero tolerance for racism, equal rights for all, all human rights for all, one-person-one-vote, justice, goodwill, reconciliation, airport-level security, nuclear weapons removal, internationally-guaranteed national security initially based on the present armed forces, and untrammelled access for all citizens to all of the Holy Land. It can and should happen tomorrow. In the face of continuing Occupation, continuing Exile, continuing Apartheid and ongoing Palestinian Genocide, the world must act against Apartheid Israel with Boycotts and Sanctions as it successfully did to Apartheid South Africa. Peace is the only way but silence kills and silence is complicity. All decent Humanity must (a) inform everyone they can, and (b) urge and apply Boycotts, Divestment and Sanctions (BDS) against Apartheid Israel and all people, politicians, parties, collectives, corporations and countries supporting this genocidally racist, nuclear terrorist rogue state.

Originally published as "70th Anniversary of Apartheid Israel: History of Violent Invasion. Chronology of Palestinian Genocide," Countercurrents, May 2018.

References

[1]. "Palestinian Genocide":
https://sites.google.com/site/palestiniangenocide/.
[2]. Gideon Polya, "Apartheid Israel's Palestinian Genocide & Australia's
Aboriginal Genocide compared", Countercurrents, 20 February 2018:
https://countercurrents.org/2018/02/20/apartheid-israels-palestinian-
genocide-australias-aboriginal-genocide-compared/.
[3]. Gideon Polya, "Israeli-Palestinian & Middle East conflict – from oil to
climate genocide", Countercurrents, 21 August 2017:
https://countercurrents.org/2017/08/21/israeli-palestinian-middle-east-
conflict-from-oil-to-climate-genocide/.
[4]. Gideon Polya, "End 50 Years Of Genocidal Occupation & Human
Rights Abuse By US-Backed Apartheid Israel", Countercurrents, 9 June
2017: https://countercurrents.org/2017/06/09/end-50-years-of-genocidal-
occupation-human-rights-abuse-by-us-backed-apartheid-israel/.
[5]. Gideon Polya, "Universal Declaration of Human Rights & Palestinians.
Apartheid Israel violates ALL Palestinian Human Rights", Palestine
Genocide Essays, 24 January 2009:
https://sites.google.com/site/palestinegenocideessays/universal-declaration-
of-human-rights-palestinians.
[6]. Gideon Polya, "Body Count. Global avoidable mortality since 1950",
that includes a succinct history of every country and is now available for free
perusal on the web: http://globalbodycount.blogspot.com/.
[7]. Theodor Herzl, "Der Judenstaat" ("The Jewish State"), 1896.
[8]. Gideon Polya, "Zionist quotes reveal genocidal racism", MWC News, 12
January 2018: http://mwcnews.net/focus/analysis/69955-zionist-quotes-
reveal-genocidal-racism.html.
[9]. Gideon Polya, "Zionist quotes re racism and Palestinian Genocide",
Palestinian Genocide:
https://sites.google.com/site/palestiniangenocide/zionist-quotes.
[10]. "Battle of Beersheba (1917) ", Wikipedia:
https://en.wikipedia.org/wiki/Battle_of_Beersheba_(1917).
[11]. Justin McCarty, "Palestine population: during the Ottoman and British
mandate period", Palestine Remembered: 8 September 2001:
http://www.palestineremembered.com/Acre/Palestine-
Remembered/Story559.html.
[12]. "Historic population of Israel/Palestine":
http://palestineisraelpopulation.blogspot.com.au/.
[13]. "Balfour Declaration", Wikipedia:
https://en.wikipedia.org/wiki/Balfour_Declaration.
[14]. Arthur Balfour, Wikipedia:
http://en.wikipedia.org/wiki/Arthur_Balfour.
[15]. William Gerhardie, "God's Fifth Column. A biography of the Age
1890-1940" (Hodder & Stoughton, 1981; The Hogarth Press, 1990, with
editing and an Introduction by Michael Holroyd and Robert Skidelsky).

[16]. Gideon Polya, "Book Review: "God's Fifth Column" By William Gerhardie", Countercurrents, 6 May, 2014:
https://countercurrents.org/polya060514.htm.

[17]. Gideon Polya, "UK Zionist Historian Sir Martin Gilbert (1936-2015) Variously Ignored Or Minimized WW2 Bengali Holocaust", Countercurrents, 19 February, 2015:
https://countercurrents.org/polya190215.htm.

[18]. Martin Gilbert (1994), "The First World War", Holt, London, 1994.

[19]. Martin Gilbert, "Jewish History Atlas", Weidenfeld & Nicolson, London, 1969.

[20]. Leon Gettler, "An Unpromised Land" (Fremantle Arts Centre Press, Fremantle, Western Australia, 1993.

[21]. Gideon Polya, "Book review: "An Unpromised Land" by Leon Gettler" – How Australia escaped becoming Apartheid Israel":
https://sites.google.com/site/bookreviewsbydrgideonpolya/gettler-leon.

[22]. "Surafend Affair", Wikipedia:
http://en.wikipedia.org/wiki/Surafend_affair.

[23]. Paul Daley, "Beersheba: A journey through Australia's forgotten war ", Melbourne University Publishing, 2012.

[24]. Tim Elliott, "Massacre that stained the Light Horse", Sydney Morning Herald, 24 July 2004: http://www.smh.com.au/national/massacre-that-stained-the-light-horse-20090723-dux9.html.

[25]. "Jews Against Racist Zionism":
https://sites.google.com/site/jewsagainstracistzionism/.

[26]. "Joel Brand", Wikipedia: http://en.wikipedia.org/wiki/Joel_Brand.

[27]. Alex Weissberg, "Advocate for the Dead. The story of Joel Brand", Andre Deutsch, London, 1958.

[28]. Lenni Brenner, "51 documents: Zionist collaboration with the Nazis", CounterPunch, 23 December 2002:
http://www.counterpunch.org/brenner1223.html.

[29]. "Lenni Brenner", Wikipedia:
http://en.wikipedia.org/wiki/Lenni_Brenner.

[30]. Gideon Polya (2011), "Australia And Britain Killed 6-7 Million Indians In WW2 Bengal Famine", Countercurrents, 29 September, 2011:
http://www.countercurrents.org/polya290911.htm.

[31]. Gideon Polya, "Jane Austen and the Black Hole of British History. Colonial rapacity, holocaust denial and the crisis in biological sustainability", G.M. Polya, Melbourne, 1998, 2008 that is now available for free perusal on the web: http://janeaustenand.blogspot.com/.

[32]. "Bengali Holocaust (WW2 Bengal Famine) writings of Gideon Polya", Gideon Polya: https://sites.google.com/site/drgideonpolya/bengali-holocaust.

[33]. Gideon Polya, "Economist Mahima Khanna, Cambridge Stevenson Prize And Dire Indian Poverty", Countercurrents, 20 November, 2011:
https://www.countercurrents.org/polya201111.htm.

[34]. Sir Isaac Isaacs, quoted by Wikipedia, "Isaac Isaacs":
http://en.wikipedia.org/wiki/Isaac_Isaacs.

[35]. Albert Einstein's letter about the Deir Yassin Massacre (1948):
http://www.ifamericansknew.org/history/ter-einstein.html.

[36]. "UN Genocide Convention":
http://www.edwebproject.org/sideshow/genocide/convention.html.
[37]. "Nuclear weapons ban, end poverty and reverse climate change":
https://sites.google.com/site/300orgsite/nuclear-weapons-ban and
https://sites.google.com/site/drgideonpolya/nuclear-weapons-ban.
[38]. Gideon Polya, "Apartheid Israel buries serial war criminal, genocidal racist and nuclear terrorist Shimon Peres", Countercurrents, 1 October 2016: https://countercurrents.org/2016/10/01/apartheid-israel-buries-serial-war-criminal-genocidal-racist-and-nuclear-terrorist-shimon-peres/.
[39]. Gideon Polya, "Dual Israeli citizenship & Zionist perversion of America, Australia, India & Humanity", Countercurrents, 30 July 2017: https://countercurrents.org/2017/07/30/dual-israeli-citizenship-zionist-perversion-of-america-australia-india-humanity/.
[40]. Gideon Polya, "American Holocaust, Millions Of Untimely American Deaths And $40 Trillion Cost Of Israel To Americans", Countercurrents, 27 August, 2013: https://www.countercurrents.org/polya270813.htm.
[41]. "USS Liberty incident", Wikipedia:
http://en.wikipedia.org/wiki/USS_Liberty_incident.
[42]. "Palestinian rocket attacks on Israel", Wikipedia:
https://en.wikipedia.org/wiki/Palestinian_rocket_attacks_on_Israel.
[43]. Gideon Polya, "Israelis kill 10 times more Israelis in Apartheid Israel than do terrorists", Countercurrents, 1 March 2017: https://countercurrents.org/2017/03/01/israelis-kill-ten-times-more-israelis-in-apartheid-israel-than-do-terrorists/.
[44]. "Hamas", Wikipedia: https://en.wikipedia.org/wiki/Hamas.
[45]. "Gaza War (2008-2009)", Wikipedia:
https://en.wikipedia.org/wiki/Gaza_War_(2008%E2%80%9309).
[46]. "Operation Pillar of Defense", Wikipedia:
https://en.wikipedia.org/wiki/Operation_Pillar_of_Defense.
[47]. "State of Palestine", Wikipedia:
https://en.wikipedia.org/wiki/State_of_Palestine.
[48]. "Palestine", Wikipedia:
https://en.wikipedia.org/wiki/Palestine_(region).
[49]. "2014 Israel-Gaza conflict", Wikipedia:
https://en.wikipedia.org/wiki/2014_Israel%E2%80%93Gaza_conflict.
[50]. United Nations, "Israel's settlements have no legal validity, constitute flagrant violations of international law, Security Council reaffirms. 14 delegations in favour of Resolution 2334 as United States abstains", 23 December 2016: https://www.un.org/press/en/2016/sc12657.doc.htm.
[51]. Gideon Polya, "Is UN Security Council Resolution 2334 the beginning of the end for Apartheid Israel?"", Countercurrents, 28 December 2016: http://www.countercurrents.org/2016/12/28/is-un-security-council-resolution-2334-the-beginning-of-the-end-for-apartheid-israel/.
[52]. Gideon Polya, "Anti-racist Jewish humanitarians oppose Apartheid Israel & support UN Security Council resolution 2334", Countercurrents, 13 January 2017: http://www.countercurrents.org/2017/01/13/anti-racist-jewish-humanitarians-oppose-apartheid-israel-support-un-security-council-resolution-2334/.

[53]. "Sharpeville Massacre", Wikipedia: https://en.wikipedia.org/wiki/Sharpeville_massacre.

[54]. Robert Inlakesh, "Gaza death toll reaches 47: Palestinians prepare for Friday demonstrations", AMN, 3 May 2018: https://www.almasdarnews.com/article/gaza-death-toll-reaches-47-palestinians-prepare-for-friday-demonstrations/.

[55]. Gideon Polya, "Sharpeville Massacre & Gaza Massacres compared – Boycott Apartheid Israel & all its supporters", Countercurrents, 6 May 2018: https://countercurrents.org/2018/05/06/sharpeville-massacre-gaza-massacres-compared-boycott-apartheid-israel-all-its-supporters/.

[56]. "List of countries by GDP (nominal) per capita", Wikipedia: https://en.wikipedia.org/wiki/List_of_countries_by_GDP_(nominal)_per_capita.

[57]. "Geneva Convention relative to the Protection of Civilian Persons in Time of War": http://www1.umn.edu/humanrts/instree/y4gcpcp.htm.

[58]. "Boycott Apartheid Israel": https://sites.google.com/site/boycottapartheidisrael/.

[59]. John Dugard, "International Convention on the Suppression and Punishment of the crime of Apartheid", Audiovisual Library of International Law: http://untreaty.un.org/cod/avl/ha/cspca/cspca.html.

[60]. "Convention on the Rights of the Child", Wikipedia: https://en.wikipedia.org/wiki/Convention_on_the_Rights_of_the_Child.

[61]. "UN Charter (full text)", UN: http://www.un.org/en/sections/un-charter/un-charter-full-text/.

[62]. "UN Declaration on the Rights of Indigenous People", UN: https://www.un.org/development/desa/indigenouspeoples/declaration-on-the-rights-of-indigenous-peoples.html.

[63]. "Universal Declaration of Human Rights", UN: http://www.un.org/en/universal-declaration-human-rights/.

[64]. "Convention Relating to the Status of Refugees", Wikipedia: https://en.wikipedia.org/wiki/Convention_Relating_to_the_Status_of_Refugees.

[65]. John Lyons, Janine Cohen and Sylvie Le Clezio, "Stone cold justice", ABC TV Four Corners, 24 February 2014: http://www.abc.net.au/4corners/stories/2014/02/10/3939266.htm.

[66]. Gideon Polya, "Horrendous Pro-Zionist, Zionist And Apartheid Israeli Child Abuse Exposed", Countercurrents, 21 April, 2014: https://www.countercurrents.org/polya210414.htm.

[67]. Yarden Skop, "Nearly half of Israel 's children suffer physical, sexual or emotional abuse, study finds", Haaretz, 13 November 2013: http://www.haaretz.com/news/national/.premium-1.557668.

[68]. Danielle Ziri, "Child abuse more prevalent than ever, report shows", The Jerusalem Post, 11 December 2013: http://www.jpost.com/National-News/Child-abuse-more-prevalent-than-ever-report-shows-331434.

[69]. Michael Brull, "The siege on Gaza: a brief guide (Part 1)", New Matilda, 5 May 2018: https://newmatilda.com/2018/05/05/siege-gaza-brief-guide-part-1/.

[70]. Diaa Hadid, "Gaza: U.N. issues warning about living conditions", New York Times, 2 September 2015: https://www.nytimes.com/2015/09/03/world/middleeast/gaza-un-issues-warning-about-living-conditions.html.

[71]. Adel Fathi, "Palestine's water crisis: 50 years of injustice", AA, 11 August 2017: https://www.aa.com.tr/en/middle-east/palestine-s-water-crisis-50-years-of-injustice/882105.

[72]. Gideon Polya, "Paris Atrocity Context: 27 Million Muslim Avoidable Deaths From Imposed Deprivation In 20 Countries Violated By US Alliance Since 9-11", Countercurrents, 22 November, 2015: http://www.countercurrents.org/polya221115.htm.

[73]. "Experts: US did 9-11": https://sites.google.com/site/expertsusdid911/.

[74]. Gideon Polya, "Palestinian Genocide-imposing Apartheid Israel complicit in Rohingya Genocide, other genocides, & US, UK & Australian state terrorism", Countercurrents, 30 November 2017: https://countercurrents.org/2017/11/30/palestinian-genocide-imposing-apartheid-israel-complicit-in-rohingya-genocide-other-genocides-us-uk-australian-state-terrorism/.

[75]. Gideon Polya, "Australian State Terrorism – Zero Australian Terrorism Deaths, 1 Million Preventable Australian Deaths & 10 Million Muslims Killed By US Alliance Since 9-11", Countercurrents, 23 September, 2014: http://www.countercurrents.org/polya230914.htm.

[76]. Gideon Polya, "Pro-Zionist, Pro-war, Pro-Opium, War Criminal Canadian Government Defames Iran & Cuts Diplomatic Links", Countercurrents, 10 September, 2012: http://www.countercurrents.org/polya100912.htm.

[77]. Gideon Polya, "UK Terror Hysteria exposed – Empirical Annual Probability of UK Terrorism Death 1 in 16 million", Countercurrents, 16 September, 2014: http://www.countercurrents.org/polya160914.htm.

[78]. Gideon Polya, "West Ignores 11 Million Muslim War Deaths & 23 Million Preventable American Deaths Since US Government's False-flag 9-11 Atrocity", Countercurrents, 9 September, 2015: http://www.countercurrents.org/polya090915.htm.

[79]. Gideon Polya, "Corporate terrorism is state sanctioned, kills over 30 million people annually and dooms humanity by lying", State crime and non-state terrorism: https://sites.google.com/site/statecrimeandnonstateterrorism/corporate-terrorism.

[80]. Gideon Polya, "Save Humanity And The Biosphere Through Zero Tolerance For Deadly Neoliberalism And Remorseless Neoliberals", Countercurrents, 13 May, 2016: https://www.countercurrents.org/polya130516.htm.

[81]. Gideon Polya, "American Holocaust, Millions Of Untimely American Deaths And $40 Trillion Cost Of Israel To Americans", Countercurrents, 27 August, 2013: https://www.countercurrents.org/polya270813.htm.

[82]. Antony Loewenstein, "Does the Zionist Lobby have blood on its hands in Australia?": http://antonyloewenstein.com/2010/07/02/does-the-zionist-lobby-have-blood-on-its-hands-in-australia/.

[83]. Gideon Polya, "Pro-Zionist-led Coup ousts Australian PM Rudd", MWC News, 29 June 2010: http://mwcnews.net/focus/politics/3488-pro-zionist-led-coup.html.

[84]. Gideon Polya, "Dual Australian citizenship & Zionist perversion of America, Australia, India & Humanity", Countercurrents, 30 July 2017: https://countercurrents.org/2017/07/30/dual-israeli-citizenship-zionist-perversion-of-america-australia-india-humanity/.

[85]. Phillip Dorling, " US shares raw intelligence on Australians with Israel ", Sydney Morning Herald, 12 September 2013: http://www.smh.com.au/national/us-shares-raw-intelligence-on-australians-with-israel-20130912-2tllm.html.

[86]. Gideon Polya, "50 Ways Australian Intelligence Spies On Australia And The World For UK, Israeli And US State Terrorism", Countercurrents, 11 December, 2013: https://countercurrents.org/polya111213.htm.

[87]. Gideon Polya, "Racist Zionism and Israeli State Terrorism threats to Australia and Humanity", Palestinian Genocide: https://sites.google.com/site/palestiniangenocide/racist-zionism-and-israeli.

[88]. "Climate Genocide": https://sites.google.com/site/climategenocide/.

[89]. Gideon Polya, "Zionist subversion, Mainstream media censorship", Countercurrents, 9 March 2018: https://countercurrents.org/2018/03/09/zionist-subversion-mainstream-media-censorship-disproportionate-jewish-board-membership-of-us-media-companies/.

[90]. Gideon Polya, "Google censorship & Zionist constraint on effective free speech threaten the Planet", Countercurrents, 9 August 2017: https://countercurrents.org/2017/08/09/google-censorship-zionist-constraint-on-effective-free-speech-threaten-planet/.

[91]. WSWS, "Google's new search protocol is restricting access to 13 leading socialist, progressive and anti-war sites", WSWS, 2 August 2017: http://www.wsws.org/en/articles/2017/08/02/pers-a02.html.

[92]. "Who controls America? Who controls Google?", The Zog: https://thezog.wordpress.com/who-controls-google/.

[93]. Kenneth E. Bauzon, "Media bias and the Israel Lobby in the United States", Countercurrents, 10 August 2017: https://countercurrents.org/2017/08/10/media-bias-and-the-israel-lobby-in-the-united-states/.

[94]. Gideon Polya, "Mainstream media fake news through lying by omission", Global Research, 1 April 2017: http://www.globalresearch.ca/mainstream-media-fake-news-through-lying-by-omission/5582944.

[95]. "Lying by omission is worse than lying by commission because at least the latter permits refutation and public debate", Mainstream media lying: https://sites.google.com/site/mainstreammedialying/lying-by-omission.

[96]. "Mainstream media censorship"; https://sites.google.com/site/mainstreammediacensorship/home.

[97]. "Mainstream media lying": https://sites.google.com/site/mainstreammedialying/.

[98]. "Gideon Polya": https://sites.google.com/site/drgideonpolya/home.

[99]. Gideon Polya, "Apartheid Israel's Palestinian Genocide & Australia's Aboriginal Genocide compared", Countercurrents, 20 February 2018: https://countercurrents.org/2018/02/20/apartheid-israels-palestinian-genocide-australias-aboriginal-genocide-compared/.

[100]. Gideon Polya, "Palestinian Me Too: 140 alphabetically-listed Zionist crimes expose Western complicity & hypocrisy", Countercurrents, 7 February 2018: https://countercurrents.org/2018/02/07/palestinian-140-alphabetically-listed-zionist-crimes-expose-appalling-western-complicity-hypocrisy/.

[101]. "Boycott Apartheid Israel": https://sites.google.com/site/boycottapartheidisrael/.

[102]. "Gaza Concentration Camp": https://sites.google.com/site/palestiniangenocide/gaza-concentration.

[103]. "Non-Jews Against Racist Zionism": https://sites.google.com/site/nonjewsagainstracistzionism/.

[104]. "Apartheid Israeli state terrorism: (A) Individuals exposing Apartheid Israeli state terrorism & (B) Countries subject to Apartheid Israeli state terrorism", Palestinian Genocide: https://sites.google.com/site/palestiniangenocide/apartheid-israeli-state-terrorism.

[105]. "Stop state terrorism" : https://sites.google.com/site/stopstateterrorism/.

[106]. "State crime and non-state terrorism": https://sites.google.com/site/statecrimeandnonstateterrorism/.

Britain Robbed India of $45 Trillion & Thence 1.8 Billion Indians Died From Deprivation

Gideon Polya

Eminent Indian economist Professor Utsa Patnaik (Jawaharlal Nehru University) has estimated that Britain robbed India of $45 trillion between 1765 and 1938. However, it is estimated that if India had remained free with 24% of world GDP as in 1700 then its cumulative GDP would have been $232 trillion greater (1700-2003) and $44 trillion greater (1700-1950). Deprivation kills and it is estimated that 1.8 billion Indians died avoidably from egregious deprivation under the British (1757-1947). The deadly impact of British occupation of India lingers today 71 years after Independence, with 4 million people dying avoidably from deprivation each year in capitalist India as compared to zero (0) in China.

Professor Utsa Patnaik is professor emeritus at Jawaharlal Nehru University, New Delhi. Utsa Patnaik is a Marxist economist and taught at the Centre for Economic Studies and Planning in the School of Social Sciences at Jawaharlal Nehru University (JNU) from 1973 until her retirement in 2010. She obtained her PhD in economics from Oxford University, UK, and has researched the transition from agricultural peasant societies to industrial societies, and food security and poverty, especially in India [1]. Utsa Patnaik's latest book, co-authored with Prabhat Patnaik, is "A Theory of Imperialism" (2016) [2]. We all know that the British rapaciously exploited India. Professor Utsa Patnaik has estimated the magnitude of the British robbing of India thus: "Between 1765 and 1938, the drain amounted to 9.2 trillion pounds ($45 trillion), taking

India's export surplus earnings as the measure, and compounding it at a 5 per cent rate of interest" [3-5].

(A) How and by how much did Britain rob India?

After the betrayal and defeat of the Nawab of Bengal, Siraj ud-daulah, at the Battle of Plassey in 1757, the British installed their own puppet, Mir Jafar, as Nawab. The British extracted huge concessions from the defeated Bengalis including land, a monopoly of trade with Europe, and exemption from taxation on internal trade. The British subsequently replaced Mir Jafar with Mir Kasim as Nawab of Bengal. The Bengalis under Mir Kasim were finally driven to revolt when he was in turn sacked by the British and replaced by Mir Jafar for a second term. The Bengalis were defeated at the Battle of Buxar in 1764, and in 1765 the Moghul Emperor Shah Alam was "persuaded" to grant the power of taxation (diwani) in Bengal to the British East India Company. The British in turn sub-contracted rapacious revenue collection to Bengalis.

Some of the revenue would go the Emperor and some to the Nawab, with the remainder being retained by the British. The British described this as "farming" the Bengali peasants (ryots), but over-taxing of Bengalis meant that 10 million Bengalis perished in the Great Bengal Famine of 1769-1770. The East India Company used about one third of the collected revenue to buy Indian goods and thus the Bengalis were in effect being paid for their goods through the exorbitant taxes applied to them. 15 years later, exorbitant British taxation led to famine in the Gangetic plain to the west of Bengal. Indeed such British excesses led to the British Parliament (unsuccessfully) impeaching Warren Hastings (first Governor General of India and father by adultery of Jane Austen's cousin Eliza) for crimes such as the violation of the Begums of Oudh – he was of course eventually acquitted [6].

By the 1840s the East India Company had dominion over most of present-day India, Pakistan and Bangladesh but the British Government was increasingly keen for greater involvement in the exploitative proceedings. In 1847 the British Government introduced a scheme whereby those wishing to buy Indian goods could only do so using Council Bills issued by the British

Crown in London. Traders would pay for such Bills in gold and silver and use them to pay Indian producers who would in turn cash them in for rupees at the local colonial office – rupees that been exacted by exorbitant taxation [5].

In his book "Inglorious Empire. What the British did to India," Shashi Tharoor describes how the British looted and de-industrialized India and thus paid for Britain's Industrial Revolution and violent global dominance: "At the beginning of the eighteenth century, as the British economic historian Angus Maddison has demonstrated, India's share of the world economy was 23 per cent, as large as all of Europe put together. (It had been 27 per cent in 1700, when the Mughal Emperor Aurangzeb's treasury raked in £100 million in tax revenues alone.) By the time the British departed India, it had dropped to just over 3 per cent. The reason was simple: India was governed for the benefit of Britain. Britain's rise for 200 years was financed by its depredations in India" ([7], page 3 [8]). This deadly and merciless taxation was accompanied by massive de-industrialization of India. Thus before the invasion by the British, India led the world in textiles, agriculture and metallurgy, but rapidly became an exporter of raw materials and an importer of goods manufactured in Britain [6- 8].

Professor Utsa Patnaik's estimate of Britain's theft from India amounting to $45 trillion (1765-1938) [3-5] can be compared with estimates based on GDP considerations. According to Wikipedia, India's share of the world economy declined from 24.4% in 1700 to 4.2% in 1950. India's share of global industrial output declined from 25% in 1750 to 2% in 1900 [9]. From available data on India's GDP and India's share of world GDP since 1700 [10, 11] one can get a very rough estimate of what India's cumulative GDP could have been from 1700-2003 if the British had not robbed and raped India.

Thus the cumulative GDP (PPP) for India is given below for 6 periods since 1700 (A) at the observed average % of world GDP, and (B) if the average Indian % of world GDP had remained at the pre-British invasion 24.0% in 1770.

1700-1820: (A) $13.1 trillion (20.3%) versus (B) $15.8 trillion (24.0%).

1820-1870: (A) $6.2 trillion (14.0%) versus (B) $10.5 trillion (24.0%).

1870-1913: (A) $7.3 trillion (9.8%) versus (B) $18.0 trillion (24.0%).

1913-1950: (A) $7.9 trillion (5.5%) versus (B) $34.4 trillion (24.0%).

1950-1973: (A) $8.3 trillion (3.5%) versus (B) $$56.8 trillion (24.0%).

1973-2003: (A) $41.5 trillion (5.5%) versus (B) $180.9 trillion (24.0%).

It has taken India 7 decades to partially recover from 2 centuries of rapacious British imperialism. The difference in cumulative GDP is $316.4 trillion (1700-2003) and $44 trillion (1700-1950), the latter estimate of India's deprivation being consonant with Professor Utsa Patnaik's estimate that the British had stolen $45 trillion from India between 1765 and 1938 [3-5].

(B) 1.8 billion Indians died avoidably from egregious deprivation under the British.

Imposed poverty kills. Poverty-derived avoidable mortality (avoidable death, excess mortality, excess death, premature death, untimely death, death that should not have happened) can be estimated as the difference between the actual deaths in a country and the deaths expected for a peaceful, decently governed country with same demographics (birth rate and percentage of children) [12]. Below are listed in rough chronological order some shocking salient features of the deadly impact of rapacious British imperialism over 2 centuries in British India, Britain's Auschwitz.

1. In the 1769-1770 Great Bengal Famine 10 million out of 30 million over-taxed Bengalis starved to death [6, 13].

2. Scores of millions of Indians perished in man-made famines between the 1769-1770 Great Bengal Famine and the 1942-1945 WW2 Bengal Famine [6].

3. Using Indian census data 1870-1950, assuming an Indian population of about 200 million in the period 1760-1870, and estimating by interpolation from available data an Indian avoidable death rate in (deaths per 1,000 of population) of 37 (1757-1920), 35 (1920-1930), 30 (1930-1940) and 24 (1940-1950), one can estimate Indian excess deaths of 592 million (1757-1837), 497 million (1837-1901) and 418 million (1901-1947), roughly 1.5 billion in total or 1.8 billion including the Native States [14].

4. Scores of millions of distant British keeping hundreds of millions of Indians on the edge of starvation was enabled by relatively small numbers of British soldiers and much greater numbers of well-fed Indian soldiers threatening requisite violence [6]. It has been estimated by Amaresh Misra that 10 million Indians were massacred in the decade after the 1857 Indian Mutiny (Indian Rebellion) as reprisals for 2,000 British deaths [15, 16].

5. Despite a very high birth rate, the Indian population did not increase between 1860 (292 million) and 1934 (292 million) [17]. This is indicative of massive avoidable deaths from imposed deprivation that can be estimated as 745 million (1860-1934) or an average of about 10 million Indian avoidable deaths from deprivation per year [14].

6. Addressing the House of Commons in 1935, racist, imperialist and mass murderer Winston Churchill made an extraordinary confession in stating of the subjugated Indians: "In the standard of life they have nothing to spare. The slightest fall from the present standard of life in India means slow starvation, and the actual squeezing out of life, not only of millions but of scores of millions of people, who have come into

the world at your invitation and under the shield and protection of British power" [6, 18, 19]. 7 years later Churchill commenced the deliberate starving to death over 4 years of 6-7 million Indians in Bengal, Orissa, Bihar and Assam as the British exported grain from India and slashed grain imports [6].

7. In the 1942-1945 WW2 Bengali Holocaust (Indian Holocaust, WW2 Bengal Famine) 6-7 million Indians were deliberately starved to death for strategic reasons by the British with Australian complicity (Australia was complicit by denying starving India food from its huge wartime food stores) [6, 12-14, 19-27]. This atrocity has been white-washed from history and general public perception by successive generations of Anglo journalist, editor, politician and academic presstitutes. Indeed perpetrator Churchill made no mention for this atrocity in his 6-volume history "The Second World War" for which he was awarded the Nobel Prize for Literature [6].

8. According to Professor Utsa Patnaik Indian per capita annual consumption of food was 200 kg in 1900, but went down to 137 kg during World War II and in 1946 [28]. This is consonant with the following data from my book "Jane Austen and the Black Hole of British History:" "The population of India at that time [1940] was about 400 million and total grain production was 50 to 70 million tons annually. The population was growing at a rate of about 5% per year and there was a requirement of net imports of about 1-2 million tons of grain per annum to make up for deficiencies ... Behrens' figures for grain shipments (in tons) for India in 1942-1945 are as follows: 1942 (30,000), 1943 (303,000), 1944 (639,000) and 1945 (871,000). The 1942 shipment involved 2 lots from Australia contracted for at the rate of 15,000 tons per month to supply the Indian Army (the balance of the demand was not shipped that year). 2.4 million men served in the Indian Army during World War 2. This estimate can be "reduced" since not all of these were in the Army at the same time, scores of thousands were in the Mediterranean theatre (250,000 served there), had been captured by the Japanese or had died. Taking the gross Indian annual grain production estimates of about 60 million tons for 400 million people, we see that the average consumption was 0.15

tons per person per year (obviously more for adults and less for children). The annual requirement for about 2 million men in the "reduced" Indian Army was therefore 0.3 million tons. We can arrive at a figure having a similar order of magnitude from the 1942 contracted requirement of 15,000 tons per month i.e. 0.18 million tons for a whole year. If we assume that an Indian Army soldier required 50% more food than the average Indian we would estimate that the annual grain requirement for a 2 million strong Indian Army would be about 0.45 million tons. The average yearly importation in 1942-1945 was 0.46 million tons and thus we can see that the grain actually imported was merely enough to feed the Indian Army" (pages 156-158, Chapter 15 [6]).

9. Shashi Tharoor in "Inglorious Empire:" "The British left a society with 16 per cent literacy, a life expectancy of 27, practically no domestic industry and over 90 per cent living below what today we would call the poverty line" ([7], page 215 [8]). As indicated in (5) above, the life expectancy of 27 years corresponded to about 10 million Indian avoidable deaths from deprivation per year.

10. Things got much better after Indian Independence. The 1.8 billion avoidable Indian deaths from deprivation under the genocidal British over 2 centuries is not that surprising when one considers that despite modern medicine, antibiotics, and the essential absence of famine, avoidable deaths from deprivation in the period 1950-2005 in India totalled 0.35 billion [14]. Annual avoidable deaths as a percentage of population fell from a genocidal 2.4% per year in 1947 under the British to 0.35% per year in 2005, but the population of India increased from 380 million in 1947 to about 1,100 million in 2005. Today 4 million Indians die avoidably from deprivation each year as compared to zero (0) in China that, unlike capitalist India, has overcome endemic poverty [11].

11. The 3 Laws of Thermodynamics that underlie Chemistry, Physics and industry are (1) the energy of a closed system is constant, (2) the entropy (disorder, lack of information content) strives to a maximum, and (3) there is zero molecular motion in

a pure crystal at absolute zero degrees Kelvin (-273.15 degrees Centigrade). Polya's 3 Laws of Economics are based on the 3 Laws of Thermodynamics and posit that (1) Price (P) – Cost of Production (COP) = Profit (p), (2) deception about COP strives to a maximum, and (3) No work, price or profit on a dead planet [29]. The major cost of production (COP) in the British Raj was the passive mass murder of 1.8 billion Indians through deadly impoverishment, and in keeping with Polya's Second Law of Economics, the British strove to deceive the world about this horror.

The capitalist perpetrator deception continues in a neoliberal One Percenter-dominated world that is existentially threatened by nuclear weapons (a nuclear winter from nuclear war would wipe out most of Humanity and the Biosphere), poverty (15 million people die avoidably from deprivation each year, 4 million in India) and man-made climate change (about 1 million people die from climate change each year but this set to increase to an average of 100 million deaths per year this century if urgent, requisite action is not taken) [30- 32]. Poverty kills. History ignored yields history repeated [6]. Peace is the only way but silence kills and silence is complicity. Please inform everyone you can.

Originally published as "Legacy of colonialism: Britain robbed India of $45 trillion & thence 1.8 billion Indians died from deprivation", Global Research, 19 December 2018.

References

[1]. Utsa Patnaik and Prabhat Patnaik, "A Theory of Imperialism," Columbia University Press, New York, 2016.

[2]. "Utsa Patnaik," Wikipedia: https://en.wikipedia.org/wiki/Utsa_Patnaik.

[3]. Utsa Patnaik in Arindam Banerjee and C. P. Chandrasekhar, editors, "Dispossession, Deprivation, and Development. Essays for Utsa Patnaik, Columbia University Press, 2018.

[4]. "How much money did Britain take away from India? About $45 trillion in 173 years, says top economist," Business Today, 19 November 2018: https://www.businesstoday.in/current/economy-politics/this-economist-says-britain-took-away-usd-45-trillion-from-india-in-173-years/story/292352.html.

[5]. Jason Hickel, "How Britain stole $45 trillion from India and lied about it," Al Jazeera, 18 December 2018: https://www.aljazeera.com/indepth/opinion/britain-stole-45-trillion-india-181206124830851.html.

[6]. Gideon Polya, "Jane Austen and the Black Hole of British History. Colonial rapacity, holocaust denial and the crisis in biological sustainability," G.M. Polya, Melbourne, 1998, 2008 that is now available for free perusal on the web: http://janeaustenand.blogspot.com/.

[7]. Gideon Polya, "Review: "Inglorious Empire. What the British did to India" by Shashi Tharoor," Countercurrents, 8 September 2017: https://countercurrents.org/2017/09/08/review-inglorious-empire-what-the-british-did-to-india-by-shashi-tharoor/.

[8]. Shashi Tharoor, "Inglorious Empire. What the British did to India," Scribe, 2017.

[9]. "Economic history of India," Wikipedia: https://en.wikipedia.org/wiki/Economic_history_of_India.

[10]. "Angus Maddison statistics of the ten largest economies by GDP (PPP)," Wikipedia: https://en.wikipedia.org/wiki/Angus_Maddison_statistics_of_the_ten_largest_economies_by_GDP_(PPP).

[11]. Angus Maddison, "Contours of the World Economy 1-2030AD," Oxford University Press, 2007.

[12]. "Gideon Polya, "Body Count. Global avoidable mortality since 1950," including an avoidable mortality-related history of every country from Neolithic times and is now available for free perusal on the web: http://globalbodycount.blogspot.com.au/.

[13]. Paul Greenough (1982),"Prosperity and Misery in Modern Bengal: the Famine of 1943-1944" (Oxford University Press, 1982).

[14]. Gideon Polya, "Economist Mahima Khanna, Cambridge Stevenson Prize And Dire Indian Poverty," Countercurrents, 20 November, 2011: https://countercurrents.org/polya201111.htm.

[15]. Amaresh Misra, "War of Civilisations: India AD 1857."

[16]. Randeep Ramesh, "India's secret history: A holocaust, one where millions disappeared," Guardian, 24 August 2007: https://www.theguardian.com/world/2007/aug/24/india.randeepramesh.

[17]. Populstat, "India. Historical demographical data of the whole country:" http://www.populstat.info/Asia/indiac.htm.

[18]. Winston Churchill, speech to the House of Commons about Indians (1935); 1. Hansard of the House of Commons, Winston Churchill speech, Hansard Vol. 302, cols. 1920-21, 1935.

[19]. N. G. Jog, "Churchill's Blind-Spot: India," New Book Company, Bombay, 1944 (Winston Churchill quoted on p195).

[20]. K.C. Ghosh, "Famines in Bengal 1770-1943" (National Council of Education, Calcutta, 2nd edition 1987).

[21]. T. Das, T. (1949), "Bengal Famine (1943) as Revealed in a Survey of Destitutes of Calcutta," University of Calcutta, Calcutta, 1949.

[22]. Gideon Polya, "Australia And Britain Killed 6-7 Million Indians In WW2 Bengal Famine," Countercurrents, 29 September, 2011: https://countercurrents.org/polya290911.htm.

[23]. "Bengali Holocaust (WW2 Bengal Famine) writings of Gideon Polya," Gideon Polya: https://sites.google.com/site/drgideonpolya/bengali-holocaust.

[24]. Amartya Sen, "Famine Mortality: A Study of the Bengal Famine of 1943" in Hobshawn, E. (1981) (editor), Peasants In History. Essays in Honour of David Thorner (Oxford University Press, New Delhi).

[25]. Cormac O Grada (2009) "Famine a short history" (Princeton University Press, 2009).

[26]. Madhusree Muckerjee (2010), "Churchill's Secret War. The British Empire and the ravaging of India during World War II" (Basic Books, New York, 2010).

[27]. Thomas Keneally (2011), "Three Famines" (Vintage House, Australia, 2011).

[28]. Prianshi Mathur, "Did you know that back in the Raj days, British looted Rs 3.2 lakh crore from India?," India Times, 16 December 2018: https://www.indiatimes.com/trending/wtf/did-you-know-that-back-in-the-raj-days-british-looted-rs-3-2-lakh-crore-from-india-358731.html.

[29]. Gideon Polya, "Polya's 3 Laws Of Economics Expose Deadly, Dishonest And Terminal Neoliberal Capitalism," Countercurrents, 17 October, 2015: https://countercurrents.org/polya171015.htm.

[30]. "Climate Genocide": https://sites.google.com/site/climategenocide/.

[31]. "Too late to avoid global warming catastrophe": https://sites.google.com/site/300orgsite/too-late-to-avoid-global-warming.

[32]. "Nuclear weapons ban, end poverty & reverse climate change:" https://sites.google.com/site/300orgsite/nuclear-weapons-ban.

Review: "Becoming" By Michelle Obama – Mainstream Lying, Genocide Ignoring & Holocaust Ignoring

Gideon Polya

"Becoming" by Michelle Obama is an inspiring, feel-good story of how a working class African-American woman became a Harvard graduate, corporate lawyer, perfect mother and thence First Lady of the US. However "Becoming" has numerous extraordinary absences e.g. the Harvard Law School years, Black felony laws, the Israel Lobby, 130,000 US veteran suicides and 30 million preventable US deaths since 9-11, pro-Apartheid America, who killed Osama, and egregious US violation of 12 countries under Obama.

"Becoming" by Michele Obama [1] is well written but it has also been very well edited to the point of massive lying by omission, genocide ignoring and holocaust ignoring. Michelle Obama comes across as a strong, smart, family- and community-oriented caring person, a hard worker, a good wife, a pragmatic idealist and an excellent mother. Her book will no doubt be an inspiration for both Black and White American children, girls, women, mothers, husbands and families. It is a feel-good, rags to riches story that attempts to validate American capitalism and the American Dream – no matter who you are and from where you come, work hard, keep your nose clean, and you too can rise to the top of the pile. The only catches are the societal realities and the statistics – thus it took 240 years after American Independence in 1776 for an African–American man to become President of the United States

(POTUS) and for an African–American woman to become First Lady of the United States (FLOTUS).

And of course this didn't happen, on top of ability and hard work, simply by serendipity, accident and good fortune. The real story of how and why the neoliberal, One Percenter American Establishment chose Barack Obama to be president will very likely never be told, notwithstanding the authoritative insider pretensions of "Becoming".

Indeed in the stuff of legend, "Becoming" has it that crucially Barack Obama asked his 8-year-old elder daughter Malia in mid-2015 for her opinion on whether he should run for president: "To this day, Malia and I still crack up about the fact that she'd been eight years old when Barack, clearly feeling some sense of responsibility, posed the question one night when he was tucking her into bed. 'How would you feel if Daddy ran for president?' 'Sure, Daddy!' she replied, pecking him on the cheek. His decision to run would alter nearly everything about her life after that, but how was she to know? She'd just rolled over then and drifted off to sleep" (page 255 [1]).

Indeed, in relation to family approval for Obama running for president, Michelle Obama further states: "Barack and I talked the idea through, not once, but many times, right up to and through our Christmas trip to visit Toot in Hawaii. Some of our conversations were angry and tearful, some of them earnest and positive. It was an extension of a dialogue we'd been having over seventeen years already. Who were we? What mattered to us? What could we do? In the end, it boiled down to this: I said yes because I believed that Barack could be a great president… I said yes because I loved him and had faith in what he could do. I said yes, though I was at the same time harboring a painful thought, one I wasn't ready to share: I supported him in campaigning, but I also felt certain he couldn't make it… Barack was a black man in America, after all. I didn't really think he could win" (page 226 [1]). In similar vein she commented: "And so I gave my approval to his first run for office [for the Illinois Senate]" (page 183 [1]).

The first half of "Becoming" was a terrific and inspiring account of the childhood, family, education and friends of an African-American woman from the impoverished South Side of Chicago. One has nothing but admiration for Michelle Obama the child and young woman, for her wonderful parents and grandparents, her music teacher Aunt Robbie (in whose house they lived), her brother Craig, her school teachers and mentors. A crucial event was Michelle Obama's mother responding to Michelle's complaints about a hopeless teacher by getting her school to shift Michelle to a better class with a competent teacher. A further key event was going to a good high school as a teenager.

However "Becoming" makes clear the economic disparities between the largely and increasingly African-American South Side of Chicago and the rest of Chicago, the real obstacles to advancement for African Americans, and the escalating gang violence in the South Side that is tragically exampled towards the end of the book by the shooting killing of 15 year old school girl, Hadiya Pendelton, shortly after she had attended the second inauguration of Barack Obama as a band member: "A professional person very dear to me had to attend an interview at the University of Chicago but as a non-American he was not aware of the deadly violence in the immediately adjacent South Side and innocently booked a room at a conveniently located South Side hotel. However the hotel would only take cash but gave him an armed escort to a nearby automatic teller machine. Throughout the night he heard the sound of gunfire" (pages 380-382 [1]).

The "political" second half of "Becoming" is an interesting "behind the scenes" account that presents Michelle Obama as a very good mother (very protective of her daughters Malia and Sasha in the bizarre but necessary presidential and political security environment), as an honest campaigner (upset by variously false and unfair denigration of her husband and even of herself by partisan commentators), and as a community-oriented person who used her position as First Lady to advance several key causes (better nutrition and exercise for American children, child ambition, child education, and better back-up for the veterans and their families).

However while "Becoming" is a feel good and inspiring account, it must be criticized for resolutely sticking to the Mainstream American narrative involving massive lying by omission, genocide ignoring, holocaust ignoring and the ignoring of a veritable Herd of Elephants in the Room. Neocon

American- and Zionist Imperialist (NAZI)- subverted US Mainstream media and US- and Zionist-subverted Western Mainstream media in general have a dominant culture of censorship, self-censorship, lying by commission and massive lying by omission. Of course lying by omission is far, far worse than repugnant lying by commission because the latter at least permits public refutation and public discussion [2-5].

Extremely pertinent here are the words of Margaret Atwood (Canadian poet, novelist, literary critic, essayist, environmental activist and author) on the unacceptability of silence (2009): "Powerlessness and silence go together. We…should use our privileged positions not as a shelter from the world's reality, but as a platform from which to speak. A voice is a gift. It should be cherished and used" [6].

Barbara Kingsolver (American novelist, essayist and poet) in her great novel "The Lacuna" (lacuna meaning hiatus, blank, missing part, gap, cavity, or empty space) has Russian Communist revolutionary and theorist Leon Trotsky (Lev) and his assistant Van having the following discussion about media (2009): "'But newspapers have a duty to truth', Van said. Lev [Trotsky] clicked his tongue. 'They tell the truth only as the exception. Zola [French novelist of 'J'accuse' fame] wrote that the mendacity of the press could be divided into two groups: the yellow press lies every day without hesitating. But others, like the Times, speak the truth on all inconsequential occasions, so they can deceive the public with the requisite authority when it becomes necessary.' Van got up from his chair to gather the cast-off newspapers. Lev took off his glasses and rubbed his eyes. 'I don't mean to offend the journalists; they aren't any different from other people. They're merely the megaphones of other people' … [Trotsky observes to his assistant Shepherd] 'Soli, let me tell you. The most important thing about a person is always the thing you don't know'" [7].

The numerous gaping absences, holes or lacunae in Michelle Obama's "Becoming" narrative are succinctly set out below.

(1). The missing Harvard Law School Years, 1981-1984. Michelle Obama got her first degree from Princeton University and deals at great length with her connections with Princeton – starting with her brother Craig's Princeton basketball

scholarship – in Chapters 5, 6 and 7, encompassing pages 59-91. However this is in stark contrast to the almost nothing that Michelle Obama has to say about her 3 years at the prestigious Harvard Law School: "I was bound for law school – Harvard Law School, as it turned out – the affirmation was overwhelming. I was applauded just for getting in, even if the truth was I'd somehow squeaked in off the wait list. But I was in. People looked at me as if I'd made my mark on the world. This may be the fundamental problem with caring a lot about what others think: It can put you on the established path – the my-isn't-that –impressive path – and keep you there for a long time. Maybe it stops you from swerving, from ever even considering a swerve, because what you risk losing in terms of other people's high regard can feel too costly. Maybe you spend three years in Massachusetts, studying constitutional law and discussing the relative merits of exclusionary vertical agreements in antitrust cases. For some, this might be truly interesting, but for you it is not. Maybe during those three years you make friends you'll love and respect forever, people who seem genuinely called to the bloodless intricacies of the law, but you yourself are not called. Your passion stays low, yet under no circumstances will you underperform. You live, as you always have, by the code of effort/result, and with it you keep achieving until you think you know the answers to all the questions – including the most important one. Am I good enough? Yes, in fact I am. What happens next is the rewards get real. You reach for the next rung of the ladder, and this time it's a job with a salary in the Chicago offices of a high-end law firm called Sidley & Austin… [much later] Next to your name [on a mentoring list] is another name, that of some hotshot law student [Barack Obama] who's busy climbing his own ladder. Like you he's black and from Harvard" (pages 91-93 [1]).
The book's missing Harvard Law School Years of 1981-1984 [1, 8] overlaps with a similar "lacuna" in Barack Obama's interrupted academic training between graduating from Columbia in 1983 and commencing law at Harvard Law School in 1988 [9, 10]. Wikipedia: "He graduated with a BA degree in 1983 and worked for about a year at the [CIA-linked] Business International Corporation, where he was a financial researcher and writer, then as a project coordinator for the New York

Public Interest Research Group on the City College of New York campus for three months in 1985... Two years after graduating from Columbia, Obama was back in Chicago when he was hired as director of the Developing Communities Project, a church-based community organization originally comprising eight Catholic parishes in Roseland, West Pullman, and Riverdale on Chicago's South Side. He worked there as a community organizer from June 1985 to May 1988" [9]. Wikipedia informs that "Business International Corporation (BI) was a publishing and advisory firm dedicated to assisting American companies in operating abroad. It was founded in 1953. It organized conferences, and worked with major corporations. It had ties to the Central Intelligence Agency (CIA)" [11]. In his book "Dreams from My Father" Obama makes scant reference to Columbia, Harvard, and British atrocities in Kenya, and no mention at all of his stint in 1983-1984 with the CIA-linked Business International Corporation.

(2) American Apartheid – wealth-based racial Segregation and Felony Laws disenfranchising African Americans.

Michelle Obama qualitatively describes the outrageous inequities of opportunity, employment, housing, income and wealth applying to African Americans (notably to her parents, grandparents and other relatives) and recounts how Barack Obama was active in Black voter registration in Chicago via Project VOTE! (page 180 [1]). However what is missing is quantitation of these inequities. Thus she describes but does not quantitate the enormous implicit wealth differential (housing is the biggest wealth asset, African American wealth is about 5 times lower than that of Whites, a $75,040 average home value for Black Americans versus $217,150 for Whites (2013) and $154,285 average household assets for Black Americans versus $783,224 for Whites (2013) [12-14]).

Indeed the Black-White discrepancy in America has been locked in for 50 years with (i) 2 times higher unemployment rate for African Americans than for Whites since 1963 (in the range from 1.8 times higher to 2.7 times higher) [14], (ii) 11.6% average unemployment rate for African Americans (1963-2012)

(5.1% for Whites, 6.7% American average during recessions), (iii) $55,000 – $32,000 = $23,000 White-Black household income gap (2010) versus $49,000 – $28,000 = $21,000 (1972), (iv) 6-fold White/Black wealth disparity in the period 1983-2010, (v) 42%/11% Black/White "below poverty line" (1966) to 23%/7% (2000) and to 28%/10% (2011), and (vi) 45% of African Americans children living in areas of concentrated poverty (poverty rate 30% or greater) versus 12% for White, 21% for Asian and Pacific Islander, 35% for Hispanic and 39% for American Indian children [12-14].

"Becoming" describes the demographic shift in the South Side of Chicago (and in schools) as White and some wealthier Black families fled to nicer, richer and safer suburbs, but the words "Segregation", "Apartheid" and "Educational Apartheid" are not used. Thus in 2009/2010, 74.1% / 38.1% of African Americans children were in in Segregated (50-100% non-white)/ Intensely segregated (90-100% non-white) schools versus 76.6% / 64.3% in 1968/1969 [12-14]. Notwithstanding the great move to school desegregation in the 1960s due to John Kennedy and Robert Kennedy, African American children today are subject to huge Educational Apartheid [15, 16]. Adam Sanchez: "One would think that the first Black president of the United States might shift course against the privatization of public education and toward desegregation and equity in our public schools" [15, 16].

"Becoming" observes that Barack Obama benefited in his various election campaigns from Black voter registration, but what is missing from Michelle Obama's narrative is what Dr. Michelle Alexander has described as "the New Jim Crow" in America based on differential wealth and disenfranchising Felony Laws. Thus 5-6 million Americans have been disenfranchised because of felony convictions and more than a million of these disenfranchised Americans are black. Felony convictions restrict 13 percent of the country's black male population from voting. Other restrictions may prevent African Americans from voting [17-19]. Dr. Michelle Alexander (author of "The New Jim Crow: Mass Incarceration in the Age of Colorblindness" [18], and former director of the Racial Justice Project of the ACLU in Northern California): "If you take into account prisoners, a large majority of African American men in some urban areas have been labeled felons for life. (In the Chicago area, the figure is nearly 80 percent.) These men are part of a growing undercaste—not class, caste—permanently relegated by law to a second-class status. They can be denied the right to vote, automatically excluded from juries, and legally discriminated against in employment, housing, access to education, and public benefits, much as their grandparents and great-grandparents were during the Jim Crow era." [19]. African Americans and Hispanic Americans have about half their "fair share" of representatives in Congress and 5-6 times less Congressional representation than Jewish Americans. Thus the ethnic mix of the United States (2010 data) is as follows: Whites (72.4%), non-Hispanic White (63.7%), Hispanic (16.4%), White Hispanic (8.7%), African American (12.6%), Asian American (4.6%), Jewish (1.7% to 2.6%), and Native American (0.9%). In 2012, the American Jewish population was estimated at between 5.5-8 million, depending on the definition of the term, with this constituting between 1.7% to 2.6% of the total US population [20]. Of the 113th Congress (100 Senators and 435 Representatives) there were 12 Jewish Americans in the Senate (12.0%; 11 Democrats, 1 Independent) and 22 in the House of Representatives (5.1%; 1 Republican, 21 Democrats) or 6.4% overall [21, 22]. However, during the 113th Congress (commencing in 2013), the Congressional Black Caucus had 1 Senator, 41 voting Representatives i.e. 7.9% of total [23]. Thus African Americans have about half their "fair share" of representatives in Congress and roughly the same representation in Congress as Jewish Americans while having a 5-fold greater population [12].

(3) No mention of Israel, Apartheid Israel, Zionism, Palestine, the Palestinian Genocide or the hugely disproportionate Jewish make-up of the Obama retinue.

Through hard work and ability (the latter possibly selected for by a millennium of persecution and pogroms in Europe) Jewish Americans (about 2% of the US population) are disproportionately represented in US government and business. Thus in 2013 Jews represented 6.4% of the US Congress (12.0% of the Senate and 5.1% of members of the House of

Representatives) [12, 21, 22]. While numerous anti-racist Jewish intellectuals are resolutely critical of the ongoing Palestinian Genocide [24-28], Western Mainstream Media variously censor or white-wash the nuclear terrorist, genocidally racist, and grossly human rights-abusing conduct of Apartheid Israel. A part explanation for this huge moral discrepancy is that the American 60% of the world's 30 biggest media companies have a disproportionately high Jewish Board membership. Jews and females represent 2% and 51%, respectively, of the US population but average 33% and 19%, respectively, of Board members of the top 18 US media companies [29]. 48% of U.S. billionaires are Jewish [30], there are 10 Jews in the Forbes list of the top 50 billionaires [31], and in 2013 the World's 165 Jewish billionaires were worth a combined $812 billion [32]. Now America has always been a very flawed Democracy that has transmuted into a Kleptocracy, Plutocracy, Murdochracy, Lobbyocracy, Corporatocracy and Dollarocracy – all terms, apart from Democracy, totally absent from the Index of Barack Obama's "The Audacity of Hope" [33] – in which Big Money purchases people, politicians, parties, policies, public perception of reality, judicial perception of reality, votes, more power and more personal wealth. The One Percenters who control 50% of the wealth of the world are disproportionately powerful politically. Numerous anti-racist Jewish activists, academics, and American humanitarians resolutely oppose the crimes of nuclear terrorist, genocidally racist, democracy-by-genocide Apartheid Israel and its ongoing Palestinian Genocide and Palestinian Holocaust (2.2 million Palestinians killed by from violence, 0.1 million, or by imposed deprivation, 2.1 million, since the British invasion of Palestine in WW1) [27, 34]. However Lobbyocracy America, US Mainstream media and indeed Western Mainstream media are dominated by immensely rich Neocon American and Zionist Imperialists (NAZIs). As with "Becoming", US and Western Mainstream media largely ignore the horrendous genocidal crimes of Apartheid Israel in its ongoing Palestinian Genocide and Palestinian Holocaust [34]. Astonishingly, given the high proportion of Jewish aides (and most likely fervently pro-Zionist) aides in the Obama Chicago and Washington retinue, "Becoming" only mentions the term "Jews" once in relation to comments by his political opponents in Chicago: "From the start of the campaign [Chicago Democrat primaries for Congress], Barack's opponents and their supporters had been propagating unseemly ideas meant to gin up fear and mistrust among African-American voters, suggesting that Barack was part of an agenda cooked up by the white residents of Hyde Park – read, white Jews – to foist their preferred candidate on the South Side. 'Barack is viewed in part to be the white man in blackface in our community,' Donne Trotter told the Chicago Reader. Speaking to the same publication, Bobby Rush said, 'He went to Harvard and became an educated fool. We're not impressed with these folks with these eastern elite degrees.' He's not one of us, in other words. Barack wasn't a real black man, like them – someone who spoke like that, looked like that, and read that many books could never be…. In March, Barack lost the Democratic primary in what ended up being a resounding victory for Bobby Rush" (pages 197-198 [1]. Elsewhere in the book Michelle Obama recounts a fellow school child asking her why she didn't talk like them.

While "Jews" gets one disputational mention in "Becoming" and "bar mitzvah" gets 1 mention, there is zero (0) mention in "Becoming" of anti-racist Jews, Apartheid Israel, Boycott Divestment and Sanctions (BDS), Gaza Concentration Camp, Genocide, Holocaust, Israel, Israeli Apartheid, Jerusalem [Al Quds], Jew, Jewish, Jewish Holocaust, Netanyahu, Palestine, Palestinian, Palestinian Genocide, Palestinian Holocaust, Passover, Seder, pro-Apartheid, Zionism or Zionist.

Yet Jewish American writer Jodi Kantor in the New York Times describes an annual Passover Seder held in the White House by the Obama's with their children and Jewish staff (2010): "In the Old Family Dining Room, under sparkling chandeliers and portraits of former first ladies, the mostly Jewish and African-American guests will recite prayers and retell the biblical story of slavery and liberation, ending with the traditional declaration 'Next year in Jerusalem.' (Never mind the current chill in the administration's relationship with Israel.) Aides like David Axelrod [Jewish] and Valerie Jarrett [African-American] will attend, but so will assistants like 24-year-old Herbie Ziskend [Jewish]. White House chefs will prepare Jewish participants' family recipes, even rendering chicken fat

— better known as schmaltz — for just the right matzo ball flavor. If last year is any guide, Malia and Sasha Obama will take on the duties of Jewish children, asking four questions about the night's purpose — along with a few of their own — and scrambling to find matzo hidden in the gleaming antique furniture" [35].

Jewish American writer Donald Harrison comments on the Jewishness of the Obama Administration (2018): "As a Jew, I empathize with the feeling that Mrs. Obama enunciates, that to members of a minority group, it feels as if one must do twice as much to go half as far. As I read her classifying people into categories of black (friendly) and white (possibly hostile), I realized that through my Jewish eyes, the world often takes on a similar dichotomous appearance. There are Jews (understanding, understandable) and non-Jews, be they Christian, Muslim, or some other religion (all possibly anti-Semitic). I read the 'Becoming Me' chapter warily, especially when I learned that one of her earliest exposures to politics was through her girlfriend Santita Jackson, whose father was the Rev. Jesse Jackson, who unfortunately will long be remembered by Jews for describing New York City as 'Hymietown,' notwithstanding anything else that may commend him. Add to that name, in the 'Becoming Us,' section, that of her and Barack Obama's minister, the Rev. Jeremiah Wright, pastor of Trinity Church, whose outbursts against white people and Jews were so well reported that they overshadowed anything good that he may have done. However, I learned from this memoir that the Obamas also had a wide network of Jewish friends, advisers, and, in the 'Becoming More' section, a considerable group of Jewish aides during their White House years. These Jews were not simply tokens; they were trusted friends and advisers, people who meant a lot to the Obamas. Reading about such people, peppered throughout the book, I found myself relaxing. If these people, whose names and roles I shall enumerate, found their way into the Obamas' hearts, then clearly the Obamas, far beyond any ceremonial Chanukah greeting, had felt real friendship for Jews, even if, as we all know, his feud with Israel's Prime Minister Binyamin Netanyahu was epic (and not mentioned in the book" [36].

Here is a short list based on references in "Becoming" [1] of the Jewish retinue and Jewish key associates of Barack Obama (BO) and Michelle Obama (MO) (with some White House Seder attendees also included [35]):

David Axelrod (Chief Strategist for BO's presidential campaigns and Obama Senior Advisor);

David Brooks (influential conservative Jewish journalist with the New York Times, considered the Obama White House's favourite columnist e.g. for "Run, Barack, Run" (page 223 [1]);

Arun Chaudhary (has a half Indian and half Jewish family, BO videographer);

Neil Cohen (husband of Susan Sher who was MO's chief of staff);

Rahm Emanuel (son of an Irgun Zionist terrorist, member of the US House of Representatives from Chicago between 2003 and 2009, Obama White House Chief of Staff from 2009 to 2010, thence Mayor of Chicago);

Sarah Hurwitz (senior speechwriter for BO and author of "Here All Along: A Reintroduction to Judaism");

Valerie Jarrett (deputy chief of staff for MO; senior adviser to the Obamas; her great grandfather was Jewish);

Sam Kass (BO's Senior Policy Advisor for Nutrition Policy, Executive Director for MO's Let's Move! campaign, an Assistant Chef for the Obamas in the White House)

Vanessa Kirsch (social entrepreneur and founder of Public Allies that employed MO in Chicago);

Michael Kors (fashion designer patronized by MO);

Eric Lesser, (former BO baggage handler and organizer of the annual White House Seder, thence assistant to David Axelrod);

Susan Sher (MO's chief of staff);

Molly Stern (edited "Becoming");

Art Sussman (in-house legal cousin for University of Chicago, employed MO's mother, helped MO get a job at the University of Chicago);

Diane von Furstenberg (Jewish Belgian fashion designer patronized by MO);

Melissa Winter (MO deputy chief of staff, former aide of rabid Zionist Senator Joe Lieberman);

Patricia Winter (the mother of Melissa Winter, and gave matzo ball instructions to White House chefs);

Herbie Ziskend (former White House advisor and one of the founders of the Obama White House Passover Seder).

Very roughly, of people named as Obama connections in the "political" latter half of "Becoming", about one third are Jewish, about one third African Americans, and one third non-Jewish White, Asian or Hispanic Americans.

We will consider the Jewish Zionist Lobby below in the section entitled "Pro-Apartheid US", noting that there is a large body of decent, anti-racist Jews (including anti-racist Jewish Americans) who speak out about the horrendous crimes of Apartheid Israel and its ongoing Palestinian genocide [24-28].

(4) 7,000 US war dead, 130,000 US veteran suicides, and 30 million preventable US deaths since 9-11 (3,000 killed).

Michelle Obama initiated 4 good causes during her time as FLOTUS, namely "Let's Move" (an anti-obesity message of good nutrition and exercise, especially for children), "Reach Higher" (promoting ambition for school children), "Let Girls Learn" (promoting female education) and "Joining Forces" (promoting better support for veterans and their families). However missing from "Becoming" were the appalling statistics relating to 1.7 million preventable American deaths annually from "lifestyle choices" and "political choices", the breakdown (with some overlaps) including (as of 2015): (1) smoking-related (440,000), (2) adverse hospital events (440,000), (3) obesity-related causes (300,000), (4) air pollution e.g. from coal burning, vehicle exhaust, or carbon burning in general (200,000), (5) alcohol-related (75,000), (6) lack of medical insurance (45,000), (7) drug-related deaths, this including 21,000 US opiate drug-related deaths annually from US restoration and protection of the Taliban-destroyed Afghan opium industry (38,000), (8) motor vehicle accidents (33,000), (9) gun-related deaths (31,000), (10) suicides, with 7,000 being US veterans (30,000), (11) avoidable under-5 year old US infant deaths (21,000), (12) homicide (15,000), (13) deaths from jihadi attack in the US (4) [37-44]

Michelle Obama laudably promoted a healthy diet and exercise to combat American obesity in her "Let's move" activism, but there was no mention in "Becoming" of the 0.3 million

American obesity-related deaths per year x 17.75 years = 5.3 million Americans who have died from obesity since 9-11 (3,000 deaths).

Similarly, Michelle Obama laudably promoted child education through "Reach Higher" and "Let Girls Learn" but there was no mention in "Becoming" of the horrendous existential realities of 15 million avoidable deaths from deprivation each year on Spaceship Earth with Neocon American and Zionist Imperialist (NAZI)-dominated America in charge of the flight deck (266 million such deaths in this Global Avoidable Mortality Holocaust since 9-11) [45]. Nor was there any mention of how a fundamentalist, state terrorist and non-state terrorism-supporting America has trashed secular governance, modernity, democracy, women's rights and children's rights in the Muslim world [46], this being associated with an ongoing Muslim Genocide and Muslim Holocaust in which 32 million Muslims have died from violence, 5 million, or from imposed deprivation, 27 million, in 20 countries invaded by the US Alliance since the US Government's 9-11 false flag atrocity [47-51].

Michelle Obama laudably promoted better care for veterans, their spouses and families through "Joining Forces" but there was no mention of the circa 7,000 veteran conflict zone deaths in the War on Terror [52], nor of the 20 veteran suicides each day since the 1960s [54], this corresponding to 7,300 veteran suicides per year and 130,000 veteran suicides since the US Government's 9-11 false flag atrocity (3,000 deaths) [37-44]. There was no mention of the 72 countries invaded by the US since 1776 (52 since WW2) [55] nor of the $6 trillion long-term accrual cost of the War on Terror [56, 57] – this huge fiscal perversion has involved committing $6 trillion to killing over 30 million Muslims abroad at the cost of 7,000 US military deaths in conflict zones, 130,000 US veteran suicides, and the preventable deaths of 30 million Americans at home from "lifestyle" or "political" choices.

(5) Pro-Apartheid America.

Michelle Obama and Barack Obama visited anti-Apartheid hero Nelson Mandela in South Africa (pages 367- 369 [1]) but there is no explicit mention in "Becoming" of "Apartheid America" per se. Indeed the message of the first Black POTUS and FLOTUS is denial of the continuing appalling reality of an Apartheid America based not on discriminatory laws but on the harsh realities of wealth inequity in a ruthless neoliberal society. Nelson Mandela and many of his anti-Apartheid associates have condemned Israeli Apartheid as just as bad and indeed worse than South African Apartheid. Thus Nelson Mandela in an address at the International Day of Solidarity with the Palestinian People (4 December, 1997): "The UN took a strong stand against apartheid; and over the years, an international consensus was built, which helped to bring an end to this iniquitous system. But we know too well that our freedom is incomplete without the freedom of the Palestinians" [58]. Anti-racist Jewish anti-Apartheid hero Ronnie Kasrils on Apartheid Israel and Apartheid South Africa: "The [Israeli] occupation reminds me of the darkest days of apartheid, but we never saw tanks and planes firing at a civilian population. It's a monstrousness I'd never seen before. The wall you built, the checkpoints and the roads for Jews only – it turns the stomach, even for someone who grew up under apartheid. It's a hundred times worse" [59].

Yet in "Becoming" there is no mention of Israel, Apartheid Israel, Israeli Apartheid, Zionism, Palestine, Palestinian human rights, or the Palestinian Genocide and Palestinian Holocaust (2.2 million Palestinian deaths from violence, 0.1 million, or from imposed deprivation, 2.1 million, since the British invasion of Palestine in WW1 [27, 34].

The Sharpeville Massacre in 1960 involved the killing of 69 Africans and the World responded with Boycotts and Sanctions that eventually brought down Apartheid in 1993 [60]. By way of comparison, the Israeli Gaza Massacre in 2008-2009 involved 1,400 Palestinians killed and 5,300 Palestinians wounded, as compared to 13 Israelis killed and 518 Israelis wounded [61]. The 2014 Gaza Massacre involved 2,256 Palestinians killed, and 17,125 Palestinians wounded, as compared to 85 Israelis killed and 2,629 Israelis wounded [62]. According to Wikipedia, the 2018-2019 Great March of Return involved 183 Palestinians killed and 9,204 Palestinians wounded, as compared to 1 Israeli killed and 11 Israelis wounded [63], but Al Jazeera estimates 266 Palestinians killed and 30,398 wounded [64].

Notwithstanding Zionist-driven Western hysteria, Palestinian rocket attacks on Apartheid Israel killed 32 Israelis in the period 2004-2014 [65]. Gaza has been devastated with massive destruction of homes and infrastructure to the point that in 2018 the UN reported that it is now "unliveable" [66].

There are now 7 million Palestinian refugees, and of 14 million Palestinians (half of them children, three quarters women and children) about 50% are forbidden to even step foot in their own country on pain of death, only 1.9 million Palestinian Israelis are permitted to vote for the government ruling all of the former Mandated Palestine, and 5 million Palestinians have zero human rights [67] as Occupied Palestinians in West Bank ghettoes (3 million) or in the blockaded and bombed Gaza Concentration Camp (2.0 million). However the "lucky" Israeli Palestinians are Third Class citizens subject to over 60 Nazi-style, race-based laws [68, 69]. The land of Palestine has now been 90% ethnically cleansed [27, 70-73].

While Indigenous Palestinians represent 50% of Apartheid Israeli subjects, nearly three quarters of them cannot vote for the government ruling them – egregious Apartheid that is declared by the UN to be a crime against Humanity [74]. Personal disclaimer – I am an anti-racist Jewish Australian humanitarian and was happily married for 52 years to a non-Indigenous Black Australian resident and thence citizen. We were, of course, utterly opposed to racism and to Apartheid in particular for obvious humanitarian reasons but also for personal reasons – if we had lived in Apartheid South Africa we would have been prosecuted for miscegeny and jailed. When we worked in the US in the late 1960s we would have been persecuted in the Deep South of Apartheid America.

The Obamas must have been aware of Israeli Apartheid and the gross violation of Palestinian human rights but political pragmatism (and indeed political survival) demanded that they go along with the fervently pro-Zionist narrative of Neocon American and Zionist Imperialist (NAZI)-subverted America. For Obama the fanatical demands of the ferocious Israel Lobby wore thin when he was publicly humiliated by Apartheid Israeli PM Netanyahu when this serial war criminal addressed Congress and received 29 standing ovations (not mentioned in

"Becoming" as noted by Jewish American journalist Donald Harrison [36]).

The public humiliation of Obama by the Israel Lobby and Apartheid Israeli PM Netanyahu is described in detail by anti-racist Jewish American Peter Beinart, a self-styled "liberal Zionist" (oxymoronic because Zionism is genocidal racism) and of Sephardic Jewish South African origin, in his book "The Crisis of Zionism" [75, 76]. He describes how Obama was influenced by the liberal Jewish tradition that was heavily involved in Black civil rights and desegregation (see Chapter 5, "The Jewish President" [75]) but when he made noises about civil rights for Palestinians he was bullied, humiliated and whipped back into the racist Zionist fold by the powerful ADL (Anti-Defamation League) and AIPAC (American Israel Public Affairs Committee) and their overwhelmingly supportive Congressional lackeys. Serial war criminal and genocidal racist Israeli PM, Netanyahu, in a speech attacking the president of the United States (Obama) received 29 standing ovations (see Chapter 7, "The Clash" and Chapter 8, "The Humbling" [75]). Obama found some courage in one of his last acts by refusing to veto and merely abstaining from UN Security Council Resolution 2334 that otherwise unanimously condemned the gross Apartheid Israeli violations of International Law in the Occupied Palestinian Territories (Trump America and US lackey Australia opposed Resolution 2334) [77-79].

Michelle Obama utterly ignored Apartheid Israel and the ongoing Palestinian Genocide in "Becoming", this astonishing omission thereby adding greater weight to the perception of the Zionist tail wagging the American dog since Apartheid Israeli acquisition of nuclear weapons in 1967 [80-85]. Senator J. William Fulbright, Chairman of U.S. Senate Committee on Foreign Relations (1973): "Israel controls the U.S. Senate. […] The great majority of the Senate of the U.S. – somewhere around 80 percent – are completely in support of Israel; anything Israel wants Israel gets" [80].

The mendacity of Zionist-subverted Mainstream media hides the deadly realities that the per capita GDP for Occupied Palestinians is a dire $3,000 as compared to $40,000 for the Israeli Occupiers [86], that Israelis kill ten times more Israelis in Apartheid Israel than do terrorists [87], and that 2.2 million

Palestinians have died from violence, 0.1 million, or from imposed deprivation, 2.1 million, since the British invasion of Palestine in WW1 as compared to 4,000 invading Zionists dying at the hands of Indigenous Palestinians since 1920 [88, 89]. Princeton and Harvard graduate and First Lady of the US for 8 years, Michelle Obama somehow didn't notice.

(6) Who killed Osama bin Laden?

The mendacious and serial war criminal Bush Administration – that according to the US Center for Public Integrity told 935 lies about Iraq between 9-11 and the illegal invasion of Iraq in 2003 [90] – claimed that the 9-11 atrocity (3,000 killed) was executed by Al Qaeda led by Osama bin Laden i.e. men in caves were responsible for this massive atrocity. Pertinently, Al Qaeda was backed by the US against Russia and Serbia; the FBI had Osama bin Laden on its most wanted list but not for 9-11; none of the 19 Bush-asserted 9-11 perpetrators were from Iraq or Afghanistan (the first Muslim countries war criminally invaded by the US after 9-11); and numerous science, architecture, engineering, aviation, military and intelligence experts conclude that the US Government was responsible for 9-11, with some cogently arguing for a key involvement of Apartheid Israel and Saudi Arabia in the atrocity [51, 52].

Neocon American and Zionist Imperialist (NAZI)-subverted Mainstream media throughout the world rapidly fell into line with the lying Bush "official version" of 9-11, brooking no dissent from the version offered by this mendacious war criminal – indeed a UK BBC TV journalist in New York with an intact World Trade Center (WTC) building 7 (WTC7) behind her, reported the demolition of WTC7 (not hit by planes and suffering only minor fires) 15 minutes before it actually happened [51]. Even President Donald Trump and former Vice President Al Gore hold blame US intelligence failures for 9-11, with Al Gore stating: "These affirmative and repeated refusals to listen to clear warnings constitute behavior that goes beyond simple negligence. At a minimum, it represents a reckless disregard for the safety of the American people" [51].

Michelle Obama's "Becoming" scrupulously and absurdly avoids commentary on world affairs but makes an exception in relation to Apartheid South Africa (pages 367- 369 [1]) and the Barack Obama-asserted extrajudicial killing of Osama bin Laden in 2011: "I knew it was coming... seven thousand miles from the White House and under cover of darkness, an elite team of U.S. Navy SEALs had stormed a mysterious compound in Abbottabad, Pakistan, looking for Osama bin Laden... Barack was coming out of our bedroom... 'We got him,' he said. 'And no one got hurt'. We hugged. Osama bin Laden had been killed. No American lives had been lost. Barack had taken an enormous risk – one that could have cost him his presidency – and it had all gone okay. The news was already travelling across the world... I'm not sure anyone's death is reason to celebrate, ever. But what America got that night was a moment of release, a chance to feel its own resilience" (pages 363-364 [1]).

However leading figures with expert inside knowledge dispute the Bush-Obama narrative parroted by US Mainstream media and thence by Michelle Obama. Thus former US-installed Afghan President Hamid Karzai (10 September 2015): "[Al-Qaeda] is for me a myth ... For us, they don't exist. I don't know if al-Qaeda existed and I don't know if they exist. I have not seen them and I've not had any report about them, any report that would indicate that al-Qaeda is operating in Afghanistan.... [re the Bush version of 9-11] That is what I have heard from our Western friends. That's what the Western media says. There is no doubt that an operation, a terrorist operation was conducted in New York and in Washington... I neither believe nor disbelieve something that I don't know about. I can tell you that Afghanistan was as much a victim of terrorism as was America, as were the people who were killed in the September 11th terrorist attacks" [51].

Seymour Hersh (famed American Pulitzer Prize-winning investigative journalist who exposed the Mylai Massacre) on the Obama-asserted killing of Osama bin Laden: "Do you think Obama's been judged by any rational standards? Has Guantanamo closed? Is a war over? Is anyone paying any attention to Iraq? Is he seriously talking about going into Syria? We are not doing so well in the 80 wars we are in right now, what the hell does he want to go into another one for. What's going on [with journalists]? … Like killing people, how does [Obama] get away with the drone programme, why aren't we doing more? How does he justify it? What's the intelligence? Why don't we find out how good or bad this policy is? Why do newspapers constantly cite the two or three groups that monitor drone killings? Why don't we do our own work?" and re the Obama-asserted killing of Osama bin Laden: "Nothing's been done about that story, it's one big lie, not one word of it is true" [51].

Dr Paul Craig Roberts (an economist, academic, former editor and columnist for the Wall Street Journal and Business Week, nationally syndicated columnist for Creators Syndicate, and author of numerous books, he served as an Assistant Secretary of the Treasury in the Reagan Administration, earning fame as the "Father of Reaganomics): "Americans live in a rigged system in which propaganda determines the public's awareness and consciousness. Americans, or most of them, live in the Matrix… Washington's phony wars based on lies and phony economy based on rigged statistics" [91]. Dr. Paul Craig Roberts re the Obama-asserted killing of Osama bin Laden: "I do not believe Hersh's story for three reasons. One reason is that bin Laden was suffering from disease that no one can survive for a decade. His death was widely reported in 2001. One reason is that even Hersh's 'true' account of 'what really happened' is contradicted by eye witnesses and the initial Pakistani TV interviews of eye witnesses. One reason is that Hersh's story is too convoluted for an assassination raid, a routine event. He exposes lies within lies, indecision within decision, payoffs within payoffs, and reports such a huge number of people with advance knowledge of the raid that it cannot possibly have been kept a secret. I could add a fourth reason–the US government's lack of credibility. Washington lies about everything. For example: Saddam Hussein's weapons of mass destruction, Assad's use of chemical weapons, Iranian nukes, Russian invasion of Ukraine. If, as Hersh reports, lies comprise 99% of Washington's tale of the raid in Abbottabad, why believe that 1% of the story is true and that bin Laden was killed. It is difficult to have murder without a body. The only evidence that bin Laden was killed is the government's claim. In my opinion, Washington's disinformation agencies have finally managed to deceive Seymour Hersh with a concocted 'inside story' that saves Washington's claim of having murdered bin Laden by proving that the US government is an extraordinary liar and violator of law. Hersh's story does prove that the US government is a liar, but it does not prove that a SEAL team murdered Osama bin Laden" [92].

On 2 November 2007 Pakistan PM Benazir Bhutto (2-time PM of Pakistan in 1988-1990 and 1993-1996 and leader of the Pakistan People Party in 1982-2007) was interviewed by Sir David Frost at Al Jazeera shortly before her murder on 27 December 2007. In this interview she said: "And he had also dealings with Omar Sheik, the man who murdered Osama Bin Laden." The same interview was published on the BBC website, but that key sentence was removed [93].

Washington lies about everything [92]. Who should we believe, President Hamid Karzai, Pullitzer Prize-winning Seymour Hersh, famed Dr. Paul Craig Roberts, 2-time Pakistan PM Benazir Bhutto … or Michelle and Barack Obama?

(7). Egregious US Alliance violation of 20 countries under Peace Nobel Laureate Barack Obama.

For all that he was awarded the Nobel Peace Prize, Obama has an appalling record of violence against numerous countries as outlined below.

(1) Afghanistan. Obama continued the Afghan Genocide and Afghan Holocaust in Occupied Afghanistan (started by his predecessor, serial war criminal George Bush) in which Afghan deaths from violence or deprivation total 7.2 million [48, 50]. The most fundamental human right is the right to life. While legitimately criticized for the one party state, the death penalty, censorship, urban air pollution and harsh treatment of dissidents, China has been hugely successful in radically reducing infant mortality and maternal mortality in Tibet and in China as a whole. In stark contrast, the war criminal US Alliance occupation of neighbouring Afghanistan continues to be associated with an under-1 infant mortality and maternal mortality incidence that is 7 times higher and 4-12 times higher,

respectively, than that in Tibet [45, 94, 95] – evidence of gross violation by the rich US Alliance countries of Article 2 of the UN Genocide Convention [96] and of Articles 55 and 56 of the Geneva Convention relative to the Protection of Civilian Persons in Time of War that unequivocally demand that an Occupier must supply its conquered Subjects with life-sustaining food and medical requisites "to the fullest extent of the means available to it" [97]. The GDP per capita is $60,000 (US), $58,000 (Australia), and $40,000 (UK) as compared to $9,000 (China) and $600 (Occupied Afghanistan) [98]. Obama and the other leaders of the US Alliance need to be taken to the International Criminal Court over passive mass murder in Occupied Afghanistan and Occupied Iraq.

Also utterly ignored by Neocon American and Zionist Imperialist (NAZI)-perverted and subverted Western Mainstream media are the 1.2 million people who have died world-wide since 9-11 due to US Alliance restoration of the Taliban-destroyed Afghan opium industry from 6% of world market share in 2001 to 93% in 2007, the breakdown (as of 2015) including 280,000 Americans, 256,000 Indonesians, 68,000 Iranians, 25,000 British, 14,000 Canadians, 10,000 Germans, 5,000 Australians (7.2 million Afghan deaths from violence, 1.4 million, or imposed deprivation, 5.6 million, 2001-2015) [48, 50].

(2) Egypt. Apartheid Israel, Afghanistan and Egypt are the biggest recipients of US military aid and this continued under Obama after the 2013 military coup that removed Egypt's first ever democratically elected president, Mohamed Morsi, who died in prison in 2019 [99] (Egyptian deaths from deprivation 1.3 million, 2012-2019).

(3) Honduras. The US has a longstanding and appalling record of interfering in Latin American countries through subversion, coups or invasions, with Honduras serving as a base for such deadly operations [45]. Under Obama the US-backed military removed the democratically-elected government of Honduras in 2009 with consequent gross human rights abuses (Honduran deaths from deprivation 40,000, 2009-2019).

(4) Iran. Sanctions against Iran by the US and its US Alliance lackeys date back to the Carter Administration response to the Iranian Revolution that overthrew the US-emplaced Shah

regime in 1979 and the subsequent US hostage crisis. Agreement with Obama America and other US Alliance powers for the Iran Nuclear Deal (Joint Comprehensive Plan of Action, JCPOA) resulted in substantial lifting of sanctions in 2015. However Trump abrogated this treaty in 2018, has re-imposed sanctions, increased sanctions and threatened "obliteration" of parts of Iran [100, 101]. While Obama deserves credit for the Iran Nuclear Deal, he must wear the egregious racism tag of imposing deadly sanctions against non-nuclear weapons Iran (that has no nuclear weapons, has not invaded any other country for centuries, wants a nuclear weapons-free Middle East, and does not occupy the territory of any other country) while lavishing scores of billions of dollars of military aid on a nuclear terrorist Apartheid Israel (that has up to 400 nuclear weapons, has invaded 13 countries and occupies the territory of 3 other countries, namely Syria, Lebanon and Palestine) [45, 102] (Iranian avoidable deaths from deprivation averaged 74,000 per year and totalled 1.3 million in the 21st century)..

(5) Iraq. US forces left Iraq in 2011 under Obama, leaving a devastated country and a bitter Sunni versus Shia divide that gave rise to IS in Iraq, thence in Syria and thence around the world. US Alliance countries (notably Saudi Arabia, Turkey, Apartheid Israel, the US, the UK, and France) variously supported jihadis (and hence IS) in their war against the Assad regime in Syria (4.6 million Iraqi deaths from violence, 1.7 million, or deprivation, 2.9 million, and 6 million refugees in 1990-2011) [48, 49].

(6) Libya. The France, UK and US (FUKUS) Coalition invaded Libya with UNSC sanction in 2011, effected regime change, and devastated what was formerly a secular state and the richest country in Africa (0.2 million Libyans killed through violence, 0.1 million, or deprivation, 0.1 million, and 1 million refugees) [48].

(7) Pakistan. Despite unanimous opposition from the National Assembly of Pakistan, the US since 2004 and under Obama has hit targets in Pakistan with drone-fired bombs targeted via the Australia-US joint electronic spying base at Pine Gap in Central Australia (6,000 Pakistanis killed with 1,000 being civilians [103] and 11.4 million avoidable deaths from deprivation, 2004-2019). (8) Palestine. For all his disingenuous talk of a "2-state

solution" in Palestine (now impossible because of the ethnic cleansing of 90% of Palestine by the genocidally racist Zionists of Apartheid Israel), Obama finished his second term as president by granting $38 billion in military aid over the next decade to nuclear terrorist, racist Zionist–run, genocidally racist, democracy-by-genocide Apartheid Israel [104]. Obama is a major player in the American Holocaust in which there have been 30 million untimely American deaths since 9-11 that are inescapably linked to the $40 trillion long-term accrual cost of Apartheid Israel to Americans [40]. Just as those supporting Nazi Germany can be reasonably considered to be "pro-Nazi" and those supporting Apartheid South Africa were considered to be "pro-Apartheid", so those supporting Apartheid Israel can reasonably be condemned as "pro-Apartheid" and hence utterly beyond the pale for decent humans. (9) Philippines. By 2009 the US had 600 military plus CIA operatives involved in counterterrorism in the southern Philippines [105] (827,000 avoidable deaths from deprivation, 2015-2019).

(10) Somalia. The US invaded Somalia in 1992 and the US Alliance occupation of a starving Somalia continues, variously involving the US, Ethiopia, and Kenya, with US lackey Australia involved in waters offshore (2.2 million Somali deaths from violence, 0.4 million, or from deprivation, 1.8 million, in 1992-2011) [48].

(11) Syria. US Alliance countries (notably Saudi Arabia, Turkey, Apartheid Israel, the US, the UK, and France) variously supported jihadis (and hence variously IS) in their war against the secular Assad regime in Syria. Under Obama the US invaded Syria without permission from the Syrian Government (1.0 million Syrian deaths from violence, 0.5 million, or from deprivation, 0.5 million, in 2012-2019 and 11 million refugees).

(12) Yemen. Since 2015 the US has been involved with drone strikes, weapons and advisers together with other US Alliance partners in the Saudi-imposed Yemeni Genocide in starving Yemen (70,000 killed, 225,000 deaths from deprivation in 2015-2019, 3 million refugees) [106].

The above is a partial list because the US Government subverts every country on earth including the US. The US has invaded about 72 countries (52 since WW2) [55], and has about 800 military bases in more than 70 countries and territories [107].

John Pilger: "Should the CIA stooge Guaidó and his white supremacists grab power, it will be the 68th overthrow of a sovereign government by the United States, most of them democracies" [108]. 15 million people die avoidably from deprivation each year on Spaceship Earth with the US in charge of the flight deck [45], and 120 million died thus during the 8 years of the Obama presidency. Obama has continued the War on Terror with sanctions, invasions and illegal drone strikes on 7 countries (Libya, starving Somalia, starving Yemen, Syria, Iraq, Afghanistan and Pakistan). It is estimated that 32 million Muslims have perished from violence, 5 million, or from deprivation, 27 million, in 20 countries invaded by the US Alliance since the US Government's 9-11 false flag atrocity in 2001 [47, 51].

It is hardly surprising that Michelle Obama should have ignored these horrendous atrocities of Nobel Peace Laureate Barack Obama in her feel-good biography "Becoming".

Final comments

"Becoming" by Michelle Obama is an inspiring, feel-good story of how an African American woman from the impoverished South Side of Chicago graduated from Princeton and Harvard, worked in a top law firm and thence in different roles in community leadership and the University of Chicago Medical School, and then as a splendid mother of 2 daughters helped her African American husband Barack Obama to achieve 8 years as president of the United States.

Barack Obama was stymied by a hostile congress but managed some action on climate change and nuclear proliferation (the existential threats facing Humanity [102]). He also managed a limited recognition of Palestinian human rights (by abstaining from UNSC Resolution 2334), and saved the lives of scores of thousands of Americans through Obamacare (45,000 Americans die annually from lack of medical insurance [37]).

Unfortunately these limited achievements of Barack Obama are all being wantonly undone by his crude, ignorant, stupid, mendacious and bullying successor, Donald Trump [37].

Michelle Obama's feel-good "Becoming" is remarkable for its niceness and the paucity of personal criticisms. Thus she very briefly refers to a really bad teacher, a boy her punched her at school, a girl who bullied her, incorrect detractors in politics (e.g. Chicago politicians Donna Trotter and Bobby Rush and various media critics such as pro-Iraq War Christopher Hitchens). However the only people she criticizes at length are journalists who quoted her unfairly and questioned her love of America (pages 262-269 [1]) and the misogynist reactionary Donald Trump (pages 407-419 [1]). The evidently very well edited "Becoming" is a book that (absences aside) could be read with pleasure and utility by people from the Democratic Left to the Republican Far Right (excepting Donald Trump) – it is a triumph of endless, feel good niceness and smart, market-informed editing. A wasted opportunity for courageous truth telling.

Famed anti-racist Jewish American writer I.F. Stone (Isidor Feinstein Stone, an outstanding US journalist, publisher of the newsletter "I. F. Stone's Weekly" and author of numerous books, including "The Hidden History of the Korean War, 1950-1951"), told journalism students: "Among all the things I'm going to tell you today about being a journalist, all you have to remember is two words: governments lie" [109, 110].

More specifically, in relation to American mendacity, Gore Vidal (a great American writer) stated in an interview with Melvyn Bragg (2008): "Unlike most Americans who lie all the time, I hate lying… This is a country of hoax. P.T. Barnum is the god of this republic, which is no longer a republic alas. It is an oligarchy and a rather vicious one" [111].

The extent of that neoconservative American Establishment deception has been cogently described by Professor Noam Chomsky (linguistics at 85-Nobel-Laureate MIT) and Professor Edward Herman (finance, University of Pennsylvania) (1988): "In sum, the mass media of the United States are effective and powerful ideological institutions that carry out a system-supportive propaganda function by reliance on market forces, internalized assumptions, and self-censorship, and without any significant overt coercion. This propaganda system has become even more efficient in recent decades with the rise of the national television networks, greater mass-media concentration, right-wing pressures on public radio and television, and the growth in scope and sophistication of public relations and news management" [112].

The most important things in history are often those that are not stated, the absences, holes or lacunae. Michelle Obama's feel-good autobiography "Becoming" has many extraordinary, Elephant in the Room absences that reflect the One Percenter-dominated Mainstream American media culture of lying by omission, genocide ignoring and holocaust ignoring that profoundly deceives ordinary Americans, including Michelle Obama, and indeed most of the West. However "Becoming" can nevertheless serve the interests of Humanity if decent folk tell everyone they can about its shocking absences.

Originally published as "Review: "Becoming" By Michelle Obama – Mainstream Lying, Genocide Ignoring & Holocaust Ignoring," Countercurrents, June 2019.

References

[1]. Michelle Obama, "Becoming", Viking, 2018.
[2]. "Mainstream media censorship":
https://sites.google.com/site/mainstreammediacensorship/home.
[3]. "Mainstream media lying":
https://sites.google.com/site/mainstreammedialying/.
[4]. Gideon Polya, "Fake news: "fake realities" and "lying by omission"",
Global Research, 18 April 2018: https://www.globalresearch.ca/mainstream-
media-fake-news-through-lying-by-omission/5582944.
[5]. "Lying by omission":
https://sites.google.com/site/mainstreammedialying/lying-by-omission.
[6]. Margaret Atwood quoted in Washingtonsblog, "5 reasons that corporate
media coverage in pro-war": http://www.washingtonsblog.com/2009/12/5-
reasons-that-corporate-media-coverage-is-pro-war.html.
[7]. Barbara Kingsolver, "The Lacuna", Faber & Faber, London, 2009, part
3, p159.
[8]. "Michelle Obama", Wikipedia:
https://en.wikipedia.org/wiki/Michelle_Obama.
[9]. "Barack Obama", Wikipedia:
https://en.wikipedia.org/wiki/Barack_Obama.
[10]. Barack Obama, "Dreams from My Father".
[11]. "Business International Corporation", Wikipedia:
https://en.wikipedia.org/wiki/Business_International_Corporation.
[12]. Gideon Polya, "Truth & Boycotts, Divestment & Sanctions (BDS) Can
Overcome Huge Inequities Suffered By African Americans Under American
Apartheid", Countercurrents, 29 September 2014:
https://countercurrents.org/polya290914.htm.
[13]. Drew Desilver, "Black incomes are up, but wealth isn't", Pew Research
Center, 30 August 2013: http://www.pewresearch.org/fact-
tank/2013/08/30/black-incomes-are-up-but-wealth-isnt/.
[14]. Brad Plumer, "These ten charts show the black-white economic gap
hasn't budged in 50 years", The Washington Post, 29 August 2013:
http://www.washingtonpost.com/blogs/wonkblog/wp/2013/08/28/these-
seven-charts-show-the-black-white-economic-gap-hasnt-budged-in-50-
years/.
[15]. "Educational Apartheid":
https://sites.google.com/site/educationalapartheid/.
[16]. Adam Sanchez, "Educational Apartheid in America", International
Socialist Review: http://isreview.org/issue/67/educational-apartheid-america.
[17]. Saki Knafo, "Voting rights of Black Americans trampled by "New Jim
Crow", civil rights advocates say", Huffington Post Black Voices, 21
September2014: http://www.huffingtonpost.com/2013/07/25/black-america-
2013_n_3647789.html.
[18]. Michelle Alexander, "The New Jim Crow: Mass Incarceration in the
Age of Colorblindness", The New Press, 2010.
[19]. Michelle Alexander, "The war on drugs and the New Jim Crow", Race,
Poverty, Environment, Vol. 17, No. 1 | Spring 2010:

http://reimaginerpe.org/20years/alexander.

[20]. "American Jews", Wikipedia:
http://en.wikipedia.org/wiki/American_Jews.

[21]. "Jewish Members of Congress", Jewish Virtual Library:
http://www.jewishvirtuallibrary.org/jsource/US-Israel/jewcong113.html.

[22]. "113th United States Congress", Wikipedia:
http://en.wikipedia.org/wiki/113th_United_States_Congress.

[23]. Congressional Black Caucus", Wikipedia:
http://en.wikipedia.org/wiki/Congressional_Black_Caucus#Senate_members.

[24]. "Boycott Apartheid Israel":
https://sites.google.com/site/boycottapartheidisrael/.

[25]. "Gaza Concentration Camp":
https://sites.google.com/site/palestiniangenocide/gaza-concentration.

[26]. "Jews Against Racist Zionism":
https://sites.google.com/site/jewsagainstracistzionism/.

[27]. "Palestinian Genocide":
https://sites.google.com/site/palestiniangenocide/.

[28]. "Apartheid Israeli state terrorism: (A) Individuals exposing Apartheid
Israeli state terrorism & (B) Countries subject to Apartheid Israeli state
terrorism", Palestinian Genocide:
https://sites.google.com/site/palestiniangenocide/apartheid-israeli-state-
terrorism.

[29]. Gideon Polya, "Zionist subversion, Mainstream media censorship",
Countercurrents, 9 March 2018: https://countercurrents.org/2018/03/zionist-
subversion-mainstream-media-censorship-disproportionate-jewish-board-
membership-of-us-media-companies.

[30]. Michael Epstein, "48% of U.S. billionaires are Jewish", Topix, 19
August 2017:
http://www.topix.com/forum/afam/TCEL6H6L79C279EVA/48-percent-of-u-
s-billionaires-are-jewish.

[31]. Gabe Friedman, "10 Jews in Forbes top 50 billionaires", Times of
Israel, 3 March 2015: https://www.timesofisrael.com/10-jews-in-forbes-top-
50-billionaires/.

[32]. "World's 165 Jewish billionaires worth a combined $812 billion",
Times of Israel, 19 April 2013: https://www.timesofisrael.com/worlds-
jewish-billionaires-worth-combined-812-billion/.

[33]. Barack Obama, "The Audacity of Hope", Vintage, 2008.

[34]. Gideon Polya, "Review: "Tales of a City by the Sea" by Samah Sabawi
– Palestinian Genocide and Palestinian Holocaust in microcosm",
Countercurrents, 10 June 2019: https://countercurrents.org/2019/06/review-
tales-of-a-city-by-the-sea-by-samah-sabawi-palestinian-genocide-palestinian-
holocaust-in-microcosm.

[35]. Jodi Kantor, "Next year in the White House: a Seder tradition", New
York Times, 27 March 2010:
https://www.nytimes.com/2010/03/28/us/politics/28seder.html.

[36]. Donald Harrison, "Michelle Obama's "Becoming" also about
belonging", San Diego Jewish World, 5 December 2018:
https://www.sdjewishworld.com/2018/12/05/michelle-obamas-becoming-

also-about-belonging/.

[37]. Gideon Polya, "14 million Americans will die preventably under a 2-term Trump Administration", Countercurrents, 22 March 2017: https://countercurrents.org/2017/03/over-14-million-americans-will-die-preventably-under-a-2-term-trump-administration.

[38]. Gideon Polya, "Movie review: "Who to Invade Next" by Michael Moore – Hammer, chisel down for social humanism", Countercurrents, 23 April 2016: https://countercurrents.org/polya230416.htm.

[39]. Gideon Polya, "One million Americans die preventably annually in USA ", Countercurrents, 18 February 2012: http://www.countercurrents.org/polya180212.htm.

[40]. Gideon Polya, "American Holocaust, Millions Of Untimely American Deaths And $40 Trillion Cost Of Israel To Americans", Countercurrents, 27 August, 2013: http://www.countercurrents.org/polya270813.htm.

[41]. Gideon Polya, "One Percenter Greed & War Means Over 1.5 Million Americans Die Preventably Each Year", Countercurrents, 19 September, 2014: http://www.countercurrents.org/polya190914.htm.

[42]. Gideon Polya, "West Ignores 11 Million Muslim War Deaths & 23 Million Preventable American Deaths Since US Government's False-flag 9-11 Atrocity", Countercurrents, 9 September, 2015: http://www.countercurrents.org/polya090915.htm.

[43]. "Stop state terrorism": https://sites.google.com/site/stopstateterrorism/.

[44]. "State crime and non-state terrorism": https://sites.google.com/site/statecrimeandnonstateterrorism/.

[45]. Gideon Polya, "Body Count. Global avoidable mortality since 1950", that includes an avoidable mortality-related history of every country from Neolithic times and is now available for free perusal on the web : http://globalbodycount.blogspot.com.au/.

[46]. Gideon Polya, "Fundamentalist America Has Trashed Secular Governance, Modernity, Democracy, Women's Rights And Children's Rights In The Muslim World", Countercurrents, 21 May, 2015: http://www.countercurrents.org/polya210515.htm.

[47]. Gideon Polya, "Paris Atrocity Context: 27 Million Muslim Avoidable Deaths From Imposed Deprivation In 20 Countries Violated By US Alliance Since 9-11", Countercurrents, 22 November, 2015: http://www.countercurrents.org/polya221115.htm.

[48]. "Muslim Holocaust Muslim Genocide": https://sites.google.com/site/muslimholocaustmuslimgenocide/.

[49]. Iraqi Holocaust, Iraqi Genocide": http://sites.google.com/site/iraqiholocaustiraqigenocide/.

[50]. "Afghan Holocaust, Afghan Genocide": http://sites.google.com/site/afghanholocaustafghangenocide/.

[51]. "Experts; US did 9-11": https://sites.google.com/site/expertsusdid911/.

[52]. Elias Davidsson, "Hijacking America 's Mind on 9/11. Counterfeiting Evidence", Algora, New York 2013, 328 pp: http://www.amazon.com/Hijacking-Americas-Mind-11-Counterfeiting/dp/0875869734.

[53]. I-casualties.org: http://icasualties.org/.

[54]. Dr. Janet Kemp and Dr. Robert Bossarte, "Suicide data report, 2012", Department of Veterans Affairs, Mental Health Services, Suicide Prevention Program, especially Figure 3: http://www.va.gov/opa/docs/Suicide-Data-Report-2012-final.pdf.

[55]. Gideon Polya, "US has invaded 70 nations Since 1776 – make 4 July Independence From America Day", Countercurrents, 5 July 2013: http://www.countercurrents.org/polya050713.htm.

[56]. Joseph Stiglitz and Linda Bilmes, "The Three Trillion Dollar War: The True Cost of the Iraq Conflict", W.W. Norton, 2008.

[57]. Joseph Stiglitz and Linda Bilmes, "The true cost of the Iraq war: $3 trillion and beyond", Washington Post, 5 September 2010: http://www.washingtonpost.com/wp-dyn/content/article/2010/09/03/AR2010090302200.html.

[58]. Nelson Mandela quoted in "Nelson Mandela quotes: A collection of memorable words from former South African president", CBS News, 5 December 2013: http://www.cbsnews.com/news/nelson-mandela-quotes-a-collection-of-memorable-words-from-former-south-african-president/.

[59]. Ronnie Kasrils quoted by Gideon Levy, "Twilight zone/Cry the Beloved Country", Haaretz, 26 January 2009: http://www.haaretz.com/hasen/spages/862911.html.

[60]. Gideon Polya, "Sharpeville Massacre & Gaza Massacres compared – Boycott Apartheid Israel & all its supporters", Countercurrents, 6 May 2018: https://countercurrents.org/2018/05/06/sharpeville-massacre-gaza-massacres-compared-boycott-apartheid-israel-all-its-supporters/.

[61]. "Gaza War (2008-09)", Wikipedia: https://en.wikipedia.org/wiki/Gaza_War_(2008%E2%80%9309).

[62]. "Timeline of the 2014 Israel-Gaza conflict", Wikipedia: https://en.wikipedia.org/wiki/Timeline_of_the_2014_Israel%E2%80%93Gaza_conflict.

[63]. "2018-2019 Gaza border protests", Wikipedia: https://en.wikipedia.org/wiki/2018%E2%80%9319_Gaza_border_protests.

[64]. Huthifa Fayyad, "Gaza's Great March of Return protests explained", Al Jazeera, 30 March 2019: https://www.aljazeera.com/news/2019/03/gaza-great-march-return-protests-explained-190330074116079.html.

[65]. "Palestinian rocket attacks on Israel", Wikipedia: https://en.wikipedia.org/wiki/Palestinian_rocket_attacks_on_Israel.

[66]. United Nations, "The Question of Palestine", 24 October 2018: https://www.un.org/unispal/document/gaza-unliveable-un-special-rapporteur-for-the-situation-of-human-rights-in-the-opt-tells-third-committee-press-release-excerpts/.

[67]. Gideon Polya, "Universal Declaration of Human Rights & Palestinians. Apartheid Israel violates ALL Palestinian Human Rights", Palestine Genocide Essays, 24 January 2009: https://sites.google.com/site/palestinegenocideessays/universal-declaration-of-human-rights-palestinians.

[68]. Susan Abulhawa, "Israel's "nation-state law" parallels the Nazi Nuremburg Laws", Al Jazeera, 27 July 2018: https://www.aljazeera.com/indepth/opinion/israel-nation-state-law-parallels-

nazi-nuremberg-laws-180725084739536.html.

[69]. "Discriminatory laws in Israel:, Adalah, https://www.adalah.org/en/law/index?page=4.

[70]. Gideon Polya, "70th anniversary of Apartheid Israel & commencement of large-scale Palestinian Genocide", Countercurrents, 11 May 2018: https://countercurrents.org/2018/05/11/70th-anniversary-of-apartheid-israel-commencement-of-large-scale-palestinian-genocide/.

[71]. Gideon Polya, "Apartheid Israel's Palestinian Genocide & Australia's Aboriginal Genocide compared", Countercurrents, 20 February 2018: https://countercurrents.org/2018/02/20/apartheid-israels-palestinian-genocide-australias-aboriginal-genocide-compared/.

[72]. Gideon Polya, "Israeli-Palestinian & Middle East conflict – from oil to climate genocide", Countercurrents, 21 August 2017: https://countercurrents.org/2017/08/21/israeli-palestinian-middle-east-conflict-from-oil-to-climate-genocide/.

[73]. Gideon Polya, "End 50 Years Of Genocidal Occupation & Human Rights Abuse By US-Backed Apartheid Israel", Countercurrents, 9 June 2017: https://countercurrents.org/2017/06/09/end-50-years-of-genocidal-occupation-human-rights-abuse-by-us-backed-apartheid-israel/.

[74]. John Dugard, "International Convention on the Suppression and Punishment of the crime of Apartheid", Audiovisual Library of International Law: http://untreaty.un.org/cod/avl/ha/cspca/cspca.html.

[75]. Peter Beinart, "The Crisis of Zionism", Melbourne University Press, 2012.

[76]. Gideon Polya, "Book Review: "The Crisis of Zionism" – Racist Zionists Ponder Substantial Or Total Palestinian Genocide", Countercurrents, 14 July, 2012: https://countercurrents.org/polya140712.htm.

[77]. United Nations, "Israel's settlements have no legal validity, constitute flagrant violations of international law, Security Council reaffirms. 14 delegations in favour of Resolution 2334 as United States abstains", 23 December 2016: https://www.un.org/press/en/2016/sc12657.doc.htm.

[78]. Gideon Polya, "Is UN Security Council Resolution 2334 the beginning of the end for Apartheid Israel?"", Countercurrents, 28 December 2016: https://countercurrents.org/2016/12/28/is-un-security-council-resolution-2334-the-beginning-of-the-end-for-apartheid-israel/.

[79]. Gideon Polya, "UN Security Council Resolution 2334 – beginning of the end for Apartheid Israel?", Uprooted Palestine, 27 December 2016: https://uprootedpalestinians.wordpress.com/2016/12/27/un-security-council-resolution-2334-full-text-beginning-of-the-end-for-apartheid-israel/.

[80]. Laurent Guyénot, "Kennedy, the Lobby and the Bomb", Voltairenet, 2 May 2013: http://www.voltairenet.org/article178401.html.

[81]. L. Michael Hager, "When dual citizenship becomes conflict of interest", The Hill, 30 April 2015: http://thehill.com/blogs/congress-blog/homeland-security/240572-when-dual-citizenship-becomes-conflict-of-interest.

[82]. Michael Hager, "Dual citizens in Congress", Counterpunch, 12 November 2014: https://www.counterpunch.org/2014/11/12/dual-citizens-in-congress/.

[83]. Gideon Polya, "Dual Israeli citizenship & Zionist perversion of America, Australia, India & Humanity", Countercurrents, 30 July 2017: https://countercurrents.org/2017/07/dual-israeli-citizenship-zionist-perversion-of-america-australia-india-humanity.

[84]. John Mearsheimer and Stephen Walt, "The Israel Lobby and U.S. Foreign Policy", Farrar, Straus and Giroux, 2008.

[85]. Gideon Polya, "Apartheid Israel buries serial war criminal, genocidal racist & nuclear terrorist Shimon Peres", Countercurrents, 1 October 2016: https://countercurrents.org/2016/10/apartheid-israel-buries-serial-war-criminal-genocidal-racist-and-nuclear-terrorist-shimon-peres.

[86]. "List of countries by GDP (nominal) per capita", Wikipedia: https://en.wikipedia.org/wiki/List_of_countries_by_GDP_(nominal)_per_cap ita.

[87]. Gideon Polya, "Israelis kill ten times more Israelis in Apartheid than do terrorists", Countercurrents, 1 March 2017: https://countercurrents.org/2017/03/israelis-kill-ten-times-more-israelis-in-apartheid-israel-than-do-terrorists.

[88]. Israeli Ministry of Foreign Affairs, "Terrorism deaths in Israel – 1920-1999", 1 January 2000: http://mfa.gov.il/mfa/foreignpolicy/terrorism/palestinian/pages/terrorism%20 deaths%20in%20israel%20-%201920-1999.aspx.

[89]. Israeli Ministry of Foreign Affairs, "Victims of Palestinian violence and terrorism since September 2000": http://mfa.gov.il/MFA/ForeignPolicy/Terrorism/Palestinian/Pages/Victims% 20of%20Palestinian%20Violence%20and%20Terrorism%20sinc.aspx.

[90]. "Study: Bush, aides made 935 false statements in run-up to war", CNN, 2004: http://edition.cnn.com/2008/POLITICS/01/23/bush.iraq/.

[91]. Paul Craig Roberts, "The attack on gold", Information Clearing House, 17 April 2013: http://www.informationclearinghouse.info/article34648.htm.

[92]. Paul Craig Roberts, "Seymour Hersh Succumbs To Disinformation", Countercurrents, 11 May, 2015: http://www.countercurrents.org/roberts110515A.htm.

[93]. BBC censors Benazir Bhutto's 2007 Frost TV interview assertion about "Omar Sheik, the man who murdered Osama Bin Laden", "Censorship by the BBC": https://sites.google.com/site/censorshipbythebbc/bbc-censors-benazir.

[94]. Gideon Polya, "China's Tibet health success versus passive mass murder of Afghan women and children by US Alliance", Global Research, 7 January 2018: https://www.globalresearch.ca/chinas-tibet-health-success-versus-passive-mass-murder-of-afghan-women-and-children-by-us-alliance/5625151.

[95]. UN Population Division, "World Population Prospects 2017": https://esa.un.org/unpd/wpp/.

[96]. "Article 2 of the UN Genocide Convention": http://www.edwebproject.org/sideshow/genocide/convention.html.

[97]. "Geneva Convention (IV) relative to the Protection of Civilian Persons in Time of War: https://www.un.org/ruleoflaw/files/Geneva%20Convention%20IV.pdf.

[98]. "List of countries by GDP (nominal) per capita", Wikipedia: https://en.wikipedia.org/wiki/List_of_countries_by_GDP_(nominal)_per_cap ita.

[99]. Farah Najjar, "Why US aid to Egypt is never under threat", Al Jazeera, 3 October 2017: https://www.aljazeera.com/news/2017/10/aid-egypt-threat-171002093316209.html.

[100]. "United States sanctions against Iran", Wikipedia: https://en.wikipedia.org/wiki/United_States_sanctions_against_Iran.

[101]. Joint Comprehensive Plan of Action", Wikipedia: https://en.wikipedia.org/wiki/Joint_Comprehensive_Plan_of_Action.

[102]. "Nuclear weapons ban, end poverty & reverse climate change": https://sites.google.com/site/300orgsite/nuclear-weapons-ban.

[103]. "Drone strikes in Pakistan", Wikipedia: https://en.wikipedia.org/wiki/Drone_strikes_in_Pakistan.

[104]. Kevin Lamarque, "Obama touts $38 billion military aid package in meeting with Netanyahu", CBS News, 21 September 2016: http://www.cbsnews.com/news/obama-netanyahu-touts-38-billion-military-aid-package-in-meeting/.

[105]. "Operation enduring Freedom – Philippines", Wikipedia: https://en.wikipedia.org/wiki/Operation_Enduring_Freedom_%E2%80%93_Philippines.

[106]. Bethan McKernan, "New fighting in Yemen threatens UN deal", Guardian, 17 May 2019: https://www.theguardian.com/world/2019/may/16/new-fighting-in-yemen-threatens-un-deal.

[107]. David Vine, "Where in the world is the US military", Politico, July/August 2015: https://www.politico.com/magazine/story/2015/06/us-military-bases-around-the-world-119321.

[108]. John Pilger, "John Pilger: The war on Venezuela is built on lies", Consortium News, 26 June 2019: https://consortiumnews.com/2019/02/22/john-pilger-the-war-on-venezuela-is-built-on-lies/.

[109] I.F. Stone, quoted in "Two words – governments lie. Iraqi oil, climate change and Tony Blair", Media Lens, 22 January 2003: http://www.medialens.org/index.php?option=com_content&view=article&id=239:two-words-governments-lie-iraq-oil-climate-change-and-tony-blair&catid=17:alerts-2003&Itemid=42.

[110]. I.F. Stone, quoted in Gideon Polya, "Iraqi Holocaust", ConScience, Australasian Science, 2 June 2004: http://www.shiachat.com/forum/index.php?/topic/33427-iraqi-holocaust/.

[111]. Gore Vidal interviewed by Melvyn Bragg on the South Bank Show", 2008: http://warincontext.org/2012/08/01/remembering-gore-vidal-change-is-the-nature-of-life-and-its-hope/.

[112]. Edward S. Herman and Noam Chomsky, "Manufacturing Consent. The political economy of the mass media", page 306, Pantheon, 2002.

US-imposed Opiate Holocaust – US Protection Of Afghan Opiates Has Killed 5.2 Million People Since 9-11

Gideon Polya

Numerous science, engineering, architecture, aviation, military and intelligence experts conclude that the US Government was responsible for the 9-11 atrocity (3,000 people killed) with some asserting Israeli and Saudi involvement, but US-beholden Western Mainstream media are united in blind belief in the official version of mendacious George Bush. However resolutely ignored is the UNODC report that 0.6 million people die from illicit drugs each year with 290,000 such deaths linked to US protection of the Occupied Afghanistan opium industry. US Government-beholden Mainstream media continue to turn reality on its head by ignoring this US-imposed carnage of 290,000 per year x 18 years = 5.2 million opiate drug-related deaths world-wide linked to US restoration of the Taliban-destroyed Afghan opium industry from about 6% of world market share in 2001 to 93% in 2007 [1-7]. Further, Mainstream media ignore the reality that Iran is the world leader in combating this deadly scourge of US-protected opiate drugs and instead beat the drums of war against Iran by the nuclear terrorist and serial invader countries of the US, Apartheid Israel, the UK and France against Iran, a country that has not invaded another country for 1,500 years [2], does not have nuclear weapons, nor any intention of building them, and repeatedly declares that it wants a nuclear weapons-free Middle East. According to the United Nations Office on Drugs and Crime

(UNODC), Iran accounts for 74% of the world's opium seizures and 25% of the world's heroin and morphine seizures. However Iran's role as a world leader in the War on Drugs and in combating opiate drugs from US-occupied Afghanistan comes at a heavy price. Thus Iran has a 900 kilometer border with US-occupied Afghanistan that produces about 90% of the world's opium under US Alliance protection. Iran has spent about $700 million policing its borders against drug movement. About 2.5 million Iranians are drug users with opium accounting for 67% of drug use. 4,000 Iranian police have been killed protecting Iran and the World from US-protected opiate smugglers [1-3].

The US Alliance restored the Taliban-destroyed Afghan opium industry from about 6% of world market share in 2001 to 93% in 2007 [1-7]. Drought reduced the Afghan share of the world opium production in 2018 to 82% [7]. UNODC (2017): "[Occupied] Afghanistan continues to be at the epicenter of the global illicit opium trade. In 2017 as highlighted in the Afghanistan Opium Survey, opium cultivation reached record levels, rising by 63 per cent compared to 2016. The survey also showed opium production increased by 87 per cent to a record of 9,000 metric tons in 2017 compared to a year earlier. The donor community and other international stakeholders in the country have expressed alarm over these record numbers" (page 32 [1]). UNODC World Drug Report (2019): "Globally, some 35 million people, up from an earlier estimate of 30.5 million, suffer from drug use disorders and require treatment services. The death toll is also higher: 585,000 people died as a result of drug use in 2017 (page 1 [7])... Global production of opium was even more affected than was cultivation by the drought in Afghanistan, which produced 82 per cent of the world's opium in 2018. After an upward trend over the last two decades, global production fell by 25 per cent from 2017 to 2018, to some 7,790 tons. Despite that drop, the amount of opium produced was the third largest amount since UNODC started to systematically monitor opium production in the 1990s (pages 8-5 [7])... Some 585,000 people are estimated to have died as a result of drug use in 2017. More than half of those deaths [over 293,000] were the result of untreated hepatitis C leading to liver cancer and cirrhosis; almost one third were attributed to drug use disorders [almost 193,000]. Most (two thirds) of the deaths attributed to drug use disorders were related to opioid use [129,000]" (page 19 [7]). Note that synthetic opioids (notably fentanyl and tramadol) are of deadly importance, particularly in wealthy North America.

UNODC (2019): "The amount of heroin seized in the Americas has shown a clear upward trend over the last decade. Most of this trafficking takes place within North America, usually from Mexico to the United States, although the heroin found in Canada originates in Afghanistan. Analysis of wholesale seizures of heroin in the United States has shown the increasing predominance of heroin originating in Mexico. Some 80 per cent of the heroin samples analysed in 2016 came from Mexico... In the case of fentanyl, for example, the bulk of the substance found on the illicit market comes from illicit manufacture, although some small diversions of fentanyl [from medical use] have been reported in the United States. The large market for tramadol for non-medical use in North Africa and the Near and Middle East also seems to be supplied by tramadol specifically manufactured and trafficked for the illegal market, but information remains limited... Outside North America, where the diversion of pharmaceutical opioids such as codeine and oxycodone from the licit to the illicit market is evident, such diversions are not reported in large quantities. This could be the result of underreporting or the limited capacity of law enforcement authorities to detect diversions" (page 18 [7]).

Global drug deaths totalled about 0.2 million in 2001 and about 0.6 million in 2019, and accordingly the average of annual drug deaths in this period was 0.4 million per year. Assuming that 90% of these drug deaths were opioid-related, that of these about 90% were due to opiates (such as opium and heroin, as opposed to synthetic opioids such as fentanyl and tramadol), and that of these opiate-related deaths 90% were linked to Afghan opium production [7], then the average global death rate from Afghanistan-derived opium in the last 2 decades would have been about 290,000 deaths per year – or a total of 5.2 million since 9-11.

For religious reasons the Taliban banned alcohol, banned smoking for public servants, and after 2000 banned opium production. Thus one can estimate that as of September 2019 –

18 years after the 9-11 atrocity in which 3,000 were killed – about 18 years x 290,000 deaths per year = 5.2 million people would have died due to US restoration of the Taliban-destroyed Afghan opium industry from 6% of world market share in 2001 to 90% in 2007.

In terms of body count one can see that Presidents George Bush, Barack Obama and Donald Trump have been the worst drug pushers in history since Great Britain's Queen Victoria who devastated China with imposed opium from British-enslaved India in the 19th century (up to 100 million Chinese died in the Opium Wars and the Tai Ping rebellion [8], with the Chinese GDP remaining almost the same between 1820 and 1950, and dropping from 30% of world GDP in 1820 to a mere 5% in 1950) [9, 10]. The Indians suffered a similar catastrophe under the rapacious British. Thus eminent Indian economist Professor Utsa Patnaik (Jawaharlal Nehru University) has estimated that Britain robbed India of $45 trillion between 1765 and 1938. I have estimated that if India had remained free with 24% of world GDP as in 1700 (like China) instead of similarly collapsing to 5% by 1950, then its cumulative GDP would have been $232 trillion greater (1700-2003) and $44 trillion greater (1700-1950). Deprivation kills and it is estimated that 1.8 billion Indians died avoidably from egregious deprivation under the British (1757-1947) [11-17].

The Neocon American and Zionist Imperialist (NAZI)-subverted Anglo-American Mainstream media, politician, commentariat and academic presstitutes lie by omission about this horrendous Occupied Afghanistan-derived, opiate-related carnage of 5.2 million people – a US-imposed Opiate Holocaust that is similar in magnitude to the WW2 Jewish Holocaust (5-6 million Jews killed by violence or imposed deprivation) [18-20]. One can well understand how the Mainstream can resolutely ignore the compelling question of who did the 9-11 atrocity in which 3,000 people were killed, and the opinions of numerous science, engineering, architecture, aviation, military and intelligence experts who conclude that the US Government must have been involved, with some concluding that Apartheid Israel and misogynistically Apartheid Saudi Arabia were also involved [21].

It gets worse. Thus the UNODC reports the annual drug-related deaths of 15-64 year olds in 2017 in the following "White" countries of the US Alliance and of the Anglosphere "5-Eyes" Intelligence Club, with opioids being the leading cause of death: the US (70,237), Canada (3,998), UK (3,394), Australia (1,899), Germany (1,333), France (257), and New Zealand (261). By way of comparison, the figures are as follows for some further entities: the World (585,000), China (25,727), Russia (7,529), Iran (3,021), Vietnam (2,184), Kenya (1,338), Indonesia (447), Myanmar (275), Uzbekhistan (220), Kazakhstan (141), Mexico (113), and Afghanistan (16) (no data for Pakistan and India) [2]. Applying a correction factor of 0.6 (to obtain average deaths in the last 2 decades) one can estimate total 15-64 year old opioid drug-related deaths in the 18 years (September 2001-September 2019) since 9-11 in these US Alliance countries and inescapably linked to the substantial worldwide impact of US-protected Occupied Afghanistan opiates (with similarly inescapably connected US synthetic opioids now very being important in the US and Canada): the US (759,000), Canada (43,000), UK (37,000), Australia (21,000), Germany (14,000), France (3,000), and New Zealand (3,000). By way of comparison, these UNODC-based figures are as follows for some further entities: the World (6,318,000), China (278,000), Russia (81,000), Iran (33,000), Vietnam (24,000), Kenya (14,000), Indonesia (5,000), Myanmar (3,000), Uzbekhistan (2,000), Kazakhstan (2,000), Mexico (1,000), and Afghanistan (170). One notes that the low figures for the major opiate producers (Occupied Afghanistan, Myanmar and Mexico; no data for Colombia) indicate that the impoverished inhabitants in these countries cannot afford to buy the opiates their fellow countrymen produce.

CIA-linked, US-backed opium production shifted from Turkey in the 1960s, and to South East Asia during the Vietnam War years [22-24], before shifting massively to Afghanistan after 9-11 and the war criminal US invasion. CIA-linked black profits aside, the strategic motivation was subversion and damage to Russia and China. Starting massively in the Vietnam War years, drugs have devastated African American communities and crippled the democratic prospect of African Americans holding the balance of power in the US (felony laws excluding large numbers of African American males from voting assisted this perversion of democracy by the White American Establishment) [25-28].

Anti-racist Jewish American journalist I.F. Stone famously stated "Government lie" [29, 30], and famed American writer Gore Vidal observed: "Unlike most Americans who lie all the time, I hate lying" [31]. Indeed the bigger the atrocity the more assiduously do Anglosphere Mainstream media presstitutes lie to the public [32, 33]. Thus patriotic Americans would generally be aware that 3,000 people were killed on 9-11, and that about 8,500 US Alliance soldiers have died in the US War on Terror [34]. However hidden from them by mendacious Mainstream media are the following appalling post-9-11 realities: 31 million American preventable deaths from lifestyle or political choices [35-40], 7 million Occupied Afghan deaths from violence or deprivation [41, 42], 4.6 million Iraqi deaths from violence or deprivation, 1990-2011 [41, 43], 6.3 million World drug-related deaths, 5.2 million World opiate drug-related deaths linked to US-protected Afghan opium production in US-occupied Afghanistan, 759,000 US drug-related deaths, and 130,000 US veteran suicides [44]. They are, of course, utterly unware of 32 million Muslim deaths from violence, 5 million, or from deprivation, 27 million, in 20 countries invaded by the US Alliance since the US Government's 9-11 false flag atrocity [45] – the bigger the US-imposed atrocity the more assiduously is it white-washed away by US-beholden Mainstream media. In my own country, fervently US lackey and resolutely "look-the-other-way" Australia, people are aware of 3,000 people being killed on 9-11 and possibly that only about 40 Australian solders have died in the US War on Terror. However they are utterly unaware that since 9-11 there have been 5.2 million World opiate drug-related deaths linked to US-protected Afghan opium production in US-occupied Afghanistan, that about 1.5 million Australians have died from "lifestyle" or "political choices" [46-50], that 21,000 Australians have died from drug-related causes (mostly opiate-related) [2], or that that 1,400 Australian veterans of US Alliance wars have suicided [44]. Interestingly, in 2008 the Australian PM Kevin Rudd suggested to a NATO meeting on Afghanistan that the Coalition should destroy the Afghan opium crop that presently kills about

290,000 people each year. His suggestion was, of course, rejected [51], notwithstanding the glaring reality that unlike Afghan combatants fighting the US and NATO Alliance, plants are sessile, cannot run away, and accordingly elaborate a huge array of chemical defences (including opiates) [52].

About 31,000 Americans die gun-related deaths each year and 558,000 will have died thus (from homicide, suicide or accidents) in the 18 years since 9-11 [35-40]. Notwithstanding this carnage and an almost weekly occurrence of mass shootings in the US, there is inaction on gun control laws due to the lobbying power of the National Rifle Association (NRA). Similarly, there are about 80,000 annual drug deaths in the 5 nations of the US-led, White Anglosphere, "Five-eyes club" (the US, UK, Canada, Australia and New Zealand), and 1.4 million will have died thus in the 18 years since 9-11 (most of these deaths being opioid-related and inescapably connected to the 18 year US Alliance war in Afghanistan). However for whatever secret strategic reason, the US Alliance will not destroy the Afghan opium crops that are killing huge numbers of US Alliance citizens.

Yet while only about 60 Americans have been killed in America since 9-11 by jihadi psychopaths, this tiny – albeit horrible – death toll provides a continuing basis for the US War on Terror in which 32 million Muslims have died from violence, 5 million, or from deprivation, 27 million, in 20 countries invaded by the US Alliance since the US Government's 9-11 false flag atrocity [45]. It gets worse because the US War on Terror has been associated with a long-term accrual cost of about $6 trillion, a vast sum that could have been used for keeping millions of Americans alive at home instead of killing millions of Muslims abroad – 1.7 million Americans die preventably each year from "life-style" or "political" choices and 31 million Americans will have died thus in the 18 years since 9-11 [35-40].

A compelling rationalization of this irrational, US-imposed Orwellian nightmare – "War is Peace, Freedom is Slavery and Ignorance is Strength… [and] 2 plus 2 does not equal 4" [53] – is that the American Establishment is resolutely committed to mendacity, subversion, violence, war and mass murder to ensure continuing American global hegemony for the benefit of the US

One Percenters. Australian writer John Menadue has cogently commented on bullying US attempts to involve Australia (and indeed other US allies) in a Cold War and potentially a hot war against China: "We [Australians and other US allies] are being softened up again step by step to support the US military and industrial complex that promotes perpetual war. The US is the greatest threat to peace in the world. It is an aggressor across the globe. It is the most violent country both at home and abroad. And people know it. The Pew Research Centre found in 2018 that 45% of people surveyed around the world saw US power and influence as a major threat... In so far as China is any sort of distant threat it would be much less so if we were not so subservient to the US. The US is determined to make China its enemy. We are cooperating in that process. The US is a very dangerous ally. It is more likely to get us into trouble than out of trouble. We are joined at the hip to the most violent and dangerous country in the world" [54].

One notes that the US subverts all countries [55, 56], has removed 67 national governments (many of them democratically elected) [57], has trashed secular government and modernity in the Muslim world [58], has collaborated with jihadi and non-jihadi terrorists around the world [56, 58], has over 700 military bases in over 70 countries [59], and has invaded 72 countries (52 after WW2), as compared to the English 193, Australians 85, France 82, Germany 39, Japan 30, Russia 25, Canada 25, Apartheid Israel 12, China 2 and Iran zero (0) [8, 60-64].

Final comments

The UN Office on Drugs and Crime (UNODC) reports that 0.6 million people die from illicit drugs each year, and it is estimated that of these about 290,000 deaths per year are linked to US protection of the Occupied Afghanistan opium industry. There are 80,000 annual drug deaths in the 5 nations of the US-led, Anglosphere "Five-eyes club" (the US, UK, Canada, Australia and New Zealand), and 1.4 million will have perished thus in the 18 years since 9-11. However Western Mainstream media resolutely ignore this largely US-imposed carnage while fervently adhering to the science-incompatible, lying Bush "official version" of the 9-11 atrocity (3,000 people killed, assertedly by technically-illiterate jihadi fanatics hiding in Afghan caves).

What can decent Humanity do in the face of this horrendous US Establishment mendacity and mass murder? Decent Humanity must (a) inform everyone they can about the largely US-imposed Opiate Holocaust, and (b) urge and apply Boycotts, Divestment and Sanctions (BDS) against all those people, politicians, parties, corporations and countries involved in this deadly assault on Humanity. The 80,000 annual US drug-related deaths are just the tip of a horror in which 1.7 million Americans die preventably each year from "life-style" and "political choice" reasons. Decent, patriotic Americans in particular who love their fellow citizens must demand at the very least that those responsible for the deception and mass murder of their fellow Americans in the ongoing Opiate Holocaust are removed from public life as utterly unelectable and utterly unfit to hold public office.

Originally published as "US-imposed Opiate Holocaust – US protection of Afghan opiates has killed 5.2 million people since 9-11" in Countercurrents, August 2019

References

[1]. UN Office on Drugs and Crime (UNODC) Annual Report 2017: https://www.unodc.org/documents/AnnualReport/Annual-Report_2017.pdf.
[2]. UN Office on Drugs and Crime (UNODC) – statistics and data: https://dataunodc.un.org/drugs.
[3]. "Afghan Holocaust, Afghan Genocide": https://sites.google.com/site/afghanholocaustafghangenocide/.
[4]. UNODC World Drug Report 2007: http://www.unodc.org/unodc/en/data-and-analysis/WDR-2007.html.
[5]. World Drug Report 2009: http://www.unodc.org/unodc/en/data-and-analysis/WDR-2009.html.
[6]. World Drug Report, Opium/heroin market, 2009: http://www.unodc.org/documents/wdr/WDR_2009/WDR2009_Opium_Heroin_Market.pdf.
[7]. UNODC, Executive Summary, World Drug Report 2019: https://wdr.unodc.org/wdr2019/prelaunch/WDR19_Booklet_1_EXECUTIVE_SUMMARY.pdf.
[8]. Gideon Polya, "Body Count. Global avoidable mortality since 1950", that includes a succinct history of every country and is now available for free perusal on the web: http://globalbodycount.blogspot.com/.
[9]. "Historical GDP of China", Wikipedia: https://en.wikipedia.org/wiki/Historical_GDP_of_China.
[10]. "Angus Maddison statistics of the ten largest economies by GDP (PPP)", Wikipedia: https://en.wikipedia.org/wiki/Angus_Maddison_statistics_of_the_ten_largest_economies_by_GDP_(PPP).
[11]. Gideon Polya, "Legacy of colonialism: Britain robbed India of $45 trillion & thence 1.8 billion Indians died from deprivation", Global Research, 19 December 2018: https://www.globalresearch.ca/legacy-of-colonialism-britain-robbed-india-of-45-trillion-and-thence-1-8-billion-indians-died-from-deprivation/5663351.
[12]. "How much money did Britain take away from India? About $45 trillion in 173 years, says top economist", Business Today, 19 November 2018: https://www.businesstoday.in/current/economy-politics/this-economist-says-britain-took-away-usd-45-trillion-from-india-in-173-years/story/292352.html.
[13]. Gideon Polya, "Jane Austen and the Black Hole of British History. Colonial rapacity, holocaust denial and the crisis in biological sustainability", G.M. Polya, Melbourne, 1998, 2008 that is now available for free perusal on the web: http://janeaustenand.blogspot.com/.
[14]. Gideon Polya, "Review: 'Inglorious Empire. What the British did to India' by Shashi Tharoor", Countercurrents, 8 September 2017: https://countercurrents.org/2017/09/08/review-inglorious-empire-what-the-british-did-to-india-by-shashi-tharoor/.
[15]. Shashi Tharoor, "Inglorious Empire. What the British did to India", Scribe, 2017.
[16]. Gideon Polya, "Economist Mahima Khanna, Cambridge Stevenson

Prize And Dire Indian Poverty", Countercurrents, 20 November, 2011: https://countercurrents.org/polya201111.htm.

[17]. Gideon Polya, "Australia And Britain Killed 6-7 Million Indians In WW2 Bengal Famine", Countercurrents, 29 September, 2011: https://countercurrents.org/polya290911.htm.

[18]. Martin Gilbert "Atlas of the Holocaust", Michael Joseph, London, 1982.

[19]. Martin Gilbert, "Jewish History Atlas", Weidenfeld and Nicolson, London, 1969.

[20]. Gideon Polya, "UK Zionist Historian Sir Martin Gilbert (1936-2015) Variously Ignored Or Minimized WW2 Bengali Holocaust", Countercurrents, 19 February, 2015: https://countercurrents.org/polya190215.htm.

[21]. "Experts: US did 9-11": https://sites.google.com/site/expertsusdid911/.

[22]. "Illegal drug trade in Turkey", Wikipedia: https://en.wikipedia.org/wiki/Illegal_drug_trade_in_Turkey.

[23]. "Opium production in Myanmar", Wikipedia: https://en.wikipedia.org/wiki/Opium_production_in_Myanmar.

[24]. "Allegations of CIA drug trafficking", Wikipedia: https://en.wikipedia.org/wiki/Allegations_of_CIA_drug_trafficking.

[25]. Gideon Polya, "Review: 'Becoming' By Michelle Obama – Mainstream Lying, Genocide Ignoring & Holocaust Ignoring", Countercurrents, 27 June 2019: https://countercurrents.org/2019/06/review-becoming-by-michelle-obama-mainstream-lying-genocide-ignoring-holocaust-ignoring.

[26]. Michelle Alexander, "The New Jim Crow: Mass Incarceration in the Age of Colorblindness", The New Press, 2010.

[27]. Michelle Alexander, "The war on drugs and the New Jim Crow", Race, Poverty, Environment, Vol. 17, No. 1 | Spring 2010: http://reimaginerpe.org/20years/alexander.

[28]. Gideon Polya, "Truth & Boycotts, Divestment & Sanctions (BDS) Can Overcome Huge Inequities Suffered By African Americans Under American Apartheid", Countercurrents, 29 September 2014: https://countercurrents.org/polya290914.htm.

[29]. I.F. Stone, quoted in "Two words – governments lie. Iraqi oil, climate change and Tony Blair", Media Lens, 22 January 2003: http://www.medialens.org/index.php?option=com_content&view=article&id=239:two-words-governments-lie-iraq-oil-climate-change-and-tony-blair&catid=17:alerts-2003&Itemid=42.

[30]. I.F. Stone, quoted in Gideon Polya, "Iraqi Holocaust", ConScience, Australasian Science, 2 June 2004: http://www.shiachat.com/forum/index.php?/topic/33427-iraqi-holocaust/.

[31]. "Gore Vidal interviewed by Melvyn Bragg on the South Bank Show", 2008: http://warincontext.org/2012/08/01/remembering-gore-vidal-change-is-the-nature-of-life-and-its-hope/.

[32]. "Mainstream media censorship": https://sites.google.com/site/mainstreammediacensorship/home.

[33]. "Mainstream media lying":

https://sites.google.com/site/mainstreammedialying/.

[34]. "i-casualties": http://icasualties.org/.

[35]. Gideon Polya, "14 million Americans will die preventably under a 2-term Trump Administration", Countercurrents, 22 March 2017: https://countercurrents.org/2017/03/over-14-million-americans-will-die-preventably-under-a-2-term-trump-administration.

[36]. Gideon Polya, "Movie review: 'Who to Invade Next' by Michael Moore – Hammer, chisel down for social humanism", Countercurrents, 23 April 2016: https://countercurrents.org/polya230416.htm.

[37]. Gideon Polya, "One million Americans die preventably annually in USA", Countercurrents, 18 February 2012: http://www.countercurrents.org/polya180212.htm.

[38]. Gideon Polya, "American Holocaust, Millions Of Untimely American Deaths And $40 Trillion Cost Of Israel To Americans", Countercurrents, 27 August, 2013: http://www.countercurrents.org/polya270813.htm.

[39]. Gideon Polya, "One Percenter Greed & War Means Over 1.5 Million Americans Die Preventably Each Year", Countercurrents, 19 September, 2014: http://www.countercurrents.org/polya190914.htm.

[40]. Gideon Polya, "West Ignores 11 Million Muslim War Deaths & 23 Million Preventable American Deaths Since US Government's False-flag 9-11 Atrocity", Countercurrents, 9 September, 2015: http://www.countercurrents.org/polya090915.htm.

[41]. "Muslim Genocide Muslim Holocaust": https://sites.google.com/site/muslimholocaustmuslimgenocide/.

[42]. "Afghan Holocaust, Afghan Genocide": http://sites.google.com/site/afghanholocaustafghangenocide/.

[43]. "Iraqi Holocaust, Iraqi Genocide": http://sites.google.com/site/iraqiholocaustiraqigenocide/).

[44]. Gideon Polya, "Australian state terrorism (4). Jingoistic, US Lackey Australia's Deadly Betrayal Of Its Traumatized Veterans", Stop state terrorism, 2018: https://sites.google.com/site/stopstateterrorism/australian-state-terrorism-4.

[45]. Gideon Polya, "Paris Atrocity Context: 27 Million Muslim Avoidable Deaths From Imposed Deprivation In 20 Countries Violated By US Alliance Since 9-11", Countercurrents, 22 November, 2015: https://countercurrents.org/polya221115.htm.

[46]. Gideon Polya, "Australian State Terrorism – Zero Australian Terrorism Deaths, 1 Million Preventable Australian Deaths & 10 Million Muslims Killed By US Alliance Since 9-11", Countercurrents, 23 September, 2014: https://countercurrents.org/polya230914.htm.

[47]. Gideon Polya, "Jingoistic, US lackey Australia's deadly betrayal of its traumatized veterans", Countercurrents, 18 May 2018: https://countercurrents.org/2018/05/26768.

[48]. Gideon Polya, "Coalition Climate Crimes & 200 Reasons Why Australia Must Dump Pro-coal, Pro-war Coalition PM Malcolm Turnbull", Countercurrents, 1 November, 2015: https://countercurrents.org/polya011115.htm.

[49]. Gideon Polya, "Pro-Apartheid Australia's New White Australia Policy

& compulsory Australian values statement", Countercurrents, 12 May 2017: https://countercurrents.org/2017/05/12/pro-apartheid-australias-new-white-australia-policy-compulsory-australian-values-statement/.

[50]. Gideon Polya, "On Anzac Day Australia ignores its complicity in horrendous war crimes & climate crimes", Countercurrents, 24 April 2017: https://countercurrents.org/2017/04/on-anzac-day-australia-ignores-its-complicity-in-horrendous-war-crimes-climate-crimes.

[51]. Louise Yaxley, "NATO commits to 'substantial' increase in Afghanistan troops", ABC News, 4 April 2008: https://www.abc.net.au/news/2008-04-04/nato-commits-to-substantial-increase-in/2392926.

[52]. Gideon Polya, "Biochemical Targets of Plant Bioactive Compounds", Taylor & Francis, 2003.

[53]. George Orwell, "Nineteen Eighty-Four", Secker & Warburg, 1949.

[54]. John Menadue, "Tugging our forelock again and again to our dangerous ally. An update", John Menadue – Pearls and irritations, 9 August 2019: http://johnmenadue.com/john-menadue-the-us-alliance-is-more-likely-to-get-us-into-trouble-than-out-of-trouble-an-update/.

[55]. John Perkins, "Confessions of an Economic Hit Man", Ebury Press, 2005.

[56]. Philip Agee, "Inside the Company: CIA Diary", Farrar Straus & Giroux, 1975.

[57]. John Pilger, "John Pilger: the war on Venezuela is built on lies", Green Left Weekly, 1 March 2019: https://www.greenleft.org.au/content/john-pilger-war-venezuela-built-lies.

[58]. Gideon Polya, "Fundamentalist America Has Trashed Secular Governance, Modernity, Democracy, Women's Rights And Children's Rights In The Muslim World", Countercurrents, 21 May, 2015: https://www.countercurrents.org/polya210515.htm.

[59]. David Vine, "Where in the world is the U.S. military?", Politico, July/August 2015: https://www.politico.com/magazine/story/2015/06/us-military-bases-around-the-world-119321.

[60]. Gideon Polya, "The US Has Invaded 70 Nations Since 1776 – Make 4 July Independence From America Day", Countercurrents, 5 July, 2013: http://www.countercurrents.org/polya050713.htm.

[61]. Gideon Polya, "British Have Invaded 193 Countries: Make 26 January (Australia Day, Invasion Day) British Invasion Day", Countercurrents, 23 January, 2015: http://www.countercurrents.org/polya230115.htm.

[62]. Gideon Polya, "As UK Lackeys Or US Lackeys Australians Have Invaded 85 Countries (British 193, French 80, US 70)", Countercurrents, 9 February, 2015: http://www.countercurrents.org/polya090215.htm.

[63]. Gideon Polya, "President Hollande And French Invasion Of Privacy Versus French Invasion Of 80 Countries Since 800 AD", Countercurrents, 15 January, 2014: http://www.countercurrents.org/polya150114.htm.

[64]. "Stop state terrorism": https://sites.google.com/site/stopstateterrorism/.

Redaction: Mainstream Media Censorship & Self-Censorship in Pre-Police-State Australia

Gideon Polya

On Monday, 21 October 2019, Australians around the country picking up their daily newspaper found that page 1 was blacked out in a facsimile of comprehensive redaction by a censor's black pen. No, pre-police state Australia had not suffered a neo-Nazi putsch or overt US takeover – the blacking out was a collective protest by Australian Mainstream media (MSM) against appalling press censorship by the mendacious and human rights-violating Australian Coalition Government. The taxpayer–funded ABC strongly supported this protest. However self-censorship by these same MSM means failure to report huge lying by omission by US-, UK- and Zionist-beholden Australian media, politician , academic and commentariat presstitutes.

In short, since 9-11, Australia has been gripped by US- and Zionist-promoted terror hysteria, Islamophobia, xenophobia and warmongering jingoism. Armed with anonymous advice from what is oxymoronically called Australian Intelligence, successive conservative Australian Governments have introduced scores of anti-terror laws and secrecy laws that variously impact on civil liberties and free speech. Thus a former Australian Intelligence officer, Witness K, and his lawyer (a former Attorney General of the Australian Capital Territory) have been prosecuted over secrecy laws. Recently the Government-instigated, Australian Federal Police raided the home of a Murdoch media journalist and also raided the ABC

(Australia's equivalent of the UK BBC) over leaked information about Australian war crimes in Occupied Afghanistan. This was finally too much for Australian MSM who quite rightly demanded protection of Australian journalists just doing their job and organized this "page 1 censorship" event to underscore this assault on press freedom by the US lackey Australian Government and by US lackey Australian Intelligence.

(1). Australia's censored and self-censoring Mainstream media and flawed democracy.

Australia is selectively "informed" by oligopoly Mainstream media, which is dominated by the gutter, right-wing and populist US Murdoch media empire (70% of Australian city daily newspaper readership plus national coverage by The Australian newspaper) and the formerly Fairfax-owned but now Channel 9-owned media empire that includes the quality and centrist publications of the Sydney Melbourne Herald (Sydney), The Age (Melbourne) and the quality Australian Financial Review (money is too important a subject to permit sloppy, incorrect or partisan reportage).

The quality and centrist UK Guardian has a major digital presence in Australia and is particularly notable for its persistent enquiry and its ethical, science-informed coverage of the worsening climate emergency. The ABC, Australia's taxpayer-funded equivalent of the endlessly mendacious UK BBC, is an important information source for Australians, particularly for intellectuals and for people in remote areas of this vast continent. The ABC (annual budget about $1 billion) is obliged to be "balanced" but in practice this means balancing reportage between anti-science right-wing populists and similarly US-, UK- and Zionist-beholden centrists (this bleak fare being leavened by the ABC's excellent Science Unit, science being utterly intolerant of lying and spin).

Australia is a multicultural country – as of 2019 about 29% of Australians were born overseas with the major source countries being England, China, India and New Zealand [1]. Indeed despite entrenched White Australian racism and the 1901-1974

White Australia Policy, today Australia is 76% White and 24% non-White but 95% of senior executive positions are held by Whites and only 5% by non-Whites [2, 3]. The taxpayer-funded ABC has a poor cousin, the Special Broadcasting Service (SBS) that has a multicultural intent but survives on advertising and an annual taxpayer subsidy of a mere $7 million [4]. It says a lot about the poor quality of Australian TV (dominated by the well-funded ABC and commercial free-to-air Channels 7, 9 and 10) that the best Australian TV in terms of world news, intelligent social issues discussion, documentaries, world movies and the world game (soccer) is provided by the impecunious SBS.

Australia is ostensibly a democracy and was one of the first parliamentary democracies in the world and one of the first to permit female suffrage. The Federal Parliament has a Lower House or House of Representatives with 151 democratically-elected MPs. Voting is compulsory and preferential (if a candidate fails to get over 50% of the vote, second preferences, etc. are taken into account). An independent Australian Electoral Commission supervises Federal elections. However this noble edifice begins to crumble on closer inspection. Thus there is an Upper House or Senate which is made up of 76 senators, with each elected to represent one of Australia's six states (12 senators each) or two territories (2 senators each). Thus Tasmania population 0.5 million) has the same number of senators (12) as New South Wales (population 7.5 million). No wonder former Australian Labor PM Paul Keating described the senators as "unrepresentative swill".

It gets worse. Thus Democracy in Australia (as in the West in general) has become a Plutocracy, Kleptocracy, Lobbyocracy, Corporatocracy and Dollarocracy in which Big Money purchases people, parties, policies, public perception of reality, votes and hence more power, and thence more private profit. Indeed the Coalition won the 2019 election on the preferences of the racist and bigoted One Nation Party and the United Australia Party that was backed in an extraordinary $60 million nation-wide campaign by mining billionaire Clive Palmer. However the good thing about Democracy is that you get a periodic change of government without bloodshed.

(2). Australia's appalling and continuing history of war criminality, climate criminality and genocide.

Before considering egregious censorship of Australian MSM by the illiberal and grossly human rights-violating Coalition Government, it is useful to briefly sketch Australian history and politics. Indigenous Australian history goes back 65,000 years. Indigenous Australians peacefully and sustainably "farmed" Australia for 65 millennia [5, 6] but this ended abruptly with the British invasion in 1788. Before the British invasion, there were 350-750 distinct languages and dialects of which only 150 remain today and all but 20 of these are endangered. The Indigenous population dropped from about 1 million to 0.1 million in the first century of colonization through massacres, dispossession, deprivation and introduced disease. The over 2 century Aboriginal Genocide and Aboriginal Ethnocide involved about 2 million deaths from violence (0.1 million) or from imposed deprivation. The Aboriginal Ethnocide continues today in racist White Australia through record removal of Aboriginal children from their mothers (a continuing Stolen Generations disaster), parlous support for remote communities, and removal of bilingual education. Indigenous life expectancy is about 10 years less than for White Australians, and Indigenous Australians suffer much poorer conditions in relation to health, education, social circumstances and incarceration [5-11]. A 1967 referendum finally permitted Aborigines to be counted and allowed laws about Aborigines to be made by the Federal Government by a change to the racist Section 51 of the Constitution [12, 13].

White Australia did not confine itself to the Aboriginal Genocide that was qualitatively the worst genocide in human history, and was matched only in this sense by the American Indian Genocide in the Americas [8]. As a UK lackey and thence a US lackey, Australians have historically invaded 85 countries as compared to the British 193, France 82, the US 72 (52 after WW2), Germany 39, Japan 30, Russia 25, Canada 25, Turkey 20, Apartheid Israel 12, China 2, North Korea (arguably none), and Iran (none since the Sasanian Empire [8, 14, 15]. Of these 85 Australian invasions, about 30 have involved genocide as defined by Article 2 of the UN Genocide Convention [16]. Australia was involved in the 2-century, British-imposed Indian Holocaust that involved 1,800 million Indians dying avoidably from imposed deprivation in the period 1757-1947, this being quantitatively the worst genocide and worst holocaust in human history [17]. Most recently, Australia was complicit in the WW2 Bengali Holocaust (WW2 Indian Holocaust, WW2 Bengal Famine) in which the British with Australian complicity deliberately starved 6-7 million Indians to death for strategic reasons [7, 8, 17-19].

Not to be confined by this appalling record, US lackey, war criminal and climate criminal Australia is disproportionately complicit in existential nuclear weapons and climate change threats that may wipe out most of humanity this century. Australia was complicit in all post-1950 US Asian wars (40 million Asian deaths from violence or from war-imposed deprivation) [8]. Through the joint US-Australian Pine Gap spying facility that is critical for US nuclear terrorism [20], Australia also targets illegal US drone strikes in 7 countries [21-23], and spies on Australians (for subsequent delivery to the US and thence to Apartheid Israel) [24]. Australia fervently opposes nuclear disarmament [20], and through its Genocide Convention- and Geneva Convention-violating occupation of Afghanistan [25] is also complicit in the US-imposed Opiate Holocaust that has killed about 5 million people since the US Alliance invasion and restoration of the Taliban-destroyed Afghan opiate industry [26]. Indeed the UNODC reported the following annual drug-related deaths of 15-64 year olds in 2017 in the following "White" countries of the Anglosphere "5-Eyes" Intelligence Club, with opioids being the leading cause of death: the US (70,237), Canada (3,998), UK (3,394), Australia (1,899), and New Zealand (261) [27]. Australia is among world leaders in 15 areas of climate criminality [28, 29] and as such is disproportionately complicit in a worsening Climate Genocide that – unless there is requisite climate action – may mean 10 billion deaths this century en route to a sustainable human population of only 0.5 – 1.0 billion in 2100 [30]. Australia has just categorically rejected the IMF proposal for a planet-saving Carbon Tax, and it can be estimated from IMF data that if all the G20 countries followed Australia's criminal example then an extra 4 million people would die from air pollution in the coming decade [29]

(3). Massive Mainstream media censorship in UK-, US- and Zionist-subverted look-the-other-way Australia.

Eminent Australia legal academic, Professor George Williams (a leading expert on Australian constitutional law and Dean of the Law Faculty at the University of New South Wales) on 70 post-9-11 anti-terror laws in Australia (2018): "One remarkable feature of Australia's response to terrorism is the sheer volume of lawmaking. In the years since September 11, Australia's Federal Parliament, and so not including the laws of the States and Territories, has enacted 70 anti-terror laws... As is clear from this list, Australia's new anti-terror laws impact upon a broad range of human rights. The laws are extraordinary in their scope and operation. It begs the question, where will this end? ... The self-restraint normally exercised by parliamentarians in respect to such areas has become increasingly absent as a political culture has developed in which it has become more acceptable to enact rights infringing statutes. This is a product not only of Australia's exceptional anti-terror laws, but also of the nation's asylum seekers policies. Unless we take a stand, it is hard to see where this will end ..." [31].

Thus, for example, it is punishable by 5 years in prison to reveal the long-term incarceration and interrogation without charge or trial of someone (e.g. a spouse). It is punishable by up to 10 years in prison to reveal illegal operations of Australian Intelligence. There are similar draconian penalties for whistleblowers revealing the truth in the public interest [31-34]. While the genocidal Zionist Irgun terrorist group (the forerunner of the Israeli Likud Party of war criminal Apartheid Israeli PM Netanyahu) was removed from Australia's list of proscribed terrorist groups. Professor Williams: "Australia's national anti-terror laws are striking not just in their volume, but, more significantly, in their reach. In particular, Australia's [laws]: define a 'terrorist act' as conduct engaged in or threats made for the purpose of advancing a 'political, religious or ideological cause'. The definition is more carefully tailored than others in some nations, but still encompasses liberation movements, such as the struggle of [Nobel Laureate] Nelson Mandela against apartheid, the armed resistance in East Timor or those seeking to bring down the Syrian government" [31]. As of 2016, Australia listed 20 proscribed terrorist organizations [35] but the list (all Muslims groups) included Hamas (overwhelmingly supported by Palestinians in the 2006 Occupied Palestinian elections held under Apartheid Israeli guns) and Hezbollah (that is overwhelmingly supported by Lebanese Muslims and defends Lebanon from genocidal and serial war criminal Apartheid Israel). While donations to support the continuing Zionist-imposed Palestinian Genocide are tax deductible in Australia (90% of Palestine has been ethnically cleansed by the Zionists with Netanyahu promising to raise this to 95%, and others demanding 100%), a donation to a Gaza orphanage could conceivably attract life imprisonment for allegedly supporting a "terrorist organization" (and indeed a major US Palestinian charity, the Holy Land Foundation, was closed down and some of its members obscenely persecuted and punished in this way by Zionist-perverted US authorities) [36].

These 70 anti-terror laws have mostly been passed by US- and Zionist-subverted Liberal Party- National Party Coalition Governments with the support of a cowardly and unprincipled Labor Opposition that is almost indistinguishable from the Coalition when it comes to defence, security, war, asserted terrorism, craven support for the US Alliance and craven, unprincipled support for Apartheid Israel and the traitorous, mendacious and deep-pocketed Zionist Lobby (indeed the Coalition and Labor are collectively known as the Lib-Labs). The Labor Party is strong on rhetoric when it comes to human rights, Indigenous rights, national sovereignty, climate change and racism but goes to water in the breach. Thus, for example, US lackey Labor is in practice grossly deficient when it comes to the human rights of asylum seekers, Indigenous Australians, Palestinians and victims of US imperialism. Labor is much stronger than the Coalition on renewable energy but has the same climate criminal policy as the Coalition of unlimited exports of coal, gas, iron ore and methanogenically-derived meat.

Former president of the Australian Human Rights Commission, Professor Gillian Triggs, declared that "[The Coalition Government] is a government ideologically opposed to human rights … Unlike almost every other comparable country Australia has no bill of rights against which government policies can be benchmarked. As there is no bill of rights, the courts are very very hamstrung in standing up for human rights" [37]. The substantially climate change denialist and totally effective climate change denialist Coalition is anti-science, anti-environment, and anti-human rights in key areas. War is the penultimate in racism with genocidal war being the ultimate crime. The right to life of the born is the most fundamental of human rights. The Coalition has been complicit in all post-1950 US Asian wars, atrocities in which 40 million Asians gave died from violence or war-imposed deprivation (Labor only excused itself from the Vietnam War and the Iraq War).

During the Cold War, Australia used to have a D-notice system whereby a government-media Defence, Press and Broadcasting Committee would ban reportage on specific security-related matters [38]. However this has been supplanted by extraordinary Federal Government secrecy, lying by omission and spin that slaps "top secret," "secret," "confidential" or "commercial in confidence" on a huge range of things, coupled with massive redaction of documents obtained Freedom of Information (FOI) requests and draconian punishment of whistleblowers "leaking" information (e.g. up to 10 years in prison for revealing an illegal Australian Intelligence operation). This massive cover-up has extended to institutions of learning and inquiry. Thus, prompted by the US, in 2012 the US lackey Labor Government passed the Australia-United States Defence Trade Cooperation Treaty-related Defence Trade Controls Bill that makes it an offence punishable by 10 years in prison for an academic without a permit to inform non-Australians (in conversation, tutorials, lectures, conference papers, scientific papers etc) about numerous technologies and thousands of chemicals and organisms listed in an over 350-page Defence and Strategic Goods List [39]. Unlike Australia, the US has the First Amendment that the guarantees freedom of expression and thus one can readily access publicly accessible, government-related information from the US whereas it is impossible and/or illegal to get the same information from obsessively secretive US lackey Australian Governments. Australian universities used to be institutions with ideals of unfettered inquiry and expression but have become corporatized entities that value their "brand" and in which freedom of expression of academics is constrained by fear and "Codes of Conduct" [40, 41].

(4). Massive self-censorship and lying by omission by Australian Mainstream media.

On Monday, 21 October 2019, every major print newspaper in Australia published a front page that was almost completely redacted, and did so (with the strong backing of the ABC and the online Guardian Australia) to draw attention to the massive constraints on the right of journalists to inform the public. The identified constraints were excessive defamation laws, draconian security laws, obsessive government secrecy and draconian punishment of whistleblowers. The Australian MSM are to be applauded for this action. However the whistle must also be blown on the stunning hypocrisy, massive dishonesty and massive self-censorship through lying by omission of Australian (and indeed Western) Mainstream media.
The horrible reality is that Neocon American and Zionist Imperialist (NAZI) subversion and perversion of Australian editor, politician, commentariat, academic and journalist presstitutes means massive fake news through lying by omission, noting that lying by omission is far, far worse than lying by commission because the latter at least permits public refutation and public discussion [42-49]. The horrendous war crimes of the American Empire and Apartheid Israel are ignored and whitewashed whereas the alleged domestic misdemeanours and illegalities of Trump and Netanyahu are reported in great detail. In US lackey Australia it is political death to criticize Zionist-subverted America or Apartheid Israel but the daily buffoonery of idiot Trump is fair game for the Mainstream presstitutes and functions like a pressure release valve on

cowardly Australian Mainstream self-censorship. However there are limits e.g. when right-wing, fervently pro-American and fervently pro-Zionist Labor leader Bill Shorten described US presidential candidate Trump as "bonkers" he was attacked for demeaning a potential leader of Australia's "great ally." Similarly, while any criticism of Apartheid Israel yields false defamation from the Zionists and pro-Zionists of "anti-Semitism" (with anti-racist Jewish critics of Israeli Apartheid being falsely defamed as "self-hating Jews' and "self-loathing Jews" as well as "anti-Semites"), there has been big coverage by Australian MSM of Netanyahu's business affairs, his alleged misdemeanours and his friendship with his next-door neighbour, Australian gambling billionaire James Packer.

Endless examples can be given of Australian Mainstream fake news through lying by omission but a powerful example relates to child abuse in Apartheid Israel, pro- Apartheid Israel America and similarly pro- Apartheid Australia that is second only to Trump's America as a supporter of Apartheid Israel and hence of Apartheid. Apartheid Israel determines that of its 50% Indigenous Palestinian subjects, 72% have zero human rights, cannot vote for the government ruling them and are highly abusively confined without charge or trial to the Gaza Concentration Camp (2 million) or to West Bank ghettoes (3 million) [50]. Apartheid is described by the UN as a crime against Humanity [51], and one can reasonably argue that people who support Apartheid are utterly unfit for public office in one-person-one-vote democracies like the UK, US, France, Canada, Germany and Australia. While there has been passionate advocacy in Australia for thousands of refugee children and their parents highly abusively and indefinitely imprisoned by successive Australian Governments without charge or trial in on-shore and off-shore concentration camps (for appalling details see [52]), there is no such outcry over the 1 million Indigenous Palestinian children bombed, shelled, shot and starved in the Gaza Concentration Camp. A Search of the ABC for "Malka Leifer" (a former Australian school principal so far successfully in 5 years of fighting extradition to Australia from Apartheid Israel over alleged sexual abuse of scores of school children) yields 82 Results but a Search for "Gaza

Concentration Camp" yields zero (0) results. Scholarly research reveals that 25% of Australian children, 17.5% of US children and 17% of Apartheid Israeli children suffer sexual abuse with horrendous consequences [53-64] but this is almost completely censored out of public perception by mendacious Australian Mainstream presstitutes. Indeed Australia has just spent $500 million on a Royal Commission into institutional sexual abuse of about 40,000 children (mainly by Catholic clergy), but overwhelmingly ignores the horrible reality that about 4 million adult Australians have been sexually abused as children (e.g. by family) [58].

And then there is child intellectual abuse whereby the one third of Australian children attending state-subsidized religious schools are brainwashed about all kinds of absurdities, obscenities and egregiously false and dangerous propositions such as misogyny, gender-based discrimination, sexism, sexual guilt, homophobia, anti-science claptrap, creationism, intelligent design, stoning to death for apostasy and adultery, miracles, life-after-death, trans-substantiation, water-into-wine, walking on water, dead-to-living conversion, virgin birth, heaven, hell, purgatory, assumption into heaven, rapturing up, divine authorship, holy book literalism, divine sanction, and the right to invade, occupy, devastate, and ethnically cleanse other countries [65, 66]. Indeed there is draconian punishment under Australian law for actually specifying what particular sects purvey these particular false, primitive and dangerous propositions. Indeed the child-abusing Australian government spends almost the same on subsidizing religion ($31 billion per year in 2013 according to the Secular Party of Australia [67]) as it does on Defence ($34.6 billion in 2019). However while an ABC Search for "child sexual abuse" yields 1,000 results, ABC Searches for "child intellectual abuse" and "intellectual child abuse" each yield zero (0) results. It must be noted that the ABC is widely regarded as a major progressive news medium in Australia.

Of course actual killing of children is far, far worse than repugnant child sexual abuse, but Neocon American and Zionist Imperialist (NAZI)-subverted and -perverted Australian (and

Western) Mainstream presstitutes resolutely whitewash the mass murder of children by the US Alliance (of which Australia is a craven member) and by other genocidal militarists. Noting that children are about 50% of the populations of impoverished, high birth rate societies, deaths in holocausts and genocides deriving from actual violence or from imposed deprivation are given in brackets as follows for the following alphabetically listed atrocities ("holocaust" means "a huge number of deaths" and "genocide" is defined by Article 2 of the UN Genocide Convention as "acts committed with intent to destroy, in whole or in part, a national, ethnic, racial or religious group"):

1788 onwards Australian Aboriginal Genocide and Australian Aboriginal Ethnocide (2 million), 21st century Afghan Genocide and Afghan Holocaust (7 million), 15th – 19th century African Holocaust (slave trade; 6 million), 16th century onwards Amerindian Genocide (90 million), WW1 Armenian Genocide (1.5 million), post-1950 Asian Holocaust due to Australia-complicit US Asian Wars (40 million), 1914-1924 Assyrian Genocide (Syriac Genocide; 0.2-0.3 million), 1769-1770 Bengal Famine and Bengali Holocaust (10 million), WW2 Bengali Holocaust, WW2 Bengal Famine and WW2 Indian Holocaust (6-7 million), 1971-1972 Bengali Holocaust (3.0 million), 1990s Bosnian Genocide (circa 0.1 million), 1969-1998 Cambodian Genocide (6.0 million), 19th century Chinese Holocaust (Opium wars and Tai Ping rebellion; 20-100 million), WW2 Chinese Holocaust (35 million), 1958-1961 Chinese Holocaust of the Great Leap Forward (20-30 million), 19th – 20th century Congolese Genocide and Congolese Holocaust (10 million), 1960 onwards Congolese Genocide and Congolese Holocaust (20 million), WW2 European Holocaust (30 million Slavs, Jews and Roma killed), 1941-1950 German Genocide and German Holocaust (9 million), Global Avoidable Mortality Holocaust (1,500 million deaths from deprivation since 1950), 1757-1947 Indian Holocaust (1,800 million avoidable deaths from imposed deprivation), 1947 Indian Holocaust due to Partition (1.0 million), 1917-1919 Iranian Genocide (Iranian Famine, Persian Famine) (2 million), 1979 – present Iranian Genocide, Iranian Holocaust (3 million), 1914-2011 Iraqi Genocide and Iraqi Holocaust (9 million), 21st century Iraqi

Genocide and Iraqi Holocaust (2.7 million), 1990-2011 Iraqi
Genocide and Iraqi Holocaust (4.6 million), WW2 Jewish
Holocaust, Shoa, Jewish Genocide (5-6 million), 1950-1953
Korean Genocide and Korean Holocaust (5.2 million), 1840s
Irish Famine (2 million), 1955-1975 Laotian Genocide (1.2
million), 2011 Libyan Genocide (0.2 million), 21st century
Muslim Genocide and Muslim Holocaust (32 million), 1900s
Namibian Genocide (0.1 million), 17th – 19th century North
American Indian Genocide (up to 18 million), WW1 onwards
Palestinian Genocide and Palestinian Holocaust (2.2 million),
WW2 Polish Genocide and Polish Holocaust (6 million), 21st
century Rohingya Genocide (circa 0.1 million), 1930-1953
Russian Holocaust under Stalin (20 million), 1994 Rwandan
Genocide (0.9 million), 1992 onwards Somali Genocide and
Somali Holocaust (2.2 million), 1930-1953 Soviet Holocaust
under Stalin (20 million), 1955-2018 Sudanese Genocide and
Sudanese Holocaust (13 million), 2011 onwards Syrian
Genocide (1.0 million), 1975-1999 East Timorese Genocide
(0.3 million), 1930s Ukrainian Famine, Holodomor (7 million),
1945-1975 Vietnamese Genocide and Vietnamese Holocaust
(15.3 million), and the 2015 onwards Yemeni Genocide (circa
0.1 million) [7, 8, 68, 69].

A Search of the ABC for the terms "Jewish Holocaust", "Shoa"
, "Jewish Genocide", "Holocaust", and "The
Holocaust"(synonymous terms in the West for the WW2
German atrocity in which 5-6 million Jews were killed by
violence or imposed deprivation) yield 19, 1, 1, 781 and 372
Results respectively. However ABC Searches for the above list
of other atrocities yield quite different results and are given
below in brackets after each term (noting that many of the
successful "holocaust"-related searches pick up results relating
to the WW2 Jewish Holocaust rather than to the national event
searched for):

"Australian Aboriginal Ethnocide" (1), "Aboriginal Ethnocide"
(1), "Australian Aboriginal Genocide" (1), "Aboriginal
Genocide" (3), "Afghan Genocide" (0), "Afghan Holocaust"
(0), "African Holocaust" (0), "American Indian Genocide" (0),
"Amerindian Genocide" (0), "Armenian Genocide" (42), "Asian

Holocaust" (0), "Assyrian Genocide" (1), "Syriac Genocide" (0), "Bengali Holocaust" (0), "Bengal Famine" (2), "Indian Holocaust" (0), "Bosnian Genocide" (2), "Cambodian Genocide" (3), "Chinese Holocaust" (0), "Congolese Genocide" (0), "Congolese Holocaust" (0), "European Holocaust" (1), "German Genocide" (0), "German Holocaust" (0), "Global Avoidable Mortality Holocaust" (0), "Avoidable Mortality Holocaust" (0), "Iranian Famine" (0), "Persian Famine" (0), "Iranian Genocide" (0), "Iranian Holocaust" (0), "Iraqi Genocide" (0), "Iraqi Holocaust" (0), "Jewish Holocaust" (19), "Shoa" (1), "Jewish Genocide" (1), "Holocaust" (781), "The Holocaust" (372), "Korean Genocide" (0), "Korean Holocaust" (0), "Irish Famine" (8), "Laotian Genocide" (19), "Libyan Genocide" (28), "Muslim Genocide" (246), "Muslim Holocaust" (1), "Namibian Genocide" (0), "North American Indian Genocide" (0), "Palestinian Genocide" (32), "Palestinian Holocaust" (55), "Polish Genocide" (24), "Polish Holocaust" (72), "Rohingya Genocide" (141), "Russian Holocaust" (123), "Rwandan Genocide" (118), "Somali Genocide" (0), "Somali Holocaust" (0), "Soviet Holocaust" (0), "Sudanese Genocide" (0), "Sudanese Holocaust" (0), " Syrian Genocide" (147), "East Timorese Genocide" (3), "Timorese Genocide" (3), "Ukrainian Famine" (11), "Holodomor" (0), "Vietnamese Genocide" (19), "Vietnamese Holocaust" (0), and "Yemeni Genocide" (23).

Memo to the politically correct racist (PC racist) and egregiously mendacious Australian ABC and Australian Mainstream presstitutes in general: "Brown and black lives matter."

Final comments

Australian Intelligence has an appalling record of criminality and mendacity ranging from the relatively minor (spying on the East Timorese cabinet meetings, spying on the Indonesian president and his wife, secret wrecking of the lives of thousands of decent and humanitarian Australians) to the major (endless false advice to Australia in the interests of malignant foreign powers, complicity in US, UK and Apartheid Israeli subversion of Australia [70], complicity in the war criminal invasion of

Iraq, complicity in war crimes, unacceptable involvement in Australian politics, complicity in the US-backed military coup in Chile, complicity in the US- and UK-backed 1975 Coup that removed the progressive Australian Whitlam Labor Government, and being accessory after the fact of the 9-11 atrocity that according to numerous science, engineering, aviation, military and intelligence experts involved the US Government and very likely Israeli and Saudi participation [71]). The draconian Australian law that provides for up to 10 years in prison for revealing an Australian Intelligence operation means that Australian Intelligence and the Australian Government can continue to commit such minor to major crimes with impunity – Australians are accordingly thoroughly entitled to think the worst of these mendacious and traitorous criminals who are now enabled by law to commit even worse crimes with impunity.

The asserted justification for the Australian Intelligence and Australian Government secrecy (lying by omission) is jihadi terrorism, but the reality is that only about 4 Australians have ever been killed in Australia by jihadi terrorists (and none before 2014) whereas 85,000 Australians die preventably each year from fiscally-impacted "lifestyle choices" or "political choices" . Indeed 1.5 million Australians have died thus since 9-11. This carnage topically includes about 80 women murdered by their partners or ex-partners each year and about 80 Australian veterans committing suicide each year [72]. The annual breakdown of this carnage (including some overlaps) is as follows: (1) 26,000 deaths from adverse hospital events, (2) 17,000 obesity-related deaths, (3) 15,500 smoking-related deaths, (4) 10,000 carbon burning pollution-derived deaths, (5) 4,000 avoidable Indigenous deaths, (6) 5,600 alcohol-related deaths, (7) 2,900 suicides (circa 100 being veterans) , (8) 1,400 road deaths, (9) 630 opiate drug-related deaths with 570 linked to US restoration of the Taliban-destroyed Afghan opium industry, and (10) 300 homicides (80 being of women killed domestically) [72-75]. Successive Australian Governments have been committing to an annual long-term accrual cost of $10 billion for the US War on Terror that is in actuality a genocidal US Alliance War on Muslims [76] – a huge fiscal commitment that could otherwise have been used to help prevent 1.5 million preventable Australian deaths since 9-11.

Further, the UNODC informs that in 2017 about 1,900 Australians died from drugs, with opiate drugs being major contributors and the US being a major player in the global Opiate Holocaust through restoration and protection of the world-leading Afghan opium industry that was largely abolished by the Taliban (down to 6% of world opium market share in 2001) [27]. Each year a mendacious, criminal and drug-pusher America is complicit in the deaths of 500 times more Australians than have ever been killed in Australian by jihadi terrorists (4, and none before 2014). Indeed it is patently obvious that jihadi non-state terrorism continues to be the greatest asset of US imperialism (which indeed has a long record of supporting jihadis from Afghanistan and Kosovo in the 20th century to Syria, Libya and Yemen in the 21st century) – thus every jihadi atrocity provides an "excuse" for American invasion and mass murder of Muslims.

In 1996, 6 years into the 1990-2011 Iraqi Holocaust (4.6 million deaths from violence or war-imposed deprivation), anti-racist Jewish American journalist Lesley Stahl asked America's UN Ambassador Madeleine Albright: "We have heard that half a million [Iraqi] children have died. I mean, that's more children than died in Hiroshima. And, you know, is the price worth it?" to which an infant blood-drenched Albright replied "We think the price is worth it." [77, 78]. Yet for nearly 30 years there has been deafening silence about the Iraqi Holocaust from Australian Mainstream presstitutes, whether male or female. A notable exception has been the ABC Science Unit that in a 2005 broadcast (and later published in a 2007 book) my detailed analysis of Australian complicity in Iraqi mass mortality [79, 80]. The Australian science journal ConScience published a similar analysis by me in 2004 [81]. However shortly thereafter, about 10 years ago, I somehow became "invisible" in Australia (US lackey Australian Intelligence and the traitorous and genocidal Zionists are most likely responsible for this censorship). However, inspired by Polish hero Jan Karski (who tried to inform a disbelieving world about the Jewish Holocaust as it was happening [82]) I resolutely continue to research, write and publish about 5,000 words each week in overseas progressive media (e.g. Countercurrents, Global Research, Media With Conscience News (MWC News), Crime & Power, and Bellaciao) about the human cost of war, occupation, neoliberalism and climate criminality.

A powerful example of the knee jerk intolerance of Australian Mainstream presstitutes to truth-telling is the case of Yassmin Abdel-Magied. In 2017 on Australia's war memorial Anzac Day (25 April), Muslim, feminist, social advocate and humanitarian journalist Yassmin Abdel-Magied (who worked for the ABC) posted the following seven (7) words on her Facebook page: "Lest we forget (Manus, Nauru, Syria, Palestine)." Savaged by public outcry, Ms. Abdel-Magied rapidly deleted the post and apologized. The ABC also apologized and a month later cancelled her TV program. Yassmin Abdel-Magied left the country. The post was correct and her silencing by rabid jingoists was and remains a stain on Australia and Australian Mainstream presstitutes and represented an outrageous attack on free speech. I published a very long, detailed and documented expansion of Yassmin Abdel-Magied's 7 inexplicit words that had initiated such national outrage. However my analysis was published overseas in Countercurrents [83], but as an "invisible" non-person in Australia my detailed and expert analysis of Australian, Apartheid Israeli and US Alliance war crimes in Syria and Palestine, and of gross Australian human rights abuse on Manus Island (Papua New Guinea) and Nauru failed to penetrate the Australian Mainstream "Wall of Silence." My "effective censorship" and "invisibility" meant that I was free from salivating, nation-wide hatred.

For sure, the Australian Mainstream media are absolutely correct in their condemnation of attacks on press free speech by the human rights-abusing Australian Coalition Government (with the collaboration of US lackey Australian Intelligence and the Australian Federal Police). However this remarkable outburst of truth telling by Australian Mainstream presstitutes hides a vastly more serious crime of the Mainstream media themselves – massive lying by omission, and indeed an endless reiteration of lying by omission about lying by omission about lying by omission … The Australian Federal Police (AFP) raids on the home of a Murdoch media journalist (Annika Smethurst) and on the offices of 2 ABC journalists was somehow connected with "leaked" revelations about war crimes by Australian soldiers in Occupied Afghanistan. Such crimes (the killing of several civilians) are serious and should certainly be exposed. However the mendacious Mainstream media, in a process of continuing and deeply racist self-censorship, resolutely refuse to report a vastly greater crime – the Australian Government's complicity in the passive mass murder of millions of Afghan women and children (and men) in gross violation of Articles 55 and 56 of the Geneva Convention in relation to the Protection of Civilian Persons in Time of War.

These Geneva Conventions unequivocally demand that an Occupier must provide its conquered Subjects with life-sustaining food and medical requisites "to the fullest extent of the means available to it". One notes that the per capita GDP is $500 for Occupied Afghanistan, $10,000 for neighbouring China, $57,000 for Occupier Australia and $63,000 for Occupier America, and that the most fundamental human right is the right to life. While legitimately criticized for the one party state, the death penalty, censorship, urban air pollution and harsh treatment of dissidents, China has been hugely successful in radically reducing infant mortality and maternal mortality in Tibet and in China as a whole. In stark contrast, the war criminal US Alliance occupation of neighbouring Afghanistan continues to be associated with an under-1 infant mortality and maternal mortality incidence that is 7 times higher and 4-12 times higher, respectively, than that in poor Tibet – evidence of gross violation of the Geneva Convention and the UN Genocide Convention by the US Alliance [25]. It is not Australian soldiers but the war criminal Australian Government politicians who are complicit in this appalling war crime. The Mainstream presstitutes are complicit in this ongoing atrocity through genocide ignoring, holocaust ignoring, genocide denial and holocaust denial.

At the 20 January 1942 Wannsee Conference in Berlin the German Nazi leadership finalized decisions on executing the Jewish Holocaust that was to claim a total of 5-6 million lives over 7 years [84-86]. On 11 October 2019 the Australian Coalition Government said "No" to an IMF-proposed global Carbon Tax, an utterly immoral act by the Australia Government that if followed by the rest of the G20 would prevent saving 4 million lives from air pollution out of the 80 million dying thus over the same period. This criminal act of adumbrated mass murder is, of course, ignored by Australian Mainstream presstitutes [29]. In 1945, the Germans adopted a CAAAA (C4A) protocol involving Cessation of the killing, Acknowledgment of the crimes, Apology for the crimes, Amends for the crimes, and Assertion of "never again to anyone". Serial war criminal and climate criminal Australia ignores all 5 elements of the C4A protocol and is blithely continuing on its war criminal and climate criminal way. This horrendous Australian criminality is aided and abetted by appalling censorship and lying by omissions effected by racist, mendacious and traitorous Australian Mainstream presstitutes. Of course Australia is a democracy of sorts with compulsory and preferential voting, and thus the 51% of Australians who voted for the Stupid, Ignorant and Egregiously Greedy (SIEG as in Dr. Strangelove and "Sieg heil!") Coalition Government have a definite complicity in this ongoing mass murder.

I have a positive suggestion for the Australian ABC and Australian Mainstream presstitutes in general, to whit that they cease lying by omission just for One Day of the Year, and no better day than the war memorial Remembrance Day (11 November, also the date of the US- and UK-backed coup that removed the reformist Whitlam Labor Government in 1975) or on the war memorial Anzac Day (25 April, and indeed famously described as "The One Day of the Year" in the Alan Seymour play of the same name [87].

The massive lying by omission, mendacity, anti-science blustering and gross human rights abuses by the war criminal and climate criminal Australian Government are self-assertedly justified by "security" and "the national interest". However rational risk management, that is crucial for societal safety and security, successively involves (a) accurate information, (b) scientific analysis involving the critical testing of potentially falsifiable hypotheses, and (c) science-informed systemic change to minimize risk. This rational, science-based protocol is sabotaged by (a) lying by commission, lying by omission, spin, obfuscation , censorship, self-censorship and intimidation, (b) spin-based analysis involving the selective use of asserted facts to support a partisan position, and (c) counterproductive blame and shame with the inhibition of vital reportage and with the ultimate irrational perversion being war [88]. On this basis, the mendacity of the Australian Government and "sacrosanct" Australian Intelligence is a huge threat to the safety and security of Australians.

What can decent people do about this massive Mainstream lying by omission? Decent people must (a) inform everyone they can, (b) do their best to penetrate the Mainstream Wall of Silence, (c) eschew mendacious Mainstream media in favour of humane and truth-telling Alternative media (such as Countercurrents), and (d) apply Boycotts, Divestment and Sanctions (BDS) against all people, politicians and parties, collectives, corporations and countries that are disproportionately complicit in this deadly perversion of truth and humanity.

Originally published as "Redaction: Mainstream Media Censorship & Self-Censorship in Pre-Police-State Australia," Countercurrents, October 2019.

References

[1]. "Almost 30% of Australians were born overseas," SBS News, 3 April 2019: https://www.sbs.com.au/news/almost-30-per-cent-of-the-australian-population-was-born-overseas.

[2]. Soutphomassane, Greg Whitwell, Kate Jordan and Philipp Ivanov, "Leading for Change. A blueprint for cultural diversity and inclusive leadership revisited," 2018.

[3]. Gideon Polya, "Review: "Leading for Change" – corporate cultural diversity deficiency & Australian financial scandals," Countercurrents, 3 May 2018: https://countercurrents.org/2018/05/review-leading-for-change-corporate-cultural-diversity-deficiency-australian-financial-scandals.

[4]. "We would have to "adjust" radio programs if budgets are cut: SBS," Radioinfo, 1 March 2018: https://radioinfo.com.au/news/we-would-have-adjust-radio-programs-if-budgets-are-cut-sbs.

[5]. "Aboriginal Genocide": https://sites.google.com/site/aboriginalgenocide.

[6]. On the back cover of Brice Pascoe, "Dark Emu," Magabala Books, 2014.

[7]. Gideon Polya, "Jane Austen and the Black Hole of British History. Colonial rapacity, holocaust denial and the crisis in biological sustainability," now available for free perusal on the web: http://janeaustenand.blogspot.com/2008/09/jane-austen-and-black-hole-of-british.html.

[8]. Gideon Polya, "Body Count. Global avoidable mortality since 1950," this including an avoidable mortality-related history of every country since Neolithic times and now available for free perusal on the web: http://globalbodycount.blogspot.com.au/2012/01/body-count-global-avoidable-mortality_05.html.

[9]. Gideon Polya, "Film Review: "Utopia" By John Pilger Exposes Genocidal Maltreatment Of Indigenous Australians By Apartheid Australia," Countercurrents, 14 March, 2014: http://www.countercurrents.org/polya140314.htm.

[10]. John Pilger, "Utopia," a movie , 2013.

[11]. Gideon Polya, " Ongoing Aboriginal Genocide And Aboriginal Ethnocide By Politically Correct Racist Apartheid Australia," Countercurrents, 16 February 2014: http://www.countercurrents.org/polya160214.htm.

[12]. "1967 Referendum (Aboriginals)," Wikipedia: https://en.wikipedia.org/wiki/1967_Australian_referendum_(Aboriginals).

[13]. "Section 51 (xxvi) of the Constitution of Australia," Wikipedia: https://en.wikipedia.org/wiki/Section_51(xxvi)_of_the_Constitution_of_Australia.

[14]. "Stop state terrorism" : https://sites.google.com/site/stopstateterrorism.

[15]. Gideon Polya, "As UK Lackeys Or US Lackeys Australians Have Invaded 85 Countries (British 193, French 80, US 70)," Countercurrents, 9 February, 2015: http://www.countercurrents.org/polya090215.htm.

[16]. Gideon Polya, "Review: "The Cambridge History Of Australia" Ignores Australian Involvement In 30 Genocides," Countercurrents, 14 October, 2013: https://www.countercurrents.org/polya141013.htm.

[17]. Gideon Polya, "Economist Mahima Khanna, Cambridge Stevenson Prize And Dire Indian Poverty," Countercurrents, 20 November, 2011: https://countercurrents.org/polya201111.htm.

[18]. Gideon Polya, "Australia And Britain Killed 6-7 Million Indians In WW2 Bengal Famine," Countercurrents, 29 September, 2011: http://www.countercurrents.org/polya290911.htm.

[19]. Gideon Polya, "Britain robbed Indian of $45 trillion & thence 1.8 billion Indians died from deprivation," Countercurrents, 18 December 2018: https://countercurrents.org/2018/12/britain-robbed-india-of-45-trillion-thence-1-8-billion-indians-died-from-deprivation.

[20]. "Nuclear weapons ban, end poverty & reverse climate change": https://sites.google.com/site/300orgsite/nuclear-weapons-ban.

[21]. Philip Dorling, "Australian intelligence "feeding data" for deadly US drone strikes," Sydney Morning Herald, 26 May 2014:http://www.smh.com.au/federal-politics/political-news/australian-intelligence-feeding-data-used-for-deadly-us-drone-strikes-20140526-38ywk.html.

[22]. Mark Corcoran, "Drone strikes based on work at Pine Gap could see Australians charged, Malcolm Fraser says," Sydney Morning Herald, 29 April 2014: http://www.abc.net.au/news/2014-04-28/australians-could-be-charged-over-us-drone-strikes-fraser/5416224.

[23]. John Stapleton, "Australia's dirty secret," UNSW Canberra, 4 December 2015: https://www.unsw.adfa.edu.au/drone-wars-australias-dirty-secret.

[24]. Philip Dorling, "US shares raw intelligence on Australian with Israel," Sydney Morning Herald, 12 September 2013: http://www.smh.com.au/national/us-shares-raw-intelligence-on-australians-with-israel-20130911-2tllm.html.

[25]. Gideon Polya, "China's Tibet health success versus passive mass murder of Afghan women and children by US Alliance," Global Research, 7 January 2018: https://www.globalresearch.ca/chinas-tibet-health-success-versus-passive-mass-murder-of-afghan-women-and-children-by-us-alliance/5625169.

[26]. Gideon Polya, "US-imposed Opiate Holocaust – US protection of Afghan opiates has killed 5.2 million people since 9-11," Countercurrents, 10 August 2019: https://countercurrents.org/2019/08/us-imposed-opiate-holocaust-us-protection-of-afghan-opiates-has-killed-5-2-million-people-since-9-11.

[27]. UN Office on Drugs and Crime (UNODC) – statistics and data: https://dataunodc.un.org/drugs.

[28]. Gideon Polya, "Millions join Global School Climate Strike – we are running out of time," Countercurrents, 22 September 2019: https://countercurrents.org/2019/09/millions-join-global-school-climate-strike-we-are-running-out-of-time.

[29]. Gideon Polya, "Australia rejects IMF Carbon Tax & preventing 4 million pollution deaths by 2030," Countercurrents, 15 October 2019: https://countercurrents.org/2019/10/australia-rejects-imf-carbon-tax-preventing-4-million-pollution-deaths-by-2030.

[30]. "Climate Genocide":
https://sites.google.com/site/climategenocide/home.
[31]. George Williams, "Sacrificing Civil Liberties to Counter Terrorism: Where Will it End?" 2018 John Marsden Lecture, NSW Council for Civil Liberties, 22 November 2018:
http://www.nswccl.org.au/2018_john_marsden_lecture_sacrificing_civil_libe rties_to_counter_terrorism_where_will_it_end.
[32]. Gideon Polya, "50 Ways Australian Intelligence Spies On Australia And The World For UK , Israeli And US State Terrorism," Countercurrents, 11 December, 2013: https://countercurrents.org/polya111213.htm.
[33]. Gideon Polya, "Terror Hysteria – Draconian New Australian Anti-Terrorism Laws Target Journalists, Muslims And Human Rights," Countercurrents, 8 October, 2014:
https://countercurrents.org/polya081014.htm.
[34]. Mark Pearson, "Journalists face jail for reporting intelligence operations – with no public interest defence," Journlaw, 3 October 2014: https://journlaw.com/2014/10/03/journalists-face-jail-for-reporting-intelligence-operations-with-no-public-interest-defence.
[35]. "Outlawed terror organisations in Australia" , Wikipedia: https://en.wikipedia.org/wiki/Outlawed_terror_organisations_in_Australia.
[36]. Joe Catron, "Brothers jailed by US and expelled to Gaza speak out," Electronic Intifada, 26 July 2016:
https://electronicintifada.net/content/brothers-jailed-us-and-expelled-gaza-speak-out/11534.
[37]. Michael Slezak, "Gillian Triggs: Australian government "ideologically opposed to human rights," Guardian, 26 July 2017:
https://www.theguardian.com/australia-news/2017/jul/26/gillian-triggs-australian-government-ideologically-opposed-to-human-rights.
[38]. "DSMA-Notice," Wikipedia: https://en.wikipedia.org/wiki/DSMA-Notice.
[39]. "Impact of the Defence Trade Controls Bill on academic freedom," NTEU: 10 October 2012: http://www.nteu.org.au/article/Impact-of-the-Defence-Trade-Controls-Bill-on-academic-freedom-13461.
[40]. Gideon Polya "Current academic censorship and self-censorship in Australian universities," Public University Journal, volume 1, Conference Supplement, "Transforming the Australia University," Melbourne, 9-10 December 2001; Free University Education:
https://sites.google.com/site/freeuniversityeducation/academic-censorship.
[41]. Gideon Polya, "Crisis in our universities," ABC Radio National "Ockham's Razor," 19 August 2001:
http://www.abc.net.au/radionational/programs/ockhamsrazor/crisis-in-our-universities/3490214.
[42]. "Mainstream media censorship":
https://sites.google.com/site/mainstreammediacensorship/home.
[43]. "Mainstream media lying":
https://sites.google.com/site/mainstreammedialying.
[44]. "Lying by omission." Lying by omission is worse than lying by commission because at least the latter permits refutation and public debate,"

Mainstream media lying:
https://sites.google.com/site/mainstreammedialying/lying-by-omission.
[45]. Gideon Polya, "Fake news: "Fake realities" and "Lying by omission,"
Global research, 18 April 2018: https://www.globalresearch.ca/mainstream-
media-fake-news-through-lying-by-omission/5582944.
[46]. Gideon Polya, "Australian ABC and UK BBC fake news through lying
by omission," Countercurrents, 2 May 2017:
https://countercurrents.org/2017/05/australian-abc-and-uk-bbc-fake-news-
through-lying-by-omission.
[47]. Gideon Polya, "Zionist subversion, Mainstream media censorship,"
JUST, 13 March 2018: http://www.just-international.org/wp/articles/zionist-
subversion-mainstream-media-censorship.
[48]. Gideon Polya, "Exposing horrendous Mainstream media lying by
omission," MWC News, 10 March 2016:
http://mwcnews.com/focus/analysis/57731-mainstream-media-lying.html.
[49]. Gideon Polya, "Mainstream media: fake news through lying by
omission," MWC News, 1 April 2017:
http://mwcnews.com/focus/analysis/64626-mainstream-media.html.
[50]. "Palestinian Genocide":
https://sites.google.com/site/palestiniangenocide.
[51]. John Dugard, "International Convention on the Suppression and
Punishment of the crime of Apartheid," Audiovisual Library of International
Law: http://untreaty.un.org/cod/avl/ha/cspca/cspca.html.
[52]. Gideon Polya, "Review: "No Friend but the Mountains" – Australia's
Manus Island Concentration Camp exposed," Countercurrents, 11 April
2019: https://countercurrents.org/2019/04/review-no-friend-but-the-
mountains-australias-manus-island-concentration-camp-exposed.
[53]. Gideon Polya, "Australian And Western Mainstream Media Ignore
Massive And Deadly Western Child Abuse In War And Peace,"
Countercurrents, 9 March, 2016:
https://www.countercurrents.org/polya090316.htm.
[54]. Gideon Polya, "Horrendous Australian child sexual abuse," MWC
News, 15 November 2012: http://mwcnews.net/focus/analysis/22859-
gideonpolya-sexual-abuse.html.
[55]. Gideon Polya, "Horrendous Child Abuse By Pro-war, Pro-Zionist,
Climate Criminal Australian Coalition Governments," Countercurrents, 4
December, 2013: http://www.countercurrents.org/polya041213.htm.
[56]. "Little Children are Sacred" Report:
http://web.archive.org/web/20070703014641/http://www.nt.gov.au/dcm/inqu
irysaac/pdf/bipacsa_final_report.pdf.
[57]. Dunne, M.P., Purdie, D.M., Cook, M.D., Boyle, F.M. & Najman,
J.M.(2003), Is child sexual abuse declining? Evidence from a population-
based survey of men and women in Australia, Child Abuse & Neglect, vol.
27 (2), pp141-152.
[58]. Gideon Polya, "Sectarian Australian Mainstream Ignores Horrendous
Child Sexual Abuse Of 4.4 Million Australians," Countercurrents, 15
November, 2012: http://www.countercurrents.org/polya151112.htm.

[59]. Jane Lee, "Child abuse victims lead "shorter lives" than other children, royal commission hears," The Age, 25 May 2015: http://www.theage.com.au/victoria/child-abuse-victims-live-shorter-lives-than-other-children-royal-commission-hears-20150525-gh8y1d.html.

[60]. Australian Institute of Criminology (1993). Second Conference on Violence (June 1993).

[61]. Brave Hearts, "Child sexual assault: facts and statistics": https://www.bravehearts.org.au/files/Facts%20and%20Stats_updated141212.pdf.

[62]. Gideon Polya, "Horrendous Pro-Zionist, Zionist And Apartheid Israeli Child Abuse Exposed," Countercurrents, 21 April, 2014: http://www.countercurrents.org/polya210414.htm.

[63]. Finkelhor, D. (1994), Current information on the scope and nature of child sexual abuse," Future of Children, 4(2), pp31-53.

[64]. David Finkelhor, "The international epidemiology of child sexual abuse," Child Abuse & Neglect, Volume 18, Issue 5, May 1994, Pages 409–417: http://www.sciencedirect.com/science/article/pii/0145213494900264.

[65]. Gideon Polya, "Australia shocked by cricket ball tampering but ignores horrendous Australian crimes from child abuse to genocide," Countercurrents, 24 April 2018: https://countercurrents.org/2018/04/australia-shocked-by-cricket-ball-tampering-but-ignores-horrendous-australian-crimes-from-child-abuse-to-genocide.

[66]. Gideon Polya, "37 Ways Of Tackling Australian Educational Apartheid And Social Inequity," Countercurrents, 22 May, 2013: https://countercurrents.org/polya220513.htm.

[67]. Chris Fotinopoulos, "Religion continues its free ride without our blessing," ABC News, 29 August 2013: https://www.abc.net.au/news/2013-08-29/fotinopoulos-why-does-the-church-still-get-a-free-ride/4918626.

[68] Gideon Polya, "Review: 'Enlightenment Now' by Steven Pinker – Climate Genocide Avoidable Mortality Holocaust ignored," Countercurrents, 7 September 2019: https://countercurrents.org/2019/09/review-enlightenment-now-by-steven-pinker-climate-genocide-avoidable-mortality-holocaust-ignored.

[69]. Gideon Polya, "Paris Atrocity Context: 27 Million Muslim Avoidable Deaths From Imposed Deprivation In 20 Countries Violated By US Alliance Since 9-11," Countercurrents, 22 November, 2015: https://countercurrents.org/polya221115.htm.

[70]. "Subversion of Australia": https://sites.google.com/site/subversionofaustralia.

[71]. "Experts: US did 9-11": https://sites.google.com/site/expertsusdid911.

[72]. Gideon Polya, "Australian state terrorism (4). Jingoistic, US Lackey Australia's Deadly Betrayal Of Its Traumatized Veterans," Stop state terrorism, 2018: https://sites.google.com/site/stopstateterrorism/australian-state-terrorism-4.

[73]. Gideon Polya, "Horrendous Cost For Australia Of US War On Terror," Countercurrents, 14 October, 2012: https://countercurrents.org/polya141012.htm.

[74]. Gideon Polya, "Advance Australia Fair" Hides Australian Racism, Theft, Genocide, Ecocide, Speciescide & Terracide," Countercurrents, 1 July 2019: https://countercurrents.org/2019/07/advance-australia-fair-hides-australian-racism-theft-genocide-ecocide-speciescide-terracide.

[75]. "Exposing Australia": https://sites.google.com/site/exposingaustralia/home.

[76]. Gideon Polya, "Endless War on Terror. Huge cost for Australia & America," MWC News, 14 October 2012: http://mwcnews.com/focus/analysis/22149-endless-war-on-terror.html.

[77]. Lesley Stahl and Madeleine Albright quoted in "Madeleine Albright," Wikipedia: http://en.wikipedia.org/wiki/Madeleine_Albright.

[78]. "Iraqi Holocaust, Iraqi Genocide": https://sites.google.com/site/iraqiholocaustiraqigenocide/home.

[79]. Gideon Polya, "Australian complicity in Iraq mass mortality," ABC Radio National, Ockham's Razor, 28 August 2005: http://www.abc.net.au/rn/science/ockham/stories/s1445960.htm.

[80]. Gideon Polya, "Australian complicity in Iraq mass mortality," in "Lies, Deep Fries & Statistics" (edited by Robyn Williams, ABC Books, Sydney, 2007).

[81]. Gideon Polya, "Iraqi Holocaust," ConScience, Australasian Science, 2 June 2004: http://www.shiachat.com/forum/index.php?/topic/33427-iraqi-holocaust.

[82]. "Jan Karski," Wikipedia: https://en.wikipedia.org/wiki/Jan_Karski.

[83]. Gideon Polya, "Yassmin Abdel-Magied censored on Anzac Day – jingoists trash Australian free speech," Countercurrents, 28 April 2017: https://countercurrents.org/2017/04/yassmin-abdel-magied-censored-on-anzac-day-jingoists-trash-australian-free-speech.

[84]. "Wannsee Conference," Wikipedia: https://en.wikipedia.org/wiki/Wannsee_Conference.

[85]. Martin Gilbert, "Jewish History Atlas," Weidenfeld and Nicolson, London, 1969.

[86]. Martin Gilbert "Atlas of the Holocaust," Michael Joseph, London, 1982.

[87]. Gideon Polya, "Review: "The One Day of the Year" – Australian Anzac Day jingoism hides genocidal war crimes," Countercurrents, 30 June 2017: https://countercurrents.org/2017/06/review-the-one-day-of-the-year-australian-anzac-day-jingoism-hides-genocidal-war-crimes.

[88] "Gideon Polya": https://sites.google.com/site/drgideonpolya/home.

Who Is Bill Gates?

Part One: How Bill Gates Monopolized Global Health

James Corbett

BILL GATES: Hello. I'm Bill Gates, chairman of Microsoft. In this video you're going to see the future.

SOURCE: <u>Hello, I'm Bill Gates, Chairman of Microsoft</u>
https://www.youtube.com/watch?v=pyg-DYm7b0A

Who is Bill Gates? A software developer? A businessman? A philanthropist? A global health expert?

This question, once merely academic, is becoming a very real question for those who are beginning to realize that Gates' unimaginable wealth has been used to gain control over every corner of the fields of public health, medical research and vaccine development. And now that we are presented with the very problem that Gates has been talking about for years, we will soon find that this software developer with no medical training is going to leverage that wealth into control over the fates of billions of people.

GATES: [. . .] because until we get almost everybody vaccinated globally, we still won't be fully back to normal.

SOURCE: <u>Bill Gates on Finding a Vaccine for COVID-19, the Economy, and Returning to 'Normal Life'</u>
https://www.youtube.com/watch?v=5oEcxMfwJnw

Bill Gates is no public health expert. He is not a doctor, an epidemiologist or an infectious disease researcher. Yet somehow he has become a central figure in the lives of billions of people, presuming to dictate the medical actions that will be required for the world to go "back to normal." The transformation of Bill Gates from computer kingpin to global health czar is as remarkable as it is instructive, and it tells us a great deal about where we are heading as the world plunges into a crisis the likes of which we have not seen before.

This is the story of **How Bill Gates Monopolized Global Health.**

Until his reinvention as a philanthropist in the past decade, this is what many people thought of when they thought of Bill Gates:

NARRATOR: In the case of the United States vs Microsoft, the US Justice Department contended that the software giant had breached antitrust laws by competing unfairly against Netscape Communications in the internet browser market, effectively creating a monopoly. Bill's first concern was that the prosecution could potentially block the release of his company's latest operating system, Windows 98.

SOURCE: <u>Bill Gates Defends Microsoft in Monopoly Lawsuit</u>
https://www.youtube.com/watch?v=kLQqPmhwcDs

GATES: Are you asking me about when I wrote this e-mail or what are you asking me about?

DAVID BOIES: I'm asking you about January of '96.

GATES: That month?

BOIES: Yes, sir.

GATES: And what about it?

BOIES: What non-Microsoft browsers were you concerned about in January of 96?

GATES: I don't know what you mean: "concerned."

BOIES: What is it about the word "concerned" that you don't understand?

GATES: I'm not sure what you mean by it.

SOURCE: <u>Bill Gates Deposition</u>
https://www.youtube.com/watch?v=GmeGPudmSjs

STEVE JOBS: We're going to be working together on Microsoft Office, on Internet Explorer, on Java, and I think that it's going to lead to a very healthy relationship. So it's a package announcement today. We're very, very happy about it, we're very, very excited about it. And I happen to have a special guest with me today via satellite downlink, and if we could get him up on the stage right now.

[BILL GATES APPEARS, CROWD BOOS]

SOURCE: <u>Macworld Boston 1997-The Microsoft Deal</u>
https://www.youtube.com/watch?v=WxOp5mBY9IY

DAN RATHER: Police and security guards in Belgium were caught flat-footed today by a cowardly sneak attack on one of the world's wealthiest men. The target was Microsoft chairman Bill Gates, arriving for a meeting with community leaders. Watch what happens when a team of hit men meet him first with a pie in the face.

[GATES HIT IN THE FACE WITH PIE]

RATHER: Gates was momentarily and understandably shaken, but he was not injured. The hit squad piled on with two more pies before one of them was wrestled to the ground and arrested; the others—at least for the moment—got away. Gates went inside, wiped his face clean, and made no comment. He then went ahead with his scheduled meeting. No word on the motive for this attack.

SOURCE: <u>Bill Gates Pie in Face</u>
https://www.youtube.com/watch?v=iK6SS8CXYZo

But, once reviled for the massive wealth and the monopolistic power that his virus-laden software afforded him, Gates is now hailed as a visionary who is leveraging that wealth and power for the greater good of humanity.

KLAUS SCHWAB: If in the 22nd century a book will be written about the entrepreneur of the 21st century [. . .] I'm sure that the person who will foremost come to the mind of those historians is certainly Bill Gates. [applause]

SOURCE: <u>Davos Annual Meeting 2008 – Bill Gates</u>
https://www.youtube.com/watch?v=Ql-Mtlx31e8

ANDREW ROSS SORKIN: I don't think it's hyperbole to say that Bill Gates is singularly—I would argue—the most consequential individual of our generation. I mean that.

SOURCE: <u>Bill Gates Talks Philanthropy, Microsoft, and Taxes | DealBook</u>
https://www.youtube.com/watch?v=_15DReQKbt8

ELLEN DEGENERES: Our next guest is one of the richest and most generous men in the world. Please welcome Bill Gates.

SOURCE: <u>Bill Gates on Finding a Vaccine for COVID-19, the Economy, and Returning to 'Normal Life'</u>
https://www.youtube.com/watch?v=5oEcxMfwJnw

JUDY WOODRUFF: At a time when everyone is looking to understand the scope of the pandemic and how to minimize the threat, one of the best informed voices is that of businessman and philanthropist Bill Gates.

SOURCE: <u>Bill Gates on where the COVID-19 pandemic will hurt the most</u>
https://www.youtube.com/watch?v=W3qz9-bxljA

The process by which this reinvention of Gates' public image took place is not mysterious. It's the same process by which every billionaire has revived their public image since John D. Rockefeller hired Ivy Ledbetter Lee to transform him from the head of the Standard Oil hydra [1] into the kind old man handing out dimes to strangers.

MAN OFF CAMERA: Don't you give dimes, Mr. Rockefeller? Please, go ahead.

WOMAN: Thank you, sir.

MAN: Thank you very much.

ROCKEFELLER: Thank you for the ride!

MAN: I consider myself more than amply paid.

ROCKEFELLER: Bless you! Bless you! Bless you!

SOURCE: John D. Rockefeller – Standard Oil
https://www.youtube.com/watch?v=sfWZeeGeLTc&feature=yo
utu.be&t=918

More to the point, John D. Rockefeller knew that to gain the adoration of the public, he had to appear to give them what they want: money. He devoted hundreds of millions of dollars of his vast oil monopoly fortune to establishing institutions that, he claimed, were for the public good. The General Education Board. The Rockefeller Institute of Medical Research. The Rockefeller Foundation.

Similarly, Bill Gates has spent much of the past two decades transforming himself from software magnate into a benefactor of humanity through his own Bill & Melinda Gates Foundation. In fact, Gates has surpassed Rockefeller's legacy with the Bill & Melinda Gates Foundation long having eclipsed The Rockefeller Foundation as the largest private foundation in the world, with $46.8 billion of assets on its books that it wields in its stated program areas of global health and development, global growth, and global policy advocacy.

And, like Rockefeller, Gates' transformation has been helped along by a well-funded public relations campaign. Gone are the theatrical tricks of the PR pioneers—the ubiquitous ice cream cones [2] of Gates' mentor Warren Buffett are the last remaining holdout of the old Rockefeller-handing-out-dimes gimmick. No, Gates has guided his public image into that of a modern-day saint through an even simpler tactic: buying good publicity.

The Bill & Melinda Gates Foundation spends tens of millions of dollars per year on media partnerships, sponsoring coverage of its program areas across the board. Gates funds The Guardian's Global Development website [3]. Gates funds NPR's global health coverage [4]. Gates funds the Our World in Data website [5] that is tracking the latest statistics and research on the coronavirus pandemic. Gates funds BBC coverage of global health and development issues, both through its BBC Media Action [6] organization and the BBC itself [7]. Gates funds world health coverage on ABC News [8].

When the NewsHour with Jim Lehrer was given a $3.5 million Gates foundation grant [9] to set up a special unit to report on global health issues, NewsHour communications chief Rob Flynn was asked about the potential conflict of interest that such a unit would have in reporting on issues that the Gates Foundation is itself involved in. "In some regards I guess you might say that there are not a heck of a lot of things you could touch in global health these days that would not have some kind of Gates tentacle," Flynn responded.

Indeed, it would be almost impossible to find any area of global health that has been left untouched by the tentacles of the Bill & Melinda Gates Foundation.

It was Gates who sponsored the meeting that led to the creation of Gavi, the Vaccine Alliance, a global public-private partnership bringing together state sponsors and big pharmaceutical companies, whose specific goals [10] include the creation of "healthy markets for vaccines and other immunisation products." As a founding partner of the alliance, the Gates Foundation provided $750 million in seed funding and has gone on to make over $4.1 billion [11] in commitments to the group.

Gates provided the seed money [12] that created the Global Fund to Fight AIDS, Tuberculosis and Malaria, a public-private partnership that acts as a finance vehicle for governmental AIDS, TB, and malaria programs.

When a public-private partnership of governments, world health bodies and 13 leading pharmaceutical companies came together in 2012 "to accelerate progress toward eliminating or controlling 10 neglected tropical diseases," there was the Gates Foundation with $363 million of support [13].

When the Global Financing Facility for Women, Children and Adolescents was launched in 2015 to leverage billions of dollars in public and private financing for global health and development programs, there was the Bill & Melinda Gates Foundation as a founding partner with a $275 million contribution [14].

When the Coalition for Epidemic Preparedness Innovations was launched at the World Economic Forum in Davos in 2017 to develop vaccines against emerging infectious diseases, there was the Gates Foundation with an initial injection of $100 million [15].

The examples go on and on. The Bill & Melinda Gates Foundation's fingerprints can be seen on every major global health initiative of the past two decades. And beyond the flashy, billion-dollar global partnerships, the Foundation is behind hundreds of smaller country and region-specific grants—$10 million [16] to combat a locust infestation in East Africa, or $300 million [17] to support agricultural research in Africa and Asia—that add up to billions of dollars in commitments.

It comes as no surprise, then, that—far beyond the $250 million that the Gates Foundation has pledged [18] to the "fight" against coronavirus—every aspect of the current coronavirus pandemic involves organizations, groups and individuals with direct ties to Gates funding.

From the start, the World Health Organization has directed the global response to the current pandemic. From its initial monitoring of the outbreak in Wuhan and its declaration [19] in January that there was no evidence of human-to-human transmission to its live media briefings and its technical guidance on country-level planning and other matters, the WHO has been the body setting the guidelines and recommendations shaping the global response to this outbreak.

But even the World Health Organization itself is largely reliant on funds from the Bill & Melinda Gates Foundation. The WHO's most recent donor report [20] shows that the Bill & Melinda Gates Foundation is the organization's second-largest donor behind the United States government. The Gates Foundation single-handedly contributes more to the world health body than Australia, Canada, France, Germany, Russia and the UK combined.

What's more, current World Health Organization Director-General Tedros Adhanom Ghebreyesus is, in fact, like Bill Gates himself, not a medical doctor at all, but the controversial ex-Minister of Health of Ethiopia, who was accused [21] of covering up three cholera outbreaks in the country during his tenure. Before joining the WHO, he served as chair of the Gates-founded Global Fund to Fight AIDS, Tuberculosis and Malaria, and sat on the board of the Gates-founded Gavi, the Vaccine Alliance, and the Gates-funded Stop TB Partnership [22].

The current round of lockdowns and restrictive stay-home orders in western countries was enacted on the back of alarming models predicting millions of deaths in the United States and hundreds of thousands in the UK.

HAYLEY MINOGUE: Imperial College in London released a COVID-19 report and that's where most of our US leaders are getting the information they're basing their decision making on. That 2.2 million deaths also doesn't account for the potential negative effects of health systems being overwhelmed.

[. . .]

The report runs us through a few different ways this could turn out depending on what our responses are. If we don't do anything to control this virus, over 80% of people in the US would be infected over the course of the epidemic, with 2.2 million deaths from COVID-19.

SOURCE: Extreme measures based on scientific paper
https://www.youtube.com/watch?v=aCpChmm1eds

BORIS JOHNSON: From this evening I must give the British people a very simple instruction: you must stay at home.

SOURCE: Boris Johnson announces complete UK lockdown amid coronavirus crisis
https://www.youtube.com/watch?v=LlJIwTd9fqI

JUSTIN TRUDEAU: Enough is enough. Go home and stay home.

SOURCE: 'Enough is enough', Trudeau with a strong message to Canadians
https://www.youtube.com/watch?v=ik5Ro3ScYXI

GAVIN NEWSOM: . . . a statewide order for people to stay at home

SOURCE: California Gov Newsom issues statewide 'SAFER AT HOME' order
https://www.youtube.com/watch?v=eMZz3ey4qxE

The work of two research groups was crucial in shaping the decision of the UK and US governments to implement wide-ranging lockdowns, and, in turn, governments around the world. The first group, the Imperial College COVID-19 Research Team, issued a report [23] on March 16th that predicted up to 500,000 deaths in the UK and 2.2 million deaths in the US unless strict government measures were put in place.

The second group, the Institute for Health Metrics and Evaluation in Bill Gates' home state of Washington, helped provide data [24] that corroborated the White House's initial estimates [25] of the virus' effects, estimates that have been repeatedly downgraded [26] as the situation has progressed.

Unsurprisingly, the Gates Foundation has injected substantial sums of money into both groups. This year alone, the Gates Foundation has already given $79 million [27] to Imperial College, and in 2017 the Foundation announced a $279 million [28] investment into the IHME to expand its work collecting health data and creating models.

Anthony Fauci, meanwhile, has become the face [29] of the US government's coronavirus response, echoing Bill Gates' assertion that the country will not "get back to normal" until "a good vaccine" can be found to insure the public's safety.

ANTHONY FAUCI: If you want to get to pre-coronavirus . . . You know, that might not ever happen, in the sense of the fact that the threat is there. But I believe with the therapies that will be coming online and with the fact that I feel confident that over a period of time we will get a good vaccine, that we will never have to get back to where we are right back now.

SOURCE: Dr. Anthony Fauci on return to normalcy from pandemic
https://twitter.com/jennfranconews/status/1247294438264586240

Beyond just their frequent collaborations [30] and cooperation [31] in the past, Fauci has direct ties to Gates' projects and funding. In 2010, he was appointed to the <u>Leadership Council</u> [32] of the Gates-founded "<u>Decade of Vaccines</u>" [33] project to implement a Global Vaccine Action Plan—a project to which Gates committed $10 billion of funding. And in October of last year, just as the current pandemic was beginning, the Gates Foundation <u>announced</u> [34] a $100 million contribution to the National Institute of Health to help, among other programs, Fauci's National Institute of Allergy and Infectious Diseases' research into HIV.

Also in October of last year, the Bill & Melinda Gates Foundation partnered with the World Economic Forum and the Johns Hopkins Center for Health Security to stage <u>Event 201</u> [35], a tabletop exercise gauging the economic and societal impact of a globally-spreading coronavirus pandemic.

NARRATOR: It began in healthy-looking pigs months, perhaps years, ago: a new coronavirus.

ANITA CICERO: The mission of the pandemic emergency board is to provide recommendations to deal with the major global challenges arising in response to an unfolding pandemic. The board is comprised of highly experienced leaders from business public health and civil society.

TOM INGLESBY: We're at the start of what's looking like it will be a severe pandemic and there are problems emerging that can only be solved by global business and governments working together.

STEPHEN REDD: Governments need to be willing to do things that are out of their historical perspective, or . . . for the most part. It's really a war footing that we need to be on.

SOURCE: <u>Event 201 Pandemic Exercise: Highlights Reel</u>
https://www.youtube.com/watch?v=AoLw-Q8X174

Given the incredible reach that the tentacles of the Bill & Melinda Gates Foundation have into every corner of the global health markets, it should not be surprising that the foundation has been intimately involved with every stage of the current pandemic crisis, either. In effect, Gates has merely used the wealth from his domination of the software market to leverage himself into a similar position in the world of global health.

The whole process has been cloaked in the mantle of selfless philanthropy, but the foundation is not structured as a charitable endeavour. Instead, it maintains a dual structure: the Bill & Melinda Gates Foundation distributes money to grantees, but a separate entity, the Bill & Melinda Gates Foundation Trust, manages the endowment assets. These two entities often have overlapping interests, and, as has been noted many times in the past, grants given by the foundation often directly benefit the value of the trust's assets:

MELINDA GATES: One of my favorite parts of my job at the Gates Foundation is that I get to travel to the developing world, and I do that quite regularly.

[. . .]

My first trip in India, I was in a person's home where they had dirt floors, no running water, no electricity, and that's really what I see all over the world. So in short, I'm startled by all the things that they don't have. But I am surprised by one thing that they do have: Coca-Cola. Coke is everywhere. In fact, when I travel to the developing world, Coke feels ubiquitous.

And so when I come back from these trips, and I'm thinking about development, and I'm flying home and I'm thinking, we're trying to deliver condoms to people, or vaccinations, you know? Coke's success kind of stops and makes you wonder: How is it that they can get Coke to these far-flung places? If they can do that, why can't governments and NGOs do the same thing?

SOURCE: <u>Melinda French Gates: What nonprofits can learn from Coca-Cola</u>
https://www.youtube.com/watch?v=GlUS6KE67Vs

AMY GOODMAN: And the charity of billionaire Microsoft founder Bill Gates and his wife Melinda is under criticism following the disclosure it's substantially increased its holdings in the agribusiness giant Monsanto to over $23 million. Critics say the investment in Monsanto contradicts the Bill and Melinda Gates Foundation's stated commitment to helping farmers and sustainable development in Africa.

SOURCE: <u>Gates Foundation Criticized for Increasing Monsanto Investment</u>
https://www.democracynow.org/2010/8/27/headlines/gates_fou ndation_criticized_for_increasing_monsanto_investment

LAURENCE LEE: The study from the pressure group Global Justice now paints a picture of the Gates Foundation partly as an expression of corporate America's desire to profit from Africa and partly a damning critique of its effects.

POLLY JONES: You could have a case where the initial research is done by a Gates-funded institution. And the media reporting on how well that research is conducted is done, the media outlet is a Gates-funded outlet, or maybe a Gates-funded journalist from a media program. And then the program is implemented more widely by a Gates-funded NGO. I mean . . . There are some very insular circles here.

LEE: Among the many criticisms: the idea that private finance can solve the problems of the developing world. Should poor farmers be trapped into debt by having to use chemicals or fertilizers underwritten by offshoot of the foundation?

SOURCE: <u>Gates Foundation accused of exploiting its leverage in Africa</u>
https://www.youtube.com/watch?v=XcMrHpLd9C4

This is no mere theoretical conflict of interest. Gates is held up as a hero for donating $35.8 billion worth of his Microsoft stock to the foundation, but during the course of his "Decade of Vaccines," Gates' net worth has actually doubled, from <u>$54 billion</u> [36] to <u>$103.1 billion [37]</u>.

The Rockefeller story provides an instructive template for this vision of tycoon-turned-philanthropist. When Rockefeller faced a public backlash, he helped spearhead the creation of a system of private foundations that connected in with his business interests. Leveraging his unprecedented oil monopoly fortune into unprecedented control over wide swaths of public life, Rockefeller was able to kill two birds with one stone: molding society in his family's own interests, even as he became a beloved figure in the public imagination.

Similarly, Bill Gates has leveraged his software empire into a global health, development and education empire, steering the course of investment and research and ensuring healthy markets for vaccines and other immunization products. And, like Rockefeller, Gates has been transformed from the feared and reviled head of a formidable hydra into a kindly old man generously giving his wealth back to the public.

But not everyone has been taken in by this PR trick. Even The Lancet observed this worrying transformation from software monopolist to health monopolist back in 2009, when the extent of this Gates-led monopoly was becoming apparent to all:

The first guiding principle of the [Bill & Melinda Gates] Foundation is that it is "driven by the interests and passions of the Gates family." An annual letter from Bill Gates summarises those passions, referring to newspaper articles, books, and chance events that have shaped the Foundation's strategy. For such a large and influential investor in global health, is such a whimsical governance principle good enough?

SOURCE: <u>What has the Gates Foundation done for global health?</u>
https://www.thelancet.com/journals/lancet/article/PIIS0140-6736(09)60885-0/fulltext

This brings us back to the question: Who is Bill Gates? What are his driving interests? What motivates his decisions?

These are not academic questions. Gates' decisions have controlled the flows of billions of dollars, formed international partnerships pursuing wide-ranging agendas, ensured the creation of "healthy markets" for Big Pharma vaccine manufacturers. And now, as we are seeing, his decisions are shaping the entire global response to the coronavirus pandemic.

Next week, we will further explore Gates' vaccination initiatives, the business interests behind them, and the larger agenda that is beginning to take shape as we enter the "new normal" of the COVID-19 crisis.

References

[1]. https://cut2thetruth.files.wordpress.com/2014/10/standard-oil-rockefeller-cartoon-monopoly-scandal-cut2thetruth.jpg?w=566&h=684
[2]. shorturl.at/hlmD1
[3]. https://www.theguardian.com/global-development/2010/sep/14/about-this-site
[4]. https://www.gatesfoundation.org/How-We-Work/Quick-Links/Grants-Database/Grants/2018/10/OPP1180191
[5]. https://ourworldindata.org/supporters
[6]. https://www.bbc.co.uk/mediaaction/about/funding
[7]. https://www.gatesfoundation.org/How-We-Work/Quick-Links/Grants-Database/Grants/2016/11/OPP1161829
[8]. https://mediadecoder.blogs.nytimes.com/2010/10/06/gates-foundation-backs-abc-news-project/
[9]. http://blogs.reuters.com/mediafile/2008/12/01/newshour-gets-35-million-from-gates-foundation/
[10]. https://www.gavi.org/our-alliance/market-shaping
[11]. https://www.gavi.org/investing-gavi/funding/donor-profiles/bill-melinda-gates-foundation
[12]. https://archive.fo/20130124180843/http:/www.google.com/hostednews/afp/article/ALeqM5h6Ih8CYz1SqAKYjI-SiowJgu8BSA?docId=CNG.07d4a47a8ce76f0e07e322726bdf65a2.6f1
[13]. https://www.gatesfoundation.org/media-center/press-releases/2012/01/private-and-public-partners-unite-to-combat-10-neglected-tropical-diseases-by-2020
[14]. https://www.globalfinancingfacility.org/bill-melinda-gates-foundation-0
[15]. https://www.gatesfoundation.org/How-We-Work/Quick-Links/Grants-Database/Grants/2017/11/OPP1180343
[16]. https://www.gatesfoundation.org/Media-Center/Press-Releases/2020/02/Gates-Foundation-Commits-10-Million-to-Support-Global-Response-on-East-Africa-Locust-Invasion
[17]. https://www.gatesfoundation.org/Media-Center/Press-Releases/2017/12/Gates-Foundation-Commits-300M-USD-to-Help-Farmers-in-Africa-and-Asia-Cope-with-Climate-Change?sf82155838=1
[18]. https://www.gatesfoundation.org/Media-Center/Press-Releases/2020/04/Gates-Foundation-Expands-Commitment-to-COVID-19-Response-Calls-for-International-Collaboration
[19]. https://twitter.com/WHO/status/1217043229427761152?ref_src=twsrc%5Etfw%7Ctwcamp%5Etweetembed&ref_url=https%3A%2F%2Fwww.foxnews.com%2Fworld%2Fworld-health-organization-january-tweet-china-human-transmission-coronavirus
[20]. https://www.who.int/about/finances-accountability/reports/A72_INF5-en.pdf
[21]. https://archive.is/vgOWw

[22]. http://www.stoptb.org/partners/partner_profile2.asp?PID=1057

[23]. https://www.imperial.ac.uk/media/imperial-college/medicine/sph/ide/gida-fellowships/Imperial-College-COVID19-NPI-modelling-16-03-2020.pdf

[24]. https://edition.cnn.com/2020/03/30/health/coronavirus-us-ihme-model-us/index.html

[25]. https://twitter.com/CNNSotu/status/1244275909944885248

[26]. https://thehill.com/policy/healthcare/491715-key-coronavirus-model-revised-downward-predicts-60k-deaths-in-us-by-august

[27]. https://www.gatesfoundation.org/How-We-Work/Quick-Links/Grants-Database/Grants/2020/03/OPP1210755

[28]. http://www.healthdata.org/about/director-statement

[29]. https://thehill.com/homenews/senate/486870-gop-senators-tell-trump-to-make-fauci-face-of-governments-coronavirus

[30]. https://www.nih.gov/file/49246/download?token=ahYMS3M1

[31]. https://www.nih.gov/file/49246/download?token=ahYMS3M1

[32]. https://www.who.int/immunization/newsroom/press/news_release_decade_vaccines/en/

[33]. https://www.gatesfoundation.org/Media-Center/Press-Releases/2010/01/Bill-and-Melinda-Gates-Pledge-$10-Billion-in-Call-for-Decade-of-Vaccines

[34]. https://www.ajmc.com/newsroom/nih-bill-and-melinda-gates-foundation-collaborate-to-develop-genebased-hiv-treatment

[35]. https://www.centerforhealthsecurity.org/event201/

[36]. https://web.archive.org/web/20100924204343/https:/www.forbes.com/profile/bill-gates/

[37]. https://www.forbes.com/profile/bill-gates/#2125194c689f

Part Two: Bill Gates' Plan to Vaccinate the World

James Corbett

POPPY HARLOW: Ten billion dollars. I mean, just speak about the magnitude of that. That is by far the biggest commitment of the foundation, isn't it, Bill? I mean, this is by far the largest.

BILL GATES: That's right, we've been spending a lot on vaccines. With this commitment, over eight million additional lives will be saved. So it's one of the most effective ways that health in the poorest countries can be dramatically improved.

SOURCE: Gates Foundation: $10 billion for vaccines
https://www.youtube.com/watch?v=m8kGz8_pC70

In January of 2010, Bill and Melinda Gates used the World Economic Forum at Davos to announce [1] a staggering $10 billion commitment to research and develop vaccines for the world's poorest countries, kicking off what he called a "Decade of Vaccines."

GATES: Today we're announcing a commitment over this next decade, which we think of as a decade of vaccines having incredible impact. We're announcing that we'll spend over $10 billion on vaccines.

SOURCE: PBS News Hour January 29, 2010
https://archive.org/details/WMPT_20100129_230000_PBS_Ne
wsHour/start/1500/end/1560

Hailed by the Gates-funded media . . .

HARI SREENIVASAN: For the record, the Bill and Melinda Gates Foundation is a NewsHour underwriter.

SOURCE: <u>PBS News Hour January 29, 2010</u>
https://archive.org/details/WMPT_20100129_230000_PBS_Ne
wsHour/start/1500/end/1560

. . . and applauded by the pharmaceutical companies who stood to reap the benefits of that largesse, the record-setting commitment made waves in the international community, helping to underwrite a <u>Global Vaccine Action Plan</u> [2] coordinated by the <u>Gates-funded</u> [3] World Health Organization.

But contrary to the Gates' own PR spin that this $10 billion pledge was an unalloyed good and would save eight million lives, the truth is that this attempt to reorient the global health economy was part of a much bigger agenda. An agenda that would ultimately lead to greater profits for Big Pharma companies, greater control for the Gates Foundation over the field of global health, and greater power for Bill Gates to shape the course of the future for billions of people around the planet.

This is **Bill Gates' Plan to Vaccinate the World**.

Given Gates' pledge to make this a "Decade of Vaccines," it should come as no surprise that, since the dawn of this coronavirus crisis, he has been adamant that the world will not go back to normal until a vaccine has been developed.

GATES: We're gonna have this intermediate period of opening up, and it won't be normal until we get an amazing vaccine to the entire world.

SOURCE: <u>Watch CNBC's full interview with Microsoft co-founder Bill Gates on the coronavirus pandemic and his work toward a vaccine</u>
https://www.cnbc.com/video/2020/04/09/watch-cnbcs-full-
interview-with-microsoft-co-founder-bill-gates-on-past-
pandemic-warnings.html

GATES: The vaccine is critical, because, until you have that, things aren't really going to be normal. They can open up to some degree, but the risk of a rebound will be there until we have very broad vaccination.

SOURCE: <u>Bill Gates on where the COVID-19 pandemic will hurt the most</u>
https://www.youtube.com/watch?v=W3qz9-bxljA

GATES: They won't be back to normal until we either have that phenomenal vaccine or a therapeutic that's, like, over 95% effective. And so we have to assume that's going to be almost 18 months from now.

SOURCE: <u>Bill Gates on Finding a Vaccine for COVID-19, the Economy, and Returning to 'Normal Life'</u>
https://www.youtube.com/watch?v=5oEcxMfwJnw&t=616s

GATES: And then the final solution—which is a year or two years off—is the vaccine. So we've got to go full-speed ahead on all three fronts.

COLBERT: Just to head off the conspiracy theorists, maybe we shouldn't call the vaccine "the final solution."

GATES: Good point.

COLBERT: Maybe just "the best solution."

[GATES LAUGHS]

SOURCE: <u>Bill Gates: Global Innovation Is The Key To Achieving A Return To Normal</u>
https://www.youtube.com/watch?v=dNiuaKKEPu8

More interestingly, since Gates began delivering this same talking point in every one of his many media appearances of late, it has been picked up and repeated by heads of state, health officials, doctors and media talking heads, right down to the scientifically arbitrary but very specific 18-month time frame.

ZEKE EMANUEL: Realistically, COVID-19 will be here for the next 18 months or more. We will not be able to return to normalcy until we find a vaccine or effective medications.

SOURCE: <u>Dr. Zeke Emanuel On The Return To 'Normal'</u>
https://www.youtube.com/watch?v=pP3-hE-DrSc

DOUG FORD: The hard fact is, until we have a vaccine, going back to normal means putting lives at risk.

SOURCE: <u>Premier Doug Ford and Ontario ministers provide COVID-19 update – April 18, 2020</u>
https://www.youtube.com/watch?v=92pgf-UpP_A

JUSTIN TRUDEAU: This will be the new normal until a vaccine is developed.

SOURCE: <u>PM Trudeau on modelling data and federal response to COVID-19 – April 9, 2020</u>
https://www.youtube.com/watch?v=h7B0scj77zM

NORMAN SWAN: The only thing that will really allow life as we once knew it to resume is a vaccine.

SOURCE: <u>Life will only return to normal when there's a coronavirus vaccine, Dr Norman Swan says</u>
https://www.youtube.com/watch?v=NcHjrI-zl44

DONALD TRUMP: Obviously, we continue to work on the vaccines, but the vaccines have to be down the road by probably 14, 15, 16 months. We're doing great on the vaccines.

SOURCE: <u>Remarks by President Trump, Vice President Pence, and Members of the Coronavirus Task Force in Press Briefing</u>
https://www.whitehouse.gov/briefings-statements/remarks-president-trump-vice-president-pence-members-coronavirus-task-force-press-briefing-19/

The fact that so many heads of state, health ministers and media commentators are dutifully echoing Gates' pronouncement about the need for a vaccine will not be surprising to those who saw last week's exploration of How Bill Gates Monopolized Global Health [4]. As we have seen, the Gates Foundation's tentacles have penetrated into every corner of the field of public health. Billions of dollars in funding and entire public policy agendas are under the control of this man, an unelected, unaccountable software developer with no medical research experience or training.

And nowhere is Gates' control of public health more apparent than in the realm of vaccines.

Gates launched the Decade of Vaccines [5] with a $10 billion pledge.

Gates helped develop the Global Vaccine Action Plan [6] administered by the Gates-funded [7] World Health Organization.

Gates helped found Gavi, the Vaccine Alliance, aiming to develop "healthy markets" [8] for vaccine manufacturers.

Gates helped launch Gavi with a $1 billion donation in 2011, going on to contribute $4.1 billion [9] over the course of the "Decade of Vaccines."

GATES: And so I'm pleased to announce to you that we're pledging an additional billion dollars to—

[APPLAUSE]

GATES: Thank you.

[CONTINUED APPLAUSE]

GATES: Alright, thank you.

[CONTINUED APPLAUSE]

GATES: It's not everyday we give away a billion dollars.

[LAUGHTER]

SOURCE: <u>Gates' mammoth vaccine pledge</u>
https://www.youtube.com/watch?v=1o8l0JQOQ5s

One of the Gates Foundation's core funding areas is "<u>vaccine development and surveillance</u>," [10] which has resulted in the channeling of billions of dollars into vaccine development, a seat at the table to develop vaccination campaigns in countries around the globe, and the opportunity to shape public thinking around Bill Gates' pet project of the past five years: preparing rapid development and deployment of vaccines in the event of a globally spreading pandemic.

GATES: If anything kills over 10 million people in the next few decades, it's most likely to be a highly infectious virus.

SOURCE: <u>The next outbreak? We're not ready | Bill Gates</u>
https://www.youtube.com/watch?v=6Af6b_wyiwI

GATES: Whether it occurs by a quirk of nature or at the hand of a terrorist, epidemiologists show through their models that a respiratory-spread pathogen would kill more than 30 million people in less than a year. And there is a reasonable probability of that taking place in the years ahead.

SOURCE: <u>Gates: Millions could die from bio-terrorism</u>
https://www.youtube.com/watch?v=6QmH3SCX0Ro

BABITA SHARMA: Many high-profile personalities have been gathering at this year's World Economic Forum in Davos, which aims to discuss the globe's most pressing issues. Amongst them is the Microsoft founder Bill Gates, whose foundation is investing millions in the Coalition for Epidemic Preparedness Innovations to help combat infectious diseases. Here's some of what he had to say about his push to develop new vaccines.

GATES: Unfortunately, it takes many years to do a completely new vaccine. The design, the safety review, the manufacturing; all of those things mean that an epidemic can be very widespread before that tool would come along. And so after Ebola the global health community talked a lot about this, including a new type of vaccine platform called DNA/RNA that should speed things along.

And so this Coalition for Epidemic Preparedness Initiative [sic], CEPI, is three countries—Japan, Norway, Germany—and two foundations—Wellcome Trust, [who] we work with on a lot of things, and our foundation, the Gates Foundation—coming together to fund . . . actually trying to use that platform and make some vaccines. And so that would help us in the future.

NARRATORS: We know vaccines can protect us. We just need to be better prepared. So, "Let's come together. Let's research and invest. Let's save lives. Let's outsmart epidemics."

Given Gates' mammoth investment in vaccines over the past decade, his insistence that . . .

GATES: Things won't go back to truly normal until we have a vaccine that we've gotten out to basically the entire world.

. . . is hardly surprising.

What should be surprising is that this strangely specific and continuously repeated message—that we will not go "back to normal" until we get a vaccine in 18 months—has no scientific basis whatsoever. Medical researchers have already conceded that a vaccine for SARS-CoV-2 may not even be possible, [11] pointing to the inability of researchers to develop any kind of immunization against previous coronavirus outbreaks, like SARS or MERS.

But even if such a vaccine were possible, serious concerns remain about the safety of developing, testing and delivering such an "amazing vaccine" to "the entire world" in this remarkably short timeframe. Even proponents of vaccine development openly worry [12] that the rush to vaccinate billions of people with a largely untested, experimental coronavirus vaccine will itself present grave risks to the public.

One of these risks involves "disease enhancement." It has been known for over a decade that vaccination for some viral infections—including coronaviruses—actually enhances susceptibility to viral infection [13] or even causes infections in healthy vaccine recipients.

ANTHONY FAUCI: Now, the issue of safety. Something that I want to make sure the American public understand: It's not only safety when you inject somebody and they get maybe an idiosyncratic reaction, they get a little allergic reaction, they get pain. There's safety associated. "Does the vaccine make you worse?" And there are diseases in which you vaccinate someone, they get infected with what you're trying to protect them with, and you actually enhance the infection.

SOURCE: Remarks by President Trump, Vice President Pence, and Members of the Coronavirus Task Force in Press Briefing (March 26)
https://ge.usembassy.gov/remarks-by-president-trump-vice-president-pence-and-members-of-the-coronavirus-task-force-in-press-briefing-march-26/

This is no mere theoretical risk. As researchers who were trying to develop a vaccine for the original SARS outbreak discovered, the vaccine actually made the lab animals subjected to it more susceptible to the disease [14].

PETER HOTEZ: One of the things that we are not hearing a lot about is the unique potential safety problems of coronavirus vaccines. This was first found in the 1960s with the Respiratory Syncytial Virus vaccines, and it was done in Washington with the NIH and Children's National Medical Center. Some of those kids who got the vaccine actually did worse, and I believe there were two deaths in the consequence of that study. Because what happens with certain types of respiratory virus vaccines, you get immunized, and then when you get actually exposed to the virus, you get this kind of paradoxical immune enhancement phenomenon, and what—and we don't entirely understand the basis of it. But we recognize that it's a real problem for certain respiratory virus vaccines. That killed the RSV program for decades. Now the Gates Foundation is taking it up again. But when we started developing coronavirus vaccines—and our colleagues—we noticed in laboratory animals that they started to show some of the same immune pathology that resembled what had happened 50 years earlier.

SOURCE: Hotez Coronavirus Vaccine Safety Testimony
https://www.c-span.org/video/?c4873497/user-clip-hotez-coronavirus-vaccine-safety-testimony

This specific issue regarding coronavirus vaccines is exacerbated by the arbitrary and unscientific 18-month timeframe that Gates is insisting on for the vaccine's development. In order to meet that deadline, vaccine developers are being urged to use new and largely unproven methods for creating their experimental immunizations, including DNA and mRNA vaccines.

KELLY O'DONNELL: For a self-described wartime president, victory over COVID-19 equals a vaccine.

TRUMP: I hope we can have a vaccine, and we're going to fast-track it like you've never seen before.

O'DONNELL: Adding Trump-style branding, the administration launched "Operation Warp Speed," a multi-billion-dollar research and manufacturing effort to shorten the typical year-plus vaccine development timeline.

SOURCE: Trump Administration's 'Operation Warp Speed' Aims To Fast-Track Coronavirus Vaccine | Nightly News
https://www.youtube.com/watch?v=EHy-GWITbxk

ANTHONY FAUCI: We're gonna start ramping up production with the companies involved, and you do that at risk. In other words, you don't wait until you get an answer before you start manufacturing. You at risk proactively start making it, assuming it's gonna work.

SOURCE: Dr Fauci Discusses Operation Warp Speed's Goal Of 100s Of Millions Of Vaccine Doses By January
https://www.youtube.com/watch?v=7bzIDqkuL1M

BECKY QUICK: You're thinking 18 months even with all the work that you've already done to this point and the planning that you are taking with lots of different potential vaccinations and building up for that now

GATES: Yeah, so there's an approach called RNA vaccine that people like Moderna, CureVac and others are using that in 2015 we'd identified that as very promising for pandemics and for other applications as well. And so, if everything goes perfectly with the RNA approach, we could actually beat the 18 months. We don't want to create unrealistic expectations.

SOURCE: Watch CNBC's full interview with Microsoft co-founder Bill Gates on the coronavirus pandemic and his work toward a vaccine
https://www.cnbc.com/video/2020/04/09/watch-cnbcs-full-

interview-with-microsoft-co-founder-bill-gates-on-past-
pandemic-warnings.html

RHIJU DAS: So the concept of an RNA vaccine is: Let's inject
the RNA molecule that encodes for the spike protein.

ANGELA RASMUSSEN: It's making your cell do the work of
creating this viral protein that is going to be recognized by your
immune system and trigger the development of these antibodies.

DAS: Our bodies won't make a full-fledged infectious virus.
They'll just make a little piece and then learn to recognize it and
then get ready to destroy the virus if it then later comes and
invades us.

[. . .]

DAS: It's a relatively new, unproven technology. And there's
still no example of an RNA vaccine that's been deployed
worldwide in the way that we need for the coronavirus.

RASMUSSEN: There is the possibility for unforeseen, adverse
effects.

AKIKO IWASAKI: So this is all new territory. Whether it
would elicit protective immune response against this virus is
just unknown right now.

**SOURCE: <u>Can Scientists Use RNA to Create a Coronavirus
Vaccine?</u>**
https://www.pbs.org/wgbh/nova/video/rna-coronavirus-vaccine/

Rushing at "Warp Speed" to develop a new vaccine using
experimental technology and then mass-producing and
delivering billions of doses to be injected into "basically the
entire world" before adequate testing is even done amounts to
one of the most dangerous experiments in the history of the
world, one that could alter the lives of untold numbers of
people.

That an experimental vaccine—developed in a brand new way and rushed through with a special, shortened testing regime—should be given to adults, children, pregnant women, newborn babies, and the elderly alike, would be, in any other situation, unthinkable. To suggest that such a vaccine should be given to the entire planet would have been called lunacy mere months ago. But now the public is being asked to accept this premise without question.

Even Gates himself acknowledges the inherent risks of such a project. But his concern is not for the lives that will be irrevocably altered in the event that the vaccines cause damage to the population. Instead, he is more concerned that the pharmaceutical companies and the researchers are given legal immunity for any such damage.

GATES: You know, if we have, you know, one in 10,000 side effects, that's, you know, way more— 700,000—you know, people who will suffer from that. So really understanding the safety at gigantic scale across all age ranges—you know, pregnant, male, female, undernourished, existing comorbidities—it's very, very hard. And that actual decision of, "OK, let's go and give this vaccine to the entire world," ah, governments will have to be involved because there will be some risk and indemnification needed before that can be decided on.

SOURCE: <u>Watch CNBC's full interview with Microsoft co-founder Bill Gates on the coronavirus pandemic and his work toward a vaccine</u>
https://www.cnbc.com/video/2020/04/09/watch-cnbcs-full-interview-with-microsoft-co-founder-bill-gates-on-past-pandemic-warnings.html

As we have already seen, in the arena of global health, what Bill Gates wants is what the world gets. So it should be no surprise that immunity for the Big Pharma vaccine manufacturers and the vaccination program planners is already being worked on.

In the US, the Department of Health and Human Services issued a declaration [15] that retroactively provides "liability immunity for activities related to medical countermeasures against COVID-19," including manufacturers, distributors and program planners of "any vaccine, used to treat, diagnose, cure, prevent, or mitigate COVID-19." The declaration was issued on March 17th but retroactively covers any activity back to February 4th, 2020, the day before the Bill and Melinda Gates Foundation announced [16] an emergency $100 million to fund treatment efforts and to develop new vaccines for COVID-19.

The plan to inject everyone on the planet with an experimental vaccine is no aberration in Bill Gates' envisioned "Decade of Vaccines." It is its culmination.

The "Decade of Vaccines" kicked off with a Gates-funded $3.6 million observational study of HPV vaccines in India that, according to a government investigation [17], violated the human rights of the study participants with "gross violations" of consent and failed to properly report adverse events experienced by the vaccine recipients. After the deaths of seven girls involved in the trial were reported, a parliamentary investigation concluded [18] that the Gates-funded Program for Appropriate Technology in Health (PATH), which ran the study, had been engaged in a scheme to help ensure "healthy markets" for GlaxoSmithKline and Merck, the manufacturers of the Gardasil and Cervarix vaccines that had been so generously donated for use in the trial:

"Had PATH been successful in getting the HPV vaccine included in the universal immunization program of the concerned countries, this would have generated windfall profit for the manufacturer(s) by way of automatic sale, year after year, without any promotional or marketing expenses. It is well known that once introduced into the immunization program it becomes politically impossible to stop any vaccination."

Chandra M. Gulhati, editor of the influential Monthly Index of Medical Specialities, remarked [19] that "[i]t is shocking to see how an American organization used surreptitious methods to establish itself in India," and Samiran Nundy, editor emeritus of the National Medical Journal of India lamented that "[t]his is an obvious case where Indians were being used as guinea pigs" [20].

Throughout the decade, India's concerns about the Bill and Melinda Gates Foundation and its corporate partners' influence on the country's national immunization programs grew. In 2016, the steering group of the country's National Health Mission blasted the government [21] for allowing the country's National Technical Advisory Group on Immunisation [22] —the primary body advising the government on all vaccination-related matters—to be effectively purchased by the Gates Foundation.

As one steering group member noted: "The NTAGI secretariat has been moved out of the [government's health] ministry to the office of Public Health Foundation of India and the 32 staff members in that secretariat draw their salaries from the BMGF. There is a clear conflict of interest—on one hand, the BMGF funds the secretariat that is the highest decision making body in vaccines and, on the other, it partners the pharma industry in GAVI. This is unacceptable."

In 2017, the government responded by cutting all financial ties [23] between the advisory group and the Gates Foundation.

Similar stories play out across the Gates Foundation's "Decade of Vaccines."

There's the Gates-founded and funded Meningitis Vaccine Project, which led to the creation and testing of MenAfriVac, a $0.50-per-dose immunization against meningococcal meningitis. The tests led to reports [24] of between 40 and 500 children suffering seizures and convulsions and eventually becoming paralyzed.

There's the 2017 confirmation [25] that the Gates-supported [26] oral polio vaccine was actually responsible for the majority of new polio cases and the 2018 follow up [27] showing that 80% of polio cases are now vaccine-derived.

There's the 2018 paper [28] in the International Journal of Environmental Research and Public Health concluding that over 490,000 people [29] in India developed paralysis as a result of the oral polio vaccine between 2000 and 2017.

There's even the WHO's own malaria chief, Dr. Arata Kochi, who complained in an internal memo [30] that Gates' influence meant that the world's leading malaria scientists are now "locked up in a 'cartel' with their own research funding being linked to those of others within the group" and that the foundation [31] "was stifling debate on the best ways to treat and combat malaria, prioritizing only those methods that relied on new technology or developing new drugs."

Kochi's complaint, written in 2008, highlights the most common criticism of the global health web that Gates has spun in the past two decades: that the public health industry has become a racket run by and for Big Pharma and its partners for the benefit of big business.

At the time that Kochi was writing his memo, the executive director of the Gates Foundation's Global Health program was Tachi Yamada [32]. Yamada left his position as Chairman of Research and Development at GlaxoSmithKline to take up the position at the Gates Foundation in 2006 and left the foundation five years later to become Chief Medical and Scientific Officer [33] at Takeda Pharmaceuticals. Yamada's replacement as head of Gates' Global health program, Trevor Mundel [34], was himself a clinical researcher at Pfizer and Parke-Davis and spent time as Head of Development with Novartis before joining the foundation.

This use of foundation funds to set public policy to drive up corporate profits is not a secret conspiracy. It is a perfectly open one.

When the Center for Global Development formed a working group to "develop a practical approach to the vaccine challenge," they concluded that the best way to incentivize pharmaceutical companies to produce more vaccines for the third world was for governments to promise to buy vaccines before they were even developed. They titled their report "Making Markets for Vaccines [35]."

ALICE ALBRIGHT: The project "Making Markets for Vaccines" was really designed to address a problem that's existed for a long time, which is insufficient research and development budgets as well as investment capacity in vaccine development and production for the third world. How do you create better incentives to get the pharma community—the vaccine community—to produce products that are specifically dedicated for the developing world.

RUTH LEVINE: Michael Kramer, a professor at Harvard, had been thinking about this problem for many years.

OWEN BARDER: He realized that if the rich countries of the world were to make a promise that they would buy a malaria vaccine if somebody produced it, that that would give an incentive to the pharmaceutical industry to go and do the research and development needed to make one. But this idea was unfamiliar. No government had made a commitment to buy a product that didn't already exist.

SOURCE: Making Markets for Vaccines
https://www.youtube.com/watch?v=fRelQxGJx7Q

When the first such "Advanced Market Commitment" was made in 2007—a $1.5 billion promise [36] to buy yet-to-be-produced vaccines from Big Pharma manufacturers—there was the Gates Foundation [37] as the only non-nation sponsor.

The Gates-founded Gavi Vaccine Alliance is an open partnership [38] between the Gates Foundation, the World Health Organization, the World Bank and vaccine manufacturers. Their stated goal includes "introducing new vaccines into the routine schedules of national immunization programmes" [39] and engaging in "market shaping efforts" [40] to ensure "healthy markets for vaccines and other immunization products."

If "introducing new vaccines" and ensuring healthy markets for them was the aim of Gates' "Decade of Vaccines," there can be no doubt that COVID-19 has seen that goal realized in spectacular fashion.

URSULA VON DER LEYEN: Let's start the pledging.

KATIE STEPHENS: The EU kicked off its fundraising drive with 1 billion euros. In the hours that followed, pledges were beamed in from across the globe.

TAWFIG ALRABIAH: The Kingdom of Saudi Arabia has pledged 500 million dollars.

STEPHENS: Even pop icon Madonna made a last-minute donation of a million euros.

SOURCE: What's behind the global €7.4 billion vaccine pledge? | Coronavirus Update
https://www.youtube.com/watch?v=vOFYcoo2p2s

MELINDA GATES: By combining the world's expertise and brainpower and resources, we can attack this disease in the way it's attacking us: globally. Our foundation is proud to partner with you and I'm pleased to announce today that we will pledge a hundred million dollars towards this effort.

SOURCE: #Coronavirus Global Response International Pledging Conference
https://www.youtube.com/watch?v=ngBTZ4xp3HM

KATIE STEPHENS: Germany was one of the leading donors, pledging over five hundred million euros. The money is earmarked for international health organizations and research networks in a bid to speed up the development of a vaccine.

SOURCE: <u>What's behind the global €7.4 billion vaccine pledge? | Coronavirus Update</u>
https://www.youtube.com/watch?v=vOFYcoo2p2s

And there, at the center of this web, is the Gates Foundation, connected to every major organization, research institution, international alliance and vaccine manufacturer involved in the current crisis.

Certainly, the Gates—like the Rockefellers—have profited from their years as "the most generous people on the planet." As curious as it might seem to those who don't understand the true nature of this monopoly cartel, despite all of these grants and pledges—commitments of tens of billions of dollars—Bill Gates' personal net worth has actually doubled during this "Decade of Vaccines," from <u>$50 billion</u> [41] to <u>over $100 billion</u> [42].

But once again we come back to the question: Who is Bill Gates? Is he motivated simply by money? Is this incessant drive to vaccinate the entire population of the planet merely the result of greed? Or is there something else driving this agenda?

As we shall see next time, money is not the end goal of Gates' "philanthropic" activities. Money is just the tool that he is using to purchase what he really wants: control. Control not just of the health industry, but control of the human population itself.

References

[1]. https://www.gatesfoundation.org/Media-Center/Press-Releases/2010/01/Bill-and-Melinda-Gates-Pledge-$10-Billion-in-Call-for-Decade-of-Vaccines

[2]. https://www.who.int/immunization/global_vaccine_action_plan/DoV_GVAP_2012_2020/en/

[3]. https://www.who.int/about/finances-accountability/reports/A72_INF5-en.pdf

[4]. https://www.corbettreport.com/gateshealth/

[5]. https://www.gatesfoundation.org/Media-Center/Press-Releases/2010/12/Global-Health-Leaders-Launch-Decade-of-Vaccines-Collaboration

[6]. https://www.who.int/immunization/global_vaccine_action_plan/GVAP_doc_2011_2020/en/

[7]. https://www.who.int/about/finances-accountability/reports/A72_INF5-en.pdf

[8]. https://www.gavi.org/our-alliance/market-shaping

[9]. https://www.gavi.org/investing-gavi/funding/donor-profiles/bill-melinda-gates-foundation

[10]. https://www.gatesfoundation.org/What-We-Do/Global-Health/Vaccine-Development-and-Surveillance

[11]. https://www.news.com.au/lifestyle/health/health-problems/coronavirus-vaccine-not-a-certainty-says-infectious-diseases-expert/news-story/00d35352f3476dd2a508f57fbd1e5425

[12]. https://www.nature.com/articles/d41586-020-00751-9

[13]. https://www.sciencedirect.com/science/article/pii/S0264410X08015053

[14]. https://journals.plos.org/plosone/article?id=10.1371/journal.pone.0035421

[15]. https://www.federalregister.gov/documents/2020/03/17/2020-05484/declaration-under-the-public-readiness-and-emergency-preparedness-act-for-medical-countermeasures

[16]. https://www.gatesfoundation.org/Media-Center/Press-Releases/2020/02/Bill-and-Melinda-Gates-Foundation-Dedicates-Additional-Funding-to-the-Novel-Coronavirus-Response

[17]. http://164.100.47.5/newcommittee/reports/EnglishCommittees/Committee%20on%20Health%20and%20Family%20Welfare/72.pdf

[18]. http://164.100.47.5/newcommittee/reports/EnglishCommittees/Committee%20on%20Health%20and%20Family%20Welfare/72.pdf

[19]. https://www.sciencemag.org/news/2013/09/indian-parliament-comes-down-hard-cervical-cancer-trial

[20]. https://www.sciencemag.org/news/2013/09/indian-parliament-comes-down-hard-cervical-cancer-trial

[21]. https://indianexpress.com/article/india/india-news-india/conflict-of-

interest-nhm-panel-raises-questions-on-bill-gates-foundation/
[22]. https://www.sciencedirect.com/science/article/pii/S0264410X10002094
[23]. https://economictimes.indiatimes.com/news/politics-and-nation/centre-shuts-gate-on-bill-melinda-gates-foundation/articleshow/57028697.cms
[24]. http://www.laleva.org/eng/la-voix-news-clipping.jpg
[25].
https://www.npr.org/sections/goatsandsoda/2017/06/28/534403083/mutant-strains-of-polio-vaccine-now-cause-more-paralysis-than-wild-polio
[26]. https://www.gatesfoundation.org/What-We-Do/Global-Development/Polio
[27]. https://www.economist.com/the-economist-explains/2018/12/19/what-is-vaccine-derived-polio
[28]. https://www.ncbi.nlm.nih.gov/pmc/articles/PMC6121585/pdf/ijerph-15-01755.pdf
[29]. https://www.thehindu.com/news/cities/Delhi/vaccine-induced-paralysis-calls-for-action-says-study/article24740588.ece
[30]. https://archive.is/vVJFo
[31]. https://www.vox.com/2015/6/10/8760199/gates-foundation-criticism
[32]. https://www.gatesfoundation.org/Media-Center/Press-Releases/2006/02/Tachi-Yamada-Selected-to-Lead-Global-Health-Program
[33]. https://archive.is/qt4OW
[34]. https://www.gatesfoundation.org/Who-We-Are/General-Information/Leadership/Executive-Leadership-Team/Trevor-Mundel
[35].
https://www.cgdev.org/sites/default/files/archive/doc/books/vaccine/Making Markets-complete.pdf
[36]. https://www.reuters.com/article/idUSL06661675._CH_.2400
[37]. https://www.gatesfoundation.org/Media-Center/Press-Releases/2009/06/Ministers-of-Finance-and-Global-Health-Leaders-Fulfill-Prom
[38]. https://www.gavi.org/our-alliance/operating-model/gavis-partnership-model
[39]. https://www.gavi.org/our-alliance/strategy/phase-4-2016-2020/vaccine-goal
[40]. https://www.gavi.org/our-alliance/market-shaping
[41].
https://web.archive.org/web/20100924204343/https:/www.forbes.com/profil e/bill-gates/
[42]. https://www.forbes.com/profile/bill-gates/#3f1766ed689f

Part Three: Bill Gates and the Population Control Grid

James Corbett

WARREN BUFFETT: Hello, everyone.

EVERYONE: Mr. B.!

DAVID ALLEN JONES: What's your secret mission about?

BUFFETT: It's not my mission, but an idea that came from our good friend, Mr. Bill Gates.

BILL GATES: Hi, kids.

RADLEY HEMMING: The real, actual, in person Bill . . . Bill . . .

ELENA RAMIREZ: He's trying to say that we're big fans, Mr. Gates.

SOURCE: Secret Millionaires Club | The Gift – Bill Gates Ep 1 | Kid Genius Cartoons
https://www.youtube.com/watch?v=YFL8-BK4QFk

It's a strange fact that Bill Gates' hagiographers—PR hacks employed, more often than not, by large corporations that receive funding from the Bill and Melinda Gates Foundation— consistently depict this drab software developer as a cartoon superhero, using his "superpower" of being very rich to help "save the planet."

JOHN BERMAN: Behind closed doors on this New York campus, a secret gathering of some of the world's most powerful people: Gates, Buffett, Bloomberg, Winfrey. It was like . . . well, it was like the "Super Friends."

[Super Friends cartoon introduction plays]

ANNOUNCER: In the great hall of the Justice League, there are assembled the world's four greatest heroes.

SOURCE: Elite Billionaires Meet in Secret (video no longer online)

But these cartoon-fueled puff pieces reveal more than they know about Gates and the other mega-rich philanthropists they are attempting to idolize: they reveal that the idea of the selfless, billionaire do-gooder is a work of fiction so unbelievable it is only fit for Saturday morning cartoon fare.

As we have seen in our first two explorations of Bill Gates' role as global health kingpin, the seemingly selfless generosity of the Gates family through their eponymous foundation has in fact greatly increased their own wealth, with Bill Gates' personal net worth having doubled in the past decade alone.

But the takeover of public health that we have documented in How Bill Gates Monopolized Global Health and the remarkably brazen push to vaccinate everyone on the planet that we have documented in Bill Gates' Plan to Vaccinate the World was not, at base, about money. The unimaginable wealth that Gates has accrued is now being used to purchase something much more useful: control. Control not just of the global health bodies that can coordinate a worldwide vaccination program or the governments that will mandate such an unprecedented campaign, but control over the global population itself.

This is an exploration of **Bill Gates and the Population Control Grid.**

From a journalistic standpoint, Good Morning America's inane report on the secretive billionaire meeting that took place in

New York in 2009 was a failure. It listed some of the meetings' attendees and their combined net worth:

BERMAN: Gates, Buffett, Bloomberg, Winfrey [. . .] Together with others in the meeting, including George Soros, Ted Turner, David Rockefeller, they're worth more than $125 billion.

It turned to the senior editor of Forbes for a sound bite about what it would be like to witness such an assembly of wealth:

MATTHEW MILLER: To have been in the room and see this meeting of the minds really would have been a fascinating thing.

And it dutifully reported the participants' own stated reason for holding the meeting. . . .

BERMAN: That much money. That much power around one table. It begs the question, what were they doing? What were they scheming? Total world domination? This group, together for six hours, was talking about charity, education, emergency relief, global health.

. . . Before wrapping up with another juvenile appeal to comic book superhero lore.

[Video onscreen of various billionaires superimposed as Superheroes, such as Batman, Superman. Etc.]

BERMAN: The new supermen and wonder woman. The superrich friends. Not fighting bad guys, but fighting for good, nonetheless. For Good Morning America, John Berman, ABC News.

Yes, from a journalistic standpoint, Berman's report was an utter failure. There was no attempt to question the participants about the meeting, no space for any criticism of these billionaires or questions about their motives, no adversarial journalism of any kind.

But as a PR piece, it was brilliant. It leaves the viewer with a vague sense that some kind of gathering took place somewhere in New York in which rich people—who, let's not forget, are superheroes—talked about charity.

One would have to turn to print sources to discover that the meeting was held at the personal residence of Sir Paul Nurse [1] then-president of Rockefeller University; that the invitation to the gathering [2] was co-written by Bill Gates, Warren Buffett and David Rockefeller; or that the aim of the meeting [3] was "to consider how their wealth could be used to slow the growth of the world's population."

Given that these extraordinarily rich and powerful men—including Warren Buffett [4], David Rockefeller [5], and Ted Turner [6]—have all expressed their belief that the growing human population is the greatest threat faced by humanity, it should not be surprising that they would convene a conference to discuss how best to channel their vast wealth into the project of reducing the number of people on the planet. Particularly unsurprising is that attendees of the meeting later dubbed Bill Gates—a man for whom population control is particularly close to his heart—as the "most impressive"[7] speaker at the event.

GATES: Here we can see a chart that looks at the total world population over the last several hundred years, and at first glance this is a bit scary. We go from less than a billion in 1800, and then 3, 4, 5, 6—and 7.4 billion, where we are today, is happening even faster. So, Melinda and I wondered whether providing new medicines and keeping children alive, would that create more of a population problem?

SOURCE: Does saving more lives lead to overpopulation?
https://www.youtube.com/watch?v=obRG-2jurz0

SCOTT PELLEY: . . . and what the developing world does not need is more children.

MELINDA GATES: And I think that was the biggest "ah-ha" to Bill and me when we got into this work. Because we asked ourselves, of course, the same hard-nosed question you'd ask, which is: "If you get into this work and you start to save these children, will women just keep overpopulating the world?" And thank goodness, the converse is absolutely true.

SOURCE: <u>Extra: Gates On Population Rates</u>
https://www.youtube.com/watch?v=7_xEn5mudP8

GATES: This is a very important question to get right, because it was absolutely key for me. When our foundation first started up, it was focused on reproductive health. That was the main thing we did, because I thought, you know, population growth in poor countries is the biggest problem they face. You've got to help mothers, who want to limit family size, have the tools and education to do that. And I thought, that's the only thing that really counts.

SOURCE: <u>Bill Gates on Overpopulation and Global Poverty</u>
https://www.youtube.com/watch?v=llAG5V7x17A

In recent years, critics have pointed to Bill Gates' own words linking vaccination programs with his goal of reducing population growth.

GATES: The world today has 6.8 billion people. That's headed up to about nine billion. Now, if we do a really great job on new vaccines, health care, reproductive health services, we could lower that by perhaps 10 or 15 percent.

SOURCE: <u>Innovating to zero! | Bill Gates</u>
https://www.youtube.com/watch?v=JaF-fq2Zn7I

SANJAY GUPTA: Ten billion dollars over the next 10 years to make it the year of the vaccines. What does that mean, exactly?

GATES: Well, over this decade, we believe unbelievable progress can be made both inventing new vaccines and making sure they get out to all the children who need them. We could cut the number of children who die every year from about nine million to half of that, if we have success on it. And the benefits there in terms of reducing sickness, reducing the population growth, it really allows society a chance to take care of itself once you've made that intervention.

SOURCE: <u>Sanjay Gupta MD February 5, 2011</u>
http://transcripts.cnn.com/TRANSCRIPTS/1102/05/hcsg.01.ht
ml

But as any number of "fact-checking websites"—not to mention Bill Gates himself—are quick to point out, this doesn't mean what it sounds like it means.

GATES: What we found out is that as health improves, families choose to have less children.

SOURCE: <u>Does saving more lives lead to overpopulation?</u>
https://www.youtube.com/watch?v=obRG-2jurz0

MELINDA GATES: The truth is that when people's lives improve—when children survive, for instance, or when girls go to school—people start making decisions based on the expectation that their children will live and thrive. The result is smaller families and slower population growth.

SOURCE: <u>Does Saving Lives Mean Overpopulation?</u>
https://www.youtube.com/watch?v=i_Z7whe-YHk

GATES: I came across articles that showed that the key thing you can do to reduce population growth is actually improve health. And that sounds paradoxical. You think, "OK, better health means more kids, not less kids." Well, in fact, what parents are doing is they're trying to have two kids survive to adulthood to take care of them. And so the more disease burden that there is, the more kids they have to have to have that high probability. So there's a perfect correlation that, as you improve health, within a half generation the population growth rate goes down.

SOURCE: <u>Bill Gates on Overpopulation and Global Poverty</u>
https://www.youtube.com/watch?v=llAG5V7x17A

Yes, the Gates' stated plan is to reduce population growth by improving health. But the idea of using vaccines as sterilization agents—even without the public's knowledge or consent—is not conspiracy lore, but documentable fact.

It its 1968 annual report [8], the Rockefeller Foundation addressed the "Problems of Population," lamenting that "[v]ery little work is in progress on immunological methods, such as vaccines, to reduce fertility, and much more research is required if a solution is to be found here." The Foundation vowed to correct this problem by funding "established and beginning investigators to turn their attention to aspects of research in reproductive biology that have implications for human fertility and its control."

This was no empty promise. By the time of its 1988 Annual Report [9], the Rockefeller Foundation was able to report progress on its funding into contraceptive research, including NORPLANT, a contraceptive implanted under the skin of a woman's upper arm and effective for five years. In its 1988 report, the Rockefeller Foundation was pleased to announce that NORPLANT—which was developed by the Rockefeller-founded Population Council—was "now approved for marketing in 12 countries."

The Rockefellers' Population Council and other research organizations joined with the World Health Organization (WHO) in 1972 to create a Task Force on Vaccines for Fertility Regulation [10]. By 1995, they were able to report [11] progress in "developing a prototype of an anti-hCG-vaccine," which works by combining an immunogen formed from a synthetic peptide of human chorionic gonadotrophin (hCG)—a hormone secreted by the surface of the early embryo to remain implanted in the womb—with a toxoid carrier molecule. The vaccine stimulates an immune reaction, causing women to develop antibodies against the hormone, thus preventing them from carrying babies to term.

But beginning in the 1990s, a series of scandals over WHO-led vaccination programs [12] in the third world led to allegations that tetanus vaccines in places like the Philippines [13] and Kenya [14] were being laced with hCG in order to implement population control by stealth. The controversy generated by these stories led global institutions to step back from the campaign to champion population control by vaccine.

But, as usual, the Bill and Melinda Gates Foundation was there to renew interest, working with the UK government to host a "London Summit on Family Planning" in 2012 at which the foundation announced their support for funding the research, development and deployment of injectable contraceptives to the developing world.

MELINDA GATES: You heard me talk earlier about Sadi, who I met in Niger. She was traveling fifteen kilometers to get an injection. But let's ask ourselves, what if she didn't have to travel to that clinic? If we put it in her perspective, how can we keep her in her village to get the contraceptives she wants? Well, Pfizer is testing a new form of Depo, the injection that she gets fifteen kilometers to get. They're now putting it in a new form, a new device that can be given—it's very, very small, it's called Uniject. I think it's going to be pictured here.

It's a high-quality product. It's effective. It's safe. It's tiny, as you can see. And it can be put in a healthcare worker's kit to give to the woman at the village level. So Sadi won't have to go fifteen kilometers any longer to get that injection.

SOURCE: Melinda Gates Keynote: London Summit on Family Planning | Bill & Melinda Gates Foundation https://www.youtube.com/watch?v=o1oZBl1w_fc

But the Gates were not content to stop there. In 2014 it was announced that Microchips Biotech, Inc., a company in Lexington, Massachusetts, had developed a new form of birth control [15]: "a wireless implant that can be turned on and off with a remote control and that is designed to last up to 16 years." According to MIT Technology Review [16], the idea originated when Bill Gates visited Robert Langer's MIT lab in 2012 and asked him if it would be possible to create an implantable birth control device that could be turned on or off remotely. Langer referred Gates to the controlled release microchip technology he had invented and licensed to MicroCHIPS Biotechnology, and the Gates Foundation granted $20 million [17] to the firm to develop the implants.

Reducing population growth has, by Gates' own admission, been a core mission of the Gates Foundation since its inception. But in order to really understand what Gates means by "population control," we have to look beyond the concept of controlling population size. At its most fundamental level, the "population control" that Gates speaks of is not birth control, but control of the population itself.

In order to understand the broader population control agenda and how it ties in to the Gates Foundation's plans, we have to look at a puzzling development that took place in 2017. In that year, Gavi—the Gates founded and funded [18] alliance that partners the Gates Foundation, the World Health Organization and the World Bank with vaccine manufacturers to help ensure "healthy markets" for vaccines—took a strange pivot away from its core mission of vaccinating every child on the planet [19] to providing every child with a digital biometric identity.

The idea was first floated by Gavi CEO Seth Berkley in a Nature article that year, "Immunization needs a technology boost [20]," where he states that the goal of 100% immunization will not be reached without "secure digital identification systems that can store a child's medical history." He then gives a specific example:

"We are working with a company in India called Khushi Baby, which creates off-grid digital health records. A necklace worn by infants contains a unique identification number on a short-range communication chip. Community health workers can scan the chip using a mobile phone, enabling them to update a child's digital record even in remote areas with little phone coverage."

This sudden interest in digital identity was no mere passing fancy for the vaccine alliance. Gavi doubled down by becoming a founding member of the ID2020 Alliance, a public-private partnership dedicated to [21] spearheading a global digital biometric identity standard. Other founding members [22] of the alliance include Gates' first company, Microsoft, and The Rockefeller Foundation.

In 2018, Gavi issued [23] a call for innovation in digital technologies "for finding, identifying and registering the most vulnerable children." The call specifically requested [24] technologies for capturing, storing and enrolling the biometric details of infants on "rugged biometric devices."

Berkley continued to follow up on this idea in public engagements as one of the new core missions of Gavi.

SETH BERKLEY: What's interesting is that people tend to think of, you know, birth certificates as kind of a major document. But, you know, the most common—as I mentioned before—is not a birth certificate, is not a death certificate, is not a marriage certificate. The most common connection—vital registration for the population—is actually a child health card, because we reach more than 90 percent of children with at least one dose of vaccine as part of a routine, so they're in the system. The challenge is that contact is not connected into the system. So, if you could connect it, then you have the ability to give them their basic identity papers. You have the ability, then, later on, if they want to own land or they want to have their rights, you're able to help them with that. But, you know, we're not currently taking advantage of that. And so the children get seen, they get enrolled in the health centers, but that information is not used for anything else.

SOURCE: Mid-term review 2018 – Michael Froman and Seth Berkley
https://www.youtube.com/watch?v=-aBE4JpHzVE

Although vaccines and identity may seem unrelated, Bill Gates has spent the last few years funding research that can bring the two ideas together.

Late last year, Gates once again turned to <u>Robert Langer and his MIT colleagues</u> [25] to investigate new ways to permanently store and record the vaccination information of each individual. The <u>result of their research</u> [26] was a new vaccine delivery method. They found that by using "dissolvable microneedles that deliver patterns of near-infrared light-emitting microparticles to the skin," they could create "particle patterns" in the skin of vaccine recipients which are "invisible to the eye but can be imaged using modified smartphones."

Rice University <u>describes [27]</u> the quantum dot tags left behind by the microneedles as "something like a bar-code tattoo."

So who was behind this development? As lead researcher Kevin McHugh explains:

"The Bill and Melinda Gates Foundation came to us and said, 'Hey, we have a real problem—knowing who's vaccinated [. . .] So our idea was to put the record on the person. This way, later on, people can scan over the area to see what vaccines have been administered and give only the ones still needed."

The microparticles that form the fluorescent quantum-dot tags are delivered along with the vaccine, but they cannot be delivered by a traditional syringe. Instead, they must be delivered by a patch of microneedles made from a mixture of dissolvable sugar and a polymer, called PVA, as well as the quantum-dot dye and the vaccine.

It should be no surprise, then, that Big Pharma vaccine manufacturers—in their scramble to produce the coronavirus vaccine that, Gates assures us, is necessary to "go back to normal"—have turned to a novel vaccine delivery method: a dissolvable microneedle array patch.

NICK HARPER: The University of Pittsburgh is where the polio vaccine was first discovered. At the medical center, researchers are now developing a vaccine that is delivered using a dissolvable patch called a microneedle array.

LOUIS FALO: Think about them as almost like a band-aid. And so the microneedle array is simply applied to the skin topically, pressed into place very shortly, and then taken off and thrown away and then the antigen is already delivered.

SOURCE: <u>Pharmaceutical companies scramble to produce coronavirus vaccine</u>
https://www.youtube.com/watch?v=StsFJgGdGhQ

As is becoming evident, this new vaccine-delivered bar- code-like tattoo is about much more than simply ensuring that children get all their Gavi-recommended immunizations.

On a recent "Ask Me Anything" thread on reddit, when asked "What changes are we going to have to make to how businesses operate to maintain our economy while providing social distancing?" Bill Gates answered [28]: "Eventually we will have some digital certificates to show who has recovered or been tested recently or when we have a vaccine who has received it."

In his answer, Gates fails to mention that he has himself been instrumental in kickstarting and funding the research into the very type of digital certificates for vaccination that he is speaking about, or that these "digital certificates"—likely, at first, to be a digital marker linked to a biometric ID—could very well one day take the form of vaccine-implanted quantum-dot tattoos.

But, as in so many other aspects of the unfolding crisis, Gates' unscientific pronouncement that we will need digital certificates to prove our immunity in the "new normal" of the post-coronavirus world . . .

GATES: Eventually, what we'll have to have is certificates of who is a recovered person, who is a vaccinated person.

SOURCE: <u>How we must respond to the coronavirus pandemic | Bill Gates</u>
https://www.youtube.com/watch?v=Xe8fIjxicoo&t=1171s

. . .is now being implemented by a number of governments. It is now being reported [29] that Onfido, a tech startup specializing in AI-based biometric ID verification, is in talks with the British government to provide the type of "digital certification" Gates mentioned, dubbed an "immunity passport." The proposed system would require would-be workers to use the Onfido-provided app to scan their face or other biometric data, link that information to a SARS-CoV-2 antibody test (or, eventually proof of coronavirus vaccination), and then have their picture taken and immunity verified every time they wish to access a restricted space or work environment.

Last month, Onfido announced [30] that it had raised $50 million in a round of investments led by Bill Gates' old company, Microsoft.

But this is not Gates' first experience with the field of biometric identity.

A decade ago, the government of India began what has been called "The Largest Social Experiment on Earth [31]": enrolling over one billion people in the largest biometric identification database ever constructed. The project—involving iris scanning and fingerprinting the entirety of the Indian population, recording their biometric details in a centralized database, and issuing them a 12-digit identity number that could be used to prove residence and access government services, all within the span of a few years—presented an incredible societal, legal and technological challenge.

It's no surprise, then, that the person who was brought in as the chief architect of the Aadhaar project when it was launched—Nandan Nilekani, co-founder of Indian multi-national Infosys—is also a long-time friend of Bill Gates and a partner [32] with Bill and Melinda Gates on a "philanthropic" venture called Co-Impact, which supports "initiatives to address major social challenges at scale."

Nilekani's involvement in Aadhaar has even made him one of Gates's "heroes [33]," featured in slick video promotions [34] produced by the Bill and Melinda Gates Foundation.

GATES: My friend, Nandan Nilekani, is one of India's best-known entrepreneurs. He led the creation of the world's largest biometric ID system. Now he's working to promote his platform to improve the lives of the world's poorest people.

NANDAR NILEKANI: There are more than a billion people around the world who don't have any kind of ID. You can't do anything in life without an ID because people are mobile, they are migrant. And wherever they go, whether they want a job, or whether they want to board a train, or whether they want to get a bank account or get a mobile connection, if the person has no way of proving who they are, then they just won't get access to those services. So the challenge we had was, how do we give a billion people, many of whom don't have birth certificates, how do we give them an ID?

Aadhaar is the world's largest digital ID system, and entirely based using biometrics to ensure uniqueness. Our enrollment was very simple: name, address, date of birth, sex, email ID and phone number if you wish, and the biometrics. The ten fingerprints of both the hands, the iris of both the eyes, and a photograph. And in a few days, he will get his Aadhaar number in the mail. And that's how a billion people got their IDs.

SOURCE: Bill Gates's Heroes in the Field: Nandan Nilekani https://youtu.be/q_I5oj9LEh8

And Gates has personally praised the Aadhar scheme as "a huge asset for India."

GATES: Well, Aadhaar is a huge asset for India. It was designed very well. The fact that you can make digital payments so easily, you can open a bank account . . . India's a leader in that. Our Foundation, you know, worked with the Reserve Bank. You know, Nandar Nilekani and a group of people that he pulled together did a great job.

But Gates is not merely an arms-length admirer of the Aadhaar experiment. He is not only personally connected to its chief architect. He is also connected to one of the key companies that spearheaded the technology that underlies the project's biometric database.

The company that provides the iris recognition technology at the core of the Aadhaar system, <u>Idemia</u> [35], also provides <u>facial recognition systems for the Chinese government</u> [36] and is currently developing <u>digital drivers licenses for use in the United States [37]</u>. Idemia even <u>created</u> the Khushi Baby identification necklaces with embedded microchips that Gavi CEO Seth Berkley touted in his Nature article. Unsurprisingly, the company receives support from the Bill and Melinda Gates Foundation through its involvement in the <u>GSMA Inclusive Tech Lab [38]</u>.

And now, Gates is funding a scheme to retool Aadhaar for a global rollout.

In 2014, the World Bank created a multi-sector working group to launch the "Identification for Development Initative," or <u>ID4D [39]</u>, which aims to "support progress toward identification systems using 21st century solutions." The World Bank cites <u>goal 16.9</u> [40] of the UN Agenda 2030 Sustainable Development Goals—vowing to "provide legal identity for all, including birth registration" in the next 10 years—as the basis for its initiative.

But ID4D was little more than a pipe dream until 2016, when the Bill and Melinda Gates Foundation provided "catalytic contributions" to launch the <u>ID4D Multi-Donor Trust Fund [41]</u>, which enticed the UK, French and Australian governments, along with the Omidyar Network, into a partnership aiming to "shape global approaches and a shared vision on identification."

Unsurprisingly, this World Bank ID4D initiative includes Nandar Nilekani—Gates' partner and the chief architect of Aadhaar—on its advisory council and Gates has said [42] that he is funding the World Bank "to take this Aadhaar approach to other countries."

This headlong rush to capture the biometric details and assign digital identification to every person on earth is sold to the public under the guise of "financial inclusion." The poorest people on the planet have trouble accessing financial services and receiving government aid because they don't have official government identification papers. In this formulation, being issued a government ID—having one's biometric details registered, tracked and databased by the government—is a "human right" that must be "secured."

It should be no surprise by this point that this "human right" also has direct benefits for big business and for the entities that are looking to exert greater control over the human population.

Gates provided insight into the real purpose of this identification control grid in a speech at the Financial Inclusion Forum hosted by the US Treasury in 2015.

GATES: Every country really needs to look through these KYC—know your customer—rules to make sure that customers are able to prove who they are. But of course in many countries you don't have any type of ID system. And the lack of an ID system is a problem, not just for the payment system, but also for voting and health and education and taxation. And so it's a wonderful thing to go in and create a broad identification system.

Again, India is a very interesting example of this, where the Aadhaar system, which is a 12-digit identifier that's correlated to biometric measures, is becoming pervasive throughout the country and will be the foundation for how we bring this low-cost switch to every mobile phone user in India. The same type of thing is happening now in in Pakistan and there's early beginnings of creating these ID programs in Africa as well.

We expect to be able to use the IDs so that when you show up for any government service—say, you walk into a primary health clinic—we'll be able to take that bio ID very quickly and bring up your electronic health record. Even if you've moved from one part of the country to the other, you will be well tracked and well served without nearly as much paperwork or waiting. And so the ID system is foundational.

SOURCE: <u>Bill Gates at the Financial Inclusion Forum,</u> <u>December 1, 2015</u>
http://www.yorkcast.com/treasury/events/2015/12/01/financial/

The ID control grid is an essential part of the digitization of the economy. And although this is being sold as an opportunity for "financial inclusion" of the world's poorest in the banking system provided by the likes of Gates and his banking and business associates, it is in fact a system for financial exclusion. Exclusion of any person or transaction that does not have the approval of the government or the payment providers.

GATES: Once financial flows go underground—where you have lots of legitimate transactions mixed in with the ones you want to track—and once they're going over a digital system that the US has no connection to, it's far more difficult to find the transactions that you want to be aware of or that you want to block.

SOURCE: <u>Bill Gates at the Financial Inclusion Forum,</u> <u>December 1, 2015</u>
http://www.yorkcast.com/treasury/events/2015/12/01/financial/

And, once again, this is no mere theoretical talk from Gates. He has been intimately involved in this process of switching the world over to a digital payment grid tied to biometric identity.

In 2012, the Bill and Melinda Gates Foundation <u>helped</u> <u>found</u> [43] the "Better Than Cash Alliance," which brings together governments, international organizations and the private sector "to accelerate the transition from cash to digital payments globally."

And, when the Indian government made a bold move to demonetize large amounts of its circulating currency in order to draw off-the-books funds back under the purview of the Indian tax office, there was Gates to praise the move as an important step toward the creation of a brave new digital economy, tied, of course, to the Aadhaar ID grid.

GATES: The bold move to demonetize high value denominations and replace them with new notes with higher security features is an important step to move away from a shadow economy to an even more transparent economy. And digital transactions really I think will rise dramatically here. In fact, I think in the next several years India will become the most digitized economy. Not just by size but by percentage as well. All of the pieces are now coming together.

One piece of this that we enjoyed consulting with the government on, making sure it comes together in the right way, is the pending roll out of payment banks. This for the first time really will mean that you have full currency capability on those digital phones. Once you have that digital infrastructure, the whole way you think about government benefits can be done differently. [. . .] Over time, all of these transactions will create a footprint and so when you go in for credit the ability to access the history that you've paid your utility bills on time, that you've saved up money for your children's education, all of those things in your digital trail, accessed in an appropriate way will allow the credit market to properly score the risk and therefore loosen up more money for investments, not only in the agricultural sector but for all the entrepreneurs in the country.

SOURCE: <u>PM at Niti Ayog's Lecture Series: Microsoft Founder Bill Gates adressing India's top policy makers</u>
https://www.youtube.com/watch?v=YFZ1bOU6Cb0

The different parts of this population control grid fit together like pieces of a jigsaw puzzle. The vaccination drive ties into the biometric identity drive which ties into the cashless society drive.

In Gates' vision, everyone will receive the government-mandated vaccinations, and everyone will have their biometric details recorded in nationally administered, globally integrated digital IDs. These digital identities will be tied to all of our actions and transactions, and, if and when they are deemed illegal, they will simply be shut off by the government—or even the payment providers themselves.

The Indian experiment in pioneering this biometric digital economy—an experiment with which Gates has been so intimately involved—also provides a perfect example of just how such a system will be abused.

In January 2018, a report in The Tribune revealed [44] that all of the details, including the name, address, postal code, photo, phone number and email, of all billion-plus Aadhaar-registered Indians, was available for purchase on WhatsApp for 500 rupees, or about USD$7. The Unique Identification Authority of India that administers the Aadhaar scheme was then forced to admit [45] that approximately 210 websites, including websites of the central government and state government departments, were displaying the list of government beneficiaries, along with their name, address, other details and Aadhaar numbers.

Even more worryingly, newly obtained documents show that the Indian government is integrating Aadhaar-collected data to create a "360-degree database [46]" that will "automatically track when a citizen moves between cities, changes jobs, or buys new property" and integrate that data into a real-time geo-spatial database built by the country's space agency, ISRO.

Only the most willfully obtuse could claim to be unable to see the nightmarish implications for this type of all-seeing, all-pervasive society, where every transaction and every movement of every citizen is monitored, analyzed, and databased in real-time by the government. And Bill Gates is one of those willfully obtuse people.

SHEREEN BAHN: A current debate that's on in India and globally as well [is] around data. Now, you've been an advocate of Aadhaar, you've supported it, you've defended it. And I think that the questions arise not on on whether it's a good idea or not, but whether it should be made mandatory for every citizen for every service possible. Because it was envisaged as people accessing government subsidy, using the Aadhaar card to avoid duplication and leakages. The question, then, is that India today is still grappling with putting in place a privacy framework, a privacy regulation, a data protection regulation. In that context, then, does it make sense, even though the matter is in court today, to link Aadhaar to every possible service?

GATES: Well, Aadhar is just something that avoids you pretending to be somebody else. That, you know, you can have, you know, fake people on the government payroll. Aadhaar, you know, prevents you being on that payroll as as a ghost worker. It prevents you from collecting things that you shouldn't collect or accessing a health record you shouldn't have access to.

So the basic Aadhaar mechanism is an identity mechanism. And so it's too bad if somebody thinks that because Aadhaar is there that in and of itself creates a privacy problem.

SOURCE: <u>Future Ready with Bill Gates (Exclusive Interview) | Bill Gates & Melinda Gates: The Philanthropists</u>
https://www.youtube.com/watch?v=a8YcDPghRx4

Gates' response is, of course, disingenuous. The very purpose of a globally integrated ID grid and cashless payment architecture is to remove privacy from our lives.

It should be no surprise, then, that this man who is not concerned about the privacy implications of a global, real-time electronic ID and digital payments grid, is also a prime investor in EarthNow LLC, a company <u>promising</u> [47] to "deploy a large constellation of advanced imaging satellites that will deliver real-time, continuous video of almost anywhere on Earth."

No, this Gates-driven agenda is not about money. It is about control. Control over every aspect of our daily lives, from where we go, to who we meet, to what we buy and what we do.

The irony is that this billionaire "philanthropist," so often depicted as a cartoon superhero for his dazzling generosity, actually resembles nothing so much as a comic book supervillain, right down to the use of his vast wealth to sponsor Harvard University research [48] into dimming the sun by spraying particles into the stratosphere.

But once again, we are driven back to the question. Who is this person? What ideology is driving this quest for control? And what is the end goal of this quest?

Who is Bill Gates?

James Corbett originally published a transcript of his videos about Bill Gates on May 1, 2020. His website is https://www.corbettreport.com.

References

[1].
https://web.archive.org/web/20100106010617/http:/www.timesonline.co.uk/t
ol/news/world/us_and_americas/article6350303.ece

[2]. https://www.nbcmiami.com/news/weird/natlbillionaires-hold-secret-
cabal-in-new-york/1861553/

[3]. https://archive.is/RAwFf

[4]. https://www.philanthropy.com/article/Warren-Buffett-Holds-
Firm/181693

[5]. https://www.youtube.com/watch?v=4tMOtR9qrRg

[6]. https://www.youtube.com/watch?v=DMgamzziQMM

[7]. https://www.theguardian.com/world/2009/may/31/new-york-billionaire-
philanthropists

[8]. https://www.rockefellerfoundation.org/wp-content/uploads/Annual-
Report-1968-1.pdf

[9]. https://www.rockefellerfoundation.org/wp-content/uploads/Annual-
Report-1988-1.pdf

[10]. https://www.ncbi.nlm.nih.gov/pubmed/1874951

[11]. http://www.biotech-monitor.nl/2502.htm

[12].
https://web.archive.org/web/20190221165650/https:/www.unicef.org/immun
ization/files/MNTE_strategy_paper.pdf

[13]. https://www.ncbi.nlm.nih.gov/pubmed/12346214

[14].
https://www.researchgate.net/publication/320641479_HCG_Found_in_WH
O_Tetanus_Vaccine_in_Kenya_Raises_Concern_in_the_Developing_World

[15]. https://nationalpost.com/news/bill-gates-funds-birth-control-microchip-
that-lasts-16-years-inside-the-body-and-can-be-turned-on-or-off-with-
remote-control

[16]. https://www.technologyreview.com/2014/07/04/74389/a-contraceptive-
implant-with-remote-control/

[17]. https://www.gatesfoundation.org/how-we-work/quick-links/grants-
database/grants/2014/01/opp1068198

[18]. https://www.gavi.org/investing-gavi/funding/donor-profiles/bill-
melinda-gates-foundation

[19]. https://www.gavi.org/our-alliance/strategy/phase-5-2021-2025/equity-
goal

[20]. https://www.nature.com/articles/d41586-017-05923-8

[21]. https://id2020.org/manifesto

[22]. https://id2020.org/alliance

[23].
https://web.archive.org/web/20180308005056/http:/www.gavi.org/infuse/call
s-to-innovate/2018/

[24].
https://web.archive.org/web/20180319101104im_/http:/www.gavi.org/uploa
dedImages/Funding_and_finance/infuse/Calls_to_innovation/infuse-2018-
graphic_source.png

[25]. https://news.mit.edu/2019/storing-vaccine-history-skin-1218

[26]. https://stm.sciencemag.org/content/11/523/eaay7162

[27]. https://news.rice.edu/2019/12/18/quantum-dot-tattoos-hold-vaccination-record/

[28].
https://www.reddit.com/r/Coronavirus/comments/fksnbf/im_bill_gates_coch
air_of_the_bill_melinda_gates/

[29]. https://www.theguardian.com/politics/2020/may/03/coronavirus-health-passports-for-uk-possible-in-months

[30]. https://techcrunch.com/2019/04/03/onfido-which-verifies-ids-using-ai-nabs-50m-from-softbank-salesforce-microsoft-and-more/

[31]. https://www.youtube.com/watch?v=SWT0TMn8t9w

[32]. https://www.co-impact.org/partners/

[33]. https://www.gatesnotes.com/Development/Heroes-in-the-Field-Nandan-Nilekani

[34]. https://youtu.be/q_I5oj9LEh8

[35]. https://www.idemia.com/press-release/idemia-ranked-1-international-nist-benchmark-iris-recognition-2020-04-06

[36]. http://www.oldthinkernews.com/2018/08/21/idemia-the-corporation-building-spy-grid-in-china-national-id-in-india-also-creates-drivers-licenses-in-the-u-s/

[37]. https://www.govtech.com/transportation/Iowa-Five-Other-States-Will-Try-Digital-Drivers-License-Projects-in-2018.html

[38]. https://www.idemia.com/news/idemia-supports-digital-and-financial-inclusion-joining-gsmas-new-inclusive-tech-lab-2019-10-09

[39]. https://id4d.worldbank.org/

[40]. https://www.un.org/sustainabledevelopment/peace-justice/

[41]. https://id4d.worldbank.org/who-is-involved

[42]. https://www.news18.com/news/tech/bill-gates-praises-aadhaar-technology-funds-world-bank-to-bring-it-to-other-countries-1737211.html

[43]. https://www.betterthancash.org/about/resource-partners

[44]. https://www.tribuneindia.com/news/archive/nation/rs-500-10-minutes-and-you-have-access-to-billion-aadhaar-details-523361

[45]. https://economictimes.indiatimes.com/news/politics-and-nation/aadhaar-data-is-fully-safe-uidai/articleshow/61725239.cms

[46]. https://www.huffingtonpost.in/entry/aadhaar-national-social-registry-database-modi_in_5e6f4d3cc5b6dda30fcd3462

[47]. https://10z325bj2404dqj6e3lhft8y-wpengine.netdna-ssl.com/wp-content/uploads/2018/04/Press_Release_18April2018.pdf

[48]. https://www.nature.com/articles/d41586-018-07533-4

Part Four: Meet Bill Gates

Computer whiz kid. Talented software developer. Shrewd businessman. Benevolent philanthropist. Global health expert.

There can be no doubt that Bill Gates has worn many hats on his remarkable journey from his early life as the privileged son of a Seattle-area power couple to his current status as one of the richest and most influential people on the planet. But, as we have seen in our exploration of Gates' rise as unelected global health czar and population control advocate, the question of who Bill Gates really is, is no mere philosophical pursuit.

Given that we are currently living through a crisis that has been "predicted" by Bill Gates, which is triggering a response from the global health organizations that the Bill and Melinda Gates Foundation has bankrolled, and driving us toward a vaccination and biometric ID "solution" which Bill Gates has been working on for years, the answer to the question "Who Is Bill Gates?" is quickly becoming one of the most important questions of our lives. That answer will not only tell us about the world that we are living in, but about the one that we are being thrust into . . . and how we can avoid it.

Today we will attempt to answer that question as we examine the motives, the ideology, and the connections of this man who has been so instrumental in shaping the post-coronavirus world.

Meet Bill Gates.

So who is Bill Gates?

Some argue that he's a genius who leveraged his natural computer savvy into a billion-dollar fortune.

JANE PAULEY: You're called a genius and I will—well, no, I don't think that embarrassed you at all. They call you a genius. Part of your genius is that you are a computer whiz, and the other is that you did have the business acumen to turn it into a working company. Are you a business genius, too?

GATES: Well, I wouldn't say "genius."

SOURCE: <u>Watch 28-year-old Bill Gates explain why he didn't see himself as a genius</u>
<u>https://www.cnbc.com/video/2019/02/25/watch-microsofts-28-year-old-bill-gates-explain-why-he-didnt-see-himself-as-a-genius.html</u>

Others insist that he is a visionary who changed our lives with his foresight and bold imagination.

ALAN GARBER: Bill had a vision—and I understand it went back even then—that computing would be ubiquitous. It would be part of all of our lives. And, indeed, as you all know, he executed on that vision. And the world today has changed so dramatically in large part due to the work that Bill has done throughout the years.

SOURCE: <u>A Conversation with Bill Gates' Q&A at Harvard University</u>
https://www.youtube.com/watch?v=ofQMbC2e_as

He has been hailed as a shrewd executive who built the Microsoft empire with his remarkable talent for business.

JAMES WALLACE: When the biographers and historians write the history of the 20th century, Bill Gates is going to go down as the best businessman of our century, and Microsoft as one of the greatest companies of the 20th century.

SOURCE: <u>Biography: Bill Gates</u>
https://www.youtube.com/watch?v=mQN8J-OIJEs

And he has been praised as a philanthropist who is selflessly devoting his wealth to improving the lives of people around the world.

JESSE KORNBLUTH: Bill, even your harshest critic would have to admit that your philanthropy work is, you know, planet-shaking incredible and could be, if you make it, a second act so amazing that it would dwarf what you've actually done at Microsoft. [APPLAUSE]

SOURCE: Steve Jobs and Bill Gates Face Off
https://www.youtube.com/watch?v=Sw8x7ASpRIY

But, like anyone of his status, he has his detractors. In the 1990s he was often portrayed as the greedy head of the evil Microsoft monopoly.

BENJAMIN WOOLEY: Bill Gates isn't content with his Windows system running just a few PCs. He wants it to run the world, spreading like a computer virus into our faxes, our phones, our TV sets, and, yes, even our toasters.

SOURCE: Bill Gates on the dawn of the Internet
https://www.youtube.com/watch?v=-uWhwmaCd00%5d

But in the age of the coronavirus crisis, he is most often treated like some sort of epidemiologist or leading health researcher.

ANDERSON COOPER: Back here with us once again to talk about this, as well as testing, treatments and more: Bill Gates, co-chair of the Bill and Melinda Gates Foundation. Bill, thanks so much for being back with us. It's been a little over a month since you were here and at that time you said the US had not hit its peak. So at this point do you think we have peaked and where do you think we are right now in kind of the arc of the pandemic?

SOURCE: Bill Gates says US system produces 'bogus' testing numbers
https://www.youtube.com/watch?v=odeq6DRVqP0

But in truth, none of these perspectives are accurate.

Microsoft's big break famously came from a deal to provide software for IBM as they moved into the personal computer market. But the deal was not the result of Gates' technical genius or amazing business acumen. As has been quietly admitted by IBM executives in the years since, Microsoft was given their shot at the chance to work with "Big Blue" as a result of Gates' mother's [1] relationship with IBM CEO John Opel.

GORAN MILIC: You remember your partnership of IBM and Bill Gates? How did it break up?

EDWARD ANDRUS: I do remember very well, actually. Bill Gates at the time at the beginning of our relationship with them was living on pizza and Pepsi Cola in Albuquerque, New Mexico. And his mother happened to be on the United Way board with our chairman and asked our chairman to help him. And you know, when the chairman comes in and tells you to go help this kid, nine hundred people get on the plane Monday morning and they all go down to try to help Bill Gates.

[. . .]

So I don't see Bill Gates as this great, creative person. I see him as an opportunist. And, in fact, in those days there was a lot of sharing of software code. People gave it away in Silicon Valley; they would share everything. He came in and he tried to control everything and put a price on it.

SOURCE: Idemo u Ameriku 2
https://www.youtube.com/watch?v=VL522xNizKs

Computer historians have long known how the basis for what became MS-DOS was not Bill Gates' brilliant imagination, but QDOS, a "Quick and Dirty Operating System" that had been thrown together by Tim Patterson, a worker at Seattle Computer Products, as a placeholder until he could sell a proper operating system to his customers. And as even Gates himself admitted, the breakthrough Graphical User Interface that became the basis for Windows was ripped off from the researchers at the Xerox Palo Alto Research Center.

As Bill would say after Apple unsuccessfully sued Microsoft for copyright infringement over Windows' GUI: "Hey, Steve, just because you broke into Xerox's house before I did and took the TV doesn't mean I can't go in later and take the stereo."

SOURCE: Paul Allen, <u>Idea Man</u> (p. 156)
https://www.goodreads.com/book/show/10139649-idea-man

And, as Gates also admits, it is not a spirit of selfless generosity that motivates his interest in vaccines and other lucrative health interventions.

BECKY QUICK: I'd like to talk to you about your approach to vaccinations. You wrote something recently, and, like you always do, you kind of looked at the problem from a scientific and business perspective on things. You've invested 10 billion dollars in vaccinations over the last two decades, and you figured out the return on investment for that. It kind of stunned me. Can you walk us through the math?

[. . .]

BILL GATES: You know, we see a phenomenal track record. It's been a hundred billion overall that the world's put in—our foundation is a bit more than 10 billion—but we feel there's been over a 20-to-one return. So if you just look at the economic benefits, that's a pretty strong number compared to anything else.

SOURCE: <u>Bill Gates: My 'best investment' turned $10 billion into $200 billion worth of economic benefit</u>
https://www.cnbc.com/2019/01/23/bill-gates-turns-10-billion-into-200-billion-worth-of-economic-benefit.html

As we have seen, Gates' "philanthropic" investment scheme has paid off well, with his $50 billion net worth having ballooned to over $100 billion after his decade of "altruism" in the vaccine market. As critics of his foundation have repeatedly pointed out, the 9,000,000 people who die every year of hunger would be best served by securing food supplies, running water and other basic necessities, not costly medical interventions for rare diseases. But there is no return on investment to be made from that kind of charity.

No, this is not about charity. It is about control. The population control grid that Gates has been quietly funding into existence for the past decade—a biometric identification system tied to a digital payments infrastructure that will be used to track, catalogue and control every movement, every transaction and every interaction of every citizen—is just now coming into view.

But the real question is: Why is he doing this? What drives a man like Bill Gates, a man rich beyond the wildest dreams of avarice, to spend his time and invest his fortune in schemes to control the population? To find the answer to that question, we have to examine Gates' family background.

Bill Gates, it should not be surprising to learn, was born into money. His great-grandfather, J. W. Maxwell [2], was the president of National City Bank in Seattle. His grandfather, Willard [3], was also a banker, and his grandmother, Adele, a prominent Seattle civic leader.

Bill Gates' mother, Mary Maxwell Gates, was a scion of the Maxwell banking family and, by all accounts, as hard-driving as her forebears. She served as a director of several companies, including First Interstate Bancorp and KIRO-TV of Seattle. She served as a regent at the University of Washington. And she was appointed to the board of the United Way of America, where, as we have seen, she persuaded IBM CEO John Opel to help her son in his fledgling software development career.

Bill's father, William H. Gates, Sr., was a prominent Seattle-area lawyer. He co-founded a powerful law and lobbying firm, helped Howard Schultz [4] in his bid to buy Starbucks, served on the boards of numerous companies and organizations, and, along the way, had a profound influence on his son's life and career.

GATES: My dad was a large presence, both physically and in terms of his wisdom. He worked very hard, so he'd leave in the mornings, often before we had breakfast, and get home in time for dinner. I always looked up to my dad in terms of how hard he worked.

At the dinner table my dad would go through various lawsuits and expect us to follow along. He had high expectations.

SOURCE: <u>Celebrating My Father's 90th Birthday</u>
https://www.youtube.com/watch?v=a2mKUoYc9OE

The young Bill Gates—technically "William H. Gates III," although his card-playing family dubbed him "Trey"—learned much from his parents. From his mother's banking family he inherited a "nose for the dollar," as one childhood friend's father called it. From his hard-driving legal-minded father, he learned the value of legalizing business arrangements. As a child, he even had a legal contract drawn up to grant him the use of his older sisters' baseball mitt.

These traits would not earn him many friends, but they served him well as he began to bring order to the anarchic software development community of the 1970s. At that time, software for the brand new personal computer market was the realm of computer hobbyists—people whose excitement about the microcomputer revolution and love of engineering and problem-solving led them to develop and share code freely with each other.

But this was no good for the young Bill Gates, who, even before Microsoft was off the ground, was already dreaming of commoditizing this hobby and turning it into the basis of a business empire. In 1976, with the ink still wet on Microsoft's first contract with Micro Instrumentation and Telemetry Systems of Albuquerque, New Mexico, the then-21-year-old

Gates wrote an Open Letter to Hobbyists [5] excoriating the early computer enthusiasts, who represented his main market, for sharing Microsoft's code for Altair BASIC.

As the majority of hobbyists must be aware, most of you steal your software. Hardware must be paid for, but software is something to share. Who cares if the people who worked on it get paid?

Is this fair? [. . .] The royalty paid to us, the manual, the tape and the overhead make it a break-even operation. One thing you do do is prevent good software from being written. Who can afford to do professional work for nothing? What hobbyist can put 3-man [sic] years into programming, finding all bugs, documenting his product and distribute for free? The fact is, no one besides us has invested a lot of money in hobby software. We have written 6800 BASIC, and are writing 8080 APL and 6800 APL, but there is very little incentive to make this software available to hobbyists. Most directly, the thing you do is theft.

SOURCE: Open Letter to Hobbyists
http://www.blinkenlights.com/classiccmp/gateswhine.html

The letter was awkward and tone-deaf, as many people have described the young Bill Gates in his social interactions. It heaped vitriol on the very people who would be the customers of any future business and tried to change an established culture of sharing software code merely by decree. Even Apple Computers, which would go on to be one of the prime purveyors of "walled garden" systems that restrict users' ability to control their own computers, scored an easy marketing victory by responding to Gates' angry letter with a reminder that "Yes, Folks, Apple BASIC is Free! [6]"

But the gauntlet was thrown down, and Gates would have his way. Although freeware and other forms of open source software development still exist, the establishment of software code as legally protected intellectual property has led to the rise of billionaires like Gates.

A "nose for the dollar" and a knowledge of how to use the legal system to get what you want were not the only things to emerge from Bill Gates' childhood, however. His parents also encouraged discussion about the family's charity work and the causes they held close to their heart.

As Gates revealed to Bill Moyers [7] in 2003, those causes included "the population issue" which sparked a lifelong interest in "reproductive health."

GATES: One issue that really grabbed me as urgent were issues related to population . . . reproductive health.

MOYERS: But did you come to reproductive issues as an intellectual?

GATES: When I was growing up, my parents were always involved in various volunteer things. My dad was head of Planned Parenthood. And it was very controversial to be involved with that.

SOURCE: **A Conversation with Bill Gates: Making a Healthier World for Children and Future Generations**
https://billmoyers.com/content/conversation-bill-gates-making-healthier-world-children-future-generations-transcript/

Gates tips his hand when he equates "issues related to population" with "reproductive health." The topic is particularly controversial, because "population control" and "reproductive health" have been used for half a century as a euphemism for eugenics, the discredited pseudoscience that holds that certain families are fit to be leaders of society by virtue of their superior genes.

As we saw in "Why Big Oil Conquered the World [8]," eugenics was a field named and codified by Francis Galton, cousin of Charles Darwin. Ostensibly concerned with heredity and what would later be known as genetics, the eugenicists believed that the rich and powerful were rich and powerful not because of luck or chance or happenstance, and certainly not from the deployment of cutthroat business tactics and underhanded dealings; no, the rich and powerful had attained their status because they came from "better stock." Conversely, the poor were poor because of their "defective germ plasm."

As transparent as it seems to us today that this ideology was a self-serving self-justification for the ruling class, it was quickly taken up as the great social crusade of the early 20th century. From Teddy Roosevelt [9] to H. G. Wells to Julian Huxley to Winston Churchill [10], there was widespread support for the eugenicist notion that society must strive to make sure that the rich and "well-born" breed as much as possible, and the poor, infirm, and "feeble-minded" be prevented from having children.

A common eugenicist argument was that the scarce resources of society should not be used to support the lower classes, as that only encouraged more of their kind. Instead, life-saving medical care and intervention should be rationed so that those resources can be best put to use elsewhere. So-called negative eugenicists even took things further, with some, like famed playwright George Bernard Shaw, calling for people to be called before a state-appointed board to justify their existence or be put to death.

GEORGE BERNARD SHAW: [. . .] But there are an extraordinary number of people whom I want to kill. Not in any unkind or personal spirit, but it must be evident to all of you — you must all know half a dozen people, at least—who are no use in this world. Who are more trouble than they are worth. And I think it would be a good thing to make everybody come before a properly appointed board, just as he might come before the income tax commissioner, and, say, every five years, or every seven years, just put him there, and say: "Sir, or madam, now will you be kind enough to justify your existence?"

SOURCE: George Bernard Shaw talking about capital punishment
https://www.youtube.com/watch?v=B-Ljkoh_vmE

But, in the post-WWII era, as the name of eugenics became tarred by association with the Nazi atrocities, the talk of death panels and other harsh eugenicist notions was dropped from public conversation. Now, the quest to reduce the size of the poor population was spoken of as "population control" and "reproductive health." Still, occasionally, these old negative eugenics ideas are revisited in moments of candor.

GATES: You're raising tuitions at the University of California as rapidly as they [sic] can and so the access that used to be available to the middle class or whatever is just rapidly going away. That's a trade-off society's making because of very, very high medical costs and a lack of willingness to say, you know, "Is spending a million dollars on that last three months of life for that patient—would it be better not to lay off those 10 teachers and to make that trade off in medical cost?" But that's called the "death panel" and you're not supposed to have that discussion.

SOURCE: <u>Bill Gates: End-of-Life Care vs. Saving Teachers' Jobs</u>
https://www.youtube.com/watch?v=03MZG9vK0W8

It is worth questioning why this man, who openly muses about death panels and the trade-offs of providing health care to the elderly, is to be taken completely at face value in his attempts to slow population growth in the third world or to handle a coronavirus health crisis that primarily affects the elderly.

That the Gates agenda is being driven by a eugenicist ideology is suggested by multiple lines of evidence, both historical and current.

As we have also seen in "<u>Why Big Oil Conquered the World [11]</u>," the Rockefeller family was instrumental in funding and promoting eugenics, both in America and overseas.

The Rockefellers helped fund the Eugenics Record Office.

The founding director of the Rockefeller Institute for Medical Research, William Welch, sat on the ERO's board [12] and helped direct its activities.

The Rockefellers sponsored the studies of the eugenics researchers at the Kaiser Wilhelm Institutes in Germany, including Ernst Rüdin, who would go on to draft Nazi Germany's forced sterilization law [13].

And, when the American Eugenics Society became embarrassed of its own name, its long-time director, Frederick Osborne, merely took over as president of the Rockefeller-founded Population Council.

This dedication to the cause of "public health" did not escape the approving gaze of Bill Gates, Sr. In a chapter of his 2009 book, Showing Up for Life, called "Walking With Giants," he writes admiringly of the Rockefellers and their influence in the field:

Every corner we've turned in the field of global health, we've found that the Rockefellers were already there and had been there for years.

When we committed to childhood immunization we found ourselves building on efforts the Rockefeller Foundation had helped launch and fund in the 1980s.

When we became interested in fighting malaria and tuberculosis, we learned that the Rockefellers had been studying the prevention and treatment of such diseases around the globe for, in some cases, as long as a hundred years.

A similar dynamic held true in the case of HIV/AIDS.

A lesson we learned from studying and working with the Rockefellers is that to succeed in pursuing audacious goals you need like-minded partners with whom to collaborate.

And we learned that such goals are not prizes claimed by the short-winded. The Rockefellers stay with tough problems for generations.

SOURCE: William H. Gates. Showing Up for Life (pp. 158-159)

As Gates, Sr., suggests, it is by working with "like-minded partners" that such "great" achievements in the field of global health can be made. For the Gates, these like-minded partners include the Rockefellers themselves. Bill Gates, Sr., got to discuss global health, agriculture and environment with the likes of David Rockefeller, Sr., and David Rockefeller, Jr., at a meeting on "Philanthropy in a Global Century [14]" at Rockefeller University campus in 2000. And Bill Gates, as we have seen, co-hosted a meeting on reducing the population with David Rockefeller in 2009.

But the most salacious hints of a deeper agenda are not to be found in the Gates' public associations, but in the associations that they have tried to hide from the public.

STEPHANIE RUHLE: Jeffrey Epstein may be dead, but this story isn't. A shocking new report from The New York Times sheds light on the connection between Microsoft founder Bill Gates and the late Jeffrey Epstein. After Gates' name came up in connection with Epstein and MIT Media Lab, Gates gave a statement to The Wall Street Journal where he insisted he did not have any business relationship or friendship with Epstein. But a new report outlines conversations with Gates and Epstein and a conversation with Bill and Melinda Gates' Foundation. A connection between their foundation and JPMorgan Chase to set up a charitable fund to benefit Epstein. You know what I want to know: Why?

SOURCE: NYT: Bill Gates Repeatedly Met With Jeffrey Epstein | Velshi & Ruhle | MSNBC
https://www.youtube.com/watch?v=WnKQ4tzg7ow

Beginning in August of last year, a string of information connecting Bill Gates to convicted sex offender Jeffrey Epstein began to emerge.

Flight logs revealed [15] that Gates had flown on Jeffrey Epstein's private jet.

An email [16] surfaced showing disgraced MIT Media Lab Director Joi Ito—who resigned from his position [17] after it was discovered that he had helped cover up Jeffrey Epstein's identity as an "anonymous" donor to the lab—informing his staff that a $2 million donation to the lab in 2014 was a "gift from Bill Gates directed by Jeffrey Epstein."

As the story gained momentum, Gates tried to downplay the relationship, with a Gates spokesperson protesting [18] that Gates "didn't know it was Epstein's plane," and Gates himself insisting that [19] "I didn't have any business relationship or friendship with [Epstein]."

This was immediately contradicted by The New York Times, who reported [20] in October of 2012 that Gates had in fact met with Epstein on multiple occasions, even going so far as to discuss the creation of a multibillion dollar charitable fund with seed money from the Bill and Melinda Gates Foundation and JPMorgan Chase.

According to the Times [21], Gates emailed his colleagues about Epstein in 2011: "His lifestyle is very different and kind of intriguing although it would not work for me."

Epstein's will even named Boris Nikolic [22]—a Harvard-trained immunologist who served as the chief scientific advisor to both Microsoft and the Bill and Melinda Gates Foundation and who appears in the sole publicly known photo of Epstein and Gates' 2011 meeting at Epstein's Manhattan mansion—as the backup executor of Epstein's estate.

It is not difficult to see why Gates would try to distance himself from his relationship with a child sex trafficker. Epstein, after all, is suspected of ensnaring high-ranking politicians, businessmen and even royalty in an intelligence-directed "honeypot" operation, recording them in the act of sexually abusing underage girls and using that evidence as blackmail.

But, as it turns out, the attempt to suppress the Gates-Epstein story may have been an attempt to suppress the revelation of an altogether different shared interest.

KRISTEN DAHLGREN: Sources say several accusers have come forward in New Mexico, where Epstein owns a sprawling ranch. According to a new report published in The New York Times—not verified by NBC News—Epstein wanted to use the ranch for controlled breeding, using his DNA to improve humanity. Citing two award-winning scientists and an advisor to large companies and wealthy individuals, the article reports Epstein surrounded himself with leading scientists and would tell them he wanted to have 20 women impregnated at a time on the ranch.

SOURCE: <u>Jeffrey Epstein Had Plan To Father Dozens Of Children, Report Says | TODAY</u>
https://www.youtube.com/watch?v=CMw-qvqbs_g

The already scarcely believable Jeffrey Epstein story took another bizarre turn in August of 2019, when it was reported that Epstein "<u>Hoped to Seed the Human Race With His DNA [23]</u>." As The New York Times explained, Epstein's plan to impregnate 20 women at a time at his New Mexico ranch in order to "seed the human race with his DNA"—a plan he told to a number of the "scientific luminaries" he kept in his orbit—put a modern gloss on a very old idea:

Mr. Epstein's vision reflected his longstanding fascination with what has become known as transhumanism: the science of improving the human population through technologies like genetic engineering and artificial intelligence. Critics have likened transhumanism to a modern-day version of eugenics, the discredited field of improving the human race through controlled breeding.

Epstein's interest in genetics led him to sponsor a number of scientists working in the field, including George Church, a Harvard geneticist whose lab received funding from Epstein's foundation from 2005 to 2007 for "cutting edge science." Church publicly apologized [24] for his connection to Epstein, which included several meetings a year from 2014 onward. This was neither the first nor the last time that this unassuming Harvard biologist, whose "cutting edge science" often strays into controversial areas, caused a public scandal. In 2019, Church proposed a "genetics dating app" which was immediately denounced as applied eugenics [25].

Church also acted as scientific advisor to Editas Medicine, a startup seeking to use [26] the genome-editing tool, CRISPR-Cas9, to eliminate diseases by deleting the parts of a genetic code responsible for the illness. In 2015, the company announced [27] it had raised $120 million from a group led by [28] Epstein's appointed backup executor, Dr. Boris Nikolic. Naturally, that group of investors included Bill Gates [29].

Yes, Bill Gates is certainly following his father's advice to collaborate with "like-minded partners."

So, the question remains: Is Bill Gates motivated by eugenics? Given that eugenics went underground over half a century ago, we are unlikely ever to unearth a frank admission along those lines from Gates himself. After all, there are no longer any card-carrying members of the American Eugenics Society; the society was rebranded in the 1970s when, as the society's founder noted [30], "it became evident that changes of a eugenic nature would be made for reasons other than eugenics, and that tying a eugenic label on them would more often hinder than help their adoption."

But there was an American Eugenics Society in the 1920s, and it just so happened to boast a "William H. Gates" on its member roster [31]. But perhaps that is just a coincidence.

And there was an American Eugenics Society in the 1960s, when William H. Gates II was preceded as head of Planned Parenthood by Alan Guttmacher, who simultaneously served as the Director of the American Eugenics Society [32].

And perhaps it was coincidence that the Bill and Melinda Gates Foundation organized their London Summit on Family Planning, at which the Gates recommitted themselves to funding population control in the third world, in July 2012, on the anniversary of the First International Eugenics Congress [33], held in London exactly 100 years prior.

And perhaps it is reaching to compare the young Bill Gates' dating preferences to the genetic-based dating favored by modern-day eugenicists.

JAMES WALLACE: I interviewed several women who had dated Bill just briefly and one told me the very first question Bill asked her was: "What did you score on your SAT test?" You know, this is not exactly what a young woman wants to hear. For Bill Gates, though . . . He had scored a perfect 800 on his math portion of the SAT and this was a matter of pride with him. And he wanted to make sure whoever he was dating, you know, had scored a pretty high grade.

SOURCE: Biography: Bill Gates
https://www.youtube.com/watch?v=mQN8J-OIJEs

No, we cannot expect an answer about Bill Gates true motives to come from Gates himself. By this point the question of Bill Gates' intentions has been buried under the combined weight of hundreds of millions of dollars of paid PR spin. Like the Rockefellers before them, the Gates have long since learned the secret of enlarging their family fortune—not to mention their control over the human population—by donning the mask of philanthropy.

There are many perspectives on Bill Gates; depending on who you ask, he is a computer savant, a genius businessman, or a saintly philanthropist. But all of these perspectives have been brought to you through PR outlets founded or funded by the Bill and Melinda Gates Foundation. Bill Gates is no longer a subject for historians but hagiographers.

Now we must confront the question of why this man is motivated to build such a web of control—control over our public health agencies—

GATES: And for all 193 member states, you must make vaccines a high priority in your health systems, to ensure that all your children have access to existing vaccines now—and to new vaccines as they become available.

SOURCE: <u>BILL GATES TO WORLD HEALTH ASSEMBLY: IMMUNIZE EVERY CHILD</u>
https://www.youtube.com/watch?v=QqePDrifFNo

Control over our identities—

GATES: And the lack of an ID system is a problem, not just for the payment system, but also for voting and health and education and taxation. And so it's a wonderful thing to go in and create a broad identification system

SOURCE: <u>Bill Gates at the Financial Inclusion Forum, December 1, 2015</u>
http://www.yorkcast.com/treasury/events/2015/12/01/financial/

Control over our transactions—

GATES: Once financial flows go underground—where you have lots of legitimate transactions mixed in with the ones you want to track—and once they're going over a digital system that the US has no connection to, it's far more difficult to find the transactions that you want to be aware of or that you want to block.

SOURCE: <u>Bill Gates at the Financial Inclusion Forum, December 1, 2015</u>
http://www.yorkcast.com/treasury/events/2015/12/01/financial/

And even control over our bodies—

GATES: We're gonna have this intermediate period of opening up, and it won't be normal until we get an amazing vaccine to the entire world.

SOURCE: <u>Watch CNBC's full interview with Microsoft co-founder Bill Gates on the coronavirus pandemic and his work toward a vaccine</u>
https://www.cnbc.com/video/2020/04/09/watch-cnbcs-full-interview-with-microsoft-co-founder-bill-gates-on-past-pandemic-warnings.html

We must confront the possibility that this quest for control comes not from a selfless spirit of generosity that never seemed to exist before he became a multi-billionaire, but from the same drive for money, the same desire for domination and the same sense of superiority that motivated him on his way up the corporate ladder.

But if the answer to the question "Who is Bill Gates" is "Bill Gates is a eugenicist," that tells us some important things about the world that we are living in.

It tells us that Gates is deceiving the public into supporting his takeover of the world with a false front of philanthropy. It tells us that the goal of the Gates, like the goal of the Rockefellers before them, is not to improve the world for humankind, but to improve the world for their kind.

And most importantly, it tells us that Bill Gates is no comic-book supervillain, single-handedly directing all of the chaos that is unfolding in the world or single-handedly bringing his own order to that chaos.

No, if Bill Gates is a eugenicist, driven by a belief in the superiority of himself and his fellow wealthy elitists, then what we are facing is not one man, or even one family, but an ideology.

This is not a trivial point. One man, whatever his wealth, can be stopped easily enough. But even if Bill Gates were to be thrown in jail tomorrow, the agenda that has already been set in motion would continue without missing a beat. An entire infrastructure of researchers, labs, corporations, governmental agencies and public health bodies exists, funded more often than not by Gates, but driven by the belief of all those millions of people working for these various entities that they are truly working in the best interest of the people.

No, an ideology cannot be stopped by stopping one man. It can only be stopped when enough people learn the truth about this agenda and the world of total, pervasive control that is coming into view.

If you have watched all four parts of this exploration on Bill Gates, then you are now one of the most informed people on the planet about the true nature of this agenda. You have seen how the takeover of public health has been used to railroad the world into a headlong rush toward mandatory vaccinations, biometric identification and digital payments. You have seen how the pieces of this puzzle fit together, and how they represent a far greater threat to the future of humanity than any virus.

Here is the good news: Armed with this information, you have the antidote to the scourge of this eugenicist ideology. The truth is that ideologies are viruses of the mind; they spread from person to person, infecting them with ideas that can lead to a disease of the body politic.

But here is the even greater truth: Inoculations do work. Inoculations of truth against the lies of those spreading their poisonous ideology.

If you have made it this far, it is incumbent on you to help inoculate those around you against the corrupt ideology of Bill Gates and all those who seek to control the population of the world. You must help to spread this information so that others have a chance to see the bigger picture and decide for themselves whether they are willing to roll up their sleeves and accept what is coming, or not.

But time is not on our side. Even as we speak, mass vaccination campaigns are being prepared:

ALLISON ARWADY: You know we are already building our plans to vaccinate the whole city of Chicago and working with others across the region on a major plan for this. We've bought syringes, we've bought cold boxes, we've planned out locations.

SOURCE: <u>COVID COACH</u>
https://www.youtube.com/watch?v=ZzsZVsSllaU

Biometric identification schemes and "immunity passports" are already being rolled out:

CARYN SEIDMAN BECKER: And so while we started with travel, at our core we're a biometric-secure identity platform, where it's always been about attaching your identity to your boarding pass at the airport or your ticket to get into a sports stadium or your credit card to buy a beer. And so now with the launch of Clear Health Pass, it's about attaching your identity to your COVID-related health insights for employers, for employees, for customers.

SOURCE: <u>CLEAR's new Health Pass service to help screen for coronavirus: CEO</u>
https://www.youtube.com/watch?v=Fw6QIQBW9ew

Programs for tracking, tracing, and surveilling the entire population are already being beta-tested:

DEENA HINSHAW: Today we are launching another useful tool that can supplement the critical detective work we are conducting in public health. Alberta Trace Together is a voluntary, secure, mobile contact tracing application to help prevent the spread of COVID-19.

SOURCE: <u>Alberta rolls out COVID-19 contact tracing app</u>
https://www.youtube.com/watch?v=Mwy-J6JANNw

And the digital payment infrastructure, the system of financial exclusion that will allow governments to turn off our access to the economy at will, is being put into place:

UHURU KENYATTA: In order to avoid the risk of transmission through physical handling of money, we encourage the use of cashless transactions such as mobile money, M-Pesa and otherwise, and credit cards.

SOURCE: <u>Uhuru: Government encourages cashless transactions to reduce risk of coronavirus transmission</u>
https://www.youtube.com/watch?v=ByQUIzYLeEM

NICHOLAS THOMPSON: People are using touchless payment systems much more than they're using cash, both because we're not interacting with people directly as much anymore and also because cash is kind of skeezy.

SOURCE: <u>A Post-Pandemic Cashless Society? Was Remote NFL Draft a Tech Success? | Tech In :60 | GZERO Media</u>
https://www.youtube.com/watch?v=xEJYTU6-kFI

We must spread the word about the dark nature of this population control agenda to as many people as we can before our ability to speak out against this agenda is taken away for good.

Thanks to the likes of Bill Gates, the virus of this population control agenda is already here. It is threatening to crash the system as we've known it.

But if Bill Gates has taught us anything, it's how to deal with a virus. It's time for a hard reset.

References

[1]. https://archive.is/qUcxP

[2]. https://www.findagrave.com/memorial/131623851/james-willard-maxwell

[3]. https://www.findagrave.com/memorial/133167234/james-willard-maxwell

[4]. https://www.youtube.com/watch?v=iDHGgiTErAQ

[5]. http://www.blinkenlights.com/classiccmp/gateswhine.html

[6]. https://gadgetspage.com/wp-content/uploads/2009/11/1976apple1-915x1024.jpg

[7]. https://www.pbs.org/now/transcript/transcript_gates.html

[8]. https://www.corbettreport.com/bigoil/

[9]. http://eugenicsarchive.ca/discover/connections/5233dd265c2ec500000000c9#!

[10]. https://winstonchurchill.org/publications/finest-hour-extras/churchill-and-eugenics-1/

[11]. https://www.corbettreport.com/bigoil/

[12]. https://www.dnalc.org/view/10950-Eugenics-Record-Office-board-of-scientific-directors-and-functions.html

[13]. https://upload.wikimedia.org/wikipedia/commons/b/b9/Reichsgesetzblatt_25_Juli_1933.jpg

[14]. https://winstonchurchill.org/publications/finest-hour-extras/churchill-and-eugenics-1/

[15]. https://www.dailymail.co.uk/news/article-7377133/Bill-Gates-REFUSES-reveal-flew-Lolita-Express-Jeffrey-Epstein-prison-release.html

[16]. https://media.newyorker.com/photos/5d72ed4faf596b00089f16ce/master/w_1600%2Cc_limit/Farrow-MITEpstein-Email4.jpg

[17]. https://archive.is/ftvZa

[18]. https://www.theverge.com/2019/10/12/20911488/bill-gates-foundation-jeffrey-epstein-meetings

[19]. https://archive.is/P9SfI

[20]. https://archive.is/76MAs

[21]. https://archive.is/76MAs

[22]. https://archive.is/ftvZa

[23]. https://archive.is/Zub3G

[24]. https://www.statnews.com/2019/08/05/citing-nerd-tunnel-vision-biologist-george-church-apologizes-for-contacts-with-jeffrey-epstein/

[25]. https://www.youtube.com/watch?v=6DRQG7HRr4Y

[26]. https://www.businessinsider.com/bill-gates-and-others-invest-in-editas-for-crispr-gene-editing-2015-8?op=1

[27]. https://ir.editasmedicine.com/news-releases/news-release-details/editas-medicine-raises-120-million-advance-genome-editing

[28]. https://www.businessinsider.com/bill-gates-and-others-invest-in-editas-for-crispr-gene-editing-2015-8?op=1

[29]. https://www.forbes.com/sites/matthewherper/2015/08/10/bill-gates-and-13-other-investors-pour-120-million-into-revolutionary-gene-editing-startup/#6392af4c6369

[30]. https://eugenics.us/frederick-osborn-birth-control-and-abortion-are-turning-out-to-be-great-eugenic-advances/256.htm

[31]. https://archive.org/details/AMERICANEUGENICSSOCIETYMEMBERS/page/n157/mode/2up

[32]. https://archive.org/details/AMERICANEUGENICSSOCIETYMEMBERS/page/n449/mode/2up

[33]. https://archive.org/details/b22439833/mode/2up/search/textsFirst+International+Eugenics+Congress

COVID-911: From Homeland Security to Biosecurity

9/11, as we were told repeatedly in the days, weeks, and months after the attack, was the day that changed everything. And now a new event has come along to once again throw the world into chaos. But whereas the post-9/11 era introduced America to the concept of homeland security, the COVID-19 era is introducing the world to an altogether more abstract concept: biosecurity. This is the story of the COVID-911 security state.

9/11, as we were told repeatedly in the days, weeks, and months after the attack, was the day that changed everything.

NARRATOR: In the span of one devastating morning, America changed forever.

SOURCE: Remembering 9/11: Never Quit
https://www.youtube.com/watch?v=-kxbwu3vkLg

KATIE COURIC: Good morning. America may never be the same and this is why.

SOURCE: Today Show – September 12, 2001
https://www.youtube.com/watch?v=6158sdfRaB8

LOU WATERS: American life will change forever as a result of this attack.

SOURCE: CNN on September 12, 2001
https://www.youtube.com/watch?v=6Z22BM41hwo

REPORTER: Nothing will ever be the same again.

SOURCE: Inside Edition – A Look Back at 9/11
https://www.youtube.com/watch?v=mHjH1sl1o9s&t=2s

JAMES ROBBINS: Nothing will ever be quite the same again.

SOURCE: 9/11 the day after – BBC1 Nightly News
https://www.youtube.com/watch?v=XocX6peVkwo

TOM BROKAW: Life will never be quite the same.

SOURCE: Dateline NBC – Sept. 18, 2001
https://www.youtube.com/watch?v=Ebf0TVQ14EI

These were no empty words. They were plain statements of fact. The world *did* change on that day.

9/11 was the carte blanche for a Great Reset, the institution of a new normal in international relations and domestic affairs. From the creation of the Department of Homeland Security and the militarization of the police to the multi-trillion-dollar wars of aggression to reshape the Middle East, our lives today are drastically different than they were before that fateful Tuesday in September 2001.

GEORGE W. BUSH: On September the 11th, enemies of freedom committed an act of war against our country.

SOURCE: <u>Sept. 20, 2001 – Bush Declares War on Terror</u>
https://www.youtube.com/watch?v=_CSPbzitPL8

TONY BLAIR: If September the 11th hadn't happened, our assessment of the risk of allowing Saddam—any possibility of him reconstituting his programs—would not have been the same.

SOURCE: <u>IRAQ INQUIRY / TONY BLAIR / 9 11 CHANGED EVERYTHING</u>
https://www.youtube.com/watch?v=B0lp17hPB1Y

BUSH: For the first time, airport security will become a direct federal responsibility.

*SOURCE: **Bush signs aviation security legislation***
https://www.youtube.com/watch?v=EroUqm5hvZg

JOHN TYNER: I don't understand how a sexual assault can be made a condition of my flying.

TSA AGENT: This is not considered a sexual assault

TYNER: It would be if you weren't the government.

*SOURCE: **Airport Body Scans Debated***
https://www.youtube.com/watch?v=dicZgQ-QihU

CENK UYGUR: The old fact sheet said, "The primary function of the FBI is law enforcement." That makes sense. That's what we grew up with. The new fact sheet says, "The primary function of the FBI is national security."

*SOURCE: **Think The FBI Is About 'Law Enforcement'? Guess Again***
https://www.youtube.com/watch?v=WDLFmNqm_4M

JANET NAPOLITANO: If you *see* something suspicious in the parking lot or in the store, *say* something immediately. Report suspicious activity to your local police or sheriff. If you need help, ask a Walmart manager for assistance.

*SOURCE: **Walmart Public Service Announcement***
https://www.youtube.com/watch?v=Czoww2l1xdw

BUSH: All of this was brought upon us in a single day—and night fell on a different world, a world where freedom itself is under attack.

*SOURCE: **Sept. 20, 2001 – Bush Declares War on Terror***
https://www.youtube.com/watch?v=_CSPbzitPL8

NERMEEN SHAIKH: The Obama administration's internal legal justification for assassinating US citizens without charge has been revealed for the first time.

SOURCE: Kill List Exposed: Leaked Obama Memo Shows Assassination of U.S. Citizens "Has No Geographic Limit"
https://www.youtube.com/watch?v=zwNsXC6OWKE

RAND PAUL: I don't know. If the president's going to kill these people, he needs to let them know. Some of the people [who] might be terrorists are people who are missing fingers. Some people have stains on their clothing. Some people have changed the color of their hair. [. . .] Or people who might like to pay in cash or people who have seven days of food on hand.

SOURCE: Senator Rand Paul exposes scary definition of 'possible terrorist'
https://www.youtube.com/watch?v=muuz-lZzEIo

DEIRDRE BOLTON: NYPD Commissioner Bill Bratton is warning that terrorists are using cellphone encryption and literally getting away with murder.

SOURCE: Social media, encryption and the spread of terrorism
https://www.youtube.com/watch?v=lupH0ivSe9M

BUSH: Every nation in every region now has a decision to make: either you are with us or you are with the terrorists.

SOURCE: Either With Us Or With The Terrorists – Bush
https://www.youtube.com/watch?v=-qdvm6h8WKg

But, nearly two decades later, 9/11 has gone from a touchstone event shaping all of the Western world's national security decisions to a fading cultural memory of a trauma that took place before the newest generation of high school graduates were even born.

9/11 is no longer a driving political issue.

But, as if on cue, a new event has come along to throw the world into chaos.

Once again we are being told that the world has changed forever.

REPORTER: This is not normal. At least it wasn't until a few weeks ago, when everything we take for granted—everything—moved just beyond our grasp.

SOURCE: Coronavirus outbreak: Can we ever return to normal during or after the COVID-19 pandemic?
https://www.youtube.com/watch?v=o6xWvJjKBDM

REPORTER: As a global community we've experienced a once-in-a-lifetime event that will shift and reshape our behaviors and perceptions for quite some time.

SOURCE: Say Hello to The New Normal Consumer
https://www.youtube.com/watch?v=ZnD22DGl1mQ

JUSTIN TRUDEAU: This will be the new normal until a vaccine is developed.

REPORTER: . . . Meaning the new normal could last for months, even years.

SOURCE: The National: COVID-19 'new normal' to last; over 1M jobs lost
https://www.youtube.com/watch?v=SCU7mzYxwQk

NICOLA STURGEON: So return to normal as we knew it is not on the cards in the near future.

SOURCE: Scotland publishes framework for coping with 'new normal' of Covid-19
https://www.youtube.com/watch?v=FKcS4PNAko0

And, once again, this is no empty rhetoric. Governments, businesses and NGOs are now coordinating at the international level on a "Great Reset" to once again completely reshape the world we are living in.

KRISTALINA GEORGIEVA: History would look at this crisis as the great opportunity for reset.

ANTÓNIO GUTERRES: The great reset is a welcome recognition that this human tragedy must be a wake-up call. It is imperative that we re-imagine, rebuild, redesign, reinvigorate and rebalance our world.

SOURCE: The Great Reset Launch | Highlights
https://www.youtube.com/watch?v=u5pxhSnDr4U

JOHN KERRY: Reset cannot mean—we can't think of it in terms of sort of "pushing a button" and going back to the way things were. [. . .] And the normal *was* a crisis. The normal was itself not working.

SOURCE: The Great Reset Initiative | 24.06.2020
https://www.youtube.com/watch?v=-h49aH8RzV8

CHRYSTIA FREELAND: I think all Canadians understand that the restart of our economy needs to be green. It also needs to be equitable. It needs to be inclusive.

SOURCE: "It's about time": Freeland speaks on being Canada's first female finance minister
https://www.youtube.com/watch?v=RUbnsuwnVHg

MARIA VAN KERKHOVE: What we're going to have to figure out, and I think what we're all going to have to figure out together, is what our new normal looks like. Our new normal includes physical distancing from others. Our new normal includes wearing masks where appropriate. Our new normal includes us knowing where this virus is each and every day, where we live, where we work, where we want to travel.

SOURCE: What the New Normal Looks Like After Covid-19
https://www.youtube.com/watch?v=7CB85HVb5o4

ALLEY WILSON: In parts of Europe, immunity passports are being considered for people who are believed to be immune to the coronavirus. While in China, some cities have already implemented QR codes that generate a color in order for officials to enable how freely an individual may move around outdoors.

SOURCE: <u>Coronavirus outbreak: Could immunity passports become the new normal?</u>
https://www.youtube.com/watch?v=PrMm6TEHNtY

Those paying attention will have already noted the parallels between the "War on Terror" declared after 9/11 and the "War on the Invisible Enemy" that has been declared on COVID-19. In fact, the security imperatives imposed by this pandemic crisis are so similar to those imposed by the terror crisis that, in many cases, the "new" security screening tools that are being put into place to combat COVID-19 are openly acknowledged to be mere upgrades of screening tools deployed after 9/11.

ANDREW ROSS SORKIN: Most people know CLEAR by going to the airport. It was born after 9/11. This is another crisis with a new component that's being born. Explain what this product is in terms of how it's going to work relating to COVID.

CARYN SEIDMAN BECKER: So, you're right: CLEAR was born out of 9/11 and it was about a public-private partnership leveraging innovation to enhance homeland security and delight customers. And that was really the beginning of screening 1.0. And just like screening was forever changed post-9/11, in a post-COVID environment you're going to see screening and public safety significantly shift.

But this time it's beyond airports, right? It's sports stadiums. It's retail, as Dana talked about. It's office buildings. It's restaurants.

And so, while we started with travel, at our core we're a biometric-secure identity platform, where it's always been about attaching your identity to your boarding pass at the airport, or your ticket to get into a sports stadium, or your credit card to buy a beer. And so now with the launch of CLEAR Health Pass, it's about attaching your identity to your COVID-related health insights for employers, for employees, for customers.

Everybody wants to know that each other is safe to start to reopen businesses and get America moving.

SOURCE: CLEAR's new Health Pass service to help screen for coronavirus: CEO
https://www.youtube.com/watch?v=Fw6QIQBW9ew

Yes, in some ways the coronavirus security state is merely an extension of the 9/11 security state. But even more disturbing parallels between 9/11 and COVID-19 are to be found at a deeper level of analysis.

It is true that, just like the response to the 9/11 attacks, the response to the COVID-19 "crisis" is being framed in terms of "security." But whereas the post-9/11 era introduced America to the concept of "Homeland Security"—security from "terrorists," individuals with identifiable intentions belonging to groups with stated political goals—the COVID-19 era is introducing the world to an altogether more abstract concept: biosecurity.

Originally employed to describe threats to the environment—the introduction of invasive species to a habitat, for instance, or the transmission of infectious diseases among crops and livestock—the term "biosecurity" was injected into mainstream political discourse when the 2001 anthrax attacks linked bioterrorism to the global war on terror. Suddenly, "biosecurity" was a pressing national security threat, and an entire architecture of national and international legislation was introduced to institute procedures for implementing medical martial law.

In the US, the Model State Emergency Health Powers Act [1] was passed in multiple state legislatures, giving governors the power to forcibly quarantine and even force-vaccinate their populations in the event of a declared public health emergency.

On the international level, the World Health Organization adopted the International Health Regulations in 2005, obligating all 196 WHO member nations to recognize declared "Public Health Emergencies of International Concern" like pandemic disease outbreaks as a global threat requiring international cooperation. Some have even argued [2] that the legislation is broad enough to allow organizations like NATO leeway to enter countries in the interest of "controlling the outbreak."

Once again, the tie between this biosecurity paradigm and the war on terror paradigm is openly acknowledged. In a 2002 paper [3] on the emerging biosecurity field, two US environmental researchers noted the way that 9/11 had opened the door for biosecurity research and legislation.

"The events of September 11 and subsequent anthrax assaults have made US policymakers and the public more aware of our vulnerability to organisms released with the intent to cause significant harm," they wrote.

In 2010, the World Health Organization issued its own information note [4] on biosecurity, stating that "The overarching goal of biosecurity is to prevent, control and/or manage risks to life and health," and—echoing post-9/11 declarations about the need for global cooperation in the War on Terror—that this goal can only be reached through "a harmonized and integrated biosecurity approach" based on "international standards."

What this predictably bland language obscures is the way that "biosecurity" is used to invoke emergency powers and install new security procedures. Just as the Homeland Security paradigm used the presumed threat of terrorism as an excuse to curtail civil liberties, so, too, does the biosecurity paradigm use presumed threats to public health as an excuse to curtail civil liberties.

REPORTER: In Hangzhou, to enter a tower block you need to have your temperature taken and registered and you must have an app on your phone into which you input your name, temperature, recent travel and ID number. The information generates a color code.

MAN: In Hangzhou, to go out of the community or to public activities you need to have a green code. This green, yellow or red code is automatically decided through the system. It uses big data to decide whether you've been to affected districts or come into contact with those people.

SOURCE: Coronavirus: China using app to track quarantined citizens
https://www.youtube.com/watch?v=JADi2Px0xAg

NARRATOR: Chinese police officers are also seen in another disturbing video nailing in wooden planks to block the front door of an apartment with people inside who had just returned home from Wuhan. Afterwards, officials are seen staking a red sign beside the front door which reads: "The people in this house have just returned from Wuhan. Don't be in contact with them." The poor people inside are heard desperately screaming, "Open the door!"

SOURCE: China is sealing people in their homes – TomoNews
https://www.youtube.com/watch?v=iuQVyvaa56M

MIKE AMOR: Melbourne is in full lockdown tonight as historic stage four restrictions take effect, forcing entire industries and shopping precincts to close. Health officials say it's the only option to stop the second wave and we'd be looking at twenty thousand cases if we hadn't shut down.

SOURCE: Coronavirus: Melbourne left desolate as stage 4 lockdown begins | 7NEWS
https://www.youtube.com/watch?v=hBcVtQCBNWM

WOMAN: Can you, like, record this? I'm in my pajamas. I have an ultrasound in an hour.

MAN: Yeah, she's pregnant, so . . .

POLICE OFFICER: Take it easy.

MAN: What's this about?

WOMAN: But I have an ultrasound in an hour.

POLICE OFFICER: Let me finish and I'll explain. It's in relation to a Facebook post, in relation to lockdown protests you put on for Saturday.

WOMAN: Yeah, and I wasn't breaking any laws by doing that.

POLICE OFFICER: You are, actually. You are breaking the law. That's why I'm arresting you.

WOMAN: In front of my children?

MAN: How can you arrest her? That's—

SOURCE: <ins>Andrews 'must go tonight' after horrible example of 'inexcusable powers': Jones</ins>
https://www.youtube.com/watch?v=hcHUGZGT9V4

PETER MITCHELL: Police are preparing to launch their aerial arsenal as part of a crackdown on covert rule breakers. High-powered drones will be used to find people not wearing masks and cars too far from home.

SOURCE: <ins>CLIP</ins>
https://twitter.com/7NewsMelbourne/status/1295277876665671681

CAMERON CHELL: Dragonfly's public health and safety system uses standard 4k cameras to provide anonymized data on social distancing, heart rate, respiratory rate and fever detection.

SOURCE: <ins>'Pandemic Drone' Conducts Initial Flights Near NYC to Detect COVID-19 Symptoms</ins>
https://www.youtube.com/watch?v=MabYf9o_2dE

RODRIGO DUTERTE: My orders are for the police, the military and the villages: Shoot them dead!

SOURCE: 'Shoot them dead': extreme Covid-19 lockdown policing around the world
https://www.youtube.com/watch?v=Z8YfSMf7S6s

MAN: Why are you surrounding my children? Please step away from my children. Please. Step away. From my children.

POLICE OFFICER: I'm just gonna take care of them, alright? Calming down, yeah?

MAN: My children are fine.

CHILD: Can we just go home?

MAN: But I've got cuffs that are too tight on my arms. All I was doing was shopping. I explained to you that I don't have to have a mask on for health reasons and then three people come up to me and start twisting my arms up. For what? Can you tell me why I'm under arrest.

POLICE OFFICER: You're not under arrest. You're detained.

MAN: You can't just detain me. Under what law?

SOURCE: Detained and Handcuffed for no MASK! White Rose Shopping Centre
https://www.youtube.com/watch?v=FMUeb0_SgL4

CRESSIDA DICK: Well, at the moment we don't have specific powers, but they will come very shortly, I'm sure. But in the British policing model, we always start by talking to people. We always start by advising people. We can talk even more firmly to people.

SOURCE: Met Police's Cressida Dick promises to crack down on people ignoring coronavirus lockdown rules
https://www.youtube.com/watch?v=NN6gT5sAtOo

MAN: Who the f*** do you think you're grabbing? Hey, who you grabbing?

POLICE OFFICER: Off the train now!

MAN: Who the f*** are you grabbing? Get off me! I told you no!

POLICE OFFICER: Get off the train or I'll get you off.

MAN: Now get off me. Now you've been told. Get the f*** off me. Oi. Who the f*** are you grabbing, mate?

POLICE OFFICER: I'll spray you, mate.

MAN: What? You're not spraying me for nothing.

PASSENGER: He hasn't done nothing wrong.

*SOURCE: **This is tyranny. It's so f*cking depressing***
https://twitter.com/RichieAllenShow/status/1301629299708104704

ELIAS CLURE: There's a significant police presence there. A number of these protesters chanting "freedom."

PROTESTERS: Freedom! Freedom! Freedom!

CLURE: We can also see that crowd. Just the size of that crowd and the number of police that have gathered. There's public order response, there's mounted police as well. Also riot police have mobilized to try and manage this crowd.

*SOURCE: **Anti-lockdown protests met with heavy police presence in Melbourne | ABC News***
https://www.youtube.com/watch?v=NVksuTZHwig

The nightmarish police state that is coming into view on the back of this pandemic panic is not a temporary state of affairs, nor is it a haphazard set of measures thrown together on an ad hoc basis; it is the creation of a new form of governance. This new form of governance relies on the perceived sense of crisis—in this case, a public health crisis—to justify constant surveillance of the public and new powers to inhibit the travel of anyone deemed a health risk.

Famed Italian philosopher Giorgio Agamben has documented [5] how this biosecurity state is being erected on the back of the panic that 9/11 and the war on terror helped induce in the public.

"We might say that once terrorism was exhausted as a justification for exceptional measures, the invention of an epidemic could offer the ideal pretext for broadening such measures beyond any limitation.

"The other factor, no less disquieting, is the state of fear, which in recent years has diffused into individual consciousnesses and which translates into a real need for **states of collective panic**, for which the epidemic once again offers the ideal pretext.

"Therefore, in a perverse vicious circle, the limitation of freedom imposed by governments is accepted in the name of a desire for safety, which has been created by the same governments who now intervene to satisfy it."

The parallel nature of 9/11 and COVID-19 as catalyzing events ushering in states of collective panic and, ultimately, new forms of governance, is seen most clearly in the area where these two paradigms overlap: bioterrorism.

The molten steel on the Ground Zero pile had not even cooled before the American public and the people of the world were confronted with the specter of bioterrorism. Beginning a week after 9/11 and continuing for weeks thereafter, a series of letters containing anthrax spores were mailed to media personalities and government officials in an apparent continuation of the terrorist attack on the US. The letters were quickly tied to both Al Qaeda and Iraq in the mainstream media:

BRIAN ROSS: Peter, from three well-placed but separate sources tonight ABC News has been told that initial tests on the anthrax sent to Senator Daschle have found a tell-tale chemical additive whose name means a lot to weapons experts. It is called bentonite. It's possible other countries may be using it, too, but it is a trademark of Saddam Hussein's biological weapons program.

TIM TREVAN: It does mean for me that Iraq becomes the prime suspect as the source for the anthrax used in these letters.

SOURCE: ABC Evening News for Friday, Oct 26, 2001
https://tvnews.vanderbilt.edu/broadcasts/639211

The 24/7 coverage of the event in the media ceased abruptly, however, when it was discovered that the strain of anthrax used in the attacks sourced not to Iraq but to the US military's own bioweapons laboratory at Fort Detrick, Maryland.

But this convergence of terrorism and biosecurity did not start with the anthrax attacks. It began in June of 2001, a full three months before 9/11 and the declaration of the war on terror itself. That was when a number of ranking US military and intelligence officials took part in "Dark Winter [6]," a high-level exercise that simulated the US' response to a smallpox attack on the homeland by bioterrorists. The drill, co-hosted by the Johns Hopkins Center for Health Security, took place at Andrews Air Force Base on the 22nd and 23rd of June 2001, and even involved fake news reports that were broadcast to the participants as the simulation unfolded.

ANGIE MILES: On day six of the smallpox epidemic, the White House confirmed that federal government officials and military personnel are being vaccinated. Three hundred people have died; at least 2,000 are infected with smallpox. Still no group claims responsibility for unleashing the deadly smallpox virus, but NCN has learned that Iraq may have provided the technology behind the attack to terrorist groups based in Afghanistan.

SOURCE: 'operation dark winter' 3
https://www.youtube.com/watch?v=BAkzNx3zFtQ

In an incredible parallel, the same Johns Hopkins Center for Health Security that co-hosted Dark Winter also co-hosted "Event 201 [7]," a simulation of a globally spreading novel coronavirus pandemic that was held in New York just months before the declaration of the globally spreading novel coronavirus pandemic that hailed the advent of the era of biosecurity. *This* exercise similarly involved fake news broadcasts:

FAKE NEWS REPORTER: It began in healthy-looking pigs months, perhaps years, ago. A new coronavirus spread silently within herds. Gradually, farmers started getting sick. Infected people got a respiratory illness with symptoms ranging from mild, flu-like signs to severe pneumonia. The sickest required intensive care. Many died.

SOURCE: Event 201 Pandemic Exercise: Highlights Reel
https://www.youtube.com/watch?v=AoLw-Q8X174

Unsurprisingly, many of the same characters that were involved in the promotion of the bioterror scare under the old "Homeland Security" paradigm have been influential in promoting the COVID-19 scare under the new "biosecurity" paradigm.

The phrase "Homeland Security" itself was popularized in Washington in the late 1990s and capitalized on by the ANSER Institute [8], which formed an Institute for Homeland Security in 1999 led by Randall Larsen, a professor and department chair at the National War College. The Institute prepared a course on "Homeland Security" which was to be co-taught by Larsen and his National War College colleague, Robert Kadlec. Coincidentally, the course was slated to begin on September 11, 2001 [9]. Part of the course syllabus included a review of the Dark Winter exercise, which the Institute for Homeland Security co-created.

The name "Dark Winter" derives from a statement made by Larsen's colleague, Robert Kadlec [10], credited as a "Bio-Warfare Defense Expert" during the exercise's fake news broadcast.

ROBERT KADLEC: . . . and the problem is we don't have enough vaccine to go around.

MILES: Meaning we don't have enough vaccine for the United States?

KADLEC: Well, I would like to think that. But we don't have sufficient stockpiles for the people in Oklahoma, Georgia or Pennsylvania, much less for the entire United States population.

MILES: Well, that certainly doesn't sound encouraging. What do you mean, exactly?

KADLEC: Angie, it means it could be a very dark winter for America.

MILES: Sobering. Thank you very much for joining us, Dr. Kadlec.

SOURCE: operation dark winter' 2
https://www.youtube.com/watch?v=VMd4z19IJU0

A career officer and physician in the United States Air Force, Kadlec would go on to contribute to the FBI's investigation of the 2001 anthrax attacks and then serve in several key biosecurity-related roles [11] in the George W. Bush White House. During this time, Kadlec helped draft [12] the Pandemic and All-Hazards Preparedness Act. Passed by Congress in 2006, the act greatly expanded federal power during public health emergencies and consolidated many of these powers in a new office, the Assistant Secretary for Preparedness and Response (ASPR). Then, in what Kadlec has called "just a coincidence [13]," Trump appointed Kadlec himself to that position in 2017.

In his role as ASPR, Kadlec oversaw a joint exercise in 2019 named Crimson Contagion [14]. The drill included the National Security Council, the Pentagon, the Department of Homeland Security and a raft of other government agencies and simulated the US government's response to a viral pandemic originating in China and spreading around the globe. Like Dark Winter, the "Crimson Contagion" exercise took place just months before the events it was simulating began to play out in real life. And, like Dark Winter, it gave participants like Kadlec the chance to argue that biosecurity was a pressing national security challenge that the country was ill-prepared to meet—an argument that he made to Congress with Dr. Anthony Fauci by his side just one week before the first reports of the novel coronavirus spreading in China.

DIANA DEGETTE: Dr. Kadlec, what keeps you up at night when you think about preparedness for the next big flu outbreak.

KADLEC: I mean, thank you, ma'am, I appreciate the question. I mean, I sleep like a baby: I wake up every two hours screaming.

DEGETTE: Much like me.

KADLEC: Yeah. But I think the key thing here is a pandemic. Quite frankly, I have a unique background on this committee or this dais. I have served two years on the Senate Intelligence Committee and looked at the many threats that face the United States, but there is no singular threat that could devastate our country through our health and our economy and our social institutions than pandemic influenza.

DEGETTE: Yeah.

KADLEC: And we had four during the last century. And even though we've had a mild one in this first century, I think the risk is that we'll have another severe one, and that would devastate our country.

SOURCE: *Pandemic Preparedness – testimony of ASPR's Robert Kadlec – December 4, 2019*
https://www.youtube.com/watch?v=rA3oi3Z5_eY

Then there's Donald Rumsfeld. As Secretary of Defense in the first term of the George W. Bush administration, there are few people more closely associated with the "War on Terror." Rumsfeld, too, has been intimately associated with the emerging biosecurity state for decades. In the 1980s he personally participated in secret meetings [15] with Saddam Hussein that resulted in anthrax, botulism, and other chemical weapons being sent from the US to Iraq. In the 1990s he was named chairman [16] of Gilead Sciences, a California biotech company that profited handsomely [17] from the scramble for Tamiflu during the bird flu scare of 2005 and which is currently profiting handsomely from Remdesivir as a result of the COVID-19 scare.

ANTHONY FAUCI: The data shows that Remdesivir has a clear-cut, significant, positive effect in diminishing the time to recovery.

SOURCE: *Fauci announces good news about coronavirus drug*
https://www.youtube.com/watch?v=SdqlNNAEju0

There are many others whose careers blaze the same trail, transitioning seamlessly from the Homeland Security state to the biosecurity state. People like Dr. Richard Hatchett [18], who served as Director for Biodefense Policy under George W. Bush, then as acting Director of the Biomedical Advanced Research and Development Authority (BARDA) and acting Deputy Assistant Secretary in the Office of the Assistant Secretary for Preparedness and Response within HHS before becoming the CEO of CEPI [19], the Bill and Melinda Gates Foundation co-founded Coalition for Epidemic Preparedness Innovations. In his position as "global health expert," Hatchett made waves back in March for his alarmist pronouncements about the SARS-CoV-2 pandemic.

RICHARD HATCHETT: It's the most frightening disease I've ever encountered in my career, and that includes Ebola, it includes MERS, it includes SARS. And it's frightening because of the combination of infectiousness and a lethality that appears to be manyfold higher than flu.

SOURCE: Coronavirus researcher accused of scaremongering for calling it 'most frightening disease I've ever encountered'
https://www.indy100.com/article/coronavirus-doctor-scaremongering-risk-spanish-flu-death-rate-9384561

That so many of the people who were there at the birth of the "War on Terror" are currently acting as midwives to the biosecurity state should come as no surprise. After all, the biosecurity paradigm is not a *replacement* for the terror paradigm; it is its *fulfillment*.

The "War on Terror" imagined a covert army of foreign invaders slipping through the defenses of the Homeland and commandeering the resources of the body politic to wreak internal havoc. The biosecurity state posits largely the same scenario, but now those foreign invaders are not "terrorists" possessed with a "hatred of freedom"; they are "asymptomatic carriers" possessed by a pathogen.

Just as the Homeland Security forces and border security agents were entrusted to protect us from the terrorists, now the "frontline heroes," doctors and nurses armed with the tools of the technocratic priest class, can protect us from the invisible enemy.

This speaks to an important aspect of the biosecurity state: ultimately, it is not about health. It is about politics.

Once again we find insight on this turn of events from Giorgio Agamben, who has noted [20] that viral epidemics are

"above all a political concept, which is preparing to become the new terrain of world politics—or non-politics. It is possible, however, that the epidemic that we are living through will be the actualization of the global civil war that, according to the most attentive political theorists, has taken the place of traditional world wars. All nations and all peoples are now in an enduring war with themselves, because the invisible and elusive enemy with which they are struggling is within us."

Governments are banning gatherings and events. Instituting new screening procedures. Quarantining healthy, functioning people against their will. Tracking and surveilling every individual. Controlling their movements. Monitoring their transactions. Make no mistake: the "War on Terror" is not over. It has just greatly expanded.

The proponents of 9/11 truth have warned for 19 years that the "War on Terror" was always a war on the public. Long pushed to the margins of the political debate, that viewpoint has been vindicated as the "terrorist" label is replaced by the "asymptomatic carrier" label and all the machinery of the police state is wielded against everyone who opposes the biosecurity takeover.

Given that those once derided as "conspiracy theorists" have turned out to be the most prescient political observers of all, perhaps it is time to learn the *real* lessons from 9/11 that mainstream discourse has always excluded:

- That 9/11 and the "War on Terror" was not a war at all, but a power grab;
- That the "temporary" measures brought in to deal with an alleged "emergency" will never be relinquished;
- And, most importantly, that unless everyone who cares about this—the most blatant power grab in history—rises up, refuses to cower in fear of the invisible enemy, and reclaims their inalienable rights to freedom of movement, freedom of association and freedom of assembly, then those freedoms will be gone for good.

This is the message of 9/11 truth: that the world was tricked into giving up their rights in the name of an endless parade of bogeymen. In reality, it was the very politicians and officials claiming to protect us from these bogeymen—the ones donning the mantle of "Homeland Security"—who were the greatest threat to the public. And now they are claiming *we* are the bogeymen—"asymptomatic carriers" of an invisible enemy," walking and talking weapons of mass destruction who must be caged in fear forever lest the virus kill us all.

This is a lie, and it exposes what the fearmongers are themselves afraid of: free humanity. Gathering. Talking. Working. Playing. Living.

It is no small irony that this year's 9/11 memorials have been disrupted by the COVID scare. The torch has well and truly passed, and the annual injunctions to "Never Forget" have been replaced by a litany of "Always Remembers." Remember to wear your mask. Remember to stay six feet apart. Remember to avoid large groups. Remember to stay home.

After 19 years, perhaps it is time to admit that 9/11 truth failed to expose the "War on Terror" lie in time to derail the homeland security agenda. But we are entering a new era, and we have a new chance to wake from this nightmare.

Knowing this, the only question is: Will we reject the "War on the Invisible Enemy" before it's too late?

Whatever our choice, we better make it quickly. A Great Reset is coming.

BUSH: Great harm has been done to us. We have suffered great loss. And in our grief and anger we have found our mission and our moment.

Freedom and fear are at war. The advance of human freedom, the great achievement of our time and the great hope of every time, now depends on us.

SOURCE: George W. Bush: Address to Congress, September 20, 2001
https://www.youtube.com/watch?v=Sr7zsgZ75FE

DONALD TRUMP: I want to assure the American people that we're doing everything we can each day to confront and ultimately defeat this horrible, invisible enemy. We're at war. In a true sense, we're at war and we're fighting an invisible enemy. Think of that.

SOURCE: President Trump says he is a 'wartime president' battling an 'invisible enemy' over coronavirus
https://www.youtube.com/watch?v=vOe4Ksoa5bk

James Corbett originally published "COVID-911: From Homeland Security to Biosecurity" on September 11, 2020. His website is https://www.corbettreport.com.

References

[1]. https://www.aclu.org/other/model-state-emergency-health-powers-act
[2]. https://www.newsweek.com/what-happens-if-who-declares-ebola-emergency-international-concern-263434
[3]. https://academic.oup.com/bioscience/article/52/7/593/248011
[4]. https://www.who.int/foodsafety/fs_management/No_01_Biosecurity_Mar10_en.pdf
[5]. http://positionspolitics.org/giorgio-agamben-the-state-of-exception-provoked-by-an-unmotivated-emergency/
[6]. https://www.centerforhealthsecurity.org/our-work/events-archive/2001_dark-winter/about.html
[7]. https://www.centerforhealthsecurity.org/event201/
[8]. https://web.archive.org/web/20080216050607/http:/www.onlinejournal.com/archive/06-29-02_Burns.pdf
[9]. https://web.archive.org/web/20011002001900/http:/www.homelandsecurity.org/ELECTIVE5994/index.cfm
[10]. https://unlimitedhangout.com/2020/05/investigative-series/head-of-the-hydra-the-rise-of-robert-kadlec/
[11]. https://www.phe.gov/newsroom/bio/Pages/kadlec.aspx
[12]. https://www.phe.gov/newsroom/bio/Pages/kadlec.aspx
[13]. https://www.acepnow.com/article/laying-the-groundwork-for-effective-disaster-response-an-interview-with-dr-robert-kadlec/?singlepage=1
[14]. https://archive.org/details/crimson-contagion-2019/page/n1/mode/2up
[15]. https://www.dailymail.co.uk/news/article-153210/Rumsfeld-helped-Iraq-chemical-weapons.html
[16]. https://www.gilead.com/news-and-press/press-room/press-releases/1997/1/donald-h-rumsfeld-named-chairman-of-gilead-sciences
[17]. https://money.cnn.com/2005/10/31/news/newsmakers/fortune_rumsfeld/
[18]. http://www.ncmbc.us/wp-content/uploads/Dr.-Richard-Hatchett.pdf
[19]. https://cepi.net/news_cepi/cepi-permanent-ceo/
[20]. https://itself.blog/2020/05/02/giorgio-agamben-medicine-as-religion/

Crimes Against Humanity

Dr. Reiner Fuellmich

I am Reiner Fuellmich, and I have been admitted to the bar in Germany and in California for 26 years. I have been practising law primarily as a trial lawyer against fraudulent corporations such as

- Deutsche Bank, formerly one of the world's largest and most respected banks, today one of the most toxic criminal organizations in the world,

- VW, one of the world's largest and most respected car manufacturers, today notorious for its giant diesel fraud, and

- Kuehne & Nagel, the world´s largest shipping company, we´re sueing them in a multi-million dollar bribery case

I am also one of four members of the German Corona Investigative Committee. Since July 10, 2020, this committee has been listening to a large number of international scientists´ and experts´ testimony to find answers to questions about the corona crisis, which more and more people worldwide are asking.

All the above mentioned cases of corruption and fraud committed by the German corporations pale in comparison in view of the extent of the damage that the corona crisis has caused and continues to cause. This corona crisis, according to all we know today, must be renamed a corona scandal, and those responsible for it must be criminally prosecuted and sued for civil law damages. On a political level, everything must be done to make sure that no one will ever again be in a position of such power as to be able to defraud humanity or to attempt to enslave us with their corrupt agendas.

And for this reason I will now explain to you, how and where an international network of lawyers will argue this biggest tort case ever, the corona fraud scandal, which has meanwhile unfolded into probably the greatest Crime against Humanity ever committed.

Crimes against Humanity were first defined in connection with the Nuremberg Trials, when they dealt with the main war criminals of the Third Reich. Crimes against Humanity are today regulated in section 7 of the International Criminal Code.

The three major questions to be answered in the context of a judicial approach to the corona scandal are:

1. Is there a corona pandemic, or is there only a PCR test pandemic? specifically: Does a positive PCR test result mean that the person tested is infected with Covid-19, or does it mean absolutely nothing in connection with a Covid-19 infection?

2. Do the so-called anti-corona measures, such as the lockdown, mandatory face masks, useless social distancing mandates and quarantine regulations serve to protect the world´s population from corona? Or do these measures serve only to make people panic so that they believe - without asking any questions - that their lives are in danger, so that in the end the pharmaceutical and tech industries can generate huge profits from the sale of PCR tests, antigen and antibody tests and vaccines, as well as the harvesting of our genetic fingerprints?

3. Is it true that the German government was massively lobbied – more so than any other country - by the chief protagonists of this so-called corona pandemic, Mr. Drosten, virologist at Charité hospital in Berlin, Mr. Wieler, veterinarian and head of the German equivalent of the CDC, the RKI, and Mr. Tedros, head of the WHO because Germany is known as a particularly disciplined country and was therefore to become a role model for the rest of the world for it´s strict, and, of course, successful adherence to the corona measures?

Answers to these three questions are urgently needed because the allegedly new and highly dangerous corona virus has not caused any excess mortality anywhere in the world, and certainly not here in Germany. But the anti-corona measures, whose only basis are the PCR test results, which are in turn all based on the German Drosten Test have, in the meantime, caused the loss of innumerable human lives, and have destroyed the economic existence of countless companies and individuals worldwide.

In Australia, for example, people are thrown into prison if they do not wear a mask or do not wear it properly, as deemed by the authorities, and in the Philippines people who do not wear a mask or do not wear it properly in this sense are getting shot in the head.

I. Summary of the facts as they present themselves today

The most important thing in a lawsuit is to establish the facts, i.e. to find out what actually happened. That is because the application of the law always depends on the facts at issue. If I want to prosecute someone for fraud, I cannot do that by presenting the facts of a car accident. So what happened here regarding the alleged corona pandemic?

The facts laid out below are to a large extent the result of the work of the German Corona Investigative Committee. This Committee was founded on July 10 by four lawyers in order to determine, through hearing expert testimony of international scientists and other experts:

1. How dangerous is the virus really?

2. What is the significance of a positive PCR test?

3. What collateral damage has been caused by the corona measures, both with respect to the world population's health and with respect to the world's economy?

1. What happened in May 2019 and then in early 2020, and what happened 12 years earlier with the swine flu?

In May of 2019, the stronger one of the two parties which govern Germany as a grand coalition, the CDU, held a congress on Global Health, apparently at the instigation of important players from the pharmaceutical industry and the tech industry.

At this congress the usual suspects, you might say, gave their speeches. Angela Merkel was there, and the German secretary of health Jens Spahn. But some other people whom one would not necessarily expect to be present at such a gathering were also there; Prof. Drosten, virologist from the Charité hospital in Berlin, Prof. Wieler, veterinarian and head of the RKI, as well as Mr. Tedros, philosopher and head of the WHO. They all gave speeches there. Also present and giving speeches were the chief lobbyists of the world's two largest health funds, namely the Bill and Melinda Gates Foundation and the Wellcome Trust.

Less than a year later, these very people called the shots in the proclamation of the worldwide corona pandemic, made sure that mass PCR tests were used to prove mass infections with Covid 19 all over the world, and are now pushing for vaccines to be invented and sold worldwide. These infections, or rather: the positive test results that the PCR tests delivered in turn became the justification for worldwide lockdowns, social distancing and mandatory face masks.

It is important to note at this point that the definition of a pandemic was changed 12 years earlier. Until then, a pandemic was considered to be a disease that spread worldwide, and which led to many serious illnesses and deaths. Suddenly, and for reasons never explained, it was supposed to be a worldwide disease only. Many serious illnesses and many deaths were not required any more to announce a pandemic.

Due to this change, the WHO, which is closely intertwined with the global pharmaceutical industry, was able to declare the swine flu pandemic in 2009, with the result that vaccines were produced and sold worldwide on the basis of contracts that have been kept secret until today. These vaccines proved to be completely unnecessary because the swine flu finally turned out to be a mild flu and never became the horrific plague that the pharmaceutical industry and its affiliated universities kept announcing it would turn into, with millions of deaths certain to happen if people did not get vaccinated.

These vaccines also led to serious health problems: about 700 children in Europe fell incurably ill with narcolepsy and are now forever severely disabled. The vaccines bought with millions of tax payers' money had to be destroyed with even more tax payers' money. Already then, during the swine flu the German virologist Drosten was one of those who stirred up panic in the population repeating over and over again that the swine flu would claim many hundreds of thousands, even millions of deaths all over the world.

In the end, it was mainly thanks to Dr. Wolfgang Wodarg and his efforts as a member of the German Bundestag and also a member of the Council of Europe that this hoax was brought to an end before it could lead to even more serious consequences.

Fast forward to March of 2020: When the German Bundestag announced an epidemic situation of national importance (which is the equivalent of a pandemic) in March of 2020 and, based on this, the lockdown with the suspension of all essential constitutional rights for an unforeseeable time, there was only one single opinion on which the Federal Government based its decision.

In an outrageous violation of the universally accepted principle audiatur et altera pars, which means that one must also hear the other side, the only person they listened to was Mr. Drosten, i.e. the very person whose horrific, panic inducing prognoses had proved to be catastrophically false 12 years earlier.

We know this because a whistleblower named David Siber, a member of the Green Party, told us about it. He did so first on August 29, 2020 in Berlin, in the context of an event at which Robert F. Kennedy Jr. also took part and at which both men gave speeches. And he did so afterwards in one of the sessions of our Corona Committee.

The reason he did this is that he had become increasingly sceptical about the official narrative propagated by politicians and the mainstream media. He had therefore undertaken an effort to find out about other scientists´ opinions, and had found them on the internet. There, he realized that there were a number of highly renowned scientists who held a completely different opinion, which contradicted the horrific prognoses of Mr. Drosten. They assumed and still do assume that there was no disease that went beyond the gravity of the seasonal flu, that the population had already acquired cross- or T-cell immunity against this allegedly new virus, and that there was therefore no reason for any special measures - and certainly not for vaccinations. These scientists include Prof. John Ioannidis of Stanford University in California, a specialist in statistics and epidemiology, as well as public health, and at the same time the most quoted scientist in the world, Prof. Michael Levitt, Nobel Prize winner for chemistry and also a biophysicist at Stanford University, the German professors Karin Mölling, Sucharit Bhakdi and Knut Wittkowski as well as Stefan Homburg, and now many, many more scientists and doctors worldwide, including Dr. Mike Yeadon.

Dr. Mike Yeadon is the former Vice President and Scientific Director of Pfizer, one of the largest pharmaceutical companies in the world. I will talk some more about him a little later.

At the end of March/beginning of April of 2020, Mr. Siber turned to the leadership of his Green party with the knowledge he had accumulated and suggested that they present these other scientific opinions to the public and explain that contrary to Mr. Drosten´s doomsday prophecies, there was no reason for the public to panic.

Incidentally, Lord Sumption, who served as a judge at the British Supreme Court from 2012 to 2018, had done the very same thing at the very same time and had come to the very same conclusion: That there was no factual basis for panic, and no legal basis for the corona measures. Likewise, the former president of the German Federal Constitutional Court expressed - albeit more cautiously –serious doubts that the corona measures were constitutional.

But instead of taking note of these other opinions and discussing them with David Siber, the Green party leadership declared that Mr. Drosten's panic messages were good enough for the Green party (remember: they are not a member of the ruling coalition, but they are the opposition!), just as it had been good enough for the federal government as a basis for its lockdown decision. They subsequently called David Siber a conspiracy theorist without ever having considered the content of his information, and then stripped him of his mandates.

2. The current, actual situation regarding the virus´ danger, the complete uselessness of PCR tests for the detection of infections and the lockdowns based on nonexistent infections

In the meantime, we know that the health care systems were never in danger of becoming overwhelmed by Covid-19. On the contrary: Many hospitals remain empty to this day, and some are now facing bankruptcy. The hospital ship Comfort, which anchored in New York at the time and could have accommodated 1000 patients never accommodated more than some 20 patients. Nowhere was there any excess mortality. Studies carried out by Prof. Ioannidis and others have shown that the mortality of corona is equivalent to that of the seasonal flu.

Even the pictures from Bergamo and New York that were used to demonstrate to the world that panic was in order, proved to be deliberately misleading.

Then, the so called panic paper was leaked which was written by the German Department of the Interior. Its classified content shows beyond a shadow of a doubt that, in fact, the population was deliberately driven to panic by politicians and mainstream media. The accompanying irresponsible statements of the head of the RKI, Mr. Wieler who repeatedly and excitedly announced that the corona measures must be followed unconditionally by the population without them "asking any questions" shows that he followed this script verbatim. In his public statements he kept announcing that the situation was very grave and threatening, although the figures compiled by his own institute proved the exact opposite.

Among other things, the panic paper calls for children to be made to feel responsible for the painful, tortured death of their parents and grandparents if they do not follow the corona rules, i.e., if they do not wash their hands constantly and don´t stay away from their grandparents.

A word of clarification: In Bergamo, the vast majority of deaths – 94% to be exact – turned out to be the result not of Covid-19, but rather the consequence of the government deciding to transfer sick patients (sick with probably the cold or the seasonal flu) from hospitals to nursing homes in order to make room at the hospitals for all the Covid patients who never arrived. There, at the nursing homes they then infected old people with a severely weakened immune system, usually as a result of pre-existing medical conditions. In addition, a flu vaccination which had previously been administered, had further weakened the immune systems of the people in the nursing homes.

In New York, only some, but by far not all hospitals were overwhelmed. Many people, most of whom were – again - elderly and had serious preexisting medical conditions, and most of whom – had it not been for the panic mongering - would have just stayed at home to recover raced to the hospitals. There, many of them fell victim to healthcare associated infections, or nosocomial infections on the one hand, and incidents of malpractice on the other hand, e.g. by being put on a respirator, rather than receiving oxygen through an oxygen mask.

Again, to clarify: Covid-19 - this is the current state of affairs - is a dangerous disease, just like the seasonal flu is a dangerous disease. And, of course, Covid-19, just like the seasonal flu, may sometimes take a severe clinical course and will sometimes kill patients.

However, as autopsies have shown which were carried out in Germany, in particular by the forensic scientist Prof. Klaus Püschel, the fatalities he examined had almost all been caused by serious pre-existing conditions, and almost all of the people who had died, had died at a very old age, just like in Italy, meaning: They had lived beyond their average life expectancy.

In this context the following should also be mentioned: The German RKI had initially - strangely enough - recommended that no autopsies be performed. And: There are numerous credible reports that doctors and hospitals worldwide had been paid money for declaring a deceased person a victim of Covid-19, rather than writing down the true cause of death on the death certificate, for example a heart attack, or a gunshot wound. Without the autopsies, we would never know that the overwhelming majority of the alleged Covid-19 victims had died of completely different diseases, but not of Covid-19.

The assertion that the lockdown was necessary because there were so many infections with SARS-CoV-2, and because the health care systems would be overwhelmed is wrong for three reasons, as we have learned from the hearings we conducted with the Corona Committee, and from other data that has become available in the meantime:

a. Lockdown was imposed when the virus was already retreating

By the time the lockdown was imposed, the alleged infection rates were already dropping again.

b. There is already protection from the virus because of cross or T cell immunity

Apart from that, there is already cross- or T cell immunity in the general population against the corona viruses contained in every flu or influenza wave. This is true, even if this time around a slightly different strain of the corona virus was at work. And that is because the body's own immune system remembers every virus it has ever battled in the past, and from this experience it also recognizes a supposedly new, but still similar strain of the virus from the corona family.

Incidentally, that´s how the PCR-Test for the detection of an infection was invented by now infamous Prof. Drosten. At the beginning of January of 2020, based on this very basic knowledge, Mr. Drosten developed his PCR test, which supposedly detects an infection with SARS-CoV-2. Without ever having seen the real Wuhan virus from China, only having learned from social media reports that there was something going on in Wuhan, he started tinkering on his computer with what would become his corona PCR test.

For this, he used an old SARS virus hoping it would be sufficiently similar to the allegedly new strain of the corona virus found in Wuhan. Then he sent the result of his computer tinkering to China to determine whether the victims of the alleged new corona virus tested positive. They did, and that was enough for the WHO to sound the pandemic alarm and to recommend the worldwide use of the Drosten PCR test for the detection of infections with the virus now called SARS-CoV-2. Drosten´s opinion and advice was - this must be emphasized once again - the only source for the German government when it announced the lockdown, as well as the rules for social distancing and the mandatory wearing of masks. And - this must also be emphasized once again - Germany apparently became the center of especially massive lobbying by the pharmaceutical and tech industry because the world, with reference to the allegedly disciplined Germans, should do as the Germans do in order to survive the pandemic.

c. The PCR test is being used on the basis of false statements NOT based on scientific facts with respect to infections

In the meantime, we have learned that these PCR tests, contrary to the assertions of Messrs. Drosten, Wieler and the WHO, do not give any indication of an infection with any virus, let alone an infection with SARS-CoV-2. Not only are PCR tests expressly not approved for diagnostic purposes, as is correctly noted on leaflets coming with these tests, and as the inventor of the PCR test, Kary Mullis, has repeatedly emphasized. Instead, they are simply incapable of diagnosing any disease. That is:

Contrary to the assertions of Drosten, Wieler and the WHO, which they have been making since the proclamation of the pandemic, a positive PCR test result does not mean that an infection is present. If someone tests positive, it does not mean that they are infected with anything, let alone with a contagious SARS-CoV-2 virus. Even the US CDC itself says this, and I quote directly from page 38 of one of its publications on the corona virus and PCR tests, dated July 13, 2020:

"•Detection of viral RNA may not indicate the presence of infectious virus or that 2019-nCoV is the causative agent for clinical symptoms."

"•The performance of this test has not been established for monitoring treatment of 2019-nCoV infection."

"•This test cannot rule out diseases caused by other bacterial or viral pathogens."

It is still not clear whether there has ever been a scientifically correct isolation of the Wuhan virus, so that nobody knows exactly what we are looking for when we test, especially since this virus, just like the flu viruses, mutates quickly. The PCR swabs take one or two sequences of a molecule that are invisible to the human eye and therefore need to be amplified in many cycles to make it visible. Everything over 35 cycles is - as reported by the New York Times and others - considered completely unreliable and scientifically unjustifiable. However, the Drosten test, as well as the WHO-recommended tests that followed his example, are set to 45 cycles. Can that be because of the desire to produce as many positive results as possible and thereby provide the basis for the false assumption that a large number of infections have been detected?

The test cannot distinguish inactive and reproductive matter. That means that a positive result may happen because the test detects e.g. a piece of debris, a fragment of a molecule, which may signal nothing else than that the immune system of the person tested won a battle with the common cold in the past.

Even Drosten himself declared in an interview with a German business magazine in 2014, at that time concerning the alleged detection of an infection with the MERS virus, allegedly with the help of the PCR test, that these PCR tests are so highly sensitive that even very healthy and non-infectious people may test positive. At that time, he also became very much aware of the powerful role of the panic and fear-mongering media, as you'll see at the end of the following quote.

He said: "If, for example, such a pathogen scurries over the nasal mucosa of a nurse for a day or so without her getting sick or noticing anything else, then she is suddenly a MERS case. This could also explain the explosion of case numbers in Saudi Arabia. In addition, the media there have made this into an incredible sensation".

Has he forgotten this, or is he deliberately concealing this in the corona context, because corona is a very lucrative business opportunity for the pharmaceutical industry as a whole and for Mr. Olfert Landt, his co-author in many studies and also: a PCR test producer? In my view, it is completely implausible that he forgot in 2020 what he knew about the PCR tests and told a business magazine in 2014.

In short: This test cannot detect any infection, contrary to all false claims stating that it can. An infection, a so called hot infection, requires that the virus, or rather: a fragment of a molecule which may be a virus - is not just found somewhere, e.g. in the throat of a person without causing any damage (that would be a cold infection). Rather, a hot infection requires that the virus penetrates into the cells, replicates there and causes symptoms such as headaches, or a sore throat. Only then is a person really infected in the sense of a hot infection, because only then is a person contagious, that is: able to infect others.

Until then, it is completely harmless for both the host and all other people that the host comes into contact with.

Once again: This means that positive test results - contrary to all other claims, e.g. by Drosten, Wieler or the WHO – mean nothing with respect to infections, as even the CDC knows as quoted above. Meanwhile, a number of highly respected scientists worldwide assume that **there has never been a corona pandemic, but only a PCR test pandemic.**
This is the conclusion reached by many German scientists such as Professors Bhakdi, Reiss, Mölling, Hockertz, Walach and many others, including the above-mentioned Professor John Ioannidis and the Nobel Laureate Prof. Michael Levitt from Stanford University.

The most recent such opinion is that of the aforementioned Dr. Mike Yeadon, a former Vice President and Chief Science Officer at Pfizer, who held this position for 16-years. He and his co-authors, all well-known scientists, published a scientific paper in September of 2020, and he wrote a corrspo0nding magazine article on September 20, 2020.

Among other things, he and they state:

"We are basing our government policy, our economic policy, and the policy of restricting fundamental rights presumably on completely wrong data and assumptions about the corona virus. .... If it weren't for the test results that are constantly reported in the media, the pandemic would be over because nothing really happened. Of course, there are some serious individual cases of illness, but there are also some in every flu epidemic. There was a real wave of disease in March and April, but since then everything has gone back to normal. Only the positive results rise and sink wildly again and again, depending on how many tests are carried out again, but the real cases of illness are over. There can be no talk of a second wave."

The allegedly new strain of the corona virus is - Dr. Yeadon continues - only new in that it is a new type of the long known corona virus. There are at least four corona viruses that are endemic and cause some of the common colds we experience, especially in winter. They all have a striking sequence similarity to the corona virus. And because the human immune system recognizes the similarity to the virus that has now allegedly been newly discovered, a „T-cell" immunity has long existed in this respect. 30% of the population had this before the allegedly new virus even appeared. Therefore, it is sufficient for the so-called herd immunity that 15-25% of the population are infected with the allegedly new corona virus to stop the further spread of the virus, and this has long been the case.

Regarding the all-important PCR tests, Yeadon writes in a piece called „Lies, Damned Lies and Health Statistics – the Deadly Danger of False Positives", dated September 20, 2020:

„The likelihood of an apparently positive case being a false positive is between 89-94%, or near certainty."

Dr. Yeadon (in agreement with the professors of Immunology Kaemmerer from Germany, Capel from the Netherlands and Cahill from Ireland, as well as the microbiologist Dr. Arvey from Austria, all of whom testified before the German Corona Committee) explicitly points out that a positive test does not mean that an intact virus has been found. The authors explain that what the PCR test actually measures is *„simply the presence of partial RNA sequences present in the intact virus which could be a piece of dead virus which cannot make the subject sick, and cannot be transmitted, and cannot make anyone else sick."*

Because of the complete unsuitability of the test for the detection of infectious diseases (it tested positive in goats, sheep, papayas and even chicken wings), Oxford Professor Carl Heneghan, Director of the Center for Evidence-Based Medicine, writes that **the Covid virus would never disappear if this test practice were to be continued, but would always be - falsely - detected in much of what is tested.**

Lockdowns, as Yeadon and his colleagues found out, do not work. Sweden with its laissez faire approach and Great Britain with its strict lockdown, for example, have completely comparable disease and mortality statistics. The same was found by US scientists concerning the different US states: It makes no difference to the incidence of disease whether a state implements a lockdown or not.

With regard to the Imperial College of London's Prof. Neil Ferguson and his completely false computer models warning of millions of deaths he says that *„no serious scientist gives any validity to Ferguson's model“*. He points out with thinly veiled contempt: *„It's important that you know most scientists don't accept that it (Ferguson's model) was even faintly right... but the government is still wedded to the model.“*

Ferguson predicted 40,000 corona deaths in Sweden by May and 100,000 by June, but it remained at 5,800, which according to the Swedish authorities is equivalent to a mild flu.

If the PCR tests had not been used as a diagnostic tool for corona infections, there would not be a pandemic, and there would be no lockdowns, but everything would have been perceived as just a medium or light wave of influenza, these scientists conclude.

Dr. Yeadon, in his piece „Lies, Damned Lies and Health Statistics – the Deadly Danger of False Positives" writes:

„This test is fatally flawed and MUST immediately be withdrawn and never used again in this setting unless shown to be fixed.“

And, towards the end of that article:

„I have explained how a hopelessly-performing diagnostic test has been and continues to be used, not for diagnosis of disease but, it seems, solely to create fear.”

3. **The current, actual situation regarding the severe damage caused by the lockdowns and other measures**

Another detailed paper written by a German official in the Department of the Interior who is responsible for risk assessment and the protection of the population against risks was leaked recently. It is now called the false alarm paper. This paper comes to the conclusion that there was and is no sufficient evidence for serious health risks for the population as claimed by Drosten, Wieler and the WHO.

But, the author says, there is very much evidence of the corona measures causing gigantic health and economic damage to the population, which he then describes in detail in this paper. This, he concludes, will lead to very high claims for damages which the government will be held responsible for. This has now become reality, but the paper´s author was suspended.

More and more scientists, but also lawyers, recognize that as a result of the deliberate panic mongering and the corona measures enabled by this panic, democracy is in great danger of being replaced by fascist-totalitarian models.

As I already mentioned above, in Australia people who do not wear the masks - which more and more studies show, are hazardous to health - or who allegedly do not wear them correctly, are arrested, handcuffed and thrown into jail. In the Philippines they run the risk of getting shot dead. But even in Germany and in other previously civilized countries, children are taken away from their parents if they do not comply with quarantine regulations, distance regulations or mask wearing regulations.

According to psychologists and psychotherapists who testified before the Corona Committee, children are traumatised en masse, with the worst psychological consequences yet to be expected in the medium and long term.

In Germany alone, 500,000 to 800,000 bankruptcies are expected in the fall to strike small and medium-sized businesses, which form the backbone of the economy. This will result in incalculable tax losses and incalculably high and long-term social security money transfers for, among other things, unemployment benefits.

Since in the meantime pretty much everybody is beginning to understand the full, devastating impact of the completely unfounded corona measures I will refrain from detailing this any further.

II. summary of legal consequences

The most difficult part of a lawyer´s work is always to establish the true facts, not the application of the legal rules to these facts. Unfortunately, a German lawyer does not learn this at law school, but his Anglo-American counterparts do get the necessary training for this at their law schools. And probably for this reason, but also because of the much more pronounced independence of the Anglo-American judiciary, the Anglo-American law of evidence is much more effective in practice than the German one.

A court of law can only decide a legal dispute correctly if it has previously determined the facts correctly–which is not possible without looking at all the evidence. On the basis of the facts summarized above, in particular those established with the help of the work of the German Corona Committee, the legal evaluation is, actually, simple for all civilized legal systems, regardless of whether these legal systems are based on civil law, which follows the Roman law more closely, or whether they are based on Anglo-American common law, which is only loosely connected to Roman law.

1. Unconstitutionality of the measures

A number of German law professors, including Professors Kingreen, Murswieck, Jungbluth and Vosgerau, have stated either in written expert opinions or in interviews –in line with the serious doubts expressed by the former President of the Federal Constitutional Court with respect to the constitutionality of the corona measures - that these measures are without a sufficient factual basis and also without a sufficient legal basis, and are therefore unconstitutional, and must be repealed immediately.

Very recently, a judge, Thorsten Schleif, declared publicly that the German judiciary, just like the general public, has been so panic stricken that it was no longer able to administer justice properly. He says that the courts of law:

"have all too quickly waved through coercive measures, which for millions of people all over Germany represent massive suspensions of their constitutional rights".

He points out that German citizens *"are currently experiencing the most serious encroachment on their constitutional rights since the founding of the Federal Republic of Germany in 1949".* In order to contain the corona pandemic, federal and state governments have intervened *"massively and in part threatening the very existence of the country"* as it is guaranteed by the constitutional rights of the people.

2. fraud, intentional infliction of damage and Crimes against Humanity

Based on the rules of criminal law, asserting false facts concerning the PCR tests, or intentional misrepresentation as it was committed by Mssrs. Drosten and Wieler as well as the WHO can only be assessed as fraud. Based on the rules of civil tort law this translates into intentional infliction of damage. The German professor of civil law, Martin Schwab, supports this finding in public interviews. In a comprehensive legal opinion of around 180 pages he has familiarized himself with the subject matter like no other legal scholar has done thus far, and in particular, has provided a detailed account of the complete failure of the mainstream media to report on the true facts of this so called pandemic.

Messrs. Drosten, Wieler and Tedros of the WHO all knew, based on their own expertise or the expertise of their institutions that the PCR tests cannot provide any information about infections, but asserted over and over again to the general public that they can, with their counterparts all over the world repeating this. And they all knew and accepted that on the basis of their recommendations, the governments of the world would decide on lockdowns, the rules for social distancing and mandatory wearing of face masks, the latter representing a very serious health hazard, as more and more independent studies and expert statements show.

Under the rules of civil tort law, all those who have been harmed by these PCR test induced lockdowns are entitled to receive full compensation for their losses. In particular, there is a duty to compensate, that is a duty to pay damages for the loss of profits suffered by companies and self-employed persons as a result of the lockdown and other measures.

In the meantime, however, the anti-corona measures have caused and continue to cause such devastating damage to the world's populations' health and economy that the crimes committed by Messrs. Drosten, Wieler and the WHO, must be legally qualified as actual Crimes against Humanity as defined in sec. 7 of the International Criminal Code.

3. class action as the best route to compensatory damages and to political consequences

The so-called class action lawsuit is based on English law and exists today in the USA and Canada. It enables a court of law to allow a complaint for damages to be tried as a class action lawsuit at the request of a plaintiff if:

- as a result of a damage inducing event

- a large number of people suffer the same type of damage

Phrased differently: A judge can allow a class action lawsuit to go forward if common questions of law and fact make up the vital component of the lawsuit.

Here, the common questions of law and fact revolve around the worldwide PCR-test based lockdowns and its consequences.

Just like the VW diesel passenger cars were functioning products, but they were defective due to a so called defeat device because they did not comply with the emissions standards, so too the PCR tests, which are perfectly good products in other settings, are defective products when it comes to the diagnosis of infections.

If an American or a Canadian company or an American or Canadian individual decides to sue these persons in the US or Canada for damages, then the court called upon to resolve this dispute may, upon request, allow this complaint to be tried as a class action lawsuit. If this happens, all affected parties worldwide will be informed about this through publications in the mainstream media and will thus have the opportunity to join this class action within a certain period of time to be determined by the court.

It should be emphasized that nobody must join the class action, but every injured party *can* join the class.

The advantage of the class action is that only one trial is needed, namely to try the complaint of a representative plaintiff who is affected in a manner typical of everyone else in the class. This is, firstly, cheaper; and secondly, faster than hundreds of thousands or more individual lawsuits, and thirdly, it imposes less of a burden on the courts. Fourthly, as a rule, it allows a much more precise examination of the accusations than would be possible in the context of hundreds of thousands or – more likely in this corona setting – even millions of individual lawsuits.

In particular, the well-established and proven anglo-American law of evidence with its pre-trial discovery, is applicable. This requires that all evidence relevant for the determination of the lawsuit is put on the table. In contrast to the typical situation in German lawsuits with a structural imbalance - i.e. lawsuits involving a consumer on the one hand, and a powerful corporation on the other - the withholding or even destruction of evidence is not without consequences. Rather, the party withholding or even destroying evidence loses the case.

Here in Germany a group of tort lawyers have banded together to help their clients with the recovery of damages. They have provided all relevant information and forms for German plaintiffs to both estimate how much damage they have suffered, and join the group or class of plaintiffs who will later join the class action when it goes forward either in Canada or the US. Initially, this group of lawyers had considered to also collect and manage the claims for damages of other, non-German plaintiffs. But this proved to be unmanageable.

However: Through an international lawyers' network which is growing larger by the day, the German group of attorneys provides to all of their colleagues in all other countries - free of charge –all relevant information, including expert opinions and testimonies of experts showing that the PCR tests cannot detect infections. And they also provide them with all relevant information as to how they can prepare and bundle the claims for damages of their clients, so that they, too, can assert their clients' claims for damages either in their home countries´ courts of law, or within the framework of the class action as explained above.

These scandalous corona facts gathered mostly by the Corona Committee and summarized above are the same facts that will soon be proven to be true either in one court of law, or in many courts of law all over the world. These are the facts which will pull the masks off the faces of all those responsible for these crimes. To the politicians who believed those corrupt people: These facts are hereby offered as a lifeline that can help you readjust your course of action and start the long overdue public scientific discussion, and not to go down with those charlatans and criminals.

Dr. Reiner Fuellmich originally published "Crimes against Humanity" in October 2020 on YouTube.

"Anyone who seeks death or destruction against anybody is an insult to Life and has no place as a leader of anybody."

Max Igan

CPSIA information can be obtained
at www.ICGtesting.com
Printed in the USA
LVHW010347240122
709144LV00001B/9